The Ballad of
Carl Drega

The Ballad of Carl Drega

🌿 🌿 🌿

**Essays on the Freedom
Movement, 1994 to 2001**

**By
Vin Suprynowicz**

A Mountain Media Book

The Ballad of Carl Drega—
Essays on the Freedom Movement, 1994-2001

Published by
Mountain Media
561 Keystone Ave., #684
Reno, NV 89503
(775)348-8591

ISBN 0-9670259-2-3

Cover Design: Scott Bieser
Page Design: Kathy Harrer

DEDICATION

How shall we count the martyrs lost so far to this War Against Freedom, struggling in inarticulate and lonely desperation to assert liberties they thought were their birthright? It depends, of course, on which "start date" — and which tyrant — we choose.

Clinton and Reno relishing the flames of Waco, 1993? Farley and Roosevelt outlawing civilian possession of gold and machine guns, cocaine and hemp (and instituting their nine-digit slave numbers) in 1933 and '34? Wilson and Palmer with their income tax and their fledgling drug war, their federal reserve and the end of the state legislatures' veto in the Senate — the whole cornucopia of evil dating from 1913? Or shall we start with America's greatest mass murderer, from his ascension in 1861?

No attempt at a comprehensive catalog is attempted here. Go to the airport. Watch the clenched teeth and the red faces of the fat ladies "randomly selected" to remove their belts and shoes and "spread 'em" for an electronic wand in the hand of a smirking illiterate (but now federally unionized) immigrant dwarf, biting their tongues and fighting back tears of rage because they know that even to crack a joke or utter a derogatory comment makes them subject to arrest. Watch their fellow passengers avert their eyes in embarrassment, glad it isn't them.

Still think you live in the "land of the free"? And to think we used to self-righteously bleat out our amazement that the German people could "just stand by and let fascism happen."

To the martyrs this book is dedicated. Let us hope that, when our turn comes, their example will inspire in us the courage to die not like cowering bitches, but charging the barricades, shouting "Today is a good day to die."

— V.S.
Las Vegas, March 6, 2002

ACKNOWLEDGEMENTS

A cynic once commented that it took a lot of money to keep Mahatma Gandhi living in poverty.

Similarly, it takes tireless effort by a devoted team of friends and associates to keep this "one-man show" on the road. Thanks for their invaluable help, advice, and labors to Rick and Kathy; to Deke; to Glen and Michael and Alan and Mikey; to Scott Bieser for capturing the vision of Sam Adams in the North Church for our cover; to everyone who wrote in (not least Widdle Stephanie and Melanie of Rutgers); to the subscribers of *Privacy Alert*, whose participation and support make it all possible ... and to Carla.

Thanks for being there.

CONTENTS

❧ ❧ ❧

March 2002

I am proud to be retained as an editorial writer and author of occasional signed commentaries by the *Las Vegas Review-Journal*, Nevada's largest newspaper. When it comes to honoring the principles of liberty and the free market on its editorial page, the *Review-Journal* is one of the top twenty newspapers in the country. However, the opinions expressed and positions taken in this book are entirely my own. They have not been reviewed or endorsed by the editors or proprietors of the *Review-Journal*, or any of the other newspapers that carry my nationally syndicated column.

Vin Suprynowicz
Las Vegas, Nevada

Introduction

"The evils of tyranny are rarely seen but by him who resists it."

— *John Hay, 1872*

"Those who make peaceful revolution impossible will make violent revolution inevitable."

— *John F. Kennedy*

"You will find that the truth is often unpopular and the contest between agreeable fancy and disagreeable fact is unequal. For, in the vernacular, we Americans are suckers for good news."

— *Adlai Stevenson, 1958*

"All progress has resulted from people who took unpopular positions."

— *Adlai Stevenson*

Calling All 'Brown-Shirt Conservatives'
🍃

On June 6, 1996, John Fensterwald, editorial-page editor of New Hampshire's daily *Concord Monitor*, wrote:

"Vin: Thanks for the latest batch of columns. Interesting, engaging and forceful writing, but too strident (brown-shirt conservative) for my taste. I'll pass."

In the course of nearly a decade syndicating my twice-a-week column into 20-odd newspapers around the country, it goes without saying more editors have rejected my submissions than have published them.

As a dedicated fan of the free market, I wouldn't have it any other way.

What stuck in my craw in Mr. Fensterwald's otherwise polite missive was not the fact that he considers David Broder, George Will, and Ellen Goodman (all able wordsmiths) to represent the full range of conceivable political opinion in America today, but this odd business about my being a "brown-shirt conservative."

I responded:

Hi, John —

And thanks for "strident." I was afraid I was getting soft.

As for my "conservatism," though, my acquaintances of the Republican persuasion, who have long torn out their hair at my incomprehensible defense of abortion rights, gay rights, and the inalienable right of young black men to openly carry machine guns without any stinking permits (the disarming of black Civil War veterans in the South, the better to deny them the vote, having prompted the 14th Amendment — a fact of which no one but a Libertarian "gun nut" is ever likely to remind you), will be somewhat surprised to hear I'm now a "conservative."

I thought a "conservative" was one who warned against too-rapid change. If that's so, the most hidebound "conservatives" around today must surely be the remaining members of the Fritz Mondale-Dianne Feinstein-Hillary Clinton Democratic Party, warning that frightening and unknown hazards await anyone who dares to carelessly disassemble their magnificent compassionate "government social safety net."

In fact, as a Libertarian, I represent the political element urging the most "radical" degree and speed of change now proposed by anyone in this country.

(Here's an easy test you can try at home: Ask the subject whether he favors organized prayer in the public schools. If she says, "No," she's a liberal. If he says, "Yes," he's a conservative. If he or she says, "Public schools? The Constitution grants the government no power to run any mandatory tax-funded youth propaganda camps," you have your hands on the wily libertarian.)

And then we come to "brown-shirt." Not yellow-dog or red-leg or blue-blood. No, I am a "brown-shirt conservative."

Can this really be a reference to the Sturm Abteilungen,

the "organized but disreputable" body of men assembled by Ernst Rohm to give the young Nazi Party the manpower it needed to beat up Jews, Communists, and cripples in the streets of Germany from 1930 to 1934, the famous "brownshirts" who introduced the very phrase "storm troopers" into the vernacular, disbanded by Hitler himself as an unnecessary embarrassment by the simple expedient of shooting Rohm and scores of his followers, sans trial, on the night of June 30, 1934?

Those of us who protest the immorality of the various current schemes of collectivist looting and income redistribution, the "centralized government control of private economic enterprise while allowing the retention of private title" (now effected under the guise of the EPA, the EEOC, the Wage and Hour Division, etc. ad infinitum), which defines fascism in my dictionary, are used to being smeared without much evidence. But here I'm really puzzled.

I'm of half-Polish descent; my late wife was half-Russian. Rohm's brownshirts used to beat up Slavs as "sub-humans" at every opportunity. I won't claim to have done time or gotten my head busted for my convictions, but I think my credentials as an advocate for individual liberties are at least average — I served for years on the board of directors of Planned Parenthood of Rhode Island, hardly a comfortable seat in the nation's only Catholic-majority state — protesters broke in and splashed the elevator with blood with some regularity.

I offer zealous support to the Peyote Way Church of God, founded by Emmanuel Pardeathan Trujillo of the San Carlos Apache, and to Jews for the Preservation of Firearms Ownership, founded by my friend Aaron Zelman of Milwaukee, Wisconsin. Presumably the embrace of such men and women is all a mere subterfuge on the part of me and my "brownshirt" buddies?

I find myself a member of the Libertarian Party, undoubtedly the political party in America with the highest per-capita percentage of homosexual members. (I expect and get no credit for being pro-Second Amendment, even though I took up gun collecting as an adult, and as a political statement. The measure of a freedom fighter is whether he'll back the right of consenting adults to smoke marijuana even though he hasn't touched the stuff for years, as well as the right of consenting adults to engage in any form of private sexual conduct they please — even if he'd just as soon not contemplate what subsequently transpires.) But apparently in New Hampshire, in the "Live Free Or Die" state, all this — along with my desire to set free the tens of thousands of minority youth unjustly imprisoned under our current racist "War on Drugs" — now qualifies me as a "brown-shirt conservative."

How interesting.

Do you support, then, Janet Reno and the president who appointed her, neither of whom has ever sought to bring to justice the subordinates who donned black ninja outfits and stormed a Texas church full of women and children, assault rifles ablaze, back in February of 1993?

If so, then I guess I could do worse than to have my stuff rejected by a "black-shirt liberal."

Have a nice year.

Hang On, Sloopy
🌿

My letter to Mr. Fensterwald will, perhaps, constitute a form of introduction to the author.

It will leave unanswered, however, the predictable charge that the writings that follow are too strident, stemming from some deep-seated bitterness over the growth of government incursions into our lives, a bitterness which rises to the surface and renders them too inflexible, too off-putting, too extreme.

As more flies are attracted with honey, I'm often advised, so I might win over more folks to the cause of freedom if only I would pull in my horns a bit, adopt a more moderate stance, soften the edges of the more frightening aspects of the truth about the blind barbarity of our burgeoning welfare-police state, afford those not yet ready to cross the bridge into the shade of the trees of liberty a chance to dawdle a while longer on the cresting tide.

Sorry — as every struggling rock band eventually has to decide whether it will, or will not, continue to take requests for "Hang On, Sloopy" and "Brandy, You're a Fine Girl," so does any writer devoted to the cause of liberty eventually have to decide whether to hang about playing touch football in the base camp of the compromisers whom author L. Neil Smith has dubbed the "Nerf Libertarians," or whether to strike out and blaze the trail as far up the mountainside as the Creator may give him the power and the vision to climb.

On March 17, 1996 — in the midst of the primary campaign for the 1996 Libertarian presidential nomination (eventually won by financial-newsletter editor Harry Browne, who was not my choice), I sat down to address this very question in an essay I called:

Doesn't Life Require Compromise?

The biggest threat today to the much-maligned and outnumbered forces who fight for freedom in the face of the endless mewlings of the collectivist mob is the siren song of "compromise."

Despite the fact it's been a pretty good decade for freedom worldwide, the compromisers whine that we're nowhere near tossing out the forces of Big Government in this country — that the vast majority of Government School graduates still prate the catechism of the Gospel of St. Roosevelt ("And then Government moved across the face of the void, and saved us from the Robber-Barons, and He saw that it was good ...") as though it were revealed Truth.

And who's to blame? Why, it must be those extremists, who continue to subject us all to ridicule as "far-out nuts" by refusing to accept "reasonable viable compromise."

After all, isn't politics the only route to power? And weren't we all taught in our government schools that politics is the "art of compromise"?

True, if you want to be philosophically pure about it, every human being has a right to defend him or herself from freelance bandits, and from out-of-control governments exceeding their assigned role of protecting individual rights. Therefore, of course, everyone's right to keep and bear arms should "not be infringed" — no government permission can be required for any of us to carry a fully automatic M-16 or a shoulder-launched heat-seeking anti-aircraft missile anywhere we please, especially to a "tax audit."

But we sound like such nuts when we say it that no one listens. So doesn't it make more sense to join with the NRA in calling for "uniform nationwide concealed-carry permits" and "must-issue" permit laws? Of course, we'd be technically acknowledging government's right to grant or withhold its "permission" (what else could "permit" mean?) for us to bear arms. But in a practical sense, isn't this the best deal we're likely to get right now from the forces of genocide and gun control?

Likewise, although the platform of the Libertarian Party calls all taxation "theft," specifically opposes any new "replacement" taxes, stridently defends reproductive freedom, and requires that the Libertarian Party's presidential candidates abide by and conform to that platform, how are we ever to get anywhere if "doctrinaire radicals" and "unrealistic extremists" continue to call for the nomination of real long-time Libertarian activists like Rick Tompkins of Arizona, in place of author Harry Browne, who was brought into the party in mid-1994 specifically as a stalking horse for the party's direct-mail fundraisers and promised he could coordinate a "done-deal" presidential campaign with his current book tour?

When Mr. Browne calls for selling off all the "federal lands" in the Western states to pay down the national debt, why sow internal dissent with "purist" quibbles about whether the federal government has any clear title or right to sell those lands?

When Mr. Browne calls for a "10 percent flat income tax" and/or a brand new replacement "5 percent national sales tax" (assuring us in his latest book that these "honor Libertarian principles") and for allowing the individual states to outlaw abortion if they please, arguing that he has to present such plans in order to prove his "political viability" and win the votes of those who haven't yet been won over to the idea that taxation is slavery and that government has no right to interfere in our bedrooms, how dare the purists stand in the way?

Wouldn't a 10 percent flat income tax or a 5 percent sales tax be "better than what we've got now"? Isn't it the "best compromise we're likely to get in the near future"?

The calls for "compromise" rise in a seeming crescendo. How could any but the most devotedly egotistical fail to ask: "Am I being too inflexible? Might they be right?"

How reassuring it was, then, to move a stack of papers in my study last week and find slipping from their midst a thin 1964 volume of essays by Ayn Rand called *The Virtue of Selfishness*.

The Looted and the Leech

It was Rand's novel *Atlas Shrugged*, of course, that taught many of us the difference between real rights and freedoms, and government hucksterism like the "right to be free of hunger," by which the statists actually mean the "right" of armed taxmen to loot half my paycheck and turn it over to what Albert Jay Nock presciently dubbed in 1935 the forces of "institutionalized mendicancy." By this he meant the allegedly poor in the New Plantation of St. Roosevelt's Projects, who far from being taught to thank me and you for these alms, are taught quite the contrary, to grow increasingly bitter at all the rest of us because we won't fork over enough to provide them with a hot daily breakfast in bed, to which (and to so much more) they're assured they are "entitled," since the fact that we have found gainful employment and they have not proves beyond doubt how we wage-earners are "oppressing" them.

Even our churchmen now endorse this perverse system of subsidized fatherlessness, urging people to pay their endless taxes without ever noting how both the looted and the leech are thus deprived of the true grace of real charity — the warm feeling of knowing one has given voluntarily, or that one has been the recipient of the voluntary kindness of others.

All this is now accepted as the norm, without anyone even asking to what extent it was government intervention that created the need for all this "welfare" in the first place — government bans on the poor entering any of a thousand professions without a "license"; government arrests for "practicing business without a license" or without a "health permit" when neighbors offer to tend each other's children or cook each other's meals; government schools that teach feel-goodism while depriving kids of the basic literacy they would easily acquire on their own if the schools were simply demolished and the tutors set to renting themselves out privately, with no double-talking psychiatric "expert" to stop the paying parents from demanding concrete results in a hurry.

I doubt I'd qualify as a "Randian," as that word is generally used nowadays. The devotees and disciples of the late novelist have a reputation for being a bit high-handed in dismissing those who aren't pure enough followers of Ms. Rand's admirable rejection of the "compassionate" collectivist state.

Nonetheless, the slim little volume that slipped into my hand last week couldn't have been more welcome if I were one of those hopelessly befuddled souls who still believed in divine intervention, especially when (I wouldn't make this up) the paperback promptly fell open to the July 1962 essay: "Doesn't Life Require Compromise?"

In this admirably brief essay, Ayn Rand wrote:

"A compromise is an adjustment of conflicting claims by mutual concessions. This means that both parties to a compromise have some valid claim and some value to offer each other. And this means that both parties agree upon some fundamental principle which serves as a basis for their deal.

"It is only in regard to concretes or particulars, implementing a mutually accepted basic principle, that one may compromise. For instance, one may bargain with a buyer over the price one wants to receive for one's product, and agree on a sum somewhere between one's demand and his offer. The mutually accepted basic principle, in such case, is the principle of trade, namely that the buyer must pay the seller for his product. But if one wanted to be paid and the alleged buyer wanted to obtain one's product for nothing, no compromise, agreement or discussion would be possible, only the total surrender of one or the other.

"There can be no compromise between a property owner and a burglar; offering the burglar a single teaspoon of one's silverware would not be a compromise, but a total surrender — the recognition of his *right* to one's property. What value or concession did the burglar offer in return? And once the principle of unilateral concessions is accepted as the base of a relationship by both parties, it is only a matter of time before the burglar would seize the rest. As an example of this process, observe the present foreign policy of the United States.

"There can be no compromise between freedom and government controls; to accept 'just a few controls' is to surrender the principle of inalienable individual rights and to substitute for it the principle of the government's unlimited, arbitrary power, thus delivering oneself into gradual enslavement. As an example of this process, observe the present domestic policy of the United States.

"There can be no compromise on basic principles or on fundamental issues. What would you regard as a 'compromise' between life and death? Or between truth and falsehood? Or between reason and irrationality?

"Today, however, when people speak of 'compromise,' what they mean is not a legitimate mutual concession or a trade, but precisely the betrayal of one's principles — the unilateral surrender to any groundless, irrational claim. The root of that doctrine is ethical subjectivism, which holds that a desire or a whim is an irreducible moral primary, that every man is entitled to any desire he might feel like asserting, that all desires have equal moral validity, and that the only way men can get along together is by giving in to anything and 'compromising' with anyone. It is not hard to see who would profit and who would lose by such a doctrine.

"The immorality of this doctrine — and the reason why the term 'compromise' implies, in today's general usage, an act of moral treason — lies in the fact that it requires men to accept ethical subjectivism as the basic principle superseding all principles in human relationships and to sacrifice anything as a concession to one another's whims. ...

"The excuse, given in all such cases, is that the 'compromise' is only temporary and that one will reclaim one's integrity at some indeterminate future date. But one cannot ... achieve the victory of one's ideas by helping to propagate their opposite. One cannot offer a literary masterpiece, 'when one has become rich and famous,' to a following one has acquired by writing trash. If one found it difficult to maintain one's loyalty to one's convictions at the start, a succession of betrayals — which helped to augment the power of the evil one lacked the courage to fight — will not make it easier at a later date, but will make it virtually impossible.

"There can be no compromise on moral principles. 'In any compromise between food and poison, it is only death that can win. In any compromise between good and evil, it is only evil that can profit' (*Atlas Shrugged*). The next time you are tempted to ask: 'Doesn't life require compromise?,' translate that question into its actual meaning: 'Doesn't life require the surrender of that which is true and good to that which is false and evil?' The answer is that that precisely is what life forbids — if one wishes to achieve anything but a stretch of tortured years spent in progressive self-destruction."

Thus ends Ayn Rand's brief essay, "Doesn't Life Require Compromise?," in a volume that — when I acquired it years ago — was available for $4.95 from The New American Library, P.O. Box 999, Bergenfield, N.J. 07621, a collection that also contains the January 1963 essay "Collectivized Ethics," by the way, in which Rand manages to completely destroy "Medicare" in a few brief pages, before the health-care Ponzi scheme was even adopted.

"'Isn't it desirable that the aged should have medical care in times of illness?' its advocates clamor. Considered out of context, the answer would be: yes, it is desirable. Who would have a reason to say no? And it is at this point that the mental processes of a collectivized brain are cut off; the rest is fog. ... The fog hides such facts as the enslavement and, therefore, the destruction of medical science, the regimentation and disintegration of all medical practice, and the sacrifice of the professional integrity, the freedom, the careers, the ambitions, the achievements, the happiness, the lives of the very men who are to provide that 'desirable' goal — the doctors. ...

"There would be no controversy about the moral character of some young hoodlum who declared, 'Isn't it desirable to have a yacht, to live in a penthouse and to drink champagne?' — and stubbornly refused to consider the fact that he had robbed a bank and killed two guards to achieve that 'desirable' goal.

"There is no moral difference between these two examples; the number of beneficiaries does not change the nature of the action, it merely increases the number of victims. In fact, the private hoodlum has a slight edge of moral superiority; he has no power to devastate an entire nation, and his victims are not legally disarmed."

Here is the philosophy of freedom, 200 proof. The compromisers must go back to drink deeply of this fountain again, and confess the error of their ways, or else go sell their bill of statist goods elsewhere. Times of great change are coming, when the victims of the collapsing frauds of Roosevelt and Johnson will cry out in the darkness for someone, anyone, to shine the faintest of lights, a single candle, on the true path back to liberty, back to a system under which each is allowed to profit by the fruit of his own works.

Libertarians are the guardians of that candle. The compromisers promise that if we will only blow out our old-fashioned candle now, there will be bright lights aplenty around the next bend ... a bend that we would never reach, of course. Since all else is darkness.

I
Live Free or Die:
How Many More Carl Dregas?

"The most difficult struggle of all is the one within ourselves. Let us not get accustomed and adjusted to these conditions. The one who adjusts ceases to discriminate between good and evil. He becomes a slave in body and soul. Whatever may happen to you, remember always: Don't adjust! Revolt against the reality!"

— *Mordechai Anielewicz, Warsaw, 1943*

"If you would achieve undying fame, attach yourself to the most unpopular righteous cause."

— *George William Curtis*
(of Harper's Weekly*), 1824-1892*

"If I Can't Pay for the Work, They'll Take My Property"
🌿

Go where the land meets the water, anywhere in New England, and you will begin to understand how deeply the region of my birth lies in bondage to the Cult of the Omnipotent State.

Town and state governments throughout New England traditionally buy and dump tons of sea sand — or whatever will pass for it — along the shorelines of their municipal beaches and parks. It doesn't matter whether the shoreline of the lake, river, or ocean cove in question was originally a reeded marshland, naturally filtering away pollutants while offering pristine habitat to waterfowl and a hundred other creatures — the kind of place I (for one) would far rather spend my time communing with nature during those nine months of the year when it's *not* "time to turn, so you won't burn."

No matter: What the majority of taxpayers want is a sandy beach for picnicking and sunbathing (in fact, precious little "swimming" ever transpires), and that is what they darned well get.

Actually, the institutionalized destruction goes much deeper than this. "Urban renewal," in New England, often includes development of new office complexes and highways on "unused" or "blighted" land. For 40 years now, the larger New England cities have bulldozed interstate highways through the "seedy, decrepit" areas of docks and profitable but low-rent private businesses that used to line their waterfronts, throwing small-business owners on the dole and erecting their new throughways atop impassable 20-foot concrete embankments, until two whole generations have grown up within a mile or two of the ocean or the navigable Connecticut River in Hartford, Springfield, New Haven or Boston, without so much as *seeing* the water that gave their cities birth, except as a distant glitter far below the highway bridge they take to work.

But let a *private citizen* try to turn a slice of his own private rocky shoreline into a boat dock, a sliver of sandy beach, or even a well-intentioned but "unpermitted" refuge for turtles and wood ducks (yes, I know of just such cases, in Connecticut and New Jersey) — let him try to similarly adjust nature to his needs or wishes — and suddenly the state authorities descend like locusts, seizing and destroying the privately held turtles, demanding to see all the required permits, showering liens and injunctions like a freak April snow storm.

What's more, the very populace who blithely speed along on the shore-destroying freeways, who consider it their civic right to lie in pure white sand where geese and fox and a hundred other creatures used to raise their young, cheer with glee as these "greedy" private "despoilers of nature" are brought low for daring to offend against the state-enforced religion of Environmentalism ... on their own property.

How dare such troglodytes tamper with sacred resources belonging to all the people, doing whatever they please with no more justification than the fact they happen to hold some bogus "private deed"?

Of course, the notion that one need only "apply for a permit" is nothing but misdirection, equivalent to telling the Jews as they boarded the trains to the east that they should be careful to "label your luggage carefully for when you return."

Big commercial developers who make big campaign contributions may well get some kind of hypocritical "certificate of environmental compliance" for *their* plans to pave and channelize the local waterfront ... requiring yet more government seizure of private property for another big "flood control project" upstream ... but the little guy faces years of hoop-jumping as his permit applications are lost, or returned for re-filing on updated forms, before they're finally denied.

At which point, the sad sack will learn to his dismay that it's too late to declare, "Well then, your whole permitting process is bogus and I'm going ahead anyway."

At that point, the long-suffering citizen will be advised by a stern-voiced judge that he waived his right to appeal the validity of the permitting process when he filed his application (way back in the days when he was told, "That's all there is to it"), thus tacitly acknowledging the right of the state to either grant or withhold its permission for the project in question!

Just ask 67-year-old carpenter Carl Drega, of Columbia, New Hampshire.

Laughed Out of Court
🌾

In 1981, 80 feet of the riverbank along Drega's property collapsed during a rainstorm. Drega decided to dump and pack enough dirt to repair the erosion damage, restoring his lot along the Connecticut River to its original size.

A state conservation officer, Sergeant Eric Stohl, claimed to have spotted the project from the river while passing the Drega property on a fish-stocking operation. (The river's natural ecology harbored huge runs of shad and Atlantic salmon, as well as native pike, pickerel, and brook trout. So most New England states — these devoted acolytes of environmental purity — now routinely stock bass, and brown and rainbow trout, none of which is native and few of which survive long enough to reproduce.)

The state hauled Drega into court, attempting to block his tiny "project."

This was piled atop earlier actions by the Town of Columbia, some dating back more than 20 years, and starting when the town hauled Drega into court and threatened him with liens, judgments, and (ultimately) property seizure over a "zoning violation" for his failure to finish a house covered with tarpaper within a time frame the town considered reasonable, former selectman Kenneth Parkhurst told the *Boston Globe*.

Drega tried for years to fight the authorities on their own terms, in court. Needless to say, as a quasi-literate product of the government schools, and no lawyer, his filings became a laughing stock both in the courts and in the newspapers to which he sent copies, begging for help.

"The dispute, punctuated by years of hearings and court orders, became an obsession for Drega," wrote reporters Matthew Brelis and Kathleen Burge in an Aug. 20, 1997 follow-up in the *Boston Globe*. Drega "filed personal lawsuits against the state officials involved and contacted newspapers, including the *Globe*, imploring them to write about the injustice being done to him."

In court in 1995, the *Globe* reports that Drega explained, "The reason I'm like this on this case, when I started my project 10 years ago I was issued permits and everything I needed. When I reapplied 10 years later, that's when Eric Stohl came in and the Wetlands Board had absolutely no records. ... I am liable for everything that's done there. In the New Hampshire Wetlands Board, if it's not done according to the plan, they can take it out. And if I don't have the money to take it out, they'll take it out. And if I can't pay for it, they'll take my property."

I sort the incoming letters-to-the-editor for a major metropolitan newspaper. The receipt of such sheafs of heartfelt illiterate pleadings from folks at their wits' end (child custody leads the list, though property rights also feature prominently), pleading for help from *someone*, has become an almost daily occurrence.

Since such tirades are too long, rambling, and "not of general public interest" to run as letters, I diligently forward them to the city desk, in hopes an editor there may occasionally assign a reporter to check them out.

They never do ... unless the author shoots somebody, at which point there ensues a mad scramble through the wastebaskets.

In newsrooms around the country, the running joke when a large number of such missives or phone calls come in on the same day is, "It must be a full moon."

Reporters cover the bureaucracy. The bureaucracy is adept at putting out its version of events in reasonable-sounding easy-to-quote form. Those who can't get with the program are generally ridiculed by reporters as "gadflies," "malcontents," and (more recently) "black-helicopter conspiracy nuts." Their rambling disjointed stories don't tend to fit well into the standard 12 inches.

By 1995, it was obvious that Carl Drega was running out of patience. Town selectman Vickie Bunnell, 42 (later appointed a part-time state judge), accompanied a town tax assessor to Drega's property in a dispute over an assessment. Drega fired shots into the air to drive them away.

(In New England, special property-tax assessments are common, and especially cruel to old folks. The courts have ruled that if the town decides to run a municipal water or sewer line along a street fronting one's property, the property owner can be assessed the amount by which the town figures the property's value has been enhanced — usually in the thousands of dollars — even if the property owner has a perfectly good well and septic system, and opts not to tie into the new municipal lines. Failure to pay can eventually lead to eviction, seizure, and auction.)

Carl Drega could see what was coming. He couldn't have been ignorant of the government tactics used to ambush and murder harmless civilians at Waco and Ruby Ridge.

He bought a $575 AR-15 — the legal semi-auto version of the standard military M-16 — in a gun store in Waltham, Massachusetts, a state with some of the most restrictive gun laws in America. He also began equipping his property with early-warning electronic noise and motion detectors against the inevitable government assault.

Too Light a Round

But they didn't come for Carl Drega at home. On Tuesday Aug. 19, 1997, at about 2:30 on a warm summer afternoon, New Hampshire State Troopers Leslie Lord, 45 (a former police chief of nearby Pittsburg), and Scott Phillips, 32, arrested Drega in the parking lot of LaPerle's IGA supermarket in neighboring Colebrook, N.H.

("Arrest" comes from the French word for "stop." Whenever agents of the state brace a citizen, stop him, and demand to see his papers, he has been "arrested," no matter whether he has been "read his rights," no matter what niceties the court may apply to the various steps of the process.)

Why was Carl Drega arrested that day? New Hampshire

Attorney General Phillip McLaughlin pulls out his best weasel words, reporting the troopers had stopped Drega's pickup because of a "perception of defects." Earlier wire accounts reported they were preparing to ticket him for having "rust holes in the bed of his pickup truck."

But Carl Drega had had enough. He walked back to Trooper Lord's cruiser and shot the uniformed government agent seven times. Then he shot Trooper Phillips, as the brave officer attempted to run away. Both died.

Drega then commandeered Lord's cruiser and drove to the office of former selectman — then lawyer and part-time Judge — Vickie Bunnell, 44. Bunnell reportedly carried a handgun in her purse out of fear of Drega. But if so, she evidently had no well-thought-out plan to use it. Bunnell ran out the back door. Drega calmly walked to the rear of the building and shot her in the back from a range of about 30 feet. Bunnell died.

Dennis Joos, 50, editor of the local *Colebrook News and Sentinel*, worked in the office next door. Unarmed, he ran out and tackled Drega. Drega walked about 15 feet with Joos still clutching him around the legs, advising the editor to "Mind your own [expletive] business," according to reporter Claire Knapper of the local weekly.

Joos did not let go. Drega shot Joos in the spine. He died.

Drega then drove across the state line to Bloomfield, Vt., where he fired at New Hampshire Fish and Game Warden Wayne Saunders, sending his car off the road. Saunders was struck on the badge and in the arm, but his injuries were not considered life-threatening.

Police from various agencies soon spotted the abandoned police cruiser Drega had been driving ... still in Vermont. As they approached the vehicle, they began taking fire from a nearby hilltop where Drega had positioned himself, apparently still armed with the AR-15 and about 150 rounds of ammunition. Although he managed to wound two more New Hampshire state troopers and a U.S. Border Patrol agent before he himself was killed by police gunfire, none of those injuries were life-threatening, either.

(Those preparing to defend themselves against assaults by armed government agents on their own property should take note that these failures do not appear attributable to Drega's marksmanship — after all, he scored plenty of hits — but rather to his dependence on the now-military-standard .223 cartridge, which has nowhere near the stopping power of the previous NATO standard .308, or the even earlier U.S. standard 30.06. Some states won't even allow deer to be hunted with the .223, due to its low likelihood of producing a "clean kill" with one hit.)

Fertilizer and Tractor Fuel
🌿

Immediately, the demonization of Carl Drega began. A neighbor told the *Globe* about seeing a police cruiser pull up to the Drega house at 2:50 p.m. and leave at 3:10 p.m., minutes before smoke began to pour from the house. Ignoring the likelihood that a uniformed officer might have been sent to see if Drega had gone home, "Authorities believe the fire was set by Drega," the *Globe* reported on Aug. 20, thereafter reporting as a matter of established fact that Drega burned down his own home.

Isn't it funny how they always do that?

Searching the barn and the remaining property later that week, "Authorities found 450 pounds of ammonium nitrate, the substance used in the World Trade Center and Oklahoma City bombings, as well as cans of diesel fuel," came the breathless Aug. 31 report by *Boston Globe* reporter Royal Ford.

Trenches on the property held PVC pipe carrying wires to remote noise and motion detectors. No remote booby-traps were discovered, though the barn and a hillside bunker contained ammunition, parts for AK-47s and the AR-15, "and a few boxes of silver dollars," as well as "homemade blasting caps, guns, night scopes, a bullet-proof helmet [sic] and books on bombs and booby traps" and "the makings of 86 pipe bombs."

"The makings," eh? I wonder how many wholesale hardware outlets in this country currently stock "the makings" of 860 pipe bombs? 8,600?

The FBI was johnny on the spot, of course, helping New Hampshire State Police Sgt. John McMaster search the three-story barn, with its "concrete bunkers" containing not only ammunition, but also "canned food, soda, and a refrigerator."

(I wonder if my basement would suddenly become a "concrete bunker" if I had a run-in with the law? How about yours?)

But it was the 400 pounds of ammonium nitrate (the estimate kept dropping during the week) and the 61 gallons of diesel fuel in five-gallon containers that gave authorities the willies.

"Realizing he had walked into the most dangerous private arsenal he had ever seen, McMaster began climbing the stairs to the second floor," reported Brian MacQuarrie and Judy Rakowsky of the *Boston Globe* on Aug. 22. "Halfway up, [State Trooper Jack] Meaney shouted for him to stop: He had just picked up a bomb-making manual opened to a chapter on how to booby-trap stairs. ...

"The large stores of dangerous materials, combined with the discovery of three instruction manuals on explosives and booby traps, helped persuade N.H. authorities that they should destroy the barn with a controlled burn and explosion," which they promptly did.

"Some federal agents initially questioned the plan to destroy the huge cache of evidence that may have shown whether Drega had links to militia groups or criminals," the *Globe* also breathlessly reported, though the paper at least had the decency to note no such affiliations were ever established.

(One wonders whether the newspaper would have given equal play to someone lamenting that they thus lost the chance to search for hypothetical links between Drega and the Irish Republic Army, Drega and the Ted Kennedy campaign staff, or Drega and the Buddhist nuns who laundered campaign contributions for Al Gore.)

Ammonium nitrate is, of course, a common fertilizer, sold in 50-pound bags to anyone who wants it — no questions asked — in garden stores in all 50 states.

Farmers all over the nation store more than 60 gallons of diesel fuel at a time, and even know how to combine the diesel fuel with the ammonium nitrate to make a relatively weak explosive, useful in blowing up tree stumps. Purchase of blasting caps for this purpose is also perfectly legal. If this and a few hundred rounds of military-surplus ammo constituted "the most dangerous private arsenal" the head of the New Hampshire state police bomb squad had ever seen, he must not get out much.

Anyway, the buildings are all burned to the ground now — just like at Waco — and the newspaper reporters, trained to just report the facts and never express opinions, had ruled within days that Carl Drega was "diabolical and paranoid," while they never got around to asking why on Earth the officers chose to detain him for having rust holes in the bed of his pickup in the first place.

That, presumably, would be "disrespectful to their memory."

The remaining question is, did government agents Vickie Bunnell, Leslie Lord, and Scott Phillips deserve to die? Did Carl Drega pick the right time and place to say, "That's as many of my rights as you're going to take; it stops right here?"

Or *is* that the right question? The problem with the question is that the oppressor state and its ant-like agents are both devious and clever: Except when faced with overt resistance and a chance to make an example of some social outcasts on TV, they rarely send black-clad agents to pour out of cattle trailers in our front yards, guns ablaze.

No, they generally see to it that our chemical castration is so gradual that there can *never* be a majority consensus that this is finally the right time to respond in force. In this death of a thousand cuts, we're *always* confronted with some harmless old functionary who obviously loves his grandkids, some pleasant young bureaucrat who doubtless loves her cat and bakes cookies for her co-workers and smilingly assures us she's "just doing her job" as she requests our Social SecurityNumber here ... our thumbprint there ... the signed permission slip from your kid's elementary school principal for possessing a gun within a quarter-mile of the school ... and a urine sample, please, if you'll just follow the matron into the little room ...

"Those are the rules," after all. "Everybody has to do it; I just do what they tell me; if you don't like it you can write your congressman."

When ... when is it finally the right moment to respond, "I'll tell you what; why don't you take this steel-cored round of .223 to my congressman? In fact, take him a whole handful, and tell him to have a nice day ... when you see him in hell!'"?

Carl Drega decided the day to finally say that was the day they came to arrest him on the private property of a supermarket parking lot, supposedly for having rust holes in the bed of his pickup.

Does anyone believe that's really why they stopped Carl Drega?

Lots More Coming

❦

I am not — repeat, not — advising anyone to go forth and start shooting cops and bureaucrats. To start with, one's own life expectancy at that point grows quite short, limiting one's options to continue fighting for freedom on other fronts.

Most of us — unlike Carl Drega — also have families to think of.

Third, there may be other solutions. Just as much of the farmland near Rome sat vacant by the fall of the Roman Empire — it simply proved cheaper to move on than to endure the confiscatory Roman taxes — so do James Dale Davidson and William Rees-Mogg predict in their book, *The Sovereign Individual*, that Internet encryption may allow many to spirit their hard-earned assets beyond the reach of this newer oppressive slave state, making "the tax man in search of someone to audit" the laughing stock of the 21st century.

And finally, such a course invites obvious risks of mistaken identity, collateral damage to relatively innocent bystanders (witness newspaperman Joos), and an end to due process ... a concept for which I still harbor some respect, even if our government oppressors do not.

What I do know is, in little more than 30 years, we have gone from a nation where the "quiet enjoyment" of one's private property was a sacred right to a day when the so-called property "owner" faces a hovering hoard of taxmen and regulators threatening to lien, foreclose, and "go to auction" at the first sign of private defiance of their collective will ... a relationship between government and private property rights that my dictionary defines as "fascism."

Carl Drega tried to fight them, for years, on their own terms and in their own courts. We know how far that got him.

This is why the tyrants are moving so quickly to take away our guns. Because they know in their hearts that if they continue the way they've been going, boxing Americans into smaller and smaller corners, leaving us no freedom to decide how to raise and school and discipline our kids, no freedom to purchase (or do without) the medical care we want on the open market, no freedom to withdraw $2,500 from our own bank accounts (let alone move it out of the country) without federal permission, no freedom even to arrange the dirt and trees on our own property to please ourselves ... if they keep going down this road, there are going to be a lot more Carl Dregas, hundreds of them, thousands of them, fed up and not taking it anymore, a lot more pools of blood drawing flies in the municipal parking lots, a lot more self-righteous government weasels who were "only doing their jobs" twitching their death-dances in the warm afternoon sun ... and soon.

When is the right time to say, "Enough, no more. On this spot I stand, and fight, and die"? When they're stacking our luggage and loading us on the boxcars? A fat lot of good it will do us then.

Mr. Jefferson declared for us that, "Whenever any Form of Government becomes destructive of these Ends, it is the Right of the People, to alter or abolish it."

Was Mr. Jefferson only saying we have a right to vote in a new crop of statist politicians every couple of years, as the pro-government extremists will insist?

No. The Declaration fearlessly declared that the Minutemen of Lexington and Concord had been right to shoot down Redcoats who were "only doing their jobs" in Massachusetts the year before. And it put the nations of the world on notice that General Washington was planning to shoot himself a whole lot more.

"You must be kidding!" come the outraged cries. "This guy shot a fleeing woman in the back."

Oh, pardon me. Did Judge Bunnell propose to fight a straightforward duel with Mr. Drega, one on one, mano a mano, to determine who should have the right to decide whether he could build a tarpaper shack on his own property or repair flood damage by sinking a few rocks and pilings along his privately owned piece of river shore?

Of course not. The top bureaucrats generally manage to be sipping lemonade on the porch when the process they put in motion "reaches its final conclusion," with padlocks and police tape and furniture on the sidewalk ... or the incinerated resister buried in the ashes.

Go watch *Escape from Sobibor*. When the Jewish concentration camp inmates finally start to kill their German oppressors, tell me how long you spend worrying that they "didn't give the poor jackbooted fellows a fair sporting chance."

Each and every one of us must decide for him or herself when the day has come to stand fast, raise our weapons to our shoulders, and (quoting *President* Jefferson, this time) water the tree of liberty with the blood of patriots, and of tyrants. Give up the right to make that decision and we become nothing better than the beasts in the field, waiting to be milked until we can give no more, then shuffling off without objection, heads bowed, to the soap factory.

Carl Drega was a resident of New Hampshire. On the day Carl Drega decided it was a good day to die — on the day they towed it away — the license plates on his rusty pickup still bore the New Hampshire state motto: "Live Free or Die."

Carl Drega was different from most of us, all right. He believed the motto still meant something.

Breeding Us a Thousand More Carl Dregas
🍃

"Why are so many Americans going nuts?" our desperate statist overseers keep asking. "It must be the guns!"

Yeah, sure. And the answer to the snakebite problem is not to teach our kids to cut your average cantankerous rattler a wide berth when spotted in the woods, but rather to launch a billion-dollar federal program to capture, anaesthetize, and defang every venomous reptile on the continent.

(Well, perhaps not all at once. We could start with "reasonable modest" reptile control — only outlawing interstate commerce in the biggest meanest-looking snakes, while requiring that manufacturers provide each new hatchling with a "fang lock.")

Shall we make a fresh try at explaining what's going on?

Many thought it was an exaggeration when a government bureaucrat in Ayn Rand's novel *Atlas Shrugged* explained to the hero that the bureaucrats' plan is to make everything illegal, the better to control honest citizens who will then live in constant fear of being charged with a "crime" for merely going about their daily lives ... especially should they ever cross an "officer."

But Ms. Rand — nee Alissa Rosenbaum — watched Comrades Stalin and Trotsky bring collectivism to her home of St. Petersburg in the years after the First World War. She knew precisely how socialism works.

Presumably the idea no longer seems far-fetched to Jim Howard, either. The 30-year resident of Kyle Canyon — a rural mountainside 40 miles northwest of Las Vegas — spent 14 days sitting in the county lockup in the fall of 1999 and was told he could be facing another 40 days after county inspectors — outraged that they've been made to look bad by recent press coverage of the case — papered him with new summonses, including one for "operating without a business license," just before his latest scheduled court appearance.

Is Mr. Howard some kind of armed desperado, or despoiler of the young and defenseless?

Well, no. What happened is that one of Mr. Howard's neighbors — they've all moved in since he set up housekeeping, you understand — complained to the county that Mr. Howard had added a dormer to his house, years ago. They also complained that — since his business is digging septic tanks and clearing snow in the winter — he was storing a dump truck and a backhoe on his property.

The nerve of this man.

And some cars. Jim Howard collects cars. A few years

ago the snow collapsed the roof of his 10-car garage, so he had 14 vehicles lined up on the property, covered with tarps.

That, and the dirt.

The "dirt" part sounds a little strange, until you realize that on rocky Mount Charleston it sometimes comes in darned handy to have a truckload of clean fill on hand to cover a septic tank or an irrigation pipe. The stuff commands a premium up there.

That's about it. That's why Dave Pollex, senior code enforcement specialist for the Clark County's Public Response Office, was called in. Pollex cited Howard for having the cars and the dirt on his property. Howard paid the fine. But Pollex returned to cite him again, waving at the dormer and telling him to "get rid of that, too."

You see, Mr. Howard hadn't bothered to make the 80-mile round trip into town to get a building permit to add his dormer, all those years ago. Mr. Howard wasn't sure why he was supposed to get rid of the window, but he took the glass out and boarded it over.

That apparently outraged Mr. Pollex, who contends he meant Howard should slice the whole dormer off his roof, and that he should have known what was meant. (Though in fact, county regulations would appear to allow for a simple inspection of the structure, in such cases, to make sure it's "up to code.")

Justice of the Peace Nancy Oesterle — whose campaign backers include a family that operates a competing snow-clearing business on the mountain — found Howard in contempt of court and sentenced him to three days in jail, plus 22 days under house arrest. Instead, he ended up serving 14 days in the clink. Some kind of "paperwork mistake," the authorities say.

For the cars. And the dirt. And the dormer.

Jim Howard has removed the dump truck and the backhoe with which he made his living. He's removed his cars — most of which were in good running order. He even says he's removed the dirt — though the county now wants him to re-move another 500 cubic yards, which Howard says will mean hauling off topsoil that came with the property in the first place. That's 500 more truckloads of dirt, a demand that leads columnist John L. Smith — who broke the story of Jim Howard's trials in the Sept. 26, 1999, *Review-Journal* — to quip, "They've ordered him to remove the *property* from his property!"

We all know what Jim Howard's real "crime" was — he got on the wrong side of an officious "by the book" county bureaucrat.

This used to be the land of the free. When an old-timer is merely conducting his life as he has for decades, there comes a time when the appropriate response is: "Lady, you did move out to the country on purpose, didn't you? We do not put people in jail for maintaining a pile of dirt."

At least, we shouldn't.

Folks like Justice Nancy Oesterle and "county officer" Dave Pollex think they can shove and shove and shove—writ-ing any of us a new flurry of citations or locking us up for "contempt" should we object — and eventually we'll all bow our heads and fall into line.

But this is not Japan, and Americans are not ants. Even for patient and long-suffering men — members of an armed populace accustomed to their freedom — there are limits.

Judge Oesterle might want to inquire what happened to the local lady judge who kept shoving around a retired New Hampshire carpenter and recluse named Carl Drega — cited and fined repeatedly over the years for "taking too long" to finish an "unsightly" tarpaper-covered barn on his property, for "filling without a permit" when he rebuilt the shoreline of his property, washed out by a flood on the Connecticut River — continually denying this man a jury trial for "failing to state a cause of action upon which relief may be granted"... that kind of thing.

I'm not celebrating what Carl Drega did. I'm not predicting Nevada's harmless Jim Howard will follow in his footsteps. Nor am I encouraging him to.

I'm just saying that occasionally, one of these old-timers who only wants to be left alone can be pushed too far.

No one's pushing Carl Drega around, anymore.

He Told Them, "If You Come on My Land, I'll Kill You"

🌿

In San Leandro, Calif., about 20 miles southeast of San Francisco, the mostly Portuguese clientele of the 78-year-old Santos Linguisa factory had grown used to the kind of signs recently displayed outside the shop by proprietor Stuart Alexander, great-grandson of the factory's founder.

"To all our great customers," read the most prominent one in June 2000, "The USDA is coming into our plant harassing my employees and me, making it impossible to make our great product. Gee, if all meat plants could be in business for 79 years without one complaint, the meat inspectors would not have jobs. Therefore, we are taking legal action against them."

In fact, on June 22 of that year, the facility had just re-opened after being closed for alleged health violations, when two state and two federal food inspectors — two men and two women, all between the ages of 30 and 50 — decided to pay Mr. Alexander another visit, ABC News reports.

Alexander, 39, surrendered without incident or attempt to flee when located less than a block from his factory. Police had been led there by the sole surviving food inspector. Police had to break a window and climb inside the factory, where they found the other three inspectors on the floor, dead of multiple gunshot wounds.

Danny Gomes, a friend of Alexander's who waited outside the police tape at the factory for news, told a reporter for the the *Daily Hayward Review* that Alexander was upset because inspectors wanted him to raise the temperature of his meat while preparing sausage.

"He was a good man, but pressure, pressure — everybody blows up under pressure," said Michael Smith, another friend of Alexander's.

In 1997, the California Legislature named San Leandro — home of a locally famous annual sausage festival — the "Sausage Capital of California."

❧ ❧ ❧

For years, Garry Watson, 49, of little Bunker, Missouri (population 390), had been squabbling with town officials over the sewage-line easement that ran across his property to the adjoining town-operated sewage lagoon.

Clarence Rosemann, whose family runs the local Handi Mart in the deeply wooded community 100 miles southwest of St. Louis, told reporters for the *St. Louis Post-Dispatch* that he and his son dug up sewer lines on Watson's property about a year back, when Watson couldn't get the city to consider fixing them. After Watson paid Rosemann to dig up the pipes, Rosemann found that the clog was, indeed, on the city's right of way, as Watson had contended.

Later, the city demanded permission to go on Watson's property to fix other sewer problems. Town residents say officials grew dissatisfied with their existing easement, and announced they were going to excavate a new sewer line across the landowner's property. Captain Chris Ricks of the Missouri State Highway Patrol reports Watson's wife, Linda, was served with "easement right-of-way papers" on Wednesday evening, Sept. 6, 2000. His wife gave Watson the papers when he got home at 5 a.m. the next morning from his job at a car-battery recycling plant northeast of Bunker. Watson — described as "white, 5 feet 11 inches, weighing 200 pounds with gray hair and blue eyes," reportedly went to bed for a short time, but arose about 7 a.m. when the city work crew arrived.

"He told them, 'If you come on my land, I'll kill you,'" Bunker resident Gregg Tivnan told me the week after it happened. "When he came home in the morning, his wife gave him the papers. Then the three city workers showed up with a backhoe, plus a police officer. They'd sent along a cop in a cop car to guard the workers, because they were afraid there might be trouble. Watson had gone inside for a little while, but then he came out and pulled his SKS (semi-automatic rifle) out of his truck, steadied it against the truck, and he shot them."

Killed in the Sept. 7, 2000, incident, from a range of about 85 yards, were Rocky B. Gordon, 34, a city maintenance man, and David Thompson, 44, an alderman who supervised public works. City maintenance worker Delmar Eugene Dunn, 51, remained in serious but stable condition at St. John's Regional Health Center in Springfield the following weekend. Bunker police officer Steve Stoops, who drove away from the scene after being shot, was treated and released from a hospital in Salem, Mo., for a bullet wound to his arm and a graze to the neck.

Watson thereupon kissed his wife goodbye, took his rifle, and disappeared into the woods, where his body was found two days later — dead of an apparently self-inflicted gunshot wound.

In the meantime, Garry Watson had gained a middle name, being thereafter referred to in all press accounts as Garry DeWayne Watson.

"Before this, nobody in town even knew he *had* a middle name, let alone what it was," says Tivnan. "All of a sudden he had this middle name, like John Wilkes Booth or Lee Harvey Oswald."

Following such incidents, the local papers are inevitably

filled with well-meaning but mawkish doggerel about the townsfolk "pulling together" and attempting to "heal" following the "tragedy." There are endless expressions of frustration by those who pretend to have no idea how such a thing could happen, pretending to ask how such an otherwise peaceful member of the community could "just snap like that."

In fact, the supposedly elusive explanation is right before our eyes.

"He was pushed," Clarence Rosemann told the big-city reporters from St. Louis.

Another area resident, who didn't want to be identified, told the visiting newsmen, "Most people are understanding why Garry Watson was upset. They are wishing he didn't do it, but they are understanding why he did it."

You see, to most of the people who work in government and the media these days — especially in our urban centers — "private property" is a concept out of some 18th century history book. Oh, sure, "property owners" are allowed to *live* on their land, so long as they pay rent to the state in the form of "property taxes" — just as they're allowed to keep custody of their own children until such time as the state decides to reclaim the custody it initially established in the maternity ward (where the infant was assigned a "voluntary" nine-digit federal ID number, with or without the parents' permission) based on any number of pretexts, from "medical neglect" (parental refusal to expose the child to the federally acknowledged risk of death or brain damage from required pertussis shots) to "mandatory public education."

But an actual "right" to be let alone on our land to do whatever we please — always providing we don't actually endanger the lives or health of our neighbors?

Heavens! If we allowed that, how would we enforce all our wonderful new "environmental-protection" laws, or the "zoning codes," or the laws against growing hemp or tobacco or distilling whisky without a license, or any of the endless parade of other *malum prohibitum* decrees which have multiplied like swarms of flying ants in this nation over the past 89 years?

There is no "mystery" about why Carl Drega and Stuart Alexander and Garry Watson did what they did.

What does it mean to say we have any "rights" or "freedoms" at all, if we cannot peacefully enjoy that property we buy with the fruits of our labors? In his 1985 book *Takings*, University of Chicago Law Professor Richard Epstein wrote, "Private property gives the right to exclude others *without* the need for any justification. Indeed, it is the ability to act at will and without need for justification within some domain, which is the essence of freedom, be it of speech or of property."

🌿 🌿 🌿

"Unfortunately," replies James Bovard, author of the book *Freedom in Chains: The Rise of the State and the Demise of the Citizen*, "federal law enforcement agents and prosecutors are making private property much less private. In 1984 the Supreme Court ruled in *Oliver vs. United States* — a case involving Kentucky law enforcement agents who ignored several 'No Trespassing' signs, climbed over a fence, tramped a mile and a half onto a person's land and found marijuana plants — that 'open fields do not provide the setting for those intimate activities that the (Fourth) Amendment is intended to shelter from government interference or surveillance' (466 U.S. 170, 179 [1984].) ...

"The core of the 'open fields' decision," Bovard wrote in the September 2000 edition of *Ideas on Liberty*, published by the Foundation for Economic Education in Irvington-on-Hudson, N.Y., "is that the government cannot wrongfully invade a person's land, because government agents have a right to go wherever they damn well please. ... And for those areas that are sufficiently fenced in, the Supreme Court had blessed low-level helicopter flights to search for any illicit plants on the ground. (*Florida vs. Riley*, 488 U.S. 445 [1989].)

"The Supreme Court decision, which has been cited in over 600 subsequent federal and state court decisions, nullified hundreds of years of common-law precedents limiting the power of government agents. The ruling was a green light for warrantless raids by federal immigration agents; in 1997 the *New York Times* reported cases of upstate New York farmers' complaining that 'immigration agents ... barged into packing sheds like gang busters, handcuffing all workers who might be Hispanic and asking questions later. ...' In a raid outside Elba, N.Y., at least one INS agent opened fire on fleeing farm workers. Many harvests subsequently rotted in the fields because of the shortage of farm workers. ...

"Police also possess the right to destroy property they search. Santa Clara, Calif., police served search and arrest warrants by firing smoke grenades, tear-gas cannisters, and flash grenades into a rental home; not surprisingly, the house caught fire and burned down. When the homeowner sued for damages, a federal court rejected the plea, declaring that the police force "only ... carelessly conducted its routine and regular duty of pursuing criminals and obtaining evidence of criminal activity. The damage resulted from a single isolated incidence of alleged negligence." (*Patel vs. U.S.*, 823 F. Supp. 696. 698 [1993].)"

Renters fare even worse. "Park Forest, Ill., in 1994 enacted an ordinance that authorizes warrantless searches of every single-family rental home by a city inspector or police officer," Mr. Bovard continues, "who are authorized to invade rental units 'at all reasonable times.' No limit was placed on the power of the inspectors to search through people's homes, and tenants were prohibited from denying entry to government agents. Federal Judge Joan Gottschall struck down the searches as unconstitutional in February 1998, but her decision will have little or no effect on the numerous other localities that authorize similar invasions of privacy."

We are now involved in a war in this nation, a last-ditch struggle in which the other side contends only the king's men are allowed to use force or the threat of force, and that any uppity peasant finally rendered so desperate as to use the same kind of armed force routinely employed by our oppressors must surely be a "lone madman" who "snapped for no reason."

No, we should not and do not endorse or approve the individual choices of Carl Drega, or Stuart Alexander, or Garry Watson. It would not be right to actively encourage anyone else to pick up a gun and shoot the next government agent who barges his or her way onto private property.

But we are obliged to honor their memories and the personal courage it takes to fight and die for a principle, even as we lament both their desperate misguided actions ... and the systematic erosion of our liberties that gave them rise.

"Just because one government agent has a piece of paper that's signed by another government agent, does that mean there's no more right to private property?" asks my friend Gregg Tivnan.

"If statists fear popular resistance," replies Jim Bovard, "perhaps government should violate fewer rights."

There remain in America — especially in rural America, where many have now made their final retreat, backs to the wall in hopes of no more than being allowed to "peacefully enjoy" life, liberty, and the pursuit of happiness — millions of Americans for whom "private property" is not some dried and dusty phrase out of a long-discarded history book, at all.

To many Americans, "property rights" remain something worth fighting — and dying — for.

Want to find out how many? Keep pushing.

Boy, Do They Ever Want the Trails End Ranch

🌿

The Donald Scott case isn't as well known as the government atrocities at Waco and Ruby Ridge. But it should be.

In October of 1992, millionaire recluse Donald Scott and his bride of two months, Frances Plante Scott, lived in a storybook wooded valley in the mountains high above Malibu, California. Trails End Ranch is almost completely surrounded by state and federal park land, and the neighboring government entities had made numerous attempts to buy out Scott and annex his property in the years immediately preceding.

Frances Scott contends the National Security Agency and NASA's Jet Propulsion Laboratories have also had a less-well-known role in the attempted government land grab — the ranch sits in the midst of a government antenna array, perfectly sited to receive data from the Pacific Missile Test Range. "My husband was the only local resident to testify against the placement of those antennas, because they cause cancer," she recalls.

Stymied in their attempt to buy the Scott ranch, government officials hit on an alternative plan. Contending an officer had seen "marijuana plants growing under the trees" during a drug-seeking overflight (though they were unable to produce any photos, which would normally have accompanied the request for a search warrant), agents from various jurisdictions gathered quietly outside the locked gate to the ranch in the morning mists of Oct. 2, 1992. After greedily studying the maps of the 200 acres of prime land they were told they'd be able to grab under federal asset-seizure laws should they find as few as 14 marijuana plants, they cut the chain on the gate with boltcutters and raced a mile up the dirt drive to the ranch, complete with police dogs.

Frances Scott was in the kitchen, brewing her morning coffee, when dozens of men in plainclothes and brandishing guns — no badges or warrants in evidence — came swarming in. Understandably, she screamed for her husband, still asleep upstairs.

Donald Scott, 63, came hurrying down the stairs in answer to his wife's screams of terror, a handgun held over his head. The officers shouted for him to lower his weapon. He did. They shot him dead.

Frances Scott contends the photograph of two plainclothes cops (County Sheriff's Deputy John W. Cater, Jr. and Los Angeles County Sheriff's Office narcotics Detective Gary R. Spencer, also identified by government investigators as the shooters) displayed at her Web site, www.savetrailsend.org, was taken mere minutes after her husband's death. The two officers wear grins of triumph.

Ventura County District Attorney Michael Bradbury, after a six-month investigation, concluded a voluminous report (www.savetrailsend.org/report.shtml) by branding the fatal raid "a land grab by the (L.A.) Sheriffs Office." He confirms the odd fact that "two researchers from Jet Propulsion Laboratories (JPL) in Pasadena" were also present for the so-called drug raid, and asks in his conclusion, "Did the Los Angeles County Sheriff obtain the warrant in order to obtain Scott's land? Did the National Park Service orchestrate the investigation or killing in order to obtain the land?"

Not a single marijuana seed or stem was ever found: "All they had to show for their trouble was this body on the living room floor," reported the *Los Angeles Times*.

The multiple government agencies — including the L.A. County Sheriff's Office, L.A. Police Department, California National Guard, U.S. Drug Enforcement Agency, the California Drug Enforcement Agency, a Border Patrol Unit of the INS, and the National Park Service — settled a wrongful death suit for $5 million.

One would think that would leave Trails End Ranch securely in the hands of the widow Scott, who has made it her life's work to see the government never gets the property. But if one assumed that, one would not be properly accounting for the creativity and plain cussed persistence of today's government land thieves.

A year after the raid and shooting, the widow Scott had to stand alongside 15 local firefighters and watch as the main house, cabins and other outbuildings of Trails End Ranch burned to the ground.

Mrs. Scott alleges that the wildfire was actually started by arson. Regardless, county firefighters arrived in plenty of time to dig a firebreak, which would probably have kept the blaze away from the ranch. But she says a county firefighter told her with tears in his eyes that a National Parks spokesman denied the firemen permission to do so, since, "It violates our rules to disturb the natural beauty of the land."

Many would have expected Mrs. Scott to depart after being burned out of house and home. Instead, she's spent the past six years camped out on the property in a teepee. Photos on her Web site show her posing amidst the ruins of the ranch building, wearing her white wedding gown, guarded by a large Winchester and a couple of stout-looking attack dogs.

Mrs. Scott's latest problem? The ranch went to Donald Scott's estate, of which she controls only a minority share, the rest going to his children by a previous marriage. The IRS appraises the ranch at $2.4 million, and wants inheritance tax on $1 million of that sum, at 55 percent.

The attorneys for the children have advised them the ranch would be hard to market — the official appraisal describes it as inaccessible, though Mrs. Scott says the mile-long access road is still perfectly functional — and that they'll be better off selling the property to pay the taxes.

Thus, on Aug. 2, 2001, a police SWAT team accompanied by two helicopters — "one a larger military model with armed personnel that landed on the mountain ridge in plain view of my teepee," arrived to evict Mrs. Scott.

Out of the $5 million wrongful death settlement, 40 percent went to the lawyers off the top, while the rest was split six ways. Once Mrs. Scott paid off her own eight years worth of legal bills, that left her barely enough to offer a $170,000 down payment to back her $1.95 million bid for the ranch in the upcoming tax auction, she says.

But now, "The lawyers have kept my $170,000 down payment for potential damages and ... I won't have a single dollar to take to this auction, so the National Park Service will be the only party to place a bid," Mrs. Scott told me in September 2001.

The widow Scott has paid out at least another $55,000 to a series of three backers who agreed to bid on the ranch in her behalf, but each has been raided or otherwise intimidated by local police and the FBI, she contends.

In one case, in January 2001, attorneys hired by Scott's adult children screamed at one of these gentlemen in court, "Are you bidding for Frances Scott? We'll investigate you fully!" Mrs. Scott contends. Within a month, she says, the man had indeed been subject to a raid by the FBI and local police, on unrelated charges.

On the telephone, Frances Scott sounds a bit paranoid — though perhaps that's understandable, given what she's been through. Responding to my e-mail messages by calling on a cellular phone, she declines to give out either a call-back number or a mailing address.

"I will not say what my current living circumstances are, 'cause they keep coming back at me," she says. "From the beginning I've said they're not going to murder my husband and get his property, too. I've been attacked militarily for nine years. I know these mountains well."

No officers were ever charged in Donald Scott's death, of course. Police are rarely charged with murdering mere civilians anymore, in this Land of the Free.

"They tell me Gary Spencer, who shot the fatal bullet, has a nervous tic now," Mrs. Scott reports. "And he's working on the bomb squad."

Mrs. Scott invites those wishing to "help save Trails End Ranch" to contribute to the Donald Scott Memorial Fund, P.O. Box 6755 Malibu, CA 90264, or c/o Bank of America, Point Dune Branch, 29171 Heather Cliff Road, Malibu, CA 90264, 310/456-6296.

License to Kill
🕊

David Aguilar, 44, retired from the military after 20 years and decided to live on his pension so he could be a "stay-at-home dad" to his five youngest children, aged 3 to 15, according to Beth Cascaddan, his neighbor in the Three Points area, 22 miles west of Tucson, Arizona.

"He was extremely devoted to his children," Ms. Cascaddan told reporter Melissa Martinez of the daily *Tucson Citizen*. Aguilar also coached youth football and baseball.

But on the early afternoon of Friday, Jan. 10, 1997, David Aguilar sensed something wrong. A man was sitting in a car parked alongside the road bordering Aguilar's property, just sitting and watching.

Only a few days earlier, residents of the neighborhood had been informed by law officers that a convicted sex offender was moving into the area, Cascaddan recalls.

The man's behavior was unusual. "Out here," Cindy Dowell, another neighbor, told reporters for the competing *Arizona Daily Star*, "people just don't sit" in cars.

Aguilar's children, including his 15-year-old son, later recalled that their father approached the man in the parked car, asking whether he was lost.

Whatever the man said, it led to an argument. Seeing that the stranger was not going to move along, Aguilar went back to the house and returned with a gun. The children told neighbor Bonnie Moreno their father was simply trying to scare the man away.

There is no indication David Aguilar ever fired. When the man in the car saw Aguilar returning, he drew his own gun and, at 2:45 that Friday afternoon, fired multiple times through his own windshield. David Aguilar died that evening in a Tucson hospital, of a single gunshot wound to the chest.

The good news is, local police know who did the shooting.

The bad news is, they won't release his name, and he has not been charged.

Detectives with the Pima County Sheriff's Office politely asked the fellow to drop by and meet with them Sunday, Jan. 12, but the newspapers reported the next day that the shooter "postponed the meeting because he had not spoken to his lawyer."

Why the incredible deference to this known killer?

It turns out the shooter is an undercover agent of the federal Drug Enforcement Administration.

Although David Aguilar and his family were not the target of any drug investigation, the unnamed agent was staking out their neighborhood.

"Investigators did not say yesterday whether the agent identified himself" to Aguilar before opening fire, the Tucson newspapers report.

Although a funeral was held Jan. 14, burial will not take place until the family raises $3,213 in funeral costs.

🍂 🍂 🍂

Ralph Garrison, 69, a video store owner, lived in downtown Albuquerque, N.M.

In a lifetime of owning small businesses, he put away enough to buy a second house next door, which he rented out.

Before sunrise on Monday, Dec. 16, 1996, Ralph Garrison awakened to hear the sounds of someone breaking into his rental property next door.

His tenants apparently were not at home.

Garrison went outside to ask who these people were and what they were doing. The men — dressed in black with no visible identifying marks, wearing black "balaclava" hoods that may have been pulled down to conceal their faces, shined lights in his eyes, brandished rifles, and yelled at him to get back in his house.

Ralph Garrison called 911. The daily *Albuquerque Journal* printed a transcript of the call on Dec. 18.

Dispatcher: "Emergency center operator 90. What is your emergency?"

Garrison: "They're breaking into my house — a whole bunch of people."

Dispatcher: "They're backing into your house?"

Garrison: "They're breaking in. Hurry up. Please hurry up."

Dispatcher: "Who's breaking in?"

Garrison: "I don't know. There's a whole bunch of people out there. ..."

Garrison gives his address.

"How many people are there?"

"Oh, about four or five."

"How are they trying to get in?"

"Oh, they're breaking in with uh, axes and all kinds of stuff."

"With axes?"

"Yes. They're breaking in hammers, and all kinds of things. Please. I've got a gun. I'm gonna go up there and shoot them."

"OK. Stay on the phone with me. I'm getting somebody out there, OK?"

Reporter Jeff Jones of the *Journal* writes that when the actual 911 tape was played at press conference later that day, Garrison's voice was "filled with fear and panic."

"Please hurry up," Garrison says. "They've got flashlights,

and cars, and trucks, and all kinds of stuff back there. Please, please hurry up. I'm gonna go out there now."

"Can you take the phone with you?"

"Yes."

"OK. Take the phone with you."

As Garrison moves toward his back door, his dog begins barking, and he complains he still can't see what's going on, because of lights shining in his face. "I've got my gun," he says. "I'll shoot the sons of bitches."

Police report that Albuquerque Police Officer H. Neal Terry and county deputies James Monteith and Erik Little — displaying no badges, dressed in unmarked dark SWAT gear and possibly wearing their black hoods pulled down over their faces — saw Garrison come to his back door with a gun in one hand, a cellular phone in the other. All three officers opened fire with their AR-15 assault rifles, discharging at least 12 rounds.

Police Chief Joe Polisar said it isn't department policy to notify 911 dispatchers before serving a warrant — in this case one under which police hoped to find "counterfeit items including checks, driver's licenses, and birth certificates."

Garrison was not suspected in connection with the "fake ID" ring. No one was arrested that day. Local papers were not told whether any false documents were found.

Officers did find it necessary to shoot and kill Garrison's Chow dog, when the animal tried to protect his master after he was down.

Garrison's wife, Modesta, was inside the home at the time police killed him.

Albuquerque police officer Howard Neal Terry, one of the three "lawmen" involved, has been a defendant in three federal excessive-force lawsuits in the past six years, the local daily reports. The city of Albuquerque has paid more than $375,000 to settle the three lawsuits.

In one case, Terry kicked an unarmed man in the head,

causing permanent brain damage, then contended the 64-year-old Mexican man "resisted arrest." In another case, the city argued (before paying up) that another Mexican man, whose home Officer Terry has invaded, was responsible for his own injuries since he failed to obey the officer's orders. In March 1993, Terry was one of two officers involved in the fatal shooting of Randy Libby, a 30-year-old man who supposedly threatened them with a locomotive-shaped cologne bottle. The city paid off the Libby family to the tune of $100,000.

Polisar and County Sheriff Joe Bowdich said they believe the officers shot Garrison in accordance with departmental policies.

The officers "couldn't look into his heart and mind," Polisar said. "They simply had to make a split-second decision."

Why do I doubt that if Mr. Garrison had shot and killed the deputies, Sheriff Polisar would be holding a similar press conference to explain why Mr. Garrison was not being charged with any crime, since, "He could not look into the hearts and minds of the unidentified black-clad men brandishing AR-15s at him on his own property. He simply had to make a split-second decision"?

๛ ๛ ๛

Pro-government extremists will argue that, in each case, if these citizens had docilely allowed armed strangers to have their way, they might still be alive.

But this does not constitute a rebuttal to my contention that we are now living in a police state. Rather, it merely constitutes advice on how we might behave if we hope to survive a little longer *in* a police state.

Short-sighted advice.

The Jews of Eastern Europe figured their best course was to passively obey the authorities in 1942. We all know where that got them.

Our judges are now issuing search warrants, which allow police to invade private property without notice and murder any law-abiding citizen they find there, on as flimsy a pretext as "searching for fake ID."

The mistake made by David Aguilar and Ralph Garrison was not in taking up arms to defend their homes, families, and neighborhoods. That is the right of every American.

They made their mistakes when they allowed themselves to be outgunned, when they failed to wear Kevlar, and when they decided to confront their violent assailants directly, rather than waiting with longer-range weapons in positions of concealment.

The people will re-learn these lessons eventually ... if only through genetic selection.

Seizure of Widow's Property
"Prohibited by the Constitution," Judge Rules
🌿

The city of Las Vegas scared away the tenants from the two downtown blocks of shops owned by the widow Carol Pappas, ordered her out in 15 days, and promptly bulldozed the place for a parking garage.

It was then up to Mrs. Pappas — for whom those rents had been the main source of income for 20 years — to come up with money for lawyers to challenge the price the city was offering for her already-demolished property — the assessed valuation of about $50 per square foot.

Furthermore, she had to do it without touching a dime of the "purchase price" the city had put in escrow in the bank — if she'd touched that money, the courts would have held she automatically "accepted their offer."

Fifty dollars per square foot. But the property lies on the

corner of Fremont Street and Las Vegas Boulevard in the center of downtown Las Vegas, long known as "Glitter Gulch" — arguably the most lucrative site for a new unlimited-license casino in all Christendom.

Once the city council (which also doubles as the Las Vegas "redevelopment" agency) transferred title to the land to a new limited liability company controlled by the biggest casino operators downtown — and they promptly did — there remained no obstacle to stop the big boys from replacing that mostly empty garage with a new casino of their own in a couple of years — or from merely keeping the land off the market, and with it the best possible site for a competing slot mill.

When they buy old buildings on the free market these days to expand the casinos up north in Reno, Nevada — a much smaller market than Las Vegas — they pay $1,000 per square foot.

Mrs. Pappas' husband opened a restaurant called the White Spot just up the street in 1931, during the Great Depression, before the arrival of any of the Johnny-come-lately casino bosses who have now received the Pappas land from their city's politicians as a virtual gift.

Then-Las Vegas Mayor Jan Jones owned stock in at least one of those casinos. So did the first local judge before whom Carol Pappas tried to take her case — though it took him many months to get around to admitting that might constitute a conflict.

In his restaurant, John Pappas served meals to the men who built Boulder Dam. Meantime, he fed the unemployed out of a free soup line out back. Then, in the 1940s, Pappas acquired the 7,000-square-feet of property now in question, on the corner of Las Vegas Boulevard between Fremont and Carson Streets.

John Pappas, who died in 1980, went back to Greece to find his bride in 1953.

For 50 years, John and his wife Carol — later the widow

Pappas and her children — kept up that retail property and paid taxes on it, knowing the rented storefronts were zoned for unlimited gaming, believing that eventually their ownership of one of the world's prime potential casino sites would handsomely repay their sacrifices.

And these were no mere absentee landlords. Carol's adult son Harry can remember carrying pails of tar up a rickety ladder to help his mother tar the roof.

🌿 🌿 🌿

When Bob Snow of Florida came to Las Vegas in the late 1980s, proposing to buy or lease the Pappas property along with others for a local version of his successful Church Street Station in Orlando, owners of the major casinos downtown fumed at public hearings that the redevelopment agency must not intercede to help him build there, since the land was not "blighted," and only "blighted" areas were subject to redevelopment.

So, Mr. Snow's project was shuffled around the corner and out of sight, next to the highway overpass at a dark corner on the inappropriately named Main Street, where it failed.

Yet by 1993, the very city that had promised up and down in 1986 hearings on its redevelopment scheme that "eminent domain will be used very, very nominally if at all" condemned the Pappas property on short notice. They told the widow Pappas she had 30 days to protest. But in fact, they actually transferred the property 15 days later, *before* the deadline she'd been given to find a lawyer and show up in court. Why? They contended — but never demonstrated — that the fully occupied block of shops was "blighted."

The city did this, District Court Judge Don Chairez has since found, without ever negotiating in good faith to buy the land and without ever demonstrating that the wealthy casino owners who wanted to build the illuminated pedestrian mall now known as the Fremont Street Experience lacked the where-withal to buy the land on the open market, themselves.

(In fact, court briefs filed by the Pappas family detail billions of dollars of new investment — "billions" with a "b" — being made both in Nevada and in gaming enterprises outside the Silver State by the very downtown hotel corporations that share ownership of the Fremont Street Experience, at the very time the Pappas property was being seized — indicating they could easily have afforded to buy the Pappas holdings outright, if they'd cared to pay a market price.)

The property was then razed and turned over to the private Fremont Street Limited Liability Company, which proceeded to build there a multi-story 1,300-space parking structure, which to this day Harry Pappas insists has "never parked 150 cars since the day it opened."

Harry Pappas — John and Carol's son — contends the parking lot was never needed to make the Fremont Street Experience a success, that the goal was to keep anyone else from building a competing casino on the Pappas property until the current occupants get around to it.

So, pooling their resources, the Pappas family went to court.

And on July 3, 1996, District Judge Don P. Chairez, of the District Court of Clark County, let the city have it with both barrels.

🌿 🌿 🌿

The Redevelopment Agency is unable to cite a single case where an existing property owner was allowed to participate in the downtown redevelopment plan — even by retaining a ground lease — as required by law, the judge found.

The city and the current occupants complained the land can hardly be given back now, with a parking garage already built. But the judge made short work of that argument, ruling, "The Plaintiff chose to file for immediate possession, knowing that there was no guarantee of ownership. ... It is the Plaintiff who bears the risk of building on another's property."

"The Agency has convinced itself that it can operate in its own world making deals without answering to the courts, the legislature or the public," the judge wrote. "They are wrong in that regard. The Court today finds that the failure of the Agency to comply with the spirit and the letter of the law render the Agency's actions void and unenforceable. ... Arranging inexpensive transfers of property between unwilling citizens and large businesses is a private taking and thus prohibited by the Constitution."

Of course, the city of Las Vegas immediately appealed Judge Chairez's ruling to the highly politicized Nevada Supreme Court ... where the case has hung in limbo, ever since.

Ever wonder why everything in a Communist country looks so decrepit? It's no accident. If the state owns everything, what would your reward be, should you fix up your apartment to look unusually attractive?

The party would immediately relocate a higher-ranking party official there, of course, rewarding you with a new slum and a bucket of paint.

The long-term health of our cities has collapsed in equal measure as more and more facilities have come under "public" regulation and control. Why would private owners here — any more than in Bucharest — continue to maintain their properties if they believed their 50-year investment can be seized at will on behalf of any new and more powerful neighbor?

Carol Pappas can remember when the German soldiers looted her home in Greece, more than 57 years ago. She can remember the Communist guerrillas in Greece a few years later.

"So everyone wants to go to the most free, the safest place, which is the United States," she says with a still-detectable accent. "But if it keeps going like this" — if City Hall is allowed to condemn and seize private property not just for roads or schools (the traditional uses of their power of "eminent domain"), but to turn those properties over to more politically connected developers at a fraction of the market price — "this country is going to be different."

As of this writing, in the fall of 2001, the Pappas family has yet to get its land back, or a single dollar in compensation. The city's "juice-job" law firm of Lionel, Sawyer & Collins still has the case "under appeal" somewhere between the district court and the state Supreme Court — where it's expected to remain in limbo until Carol Pappas finally dies.

A Loyal Reader Wrote to Me in September 2001:

"Vin, I love your column and read it every week. Could you write one on the murder in Michigan of a hemp activist to steal his land like the Don Scott outrage? Below is an excerpt from a Michigan paper:

"Friends of Campground Victims
Praise the Men and Their Place"

"Saturday, September 8, 2001 ASSOCIATED PRESS

"VANDALIA — Friends of the two men killed by lawmen say they will cherish their memories of the pair and their 34-acre campground. Grover T. Crosslin, 46, died Monday after he was shot by an FBI agent at the Rainbow Farm Campground. Rolland Rohm, 28, was shot and killed by a Michigan state trooper on Tuesday.

"Authorities said both men were pointing guns at officers when they were killed.

"Family, friends and supporters of the two men and their way of life gathered here to keep a vigil over the property. Against a backdrop of burned buildings and an American flag flying upside-down at half-staff, they recounted the good times they had at the campground.

"'I only ever had a chance to come here to stay one time,' said the Rev. Steven Thompson, director of the Benzie County chapter of the National Organization for the Reformation of Marijuana Laws.

"'And as soon as I drove in, I felt like I had come home.'

"Thompson acknowledged that he and his friends had smoked marijuana while at the campground's "Whee 2000" festival, but he said the campground had a friendly atmosphere and that he never saw the sale of drugs, use of hard drugs, or sexual acts out in the open.

"Maurice Williams, a retired 40-year veteran of the Chicago Police Department, sold the campground to Crosslin in 1993. He said he and Crosslin were close friends for many years.

"'Oh, I came up here to visit all the time,' he told the *South Bend Tribune.* '[Crosslin] always made up a place for me to stay in the house. I was a V.I.P.'

"Williams, who still lives in Chicago, said he leased the land to farmers for more than 40 years. He said he intended to retire there, but decided to sell the land to Crosslin instead.

"The future of Rainbow Farm is unknown. A civil forfeiture proceeding initiated last spring against the property is still ongoing, which means the land may still be seized from Crosslin's family.

"Visitation and funeral services for Crosslin were expected to take place Saturday. Visitation services for Rohm are scheduled for Monday, with funeral services on Tuesday."

To the fellow who sent in this all-too-familiar story, I replied:

Hi —

One of the great failures of this generation of the American press is that they/we insist on treating such incidents as isolated and inexplicable, as though they were random acts of nature — instead of at *least* honoring these martyrs by reporting, "This weekend, the 216th American finally decided to stand up for his rights in hopeless resistance against the tax men, the regulators, the planners and zoners and drug police, and — since such actions are of course always spontaneous, leaderless, and unorganized — was promptly mowed down without remorse, pity, or honor ..."

As little as a year or two ago, we seemed to have one of these every couple of months, and I did my best to keep up with them. Over this (2001) Labor Day weekend, we had not only the one you refer to below, but also an ex-cop burned to death in his home in Los Angeles for the suspected offense of "gun hoarding." His dog burned to death with him (you'd think at least *that* would bring some kind of outcry); the AP lied and said his body was found lying atop an "assault rifle" (I'll bet dollars to donuts it was a *semi*-auto AR-15 Sporter); and in a final irony the press reported it was "unclear" whether the place caught fire due to cops launching so many pyrotechnic gas and incendiary flash-bang devices in through the windows, or whether the guy set the fire himself ... which in my book equates to reporting it's "unclear" whether the residents of Auschwitz were killed by the Nazis on purpose, or simply raced into the gas chambers and committed mass suicide despite the best efforts of their German "caretakers" to restrain them.

At least in last weekend's L.A. event, the victim managed to take one cop with him (though, of course, that will only lead to further calls to authorize cops the freer use of tanks, flamethrowers, Kevlar, and poison gas — while "civilians" will now be barred the possession of slingshots, starter pistols, and kids' archery equipment).

I'm swamped and saddened. But please do send me some further photocopied clips from your local papers.

I then proceeded to write the following:

Incinerated For the Crime of 'Stockpiling Weapons'

🌿

Today's reading begins with the 13th Amendment to the Constitution: "Neither slavery nor involuntary servitude, except as a punishment for crime whereof the party shall have been duly convicted, shall exist within the United States, or any place subject to their jurisdiction."

No, we're not talking here about the income tax — though this 1865 amendment certainly would seem to ban any such redistributionist scheme, especially since the subsequent and curiously worded 16th Amendment didn't bother to specifically *revoke* any part of the 13th.

(Those who would turn us into Treasury Department sharecroppers get around this, you understand, by insisting we all "volunteer" for the "payroll benefits tax" when we sign our W-4 "Requests for Withholding." If you choose to commit perjury by swearing at the bottom of Form 1040 that you're subject to some kind of "income tax" — generally defined by statute as an excise on a privileged activity — you can hardly expect the *IRS* to set you straight. Do you have any idea how busy they are, keeping up with the latest Internet porn sites and poking through celebrity tax returns looking for some hot child-support gossip?)

Anyway, the importance of this simple sentence from the 13th Amendment to the advocates of our God-given right to self-defense lies in that phrase "except as a punishment for crime..."

What's that doing in there? Surely common sense would have made it clear to everyone that convicted criminals could still be locked up and committed to "involuntary servitude," right?

Actually, no. The kind of folks who write Constitutional Amendments understand that their words are going to be subject to what the lawyers call "restrictive construction" — they're going to be read in a way that grants the government as little power as possible.

That's why, for instance, Richard Henry Lee and the other guys who drafted the *Second* Amendment made sure to write: "A well-regulated Militia, being necessary to the security of a free State, the right of the people to keep and bear Arms shall not be infringed, except as a punishment for crime whereof the party shall have been duly convicted, which punishment may persist indefinitely, even after said party shall have paid his fine or served out his sentence, unless this privilege be restored in writing by the governor of the state wherein the party shall reside."

Right? Isn't that what the Second Amendment says?

Um, no. Sorry. It just says "... the right of the people to keep and bear Arms shall not be infringed." That other stuff isn't in there at all. I just made it up. Or *someone* did.

Which means the Second Amendment rights of the convict are restored immediately upon his or her release from prison, the same as his or her rights under the First Amendment, or the Fourth Amendment, or the Sixth, or any of the others.

Shall we imagine how the liberal left would respond if anyone in power in this country asserted a former convict who's served out his sentence no longer retains, say, the freedom to attend worship services at the church of his choice ... unless and until that right is specifically restored in writing by the governor?

If a convicted felon is too dangerous to be allowed to wander about with weapons, the solution is to execute him, or exile him, or keep him locked up.

It's also against current law for convicted felons to commune with their former cellmates in taverns — does this mean all of us entering taverns have to fill out some kind of federal "yellow form," swearing on penalty of perjury we've never renounced our U.S. citizenship or been locked away in the local filbert factory, thereupon submitting to some kind of telephone "background check" before the bartender is allowed to pour us a tall one?

The question of "former felons" arose again over the recent Labor Day weekend, 2001, when "neighbors" supposedly called Los Angeles County deputies to snitch on former Arcadia, Calif., police officer James Beck, 35 (most recently of Santa Clarita, Calif.), for the alleged crimes of falsely claiming to be a U.S. marshal and of "stockpiling weapons."

Really. That's what the Associated Press reported Mr. Beck was suspected of: "Stockpiling weapons."

If that's a crime, I'd be convicted before the arresting officers ever made it out of my bedroom. But the cops found it necessary to lay siege to Mr. Beck's home while on holiday overtime, peppering the premises with incendiary tear gas rounds. The house burned to the ground on Friday, Aug. 31, with remains believed to be those of Beck and his dog being found the next day after the rubble cooled, "lying on top of an assault rifle," the AP reports.

About that semiauto AR-15 Sporter. I doubt it was an "assault rifle." True selective-fire assault rifles are a little hard to come by in California these days, especially for a fellow previously convicted at least three times for such offenses as burglary, receiving stolen property, and impersonating a police officer.

No, I'm not holding up James Beck as a hero — he sounds pretty squirrelly to me. But the question remains whether "impersonating a U.S. marshal" is now a crime for which we incinerate citizens without trial.

So long as the Second and 14th Amendments are still in force, there was no "gun crime" here. So why are both Beck and veteran L.A. County Sheriff's Deputy Hagop "Jake" Kuredjian, 40, the uniformed gun-control assailant Beck took with him, now dead?

You'd think my brethren among the nation's ink-stained wretches could *at least* honor these martyrs by reporting, "This weekend, the 216th American in recent years finally decided to stand up for his rights in hopeless resistance against the tax men, the regulators, the planners and zoners and victim-disarmament thugs, and — since such actions are of course always spontaneous, leaderless, and unorganized — was promptly mowed down without remorse, pity, or honor."

Seen Here Together for the First Time in Print
🌿

What is the significance of the deaths of Carl Drega, Garry Watson, Donald Scott, Grover T. Crosslin, Rolland Rohm, James Beck, David Aguilar, Ralph Garrison ... ?

The real significance, I believe, lies in the fact you've never heard of them. Or — if you have — that no magazine writer, no TV reporter, no documentarist has ever before juxtaposed all these deaths at the hands of the regulatory state (along with scores of others — my personal catalogue is anecdotal, including only those I had time to research for my weekly column as they came to my attention, not comprehensive by any means) and asked ... what do they mean?

Imagine with me that scores of zoning-enforcement officers and miscellaneous government regulators were to fan out across America tomorrow, each accompanied by a pair of armed firm-jawed SWAT guys primed and ready to kick ass, intent on serving papers on a few dozen troublesome "gadflies" who have raised official ire by refusing to comply even after repeated notices of violation, instead upsetting everyone, throwing a wrench in the gears, creating nuisances unsafe and unsightly while raising an endless stream of rambling, poorly articulated, off-the-wall defenses and badly Xeroxed briefs centering around the claim that they possess various natural, human, constitutional, and God-given liberties and property rights *pre-dating* the zoning codes; that the courts and municipalities in question have no proper jurisdiction over them because they have rescinded any voluntary submission to that jurisdiction they had ever implied by their agreement to accept a Social Security Number, or to voluntarily apply for any government benefit, or otherwise make themselves the subject of any government regulatory or licensing scheme; that any remaining supposed jurisdiction of that court or municipality has been fraudulently manufactured through a series of myths and frauds involving legal terms of art, improper convening of an admiralty court, the creation of a fictive parallel legal entity consisting of the defendant's name spelled in all capital letters and thus presumed to be a subject of the plenary jurisdiction of Congress over the District of Columbia and the island territories, further perverted by the presumptive application of the Uniform Code of Commercial Conduct, defendant having been given no opportunity to rebut these legal presumptions since the court and municipality won't even answer his simplest and most basic jurisdictional questions ... et blooming cetera.

Defendants answer their doors and are informed the officers have executive warrants and orders in hand to transport them to the nearest county medical facility, for the administration of a local anaesthetic, to be followed immediately by their involuntary castration.

After a brief period of attempting to laugh off this proclamation as a joke, defendants scramble for their guns, each killing at least one officer of the law, whereupon they are, themselves, either shot dead or surrounded in their homes and burned to death.

Remember, in this hypothetical example of mine, all these deadly gunfights and "standoffs" and deaths would occur *on the same day.*

I submit the media would be hard pressed to ignore such a wave of events ... though they'd try. "Mad Killers in Our Midst," the while-you-wait custom-crafted logos on the news specials would proclaim. "How did this happen?" "Isn't it finally time for sensible, effective gun control?" "Why aren't our zoning enforcement officers better armed and protected?" But then, gradually, the news documentaries would also find it hard not to ask, "What is zoning? Where did it come from? Do low-ranking government regulators really have the authority to castrate us without so much as a trial?"

By the weekend the talking-head shows would be full of "legal experts" and desperate pundits (including the token woman in the red dress) shouting at each other that since in this modern world we must all be willing to sacrifice a few so-called "rights" for the greater good and the smooth functioning of an urbanized society far removed from the bucolic rural world of the 18th century Founding Fathers, the proper course of action in such a circumstance is to go along peacefully and have your balls cut off, thereafter following proper legal procedures to seek compensatory and punitive damages in court, the place where — in a civilized nation — all such matters are properly resolved.

On talk radio and the Internet, however — they'd never be allowed on TV — Anne Coulter and Phyllis Schlafly and a small cohort of men who still had their testicles would come forward, first hesitantly and in small numbers, then with growing confidence and in ever larger numbers, asserting that there *is* an actual right to shoot any officer who comes to our door to castrate us.

Why is no such debate now joined in the real world? Because our castrators have been devilishly clever, that's why. They subdue and unman us gradually, starting with the dulling down of children in their government propaganda camps, where (in the words of Buffalo attorney James Ostrowski, writing in *The Free Market*), "The religion taught ... is that interventionist government is the ultimate human value. Government schools forbid the teaching of any religion but state worship. ... These students 'know' that we needed the Constitution because the nation was in chaos, FDR saved us from the Great Depression, and TR saved us from the 'robber barons.' Such ideas and worse are inculcated in young minds when they are soft and malleable. They gradually harden like concrete long before any of our libertarian institutions can supply an antidote. ... Government schools introduce and reinforce the bureaucratic mentality, the opposite of a free and spontaneous attitude toward life. To the bureaucratic mind, life is about unthinking adherence to a set of arbitrary rules of behavior established by superiors in a chain of command."

Our castration is more like the chemical sort to which "members of the transgender community" subject themselves when they want to grow breasts to complete "the change." This gradual transformation works by progressively isolating, ostracizing, and demonizing anyone who won't get with the program and paint his front door the proper color, alleging that such a nonconformist is a repulsive Neanderthal, a chauvinist troglodyte with anti-Semitic militia sympathies, a dangerous anti-government loner and black-helicopter conspiracy nut.

They press and press and press these characters, no matter how they struggle to move to the edge of town and keep to themselves and avoid entanglements with "May I see your photo ID; Social Security number please" authority.

Finally they snap, and we get another six-inch story buried on page 12: "No explanation as crazed loner kills cop, dies in shoot-out with authorities."

Who can explain such events? They're as random and unpredictable and therefore finally meaningless as tornadoes and hailstorms ...

Let's Try

🌿

Americans are fond of prattling on about how we live in the freest country in the world. But Carl Drega and James Beck, Garry Watson and Donald Scott, Grover T. Crosslin and Rolland Rohm, David Aguilar and Ralph Garrison seem to have taken curiously little comfort from this assertion that they were statutorily better off than people in Afghanistan or Mongolia, in Paraguay or the Sudan.

There are several factors at work. For one, measuring freedom by reading the statute books ignores wide disparities in enforcement. Whether or not private ownership of arms is technically illegal in Afghanistan appears to be a moot point — every time there's another war there, our TV and newspapers are full of photographs of happy 13-year-old mujahadin trekking the mountain trails with machine guns and rocket-propelled anti-tank rockets over their shoulders. The fact that they lack the "freedom" to write a letter to their congressman encouraging more arts subsidies and to thereupon receive a generic form letter in reply does not seem to weigh down too heavily upon them, any more than the fact that after voting down a tax-subsidized ballpark they lack the opportunity to watch the local city fathers create a "special-use district" and push it through anyway ... the ongoing charade that our golden-coiffed talking heads chirpily refer to as our current proud "democracy."

Yes, presumably the lives of these young men are hard and their diets frugal. Yet they always look cheerful enough, and I doubt many of them have to have their attitudes "adjusted" with Luvox or Prozac or Ritalin.

Just because we brag that our teen-age boys are "free" to sit bored to tears in government classrooms, "getting a free education courtesy of the taxpayers," are we really so certain their lives are so much "better," on balance, than those of their counterparts, given adult responsibility to watch over the family sheep and marry as soon as they reach child-bearing age, somewhere high in the Andes or the Pyrenees or the Hindu Kush?

Which culture has the highest teen suicide rate? The highest rate of out-of-wedlock births? Of failed marriages? In countries where the opium poppy and the hemp used for hashish are grown openly, do teenagers indulge in irresponsible use of these drugs more than in America, or less? Which 13-year-old is better able to pick up a weapon and defend his mother and sisters? To stalk and kill and butcher an animal and bring it home to the table? To practice his father's trade? To go to market and make a decent profit selling some family heirloom? Which better knows how to clean and roast a rabbit; how to identify wild edible plants from poisons; how to disinfect and stitch a wound? Which, in short, knows full well that he is a deadweight burden on those around him, and which that he is not?

What drives people crazy may be not so much the opportunities, the wealth, and even the luxuries they do or don't have, as the yawning chasm between the degree of freedom and self-responsibility they've been *told* they possess (or ought to), and what they run into in real life — increasingly, here in the "land of the free," a web of depersonalized institutional constraints as carefully designed as a spider web, gradually cinching up tighter and tighter as its victims protest and struggle to escape, leaving them no single appropriate target within reach at which they can strike out or fight back.

Propose to the average American today that the residents of just one of the 50 states — hell, just one *county* among our 3,066 — be allowed to live with the degree of freedom enjoyed by every one of our great-grandparents in 1911, and (as soon as you rectify their government-school ignorance about conditions 90 years ago) they'll lash back with a vindictiveness that can't be born of anything but raw panic and terror.

No planning and zoning? No building permits? So you

want the houses to fall down around our ears and your neighbors to erect slaughterhouses and nuclear reprocessing plants in residential neighborhoods?

No restrictions on the use or possession of cocaine, heroin, marijuana and machine guns? So you want 13-year-old boys to be free to shove .357 Magnums in their belts, stop by the tavern to buy a bucket of beer, and haul it to their dad on his lunch hour down at the plant?

(To be read with increasing speed and shrillness:) And are we to suppose it would be "just fine" to lynch or turn firehoses on "uppity Negroes" so long as they were occupying the property of a person who saw fit to deny them service — just like would have been done in 1911? You want everyone to go about armed, so we'd have deadly shoot-outs after every minor parking-lot fender bender?)

Each of these absurdities can be answered individually ... but calm explanation is *so* much more tedious, so much less fun, than indulging in squawking paranoia, isn't it?

The newsreel footage many of us saw from the Deep South in the 1960s portrayed police officers using firehoses to break up non-violent demonstrations by civil rights marchers (of several skin colors) in public places ... violating the constitutional guarantee that the people's right to assemble and petition for a redress of grievances shall not be infringed.

This was an unconstitutional use of police powers, which Libertarians and other Constitutionalists should and would oppose. This was, therefore, a question of energetically enforcing our constitutional rights as they existed long before 1912 — calling for a return to the level of freedom we enjoyed in 1912 doesn't mean that we wouldn't punish crimes that were crimes even then. (Anyway, name me a Southern police officer who ever did jail time for breaking up a civil rights march, even after our current proud "civil rights" laws were enacted.)

Yes, most of us who believe that the Constitution guarantees us all the "freedom of association" also believe this has to include a "freedom *not* to associate." A private business owner is and should be free to turn away customers because of their age, race, or sex ... just as the NFL seems to violate all kind of federal "civil rights" and "equal employment" laws by refusing to allow women or extremely short, fat, or elderly men to play on its football teams ... just as the Miss America Pageant similarly would appear to violate all kind of federal statutes by refusing to allow entrants who are men ... or young mothers ... or who have had sex changes.

I don't see that this means a call to the freedoms of 1911 means a call for renewed racial discrimination — or assaults on black demonstrators. Even Jesse Jackson admits he'll cross to the other side of the street if he's approached by three young black men in a bad neighborhood at night, faster than if the young men are white ... a clear case of prophylactic self-preservation through sensible "discrimination."

Current "anti-discrimination" statutes are a hypocritical, inconsistent, unconstitutional maze designed to allow certain select minorities to use the threat of federal force for what the economists call "rent-seeking." Pulling out the shopworn cliche that anyone who sees a danger in our current regulatory spider web "must want a return to racial discrimination" (or to take away the vote from women, or whatever bogeyman promises to outrage the wide-eyed throng at present) ignores (among other things) the historical fact that much of the black middle class was prospering better — with lower rates of illegitimacy, higher rates of complex literacy, faster growth curves in income and home ownership, and far better success at holding families together — *before* the birth of the current "compassionate" welfare state in the mid-1960s.

Racial discrimination is reprehensible and the best solution is to allow the free market to bankrupt those who foolishly turn away a large part of their potential customer base under a system of free competition.

Since "Jim Crow" laws, which instituted racial discrimination at the state level via government force, interfered with the free market, they were indeed unconstitutional and almost certainly deserved and needed to be overturned. But at *that* point the competitive forces of the free market should have been allowed to reward those wise enough to break the color bar (as happened very quickly once the other baseball team owners realized they were likely to *lose* by playing all-white teams against folks like Jackie Robinson and the scores of other great black athletes who everyone knew would follow in his path.)

The last thing we needed was to harness the *same* process of fascist government coercion, this time to impose our current racial quota system.

There, now. Wasn't that tedious? See how our feet drag and grow heavy as though trudging through the Russian mud when we take time to systematically rebut just *one* of these absurd "throw-stuff-at-the-wall" allegations as to the deadly dangers of freedom? Meantime, what have the freedom-haters succeeded in distracting us from? Why, the very question of *why* our neighbors become so shrill when we present evidence of just how *un*-free we have grown since 1912 — not *denying* all these new government straightjackets that bind us, mind you, instead merely asserting that the straightjackets are well-intentioned and wholly necessary, that it's really *freedom* that would be dangerous and insane ... at the same time they smugly purr that we remain the "freest country on Earth."

Well, which is it? Or have we now redefined freedom to mean not "the freedom to do as thou wilt, so long as thou harm no other," but instead, "the freedom to be protected from all worry and danger by our great father, the state"?

In which case, let me take this occasion to remind us of the only two things that can protect us from worry: heroin and death.

Why do those of us who love freedom foolishly allow ourselves to be drawn into wasting *far* too much time rebutting such absurd hypothetical constructs — such "reductios ad absurdum" — over and over again?

Shall we now spend *another* nine or 10 paragraphs discussing whether the "right to keep and bear arms" means I should be "allowed" to own a cannon? Whether the Ninth Amendment means 12-year-olds should be "allowed" to buy heroin in the grocery store?

The purchase and ownership of heroin and machine guns by 12-year-olds were perfectly legal in this country in 1911 and for many years previous — examine a year's worth of newspapers from those years, searching for any documented incident of stoned children murdering anyone with powerful military-style weapons ... or even any expression of editorial opinion that this was a *potential* problem worth anyone's time. Either we love freedom and are willing to seek *non-coercive* mechanisms to solve these imaginary "problems"... or else we love our current state of slavery, and will continue to seek or invent hypotheticals to defend a status quo that led to the maddened frustrated killing sprees — and/or the deaths — of Carl Drega and James Beck, Garry Watson and Donald Scott, Grover T. Crosslin and Rolland Rohm ...

Shall we restore our constitutional and God-given natural rights and liberties? Or shall we allow government thugs to coerce our neighbors only when it's a "really good cause" ... with politicians and non-elected bureaucrats allowed to decide when it's "really necessary"?

If the latter, we have just described today's status quo. Let us, then, take a somewhat more detailed look at how that's been working out, of late.

II
Death by Levy:
The Tyranny of Taxation

The Questions That Are Never Asked
〵

The day-after-Christmas Year 2000 shooting spree by bearded 42-year-old misfit Michael McDermott in Wakefield, Mass., will doubtless bring yet more calls for more and harsher "gun control."

In fact, Massachusetts already has among the harshest "gun control" laws in the country. McDermott (don't get me wrong — what he's accused of doing that snowy Tuesday was evil and unjustified and wrong) appears to have blithely violated many of those laws without experiencing any noticeable impediment to his plans. Massachusetts, you will remember, is the one state in the nation (so far as I know) where the "welcoming" billboards on state highways depict a handgun with the huge legend: "Have a gun, go to jail."

Perhaps Mr. McDermott's dead victims will be gratified to learn he's now in jail ... though I doubt it. Virtually every firearm in the Bay State must now (by law) be registered, the most noticeable affect of that law to date being that the commonwealth's law-enforcement agents are now months or even years behind in processing all those hampers full of registrations and requests for registration, to the point where they started whimpering more than a year ago that without federal help and manpower (which would be unconstitutional, as though that stops anyone, anymore) they may simply *never* get caught up.

Actually, I misspoke — there are two other results of such

feel-good laws. 1) They do take cops off the streets to handle all the paperwork. Confident you don't need a gun in your workplace because you can always dial 911? Workers at Edgewater Technology — McDermott's ill-fated workplace — dialed 911. Wakefield isn't way up in the Berkshires, either — it's in the densely populated silicon suburbs of Boston. Yet it took cops so long to respond that Mr. McDermott had finished killing everyone he was after, and was calmly sitting in the reception area waiting to be arrested, when police finally finished donning all their fancy SWAT gear and stormed in. (See the fine book *Dial 911 And Die: The Shocking Truth About The Police Protection Myth*, by attorney Richard W. Stevens, www.libertymall.com).

2) The second result of Massachusetts "gun control" — which would thus be better dubbed "victim disarmament" — is that McDermott was virtually assured none of his law-abiding victims would be armed in their own self-defense.

The Wakefield shootings prove "gun control" will never work, unless the advocates believe they can eliminate guns as thoroughly as the king eliminated all the needles from his kingdom in the fairy tale "Sleeping Beauty." The problems with that scheme being: 1) the king failed; 2) real-life bad guys never live up to such agreements, either (see "The Rhineland, 1936"; "Poland, 1939"); and 3) I keep asking gun-control advocates if, as an initial three-year experiment, they'll agree to start by taking all the guns away from the police and the army. They never respond.

Meantime, the Wakefield shootings do raise one other, more important, issue. Most folks are wailing, as usual, that there was just "no imaginable reason" for this poor nut to go off the deep end.

Leave aside for the moment the fact that McDermott's friends testify he was a normal well-balanced fellow until he spent time in the U.S. military — like Timothy McVeigh and Lee Harvey Oswald. Leave aside for now the question of whether he'd been recently under treatment with psychoactive drugs akin to Luvox or Prozac (like one of the shooters at Columbine High School, as well as that Kip Kinkel kid up in Springfield, Ore.).

More importantly, McDermott bypassed several other possible targets to single out and kill seven members of the firm's accounting department. That accounting department had recently informed McDermott they would start seizing his paychecks and sending them to the IRS for "back taxes." The AP delicately reports the IRS had issued a "request to garnishee his wages" and that the firm had "agreed not to begin taking money from McDermott's paycheck until after the holidays."

🌿 🌿 🌿

But that's bull. The IRS does not "request"; it demands. Employers do not merely "take" a little extra from each paycheck; they are routinely instructed under the Notice Of Intent To Levy (Form 668-W) to seize and send every dime to Washington, stealing every cent of a working-man's living — the very thing the Constitution with its careful limits on "direct taxation" (not to mention the Bill of Rights with its Fourth and Fifth amendments) were designed to prevent the central government from ever doing.

Imagine being told that — no matter how hard you work — you will never see another dime of your own earnings. The miracle is not that an occasional IRS victim goes homicidal here and there, but that so *few* of them do.

These thoroughly illegal paycheck seizures are done to create an "incentive" for the worker to crawl on bended knee to the local IRS office, where he is expected to bare his financial soul (bringing along a year's worth of utility bills, grocery receipts, car repair bills, etc.)

At that point, supercilious IRS drones will decide how many of those expenses to "allow" (yes, in many cases they will actually "not allow" one to retain as much as one can demonstrate one has been spending on car repairs, for instance — recall that those subject to IRS liens can neither buy new cars "on time" for a decade, nor save up any money in a bank account for that purpose — their bank accounts being regularly cleaned out and seized). These simpering IRS weasels — one pretending to be the victim's "advocate" — then determine how much of his paycheck the worker "needs to live on" and draw up a formal written agreement allowing him to retain only that amount ... the final reductio and goal of any socialist system of income redistribution.

Thereupon, the "taxpayer" must "voluntarily" sign a waiver of his or her right ever to contest this "agreement" or the underlying assessments — along with an arbitrary extension of the statute of limitations that would normally allow him to go free after a mere 10 years. If he fails to sign he will be dubbed "uncooperative" and the seizure of every penny from his bank accounts and paychecks can continue indefinitely.

During this entire process, are either bookkeepers like those at Edgewater Technologies of Wakefield, Mass., or "taxpayers" like Michael McDermott told that wage and employment taxes are voluntary in America — that there's absolutely no statutory or legal requirement that in order to assume employment in this country a citizen needs to "request" withholdings by applying for a Social Security Number, or to fill out a W-4 "request for withholding"?

Were the Edgewater Technology bookkeepers — who have now paid the ultimate price for their officious and uncaring ignorance — aware that IRS "notices of intent" to seize paychecks or bank accounts are not legally binding unless accompanied by a court order signed by a judge, who is required to give someone like Mr. McDermott the benefit of a due-process hearing, determining whether the IRS has statutory authority to apply such methods to said specific "taxpayer"?

Did they bother to ask why "paragraph A" of the legal

code citation is always deleted from the "authorizing" fine print on the back of the IRS' standard "seize-his-paycheck" Form 668W (it starts with "paragraph B") — the reason being that paragraph A specifies that said law authorizes the use of such onerous methods only against employees of the federal government? [Here is that carefully deleted paragraph: "Sec. 6331. Levy and distraint. TITLE 26, Subtitle F, CHAPTER 64, Subchapter D, Sec. 6331

"STATUTE: (a)Authority of Secretary

"If any person liable to pay any tax neglects or refuses to pay the same within 10 days after notice and demand, it shall be lawful for the Secretary to collect such tax (and such further sum as shall be sufficient to cover the expenses of the levy) by levy upon all property and rights to property (except such property as is exempt under section 6334) belonging to such person or on which there is a lien provided in this chapter for the payment of such tax. Levy may be made upon the accrued salary or wages of any officer, employee, or elected official, of the United States, the District of Columbia, or any agency or instrumentality of the United States or the District of Columbia, by serving a notice of levy on the employer (as defined in section 3401(d)) of such officer, employee, or elected official. If the Secretary makes a finding that the collection of such tax is in jeopardy, notice and demand for immediate payment of such tax may be made by the Secretary and, upon failure or refusal to pay such tax, collection thereof by levy shall be lawful without regard to the 10-day period provided in this section."]

(See the Web site www.getawarrant.com — which contains a citation from Clark County (Nevada) Magistrate Victor Miller's historic opinion in *Williams vs. Boulder Dam Credit Union.*)

🍃 🍃 🍃

Furthermore, the U.S. Supreme Court in its decision in *Gould vs. Gould*, 245 US 151 (http://caselaw.lp.findlaw.com/scripts/getcase.pl?court=us&vol=245&invol=151), ruled: "In the interpretation of statutes levying taxes it is the established rule not to extend their provisions by implication beyond the clear import of the language used, or to enlarge their operation so as to embrace matters not specifically pointed out. In case of doubt, they are construed most strongly against the government and in favor of the citizen."

Lawyers tell me this means that, for instance, the word "includes" in a tax law is a "term of limitation" — it means "includes *only*."

Thus, the paragraph above means paycheck and bank-account levies can be made *only* against "any officer, employee, or elected official, of the United States, the District of Columbia, or any agency or instrumentality of the United States or the District of Columbia."

Furthermore, under Title 26, United States Code, the Social Security tax is imposed in chapter 21, subtitle C, in which Section 3121 defines "employment" as "any service, of whatever nature, performed (A) by an *employee* for the person employing him, irrespective of the citizenship or residence of either, (I) *within the United States*" ... and then continues in Section 3121(e)(2) to declare that, for purposes of this specific statute, "The term 'United States' when used in a geographical sense includes the Commonwealth of Puerto Rico, the Virgin Islands, Guam and American Samoa."

"Includes only."

How can this be?

"The FICA tax is administered by the IRS as if it were a direct tax on individuals," responds Gordon Phillips of the tax-education group Inform America (www.informamerica.com.) "To be constitutional, any direct tax on individuals must be imposed by law" only *outside* the 50 states of the Union: i.e., only in the four island possessions ... despite the IRS' deception of the public into falsely believing the tax applies "*within the 50 states of the union.*"

So, under the bizarre definition of "United States" adopted to purposely mislead us in this part of the Internal Revenue code, it would appear neither Michael McDermott, nor most of the rest of us, live in "the United States" as defined for this section — or thus fall under its requirements.

Besides which, the tax regulations to enforce the aforementioned paycheck seizure statute — applying only to federal employees — are not promulgated under 26 CFR (the Code of Federal Regulations for Title 26 — the "Internal Revenue Code"), but appear instead under 27 CFR "Alcohol, Tobacco and Firearms." Thus, "It applies only to taxes due on those excise taxable products, anyway," Phillips explains.

"None of us in the tax-education division of the constitutional revival movement have ever heard of any recrimination or retribution whatsoever befalling the plucky participating employer [who voluntarily applied for and chooses to use an Employer Identification Number] who dishonors — that is to say, refuses — a 'Notice Of Intent To Levy' based on the IRS' failure to include the Warrant of Distraint — the court order as required by law before the government can take the property of a citizen," Phillips goes on.

But, "Ninety-nine percent of all American employers are, as are most loyal Americans, deeply chicken. ... Upon receiving the bogus 'levy,' they drop their pants to their ankles, snap briskly to attention, smartly salute the IRS and, fearing that *they* may be audited for failure to comply, begin shoveling the hapless worker's daily bread to the government as fast as their busy little fingers can cut the checks to the IRS. Can you spell 'due process'?"

Yet is any reporter calling the IRS today, asking them, "How do you feel about the outcome of your purposeful misapplication of the tax laws in the case of Michael McDermott of Wakefield, Mass.? By the way, is it true you have this fellow's employment coded as 'manufacturer of truck axles' or 'handler of investments for foreign nationals'? Could you take a moment to explain to our listeners why all Americans are thus coded in the IRS computers as being involved in excisable activities? Is it also true that the suspect Mr. McDermott was under no legal *obligation* to apply for a Social Security number or fill out a so-called 'W-4' form, in order to take a job in one of the 50 states, in the first place? That he may well have been assessing himself for the income tax in error?

"When the employer's bookkeeper called and asked you what to do about your seize-the-paycheck notice — the notice you sent out that led directly to these seven deaths, without telling them you're only authorized under that statute to seize paychecks of federal employees — did you point out to them it's not valid or binding without a signed *court order*? Do you have that court order and could you show it to us, today?"

But of course, these are the questions that are never asked.

How I Came to Understand the IRS
🌿

As soon as the local (largely blue-collar) economy started to tank and a couple of our best advertising salesmen jumped ship, hindsight tells me we should have spun off our weekly newspaper in Providence, Rhode Island — sold it, parceled it off, closed it, whatever.

But we were young and naive, and possessed of a fairly silly reluctance to be branded "quitters." We'd been able to scramble to keep our heads above water for another year or two after the start-up capital ran out in 1982, but the publication — while enormously popular in the capitals of business and government for its irreverent commentary — had never shown any real profits.

Did we make any other mistakes? How much time do you have?

I figured only con men and grifters bothered to set up multiple trusts and partnerships and corporations, billing the newspaper for equipment rentals and "marketing and consulting services" — all the ways clever business folk shift proceeds out of a business to leave it *looking* like it's about to gasp its last (for the benefit of taxmen, labor organizers — anyone who might like to see the books), when in fact some other bank account, somewhere, is growing pleasingly plump.

But most of all, when we went to the accountants and lawyers to set up our corporate entity, they advised us from day one to apply for tax numbers, volunteer to become unpaid tax collectors and remitters (I was so naive that for a time I couldn't even *grasp* why we were supposed to "match" all those payroll withholdings — it had to be a mistake; were we to be taxed as some kind of punishment for having the nerve to create new private-sector *jobs*?).

By the fall of 1984 there was little left to do but watch the wreck settle by the bows. Exhausted and broke after four years of 80-hour weeks, where we'd had a dozen employees we were left with three or four grinding out the last couple of issues in a kind of catatonic dance.

We locked up for Christmas 1984. There wasn't enough left to pay the attorneys to file bankruptcy. In late '83 and early '84 Jeanne had been filing those withholding-tax returns and making payments, but she'd been unable to pay the full amounts — she'd merely been submitting partial payments. By late 1984 we couldn't even afford bookkeepers and accountants to keep making the filings at all.

I'd been brought up a good Democrat, believing the government was just there to help. The IRS did indeed prove helpful. Men with guns came to take all our desks and equipment, hauling it away and storing it in private warehouses that weren't bonded — more on that in a minute.

The IRS graciously filled out the missing tax returns *for us*, for the last couple of quarters we were in business, assuming we had the same number of employees in late 1984 as we'd had back in 1983. I pointed out this was wrong. We were told in no uncertain terms that if we didn't sign a form admitting our personal liability for the $30,000 delinquent tax bill they'd guesstimated, "It could become a criminal matter."

Knowing what I know today, I should have said, "Really? We can go into criminal court where we'd have a presumption of innocence? Great! Then I'm not signing anything; when's our date in federal criminal court?"

They hate it when you actually ask to be thrown in the briar patch.

But we were good, docile, beaten-down little tax slaves. We signed on the dotted line. The cackling agents then told us about the "automatic personal doubling penalty." Although we'd signed that we owed $30,000, Jeanne and I now owed $60,000.

IRS Special Agent Dominic Cambra (yes, that's his real name) of the Providence office told me our seized stat camera — worth about $5,000 — would be sold at auction for a minimum bid of $500 unless I could find someone to approach him with a higher bid — in which case, he encouraged me, the added sum would be credited against what we "owed" the IRS.

I knew an old-timer named Ben Weiss — a self-made entrepeneur who had started working part-time jobs as an underage bellboy in the Great Depression and bootstrapped his way to success without much formal schooling. Ben owned low-rent housing (many had less kind names for him, though he was always good to me) and ran a little all-advertising weekly "shopper" tabloid. I told him he could get the camera — a huge piece of equipment used to produce art for advertisements — for about $600 if he'd like to call the IRS agent.

Agent Cambra told Ben to show up with a money order at his office at 4:30 p.m. Payment in hand, Agent Cambra told

old Mr. Weiss the camera was stored at a warehouse across town and he couldn't possibly get there before it closed; Mr. Weiss should pick it up in the morning.

When old Ben Weiss showed up bright and early the next morning, he was told there'd been a break-in and the camera had been stolen — although there were no signs of anything else missing, nor any ongoing police investigative presence, nor any other indication that this was true.

Ben Weiss called me and I called Agent Cambra, asking if the warehouse wasn't bonded to cover Ben's loss. Agent Cambra gleefully told me it was not, and that there was no statutory requirement that the IRS use bonded warehouses; "we" were simply out of luck.

In hindsight, I'm sure Agent Cambra thought I'd handed $600 of hidden loot to my front man, Mr. Weiss, and that he'd thus tricked *me* out of this sum, rather than victimizing an old man who had grown up an orphan, building up his nest egg by working three jobs before he was 15 on the mean streets of Providence.

Throughout, the IRS agents repeatedly called us in to sign, under penalty of perjury, statements that we didn't have any cash, furs, jewels, art treasures, valuable sports cars, or other meaningful assets squirrelled away, either in this country or abroad. They always shared sly smiles amongst themselves as we signed these bizarre forms — obviously convinced that *anyone* who had ever owned a business and then closed it down, supposedly "broke," must have an Aladdin's cave of treasure secreted away somewhere. When they found it, obviously, they assumed they'd have us dead to rights on multiple counts of perjury — these signed statements being their prima facie evidence.

When a payment was due, they'd insist we bring it down in person and put it in their hands. No amount of personal inconvenience and humiliation seemed to satisfy them.

But of course, these folks often seem to work about two

hours in the morning and an hour in the afternoon, with at least one day off each week. So I'd end up handing the on-deadline payment to someone else, who "promised" to give it to "our agent" the next time she saw her. I would then be accused of missing the "payment deadline" unless I'd been smart enough to make a note so I could prove "Mrs. Grabonzo — the fat woman in the bright orange dress — took the money order at 2:35 p.m. Friday afternoon. I noticed this was witnessed by a frog-like man in thick glasses wearing a nametag that said 'Mr. Girlyboy.'"

Their tax liens meant our lives were hand-to-mouth, of course. I gradually learned to start hiding small amounts of cash where the G-men couldn't find them. The revelation that our banks in this country are merely quasi-private IRS collection centers (they don't even bother to insist the IRS deliver true tax liens, signed by a judge after a due process hearing as required by law) came as an early and important revelation.

The idea that if they simply left us alone to earn a living and accrue some savings, making new investments on which we might earn a return, we could probably have done a better job paying off our "obligations" than through this mechanism of emptying our bank accounts in surprise raids every year or so, never seemed to occur to them.

I'm a slow learner. I'd already noticed the arrogant way the Rhode Island state environmental inspectors threatened to jail us unless we provided evidence of the proper disposal of the solvents used to clean our presses — wouldn't take my word for it that a little weekly tabloid *rented* press time on other people's presses and couldn't *possibly* afford the million-dollar investment required for an offset press of our own. That went on until the state DEP pulled a snap inspection, going so far as to crawl about our basement with flashlights to make sure we didn't have a multi million-dollar Goss Metroliner hidden away down there, their sharp disappointment clear as they left without finding any way to even issue me a citation of violation, let alone haul me away in chains. But only now did I begin to realize just how much these professional state-socialists hated capitalism and all its practitioners. It didn't seem to matter that my father's parents had arrived penniless on these shores in 1912, that my mother's people had hunted raccoon and possum for food and worked in the coal mines and the hardscrabble farms of Ohio and Minnesota — Grandpa Higginbotham raising and slaughtering his own hogs for food to eke out a living through the Great Depression. It didn't seem to matter that I'd borrowed money at interest from friends to launch our little publishing venture, created a dozen jobs, paid untold local taxes, and performed our First Amendment duties as best we could for four years, offering Rhode Islanders some responsible alternative to the smug monopoly Republican a.m.-p.m. daily.

Nope: I was a symbol of corporate greed, and my misery and humiliation would somehow compensate these folks for whatever indignities they felt their own parents or grandparents had suffered at the hands of the mill owners of Pawtucket and Fall River. (I never bothered to ask them if their dads hadn't taken those jobs *voluntarily*.)

Ruined, I moved west to Arizona to find work. Jeanne followed. The IRS contacted me from time to time to put me on a payment plan. The way they do this is, people start calling to complain that checks you have written have bounced. You call your bank and are told, "Oh yes, the IRS levied your bank account last Friday and we've been bouncing all your checks since then. You'll be getting a notice in the mail in a few days." You go down to the IRS office and sign a new payment plan under the threat that otherwise your checks will continue bouncing — running up more hundreds of dollars in bounced-check fees — indefinitely, unless you "cooperate."

(Aren't all those bounced-check fees lost to the Treasury Department? Isn't that money they could have insisted we pay them, instead? Of course. But that doesn't matter. This is all a ritual — the way the police have to knock on your door at dawn and haul you out in handcuffs in front of the neighbors on some bogus procedural charge, even when your attorney had volunteered to bring you in for processing and posting of bond whenever they want to see you. The formal and awesome majesty of the state's power must be demonstrated before all else.)

Over the years, I paid many times the $30,000 Jeanne and I originally agreed to pay. Yet at years' end — given the high effective monthly interest rates — I would still end up owing more than I had the year before, the bill eventually exceeding $100,000.

When Did It End?

When the original assessments were filed in 1983 and 1984, the statute of limitations on our "crime" of failing to withhold and remit enough out of our employees' paychecks (try to get the IRS to give you a straight answer as to whether this is mandatory, or whether we've all been simply "volunteering" to do this, all these years) was six years. Only the next year was the law amended to extend the time limit for pursuing that "offense" to 10 years.

So, after the law was changed, the IRS simply *re-filed* their claims (within the *previous* six-year limit), insisting the 10-year statute extended from the time of their *re*-filing ... despite the constitutional restriction on applying any law retroactively.

(This would be like passing a law against having more than three children, and then arresting you because you had a fourth child *two years before the new law was enacted*.)

When *that* 10 years was about to expire, IRS agents then called to inform me of a wonderful "new" program called the "offer in compromise," in which one is invited to offer a lesser amount to pay off all "obligations." I went to the trouble to read the "offer in compromise" papers in detail and to retain a semi-retired Arizona attorney to (supposedly) help and advise me. (I called the Bar Association for a referral. Never do that.) We both agreed the paperwork said the statute of limitations could be frozen or held in abeyance by the "Service" for only that length of time during which my offer was "under consideration," although it did say they could keep the offer "under consideration" for as long as two years.

My offer (all the money I had in the world) was flatly rejected over the phone by the Phoenix, Ariz., agent handling my case — who literally laughed at me over the phone — within 72 hours. When I told him, "No problem, now that you've rejected my offer, the statute of limitations continues to run as from today, and it'll toll in a few months," he replied, "Oh, no. We interpret that language to mean you've just voluntarily extended the statute of limitations on your case by two more years, no matter how long your offer was seriously 'under consideration'."

This is how our government works. After all, they're just there to help us and to enforce the letter of the law ... however they choose to "interpret" it.

Interestingly enough, after you finally call their bluff and say, "Do whatever you want; I'm going to sit here with my arms crossed and never sign or agree to another thing; I'll just sit here and eat cookies from your vending machine for the next six months if you like ..." they look hostile and pretend to be "going upstairs to see if more aggressive collection steps may be in order" for a few minutes. But when that doesn't work — and I find the best response is to pretty much put your head down on the table and start to go to sleep, after asking them to *please* just kill you if they have any authorization to do so, because you're just too *tired* to play the game anymore ... they're simply out of things to do.

They tell you to go, ominously promise you you'll be hearing from them, and a few months later you get a little yellow self-duplicated 8-by-10-inch form in the mail, called a "Notice of Release of Federal Tax Lien," citing as the reason "expired." It's kind of like loading your M-203 grenade launcher and storming in on a suicide mission to take out the Wizard of Oz ... only to find there's really no one behind the big curtain. All your fear has been self-generated.

Once they've got your bank account, and you tell them, "Hey, my sixteen-year-old car with the crumpled fenders still has a Blue Book value of four hundred dollars. You want to know where it's parked so you can tow it away? You want my shoes? I'll gladly give you my shoes and leave here barefoot" ... it turns out the weasels are 99 percent bluff and bluster. I *guarantee* you they'll whine and wiggle and shriek and pee their pants and cry out for their mommies when it finally comes time to hang them — there's not a *one* who will stand up like a Marine and say, "What I did was right and I'm proud of it; I'm not going to claim I did it just because they told me to; I'd do it all again if I had the chance; I'm proud to die today for the righteousness of the progressive income tax; Long Live Socialism and the Dictatorship of the Proletariat." No, instead it'll be, "It wasn't *me*, it was some *other* 'Dominic Cambra'! You want my *cousin* Dominic. Not me, not me! I have allergies! Who will feed my kitty-cat? Pleeeeease!"

Of course, it would still have been much better if I'd known not to sign anything in the *first* place. They accustom us to signing first our W-4 "requests for withholding," then our 1040 "self-assessments" in which we swear on penalty of perjury that we owe a tax that really only applies to foreigners working in the U.S. or to investment advisers handling the funds of foreign nationals, and then our "quarterly returns" when we open a business. ...

So it only seems natural to sign every other self-incriminating "form" they place in front of us, absolving them of the need to actually prove us guilty of anything. The wonderful truth is, you can and should stop signing things at any time, simply asking, "Does the Fifth Amendment apply, here? Can anything you're asking me to sign be used against me in a court of law? It *can*? Then shouldn't you be reading me my 'Miranda' rights — the guys with the guns in your Criminal Investigations division read folks their 'Miranda' rights, telling them they have a right to remain silent, don't they? Joe Banister told me they do — you guys ever hear of an IRS agent named Joe Banister?

"Wouldn't that include a right not to sign anything, especially this form, which looks kind of like a confession to me? In fact, you know what? I'm not signing anything else for you guys, ever. I'm done. What's that you say? My failure to sign this confession form could 'turn this into a criminal matter'? Well, now we're getting somewhere! Wait while I make sure my little tape recorder is running — now, tell me again your name and rank, under what authority you can declare this a criminal matter, and when I get to show up for my first court date in federal court — not a so-called 'tax court' with an IRS agent pretending to be a judge, but a real criminal court where I have a 'presumption of innocence'? No, no, there's no need to 'go upstairs.' See, right here — just repeat that 'criminal matter' stuff you said a moment ago into the little tape recorder."

And I should also note that giving up, folding your arms, and falling asleep on the table only works if you really *have* nothing left to lose. Being a slow learner, it took me years to learn that in America today you don't *want* a new car in your name, you can't *afford* to own a house with lots of equity in your name, they've turned the "benefit of property ownership" on its head.

The hardest part of developing some modest income streams outside of your "in-the-system" paycheck — some modest hard assets stored anywhere but down at the FDIC-regulated bank (which is really just a thinly disguised subsidiary of the IRS) — is getting yourself to believe this is all really necessary, in what we once thought was a free country that celebrated and *rewarded* hard work and the traditional trappings of success. But believe me, our current environment is little different from that of Stalinist Russia, where you didn't dare actually own anything and let it be seen in public, lest some jealous neighbor "turn you in" to an equally jealous and fastidious Party apparatchik.

Get used to it — thanks in large measure to the unionized government-school workforce, we now live in the midst of two entire generations taught to ridicule and sneer at the notion that "government exists to protect the Haves from the Have-Nots" (their cynical formulation for what we used to call "property rights" — now to be further eviscerated by barring "greedy" rich folks and corporations from "buying" political protection with their extorted campaign "donations").

In the face of this Through-the-Looking-Glass attitude toward wealth and property — the very things that made America the rich and successful envy of the world — we now face our own "going back to school" process, which is actually most painful and frustrating to precisely those of us old-timers who did well in school and were brought up to "play by the rules" — never realizing that half of what teacher taught would eventually become (if it wasn't already) a seductive pack of lies. And it's a minefield that's made even harder to navigate by all the new well-meaning "tax gurus" springing up out there, whose $119 cassette tapes full of partial truths can end up doing us as much harm as good.

In the end, it was a self-educational odyssey that led to the founding of my newsletter, *Privacy Alert*, where I and a few other interested souls are still learning and sifting through this stuff on a monthly basis. So don't get me wrong — they've spent 88 years perfecting this life-sucking maze, and finding a way out isn't easy.

As a matter of fact, I still hear from greasy offal-fattened "former" IRS agents and prosecutors — expecting me to thank them and pat them on the back — who have now gone into private practice, supposedly "helping" taxpayers by reattaching the collar of illegal taxation around their necks, leading them back into the slaughterhouse and getting them to sign perjurious documents under which they claim all these taxes apply to them in exchange for the hope that the "Service" will accept their 20-percent-off "offers in compromise"!

These scum, which is to say (with the possible exception of those who have publicly renounced and actively fought the IRS tyranny, like former Special Agent Joe Banister; see his Web sight www.freedomabovefortune.com) anyone who has ever drawn pay from the IRS or served as their civilian procurers and enablers — by the same standard the Israeli courts applied to Adolf Eichmann, who insisted he was "an old man now" and had only been involved with that distasteful Nazi stuff "many years ago" — should be arrested and tried for fraud, conspiracy, extortion, grand theft, treason, depriving their fellow citizens of their civil rights under color of law, and the murder of anyone who ever committed suicide while suffering under this systematic regimen of inquisition and extended torture. Only if unanimously convicted by a randomly selected jury of former IRS victims, they should then all be hanged by the neck until dead.

That's the way the French solved the problem with *their* entrenched and arrogant aristocracy, in 1793.

Or do you really believe the IRS will pull in their horns and restore our financial freedom if Congress holds just one more round of hearings, waves its fingers just one more time, passes just one more package of "tax reforms"?

IRS Fine at Asking Questions,
But Not Answering Them
☙

Outfits like the Internal Revenue Service and the United States Dept. of the Treasury routinely insist they're only enforcing the law; they have no choice.

Let a victim of their abuses and usurpations haul them into court and demand that they present the very laws and authorizations under which they claim to be operating, however, and suddenly it's a very different story. Suddenly the court is informed that all these demands are "moot " and "frivolous"; that the plaintiff has no "standing" or cause to seek relief; that the answers to all his questions are "self-explanatory."

Laws? We don't have to show you no stinking laws.

Case in point: the action of Steven M. Beresford, Ph.D., a British subject now residing as a legal alien in the state of Oregon, whose case against the IRS and Dept. of the Treasury is being recorded in real time on the Internet for anyone who wants to watch the way the federal government conducts and explains itself, at http://www.beresford-v-irs.com.

Mr. Beresford went to court on Feb. 28, 2000, asserting he is a British citizen who has been a legal resident alien in the U.S. since 1987. He advised the court that "Soon after taking residence in the U.S., it came to his [Beresford's] attention that the American income tax system is based upon voluntary compliance. Plaintiff believes that he cannot be legally compelled to obey any law that is voluntary, and that he therefore has no legal obligation to file or pay income taxes."

However, "At the beginning of 1996, plaintiff received a letter from defendant requesting payment of overdue income taxes for 1987, 1988, 1989. Plaintiff responded by writing to defendant stating that since the income tax system is based on voluntary compliance, he had voluntarily chosen not to comply.

"During the next year or so, plaintiff contacted the IRS

offices in Portland and Seattle by telephone and certified mail on numerous occasions asking for an explanation of the term 'voluntary compliance' so that he could determine his legal liability and comply with the law if required to do so. Defendant ignored these requests and issued an involuntary federal tax lien against him ... for the sum of $7,256."

Predictably, by 1999, "The sum of $14,609 was subsequently withheld from the sale of plaintiff's home at 701 N. Winchell St., Portland. ... Finally, on 1/3/00 defendant notified plaintiff that his request for a due process hearing had been denied."

Where does Dr. Beresford get this "voluntary" nonsense?

From the horse's mouth, as it turns out. In his "points and authorities," he cites:

"The tax system is based on voluntary compliance" — Federal Tax Regulations, Section 601.602.

"Taxpayers in the United States assess their tax liabilities against themselves and pay them voluntarily. This system of assessment and payment is based on the principle of voluntary compliance" — Internal Revenue Manual, Section 20:123 (July 15, 1996).

"Of course, the Government can collect the tax from a District Court suitor by exercising its power of distraint — if he does not split his action — but we cannot believe that compelling resort to this extraordinary measure is either wise or in accord with congressional intent. Our system of taxation is based upon voluntary assessment and payment, not upon distraint" — U.S. Supreme Court, *Flora vs. United States*, 362 US 179, 80 S.Ct. 630 (1960).

"Let me point this out now. Your income tax is 100 percent voluntary tax, and your liquor tax is 100 percent enforced tax. Now the situation is as different as day and night. Consequently, your same rules just will not apply" — Testimony of Dwight E. Avis, Head of the Alcohol and Tobacco Tax Division of the Bureau of Internal Revenue, before the House Ways and Means

Committee on Restructuring the IRS (83rd Congress, 1953).

This, of course, leads to the obvious question: What does the word "voluntary" actually mean? Here, too, Dr. Beresford appears to have done his research, advising the court:

"Neither the Federal Tax Regulations nor the Internal Revenue Code define the term 'voluntary compliance.' Hence plaintiff relies on the definitions of 'voluntary' given in Corpus Juris Secundum (C.J.S. 92: 1029, 1030, 1031):

"The word 'voluntary,' which connotes an agreement, implies willingness, volition, and intent. It suggests a freedom of choice and refers to the doing of something which a person is free to do or not to do, as he so decides.

"Although for legal purposes the word 'voluntary' is considered to be so simple and in such general use that it need not be defined, it has been defined variously as meaning acting by choice, acting of one's self, without compulsion, or without being influenced by another; acting with willingness; done by design or intention; purposed; intended; done of his or its own accord; done of or due to one's own accord or free choice; produced by an act of choice; proceeding from the will or from one's own choice or full consent.

"'Voluntary' is further defined as meaning free; willing; not accidental; spontaneous; proceeding from the free and unrestrained will of the person; proceeding from the spontaneous operation of the party's own mind, free from influence of any extraneous disturbing cause; of one's own will without being moved, influenced, or impelled by others; unconstrained by external interference, influence, or force; unimpelled by another's influence; not compelled, prompted, persuaded, or suggested by another; acting without constraint by extraneous force; without compulsion. ..."

Dr. Beresford then requests of the IRS and Dept. of the Treasury certain documents, which one would think they would have no trouble producing ... if in fact they are acting according to law and properly delegated powers, as they claim.

Yet, instead of answering substantively this most serious question, U.S. attorney Kristine Olson of Portland, Ore., and U.S. Dept. of Justice Tax Division Trial Attorney Jian H. Grant, of Washington, D.C. — acting almost as though they have something to hide — instead ask the court "to dismiss the Complaint for lack of subject matter jurisdiction and failure to state a claim upon which relief can be granted."

(Here's a hint, Kristine; Jian — you could give the guy his money back.)

Then in early June 2000, the government mouthpieces got even more clever, sending a Motion to Stay Discovery (which gets them out of answering any of Dr. Beresford's troubling questions, you understand) to the judge via overnight delivery, while the copy they were required to send to Dr. Beresford lingered in the snail mail.

"Just like before," Beresford writes to his Internet audience, "since the motion was unopposed, Judge King granted it, meaning that all discovery is halted until the judge rules on the Motion to Dismiss. This is absolutely scurrilous. ... These IRS attorneys are despicable. They are resorting to one piece of trickery after another to avoid answering the questions I have posed them. These are sleazy people determined to evade the truth," whose "trickery shows how desperate they are. My Request for Admissions has evidently touched a raw nerve."

Among the documents Dr. Beresford has demanded?

— Copies of any and all documents that establish the Internal Revenue Service as an agency of the United States Government other than in the District of Columbia, insular possessions of the United States, and maritime jurisdiction of the United States.

— Copies of any and all documents that authorize the Internal Revenue Service "to seize property in the State of Oregon other than under authority of 26 U.S.C. No. 7302 & No. 7327 and 26 CFR No. 403. (Do not include authority authorized by 26 U.S.C. No. 7701(a)(12)(B) and other authority relating exclusively to the District of Columbia and/or insular possessions of the United States)". ...

— Copies of any and all laws requiring an individual to sign a federal income tax return. ...

— Copies of any and all delegation orders from the Secretary authorizing the federal tax lien that was filed against plaintiff during the years material to this case.

— Copies of any and all delegation orders from the Secretary authorizing the notice of levy that was issued against plaintiff during the years material to this case.

— Copies of any and all court orders authorizing the federal tax lien that was filed against plaintiff during the years material to this case ...

What's the matter Kristine; Jian? Missing a few documents?

"It's the Duty of Those Who Have to Take Care of Those Who Do Not ..."

Is it the natural right of a Nevadan to set him or herself up in business to make a living? Or is this a "privilege" that must be granted by the state?

(Pardon me for using so many Nevada case histories in this volume, but the Silver State *is* where I've labored in the journalistic vineyards lo these past nine years, gaining a painfully intimate familiarity with such petty tyrannies — and recording some home-grown rationales for redistribution downright charming in their provincial lack of guile. I could point out the number of readers who write from around the country, saying, "Vin, you could have been talking about my own city council or state assembly right here in Palookaville; they've been doing exactly the same thing!" But truth be told, the aspect of Nevada that makes these examples so poignant is the fact that Nevada is *not* a typical state.

Nevada was for decades the only state where prostitution and casino gambling were legal and "no-fault" divorce quick and easy; to this day liquor is peddled 24 hours a day, the state constitution bans any state income tax, and it's still legal to pack a sidearm openly on your hip without a permit except in downtown Las Vegas, where the Clark County sheriff unfortunately now defers to a bunch of hoplophobic out-of-towners in shorts and sandals. In short, redneck Nevadans are enough to give your typical East coast schoolmarm a bad case of the flutters, so when we see this kind of stuff starting to happen *here*, where you got left to run?)

The Nevada State Education Association (the teachers union) informs us on page 7 of its new 28-page tax proposal that going into business — even setting out to make a profit as a private person or partnership — is a "privilege" for which Nevadans should pay the government a levy starting at 4 percent ... though we all know where tax rates tend to migrate over time.

(Or were you under the impression the federal government *kept* its 1912 promise that the federal income tax would never exceed 1 or 2 percent, and would apply only to millionaires?)

NSEA executive director Kenneth Lange called for an appointment and trouped into the editorial offices of the *Review-Journal* with union president Elaine Lancaster and two retainers on May 8, 2001, to present the union's tax proposal.

Like Goldilocks in the fairy tale, the union folks explained that a 4 percent business profits tax rate will be "just right." Any less wouldn't raise the $250 million in new school funding the union seeks. But, "We figure that at 4 percent, the economic theory is that Macy's or United Airlines won't raise their prices on services to people in Nevada based on a 4 percent business tax," Mr. Lange explained.

Greedy corporations don't pass taxes along to their customers, you see — so long as they're "just-right" taxes.

The question then arose as to whether — by adding this levy to the state's nine-year-old business tax (which penalizes Nevada's small businesses for each new employee they hire) there might not be a risk of eventually breaking the camel's back.

"That's what we heard when they proposed the Business Activity Tax," responded Al Bellister, the union's director of research. "But businesses continued to expand and prosper in this state after that tax was enacted; none of the Chamber's predictions of gloom and doom came true."

Listening to Mr. Bellister, who like Mr. Lange came to visit sporting a tweed jacket and a goatee, it was hard not to think of Hank Rearden's meeting with Wesley Mouch and the rest of the "Steel Unification" gang (page 906 in my paperback edition) in Ayn Rand's classic novel of the collapse of the welfare state, *Atlas Shrugged*:

"Then Lawson said softly, half in reproach, half in scorn, 'Well, after all, you businessmen have kept predicting disasters for years, you've cried catastrophe at every progressive measure and told us that we'll perish — but we haven't.' He started a smile, but drew back from the intensity of Rearden's eyes. ...

"'It's only a matter of gaining time!' cried Mouch.

"'Oh, you'll do something!' cried James Taggart. ...''

Nevada voters in the 1980s enacted a constitutional amendment banning any state "income tax ... levied upon the wages or personal income of natural persons." Presumably the teachers union would argue that applies only to a "personal" income tax, leaving the field wide open for their proposed "business" income tax. Note, however, that the teachers' proposal specifically defines "businesses" to include "independent contractors, partnerships, limited liability partnerships, business associations," and even private persons who file IRS tax forms

Schedule C or E ("Profit or Loss from Business"; "Supplemental Income and Loss.")

The union insists "a $50,000 deduction will protect small businesses." But their measure specifically requires that "a natural person subject to taxation as a business under this chapter ... shall make a return to the department" ... regardless of whether he or she falls below the $50,000 cut-off.

Interesting.

Anyway, let's assume for now that no successful constitutional challenge is raised, and this ballot initiative succeeds, providing Nevada's mandatory government youth propaganda camps with the fresh cash-flow here promised. That money would be dedicated to increase the cash flow to the government schools — the union insists the legislature would be specifically forbidden to shift any current school funds elsewhere (though who would arrest a legislative committee chairman for violating this edict in the traditional shell-game of fungible funds remains unclear.)

Clark County residents recently saw what a much smaller dedicated tax could do when it came to funding local libraries. Southern Nevada's new libraries are architectural showpieces, full of vast and impressive aquariums, marble statuary, and professional-level theaters (one of them even had to be partially torn down and re-built when it turned out *its* theater wasn't as big as the theater being built across town in a newer, wealthier, whiter neighborhood.)

Not many books, of course. Try to get an accounting of why there weren't more thousands of books purchased — perhaps even truckloads of castoffs from other libraries — and the benighted amateur was merely treated to a supercilious lecture on how "libraries are a lot more than books, these days."

Would the new Teacher Tax be the same? Vast sums for teacher and administrative salaries and glorious architectural monuments — while Nevada's Janes and Johnnies would still sally forth, unable to spell and do sums?

NSEA Executive Director Kenneth Lange says no — "That's why we built the accountability into this document, where we'll at least have a quarterly report, and with luck even a quarterly discussion."

That's right. "Accountability," as covered in Section 15 of the new Teacher Tax proposal, simply means that every three months, the clerk of the county school board "shall cause to be published an accountability report detailing the amount of money received by the district during the preceding quarter" and "expenditures made by the district."

Then, within 14 days, the school board "shall hold a public hearing at which citizens may: a) Offer testimony as to whether money received by the district ... was used in a manner most beneficial to students in the district; and b) Make recommendations as to how the money should be spent in ensuing quarters."

Isn't that nice? In 1995, the U.S. Supreme Court decided the case of *Missouri vs. Jenkins*, in which a single federal judge in 1985 had taken control of the school district in Kansas City, Mo., mandating a local school tax increase and forcing the schools to spend an extra $1.5 *billion* on state-of-the-art school greenhouses, athletic arenas, radio and TV studios, a planetarium, and computers in every classroom.

The result? As summarized by the Separation of School & State Alliance: "No measurable improvement in academic achievement, a fallen attendance rate, and a dropout rate that remains at 60 percent for high-school students."

On May 3, 2000, the Missouri state Board of Education finally stripped the troubled Kansas City School District of its accreditation. Despite all the billions spent, it turns out the district "has not met any of 11 state performance standards," The AP reports.

Utter failure. But at least the U.S. Supreme Court came to the rescue of Kansas City taxpayers after a mere decade. Nevada's new Teacher Tax, on the other hand, would never sunset no matter *how* badly the schools should fail. The union's version of "accountability" contains no provision for an end to the money river in the event of failure by *any* definition.

"The Legislative process buys you three years," explains NSEA Executive Director Kenneth Lange. "That would probably be a window to decide how to judge what are reasonable standards by which to judge student performance, teacher performance, and so forth."

In other words, *after* the new tax is put in place, the unions might agree to sit down and figure out what — if any — standardized tests may be used in judging whether they succeed or fail.

And then? Even if they fail by their own standards — yet to be revealed — we just keep throwing more money down the black hole?

"I've always said, 'Don't just throw money at the problem,'" answered NSEA President Elaine Lancaster, during that May 8 sojourn to the *Review-Journal* offices. Instead, "The answer is to give us as much money as we think we need to solve the problem, and then if we fail, take it from there."

And what does Ms. Lancaster mean by "take it from there"? If all the new spending fails, we finally close the failed government school in question?

"No, you wouldn't do that," she responds.

Ah. So when she says, "then you take it from there," Ms. Lancaster means that in the result of failure (remember, this is after the union has been given "all the money we think we need to solve the problem,") all the teachers and administrators in the failed school in question would be dismissed — never allowed to work in the system again?

"No, we wouldn't do *that*," Ms. Lancaster responded.

Ms. Lancaster was clearly getting a bit testy, on several occasion muttering things under her breath as the more diplomatic Mr. Lange answered our questions, jerking her head and staring at a point high up on the wall as she added her *sotto voce* comments, for all the world like some shopping-cart lady.

But I considered it important enough to keep seeking an answer: What did she mean by "and then if we fail, take it from there"?

"You might bring in some people from the state to discover what's going wrong," she snapped, rolling her eyes up and away from me.

Aha. So, "Then if we fail, you take it from there" simply means "you keep on giving us more money, no matter what"?

"Well, you can put those words in there if you want," Ms. Lancaster huffed, "but that's not what *I* said."

Ms. Lancaster also wouldn't comment on the case of *Missouri vs. Jenkins*, in which the education bureaucrats really *were* given "all the money they thought they needed" — for more than a decade — and still failed to show any measurable improvement.

"I'm not familiar with that," says the head of Nevada's teachers union of one of the most famous school cases of the past decade.

She did prove willing to respond to editor Thomas Mitchell's question on the way all state tax monies are divvied among the school districts, however — redistributing funds into poorer districts from areas where people earn more money and tend to buy nicer houses.

After all, in a capitalist system, what is the great incentive for folks to complete their own educations, get married, work hard, save, and invest? Isn't it the fact that such behavior is rewarded by the ability to buy their children better things — including a better education? Is it really wise to completely eliminate this link between work habits and the ability to provide for one's children? If schools for the kids of folks who *don't* do these things receive funding redistributed from the richer folks across town, what does that make those who continue to work hard — mere suckers? Is it really to be "from each according to their ability, to each according to their needs?"

"Well, it may be politically incorrect to say it," replied Ms. Lancaster of the teachers union. "But yes, it's the duty of those who have to take care of those who do not."

Actually, of course, it's perfectly politically correct to advance this view in America today. All that's politically incorrect is to give this belief its proper name. Only today, after half a century, are "mainstream" economists beginning to acknowledge Ludwig von Mises and F.W. Hayek were right, in their mighty books *Human Action* and *The Road to Serfdom*, when they demonstrated that there can be no stable "mixed system" between capitalism and its opposite. Euphemize it as "progressive socialism" all you want, but the doctrine union president Elaine Lancaster embraced in our offices on May 8 is that of Karl Marx, and its proper name is communism.

Growing from this rotten root, it should be no surprise that today's "public schools" dope up a fifth of their students to treat the disease of "boyhood," while indulging the absurd "leveling" theory that — instead of expelling the troublemakers and allowing brighter students to move ahead at their own pace — every standard should be dumbed down, the laziest and least adept students finally awarded their surgeon's scalpel or their pilot's wings, since any other course of action would be "unfair," and might "damage the child's self-esteem."

"Accountability?" Once this new Teachers Income Tax opens the floodgates of dedicated school funding, you might as well try to block the Hoover Dam spillways with a spoon.

The Tides of History

🌿

Correspondent J.P. wrote to ask if it's an official Libertarian Party stance that "taxation is theft," reporting he has read one recent reviewer "using this argument to ridicule the Libertarian Party and to suggest that it has been taken over by anarchists."

Long-time Arizona Libertarian Party Chairman Rick Tompkins, who would never claim to speak for the national Libertarian Party as a whole, replied:

"On the contrary, I suggest the party has been taken over by 'Nerf Libertarians' who, in the well-traveled tradition of politicians everywhere, are more concerned with being 'ridiculed' than with standing for principles.

"I suspect the 'official party stance' on this issue, if articulated by the Libertarian Party of the United States, would be fairly equivocal, and hardly compatible with the principle of non-aggression. I have no fear of being ridiculed by collectivists, no matter the size of their mindless cheering section. Rather I consider it a sign of honor to me.

"Your reviewer sounds as if he basks in the glory of agreement with all the tyrants of history, from Pol Pot to Hitler and Mussolini, from FDR and Stalin to William Jefferson Clinton. And let us not leave out our current Congress — the Great Republican Revolution!

"I take the term 'taxation' to mean the confiscation of money or other property from people without their express consent as to the amount, the time, and the purpose. In other words, it is a classic example of the initiation of force.

"To say that taxation is merely theft is to understate the issue and to downplay the truth. A thief, in most cases, strikes a given victim very few times, most often only once. And a typical thief does not try to convince the victim that it's her patriotic duty to submit to the theft, or that it's for 'the good of all' (those who apologize for taxation are normally reluctant to say 'for the good of the collective' which means, of course, for the good of those who wield political power).

"Taxation is far greater an evil than theft. It is a form of slavery. If you cannot choose the disposition of your property, you are a slave. If you must ask permission to work, and/or pay involuntary tribute to anyone from your wages, you are a slave. If you are not allowed to dispose of your life (another way of defining money, since it represents portions of your time and effort, which is what your life is composed of) in the time, manner, and amount of your choosing, you are a slave.

"How is it that so many have so much difficulty with this?

"And spare me the arguments that begin with, 'But how could we (whatever) if there was no taxation?' If a person will not concede the moral wrongness of forcible confiscation of property, no fruitful discussion on this subject is possible. Without first getting an understanding that taxation is wrong, no serious effort will be made to find an ethical and moral way to do 'whatever.'

— R.T.

Though Mr. Tompkins needs no help, I took the liberty of adding:

Furthermore, those who want to enjoy the "benefits" of taxation (a "free" school, a "free" highway) generally prefer to do so without acknowledging the uncomfortable fact that they supported the underlying convenient theft. Thus, the taxmen and their supporters inevitably drag us into a culture of lies and deceit, which must in the end corrode and destroy all that is good in any culture, finally rendering the language so twisted and full of euphemism and misnomer that it becomes almost impossible to even *describe* a moral system of exchange and equity, let alone claw our way out of the pit to rediscover one.

"But all taxation is based on voluntary compliance," we are often told.

OK: Let us pass ordinances that dictate all tax collectors, from your local town clerk to the IRS, may only open the envelopes that arrive in the mail, deposit the receipts in the government accounts, and report the totals to the appropriate spending body — be it City Council or Congress.

They shall no longer be allowed to carry guns, knock on doors, issue liens or levies, send threatening letters, order cowering citizens to report "under threat of compulsory process," buffalo any employers into the form of third-party tribute extraction known as "withholding," operate kangaroo "tax courts," seize and auction off homes, cars, and bank accounts, suborn bank clerks into spying on and reporting our transactions under threat of "license revocation," etc. etc.

What do you think would happen to your level of "voluntary" compliance after one year? After two?

(Frankly, I believe it might remain surprisingly high, when it comes to *local* levies to support the local firehouse, or snow-clearing by the local township, or whatever — proving that the citizens *will* voluntarily pay reasonably realistic fees for necessary local services without coercion. But I assume the *federal* government, as we know it, would be gone within three years, at least west of the Alleghenies. While it might receive the same approximate percentage of the GNP as it received in the years 1790-1825 — plenty to maintain the kind of small defensive Navy that won the War of 1812 — can anyone imagine the kind of wailing and rending of garments this would bring from the modern-day Potentates of the Potomac, and their lapdog press?)

"Voluntary" payments for goods or services received is indeed the answer. But by corrupting the very meaning of such words, the taxmen land us in a morally topsy-turvy purgatory, where we're too busy racing to the front of the trough before the gruel runs out to even recognize how wanting to feed our own family with our earnings has been redefined as "greed," how "rights" have been redefined from things the government can't interfere with into various forms of succor the government is "obliged" to provide to the protected classes through income-transfer schemes, etc.

If you take my property by force, or under threat of force, that's theft (or robbery).

If you get 51 percent of my neighbors to "vote" that it's OK with them for you to take my property by force or threat of force, that's still theft or robbery.

Constitutional republics sharply limit the possible government actions that can be "put to a vote," granting government only a short list of proper functions, while acknowledging private rights, uninfringeable by government (even by a vote of a million-to-one), which remain virtually innumerable.

Totalitarian slave states allow the gang in power to tax anything it wants, at whatever level the "traffic will bear," to raise funds for any purpose they can dream up, and cloak it all in legitimacy with vague phrases about "the greater good of the people." The individual's life and labor belong to the state, which informs him what portion of his time and earnings he is allowed to use for his own purposes ... *this* year.

Totalitarian slave states are characterized by maintaining registration systems for compulsory military service; by progressive limitations on the rights to self-defense and "dissident" speech and religious practice (including the use of "forbidden" hallucinatory sacraments); by the operation of ever-expanding archipelagos of mandatory government youth propaganda camps to break down the intergenerational transfer of the "old ways of thought" about morality and the like (turning the younger generation into a legion of spies on their own parents); by the gradual conversion of banks and other previously "private" institutions into de facto agents of government supervision and administration; by the increasingly sophisticated and intrusive numbering and tracking of all citizens, who can be called in on pain of arrest at any time and required to prove that they've been "contributing their fair share" to the state.

Totalitarian slave states and their adherents are also characterized by a progressively more irate refusal to acknowledge that "taxation is theft."

J.P replied:

Vin and Rick —

The original reason I asked the question regarding taxation being theft is that I see it often being used in the context of a slogan used during demonstrations, but I was unclear if this was an official party position. This is one of the supporting arguments H. is using to equate Libertarianism with Anarchism.

Personally, I believe that the vast majority of the money that is plundered from my paycheck is theft, but I don't believe that taxes used to fund legitimate (Constitutional) government activities constitutes theft.

While it would be nice if government could be funded by donations, I am doubtful that it would be sufficient to fund a government able to protect individuals and their property. Even if it were possible to fund government through donations, there would still be the problem of free-riders benefitting at the expense of others.

One final time, I wrote:

Hi, J.P. —

Surely you won't deny that feeding my family is one of my "legitimate functions."

Send me your home address, and I'll stop by shortly to borrow your ATM card and access code number.

Don't worry — I'll only take out of your bank account the amount that I need to supplement my "legitimate functions" as a breadwinner ... each week.

If I don't have a right to arrange said transaction at gunpoint — because it's "theft" — then how can I delegate to a group of men we call "government" the right to do something that I, myself, have no right to do?

And if no individual citizens can "delegate" such a right to government, because they do not *have* such a right in the first place, where do we suppose "government" gets the power to leech from our paychecks (without asking our deniable permission) those sums to which it alone decides it has a "legitimate right?" Does our government have some powers that are not delegated to it by the people? Where did it get those powers?

Or am I free to withhold all "requested" tax payments,

other than those that I decide are for "legitimate purposes?" Please explain how that would work, without resulting in the levying of my bank account and paychecks and the seizure of my car by armed men, charged to arrest or shoot me should I resist.

It's an endless circle, this pretense that "It's not theft as long as they take it from unwilling victims to fund something really *important*.

Yes, there is a doctrine of law that — whereas it would usually be a crime to untie someone else's boat and row it across the lake without his permission — I may be forgiven if it was the only way I could race a snakebite victim to the hospital.

But no, you may not extend this principle to the federal government systematically lining up every taxpayer in the land, every year, and shaking them down for the money necessary to fund the bee and mohair subsidies and the National Endowment for the Arts.

Minarchism verges on anarchism, and can certainly look like anarchy to those who have been living in slavery too long. I acknowledge the need for a minimal system of courts, where property rights can be defended, contracts enforced, and so forth. Is it impossible to fund such a system through voluntary subscriptions, premiums, and fee structures? How can we know until we try? Certainly many civil arbitration systems do indeed survive by such fees and assessments, mutually agreed upon, right now.

But the real source of trouble here is: "While it would be nice if government could be funded by donations, I am doubtful that it would be sufficient to fund a government able to protect individuals and their property."

Similarly, "While it would be nice if a large enough army to defend democracy could be raised through accepting volunteers, I am doubtful that it would be sufficient without the aid of conscription."

And, "While it would be nice if we could depend on the common sense and decency of the populace to remain sober enough to safely staff the factories and raise the children, I am doubtful that it would be sufficient without the threat of jailing anyone found consuming opium without a prescription."

How far, then, to: "While it would be nice if an armed populace could be trusted to maintain a peaceful and civil environment, I am doubtful that it would be sufficient without armed government SWAT teams authorized to break into private homes with blank search warrants, seizing all private weapons and killing anyone who resists such a seizure ..."

And, "While it would be nice if we could depend on enough people volunteering for vital defense work, I am doubtful that it would be sufficient without some central-government commissariat assigning and delivering boxcar loads of workers in striped uniforms to the industries where they are most needed. ..."

Once we accept the use of force for any purpose that government deems "legitimate," with said legitimacy to be decided by a majority vote of any given group of political functionaries ... or even by a majority vote of the whipped-up mob as a whole ... where do we think it will end?

The Russians found out in the 1930s. The Germans found out in the 1940s. The Chinese found out in the 1950s. The Cambodians found out in the 1970s. And it appears we are about to find out, too.

If people won't voluntarily pay for enough "government" to protect the innocent and to help enforce property rights, then they shall not *have* enough government to perform those functions. The alternative — "forcing them to pay us to keep them good" — will fail, with all the good and noble functions of government being torn down and thrown on the pyre along with the evil. In Paris from 1789 to 1793, did the mob carefully discern and preserve the king's "good works"? Did they spare the tax collectors who had only collected enough to fund "legitimate functions"?

Having seen what it is to live without that much government — after the systematic hunting down and mass execution of tens of thousands of past and current government employees, deserving and otherwise — the people can then be expected to voluntarily gather together and re-establish such minimal functions, and delegate to a few men the power to carry them out, voluntarily subscribing to pay their salaries and costs. Then ... for a time ... we shall again have a constitutional Republic.

Blood will be shed in the process. Jefferson warned us that we must be willing to pay this price if we are to have freedom. I am willing to shed my blood — to give my life — if it means my family can again live in freedom. How many others will?

One need not *favor* anarchy to predict that anarchy is the inevitable result of the current relentless growth of faceless tyranny. Though, mind you, if I be branded an "anarchist" I won't lose an hour's sleep. What government irrationally fears, it inevitably creates. As one harmless militia leader after another is framed by government *agents provocateurs*, railroaded, and imprisoned for decades, does anyone believe the public — particularly in the West and South — will become *less* restive, *less* prone to acts of defiance and rebellion, *more* docile in their "voluntary compliance"?

Let the most skilled lawyer or pedagogue stand before the rising tide and try to convince the ocean by clever definitions, rationales, and syllogisms not to wet his knees, not to finally rise to his waist and knock him from his feet.

The tides of history will decide who has been a "thief" ... and from that judgment there will be no appeal.

Senator Harry Reid Gets Right Down to Work

Was someone just discussing "the use of taxes to fund legitimate government activities"?

Today's lesson in the kind of pared-down tight-fisted federal government now being starved into shape by the mean penny-pinching Republicans — with, let's be fair, plenty of help from the moderate "new Democrats," a far cry from those "big-spending liberal Democrats" of olden times — comes to us from the Harry Reid Center for Environmental Studies at the University of Nevada, Las Vegas.

(Why this playground for those who would use government money to engineer more restrictions on our property rights is named for a living politician will become clear in the course of today's discussion.)

Anyway, at UNLV, bureaucrat Donald Baepler had a dream.

Mr. Baepler, one of the environmental center's poobahs, thought it would be grand if the center had one of those fancy DNA analyzers we see the FBI using to identify suspects and orphans on prime-time TV.

But there were a couple of problems. First, the machine costs $200,000, and another $100,000 would be required just to pay someone to operate it. Then, strictly speaking, the machine is of no use whatsoever in pursuing the goals of the federal Department of Energy, the outfit from which Mr. Baepler chose to seek his latest hand-out.

Research grants from the DOE are supposed to "support our nation's energy security, national security, [and] environmental quality." But the best Mr. Baepler, an ornithologist, can do is to claim the DNA analyzer will help "enhance our ability to understand avian species, distribution, migratory routes, and wintering areas."

He wants the machine to study birds, you see. That's what

ornithologists do. And nowhere in the charter of the federal Department of Energy does it say anything about studying birds. Nuclear power, sure. Solar power, fine. Even oil shale. But one thing on which DOE fans and opponents can agree? No birds.

Furthermore, not only was Mr. Baepler's dream not a very good fit to the purposes for which Congress supposedly funds the DOE, but the proposal itself is "gobbledygook," according to Larry Paulson, a limnologist who worked at UNLV's research center from 1985 to 1989.

"Anyone could sit down and write that in 15 seconds," Paulson told a reporter for the *Las Vegas Review-Journal* the week the grant was announced. "It's vague, nebulous, and so, too, will be the results.

"In terms of advancing science, I don't think we want to operate in this direction," added Paulson, who left the center after a falling out with Baepler. "We really need to get back to a rigorous competitive research process. We need more accountability from a scientific and an economic standpoint."

Well, don't expect it from the Harry Reid Center for Environmental Studies. David Thomassen, a program coordinator for the DOE's office of biological and environmental research, admits if the $300,000 grant request had come through regular channels "we would have sent it back and said it was not relevant to our mission. We don't do bird research. ..."

But bureaucrat Baepler didn't go through regular channels. He knew better than that. Instead, he went directly to the center's namesake, U.S. Sen. Harry Reid, for his porkbarrel grant — the way smart operators in Elizabethan England knew enough to name their theater troupes for some patron well-connected at court, constantly flattering his lordship in order to keep the subsidies flowing.

The senator interceded, and in the autumn of 1998 the DOE duly issued the bird grant under the category of "congressional earmarks" — a Washington code word for pork barrel spending.

Should anyone be surprised? Senator Reid had just won a close re-election race by vowing to be the guy who could continue bringing home that bacon for Nevada. A few too many Nevadans (about 200) voted for him, and this is what we get.

So the next time you open your paycheck and wonder at how much the government takes and how little is left for you and your family, don't fool yourself that the federal government "needs" all that loot to maintain the courthouses and the post roads and to mint the coin of the realm.

Nope — it's going to provide bureaucrat Baepler with the nicest shiniest new $200,000 machine he could possibly ask for, for his vital bird-migration research ... and to a hundred other projects just as vital, as Sen. Reid repays this favor by voting in turn for budgets featuring hogpen redesign projects in Arkansas, endive inquiries in Massachusetts, mollusk research at the Claiborne Pell Center for Quahog Studies ...

Senator Reid Fears We'd Only "Squander" Proposed Bush Tax Cut

〰

One thinks of some bizarre old horror film, in which the aging animal-trainer cannot imagine giving up either his furry friends or the little act that has supported him through the years (delighting young and old alike). So he insists on going through the motions of setting up his little horns and balls and flaming hoops, at which point (to the sound of pre-recorded drum roll and fanfare) he brings out and begins issuing loud and cheerful commands — the crowd first murmuring and then recoiling in dawning awareness and escalating horror — to the stiff embalmed remains of his long-dead animal friends.

Speaking before about 1,000 municipal officials gathered from around the country at the Washington Hilton Hotel on

March 12, 2001, U.S. Sen. Harry Reid, D-Nev., tried to re-stage the old Democratic dog-and-pony show about the evils of tax cuts, asserting, "To take all this money that we have in the way of surpluses and squander it on the tax cut is really the wrong way to go. ... Don't you think it's a better idea to spend that money on our water systems and sewer systems than to give Bill Gates a bigger tax break?"

Senator Reid's remarks reportedly drew applause "from sections of the audience" — a group well chosen to appreciate promises of renewed federal largesse — as he added promises of more federal aid to repair derelict schools, roads, and bridges.

But the dogs are still dead, and one feels increasingly embarrassed for aging redistributionists like Sen. Reid as they try to prop them up in their tattered pastel tutus and shove them through the hoops one more time, bowing to draw that increasingly reluctant little scattering of applause.

One is put in mind of the hypothetical "ideal Democratic plan" to compensate the fans of a rained-out baseball game — fortuitously e-mailed to me recently by Connecticut Republican legislative staffer Mark Anderson:

"The team was about to send out refunds when the Democrats stopped them and suggested they send out refund amounts based on the Democratic interpretation of fairness. After all, if the refunds were made equally to the people who paid for the tickets, most of the money would go to the top 2 percent who bought the most expensive seats. The Democrat's Plan:

"— People in the $10 seats will get back $15, because they have less money to spend.

"— People in the $15 seats will get back $15, because that's only fair.

"— People in the $25 seats will get back $1, because they already make a lot of money.

"— People in the $50 luxury seats will have to pay another $15, because they have so much to spend.

"— And the people driving by the stadium will get $10

each, even though they didn't pay anything in, because they must need the most help."

In America, such taxes as are necessary are supposed to be capitized equally among the citizens. The doctrine that more should be assessed from those who have worked hard and gathered together enough capital to set up a business and create jobs, "from each according to his ability," belongs to quite a different school of economics, Senator Reid, one that's spread poverty and desolation across half the globe in the past 80 years.

Senator Reid believes that if the Nevadans — all the Americans — who work so hard to earn their pay are allowed to *keep* a little more of those earnings, we will "squander" them ... who knows, probably on such frivolities as groceries, children's clothing, housing, and utility bills.

But let Sen. Reid keep his hands on that loot, and he'll put it to much better use — on such projects as (here I cite the spending items for which Sen. Reid was "honored" in the latest annual pork report of the Citizens Against Government Waste) a $2 million UNLV study of remote airport check-in sites and another $36 million in dubious and unsolicited "energy project" grants to both of Nevada's major state universities.

Every six years, big-spending Washington Democrat Harry Reid kisses his buddies Chuck Schumer and Dianne Feinstein and Ted Kennedy on the cheeks, pulls on a plaid shirt and a pair of blue jeans, travels back to Nevada, and has himself photographed sitting on a hay bale telling us he's a conservative Nevadan. In fact, if he and his tax-and-spend brethren had their way, they'd be taking more than *half* our income, rather than leaving us even as much as we're now busy ... in their view ... "squandering."

And He's Taxing the Stairway to Heaven ...

〽

State and local governments are rolling in money these days. The combination of a booming economy and confiscatory tax rates have combined to saddle governments everywhere with the kind of problem politicians love — finding ever more black holes into which they can shovel the embarrassing surpluses that otherwise keep piling up in excess of inflation and population growth, combined. (See *The Government Racket* by Martin L. Gross, Bantam Books; and *Adventures in Porkland* by Brian Kelly, Villard Books.)

In this context, one wonders why the taxmen would continue to seek out new things to tax. But in the end, that's like asking why the scorpion stung the frog — it was just in his nature.

When Popeye the Sailorman came ashore at Sweethaven, he wanted to ask a question about all the port and docking fees he was being required to pay. The response was that he was welcome to ask his question — as soon as he paid the question tax.

The year 2001 Sweethaven Award must surely go to Los Angeles County Assessor Rick Auerbach, who was shocked — shocked! — to learn that Hughes Electronics of El Segundo, Calif., owns hundreds of millions of dollars worth of property on which it's not paying the county any property tax.

"Reaching 22,300 miles above the equator," reported staff writer Nancy Vogel of the *Los Angeles Times*, "boldly going where no tax collector has gone before ... Auerbach is angling to impose property taxes on several satellites.

"Though never done before in California, the move is legal, say state and county tax attorneys. That's because, they say, nobody else is taxing the satellites. ..."

One might want to take a moment to savor that logic. If

it's legal and appropriate to tax something just because no one else is taxing it, does that mean it's OK to steal a car from a dealership as long as no one else has bought it yet? To rape a woman as long as she's a virgin?

The eight satellites, launched from either Cape Canaveral or French Guyana, serve a multitude of functions, from beaming HBO movies into American homes to speeding up credit-card processing for motorists who pay at unmanned gas pumps. And they "could bring in millions of dollars a year in taxes to schools and government," the *Times* goes on.

Fortunately, it appears the aerospace giant may not take this lying down. Brian Paperny, Hughes vice president of taxes (another moment of silence, please, in sober contemplation of the fact that such a post is now necessary), described the company's executives as "very concerned with the concept of a tax being assessed on a stationary object 22,300 miles away from the Earth, which is residing in a fixed parking slot ... over the equator, far far away from Los Angeles County and the borders of California."

Auerbach responds that satellites are no different from other movable personal property that he has authority to tax — like boats, construction equipment, and ice-skating costumes.

(Yes, in a 1976 case, a judge determined that the property of the Los Angeles-based Ice Capades could indeed be taxed by Los Angeles County, even though it spent most of the year "on the road," as it were.)

"The property in question here is geostationary," protests Larry Hoenig, a San Francisco attorney representing Hughes Electronics. "Geostationary satellites sit above the equator in a fixed position; they do not rotate around the Earth. So the satellites we're talking about here are not movable property."

A somewhat dangerous distinction, surely. Shall counties begin to tax aircraft as they fly overhead? Might they even collect liquor taxes on cocktails poured at 30,000 feet?

For that matter, don't a number of churches still preach

that by doing good deeds, their parishioners are piling up "treasure in heaven"? Whether or not said treasure is technically located in this "heaven" place, couldn't it still be said to fall under the "ownership and control" of the local churchgoers?

There are precedents for "presumptive assessments," when property is not conveniently available for inspection. (Surely no one expects Mr. Auerbach to have access to the locale in question.) Couldn't Mr. Auerbach thus set a presumed value on all that loot, giving parishioners 30 days to show cause why their "treasure in heaven" is worth less than estimated? Doesn't he, in fact, have a fiduciary *duty* to do so?

Mr. Auerbach insists he's duty bound to tax the satellites. "I've read the opinions," he said, "and it's pretty clear in my mind that it's taxable."

He does admit one likely outcome, however: "I do believe this will eventually end up in the courts."

Ah, yes. The "lawyer tax."

The Ballad of Carl Drega

III
The War for the Western Lands

Second only to the problem of the government schools (though directly linked to those youth indoctrination camps, since that's precisely where the problem starts), tackling the real agenda of the modern "environmental movement" presents the greatest challenge to anyone hoping to defeat years of indoctrination fed into the minds of virtually any American under the age of 40 ... during precisely his or her most tender and impressionable years.

Just check out the look of amazement on the face of any such youngster once they actually figure out you're not joking — you actually expect them to believe the modern green extremist operates from a sinister set of premises; is dead wrong; has rejected the idea that we should take joy and pride in the achievements of mankind and with it (whether consciously or otherwise) virtually all the other Judeo-Christian values that have made our civilization great and free; is out to destroy our civilization and throw mankind back to an era with no dental care, no washing machines, no clean underwear, and a life expectancy of 40.

In the experience of your young listeners, the only person they will ever have heard say such things is the evil factory owner swirling his black cape in the "Green Rangers" Saturday morning TV show, twirling his handlebar mustache and plotting to dump toxic pollutants in the nearest river just for the fun of it.

The forces of darkness have arranged a nice little Catch-22 for us here ... and it's the same one you'll confront when you set out to demonstrate that the government schools — indispensable reproductive organ of the socialist state — need to be closed and done away with if there's ever to be a rebirth of freedom and free thinking, of self-sufficiency and self-confidence, in this land.

Fail to offer enough specifics and you'll be laughed off (in the one case) as an anti-social kook who hates children, hates learning, and is merely too greedy to pay your "fair share" of the school taxes now that you've got *your* precious fancy-pants education, or (in the second case) as a depraved lunatic who hates clean air and clean water, and has doubtless sold his soul to some ghoulish flesh-eating corporate master, agreeing to shill for one form of pollution or another (allowing your own children to writhe and die as they waste away from one form or another of chemical or radioactive rot) in exchange for your filthy 30 pieces of silver.

(Did I mention the greens are, inevitably, also anti-capitalist, attempting to paint any opponent with the broad brush of "greed," always juxtaposed against their own purported altruism? Since capitalism is the only economic system under which energy and innovation and bettering the living standard of your fellow men are justly rewarded, this is hardly a coincidence.)

On the other hand, start to pile up specific case histories in which children are dumbed down and made worse off in a hundred ways by the institution of state schooling — or in which the lives of honest and hard-working American miners, ranchers, and lumbermen are ruined by the bizarre legislative enactments of the eco-freaks, and you will hear (over and over again, to the point of nausea):

"OK, we can all agree the schools (the environmental management bureaucracy) can make mistakes. There's always going to be room for improvement and reform in any enterprise this large. But won't you help try to build our children up (save the last remaining green places), rather than just stand there as a heckler, a cynical, negative, and destructive force? After all, the problems you've shown us here are just an example of one single bureaucrat being a little overzealous in the pursuit of her duty. I'm sure she would have done better if they'd only given her more money and staff to work with. Yes, it's too bad this one child's brain was rotted away on Ritalin (hard-working rancher had to sell out, move to town, and die of alcoholism), but why can't you look at the *big* picture?"

OK: here's the "big picture":

They have changed the meaning of "pollution," and we need to call them on it.

Although there's good evidence that the free-market economy (and the vitally necessary wealth and heightened social expectations it alone can produce) had already made great strides toward cleaning up the North American environment before any government "environmental-protection agencies" got started in the 1960s, 40 years ago there was, at least, a sensible consensus as to the goal at hand:

The skies over the mill towns of Ohio and southern Michigan and western Pennsylvania were sometimes so orange and brown with coal smoke you couldn't make out the noonday sun. Rivers that flowed past chemical plants or pulp mills were dyed bright primary colors by the raw pollutants poured forth into them, with fast-vanishing fish populations floating belly up even miles downstream.

The rivers that were spared this industrial pollution often served as the default over-capacity outflows for old-fashioned inadequate municipal sewage-treatment facilities, so that after a heavy rain people dared not swim or boat in these waters, where human turds could be seen floating by in vast numbers.

The job at hand was clear: The crises of the Second World War and Korean War were past — time to turn our attention to cleaning up the air and waters so as to make them again usable and enjoyable to the (increasingly affluent) outdoorsman, boating enthusiast, fisherman, and swimmer.

And guess what? In a remarkable couple of decades, we did it. Salmon now run again in waters where that seemed an impossible dream a mere 40 years ago. That job is essentially done, and *has* been done for more than a decade.

We wiped out pollution.

So, when was the victory party? Are the federal EPA and her various sister agencies winding down, phasing out, reducing their strength to a kind of "caretaker" status?

You must be joking. Like any government bureaucracy, they just continue to grow and grow and grow.

Which could present a problem, of course. With their original mission accomplished, what should they now *do*?

The answer was fiendishly simple.

Just as "anti-discrimination" agencies with no more segregated lunch counters to integrate now busy themselves fining newspaper publishers who accept real estate ads for houses with "fine city views" because that wording discriminates against blind home-buyers (no, I'm not making that up, a reader sent me the case history from Pittsburgh) — just as "anti-poverty" agencies just keep "re-norming" the poverty standards to convince themselves that single moms living in homes with carpets and color TVs and hot and cold running water and driving cars with automatic transmissions and talking on cell phones need "public assistance" so they won't have to debase themselves by actually, you know, *marrying* the fathers of their children — so the "environmental" storm troopers just shifted their mission ever so slightly ...

By redefining the definition of "pollution."

We used to clean up pollution to make the land and air and water more enjoyable and easier to use *by* people.

Now, pollution *is* people ... and there ain't much chance of our running out of them.

What is the real agenda of "endangered species preservation," when the green bureaucrats will frankly admit, off the record, that they can go into any ecosystem and identify a population of some plant or animal that's endangered or threatened *within* that ecosystem?

Why, to drive away mankind and to bar his use of the

land, since man is an interloper, a "polluter" of all that's right and pure in nature, of course.

What is the agenda of "wilderness preservation?"

Why, to bar *people* from ever vaster swatches of acreage, since mankind is not a natural creature, but rather a hostile, foreign, and alien force upon the land, a destructive and polluting influence that must be driven away if the Earth is ever to be healed from his frightful assaults upon her dignity and her chastity, ever to return to her pristine beauty in a state of nature.

Not to clean up the Earth in order to make it more useful and enjoyable to man, any longer, but (like that depraved satellite in the first *Star Trek* movie) to clean mankind *off* the Earth, since mankind *is* pollution.

I will leave it to others to debate whether this bizarre cult of self-hate is a psychological aberration; a plot by the otherwise discredited Marxists (Lew Rockwell refers to the commerce-hating green extremists as "watermelons" — green on the outside and red on the inside); or something even more difficult for those who reject a literal interpretation of biblical teachings to accept ... though our more observant religious brethren may have less trouble identifying for us a force abroad upon the land that seeks to gain control of men's minds, twisting them to believe that mankind — far from being a creature cast in God's image — is a dirty shameful race whose works are despicable in the eyes of the heavenly host — that our only proper fate is to be ground down into the mire for our sins of aspiration and presumption.

Whatever their motivations (conscious or otherwise), if you doubt this is what the cynical federals are up to, let me narrow down the beam and share with you a few stories of what they've been doing in the West, of late. Just look through this little eyepiece right here ...

April 24, 1994 — So Happy Together
☙

Armchair environmentalists who go to bed confident the 20-year-old Endangered Species Act is hard at work, efficiently protecting the last few grizzlies in Montana or the last flight of bald eagles in New Mexico, should probably count themselves lucky that they weren't in Las Vegas to witness the Desert Tortoise Affair of the 1990s.

Clark County, Nevada, and the desert tortoise have been cited more than once — by former Interior Secretary Bruce Babbitt, for one — as an example of how a peaceful compromise can be worked out between development and preservation interests, defusing potentially explosive conflicts. Back during the Clinton administration, Babbitt said he would like other preservation conflicts resolved on the model of Clark County's.

Heaven help us.

Clark County's struggle started in 1989, when the U.S. Fish and Wildlife Service unexpectedly exercised its powers under the Endangered Species Act to list the Mojave Desert Tortoise as an endangered species, based on studies showing population densities of the creature had dropped precipitously since the 1950s. The agency followed that initial designation in 1990 with a final designation of the tortoise as "threatened."

The government decided that 200,000 tortoises had to be preserved on 6.2 million acres (roughly 10,000 square miles) in four states, to assure the species' survival. Cattlemen, protesting that there was no evidence cattle grazing reduced tortoise populations and thus outraged at proposals that their grazing rights be restricted even outside the 6-million-acre set-aside, asked why as few as 2,000 tortoises weren't sufficient, accusing government biologists of picking the 200,000 figure out of thin air. Which was pretty much true, though preservationists prefer to refer to this as "erring on the side of caution."

The problem was that the government faced more than

the usual sparse population of ranchers this time around. Las Vegas, with a population approaching one million, was then and is still the fastest growing city in America. And almost all that growth involves development of previously untouched desert scrub lands — habitat of the tortoise.

Stopping the city's growth overnight would have been economically devastating and politically insupportable. So the FWS bought into a compromise: 22,000 acres of tortoise habitat in and around Las Vegas would be okayed for further development, providing developers ponied up $250 to $550 an acre for a fund earmarked for tortoise preservation. Those funds — totaling more than $10 million to date — would be used by Clark County to buy grazing rights on federal land, or to purchase private land outright, to make up a 400,000-acre turtle sanctuary to the south.

No one was sure whether cattle grazing put tortoises at risk, so cattle grazing was banned on the 400,000 acres just to be safe, along with off-road vehicle use. Harsh fines were imposed on anyone molesting or even touching a tortoise: Urban homo sapiens who crossed paths with one of the shelled creatures were required to turn over the beast to county authorities, who shelled out $52,000 to build special pens to house up to 40 turtles while waiting to turn them over to zoos, restore them to the wild, or whatever.

Up to 40 turtles.

Skeptics pointed out at the time no one was sure exactly how many Mojave desert tortoises there are, even assuming there was a distinct "Mojave Desert Tortoise," any more than Oregon harbors a separate species designated the "Northern Spotted Owl." (There isn't, and it doesn't.)

In fact, there are plenty of spotted owls in America, just as there are plenty of desert tortoises. All the designations really mean are "Spotted Owls that live north of California" and "Desert Tortoises that live in the Mojave." What the casual weekend environmentalist doesn't realize is that Green activists now identify "subspecies" at the drop of a hat, interpreting the law to mean that not merely the species, but the species in each of its individual *habitats*, must be protected.

There may be 50 million pigeons in New York. But if two lonely nesting pairs are found to have blown off course and taken up residence in the New Jersey Pine Barrens, the law allows — even encourages — those opposed to development of the planned Pine Barrens Multiplex Cinema and Warehouse Food Mart to seek official listing of the "Threatened New Jersey Rock Dove," a biological treasure whose chromosomes, hushed congressional hearing rooms will be assured, may hide the secret of the cure to cancer.

The Wildlife Federation folks pretty much admit this. The species singled out for preservation are mere "markers," used to protect entire ecosystems from human interference, in an oddly blindered version of the science of ecology that manages to see a world in which humans have no place at all, while adopting the positively weird notion that we are both capable and duty-bound to halt the endless parade of extinctions and new-species evolution that has been underway since long before mankind came upon the scene, all to show our "respect for nature."

Anyway, no one had an accurate count, or even a good estimate, of how many "threatened" tortoises were really out there in the Mojave. So the Clark County staff's plans to handle up to 40 orphan tortoises seemed as good a guess as any. After all, there turned out to be only 16 California condors left in the wild by the time preservation efforts were begun on their behalf. And the tortoise was "threatened," wasn't it? The federal government said so.

Two years after the plan was adopted, on March 28, 1994, the Clark County manager reported to the county commissioners on how many tortoises had been rescued and turned in.

Eight? 16? 32?

As of that date, 946 tortoises had been turned in. Museums took exactly zero: Turns out that anyplace with a suitable climate already has tortoises coming out its ears. Sixty were placed in research programs, 387 were allowed to be adopted by private parties (imagine placing grizzlies or bald eagles for "adoption"), and 175 were reported to have "died or been euthanized because of injury or illness," often as minor as a runny nose.

County facilities are currently overstrained with 296 captive turtles, which the keepers are afraid to release into the wild lest they carry a contagious respiratory infection back to their wild brethren. The market for adoptions seemed to be pretty well saturated, and another predictable problem now arose: The 296 captive animals were breeding quite happily, and "can be expected to produce progeny numbering over 100 each year," in addition to the new rescue cases coming in daily, County Manager Donald Shalmy warned the County Commission in his March 1994 report.

Since desert tortoises live at least 50 years, the county staff at that point predicted they could end up housing 8,000 to 10,000 turtles over the next 20 years, at a cost of $6 million to $9 million.

And those are just the ones that wandered in. No one has yet extrapolated how many that leaves out there in the wild, though figures in the high six digits don't seem unreasonable.

The staff further estimated it would cost $745 *per* turtle to relocate the healthy specimens back into the wild, leading the *Las Vegas Review-Journal* to quip that they must be planning to fly the reptiles to Paris on the Concorde.

The county staff's solution? Since preservationists already consider the turned-in tortoises to be "lost" from the wild population, anyway, they want permission to "euthanize" their captive tortoises. Put them to sleep. Send them to turtle heaven.

"Tortoise: Kill It to Save It?" cried the headline in the afternoon *Las Vegas Sun* March 30.

"Only government could concoct a scheme to collect

millions of dollars to save a species by killing it," Clark County Commissioner Don Schlesinger, who was running for re-election, responded on March 29. "I feel like letting them loose and telling them 'Run for your lives!'"

Where on Earth were all these turtles coming from?

● ● ●

Rancher Cliff Gardner of Ruby Valley has researched the question as well as anyone — better than the professional biologists who might have been expected to do so earlier, some would suggest — in a 40-page annotated report titled, "The Plight of the Desert Tortoise: A Surrogate for Social Change." Gardner traces the momentum to list the tortoise to a 1979 article by Dr. Kristin Berry in the *Nature Conservancy News* titled "Tortoise for Tomorrow." Berry interviewed Nevada old-timers who remembered thick populations of tortoises in Nevada valleys from the 1920s to 1950s — thicker numbers than they saw in the '70s.

But Gardner contends the turtle boom during the early years of this century was atypical, caused by government agents busily poisoning predators with strychnine baits dropped from airplanes as an aid to sheepmen who had been losing lambs to coyotes. The result was a drastic reduction in the populations of coyotes and ravens (which eat baby tortoises by the score), resulting in a population boom among the tortoises.

When the predator-control programs were curtailed or eliminated in 1972, the return of the coyote started to bring the tortoises back into balance, Gardner argues.

Gardner points out that there is practically no mention of these huge herds of tortoises in the journals of early explorers, who repeatedly remarked on how little edible game there was in the area, in part because the Paiutes ate every turtle they could find, after which they subsisted on a fairly miserable diet of grasses and seeds.

And far from harming the tortoises, Gardner cites impressive sources for his contention that cattle have merely replaced the buffalo that used to provide friendly turtle habitat by cropping the grasses to produce the new young sprouts required by the toothless tortoise.

Gardner cites government reports — and attaches signed affidavits from Vernon Bostic (who took a degree in Range Management from Colorado State University in 1935) and seven other desert old-timers — to support his contention that cow droppings crust over but stay moist inside for long periods even in the desert heat, and actually constitute a vital source of protein and stored water that desert tortoises ingest avidly throughout their range. The old-timers also insist the respiratory infection that so worries today's biologists has always been with the tortoises, and was commonly known in the old days as "white-eye."

Gardner quotes Bostic's recent thesis, *Ecology of the Desert Tortoise in Relation to Cattle Grazing*: "On the Nevada Test Site where cows have been excluded for many years, tortoises have a tough time making it every year. The greatest death loss in Nevada in 1981 (a severe drought year) was in a pasture (Crescent Valley Allotment) where cows had been excluded all year. On the adjoining Christmas Tree Pass allotment, which was grazed (by cattle) all year long, the tortoises were relatively unaffected by the severe drought. ... The reason is very simple: Cows provide tortoises with both food and drink."

So why did government scientists ban cattle grazing on the whole 10,000-square-mile tortoise preserve (Clark County's 400,000 acres is just a portion of the 6.2 million acres the federals covet for the purpose in four states)? Unless they intend to replace the cattle with enormous herds of indigenous buffalo and antelope to recreate conditions as they may have existed in the 18th century or before, shouldn't they have made a thorough study of the possible symbiosis between cattle and turtles before upsetting that existing balance? Isn't that what environmental science is all about?

Or is it about getting the cattle off the land regardless of whether they actually help or harm other animal life, based on the quasi-religious notion that cattle were brought by the white man and are therefore "bad"?

Bingo.

🌿 🌿 🌿

Since it never rains but it pours, Nevadans should have figured their environmental plate was due to grow even fuller at this point: Also on March 28, 1994, the U.S. Forest Service announced that a wildlife biologist surveying the Toiyabe National Forest for a planned timber harvest east of Lake Tahoe last July spotted the first-ever spotted owl in Nevada.

Biologists announced they would search 26,000 additional acres of Nevada forests for more spotted owls. No timber would be cut anywhere owls are sighted.

Why was the announcement delayed for eight months? For fear some irate logger would kill the owl, of course.

Such popular uprisings against the Act must be spreading. Congress was scheduled to convene hearings in April 1994 to consider reauthorizing the 1973 Endangered Species Act, but the *Washington Post* reported that March that a memo circulated to the heads of most major environmental groups by Erik D. Olson, staff member of the Natural Resources Defense Council, urged that reauthorization of the ESA be "taken off the table" that year, "apparently because congressional opponents are mounting a strong and popular campaign to weaken it." (In fact, it's been "off the table" ever since.)

"There is a feeling among enviros," reported Tom Kenworthy of the *Post*, "that the administration, while with them on many of these issues, is not in a position to help in this session given some of the distractions caused by other initiatives on health and welfare reform and the Whitewater tangle."

And, who knows, maybe even by loggers stalking the Toiyabe with guns in hand, and the tortoise-keepers of Clark County, up to their armpits in 296 "threatened" desert tortoises.

February 1, 1995
This is Clearly a Jurisdictional Case
🌾

Before he found his career in the army, young George Washington sought the esteem of his countrymen by paddling upstream on the James, drawing charts, and proposing the removal of obstacles to navigation.

These days, seizing on its constitutional authority to manage "navigable waterways," the federal government will declare any creek a "navigable waterway," the better to seize control of "national forests" under the guise of protecting the watershed of said rivers.

One of those forests is the Tonto National Forest, through which flow the headwaters of the Salt River northeast of Phoenix, Arizona.

That far upstream, the Salt is only "navigable" by whitewater rafters in rubber boats. Even then, in May 1993, two experienced California rafters, Richard Panich, 44, of Manhattan Beach, and Jerry Buckhold, 43, of Chico, tried the rose quartz ridge known as Quartzite Falls, where a massive undertow can suck logs, cows, even 16-foot boats to the bottom and hold them down for 30 seconds. Both men died.

That was enough for William "Taz" Stoner, a 34-year-old construction engineer from Mesa, Ariz., who earns a few thousands dollars each spring leading rafting trips down the Salt. He, fellow engineer Rich Scott, 39, and a group of six rafting friends legally purchased 145 pounds of commercial binary explosive and blew the 21-foot lip off Quartzite Falls.

"I did it to save lives ... to make it safer for the public to pass through there," Stoner explained to reporter Paul Dean of the *Los Angeles Times*, before his attorney told him to shut up. But despite the fact no one was endangered, and that Stoner's pro bono work only made the river more "navigable" — the crucial requirement for the feds to maintain even a tenuous authority there — the U.S. government tracked down Taz Stoner and the "Quartzite Eight" and, goaded by an outcry among eco-extremists, charged them with destruction of government property. Stoner pleaded guilty in December 1994 and faced a sentence of up to 18 months.

I asked Stoner's attorney, Charles McNulty, whether he looked into challenging federal ownership of the rock in question.

"The U.S. Code he was charged under ... Title 18 Section 844-F, ... deals with use, not just ownership," McNulty responded.

"So you can be guilty of destroying government property, even if the government is just 'using' the property?" I asked.

"If you'll read the statute you'll see it's clear he violated it," McNulty answered impatiently.

Angus MacIntosh of Safford, Ariz., is not a lawyer, but he did work for the federal government for 12 years, resigning from the U.S. Forest Service in disgust just last November [1994]. And Angus McIntosh, now head of the Arizona branch of the County Alliance to Restore the Economy and Environment (CAREE), disagrees with attorney McNulty.

"This is clearly a jurisdictional case," McIntosh says. "If they do not own the land, if they cannot prove ownership, then they cannot bring the case. That's an element of the crime. ...

"Where it happened was in the Tonto National Forest, and as it happens I just got back the response to an FOI request I sent in a couple of months ago (in a separate case) seeking titles to any land the federal government claims to own there, and any enactments of the state legislature authorizing them to buy the land. ...

"Their response was ... they don't have those documents, they don't have any enactments, they don't need to seek permission from the state legislature to buy land, and they didn't seek permission. Which isn't true, of course."

The U.S. Constitution clearly states the U.S. government may own land within the states only for such "necessary buildings" as post offices, naval yards, and the like, *after* the purchase of said lands is authorized by the state legislature.

The argument that lands now controlled by the federal government in the Western states really belong to the states is known as the "equal-footings doctrine," referring to the fact that new states enter the union on an equal footing with the original 13.

"There is a lawsuit in federal district court in Phoenix challenging the ownership of the Tonto Forest, called *U.S. vs. Haught*," McIntosh relates. "This is the first case where they've filed a response to a claim under the equal-footings doctrine. They usually drop them because they've received advice not to let it be tested in court, because they'd lose. But they've spent years trying to make an example of this elderly gentleman, and they knew he didn't have a lawyer, the brief he filed was a homemade kind of thing, so they must have figured this would be an easy place to score a win against the equal-footings doctrine."

But Carrel Haught didn't go unrepresented by counsel for long. Not only did CAREE take an interest in his refusal to file a "Mining Plan of Operations" on claims proved up by his father long ago, but MacIntosh reports noted attorney John Howard of the Los Angeles-based Individual Rights Foundation agreed to represent Haught in federal court.

So why on Earth wasn't William "Taz" Stone advised not to plead guilty until the federal claim to ownership of the Tonto could be resolved by the ongoing *U.S. vs. Haught*?

I don't know. Attorney McNulty answered all the rest of my questions with "No comment." And Taz Stoner has been advised by his attorney not to have any more conversations with the press.

Early in 1995, Taz Stoner failed to appear for sentencing. The last I heard, he was still listed as a fugitive. I hope he found a better life, in a freer land.

October 19, 1994
In the Canyons of Nevada,
the Men in Green Are on the Run
🌿

"Where this whole thing started was on the Smith River in northern California, when Congress passed the Six Rivers National Recreation Act in 1990," says Ed Presley, holding forth to a half-dozen rapt northern Nevadans seeking shelter from a freezing fog that's rolled up the canyon following the early October snow. It's snug enough, though, in the Toiyabe Cafe on a Saturday night in Austin, Nevada.

"I had claims on the Klamath River in Siskiyou County. I wasn't an owner of Bluewater Mining, but I knew the three guys who owned those claims, Gene Lilly and Bill Clark and John Malczewski. So when Congress passed the Six Rivers National Recreation Act, the Forest Service came in and told the miners they wanted them to prove up their claims, and in talking with them they said, 'What do we do about this?'

"I said, 'We're not going to do any operating plans for them or prove up for them. You've already filed these claims down at the county seat and that's all that's required.' We took in a tape recorder, that's the first time we did that, and we told Karen Jo Caldwell, the acting chief ranger, that they didn't have any jurisdiction over us. They wanted to know where we were going to dredge and we refused to tell them. So they said, 'In that case we're going to have to come down and write you a ticket,' and we said, 'If you do that, we'll sue you personally.'

"Well, Bluewater Mining had 57 claims, and they're the only ones still there, the feds badgered all the others out. They said, 'We want to know what those claims hold,' and we said, 'It's none of your damn business. We're not going to disclose our worth to you. The fact that we're willing to work them is enough to prove they have value.'"

Eventually, Presley says, "The acting district ranger, Karen Jo Caldwell, got so scared she wanted a transfer, and when she couldn't get one she left the Forest Service."

Gene Lilly, in Happy Camp, California, confirms Presley's recollection. "Caldwell left because she couldn't get the protection like she thought she could after she stepped beyond her written authority. There's been about a 97 percent reduction in mining claims in the Six Rivers area; the only ones who still have claims over there, besides ours, are the ones who listened to us. If you let them do a validity test then your claim is invalid. One guy showed $30,000 in gold and it was still declared invalid."

The Forest Service does this, Lilly explains, by holding that claims have to be valuable enough for each owner to make a $15-per-hour profit, an almost impossible standard for placer deposits, where gold concentrations vary widely from one underwater gravel bed to the next.

🌿 🌿 🌿

It was October 1994, and Presley was in Austin, a picturesque old mining town and Pony Express stop with an 1869 brick courthouse tucked among piney hillsides, for the second road opening of the year by county commissioners in Central Nevada. Dick Carver of the Nye County Commission opened the Jefferson Canyon Road with a Nye County bulldozer on the Fourth of July. On Oct. 15, braving intermittent snow and sleet, road crews from both Nye and Lander counties joined to fill in three enormous pits in the middle of the San Juan Canyon Road south of Austin. The pits had been dug two years back by the Forest Service to block traffic up the aspen-studded canyon, on a gravel road for which the patent was signed by President Ulysses S. Grant in 1874.

In each case, first in July and then in October, Forest Service personnel advised county officials not to re-open the roads through the National Forests. On Oct. 13, District Ranger Dayle Flanigan wrote the two county commissions, warning they could be "subject to criminal penalties" if they opened the San Juan Canyon Road, supposedly closed to protect "numerous archaeological and historic artifacts, ... as well as sensitive riparian vegetation and habitat."

But Flanigan was present when the operation started — as were about 90 local ranchers and several county deputies with orders to arrest any federal agents who interfered. No arrests took place.

"They left rather than confront me," said Carver, a bit of a twinkle in his eye. "I was going to ask them, 'Can you provide me proof of ownership of this land?' Which they wouldn't be able to do, of course, because what I'd want to see would be a deed recorded in the Nye County courthouse, and there isn't one."

Ray "Bubby" Williams, chairman of the Lander County Commission, started out operating the backhoe "until they got done taking pictures." Once the Forest Service shutterbugs left, the 90-odd locals in attendance started a bonfire and made a barbecue of it.

Why does he think Ranger Flanigan made no arrests, I asked Presley, a bearded tobacco-chewing Ohio native who now lives in Las Vegas and sports a Stetson Paloduro.

"We asked the Forest Service under the Freedom of Information Act if they had criminal jurisdiction in Nevada, and their lawyer said, 'No,' they don't. If the feds violate the law, they're stripped of their sovereign immunity, and they're common criminals. Does a Forest Service guy have sovereign immunity to go in wearing his uniform and rob a liquor store? You don't argue subject matter with these guys, you just ask do they have jurisdiction *here*. Why don't they go up to Canada and enforce their rules and protect the forests? Because they have no jurisdiction."

Under Article 1 Section 8 clause 17 of the U.S. Constitution, the federal government is granted exclusive criminal jurisdiction over the District of Columbia, territories like the Virgin Islands, and pieces of property specifically sold and deeded to the federal government by state legislatures for post offices, dockyards, and other "needful buildings." The key to the land-rights movement now sweeping the West is the conclusion that federal agents have criminal authority *only* in those places — that the feds can protect endangered species or "sensitive riparian habitat" to their hearts' content at the Washington Monument, or on Guam, or on the post office lawn, but that any claim they make to law-enforcement authority elsewhere within the several states is nothing but an enormous bluff.

🌿 🌿 🌿

I asked Presley, honcho of the Las Vegas-based County Alliance to Restore the Economy and Environment, if he thought Ranger Flanigan violated the law with his Oct. 13 letters, threatening the Nye and Lander County commissions with criminal penalties.

"I believe he has, under the delegation of power. He has no power to determine when a criminal violation has occurred."

Bubby Williams' wife, Jennifer, owns the Toiyabe, which is the best breakfast spot in Austin (competition at dinner time is stiffer, with Carol's Country Kitchen down the street having its adherents). Joining Presley for dinner at the cafe — the kind of place decorated with an oval mirror set in a horse collar and a sign that promises "Free Beer Tomorrow" — Bubby Williams explains that rural Nevadans feel the federal government has given them no choice but to start calling the bluff of federal "ownership" of 87 percent of Nevada.

"We've got a road to the municipal well" about 50 yards off the main highway, Bubby explains. "This year the Bureau of Land Management said they want $29 a month rent for that right-of-way. Well, we refused to pay. The BLM guy asked me, 'Why do that? It's going to cost you more in legal fees than that rent could ever add up to.' But the rent on the Austin airport used to be $20 a year," Williams explains, referring to the unmanned one-strip field built as a Navy auxiliary facility during the Second World War, "and this year when we got the bill, they'd reappraised it at 'fair market value,' and they wanted $15,000."

The locals aren't paying that, either.

"I went over to the Forest Service office Friday to ask Dwayne if they were going to have helicopters over there today when we opened the road, a SWAT team, a tank, or whatever, but it turned out Dwayne was down at the sheriff's office to deliver his letter to me," threatening criminal penalties, William recalls.

"It's hard on these guys. Their wives live here; they're active in the sororities. They're active in the LIONS and the gun clubs. Then this comes up and they get their orders and it puts a lot of stress on them. It doesn't bother *us*," says Bubby Williams.

November 30, 1994
A Few Rotting Shacks, Some Gravel,
and a Rust-Colored Streambed
ⵞ

Over the slow Thanksgiving 1994 weekend, a number of papers around the country ran a series out of the *Chicago Tribune*, expressing shock that some Westerners have been threatening violence against federal officials sent to enforce well-meaning "environmental regulations," while simultaneously pleading the case for "reform" of the "outdated" Mining Law of 1872.

"Less than three miles" from the border of Yellowstone National Park in Cooke City, Mont., the Chicago paper reports with thinly disguised horror, "fresh surveying stakes are evidence of plans by Noranda Minerals Inc. of Canada to renew digging for recently discovered deposits of gold, silver, and copper worth $600 million."

One might think this would be a cause for celebration — new wealth to be created out of previously worthless hillsides, creating many highly paid jobs in tiny Cooke City, today described as nothing but "a fly-by for tourists" dependent on taverns and ski rentals.

But, "Not so fast, say environmentalists," who "point at a rust-colored streambed, rotting shacks, and piles of gravel from abandoned mines on Henderson Mountain as illustrative of how federal property has been abused" in the past. "Despite the public stake, the U.S. government will charge the company only $130" for the 26 acres Noranda wishes to patent, the *Tribune* reports.

In a free country, of course, the only proper role of government is to facilitate the orderly establishment of private-property claims, and then to protect them. We give a different name to a system where everything belongs to the government, and private "exploitation" of such resources by "greedy capitalists" is criminal.

But so what if a few environmental extremists and the government agents who serve them pine for the political atmosphere of Leningrad in 1920? What can they really do to affect the ability of hard-working Americans to make a living?

Well, let's look at the case of one small town surrounded by a national forest near California's Oregon border — the optimistically named hamlet of Happy Camp.

Up through 1990, Happy Camp's 1,500 souls eked out a decent living through a combination of mining and logging. But with the passing of the Reagan era and the renewal of the federal regulatory buildup under Bush and Clinton, that began to change.

I detailed earlier how federal officials worked an organized scam to expel nearly all mining operations from the nearby Smith River system after Congress passed the Six Rivers National Recreation Act in 1990, setting such a high definition for "profitability" that hundreds of working claims were declared of "unproven" value and shut down.

Next came logging. In 1990, more than 90 percent of the lumber processed in the Happy Camp sawmill came from nearby public lands. By the spring of 1994, logging restrictions designed to "save" the spotted owl (which isn't endangered, and turns out to nest perfectly well in new-growth forest) had reduced the percentage of lumber reaching the Happy Camp mill from public lands to 4 percent.

But that wasn't the end of the "death of a thousand cuts" the Forest Service had planned for logging in the Klamath National Forest. Dale Andreasen, publisher of the *Siskiyou Daily News* in nearby Yreka, recalls that rent for an "easement" to allow logs to be hauled across one piece of Forest Service land in the Klamath increased over a short time to a prohibitive "market rate" of $15,000 per month.

The result was predictable. The Stone Forest lumber mill in Happy Camp closed this September, throwing 80 families out of work.

Today, the United States Forest Service is the biggest employer in town, followed by the county government. With both mining and lumbering effectively at an end, some families had nothing to fall back on but hopes of picking and selling matsutake or "tan oak" mushrooms, which grow wild in area forests in the fall. Jobbers arrive in the area in November to buy the mushrooms in volume and haul them back to San Francisco, where they command a considerable price.

So guess what? The Forest Service has now instituted a mushroom permit program, $10 per day with a five-day minimum, to take any more than one gallon of mushrooms "for personal use" — though local Indians are still free to pick and sell as many as they please.

I asked the folks at the Ranger Station in Happy Camp to send me a copy of the new mushroom regulations. They came with a little happy face drawn on the back of the envelope.

"Since money's real tight now, what the locals would have done is bought a five-day permit and picked enough to make some money to buy a permit for the rest of the month," explains local miner Gene Lilly. "But since it's first-come first-served, we're afraid the commercial pickers who move south with the harvest will show up the first day and buy up all the 30-day permits."

At last report, cold rains and early snow had snuffed the fall mushroom harvest, anyway. The laid-off mill workers have gone, the town's population now estimated at fewer than 1,000 souls, with most of the rental housing already empty or boarded up for the winter.

So, are the Forest Service men in green — and their state counterparts from California Fish & Game — finally done?

"The biggest story now," answers Sherryl Lilly, "is that the Highway Patrol, the Fish & Game people, and the Forest Service rangers are all pulling people over and ticketing them for out-of-state plates. The Fish & Game men are even writing the tickets on their Fish & Game ticket books, which is illegal.

They don't have any authority to enforce motor vehicle laws."

A pickup truck that costs $1,600 to register for two years in California can still be registered for just $32 across the line in Oregon, Mrs. Lilly explains, "and with money being so tight now, a lot of people are doing it."

Why on Earth would the federal rangers — and even California's own Fish & Game wardens — want to turn a hardworking town like Happy Camp into little more than "some rotting shacks and a rust-colored streambed"?

"They're not from around here," responds Gene Lilly. "You meet these people, and they're all longhairs. They look like the people you would have met in Berkeley 20 years ago."

The people of the West are being pushed to the limit. The surprise is not that they are finally talking about taking up arms to defend their way of life ... but that they have waited so long.

August 24, 1994
"I'd Like an Open Area on a Lake
With a View of the Mountains"
ℳ

In the East, lush rain enables a family to make a living on some multiple of the proverbial "40 acres of bottomland." So when Easterners thought up schemes to encourage the settling of the West, they thought in terms of allotments of 160 acres.

But you cannot graze enough animals to support a family on 160 acres in most of the arid West.

So, in the 19th century, a politically viable compromise was reached. While Western ranchers could only claim land in small allotments around creeks or springs, their need for thousands of acres of additional graze would be handled by granting them "grazing rights" on adjoining waterless — and therefore worthless — federal land.

Similar schemes allow those who found anything of use to file claim for the mining rights, or timber rights, or water rights, on a given piece of land. A complex mosaic of overlapping property rights was thus established, suited to lands that would never support 40-acre homesteads.

The compromise worked for a century. But now in the East arises a new form of Utopianism, which preaches that all lands (except those on which the Greens themselves live) should be returned to a state of nature, with every bug and weed held sacred. The Western rancher, miner, or logger, these acolytes now discover, has been "ripping us off" for years, paying token fees to "rape" the public land of its resources.

A clear example of this came when Interior Secretary Bruce Babbitt made a big show in May 1994 of protesting the fact that a Canadian mining company was being allowed to claim valuable gold reserves in central Nevada for "only $5 an acre" under the Mining Law of 1872. Billions in gold would thus be stolen by these dastardly foreigners, announced Babbitt as he held up an enormous dummy check, purporting to represent the "$410 billion" the law required him to "give away."

Unmentioned was the fact that the rock at the Goldstrike Mine holds such a low concentration of gold that no one could figure out how to mine it at a profit, at all, until Canadian-based American Barrick Resources (which actually bought the claim from another firm for $62 million in 1987) invested millions in new technology. And millions more must still be spent — money that will flow into Nevada for equipment and salaries — before any profit is realized.

Having heard Babbitt's posturing, Dick Swainbank of Fairbanks, Alaska, wrote a puckish letter to the secretary on June 10, 1994:

"There has been a great deal of publicity recently about the fact that the U.S. government is selling the rights to mining claims for only $5 an acre. ... Enclosed, please find a cheque in the amount of $5 for my purchase of mining land, preferably in Alaska. I would like an open area on a lake with a view of the mountains. If I have a choice, the claim should have gold, platinum, or scandium. ..."

Paul Politzer, chief of the Interior Department's Division of Solid Minerals, responded to Swainbank on July 8: "Thank you for your letter of June 10. ... As you know, the patenting of land under the Mining Law of 1872 is not as easy as simply writing a check. The Mining Law of 1872 provides a method of acquisition of federal land for the sole purpose of mining and producing minerals for the wealth of the Nation. ... For most individuals, the exploration process leading to the discovery of a valuable mineral deposit may cost several hundreds of thousands of dollars per claim for drilling and sampling expenses and that expenditure may lead to nothing if no minerals are found. ... We are returning your check and enclosing a brochure which describes the administration of the law by the BLM."

What? Secretary Babbitt certainly didn't mention any of that stuff. No, holding up a big fake check the size of a surfboard, he made it perfectly clear that greedy corporate interests could just claim all the best stuff for a mere $5 an acre.

The Mineral Resources Alliance, which lobbies for miners in Washington, was good enough to send me copies of Swainbank's correspondence. The admission that, "The patenting of land under the Mining Law of 1872 is not as easy as simply writing a check," illustrates "the deceptive nature of the public misinformation campaign being waged by Mr. Babbitt against the mining industry," the folks at the MRA conclude. Furthermore, the MRA notes, "While Mr. Babbitt downplays the economic contributions of the mining industry, his department has a greater appreciation for domestic mineral production as a key contributor to the 'wealth of the Nation'."

Here is the key, and it's a concept no longer explained in our government schools: The wealth of the nation does not consist of the holdings of the federal government. Since the federal government is a parasite, its holdings must properly be deducted from the tally of that wealth. The wealth of the nation consists of resources developed and held by the private citizens.

To propagandize that private entrepreneurs developing wealth where previously no one could see anything but worthless dirt are somehow "ripping off the nation" by taking what would better be retained by the government in the name of "all the people," even if it were therefore never put to any profitable use at all, is a theory that has a name, as out of fashion as it may be to pronounce it. This totally failed alternative to property rights is called ... "communism."

December 6, 1998
Forest Service Maneuvers to Further Limit Access to the Land
🌿

For decades, those heading west had few maps. They followed the wagon ruts of those who had gone before. It worked fine.

But the U.S. Forest Service doesn't like things that way. Much too undisciplined, you see. Did any bureaucrat *approve* all those roads?

The Forest Service seems particularly agitated these days over "ghost roads" — small trails usually left by all-terrain vehicles moving across the empty lands. Such man-made scars upon "their" land disturb and threaten wildlife, trample plants and grasses, and even pose a threat of flood and fires, the Spruce Troopers insist. (Never mind that such lightly used roads can actually show fire crews the best way to *get* to a fire.)

So, beginning in late 1998, the Forest Service undertook

to begin "erasing" thousands of miles of "ghost roads" (along with old logging roads and historic sheep-herding trails) in the Tonto National Forest in Arizona ... at an estimated cost of $1,500 to $2,500 per mile "erased," or more than $1 billion for the Tonto alone.

Do the Geese Police set forth with brooms to sweep the trails away? It's weirder than that, actually. In order to cut off members of the public — in whose behalf and at whose expense all this is undertaken — from their habitual and established uses of these lands (camping, shooting, rock collecting, whatever), the greenies propose to dig huge tank traps, pile immovable boulders and logs, or plant trees and cacti so as to block access to these pathways from the trailhead.

So much for "leaving things the way we found them."

And K.M. Larney of the Nevada Policy Research Institute reports Nevada's Toiyabe-Humboldt National Forest may well be next ... at a cost to taxpayers of another cool billion, in all likelihood.

Are they mad?

Well, there certainly is a question whether the de facto religion of environmentalism — which holds that the sanctity and quiet repose of sundry bugs and weeds takes precedence over the pursuits of mankind — is here being "established" in violation of the First Amendment.

But if there's madness here, there's also method in it.

In order to declare vast new tracts of land to be official "wilderness" — and thus effectively shut them off from any human use forever — the law requires that these simpering "stewards" demonstrate that areas to be walled off from the taxpayers contain no roads or human habitations.

Thus, when old miner and Indian cabins are quietly disassembled and removed and the ghost roads themselves made to "disappear" — what shall we conclude the Forest Service has in mind?

February 5, 1995
"Your Hearts Are Not Wrong,
There's Just Much Much More to Know"
🌾

Anyone who has ever ventured to express an opinion on overgrazing, the need to return Western range to its "pristine state," or the "cowboy welfare of below-market grazing fees," should run, not walk, to the nearest post office and send off $19.95 ($27.95 Canada, $39.95 other, in U.S. funds) to the Range Education Foundation, P.O. Box 639, Carson City, Nev. 89702-0639, for a year's subscription to a surprisingly attractive, readable, down-to-earth quarterly magazine called *Range*, and subtitled "Cowboy Caretakers on America's Outback."

That is, providing you can tolerate a few facts mixed in with your cherished environmental myths, superstition, and assumptions.

Where else would I have learned (as I did from the "Amazing Facts" column of the Summer 1994 edition) that the Canadian government managed to reduce forest reseeding costs to five cents per tree, while almost doubling tree-survival rates, when they switched from toxic herbicides for clearing underbrush to ... sheep?

Did you smile with satisfaction — picturing the return of rivers alive with fish — at the news that the Seattle office of the Sierra Club Legal Defense Fund had brought suit against the U.S. Forest Service, seeking to remove all 18,000 cattle now grazing on public lands in the headwaters of the Snake River in eastern Oregon?

Then you'll read with amazement Colorado writer Gavin Ehringer's personal tour of the lands in question in "An Oregon Fish Story" (Fall 1994), where it's revealed the permitees now move their cattle off their own private lands onto the Forest Service's higher summer range thousands of feet above the tributary creeks during the crucial summer months. Throw those cattle off the Forest Service allotments, as the environmentalists demand, and ranchers will be forced to hold them on their own lands — directly adjoining the creeks in question.

"Makes you wonder if they have the best interests of the salmon in mind," comments 43-year Wallowa Valley rancher Mac Birkmier.

But the stories I'm busiest Xeroxing and circulating these days are the Fall '94 essay by Christopher McKellar titled, "Confessions of a 55 mph Environmentalist," and a back-up essay in the same edition by Utah rancher and range consultant Steve Rich titled, "National Park Syndrome: Long-Term Rest in Climates Typical of Most of the Western U.S. is a Biological Disaster!"

Rich's data-filled essay makes the simple point that "resting" dry Western land doesn't return it to health ... it turns it into desert. Why? Because Western grasslands evolved in conjunction with hoofed grazing animals, whose cropping is necessary to remove dead growth and allow new grass to sprout, and whose hooves punch seeds into the dry crusted soil to allow re-seeding.

"Humankind has believed for centuries that rest would heal damaged land," Rich writes. "And it will, in Northern Europe, the eastern coastal areas of North America, and places like that. ... (But in) Utah, years of rest will only deepen the desert."

But why believe Rich? Instead, read the essay by Mr. McKellar, the principal violinist of the Utah Symphony by profession, and a dues-paying member of the Sierra Club, the Southern Utah Wilderness Alliance, the Grand Canyon Trust, and Ecology Action.

Driving past cattle on dusty windblown soil, he used to think, "If only they'd let the land rest, it would be covered in healthy, tall, soil-holding grass." Angry, McKellar says he used to "hope my environmental club dues would do something to stop the destruction."

But following a chance meeting with Steve Rich and a

two-day visit to Rich's family ranch, the Bar Z, McKellar is big enough to admit, "What I saw in those two days turned my world upside down.

"The green highway side of the fences where cattle had been excluded for 40 years turned out to be tumbleweeds covering, in many instances, the skeletons of widely spaced dead grass plants. Inside the fence I saw live, closely spaced native grass plants. ...

"I learned how grasses in dry climates gradually choke themselves off from the sunlight with their own previous years' growth. Such overrest produced the grass skeletons I'd seen on that first day. ... Hundreds of hours of observation and study have since confirmed everything I saw and that Steve so patiently showed me. ... This has led me to the inevitable conclusion that dry grass and shrub land needs hoofed grazers to plant the seeds, fertilize the plants, and make the growth points of the grass available to the sun. ...

"It makes sense: The herds and the grasslands grew up together. ... [But] we cannot just turn all the land back to the native herds [of bison, bighorn sheep, elk, and antelope], hoping for restoration. There are not enough herds left. ...

"We and our herds can fit in by doing the work of the missing wild herds. In order to maintain my integrity as an environmentalist, let alone a human being, I cannot say otherwise. Nor can I remain silent. ... I see ranchers in the position to be the actual guardians of the land."

If ranchers are forced out of business, McKellar warns, "Let's not kid ourselves into thinking that ... preservation groups will buy up all the private land involved. ... Developers will cover the places with ranchettes and condominiums, paved roads and fences. ...

"Environmentalists, please become wise enough to know that you can't tell much from a car window even at an environmentally sound 55 mph. Your hearts are not wrong, there's just much much more to know. ..."

January 14, 2001
The State-Established Religion
of Environmentalism
🌿

Bruce Wilkin is a Pioche native and 1958 Nevada high school graduate who came back to Ely to practice medicine in 1975.

Like many long-time Nevadans, Wilkin remembers when the game herds were thick on the land those animals shared with Nevada's cattlemen. He's seen the campaign by government regulators to move the cattle off the land (Clark County retains only two of what were once 50 ranching families — and the federals have been trying to run Cliven Bundy off his Mesquite allotment for eight years now) ... walling off human access to swatches of real estate the size of New England states under a brand of "environmental protection" that forbids cattle or sheep from grazing back the forage, which subsequently dries out and leads directly to our current wave of cataclysmic wildfires.

Furthermore, Bruce Wilkin the country doctor has done the studies and can show the graphs proving it's not cattle that are responsible for these bigger and more destructive wildfires or for the thinning of game species like the deer and the sage grouse.

Dr. Wilkin's graphs (based on the state's own data) show Nevada's deer herd was healthiest precisely when the most cattle were run on the range — from about 1948 to the early 1970s — and then dropped precipitously when the poisoning of coyotes was halted during the Nixon and Ford administrations.

Further, while government regulators claim ranchers and hunters are to blame for the thinning of the sage grouse, the good doctor hands me a copy of the 1990 study, which he says the Nevada Department of Wildlife has "buried" ... precisely because it shows the problem is not the cattle, but the end of programs to control the now-exploding populations of coyote, raven, and mountain lion.

The official October 1990 report, "Sage Grouse Production and Mortality Studies," prepared as the final report of the Federal Aid in Wildlife Restoration Project W-48-R-21, Study XVII, Job 1, edited by San J. Stiver and prepared by Don Klebenow, Gary Zunino, and others, demonstrated (by using chicken eggs to set up mock sage grouse nests near typical raven habitat) that the decline in sage grouse populations can be entirely attributed to raven predation of the nests.

"At the completion of the 15-day period, all 1,400 eggs were destroyed in both study areas," the report concluded. "On the Grassy Meadows Study Area in Surprise Valley, 84 percent of the nests were destroyed in the first three days. Ravens were believed to be the chief nest predator."

The 1990 study only confirmed earlier studies such as that of researcher Warren Allred, who found that in Wyoming in 1942, "Eighty percent of all sage grouse nests were being destroyed by predators — of which 23 percent were attributed to ravens and 14 percent to coyotes. It was found that even in areas completely protected from hunting, sage grouse were steadily declining."

In fact — here Dr. Wilkin agrees with such long-time Nevada ranchers as Cliven Bundy and Cliff Gardner — the journals of the first white men to cross Nevada found it so bereft of game the Indians were reduced to eating insects, while the travelers often considered eating their pack animals to make it through.

Thick herds of deer and flocks of game birds showed up only after ranchers moved in to improve the water features (clearing springs, building tanks and ponds); set their cattle to improving ground cover by cropping plants that evolved in an ecosystem dependent on large ungulates to clear room for new growth and to help the plants re-seed; and finally completed the equation by severely thinning out such predators as the coyote and the raven — all now "protected" by muddle-headed "environmentalists."

But because information like the Klebenow-Zunino report doesn't mesh with the current drive to force ranchers and hunters from the land in keeping with the new state-established religion of Environmentalism (which designates "untouched wilderness" as its cathedral), the 1990 study was "buried" by Willie Molini's state Department of Wildlife, Wilkin insists.

Over dinner at the Prospector restaurant in the Ely Holiday Inn, Wilkin — glancing occasionally at his pager in case he should be called back to the ER — hands me an invitation to the "Nevada Land Use Summit 2001," being put on by Assemblywoman Marcia de Braga and Sen. Dean Rhoads in Carson City Feb. 23 and 24, which intended to focus on the interrelated issues of noxious weeds, wildland fires, and Nevada's sagging sage grouse population.

Wilkin points out a section on page 2, underlined by the organizers: "There have been questions about distributing materials other than those provided by the 2001 Summit. We respectfully request [that] *no* outside materials be brought in by any individual or group for distribution."

This is so the state wildlife bureaucrats can make sure no one presents copies of studies — even *their own* studies — that contradict the current myths about hunters and ranchers, Dr. Wilkin says.

I called both Assemblywoman De Braga and Sen. Rhoads — both of whom are in the ranching business — to ask about that. Both denied it was their intention to ban any such relevant material.

I asked if Dr. Wilkin or Cliven Bundy or Cliff Gardner has been invited to address the meeting. Ms. De Braga said there "are no specific invitations, we're not going to have many actual speakers." (Actually, two hours are set aside Friday morning for a motivational talk by "renowned facilitator" Susan Carpenter, on the topic, "How to Get to Yes.") "But certainly anyone is welcome to attend."

Cliff Gardner says he has no intention of showing up where he's not wanted. "They don't want Cliff Gardner and his stuff; they don't want the truth. What do you suppose that 'no outside materials' rule is all about? I've got more scientific evidence about what's happened to the sage grouse than anyone else in this state, but do you think Cliff Gardner is welcome there? All it is is a PR event for the [Department of Wildlife] bureaucrats."

January 21, 2001
"Now They've Made It All 'Wilderness' and There's No Deer Left"
🌾

Joining me and Dr. Wilkin for our Friday dinner in Ely was Harry Pappas, who was appointed by former Congresswoman Barbara Vucanovich to the BLM Citizen Advisory Council and later represented the State Rifle & Pistol Association on the Clark County Tortoise Advisory Council. Harry chimed in with a few tales of the absurdities he's witnessed over the years.

"They told us the tortoises were threatened, so they had to fence off these huge areas and shut out all the cattle, which means no one is out there shooting the coyotes and the ravens or trapping the lions anymore, so of course that wrecked the hunting. They said anyone who found a tortoise had to turn it in.

"So what happens when people start turning in these 'threatened' tortoises? Hundreds of them start to come in, more than they had room for, so they told us they were going to start euthanizing them. I said, 'Hold on a minute, here. You told us they were threatened, and now you're going to euthanize them?

Why don't you just put them back out in the desert somewhere?'

"And they go, 'Oh no, we can't do that, because they'd fight and the little tortoises would kill each other. After all, the range is currently at saturation.'"

"'It's at saturation? First you tell us they're endangered, or threatened, or whatever, but now you're telling us there are so many tortoises out they're that the population on all these ranges is at *saturation*?'"

Harry recalls a wildlife biologist from California who, years earlier, spoke before the BLM's Citizen Advisory Council (on which Harry also served), bringing in "two huge plastic garbage bags full of baby tortoise shells — there had to be hundreds of them. Heck, he had thousands of them. And each and every one of these shells had a hole pecked through the top where the ravens had brought the baby tortoises back to their nests and pecked through the shell and eaten the baby tortoise right out of the shell, and he said they picked these up in middens around the raven nests, just thousands of them. It's the ravens and coyotes that kill the tortoises, and this guy had the proof.

"Well, he showed up once, and then we never saw or heard from that guy again."

In fact, when "desert tortoise preservation" became the main rationale for pushing most of southern Nevada's cattle ranchers off the land, Harry remembered the ranger from California with his bags of tortoise shells, and asked if he couldn't be brought back to address the Tortoise Advisory Council. "At that point they said they didn't know who I was talking about; they couldn't find him.

"I followed him out to his truck that night and asked if I could have one of those shells, as a souvenir. He didn't want to do it, but I talked him into giving me one." Harry had with him a photographic slide showing the baby tortoise shell with the hole pecked in its back. He delivered it to Cliff Gardner at the Gardner Ranch in Ruby Valley the next day.

"But now they say the tortoises are endangered because

of the cows, because they get stepped on by the nasty old cows, when the biggest tortoise populations we ever had were in the '50s and '60s, when you had plenty of ranching, and plenty of hunting, and plenty of predator control," Harry continues, turning back to his spaghetti and meatballs, while eyeing with considerable skepticism the carrot and cauliflower vegetable medley.

"So when any evidence comes up to the contrary, they just bury those studies and don't let anyone see them any more.

"I hunted the Star Valley (west of the Rubies) for 10 years. There used to be lots of deer there, but now they've made it all 'wilderness' and there's no deer left. But where Cliff has his cattle running up and down the east side of the mountain, there's plenty of deer." (Harry turned out to be right; the next day we spotted more than 80 deer — mostly does and fawns, and the tracks of a 150-pound lion — just driving the snowy road through Harrison Pass with Walt Gardner, who hires out as a hunting guide.) "You don't have to be a rocket scientist to figure it out."

"The Fish & Game data show they're losing 60 to 80 percent of the fawn crop each year — not to hunters, to predators," Dr. Wilkin concludes. "A lion will take one deer a week; 50 in a year. You can't sustain a herd at that rate. Not without predator control."

January 28, 2001
Eviction of Western Ranchers
"Amounts to a War of Religions"

🌿

On Feb. 21, 2001, Ruby Valley rancher Cliff Gardner was due to appear for sentencing before Chief U.S. District Judge Howard D. McKibben in Reno. Despite an affidavit from his attorney that it was impossible to prepare a defense in the face of the court's refusal to clarify its rules or jurisdiction, Gardner was convicted Nov. 17 in federal court in Reno of grazing his cattle from time to time on government land near his Ruby Valley ranch without permission.

He faced up to a year in prison and $10,000 in fines.

Gardner makes no bones about the fact he places cattle on that land from time to time, as his family has done for 130 years — since Mexican War veteran William Gardner "was discharged out of Fort Douglas there in Salt Lake in 1872 — he came west with an old gun, a wagon full of kids, and a handful of scrip that the government give him to claim some land."

In arid Nevada, no rancher can make a go of it on the 160 or 320 acres his grandparents were allowed to homestead. To run even 300 to 500 head of red Angus, as the Gardners do, requires thousands of acres. Thus, Western ranchers have always grazed their cattle on the adjoining public lands.

The question is: What does "public" mean? Do the ranchers have an established property right — a grazing right — just as both state and common law across the West acknowledges private citizens may have legitimate mining or water or right-of-way claims on that land, established both through paperwork "filings" and through years of habit and custom and adverse possession, which cannot be overturned by mere bureaucratic whim?

Or does the federal government — as Judge Johnnie Rawlinson has brazenly asserted in the similar case aimed at driving Clark County cattle rancher Cliven Bundy off his Mesquite Allotment — literally own all this land, with "plenary" rights to kick anybody off, any time they please?

The way Bill Clinton spent his final weeks in office waving million-acre parcels of these "public lands" off limits to human trespass with each flourish of his pen, it would certainly appear the federal government owns these lands and can use them — or bar them from human use — as they see fit.

There's little doubt the federal government did exercise precisely such imperial authority when these lands were territories — just as Washington City can still do as it darned well pleases with the "public lands" in places like Puerto Rico and American Samoa. (Just ask the Puerto Rican folk unhappy with that little naval gunnery range on Vieques Island.)

But did the Founding Fathers really intend for the federal government to permanently own 87 percent of Nevada ... 68 percent of Utah ... 50 percent of the land mass of California ... for as long as the sun shall shine?

Why? To meet what goal of a "limited government" instituted solely to "secure the rights of all Men"? To keep these lands out of the hands of settlers, miners, ranchers, loggers — out of the hands, in short, of the American people themselves?

To what purpose?

Mind you, no one objects to setting aside a few areas of particular scenic beauty as National Parks. But we're not talking here about building Wal-Marts in Yellowstone — we're talking about sealing off hundreds and hundreds of miles of desolate desert scrub from the only activity for which they've ever proven to be of the slightest use — grazing cattle.

When did the federal government buy these lands? Where are their deeds recorded? To whom do they pay property taxes? Or, if they're held "in common for all the people," how do I identify my one part in 250 million, so I can rent it to Cliff Gardner?

Cliff Gardner is quiet about it — he's not the kind of man who shouts much. Nor does he even have unanimous support among the state's other ranchers. ("Too many of them are doing too well with the federal handouts and subsidies that are coming down," explains his wife, Bertha. "They don't want to rock the boat.")

But make no mistake. Unassuming Cliff Gardner is taking on the entire majesty of the federal government — a federal government that *Range* magazine reports has succeeded in reducing livestock production on Western public lands by 20 percent in the past eight years; a federal government that — the Reno-based magazine argues — has embraced the visionary "Wildlands Project ... an almost unbelievable scheme to favor wildlife over human habitation ... (that) fully implemented suggests a reduction in human population in the West by one-third."

Defiant, Cliff Gardner declares he can find "no authority whatsoever" for the federal government to "hold and manage lands within an admitted State," aside from the power granted in Article I Section 8, to purchase specific parcels "by the Consent of the Legislature of the State in which the Same shall be, for the Erection of Forts, Magazines, Arsenals, dock-Yards and other needful Buildings," which would hardly seem to apply to the millions of acres of Western grazing land.

It was "for these reasons, in 1994, that the Gardners chose to turn their livestock out upon their allotment without a permit — just as he and his forebears had done prior to the establishment of the Forest Reserves," Gardner explains in the two-page written summary of the case which he'll hand to anyone willing to read it.

All Americans should be concerned, Gardner warns in the prepared summary, that "more than a third of the land surface of the United States of America is now being policed under Article IV jurisdiction" — never intended for use within the 50 states, and under which the courts will not acknowledge any obligation to grant accused citizens their constitutional rights, including their "Sixth Amendment right to be informed of the nature and cause of a prosecution ... in order that they may prepare a defense."

(As a matter of fact, if the current governor and attorney general of Nevada really want to stop the proposed federal nuclear waste dump at Yucca Mountain — if Gov. Kenny Guinn really means to leave "no battle unfought" against the waste dump, as he declared in his 2001 State of the State speech last week — one has to wonder why they're not joining this suit on Gardner's side. No private landowner would ever be allowed to set up a nuclear facility within the state's borders without state permission. It's only this presumption that the federal government has unlimited, extraconstitutional, territorial jurisdiction over 87 percent of Nevada — precisely the presumption Gardner is fighting to expose and refute — that makes such federal arrogance even remotely thinkable.)

"This question is of particular concern now that the federal government is poised to buy up all the remaining rural lands within our state," Gardner concludes. "With the money the feds will be receiving from the CARA legislation and the Southern Nevada Public Lands Act, they will have more than enough money to purchase all the remaining ranch and farm lands that lie within the State of Nevada."

🌿 🌿 🌿

It was in the winter of 1999 when I toured the Mesquite Allotment — 60 miles northeast of Las Vegas — with one of Clark County's last two cattle ranchers, blue-eyed Cliven Bundy. (Needless to say, the federals have been working to drive Cliven out of business for even longer than they've been after Cliff Gardner — seven years for Cliff; eight years for Cliven. Cliven responded by "firing" the BLM — "I don't sign their contracts and I don't pay their fees and I don't expect any services from 'em," he declares. And these guys all know each other; Cliff refers to Cliven having dropped by to do some deer hunting a few years back.)

At the time, Cliven and I squatted to examine some mighty spindly ground cover, the third-generation rancher explaining to me how the browsing of the plant by cattle clears room for the new green shoots to come in each spring.

I must have expressed some amazement at the idea that

cattle could survive by eating such stuff in the first place.

"A calf only learns what to eat out here because his momma shows him what to eat," Cliven responded, seriously. "At one point the tortoise people came in here and said I should just pull my cattle off the range for a few months in the spring, when the tortoises were breeding. I told them the only way I could do that would be to haul my herd to St. George and sell it, then buy new feed-lot cattle and put them out here come summer. They couldn't see why that would be a problem. I had to explain to them that when you put cattle out on land like this, if their mommas haven't taught them what they can eat out here, they starve."

Cliven showed me areas where he'd bulldozed dirt across an occasional wash, which then filled up and became a muddy watering pond not only for his cattle, but for the quail and other wildlife that subsequently thrived there in much larger numbers than had been seen before.

Left in its natural state, the salt cedar will move in and clog a spring till there's no more surface water for wildlife or cattle, Cliven explained. Only the rancher has the incentive to dig the spring back to bedrock, install piping, and run the water to a tank where it can then be used by deer and wild sheep, as well as domestic stock.

Cliven explained to me how the process works now, if a farmer grazing the public lands tries to follow the rules when he brings in his own bulldozer for such a one-day job — or even to run a piece of galvanized pipe under a dirt road. He must call the Forest Service or Bureau of Land Management, asking for an officer to come out, do a survey, and sign off that in performing such a "range alteration" he will not be dangerously infringing on the habitat of any threatened or endangered species.

(Five hundred ninety-six species were listed as "threatened or endangered" by the federal government in 1990. By 1999, the list had grown to 1,205, many of them weeds and bugs, the vast majority of them in the Western states, and many of those newly "discovered" for the sole purpose of halting development or blocking the traditional use of some swatch of land once valued for timber, cattle, or mining, but now attracting the attention of our modern-day Luddites, the "watermelon" environmentalists who mask their anti-commerce, anti-capitalist, anti-human-race agenda under a thin but trendy "green" skin.)

Having won an "endangered species sign-off" for his one-day culvert project, the naive rancher might then assume he could proceed to do the job (at his own expense, of course).

Oh no.

"You can't do a thing till they send out another guy, who has to do another survey to find out if you might be 'damaging any potential archaeological sites.' " Cliven explained. "I used to ask them, 'Gee, couldn't that guy have come along with you at the same time?' But no, you have to wait more weeks before you see that guy."

🌾 🌾 🌾

Back up near Elko, Bertha Gardner tells me they've been waiting "10 years" for a simple adjudication of the water rights to one of the seasonal creeks that flows under the road near their ranch in the Ruby Valley. Trying to play by the bureaucrats' rules is like Chinese water torture for such can-do folks. One might even begin to suspect the slow-downs are part of some calculated plan, as the federal government systematically reduces and abrogates grazing allotments across the West.

"They'll put me on the stand and ask how many years I have studied ecology, what college degrees I have," says Cliff Gardner, both describing his past treatment and predicting the way things are likely to go, come February in Reno.

"I'll tell 'em I've got a high-school education so they'll discredit me, see. But what I plan to testify is these people here — there'll be a lot of ranchers in the audience — are my peers, they have the know-how to manage the range and make it pay or they'll be put into bankruptcy and driven off the land. But these BLM and Forest Service people, they get their degrees and then they come out here and they're the experts — they don't have to test their theories against reality the way we have for three and four generations — that's the real teacher. They can be wrong and it doesn't matter. All they have to do is get more money for their department, grow the bureaucracy. And the way to do that is to create a villain, which is the rancher, and drive him off the land.

"So they become spin doctors. If the studies show what would really help the deer and the sage grouse is more predator control, that the wildlife does better when there's cattle on the land and their so-called preserves go to waste when they fence the cattle off, they just bury those studies, they never see the light of day if they don't match up with their theories.

"They say we can't know what we're talking about because we don't have any 'peer-reviewed studies.' Well, there can't be any 'peer-reviewed studies' because any of the ones that didn't fit their theories were all suppressed and hidden. I've had a lot of people sneakin' me studies who worked for the BLM and the Soil Conservation Service, because the agencies didn't want the public to know about 'em."

Cliff will stage his slide show at the drop of a hat, documenting the way Western wildfires have become more severe of late — not only larger and more frequent, but burning hotter and destroying even mature plants that might have survived earlier milder fires — a phenomenon that Cliff links directly to the ever larger areas now closed to cattle grazing, thus allowing excess plant growth to go unused, the excess drying into fuel, awaiting the first lightning strike or careless campfire. (He might add the vast expanses now closed to logging — even to clear away deadfalls.)

"And will they ever admit, 'Gee we made a mistake?'" Cliff asks. In answer, he shows slides of the impromptu truck parking lots and tent cities that spring up as federal contracts feed the growth of the new Western "fire suppression industry," whose participants he and Bertha describe as often more interested in lackadaisical "fire-watching" than fire-fighting.

Bertha relates the story of a young woman of their acquaintance who was hospitalized for third-degree burns, acquired saving her ranch from a wildfire that Cliff had helped the new firefighting teams "knock down the night before," but sprang back to life when the government contract laborers failed to watch it through the night, as the local men had advised.

"The plants developed in an ecosystem where they need to be browsed to clear room for the new growth each year and all the studies show this, so they bury the studies and just declare, 'The cows cause erosion; the cows drive the deer and the birds away,'" Cliff continues. "Well, why do they need to keep buying up more land to expand their preserves? The birds abandon their preserves and go where the cows are grazing, because the cows fertilize the water and churn the sediments and stir them up, and that's where you get your insect growth; ungulates are a vital part of the ecosystem. [But] do you think they'll let me testify to all that?"

🌱 🌱 🌱

What Cliff Gardner is insisting on is that — even if we agree the federals are to "administer" all these lands, punishing "trespassers" like Cliven Bundy and Cliff Gardner — we must still ask under what jurisdiction their courts and other officers are to operate as they do so: under Article III of the Constitution, which establishes the Supreme Court "and such inferior Courts as the Congress may from time to time ordain and establish" ... in which case defendants like Cliff Gardner have a right to a trial by a jury of their peers, a right to due process and equal protection — all the rights guaranteed by the Bill of Rights?

Or is the federal jurisdiction over these lands in fact a "territorial" jurisdiction, as established under Article IV, Section 3 of the Constitution, which would appear to set no such due-process restrictions on the power of Congress to "dispose of and make all Needful Rules and Regulations respecting the Territory or other Property belonging to the United States; and nothing in this Constitution shall be so construed as to Prejudice any Claims of the United States, or of any particular State"?

(Such "territories" being originally assumed to contain little but ... not to put too fine a point on it ... rogue French trappers and rascally redskins.)

Most Nevadans — most Americans — would doubtless respond that folks like Cliven Bundy and Cliff Gardner (Americans born and bred) are citizens of both the United States and the sovereign state of Nevada, and that in any action brought against them by the U.S. government, of course they enjoy all the constitutional rights to due process guaranteed by the Fourth, Fifth, Sixth, Eighth and Ninth Amendments.

Cliff Gardner keeps trying to get Judge McKibben to confirm that. But for some curious reason, whenever Gardner makes a court filing asking for just such a confirmation of his due-process rights, Judge McKibben — he just lay low and don't say nothin'.

Motion denied without comment. Motion denied without comment. Motion denied without comment.

"Before we can argue about how many cows are on the land, we need to know whether we have constitutional rights under the Sixth Amendment; is this an Article 3 or an Article 4 court?" Gardner says. "We need to know the rules and the jurisdiction.

"I ask: 'Will Gardner's constitutional rights be respected?' They respond: 'Mr. Gardner has what he has and I'm not going to get into that.' ... They don't want to rule that constitutional rights don't apply; they just keep denying motions to answer that question. They certainly don't want to say it's an

Article 3 court, because then state law applies. And the state recognizes grazing rights; we wouldn't then be under the Taylor Grazing Act, et cetera.

"So how can I prepare a defense?"

It sounded to me like a question the judge should be able to answer — after all, how can any government agency commence exercising its powers without first agreeing to cite chapter and verse of its constitutional authority and jurisdiction, without first clarifying the extent — and limits — of its authority?

I called Judge McKibben. The judge explained he had taken my call as a courtesy, but that he couldn't answer any questions about a pending case. "You could present to me a summary of his concerns and I could take them under consideration, but I wouldn't be able to comment," the judge explained.

"And that would include the jurisdiction?" I asked. "Mr. Gardner says he can't get an answer as to whether his case in your court falls under Article 3 jurisdiction or Article 4 jurisdiction. So when you say you can't comment, would that include telling me whether this case falls under the jurisdiction of Article 3 of the Constitution or Article 4 of the Constitution?"

"What it includes is that I can't comment on the case," Judge McKibben replied. "You have expressed to me what his concerns are. I can tell you this, that if you file something in court, I always prepare an order and you can read that order. But I don't want to be quoted on that."

"So you can't even say whether — just speaking in general now — all defendants have their due-process rights under Article 3 and the Bill of Rights when they appear in your court?"

"The canon of ethics prevents me from speaking about a pending case, and we have an ethical obligation not to do that," was all the answer Judge McKibben would give me.

And I'm quoting him on that.

❧ ❧ ❧

Tim Findley, former chief investigative reporter for the San Francisco *Chronicle* and assistant editor for *Rolling Stone*, who for more than a year has been covering the Gardner case for Reno-based *Range* magazine (for a sample copy, dial 800-RANGE4U), says the struggle between ranchers like Cliff Gardner and Clark County's Cliven Bundy on one side — federal regulators and "land managers" on the other — amounts to a war of religions.

Gardner and his Clark County counterpart Cliven Bundy are Mormons, Findley points out. They believe that taming the wilderness is a noble cause and raising their children close to the land has been good for their families and their society.

"On the other side we have the arrogant practitioners of an environmental religion, endeavoring to use federal force — in blatant violation of the First Amendment — to 'establish' and impose across the West the religion of environmentalism, which holds that cattle — and lumbering and mining, for that matter — are unnatural desecrations of nature's temple, a wilderness from which all human activity must be banished so that the lands can be held in permanent trust in their wild splendor."

I mentioned to Findley the fervor with which Cliff Gardner will present his slide show at the drop of a hat — it's the first thing he did when I arrived at the Slash-J Ranch for a visit over New Year's weekend, the ranch's muddy turn-in looking like market day in the county seat as a free-lancer for *Range* magazine also showed up to take some photos of Cliff for the February issue and got offered a chair — showing the photographic evidence he's gathered over the decades, before-and-after photos demonstrating that the lands are in better shape where they've been grazed by cattle than where they've been fenced off for years as sterile "wilderness."

"Cliff has more than anecdotal evidence for his claims,"

Findley responds. "He's been out there taking pictures for more than 20 years and he built a very convincing case. Cliff contends these forage plants evolved to need large ungulates to graze them, whether that be cattle or some other animal, and the cattle are a vital part of the ecosystem. Where the cattle graze you see an enormous beneficial growth of the game species, the deer herds, and so forth. Where they fence the cattle off the land you see the land go to waste; you see a build-up in fuel so you get more and harsher range fires.

"It becomes a kind of matter of faith to these [government] people. They really don't understand what they're doing to destroy the lives of people with equally good hearts. The Nature Conservancy had grabbed off two-thirds of that land (near the Gardner Ranch in the Ruby Valley) and they desperately want Cliff's chunk. It's really extortion.

"With Cliven and Cliff you have the Mormon influence, and they're going up against an equally strong belief on the part of the government types in an environmental faith that all the cattle should be off the land and everything should be preserved. So what's underlying this is a really cynical kind of land grab and Cliff doesn't mention that much; I don't think he gives enough emphasis to the way the Nature Conservancy is behind all this, using everyone's good intention for a really cynical land grab."

I asked Findley what he expects to see in Judge McKibben's court on Feb. 21.

"McKibben isn't going to be kind. He isn't going to allow Cliff to present either his constitutional case or the environmental case he wants to present. I have a lot of sympathy for Cliff. People are saying he's making a martyr of himself, but I don't know, I think there's something else going on here. He used to have dinner with these guys; when he was a kid on the ranch the forest rangers would come visit his father and stay overnight at the ranch and Cliff really respected them and looked up to them, so I think there's a lot of personal disappointment now in the way they're acting and the fact they won't look at his evidence and listen to folks who have been on the land for generations and learned how to manage the land and are willing to share that knowledge; instead all you get from the federal side is arrogance."

Findley, the transplanted Californian, has been in Nevada for 10 years. "I came here looking for a place to raise a young son and moved to Fallon and got caught up in the water wars," he explains.

"Ranchers like Cliff remind me a lot more of the Black Panthers. Those were also people who tried to stand up for their rights, but they were pushed around because they were minorities. I try to explain to my friends [back in California] that these ranchers are now being pushed around and terrorized and threatened with jail and the loss of their livelihoods for standing up for their rights in exactly the same way the Black Panthers were; I don't see any conflict between what we used to write about back then and what I'm doing now.

"What drew the Black Panthers to public attention is one day they went to Sacramento to the Capitol and walked around carrying shotguns, which it was perfectly legal for them to do. We didn't know then and we will never know whether they were loaded. But because they were all black and all dressed the same the police then started to terrorize them — they were all arrested, and the state terrorism against them began.

"The Black Panthers were never charged with robbing banks or anything like that. They said, 'We have these rights,' and the state said, 'Not to exercise them when you're all black and you all dress the same, not to exercise them in this militaristic fashion.' So the police terrorized them. If you start with people like Cliff Gardner becoming political prisoners, that's when you're going to see more resistance and more real tragedy. They're saying we have constitutional rights and the government is saying well, you have to give up your livelihoods if you try to exercise those rights. ... I don't know what the others will do if they put Cliff Gardner in jail."

Does Findley think McKibben will jail Gardner?

"I think what McKibben will do is impose some kind of house arrest or some form of economic restraint that'll cripple what Cliff can do. I doubt he'll risk going so far as to put him in jail and give this movement its martyr and its political prisoner."

🌿 🌿 🌿

Spending a weekend at the Gardners' Slash-J Ranch is like stepping back 40 years in time — except for the cordless phones, of course, and the fact that everyone in the household seems to have his or her own personal computer.

This city slicker was pretty proud of himself, rousing out of bed and brushing my teeth soon after first light. The dawn was barely breaking as I reached the kitchen ... to find half the household chatting about a proposed coyote hunt over the fast-cooling remains of breakfast. (Bunny-huggers can relax — our wily brothers sang back to Walt and Harry, but none loped near enough to come to harm.) Bertha graciously handed me the last of the sausage and fried eggs, though she warned, "I can't guarantee they're still warm." City boys: sleeping in till almost dawn.

By 10:30 the woman of the house had finished doing her accounts at the kitchen table and moved on to preparing lunch — three huge hot meals being the order of each day. She chatted with me as I jotted a few notes at the table, but not about her elder son — though the Gardners are obviously proud of Charley, the champion rodeo cowboy whose trophies crowd the house till there's no place left to hang the huge poster for last summer's Reno rodeo, which featured a picture of Charley himself, on a bucking bronc.

No, as I made friends with the gray cat, sole survivor of a long-ago litter, Bertha fell to talking about her younger son Walt, who now bears the major load of helping his dad with the ranch, what with Charley being away on the rodeo circuit.

Walt is a big healthy lad who not too long ago brought home a lovely bride with a 15-year-old stepdaughter, both of whom the Gardners treat as their own. The family shares stories of Walt and Charley racing each other "up the hill" behind the ranchhouse — the "hill" being one of the larger peaks in the 11,000-foot Ruby Mountains, which stretch both north and south outside the window and just across the road, as far as the eye can see.

"One day Charley says he ran up the hill so fast his heart stopped," Walt says with a smile.

"What did he do?" I asked.

"Oh, you just wait for it to start again."

Walt guided me and Harry Pappas on an impromptu late afternoon drive through 7,200-foot Harrison Pass, spotting at least 80 deer through Harry's binoculars — only three or four of them bucks, and among them only one that would have been suitable for harvest, by Walt's standards — they prefer to wait till a deer's antlers are over 20 inches.

Walt, in his element, spotted a set of lion tracks from the moving car. As we emerged to join him, he told us how long ago the 150-pound lioness had crossed the road.

"Now, how do you know she's a female?" asked a skeptical Harry.

"Well, do you see any marks where his balls were dragging?" answered Walt, his sly smile following his punchline by a few seconds, as usual.

Walt speaks offhand of a hunter who — it turned out — couldn't hit a tree at 50 yards with either his rifles or his guides', emptying the magazines of two rifles before one particularly lucky mulie managed to get away unharmed. He recalled another fellow for whom Walt had worked all day, positioning him for a clear shot at a trophy buck.

"Now, in a minute here, there are four deer going to come over that ridge," Walt recalls instructing the fellow. "I've been watching them, and if you'll shoot the second deer, that one's your trophy."

Sure enough, the four bucks soon came strolling up over the rise, the second of the four sporting an enormous rack of well over 20 inches.

The hunter fired, and the third deer in the group — a legal prey but with a pitiful six-inch rack — tumbled down the slope.

"I got it! I got it!" the hunter yelled, literally leaping up and down.

"Yep, you shot it," Walt recalls, deadpan. "But you shot the wrong deer. I said to shoot the second one."

"That *was* the second one!" the hunter insisted.

"Counting from the front ... or the back?" Walt asked.

"From the back!"

His mom is doubly proud of Walt, who hires out to guide lion hunts in the mountains, speaking with awe of old-time hunters who were known to "walk down a cat." (While mountain lions can demonstrate awesome bursts of speed for short periods, a man and a dog can exhaust them till they have to either tree or turn, if they can just demonstrate the persistence — and endurance — to stay on their trail for enough days and nights in the frozen mountains.)

Bertha's pride in her second son comes in part from the fact things didn't look so good for him when he started out in life.

"He was born allergic to milk, and they didn't think he was going to make it. They handed him back to me in that hospital in Reno and said, 'We've done all we can for him; you need to take him home now.'"

As farm folks, the Gardners had no medical insurance. The clear message was that there was little else the doctors could — or would — do. Nature was supposed to take its course with Little Walt at home, out of sight and out of mind. These things happen.

"My pediatrician said to put him on Coca-Cola. That was all he could tolerate, so we did. He's only alive today because of Coca-Cola." Later, more competent specialists in Salt Lake found the boy could indeed tolerate soy milk, though the folks at the Reno hospital had scoffed at the idea.

Walt was also born with club feet, which required surgery. "He didn't go to sleep without shoes on till he was nine years old," Bertha relates. "He still doesn't have the flexibility in his ankles that most people do. But he can jump up into the bed of a pickup truck from a standing start."

Walt also progressed slowly at school. Bertha decided to tutor him at home, long before most folks had even heard the term "home schooling."

I believe there's a point to Bertha's story of her younger son turning out fine.

In some big city school, Walt could have slipped through the cracks — who knows, maybe even been doped up on Luvox or Ritalin before he was through. But not on the ranch. On the ranch, he was just Walt. On the ranch, where the physical demands of the work suited him, he grew to be strong, affable, confident — a man sought out and paid for his endurance and his special knowledge of the high country — a man with whom I'd gladly climb the mountain.

Farm and ranch families like the Gardners know that raising their children close to the land, in an environment where the harsh necessities of nature provide the best task-master, breeds sturdy men of strong character from even the most unpromising of material.

Bertha Gardner raised up strong sons. But it is also the land that raised these children — the very land from which the federals would now push the small ranching families — and all other Americans, truth be told.

I asked Cliff whether he thought his four kids — both girls have now married and moved out of the county — would have turned out as well if they'd been city-bred.

"Of course not. There's nothing like the opportunity for children when they're being raised, learning to be around cattle and do chores, to be around wood and land and iron at a young age, learning to work. That's probably the biggest reason that we stay in the ranching business, is that reason.

"That's why I want my grandkids around. ... It's pretty hard for a government agent to pull the wool over someone's eyes that's ever had to deal with fire and rain and wind and snow and all the other elements. My kids started working right at my side fighting fires, moving cattle at 11 or 12 years old. ...

"You don't just feed cows or chickens; you have to feed 'em right or they don't produce, and that's a discipline that's learned, that's what they learn very young. Not like a bunch of bureaucrats who live in an imaginary, abstract world. We have to live in the real world. If we don't adhere to and work with nature, we get cold pretty danged fast. Someone who works for the government because they've got a degree might get away with ignoring the truth, but anyone in the ranching business, we haven't been here for four generations because we ignored the truth and didn't work with nature."

"There's a philosophy of life that I have," adds Cliven Bundy of Mesquite, blue eyes sparkling beneath his Navajo silver hatband. "All these resources — the brush, the game — are put here for man's use. If you don't get any use out of it, what use *is* it? They say they want to protect the ecosystem, but man has to be part of the ecosystem. If man manages the predators so they only eat half the quail, and half are left for man, think of all the dutch-oven meals that makes. Everything here on the Earth is made for man. This land would be better off if you let people use it and work it and improve it."

In the snide phrases of the coffeehouse environmentalist, these families that have worked from dawn to dusk for 130 years — no "calling in sick" when it's 30 below — are "welfare ranchers," taking advantage of the rest of us by leasing federal scrubland for "less than market rates" ... as though anyone else is chafing at the bit to pay good money to use this God-forsaken scrub, risking their savings against the bank, the sheriff, and the bankruptcy court.

I didn't see any welfare cases on the Gardner ranch.

❦ ❦ ❦

Cliff's theme doesn't change as he's bidding me goodbye on Sunday morning — our route about to take us past miles and miles of the fenced-off cattle-free Franklin Lake "water-fowl sanctuary," where we manage to spot precisely one bird, a majestic blue heron.

"Thomas Jefferson's vision of happiness was being able to devote your life to your livelihood, not having to fight the government all the time. He said if we could get that kind of freedom the country would grow rich. ... Government is set up to resolve disputes between individuals, but now 90 percent of the disputes are between individuals and the state. Bertha and I are now enemies of the state. ...

"How can they say there's equity in these courts when they won't even answer my questions about jurisdiction and the constitutionality of the statute? Those are the first questions they should answer, before they move on to anything else. Instead they say, 'You can bring that up on appeal, at the appellate level.' But what good does it do, even if the high court does finally remand these questions back to the lower court and tell them to answer them, if by that time I've expended my resources, and then I face another five or six years of working my way back up through the system? How can they say there's justice there? How can they say there's equity?"

Some say the wealth of America lies in her coal mines and her forests, her wheat fields and her factories. But they are wrong.

I have seen the wealth of America. It lies in the hearts of Cliff and Bertha Gardner. It lies in the spunk with which they will continue to fight their hopeless fight for as long as they draw breath. It lives in their naive faith that some judge, somewhere, will hear them out, answer their questions, acknowledge the limits of his jurisdiction, search his conscience, see justice done.

They're wrong, of course. There will be no justice. They will be beaten down, and driven from the land.

But the funny thing about their kind of faith and strength is that you cannot steal these things away. You cannot load them up in a trailer and alter their brands and claim them for your own.

Instead, when they have finished driving the Cliff and Bertha Gardners off this land, they will find the America they claim to be "protecting" ... is gone.

❦ ❦ ❦

Land-rights activists report the letters poured in to Chief U.S. District Judge Howard McKibben in the weeks before his Feb. 21 sentencing of Ruby Valley rancher Cliff Gardner.

One also wonders if His Honor didn't raise a finger and sense a change in the wind when the U.S. Forest Service — now serving a very different master in the incoming Bush administration — last week folded its tents entirely in the five-year struggle to close off the Jarbidge Canyon Road (also in northeast Nevada) to all human access.

("We received threats and intimidation from the government up until election time, and then they [federal officials] became cooperative," says Nolan Lloyd, chairman of the Elko County Commission.)

Finally, some 75 people — mostly ranchers rooting for the defendant — packed McKibben's courtroom Wednesday to see if the judge would make a sacrificial lamb of Gardner in the ongoing federal campaign to drive the West's small, family ranchers off the land.

And suddenly, the judge's demeanor began to change.

Where Gardner had previously been told he would not be

allowed to stage his slide show in the courtroom, presenting his case that grazing cattle on the lands actually increases crop diversity and wildlife yields (while challenging federal jurisdiction over the lands in question), Judge McKibben announced at the last minute that Gardner would be given half an hour to speak his piece.

"He told him he'd only let him run it for half an hour, but I think it ran 45 minutes or an hour," says Gardner's son Charley, reached at the Slash-J Ranch. "They let him do the whole slide show and it came off real well."

In the end, the judge imposed a $1,000 fine, suspended pending appeal — a minimal penalty — and ordered the Forest Service to sit down and work with Gardner. Another witness describes prosecutors and other government agents on hand looking "stunned — and not in a happy way."

October 8, 2001
Half-Measures in the Klamath Valley

Hundreds of thousands of acres of the Klamath Valley in southwest Oregon have gone without irrigation water this summer; most of the 1,500 affected farm families have suffered total crop loss and those losses may total $250 million — dwarfing a $20 million emergency federal aid package.

But the problem isn't drought — there's plenty of water behind the dam the federal government built in 1909, thereafter holding "land lotteries" for veterans of both the First and Second World Wars, encouraging the winners to settle the valley and set up farms by signing contracts that promised irrigation water would always be provided.

"It was a beautiful trade-off until a month ago, when the Bureau of Reclamation broke the contract, leaving 90 percent of the farms — some 200,000 acres of land — without water," the *Wall Street Journal* editorialized last May.

"What caused the U.S. government to condemn 1,500 farms, a $250 million industry, to oblivion? To save sucker fish, a bottom-feeding scavenger that got on the Endangered Species Act in 1988. ...

"The Bureau of Reclamation is hiding behind biological opinions issued in April ... that say the sucker needs more water," the *Journal* continued. "But the Bureau's maddening folly is that it abides by science already proven an abject failure in that other great Northwest fish story: salmon."

Although "Environmentalists ... saw this was a perfect way to pursue their broader antigrowth agenda — to force farmers off the land, blow up dams, get rid of barges," attempts to restore salmon runs by increasing water flows past the region's many dams have been an abject failure, the *Journal* reports.

But if this isn't really about saving fish — a "trade fish" we used to be encouraged to clean out of Connecticut's trout streams with frog spears when I was a boy — who would want to see these farmers driven off the land? The Oregon Natural Resources Council, for one. That group has drafted a plan under which the federal government would buy much of the basin's farmland and set it aside as a "desert preserve."

Environmentalists like Andy Kerr of the ONRC hate the region's very lushness because it's artificial — what had once been a high desert was transformed into a garden spot by the intervention of mankind, you see, damming and diverting the Klamath River in a massive public works project completed in 1909. In direct opposition to the ancient biblical notion that it's man's proper role to make the earth fruitful, eco-extremists hate such interventions as "unnatural."

"Environmentalists often say their use of the Endangered Species Act is for the benefit of humanity," points out Glenn Woiceshyn of the Ayn Rand Institute. But, "whenever man's needs conflict with the 'interests of nature,' as they now do in

Klamath Basin, environmentalists always take the side of nature.

"The environmentalists subscribe to an 'intrinsic-value' ethic, which means that nature must be valued — not for any benefit it brings to man, but because nature is somehow a value in and of itself," Mr. Woiceshyn continues. "Hence, nature must be kept pristine despite the harm this causes man. We must halt activities beneficial to us, such as farming, forestry, and the treatment of disease, in order to safeguard fish, birds, trees, and rats. We are being told to sacrifice our lives to nature. ..."

In a wave of civil disobedience, hundreds of local farmers seized the headgates of Klamath Lake, using saws or blowtorches to open the valves to feed irrigation water into their canal on at least three occasions in June and July. Bureau of Reclamation officials closed them again, turning to federal marshals and the FBI to help them keep the gates closed after the local sheriff refused to intervene.

"Already, in towns like Klamath Falls, population 17,000, and Tulelake, Calif., population 1,000, businesses have begun to close and school populations have plunged by as much as 30 percent, reflecting an exodus of farm workers," *The New York Times* was reporting by June.

Actually, the Endangered Species Act offers opt-out provisions designed to get around such travesties as what's been happening in the Klamath Valley. The Endangered Species Committee — a panel made up of seven cabinet-level officials and informally known as the God Squad — is charged with weighing economics against the risks of extinction and has the power to override provisions of the law that promise primacy to the protection of listed plants and animals. But Interior Secretary Gale Norton has resisted pressure to convene the "God Squad."

Instead, the Interior Department agreed to an independent review of the scientific findings that led to the virtual shutdown of water to farmers in the Klamath Basin. Interior Secretary Norton said the National Academy of Sciences will review scientific and technical information regarding the two types of endangered sucker fish in Upper Klamath Lake, as well as the coho salmon downstream.

"It's good news, but it's not going to be in time for next year's growing season," points out Mike Byrne, who farms alfalfa and barley in Tulelake. "People are already trying to figure out what to do next year. They have to deal with their bankers."

The findings of credible scientists hired by the Klamath irrigators suggest the suckers are doing far better than federal biologists have suggested. Their populations, which numbered about 5,000 in the lake when the species were listed as endangered more than a decade ago, have swelled to at least 100,000, and might actually be harmed by excess water behind the dam, according to those reports — which federal courts have so far refused to consider.

"In the dry years we always shared our water with the fish and the Indians. I don't think any fish died," local horse-radish farmer Paul Christy (who came to the Klamath Basin after serving in World War II, attracted by the federal government's offers of land and water) told Pat Taylor of CNS News in May. "The people who passed the Endangered Species Act had a good idea, but now it's being used as a club against the farmers."

The ESA was due for renewal by the Congress in 1990, but revisiting the Act has been blocked by the very eco-Luddites who originally sponsored it, out of understandable concern that common-sense legislators — now aware of the extremists' real agenda — would take the opportunity to moderate its most bizarre and anti-human impacts.

"Rather than spending tax dollars to mitigate the damaging effects of one of its own laws, Congress should amend the ESA to add protection for endangered farmers and ranchers," suggested Gretchen Randall of the National Center for Public Policy Research in a recent position paper. "It could prohibit any government agency from taking action that diminishes the value of private property or require that compensation for damages be paid. Congress could also require an independent scientific review of all proposed listings of threatened and endangered species. ..."

Indeed, that's the kind of radical reform the Bush administration *ought* to be pursuing.

In the Klamath Basin, "The damage is done," concludes Anne Hayes, an attorney with the Pacific Legal Foundation, which represented water users in an attempt to get the governors of California and Oregon to petition for the "God Squad" to be convened this summer.

For Secretary Norton to order an Academy of Sciences review at this late date is really "a cop-out," attorney Hayes said Wednesday. "The God Squad is the *only* method for people to sit down and solve a resources-allocation problem — 'How do we do this in a way that doesn't harm the farmers, that doesn't harm the fish?' ...

"When it comes to protecting species it does so in an extremely costly and ineffective way and people don't matter. But for the environmentalists it's an extremely useful tool toward achieving their real goal, which is stopping the resource industries: farming, mining, lumber. We call it 'toad-throwing.' If you want to stop your neighbor from doing something you just call Fish & Wildlife and throw down a toad on their property ..."

All that's really being decided in the ongoing arbitration in the Klamath Basin is "how much land will go to the Indians, how much will go into the reserve ... and that was the whole purpose in the first place," attorney Hayes explains. "As one of the farmers put it, 'Rural Cleansing,' to take some of the farmland out of production. ...

"What happened up there got a lot of attention from the American public, they're finally seeing just how harsh the Endangered Species Act can be ... And you're going to have results like that repeated over and over and over again, as long as we have the Endangered Species Act. It's just a bad law."

The kind of law the American people elected a new Republican administration to radically reform or repeal.

They're still waiting.

December 1994
Things I'd Like To See
〵

Westerners will never make any headway against thumb-sucking Eastern eco-nuts so long as they remain on the defensive, trying to explain how noble-sounding efforts to "protect and preserve delicate Western ecosystems" in fact means driving productive ranchers, miners, and loggers from the land, at which point such nationalized resources will be promptly plundered and mismanaged by arrogant and corrupt officials, as has happened in every socialized regime from Kenya to Kazakhstan.

Instead, lawmakers from the Western states should pool their votes to pass some "environmental-protection" measures designed as mirror images of those now being imposed on the West.

How could an environmentally sensitive congressman from Massachusetts possibly object to the Bureau of Land Management setting out surveying stakes in preparation for the demolition of every privately owned home and business in Barnstable, Hyannis, and Yarmouth, Mass., as required by the stipulations of the 1995 Cranberry Bog Restoration and Protection Act?

(Heck, what ever happened to the Eastern woodland bison? Let's genetically engineer some of the shaggy beasts and set them to roaming the restored woodlands of Newton,

Scarborough, Grosse Pointe Farms, and Chevy Chase, with a couple hundred ravenous gray wolves to chase them.)

How could a senator from Maryland possibly object to 200 years' worth of delinquent assessments at "market rates" being levied against the dorymen who have been "ripping off a precious public resource" by pulling shellfish out of the Cheasapeake Bay without paying a royalty to the federal government? Aren't the beds of clams and oysters there a unique natural treasure properly preserved for the entire nation? Are we to allow a few greedy locals to profit from the accident of their birthplace, receiving "federal subsidies" in the form of harvesting fees left uncharged?

Needless to say, the appropriate federal agencies must be instructed to start enforcing the Chesapeake Bay Shellfish Protection Act within the districts of congressmen now proudly displaying perfect environmental voting records. ...

June 28, 1995
And Address It c/o The Colonial Ministry, Times Square ...

In the West, ranchers know that wolves re-introduced to Yellowstone Park haven't stayed in the park, but roam hundreds of miles, killing sheep and calves in far greater numbers than they need for food. (The Summer 1995 edition of *Range* magazine, out of Carson City, has the names and photos.)

Yet Easterners who have never seen a wolf except in a Disney movie think restoring the ecosystem of the Great Plains to the state depicted in *Dances With Wolves* — vast restored herds of buffalo migrating across an unfenced plain from Saskatchewan to Amarillo — would be nifty. If there are a few hundred thousand private-property holders in the way, so what

— they stole the land from the Sioux and the Comanche, didn't they?

So rationalizes the Easterner, mowing his suburban lawn on land stolen from the Pequot, the Mohawk, the Oneida, and the Mohegan.

How much does such arrogance really differ from the rationale of Joe Stalin, packing up whole peoples and exiling them to sure death in snowy Siberia because they clung to land for which Mother Russia had other plans?

If Easterners like wolf restoration so much, let's put a few dozen 175-pound six-foot-long timber wolves in Central Park and ban New Yorkers from shooting them even if they're spotted hauling away their toddlers.

In a June 18, 1995, editorial titled, "The Endangered West," the esteemed *New York Times* reported, "What we are seeing is an updated but more ominous version of the Sagebrush Rebellion of the early Reagan years. That revolt was dominated by ranching interests protesting federal regulation of public lands. The present explosion embraces not only those familiar despoilers but mining companies, timber barons, developers, big commercial farmers, and virtually anyone else who stands to profit from relaxation of environmental controls."

"Despoilers"? This from writers sitting in the midst of thousands of acres of concrete, wealthy beyond belief because their grandfathers "developed" everything in sight without tolerating a single "environmental control." Did any editorialist in 1840s London ever speak so patronizingly of the ineffectual struggles for independence of their "little Brown Brothers" in India or Asia?

Ironically, writing in the year 1776 in *Common Sense*, it was Americans of the West and South whom Thomas Paine called to the aid of New Englanders, warning: "It is the good fortune of many to live distant from the scene of present sorrow; the evil is not sufficiently brought to their doors to make them feel the precariousness with which all American property is possessed. But let our imaginations transport us a few moments to Boston; that seat of wretchedness will teach us wisdom, and instruct us forever to renounce a power in whom we can have no trust."

Americans of the South and West heeded this call and came to the aid of their blockaded brethren in New England. But when we cry out now that we face precisely the same treatment by a distant haughty tyrant, how do our brethren in New York and New England respond?

Turning on its head the ancient guarantee that all local matters would be left to the states, my esteemed brethren at *The New York Times* protest, "Back in Washington, an Idaho Republican, Dirk Kempthorne, is leading the Senate charge to cripple the Endangered Species Act, which provides what little protection the salmon have. If Senator Kempthorne succeeds in transferring protection of endangered species from Washington to Boise, it will be goodbye salmon, with grizzlies and wolves to follow."

Why Idahoans would want to exterminate their lucrative and beloved salmon fishery is unexplained, because it is unexplainable. Secondly, Idahoans are advised to turn over protection of their waters and game species to those who rendered the Charles, the Housatonic, the Delaware, and the Cuyahoga the stinking sewers they are today. But last and most important, if the people of Idaho should indeed decide to exterminate every salmon within their borders, what conceivable business is it of anyone in New York or Washington City?

Washington has an "overriding national interest in preserving the public lands and forests from exploitation," these Times Square cowboys assure us, and the power to do so because, "At no time have the Western public lands belonged to the states. They were acquired by treaty, conquest or purchase by the Federal Government acting on behalf of all citizens of the United States."

But weren't Indiana and Missouri and Florida acquired

in just the same way? Doesn't it follow that all lands in those states should also be administered by federal bureaucrats "in trust for all the people"?

None have gone so far since Prince John forbade the Saxons to hunt the deer in their own forests, declaring that all deer are the king's deer.

Once, brave men came to this continent to escape such tyranny. Such men were the ancestors of Arthur Ochs Sulzburger, Joseph Lelyveld, and Howell Raines. But Thomas Paine could have been speaking of the way such latter-day Tories shrug off the massacres at Waco and Ruby Ridge when he wrote: "If you say you can still pass the violations over, then I ask, hath your house been burnt? Hath your property been destroyed before your face? Are your wife and children destitute of a bed to lie on, or bread to live on? ... If you have not, then are you not a judge of those who have. But if you have, and can still shake hands with the murderers, then you are unworthy the name of husband, father, friend, or lover, and whatever may be your rank or title in life, you have the heart of a coward, and the spirit of a sycophant."

IV
Mean Greens: Environmentalism as a State Religion

Burned Alive by the Endangered Species Act

Citing as their source Congressman Scott McInnis, R-Colo., and chairman of the House Resources' forest subcommittee, the *Seattle Times* reported Aug. 1, 2001, "Confusion about rules related to threatened fish may have delayed aerial delivery of river water to last month's Thirty Mile Fire, in which four firefighters lost their lives."

"Before the Thirty Mile Fire turned deadly July 10, dispatchers delayed sending a helicopter to drop water on the flames because they were unsure whether they needed permission to draw water from a river containing threatened fish," the U.S. Forest Service told *Seattle Times* reporter Chris Solomon in late July.

Fourteen firefighters and two hikers were trapped late that afternoon by the fire along the Chewuch River in Okanogan County. Four of the firefighters died.

McInnis suggested that concerns about Endangered Species Act protections may have contributed to the deaths.

A nearly two-hour delay did occur that day, but not because of the strictures of ESA, according to Elton Thomas, fire-management officer for the Okanogan and Wenatchee National Forests.

"Water can be plucked from a river without permission from wildlife agencies during such an incident," Thomas told the *Times*. "However, in the water- and fish-sensitive Methow Valley area, dispatchers may have been simply 'trying to do the right thing,'" he said.

One firefighter trapped that day believes the delay was critical.

"If we'd had the water when we'd asked for it, none of this would have happened," Ellreese Daniels, a 24-year firefighter, told the *Times*. When the water did arrive, it was too late to be useful, he said.

Out of Balance

In recent years, mountain lions have been padding into suburban back yards in California, hauling off family pets and terrifying the mothers of small children.

In a couple of cases, lone adult humans — usually small women — have actually been attacked and killed by the highly efficient predators, in parks or recreation areas where Californians are no longer allowed to carry firearms.

Now, even wildlife biologists are worrying that predation by mountain lions that suddenly overrun their established ranges may endanger the dramatic and welcome comeback of another previously endangered species — the bighorn sheep.

What's going on?

Often blamed for the increasing frequency of human-cat contact is suburban sprawl. Of course, that's a factor. But more importantly, a misguided 1990 California ballot initiative banned all hunting of the cougar in that state. It's now illegal to kill a mountain lion unless it directly threatens people or livestock. Even then, you're likely to do more time than O.J. Simpson.

"They have no vision of conservation," complains biologist John Wehausen, a cougar expert at the University of California's Mountain Research Station, referring to those who promoted the 1990 initiative.

"We are concerned with habitat preservation and maintaining rich biodiversity, but they're concerned with the life of a particular animal in a particular place," Mr. Wehausen continues. "They essentially reject science."

Precisely. No one wants to see either the big cats or the wild sheep driven to extinction. They're both vital parts of our wild heritage.

But they are just that — wild. The idea that nature lovers can or should walk peacefully, shoulder to shoulder, with these deadly predators is the kind of fantasy that can be deadly, especially to children.

California wildlife officers lecture elementary-school classes these days on what the children should do if they encounter a lion: Don't run, which will only draw a charge. Instead, stand tall, shout, and wave your arms.

Passable advice as a last resort, since no child is likely to outrun or outclimb one of these cats.

But how about starting with: "Don't go into cat country without an adult, and make sure that adult is carrying at least a medium-bore firearm full of soft-points. If you see a mountain lion stalking you or poised to spring, shout, 'Daddy, Mommy, shoot the cat!'"

Environmental absolutism is a far cry from a true understanding of the science of ecology, and is bound to have bizarre and unintended consequences.

Ecology is the study of the way all the parts of a biological system fit together. Though it may not make for fuzzy heartwarming cartoon shows, such systems inevitably include predation, and often a necessary culling role for man the hunter (we keep forgetting that Nature put *that* creature here, too) — especially where such other top predators as the grizzly are long gone.

The solution is not to take away the power of the referendum, but rather to better educate the discretion of the populace. The more detailed our understanding of a complex ecosystem, the more we are likely to abandon the hubris that ever led us to believe we could fine-tune every aspect of nature to suit our romanticized wishes, "preserving" at a randomly selected moment in geologic time a biological status quo that Nature herself has placed in a state of constant change.

Leaving a place for wildlife is an estimable goal. Once we are rid of the warping of land uses caused by the dual tyrannies of the property tax and "government land ownership," there's no reason private entrepreneurs can't buy up and preserve vast wilderness areas for the enjoyment of hikers, hunters, birdwatchers ... anyone who will pay the admission charge.

But (in the meantime) modest sensible wildlife management is never likely to succeed, so long as it is based on popular votes to determine which animals look more cuddly.

And They Worshiped the Dragon ...

A couple of decades back, when members of Congress raced to placate "green" voters by coupling with the extraconstitutional Endangered Species Act, there was a lot of talk of making sure our grandchildren would still be able to view an American bison, a grizzly bear, and a bald eagle in the wild. No one wanted to be responsible for the extinction of those species, which are virtual "totems" of the American frontier.

Those species now appear "saved" — though it's still debatable whether more might have been done, sooner and at lower cost, by simply encouraging private parties to establish and maintain private hunting and photo-safari preserves.

Now, however, the permanent bureaucracies created under the rubric of "species preservation" (far from patting themsleves on the back and folding their tents) have taken on a life of their own, and are starting to make clear the real cost of signing away Americans' private-property rights in favor of such fatally vague government goals.

If anyone had warned, back then, that the state and federal bureaucracies put in place to "protect endangered species" would someday attempt to ban window screens because they block "threatened" mosquitos from enjoying their "habitual feeding grounds" — our children's flesh — he or she would surely have been hooted down as a ridiculous alarmist with no grip on reality.

But let us now consider who has actually lost his grip on reality and common sense — and in a case involving a predator far more deadly than the mere mosquito.

In Fishkill, New York, The Associated Press reported in March 1999 that Jay Montfort has erected a waist-high wire-mesh fence around the wooded property owned by his family's quarry and cement-block business, to keep out the rattlesnakes.

"They're rattlesnakes," Mr. Montfort says. "They're poisonous. They're deadly. It seems pretty fundamental that you should be able to keep deadly things off your property."

Not in New York. The state Department of Environmental Conservation went to court last week, seeking to have the fence removed as a violation of the state's Endangered Species Act.

The fence could have the effect of "disturbing, harrying and worrying" the "threatened" timber rattlers, according to Theodore Kerpez, a state wildlife biologist. It would do that by blocking the snakes from areas where they are (presumably — no one has actually asked them) accustomed to hunt, bask, and reproduce. The fence could thus cause the snakes "physiological stress," Kerpez argues in court papers.

(A "threatened" species, you understand, is a species that does not meet any definition of "endangered," but whose presence is cited by the state to block otherwise legal private land uses, anyway. Though no one has ever counted the rattlesnakes of upstate New York, it seems a safe bet there are a million of 'em out there.)

"We have an obligation to protect not only the attractive species, but the rattlesnakes and the other less cuddly animals that make up the biodiversity of the state of New York," agrees Richard Brodsky, chairman of the state Assembly's environmental conservation committee.

Funny: Here I thought their only obligation was to protect and defend the rights of their human constituents — including the right to quiet enjoyment of privately deeded property — as guaranteed by the Constitutions of the United States and the state of New York.

But even if the current law in New York is so weird as to "establish" the religion of Extreme Environmentalism by making it illegal to "disturb and harm" rattlers, surely that would refer to purposely seeking them out and killing them in their dens, attempting to wipe out animals that keep to themselves and offer little offense. Once such laws are interpreted to mean you can't even screen such pests off your property, can a ban on window screens because they cause "worry and stress" to "threatened" mosquitos be far behind?

And at that point, what about those poor little smallpox germs, cooped up for all these years in a couple of jars in Moscow and Atlanta? I ask you, is that fair? Weren't they also "born free"?

"I Wouldn't Trust the Market ..."
🌿

My column of March 26, 1999, on New York state "endangered species" bureaucrats fighting efforts by a business owner there to fence rattlesnakes off his property brought the following from an Eastern reader:

"One of the worst columns that I've read from Vin. Libertarians have never been able to address species loss and extinction well. Applying 'property protection' to species protection has never been shown to be a viable method of species recovery. Animals do not recognize property lines and do not neatly fit into game parks and reserves, regardless of ownership.

"The answers are never short and sweet. That irritates ideologues.

"One idea of incorporation of a species and allowing this corporation the right was derided in this (Internet) discussion group. Remember the 'turtles can sue' thread?

"Rather than being blinded by ideology, I suggest that policy makers look at the solutions that are most effective at protecting species. Not all species are readily marketable; consequently, I wouldn't trust the market to preserve unpopular species. Relying on the whims of short-sighted marketeers is not good public policy and merely shrugging shoulders when a species is threatened due to human activity is not an option."

I replied:

Welllllllll then: If we can't figure out a way to award voting and property rights to animals, we're now branded as "ideologues."

How about this for "addressing species loss and extinction well":

Nature's God tries out thousands of new species, all the time, and in this process of trial and error thousands go extinct and are "lost." This is a good thing. If this process weren't ongoing, sudden environmental changes could easily wipe out all life on Earth. Thank goodness there were a few little mammals around to take over, after the meteor wiped out all the dinosaurs. But didn't those mammals probably fill an environmental niche created when an earlier less successful form of saurian went extinct? Do we really wish that little misfit lizard had been "preserved," leaving no niche for our "fuzzy rodent" evolutionary ancestors?

This process seems to have worked out just fine for many

millions of years, before it ever occurred to any smug city dweller with time on her hands to try and interfere. There wouldn't have been room for homo sapiens and some of our favorite eating species, like cows and piglets, if Nature hadn't wiped out all kinds of dinosaurs and trilobites and slimy crawling things to make room.

Now some will say, "Those earlier species were a mistake." But "mistake" is an odd attempt to impose a moral judgment on a natural process. Thomas Edison (who I do not mean to compare to "God," in any other sense) didn't make "thousands of mistakes" in trying to find the right stuff from which to manufacture light-bulb filaments. The failures were not "mistakes," but part and parcel of the natural process of trial and error.

Besides, earlier species were able to keep "life" going when the world presented a totally different environment, then pass the torch along to species better suited to new conditions ... as our species doubtless someday will, whether we like it or not.

This "species loss and extinction" is natural, and part of the "will" (or natural evolution) of God or Nature, which ever name you prefer. Certainly, we are free to attempt to educate our fellow men in the concept that shooting every individual of a given rare animal for its fur or plumage is short-sighted. We can urge them to establish private-property claims, then husband these resources in a way that will enrich their progeny.

But to attempt otherwise to interfere in any way with this process of ongoing "species extinction" is stupid, hopeless, evil, prideful, counterproductive, likely to be used to justify terrible tyrannies by smug "green" zealots self-assured in the righteousness of their bizarre cause, and an unjustified interference with the will of Nature's God, by creatures too stupid to have any *chance* of understanding what results their interference might produce ... assuming they had any real power to stop such processes, which is highly doubtful.

The argument is made that some minor species may yet turn out to contain a biological ingredient that can cure cancer. (Not a hint of anthrocentrism there, I hope?) But this only reveals much of the fraud of "species protection" as now practiced. There is *no* genetic difference between the Northern Spotted Owl and spotted owls in general — the only difference is where they live, and some minor variations in coloring, probably due to climate.

Therefore, given that "southern" spotted owls are plentiful, the "species protection" folks, if they were honest, should be telling us, "OK, the genetic heritage is secure; you can go ahead and shoot and kill every Northern Spotted Owl you find."

But they don't. Oh no. Instead, "species preservation" is expanded to mean that the "species" must be preserved in every micro-habitat where it's now present (no matter by what historical accident — like "threatened" non-native horses in Nevada). In truth, this is merely an excuse to block all further land development for human use, anywhere — a blatant cheat, scam, and fraud.

(Besides which, we are presented in effect with a choice of sharing our world with only one of two distinct groups of species — those feeble failing critters that will soon go extinct, and the stronger more robust ones that would subsequently develop to fill their empty ecological niches. By "preserving" the first set, we prevent the second set from ever being born. Now: If we're going to be pragmatic about this, in which group of species are we more likely to find our proverbial "cure for cancer"? Here's a hint: You have a choice between two piles of pearl oysters. One has already been shucked. The other is fresh and unopened ...)

🌿 🌿 🌿

Why should "policy makers" be encouraged or empowered to "find effective means to protect species"? "Protecting species" is the goal of a religion known as Environmentalism and its zealots. Our Constitution forbids our government from doing anything to promote the causes of (to "establish") any specific religion.

"The market" is simply a way of describing the results of an endless series of private voluntary transactions judged to be mutually beneficial by free (human) traders. The market does a great job of preserving species. Once uses were found for cattle and goats and carrots and various types of mushrooms, human beings voluntarily took it upon themselves (as a source of "profit") to propagate and preserve these species, to develop endless genetically engineered varieties of them, to protect (by buying and putting up "private-property" signs) the habitats of those species that cannot be easily propagated "in captivity," etc.

As long as private-property ownership is allowed, hardly anything of real value ever vanishes. Even in Africa (and directly contradicting our correspondent's claim that "Applying 'property protection' to species protection has never been shown to be a viable method of species recovery,") relatively free Tanzania finds it no longer has any threat of looming elephant extinction since it allowed villagers to claim a "private-property right" in the nearest elephant herd, charging fees for those who wish to hunt or merely photograph them. Only in socialist Kenya, where no private ownership of elephants is allowed, does poaching continue to threaten the extinction of the local herds. (See Ike Sugg's *Elephants and Ivory*, available from Laissez Faire Books in San Francisco for $12.95; 800-326-0996.)

"The market" again turns out to be the answer, whereas the model of "selfless government protection unsullied by the dirty profit motive" proves a disaster at every turn.

Private "tiger farms" have been proposed in Southeast Asia, where owners could raise tigers in a semi-wild state, harvesting only at sustainable rates to fill the needs of the Chinese medical market, zoos, etc. Their incentive to preserve viable prides (OK, tigers don't form "prides" — what do I call them, "clutches"?) to pass on to their heirs would be enormous, and their private security against poachers would doubtless be formidable. Of course, "conservationists" — who are really only state-socialists in a green cloak — have fought this proposal tooth and nail, asserting that such "ownership" of animals is inherently evil — thus helping to drive the tiger near extinction in many areas, since what no man may own will simply be used up by the first poacher, in a race to beat the second poacher, no matter how many "laws" are passed.

🌿 🌿 🌿

The free market allows bunny-huggers to pool their funds and buy any land they consider "environmentally sensitive" — as the Nature Conservancy often does. However, that would require these "greens" to put their own money where their mouths are, giving up some of their vacations and BMWs in exchange for part ownership of some desolate desert canyon or mosquito swamp. Not only that, faced with the economic reality that they can't buy and "save" *everything*, they would then have to set priorities and *choose* whether to spend millions buying prime commercial real estate in Southern California to save the Delhi sands-loving fly, or rather to let the miserable maggots go and instead spend their money buying up some peaceful riverbank near Tucson, thus preserving dozens of rare songbirds.

(I'd go with the brightly colored songbirds, myself. At least you could enjoy an occasional picnic.)

But they don't want to *choose* and back the real-world economic costs of their choices with their own bank accounts, do they?

Instead, "I wouldn't trust the market to preserve unpopular species" is merely another way of saying, "I propose to hire armed bully-boys and authorize them to force others to fund my casual warm and fuzzy whims, seizing money from the unwilling to use in forcing private-property owners to kneel before and honor (however reluctantly) the dictates of my particular religious priesthood, by having armed agents threaten them with jail if they do anything with their own land that threatens to harm or even irritate the snails, bugs, weeds, and venomous pests living there, since under my religion — which I now want armed government agents in really big trucks to impose by force — the survival of these obscure molds and leeches is more important than the so-called 'liberty' of a property owner to do what he wants on and with his property, so long as he harm no other human."

"Merely shrugging shoulders when a species is threatened due to human activity is not an option," we are told. Ah, but throwing California farmers in prison for running over rats with their farm machinery *is* "an option," apparently, and a darned good one.

Oh, these statists, these acolytes of the Cult of the Omnipotent State. It wasn't the *methods* that were the problem, apparently, when an earlier generation of big-government goons said, "Rather than being blinded by ideology, I suggest that policy makers look at the solutions that are most effective at eliminating Jews, Slavs, and other subhuman races from our midst," or "I wouldn't trust the market to force these darned Ukrainians to give up their precious private-property deeds and join in our cooperative farming schemes, as laid down by Comrades Marx and Engels. No, relying on the whims of shortsighted marketeers is not good public policy, and merely shrugging shoulders when these stubborn Kulaks stand in the way of our grand scheme for a workers' paradise is not an option."

No, no, the only problems were the *goals* of Herrs Hitler and Himmler, Comrades Stalin and Dzerzhinsky — eliminating various non-Aryan races, or imposing that earlier less subtle form of communism. *Those* were evil. But the *methods* these

gentlemen pioneered for government agents to use in imposing a "brave new vision" on an unwilling populace — propagandizing children in the government schools to memorize sim-
plistic slogans and snitch on their elders, etc. — weren't so bad
at all. We just need to marry those methods of government
force and coercion to a more *noble* goal, *my* goal, which this
month happens to be "species preservation ..."

How easy it is to say, "I don't think we should allow ..."
when you don't actually envision *yourself* beating the helpless
nonconformist to the ground with your rifle butt, forcing him
to drag himself on bloody hands and knees onto the cattle car
as his weeping wife and children are led away, never to see
him again.

"Allow?" "Allow"? The only alternative to the "free market" is a market in which those who enter into transactions of
which you disapprove are arrested, beaten, and — if they continue to show any spunk — shot in the head and dumped in a
mass grave.

In the end, that is what it means — that is what it *always*
means — to "not trust the free market."

Environmentalism as a State-Established Religion

*(from an address to the Doctors for Disaster Preparedness, Las
Vegas, Nevada, July 2001)*

The First Amendment says Congress shall make no law
regarding an establishment of religion. That's generally interpreted as: "There shall be a separation between church and
state." It doesn't really say that, but that's the shorthand way in
which it's often interpreted. And what it means is the teachers
on the public payroll in the government school should not be

proselytizing Scientology or Catholicism or Methodism. We all understand that, and it's actually well enforced up to a point. Our Supreme Court will spend hours listening to arguments about whether a schoolteacher in Tennessee is allowed to display the Ten Commandments in his classroom.

But what did they really mean, the Founding Fathers, when they said that Congress shall not pass a law respecting an establishment of religion? What is an establishment of religion? Well, you go back to the 18th century and you see what these people were used to, having grown up under British colonial rule. In England to this day, the queen is not only the head of the state, but also the head of the church and the defender of the faith. It says so right on the coinage in abbreviated Latin that no one can actually read any more, "Fidele Defensor — Defender of the Faith."

If you weren't a practicing member, or at least pretended to be, of the Orthodox Anglican Church and you were in the British colonial hierarchy, you weren't generally going to get very far. And the British took it upon themselves to actually outlaw other religions. We tend to think they're rather liberal-minded in Britain, but they outlawed the Quakers, for instance. And a great case that resonates down through history from the 1600s is known as the *Bushell* case. Edward Bushell was the jury foreman in that case. They had closed the Quaker meeting houses in London, so the head of the Quaker denomination in London preached his sermon out in the streets and was arrested for preaching an illegal sermon and hauled into court. They rounded up this randomly selected jury, and the jurors then selected as their foreman Edward Bushell.

And the court instructed them, Look, it's against the law to preach a non-Anglican sermon, especially these Quakers, whatever they are. It's banned. The fellow was caught preaching a sermon in the street. Many witnesses say he did so. He doesn't even deny it. So what you have to do is convict him, and we'll put him in prison.

The jury retired to deliberate, and they came back and they found him not guilty. And the judge said, What part of this do you not understand? We told you what the law is. It's against the law to preach a Quaker sermon. We can't have that — pretty soon we'd have every kind of dangerous dissident sect out there, maybe even Catholics. The magistrates, the enforcement officers, found him preaching the Quaker sermon in public on a Sunday morning in the public streets. He does not deny that he did this. You have to convict him.

They locked the jury up for a week with no food, no water, no toilet facilities. I mean, their friends were passing them jugs of water on poles through this upstairs window so they could survive until they would find him guilty. Edward Bushell and the rest of the jury refused. And this case found its way to the Court of Common Pleas in London. In our system, the Court of Common Pleas is a lower level of court. But in the English system it's the highest appellate court, or court of appeals. And in a decision that rings down through the ages, the highest court in England ruled, no, the jury has a right to find according to its own conscience. It doesn't matter what the law says. It doesn't matter what the facts of the case say. The jury is perjured of its verdict — in other words, they're lying — if they do anything but bring a verdict according to their own conscience regardless of the law or the instructions of the judge. You have to let the guy go. He's been found innocent.

This is where we get our right to a jury trial. This is what the Fully Informed Jury Association has been trying to remind people about in this country: The power of jurors to nullify bad laws. That's why they could never get a conviction under the Fugitive Slave Act in this country in the 1850s. With a randomly selected jury, you'd always have at least a couple of abolitionists going, "This law is stupid." Now, there wouldn't be any question about the facts of the case. They didn't think those black people wearing striped clothes with the manacles on their wrists who were found in the church basement were the minister's visiting relatives from New Hampshire. There was no doubt about what was going on. They just found them innocent because they felt the law was "a ass." The law was bad. It violated their conscience. They wouldn't enforce it.

The power of juries comes down from the *Bushell* case, as does — less directly — our freedom of religion and the notion the founders of this country had that they didn't want people to be put on trial for preaching illegal sermons. It's no coincidence that after the defendant in that case was set free, he migrated to these shores. He founded a colony on the shores of the Chesapeake. They named it after the defendant in the *Bushell* case, William Penn. It's called Pennsylvania. That's where the Founding Fathers met to write the Bill of Rights in 1787. And that's why they said that Congress shall not establish a religion — not make laws respecting the establishment of religion.

So the question is — religion is not taught in our schools, but environmentalism is — so, what is environmentalism? We're told it's a science. Well, if you want to teach the scientific method to precocious 11- and 12- and 13-year-olds, I would say that's fine. You sit them down and you say, the scientific method, it's just logic. If you think about it, we observe phenomena. When we turn on the heat under the kettle and steam comes out, what is going on? That's an observed phenomenon. We can all agree it's a reproducible result. No matter how many fires you light under how many kettles, unless you're at extremely high altitude or under the ocean or something, under normal circumstances you're going to get steam. It's an observed, verifiable, repeatable phenomenon.

Now we come up with a theory to try to explain it. It has something to do with the heat; maybe the water is made out of molecules that are converted to a gaseous or vaporized form under heat, and the vaporous form takes up more room than the solid form, so the resulting steam builds up pressure in the vessel — whatever your theory is. Then you come up with ways to test your theory. You know, let's come up with other things to do with water, and let's see if it behaves in ways that meet this theory that it's made out of little molecules or something. We test our theory scientifically.

Now, what about environmentalism? You've heard speakers here talking about global warming. Our kids are taught in the school there's a landfill crisis. There's no place to put our garbage. That's why they have to sort and recycle our garbage. Can we go through those three steps? Is there an observed phenomenon that we can all agree on? Do the data show there's global warming? Well, the whole case falls apart immediately, because even the guy who runs the satellite program for NASA says he can't figure out where they're getting the data. There is no global warming to begin with. So before we even come up with a theory to explain it, you might want to establish that it's an observed phenomenon that can be verified.

But then even if we were to concede that global warming exists and that there's a landfill crisis — which is absurd; you could fit all the garbage this country will generate in the next 50 years in a one-mile-square hole in North Dakota. There may be a political crisis over where to site landfills, but we don't have any shortage of room in which to dump our garage. But even if we just stipulate that the crisis exists, for the sake of argument, then you try to come up with a theory that explains what causes it and a test to see if you can affect the results. And you look at the proposed solutions.

Let's say we agree to cripple our entire industrial economy by reducing our emissions of greenhouse gases by a third. Then we ask how that could possibly affect the atmosphere, even in a best-case scenario. Well, if 85 percent of the bad stuff in the atmosphere comes from natural sources, then reducing man-made emissions by a third — which would cripple our industrial economy, even if everyone followed the rules, and the rules of the Kyoto treaty already exempt the "poor nations," like Red China and India, by the way, but we're pretending here that we could reduce man-made emissions by one third

— well, that would still only improve atmospheric levels by 5 percent. Is it even worth trying?

These are the kinds of skeptical tests that would be applied if this were a science. But I'm here to submit that environmentalism is not a science. Not only do the practitioners refuse to abide by any of these principles of the laws of scientific evidence, they outright reject evidence when it contravenes what they want to teach the kiddies.

Now, I should say as an aside that everybody likes clean air and clean water. Nobody here is in favor of making the skies brown with soot and having the rivers run with raw sewage. And, in fact, my father can remember a day — I'm old enough I can remember a day — when the sky was blocked out with orange clouds in Pittsburgh and Weirton and in Washington, Pennsylvania. And my father would take me down to the Connecticut River where he used to fish as a boy, and the sewage treatment plants were so primitive that when there was a heavy rain they would flood, it would exceed their capacity, and raw sewage would flow into the river.

But what's interesting is our industrial civilization started to clean that up in the '40s and '50s and '60s, long before there was a federal Environmental Protection Agency. So I think there is a defensible case that can be made that it is prosperity, brought about by capitalism, which allows that surplus income that allows us to clean up our environment. And that corporations do this because they want good public relations and they want to please their customers. And it reaches a point where it's cheaper to buy and burn oil than it is to burn coal and pollute the atmosphere.

And the notion that collectivism somehow is the solution? Well, go to the Soviet Union. Large sections of the former Soviet Union, from Chernobyl to the nuclear-waste dumping grounds under the Arctic Ocean, are now toxic graveyards. The notion that because they were acting on behalf of all the people, those nations should remain pristine ecological paradises? Again, you just test the theory against the observed result. And collectivism didn't have a great result. If we're going to be scientists, isn't that what we want to do? We want to look at what really works in the real world.

I don't generally like to read passages, but just in searching the Web for a week preparing to come to speak to y'all, it was very interesting how much material is moving on this subject, how easy it is to make this case if you just look around you. There's a freelance journalist in New York named Joseph Kellard, and he noted in a piece on July 8th — and most of these refer to the ABC News Special that John Stossel put on two weeks ago, late June, called "Tampering with Nature," in which he examined the way children are being educated about environmentalism in the schools.

And Kellard writes, "In his hour-long report [throughout the program], Stossel used facts to debunk many environmentalists' claims, such as that the Earth is catastrophically warming. One example of this came when he interviewed a class of elementary-school students. He told them the Environmental Protection Agency says air quality in America has improved over the past 30 years. 'No,' the children yelled, 'they're wrong, they're lying.' In part this exchange demonstrates how environmentalism has become a largely unquestioning movement, not viewed as what it really is: a crusade that invariably manipulates facts in order to charge human beings with, quote, destroying the planet."

Then he quotes an interesting speech given by Dr. Andrew Bernstein at an Earth Day rally — well, an Industrial Technology Day rally. It's the right-wing answer to the Earth Day rally. You know Earth Day is held on Lenin's birthday, right? It is. It's no coincidence. And Dr. Bernstein, who's a senior writer at the Ayn Rand Institute, presented the following facts, quoted here by Kellard, the journalist. Quote, "At the time the Clean Air Act was passed in 1970, our air was becoming progressively cleaner, not dirtier; had been doing so for a long time, precisely because of industrial progress. According to Professor Matthew Crenson at Johns Hopkins, sulfur dioxide pollution had been declining for decades."

In 1971, just about the time the EPA's getting rolling, Crenson of Johns Hopkins writes, "In some cities the sulfur dioxide content of the air today is only one-third to one-fourth what it was before World War II. Measurements in 14 U.S. cities in 1931 showed an average particulate concentration of 510 micrograms per cubic meter. In 1957, it was down to 120 micrograms. In 1969, the measurement stood at 92 micrograms per cubic meter. The major reason for this positive trend was the conversion to cleaner burning fuel, such as oil and gas, from coal or wood. Improvements in technology in a free market caused this trend, not environmentalists' propaganda or government legislation."

Again, this was long before the EPA got going in 1969 and '70. And Kellard concludes, "Stringent pollution standards ultimately cost Americans billions of dollars in retarded or halted technological development which is the best means to keep or make air and water clean. In reality, environmentalists set the philosophical foundation policy at the EPA."

I love this. Here's something we ran in our own paper, in the *Review-Journal*, July 3, 2001. It's by Robert Tracinski, editor of *The Intellectual Activist* and also associated with the Ayn Rand Institute in Southern California. And he, again, is writing about John Stossel's special.

"On Friday, ABC news correspondent John Stossel aired a hard-hitting report challenging the environmentalist movement and suggesting that 'tampering with nature' makes human life better — that such 'unnatural' phenomena as clean water, heated homes and modern medicine are an advance over living in a mud hut and foraging for berries.

"The environmentalists, however, have gotten used to treating the press as a wholly owned subsidiary — so they did their best to sink Stossel's special. Under the auspices of the

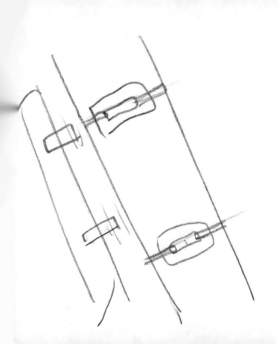

2 c flour
3 tsp B. pwdr
sugar
1/2 tsp salt
1/2 c shortning
2/3 c milk
1/2 cream tarter
450° 10-12 min

Environmental Working Group, several parents who had allowed their kids to be interviewed for a segment on environmental education announced that they were revoking their consent.

"One parent, Brad Neal, complained that he agreed to the interview because he thought it would be about 'sharing our children's thoughts on the environment' — but he changed his mind once he discovered the show's 'negative slant.' Apparently, he only allows his children to be exploited for the correct causes.

"Revealing its exact degree of journalistic independence, ABC caved in to the greens and cut the segment. ..." [Meaning that the interviews with the California kids had been deleted from the preview tape of the show.]

Now, Tracinski wrote this before that show aired. Mr. Stossel was actually a little more creative than that. He went out and found some schoolchildren in New York and duplicated the same research and asked them about environmentalism. And I've reported the results. They were screaming at him, "No, no, the air's getting dirtier." These sound bites, this mantra, this catechism that they memorize in school. But what I liked about Tracinski's piece — he's not a professional journalist and yet he does the first thing a journalist should do, he goes to check something out himself. He says the kids Stossel initially interviewed were found at an Earth Day fair held for school children in Los Angeles. Again, this is Tracinski writing:

"I attended that event, and what I saw was an exercise in manipulation so cynical that it must be exposed. If Stossel won't be allowed to expose it, I will.

"The children, ranging in age from 6 to 15, were bused in by the hundreds. It was an official school field trip, supported by the park service and the City Council.

"The students were told that Earth Day was like Mother's Day, that we celebrate Earth Day to show that we 'love our mother.' What would you think of someone telling your eight-year-old that if he doesn't accept a certain political agenda, that means he doesn't love his mommy?

"The children were asked to sing along with the 'Please Conserve' song, with lyrics like, 'They want to drill our parks for oil/That will pollute our sea and soil.' I'm not sure which is worse: children at a school-sponsored event being drafted to take sides on a current political controversy — or the presentation of these serious issues, which ought to be debated by thoughtful adults, in the form of a simple-minded children's song.

"The practical purpose of the event was to push 'green power,' as opposed to coal, oil, and nuclear, which were condemned as evil and 'dirty.' The students were told repeatedly that solar power is the wave of the future. As the event's organizer declared, 'If anyone ever tells you that (solar power) won't work, tell them that you were here at Earth Day and you saw it work.'"

So Mr. Tracinski then does a little research. "He did not tell them that, although 100 percent of the nation's central-station solar power plants are located in California, they generate less than 200 megawatts, a measly 0.3 percent of the state's power supply. Had he given them these facts, they might have been able to decide for themselves whether solar power really works.

"Or perhaps not. To assess the merits of a new source of power requires a basic background of scientific, technological and economic knowledge. The real absurdity is that the pro-solar propaganda was being pushed to children who are too young to know what a megawatt is or even what a percentage means. These children are being indoctrinated in environmentalism before they have any capacity to grasp its meaning and judge it for themselves. And they are being taught this dogma as a substitute for learning what they would need to know to become rational, informed adults."

Lou Rockwell works now with Hans Herman Hoppe, who teaches economics here at University of Nevada Las Vegas and who worked in the past with Murray Rothbard, who also held a chair in economics here at UNLV. Lou Rockwell runs the Ludwig von Mises Institute in Auburn, Alabama. And when I first heard Lew use the term I didn't understand it. He called these environmental — and again, it's not everyone who's concerned about the environment. We all have some concerns. But what would we call them, then? Eco-extremists? He called these people watermelons, and I had to ask him what he meant. He said, "Well, they're green on the outside, but they're red on the inside." And I don't think that's stretching it too far. Their agenda is anti-capitalist. It's anti-private property. Look at the elephants.

Ike Sugg has written a nice little book that Laissez Faire Books in San Francisco will sell you for a very modest sum, on the movement to save the elephants in Africa, which I highly recommend. And to oversimplify it grossly — but we're trying to move along briskly here — he looks at Kenya and he looks at Tanzania.

Kenya is a socialist country where the elephants are held to be the property of the government, being held on behalf of all the people. I mean, how often have we heard that about our park lands and our forest lands in this country? And so the country protects the elephants. But not very well, as it turns out. They're seriously endangered. Poachers are killing elephants all the time.

And the notion that these poachers can get in the preserves and kill the elephants, I mean, it's not quite like sneaking in and stealing eggs. An elephant is a really big thing. And they have to get in there with these very large weapons. I mean, they don't shoot them with handguns. They've knocked the elephant down with a 50 caliber bullet that sounds like a cannon going off; you can hear it from a couple of miles away. They then go at the elephant with chain saws to cut off its tusks and load them on trucks and run them out. And the notion that these people can't be found and caught is absurd. Clearly, they're bribing the government functionaries to stay out of that particular sector when they decide to kill the elephants, or else the guards are so incompetent the poachers just check their patrol schedules on the bulletin board.

And so Kenya has a terrible elephant shortage. They're all dying off. They're importing elephants from elsewhere to bring them in to keep the poachers supplied, as opposed to what's happened in Tanzania. I don't want to praise Tanzania as the ultimate libertarian republic. It's in Africa, for heaven's sake. But compared to Kenya it's a free-market paradise, because they came up with a very different solution, in part because they were broke and they couldn't afford to set up all these parks with all these rangers. So in Tanzania they just said, Look, we have no other option, let's go to the villagers in the villages closest to where these elephants run around and try this: We'll just tell them, here is a deed, you own the elephants, they're yours, do with them as you please. If they're trampling your corn fields and you don't like it, shoot them, kill them, we don't care. They're yours, you really own them.

On the other hand, you might want to charge tourists to come look at them. And you're free to do that. You can charge the tourists. You can run a little safari. They're your elephants, you own them. And if occasionally one gets old and you have to kill it and cut off its tusks and sell them for ivory, maybe that's a sustainable, renewable harvest that you villagers could make money with for generations to come.

And the Tanzanian farmers ask, "They don't belong to the government? If we do harvest some ivory, we don't have to give it to you?" No, no, no, you sell it, keep it, whatever you want. "And we can charge people to come look at the elephants? We can run the tours, run the safaris? We can sell a hunting license, let someone shoot one occasionally?" Sure, they're yours.

Well, of course, Tanzania has elephants coming out of their ears. There's no shortage of elephants in Tanzania. And when the poachers go in there, it's the poachers who get killed. I mean, if you owned a valuable resource and it was something really big and easy to keep track of and someone arrived and tried to shoot it, you'd kill the poacher. They're dragging out poachers by the heels behind their trucks, all over Tanzania. There's no problem keeping the elephants. It's a private property solution.

And yet, you go to the UN and you go to these environmental groups and say, "Look, the tiger is endangered. The Chinese are willing to pay all kinds of money for the internal organs of tigers. They're nuts. They think they promote longevity, or give you sexual stamina, whatever. We don't care why they want the stuff. The key is, why don't you let people in Borneo and Malaysia and places where the tigers are endemic, set up tiger preserves and farm them, just raise them for profit and harvest them at a sustainable level. I mean, if you own them, you're not going to kill them all in one year and not have any to breed next year. Let these people sell them to the Chinese for their medical uses. And the environmentalists go, "No, no, that's an unacceptable solution."

Why? It would save the tigers. We have economic uses for carrots and chickens. Is anybody worried that the carrot is endangered and that we're going to run out of them? We have an incentive to breed more carrots. Chickens are not going to be extinct. We have found commercial uses for them. If you let them set up tiger farms, there will be no problem with tiger extinction. But the environmentalists are opposed to that because it's a free-market, private-property-oriented solution. They show their real agenda when they won't adopt a solution that would work. Instead they talk about "animal rights," and how it's wrong to "make an animal a slave by owning him." The truck farmers of New Jersey are apparently operating carrot slave camps.

I'll read you one more piece. This is from World Net Daily, one of those Internet news sources, so you start out taking it with a little skepticism. But in fact, Paul Sperry, their Washington bureau chief, does some good work. And I think this is a hopeful sign, that talk radio and the Internet are allowing access now to this kind of data that the — what shall we call them — the regulators at CBS News and the *Washington Post* and the *New York Times* used to try to keep us from getting access to. There's an end-run being done around those establishment media these days.

Paul Sperry at World Net Daily writes, just recently, again about John Stossel's special (thank goodness for Mr. Stossel), "The hidden message in the environmentalist movement is anti-capitalism; anti-individualism; anti-God; and ultimately, anti-America, since it's all these things upon which this country was founded. 'Global warming' alarmists have convinced kids, not to mention many gullible politicians and journalists" — if in fact there's a difference, someone earlier called these politicians delightfully childlike in their innocence — "that CO2-spewing factories are causing a, quote, 'greenhouse effect' that will overheat the planet and trigger a chain of disasters.

"Who's the villain? Industry. And why does industry pollute? To make profits. Of course, volcanoes have been spewing heat-trapping greenhouse gases since the Earth's mantle was formed. All the smokestacks and tailpipes in the world couldn't compete with Mount St. Helens' or Mount Pinatubo's carbon belches. Fact is, 85 percent of the CO2 in our atmosphere comes from natural sources. Man's activities produce the rest. But public school teachers skip that chapter."

And I'll interject that I know this first-hand. I think it was a year and a half ago at the newspaper, we received a report from one of these environmental groups — a very fancy, full-color, printed on coated paper report — on the evils of the greenhouse gases. And what it did is it graded the nations. It had the nations ranked according to the amount of greenhouse gases they produce. You can picture it forming this curve where the evil nations were off over on this side of the chart. Of course, the United States was way up there, along with West Germany and Great Britain. You know, huge emissions of greenhouse gases. I don't remember if it was gross or per capita. It might have been per capita.

And in the graph was this nice sort of ski-slope curve down to the good countries. The good countries like Sri Lanka and Zaire. Ceylon is Sri Lanka now, you have to keep track. And Bangladesh. Bangladesh was way down there. And the Philippines. The Philippines was way down at the low end of the chart, very small emissions of greenhouse gases per capita. And I looked at the date on the study on which this was based, and I thought maybe my memory was slipping. But it's wonderful to have computers on your desk these days. I did a search under Mount Pinatubo. The date for which they took their readings of the greenhouse-gas emissions per country was the year that Mount Pinatubo blew up in the Philippines. And I knew that must have dumped just enormous quantities of greenhouse gases into the atmosphere that should have put the Philippines up at least even with the United States or probably far higher, according to these statistics that 85 percent of this stuff is naturally occurring.

So I called up this particular environmental group, at their headquarters in Washington. And I said, there's something wrong here. The Philippines is listed with this tiny level of emissions of chlorine gases and greenhouse gases: sulfur dioxide, carbon monoxide, all this stuff. And yet your base data year is the year Mount Pinatubo blew up. And he goes, their press person goes, "Oh, look at the footnote." I said, "What?" He said, "After the legend at the top that says greenhouse gas emissions, there's an asterisk. Go to the bottom for the footnote." So I look at the bottom. It says "from man-made sources." Well, what, the ozone hole is going to know whether these gases are emitted by a volcano or by somebody's tailpipe? I mean, there's clearly an agenda here to demonize industrial nations for having this huge level of bad stuff they pour out. But we don't count volcanic gases emitted by Mount Pinatubo; somehow they're different.

To me that's just stoned evidence that we're not looking for the scientific facts. We've got a political agenda, which is anti-industrial development, basically. And the notion that we should all go back to pedicabs; we should all live in a world the way Alfred the Great knew it in the 9th century without any of the modern conveniences brought about by the industrial revolution. You know, these people should have to come face-to-face with what they're really proposing.

Anyway, to finish with Mr. Sperry's piece from World Net Daily, "After school, children's minds are polluted with more industry-bashing green propaganda, thanks to Hollywood nature nuts, like capitalist-turned-socialist Ted Turner."

In his TBS cartoon, quote, "'Captain Planet and the Planeteers,' industrialists aren't just greedy, they're downright evil, polluting just for the hell of it until the Team Green superheroes rescue the planet from their dirty mitts. Reduce, re-use, recycle." In some schools this pledge to recycle is recited more often than the Pledge of Allegiance. But what kids aren't taught is that most recycling doesn't work and makes no economic sense at all. If you recycle, chances are you're wasting your time. Because plastics are so hard to sort and separate, only about 2 percent of bottles and other plastics ever get recycled. Sorting costs can run as high as $1,500 a ton, far outstripping any potential revenue.

"Companies and cities just have no incentive to do it, so backlogs grow higher and higher. Some cities actually have to pay recyclers to take newspapers because it's too costly to invest in the de-inking machines and other equipment used in recycling them. Recycling a newspaper is 10 times as expensive as dumping it in a landfill. Only recycling aluminum cans makes sense."

There's a wonderful report — I couldn't find the clip in

my files; it's been a couple of years — but there was a fine report by a lady reporter for the *Mercury News* in San Jose, California. She was invited out to do one of these standard heart-warming little stories, the little features that run Saturday or Sunday in the feature section about an honors class in the local high school which was donating an hour after lunch each day to sort garbage, basically, as their environmental project. They would go into the cafeteria and they would carefully sort the cardboard from the plastic and the plastic from the bottles. I think they actually sorted the white glass bottles from the brown from the green.

So she shows up with their photographer, and they take a picture of the proud teacher with her honors class. Isn't it wonderful the kids are willing to volunteer their time to help the environment? And then everybody shakes hands, and they told her she was free to go. And I think the photographer actually left. But this reporter was smart enough, and too few of us these days will even do this, she stuck around and didn't leave. She had one more person she wanted to talk to in that high school. And she found him. She found the head janitor — head custodial engineer, pardon me.

She said, "What do you do with the stuff after the kids finish sorting it into these various barrels, the cardboard and the plastic and the green glass?" And he goes, "Oh, yeah, we throw it in the dumpster out back." And she goes, "dumpster," like singular "dumpster?" He goes, "Sure." He says, "You know, it doesn't pay to recycle that stuff." The guy actually knew more than the teacher. The janitor's telling her, "You know, we're here on the Pacific Coast. I used to see barges heading out to sea. The Japanese would buy our used pasteboard, at least. Well, the market got saturated. They don't want it anymore. I mean, there's only so much you can chip and turn into fiberboard or whatever they did with it. It's just that we've saturated the market. Nobody will buy this stuff anymore. Recycling is a sham."

She asked, "Well, why don't you tell the kids?" She went back and phoned the teacher. And it turned out the teacher knew this, but wasn't going to tell the press. She was kind of upset that they had learned this. And she asked the teacher, "Why don't you tell the kids?" And the answer was, "Well, the main thing is that they feel good that they're doing something for the environment. It would only upset them if we told them that it didn't really do any good. It would destroy the lesson we're teaching them." And that's the level of fantasy you're dealing with.

There was a similar story just within the past year that started in the *Denver Post*. They did a feature about this class in one of the suburban schools around Denver where the teacher had been reading news accounts to the kids until they had tears in their eyes. They were literally crying about this terrible slavery that persists in Africa, human chattel slavery, where in these minor wars people are captured and still to this day sold on the slave markets in Sudan, or is it The Sudan, I lose track. And I don't mean to make fun of the fact that slavery still exists. But these kids were so concerned, they asked the teacher what could they do.

So they started holding paper drives and selling candy bars after school, all the various methods to raise money, to send money to Africa through this guy who runs a program out of Switzerland to buy slaves and set them free. So they were raising money to set the slaves free. They were doing this for a year.

And then the feedback starts coming back from the — what's the name of the French organization? Doctors Without Frontiers, Les Medicins sans Frontieres — that actually what was going on was, the laws of free-market economics began to apply. Money is coming in through this fellow who's collecting money from schoolchildren to buy slaves. So the slave markets are running short of the product, so they're going out and capturing more people and putting more slaves on the block because there's a demand that they can't fill.

And the reporter from the — I don't think it was the *Denver Post*; it may have been the competing *Rocky Mountain News* — went back to the same teacher and asked, "Have you heard what they're saying, that because you're sending money over there, more slaves are being captured and sold? Doesn't this concern you? Are you going to stop doing this?"

And the teacher thought about it and said she was very troubled. But in the end she decided, no, it was so important to the children to feel that they were doing something to solve the problem that they were not going to stop sending money to buy slaves and set them free.

Now, of course, many of those "set free" are immediately recaptured and sold again. This is the law of unintended consequences that comes into play when you try to override what happens in a real free-market economy. Again, this is not to say I'm in favor of buying or selling slaves. But what shall we make of this reluctance to accept real-world results as evidence that you might want to go try something new? It's a kind of magical thinking, which holds the purity of your intention counts for more than real-world results, even if the results are the opposite of what you intended.

So why do I say this is a religion? Let's compare this to a teaching, something we would never deny is a religion. Children are taught about heaven and hell. And this, of course, comes down to us from the Greeks who believed that the gods lived on Mount Olympus and that there was an underworld called Hades that you could physically get to.

Hercules is supposed to have climbed down through the Cracks of Doom into the bowels of the Earth and bribed Charon, who runs the ferry across the Styx, to take him to see his dead wife in Hades. You could get there if you tried hard enough, this was a real, physical place.

But as we enter the modern era, you get to a point a few centuries ago when people started to realize — and now we've got satellites; we've sent probes as far as Neptune — we know that there are no angels with wings living just above the clouds. We're pretty sure there's no physical hell just under our feet. And yet, children are still taught this as sort of a separate parallel belief system that they can cling to, and the excuse, explanation, or whatever — I don't mean to dismiss all religion here as valueless, by any means — but these constructs are just supported on the theory that, "It's useful if people believe these things, because it affects their behavior."

And so what difference does it make that physically we can demonstrate that you don't get a harp and wings and live just above the clouds? Heaven is this construct that has a philosophical reality. It doesn't have to link to our physical reality. So that's the way religious belief can sustain itself even when it seems to be contradicted by the evidence of physical reality. Which is fine in church or temple — I just thought government agents were banned from using tax money to promote one of these belief systems, one of these religions to the exclusion of any of the others.

If a teacher in the government schools started telling the kids that man is meant to be the steward of the Earth and have mastery over the animals, which have no souls, and the way we know this is because it says so right here in this book, the Bible, that teacher would be called to account, called in and told, "Not all these kids necessarily come from homes that share your faith, so knock it off," and if she persisted she'd be fired. Right?

Yet environmentalism, which is being taught in the schools pretty much exclusively and not with any notable degree of skepticism, has all the earmarks; it's the catechism of a religious faith that's being taught to these children in violation of the First Amendment.

So, what's the solution? This is where I think 95 percent of our neighbors go wrong. You explain this, and even if they buy what you're saying up to this point, they blow it. They go,

"Well, we'll just go protest to the school board. We'll write a letter to our congressman." And what will happen? Committees will be formed and reports will be written and a new edict will advise teachers to teach only established facts and not their religious beliefs. And who's going to actually get called before the new board of inquiry for violating this rule? It's that one-in-a-hundred teacher who teaches that Americans are free because of guns and gold and capitalism. He's the one who's going to be accused of promoting his own beliefs. Because, after all, that's abhorrent; it's environmentalism that everyone knows is true. So it's a vicious cycle.

I think John Taylor Gatto has it right. He was the New York State Teacher of the Year some years back. And he's written a wonderful book. His first little book was called *Dumbing Us Down*. His latest book, I think, is called, *The Underground History of American Education*, from Oxford Village Press. And Gatto, again, was a Teacher of the Year in the public schools. So he's not an outsider. He's someone who did very well in that system, who's now telling us, no, the government schools cannot be reformed, because they're not doing anything badly; they're doing exactly what they were built to do.

They're based on the Prussian model. After the Prussians lost to Napoleon in the early 1800s, they set up their school system in the 1820s and '30s to train better soldiers and better citizens to work in the wheels of industry. The whole idea was to create a docile underclass of people who had some reading and writing — they had to be able to read the instruction manuals for the machinery and to operate the rifles. But we didn't really want them educated the way the upper classes were educated in skeptical thought. They would just be dragooned into the government gynmasia and grouped by age and sent to the showers together and sent to physical education together.

They would be taught knowledge in small 50-minute bursts, and then the bell would ring and they would go to the next room. Because we were training them, after all, to be factory workers who report to the proper station when the whistle sounds in the factory.

That's the model of Prussian education that people like John Dewey and Horace Mann brought back to this country from Germany — Gatto documents all this — in the 1850s and '60s into Massachusetts. That's where the current set-up of our government schools comes from. And as McLuhan said, it's the form that dictates the function. Getting all these kids together by age, stripping them away from their mommy's apron strings, having them indoctrinated by the government, standing up and marching around to the sound of bells is what the government schools are about.

And trying to reform them back, supposedly back, into institutions that teach critical thought defies the very reason they were set up. They are there to civilize the children of the lower classes. The Bolshevik immigrants pouring in from third world countries like Ireland and Italy and Yugoslavia that had to be taught the Protestant work ethic, but also had to be trained into useful little soldiers and factory workers. And the idea that you can reform these schools is, I think, pointless.

We need to get rid of the government schools. Home schooling or private schooling of some kind without any government infringement is the only solution. I think Marshal Fritz is right. He runs the Separation of School and State Alliance out of Fresno, California. And he says the idea that we can reform our way out of this problem is nonsense. The government schools are just showing their true colors. If you ban environmentalism, they'll just find a new colored fruit to wrap around the red innards. It's socialism and it's anti-capitalism. It doesn't value our tradition of property rights and liberties. And the government schools cannot be part of the solution because they are the problem.

(Editor's Note: Even from within the Green Extreme, whistleblowers are now beginning to surface, confirming Vin's thesis here. See Appendix I.)

V
Sept. 11, 2001

"All We Are Asking Is Give War a Chance."
— *Cal Thomas*

September 14, 2001
The Passengers Were All Disarmed
🌱

In *The Adventure of the Silver Blaze*, the clue that helps Sherlock Holmes solve the case is "the curious incident of the dog in the night-time."

"The dog did nothing in the night-time," protests Inspector Gregory.

"That was the curious incident," Holmes replies.

Because the stable dog had not barked, Holmes knew that the night visitor must have been a member of the household.

On Sept. 11, 2001, as a shocked America watched our real-life disaster film unfolding at the Pentagon and in the burning skyscrapers of New York, I waited for the dog that never barked.

For years, American air travelers have suffered the indignity of being run through metal-detectors, being made to empty our pockets and our purses, remove our belt-buckles and our steel-insoled boots, run our bags through a scanner and submit them to "random searches," answer rote questions about whether we've stupidly let some guy in a turban insert in our bags a "gift for his sister in Boston," warned that we can be imprisoned for telling a joke because "security is no laughing matter."

All of this has cost us millions of productive hours wasted, not to mention billions in salaries for these laughably ineffective goons in their ill-fitting jackets.

I have long warned the only reason no plane was hijacked in this country in the past decade was because no serious terrorist had tried — that the only real purpose of this system was to accustom the residents of a once-free nation to showing our "government-issued photo IDs," to being disarmed on penalty of imprisonment, to random searches on demand — that what I've always called the "Fred and Ethel Mertz security system" would have zero impact on anyone serious enough to plan ahead and plant a "mole" among the minimum-wage employees who load the TV dinners aboard our aircraft.

On Sept. 11, I hoped I was wrong. As it quickly became clear that terrorists had boarded four transcontinental flights taking off from Eastern airports with an aim to use those fueled-up jets as flying bombs, I waited to hear in how many cases our crack security operatives had polished off the would-be terrorists before they ever made it onto the plane.

Had our security system stopped three-quarters of the would-be terrorists? Seventy-five percent might be considered a "passing grade."

Nope.

Had all the metal detectors and bomb-sniffing wands and random bag checks and "may I see your travel papers please" stopped one in four? Come on, surely one in four of the terrorist teams lay bleeding to death in an airport concourse somewhere. Think of all the years we've put up with this crap. One in four would not be an *acceptable* level of success, mind you. But it would at least be a *token* level of success.

Nope. The Fred and Ethel Mertz security system stoppeth not even one in four. And the only reason one of the four planes failed to hit its target — it now appears from passenger cell phone calls made from the plane that crashed near Pittsburgh — is that three brave American men decided to "do something," counterattacking their captors despite the fact these red-blooded American heroes had been *disarmed* by the very White House (and/or Capitol) they gave up their lives defending.

So what will Congress and the FAA and the airlines do in the months to come?

Will they conclude, "Well, we tried disarming law-abiding Americans; that obviously didn't work. What the heck, we might as well try the Archie Bunker plan — it couldn't possible do any *worse* "?

No. That could only happen in a free country ... like America before 1934.

Instead, what we're going to do now is pass more victim-disarmament laws and make our law-abiding disarmed victims wait in even *more* interminable lines while we search their bags and persons really, really, really well.

For little knives and nail-clippers.

"That's not gonna do any good; it's the minimum-wage employee comin' in the back door who did this," exclaimed my friend Pete the pilot (he didn't want me to use his real name). Pete flies 757s and 767s for a major airline back East.

Today's commercial aircraft swarm with people in the hours before they take off, Pete explained to me on the afternoon of the Sept. 11 disaster. From the janitors who vacuum out the planes to the employees of the contract catering firm who load the TV dinners and soda pop into the pantries, these tend to be minimum-wage employees, often recent immigrants, in high-turnover jobs. Background checks on these workers are minimal to non-existent, Pete explains. A mail-order driver's license would get Osama bin Laden's nephew one of these jobs, whereupon he could merely wait to be told which night to leave the knives and box-cutters — or the full-auto Uzi, for that matter — in with the ice cubes (though there's no evidence any firearm was used in the Sept. 11 attacks; Sarah Brady must be *so* frustrated; how on Earth are they going to justify more gun control when all the terrorists used were *knives*?).

But that won't be fixed. Instead, Pete warns, "It'll all be, as it always has been, public-relations sort of stuff; they'll make it *appear* that they're doing something. ... I worry they'll take more Draconian restrictions on our liberties that aren't gonna make us any more secure."

❧ ❧ ❧

"Now Is the Time for Americans to Defend America," wrote Aaron Zelman in a Sept. 11 press release from Milwaukee-based Jews for the Preservation of Firearms Ownership.

"We know: 1) The World Trade Center was undefended against any air attack; 2) the Pentagon was undefended against unexpected air attack; 3) the airliners carried nothing but unarmed and undefended people," Aaron continued. "The common factor: 'undefended.'

"What renders Americans undefended?" the JPFO press release goes on. "The culture of disarmament ... delivered to the terrorists many thousands of potential aircraft full of people who had *no* means to stop an onboard terrorist. Even the pilots and crew were federally guaranteed to be unable to resist hijackers by force. ...

"You will soon hear proposals to impose 'heightened domestic security.' ... Many more will urge complete disarmament of Americans, 'just to make sure' that the terrorist threat is reduced.

"We will hear 'this event changes our ideas about how free a free society can be.'

"Wrong," the JPFO concludes. "Now is the time, not to disarm ourselves and resign to government protection, but to arm Americans against terrorist attacks. ... Terrorists must learn: Americans don't get terrorized — Americans get prepared to fight back."

❧ ❧ ❧

My friend, Libertarian novelist L. Neil Smith of Colorado, went further in an essay also penned Sept. 11 and titled "While Norman Leared."

"Professor John Lott wrote a book a few years ago, called *More Guns: Less Crime*," Neil begins, "in which he said things — the mere title was enough — that still have the victim disarmament crowd screaming and weeping. Today, after horrifying attacks on the World Trade Center and the Pentagon, we can now safely observe that no guns means the ultimate crime.

"When I started writing my first novel, *The Probability Broach*, in 1977, I was just back from a national Libertarian Party convention where I was almost laughed off the platform committee I was a member of, because I introduced a plank warning that airport security featuring metal detectors, X-ray machines, and Air Marshals — which was a relatively new thing back then — represented the seeds of a police state. Each year that's passed since then has only proven that I was right. ...

"One of the features of *The Probability Broach* that was fun to write ... was a scene in which the hero, a cop from our world, boards an aircraft with his friends and is startled when representatives of the company merely want him to demonstrate that the ammunition in the guns he carries is designed not to harm the aircraft.

"I confess that I got this idea, way back then, from an episode of 'All in the Family' in which Archie Bunker proposes arming airline passengers to prevent hijackings. Norman Lear obviously thought the notion represented the very height of right-wing absurdity. But somebody tell me — now — how an aircraft full of well-armed people could be hijacked and used against civilization the way four were today. ...

"Everyone who died today ... was, first and foremost, a victim of Thomas Dodd, Howard Metzenbaum, Pete Shields, Sarah Brady, Charles Schumer, Diane Feinstein, Diana DeGette, and anybody else who ever strove to disarm victims of crime . ... (In) an armed society — a society consisting of armed individuals — today's acts would simply have been impossible to carry out successfully," L. Neil concludes.

"It's company policy that the pilots can't be armed on the

airplane," explains my friend Pete the pilot. "Now we've seen from recent events that that makes us sitting ducks.

"I know there's other pilots that are willing to carry guns. I can say that as a professional pilot I wouldn't be uncomfortable with my passengers being armed. ... I just can't help believing that if a random factor of armed passenger or crew members being on that plane were inserted in the equation ... maybe at least one of those towers wouldn't be gone today."

Flashback: My Airline Security Column of March 13, 1999

Back to the Drawing Board

During recent surprise exercises to find out if all the expensive, confoundedly demeaning security procedures at America's commercial airports are really doing any good, federal agents made the not terribly surprising discovery that they could sneak through supposed "security" doors 46 times at four major airports, and even board empty airliners at will.

"Without displaying any identification, the agents roamed the air operations area, passing 229 employees, but were challenged only 53 times," according to retired Adm. Cathal Flynn, the Federal Aviation Administration's associate administrator for aviation security.

Unstated is the obvious corollary, that even after being discovered the agents were always able to talk themselves out of trouble by flashing easily counterfeited ID cards. I mean, we would have heard if any had been shot and killed, right?

Admiral Flynn has subsequently warned airport officials nationwide by letter that, if this problem cannot be solved, it may become necessary to order a guard posted at every airplane.

Hundreds of planes per airport, 24 hours a day?

Though his real-life adventures are by now well melded in the public mind with the fictional embellishments of his popular *Rogue Warrior* novels, the original claim to fame of 30-year Navy Cmdr. Richard Marcinko, a Vietnam special forces veteran who helped run SEAL counter-terrorist operations in the 1970s and '80s, stemmed from his similar "red team" assignment to test out security at such facilities as American embassies abroad.

Commander Marcinko writes that it turned out such facilities could often be easily penetrated by someone who spoke English, wore a uniform, and simply acted as though he belonged there, by such simple expedients as entering through a patio "smokers door" left propped open for the convenience of employees not allowed to smoke inside the building.

And that's without even mentioning the U.S. Marine embassy guards in Moscow who were recently discovered to have Russian girlfriends — girlfriends not reluctant to share their pillow talk with their KGB handlers.

If security measures enforced by armed U.S. Marines with orders to shoot to kill can be so easily defeated in such relatively small, highly secure facilities, the notion that legions of civilian Fred and Ethel Mertz security staff in ill-fitting uniforms running us through metal detectors and asking us to remove our belt buckles can secure airports with dozens of miles of unsupervised perimeter fencing is absurd.

"It's like putting a steel door on a grass hut," one airport official told the *Dallas Morning News* last week.

Airline flight crews tell me they're routinely picked up at their motels by drivers whom they have never met before, and driven (their personal luggage uninspected) through gates that open automatically in front of these vehicles, directly to their planes. Any four people who showed up in that motel parking lot at the right time, with good haircuts and wearing the right uniforms, would receive the same courtesy.

But rather than panicking and slapping on ever more expensive and intrusive layers of this so-called "security," might it not finally be time to ask why millions of airline passengers are inconvenienced waiting to pass through metal detectors and body searches — conditioning Americans to tolerate as routine these ever more repressive violations of our persons and property — if the whole procedure turns out to do no good?

No one is saying airports should have no security. But one begins to wonder if the threat of "terrorism" isn't more often used to compromise our Fourth Amendment rights for the mere convenience of those trying to fight the War on Drugs, or even the War Against Moving Money Around.

Routinely harassing millions of blameless passengers to theoretically stop the one-in-a-million criminal isn't the American way. Israel's security services seem to have solved that nation's historically much larger problem by merely salting their flights with armed plainclothes officers.

Perhaps it's finally time to seek out methods both less intrusive and more effective (or — gasp — even to get government out of the loop entirely, allowing the different independent airlines to try their own schemes, under the goad of free-market liability insurance premiums) ... rather than merely doing more of what we already know doesn't work.

September 19, 2001
A Nation of Primping Fauntleroys
Readies for War

I worry our adversaries may have it right — America is no longer virile enough, America no longer has the resolve, America has become too silly and "mommified" and caught up in Politically Correct fibs and fripperies to win a protracted struggle for our very existence against a force as elemental as the Islamic fundamentalist drive to destroy capitalism, Western values ... the modern world as we know it.

Last Friday evening, after 84 hours, CNN and the other networks started to scrape bottom in their attempts to fulfill their "24-hour" commitment to covering the destruction of the World Trade Center. One of the network talking heads was interviewing a spokesman for the New York Police Department, and asked a question that made the fellow look temporarily uncomfortable.

"What about profiling?" she asked. "Some of our callers have expressed concerns about profiling" of Arab-Americans.

"We're going to do whatever's necessary to protect America," the crewcut fellow replied. "But we'll stay within the letter of the law."

An adequate response as far as it goes — and I know how hard it can be to "think on your feet" in those circumstances.

But a missed opportunity to say, "You know, Michele, I've instructed all my men, and I want to say to the American people here tonight, that there are plenty of good loyal Americans who are of Middle Eastern origin or Arab extraction. I hope this country learned from our mistake of 1942, when they rounded up and interned all the Japanese immigrants, and even American citizens of Japanese extraction.

"That was a mistake; we've rightly apologized for that as a nation; and I hope we never do anything like that again. Just because someone has an Arabic-sounding name or a Middle Eastern accent doesn't make them a criminal. Unless such a person is found to be in this country illegally, he or she has just as many rights as the rest of us.

"But having said that, let's suppose for a minute you're about to board a transcontinental flight, and I'm the security officer assigned to spend a few minutes interviewing your fellow passengers, and there are three people who have attracted my attention, either because they appear nervous, or there's something unusual about their ticketing arrangements, or whatever.

"One of these passengers is an Asian woman whose accent tells me she was raised in Texas. One is a black man whose accent tells me he was raised in Boston, Massachusetts. And the third passenger who's caught my interest is a visitor to our country from Saudi Arabia, whose name is Mahmood.

"Now, I don't have the luxury of sitting down each of these people for an hour and getting on the phone and checking their stories, as my opposite numbers might do in Israel. I've only got three minutes, and your life could depend on the decision I make in the next three minutes, because you're about to get on that plane, Michele.

"So, knowing no female person has ever attempted to hijack an American aircraft, that no Asian or black person has ever attempted to hijack an American aircraft, would you want me to spend exactly one minute apiece with each of these three passengers ... or do you think maybe I ought to spend most of my time chatting with Mr. Mahmood?

"Because if you chose option 'b,' you've just endorsed 'profiling.' You see, 'profiling' became an issue in this country because of the allegation that police are more likely to stop and question young black men when they see them somewhere where they appear to be out of place, on the theory that young black men commit more than their fair share of crimes. The problem is, young black men *do* commit more than their fair share of crimes. And like it or not, Mr. Mahmood *is* more likely to be a hijacker."

Political correctness costs lives, and lies and euphemisms and double-talk invite confusion and mistakes. If our limited security resources are expended tossing the luggage of every black and Asian and Scandinavian air passenger in a relentless search for deadly toenail clippers and plastic picnic knives, those resources will *not* be available to run a better background check on a young minimum-wage contract janitor named Fatima Mujahadeen, who's going to be alone in your plane later tonight, vacuuming the seat cushions.

A Nation Gone Daffy

Have "things in America" really changed? Let's suppose a common-sense employer actually summons up the nerve tomorrow to tell an applicant for a job on the 80th floor of the Sears Tower in Chicago, "Miss, you're the best qualified person for this job, but I'm not going to give it to you, because you're in a wheelchair, and in an emergency like Sept. 11 we'd all have to leave via the stairwells, and you wouldn't make it, and not only that, *other* employees here might lose their lives coming back to help you, as happened at the World Trade Center."

Do you think the courts and the federal anti-discrimination agencies would tell that aggrieved job-seeker, "He's right, honey. Things in America changed last week; we're now gone back to operating on a much older principle, called 'common sense'"?

Or would that straight-talking interviewer lose his job as the company still got dragged through the courts in another million-dollar "Americans with Disabilities Act" lawsuit, as though nothing had changed at all, and we're still willing to sink giggling into the sea, counting angels on the heads of pins and finding new grievances and liabilities everywhere, even as our enemies plot their next attack?

In a nation where "right-thinking" environmentalist Luddites and human-haters are actually willing to throw whole towns on the dole (and the health of the economy be damned) by shutting down sawmills and mines and cattle operations to "protect the endangered Northern Spotted Owl" or some other weed or bug that's not really in danger of extinction at all — merely "threatened in this limited ecosystem" ... in a nation where urban moms are afraid to let their boys play with icky toy guns and there's a systematic campaign afoot to demonize the ownership of firearms or skill with firearms while leaving no public lands open to target practice ... where does anyone imagine we're going to find the skilled marksmen needed to *fight* a war for our very survival?

Why are we raising generations of sociopaths? Our womenfolk have been taught to take their children to the shelter and raise them without a dad (Uncle Sugar offering to obligingly seize their sustenance from the abandoned dad's paycheck, tracking even childless American wage-earners by nine-digit slave numbers for this purpose) the first time some troglodyte suggests that, if he's bound to certain previously undisclosed financial obligations by an "unwritten traditional marriage contract," his wife is similarly bound to fulfill her half of that contract as understood by our ancestors going back a thousand years.

With fathers thus largely eliminated from the picture (or threatened with jail should they discipline their sons), the schoolmarms resort to doping up half our young men on Ritalin and Prozac and Luvox to keep them still in their seats, dumbing down the reading tests till a caged parrot could get a high school diploma. And now, with this raw material, we propose to win a cultural war to the death?

I've been accused of sounding somewhat bellicose of late. In fact, I hate war. "War is the health of the state," as Mr. Bourne warned us. I despise the opportunists who will likely use this handy excuse to enact their canned agendas of more victim disarmament ("gun control"), more demands that we show internal passports ("government-issued photo IDs") to move around within our once free country, etc. etc.

By now the citizens of a truly free and virile nation would

have been advised to strap on our .45s and fly armed ... the president warning the bad guys, "We're ready for you now ... just try us."

Instead, our airlines are being systematically bankrupted (that is to say, consolidated into two or three state-franchised, state-subsidized, state-regulated, quasi-public utilities) and millions of man-hours wasted as law-abiding Americans search each other for deadly *toenail clippers*.

I don't want war. It's no surprise a statist like John Ashcroft sees today's crisis as a good opportunity to call for expanded FBI power to snoop on every e-mail and voicemail message of every American. I've long said we should allow everyone to carry guns on planes and that we should stop meddling in a hundred global "hot spots" from Bosnia to the Horn of Africa where we can accomplish little but to make ourselves new enemies ... and I suspect we'd be a lot better off today if someone had listened.

But, that said, I also agree with the late Barry Goldwater that — when you've done all you can to avoid war and war has been thrust upon you anyway — the thing to do is to fight to win, to kill as many of the enemy as you can as fast as you can, no matter how many mewling Johnson-McNamara gradual-escalation liberals ridicule you for "viewing the world through a rose-colored bombsight" (an actual campaign slogan of that renowned 1964 "pacifist," Lyndon Baines Johnson).

Who Is "the Main Sponsor of the Taliban?"

Are we serious about winning a "war against terrorism"? President Bush could begin by declaring an end tomorrow to the fruitless and expensive "War on Drugs," abrogating all American drug laws and releasing that half of our enormous prison population currently in stir for victimless non-violent "drug crimes."

If heroin and morphine were legal, their prices would quickly drop by more than 90 percent. What do you suppose *that* would do the profitability of the Afghan poppy crop?

Think of how many police and intelligence resources could be immediately diverted to tracking murderous mullahs.

And how would that compare to the effects of the administration's current "War on Drugs" hysteria?

"Enslave your girls and women, harbor anti-U.S. terrorists, destroy every vestige of civilization in your homeland, and the Bush administration will embrace you," wrote columnist Robert Scheer in the *Los Angeles Times* of May 22, 2001, in an essay titled "Bush's Faustian deal with the Taliban."

"All that matters is that you line up as an ally in the drug war, the only international cause that this nation still takes seriously. That's the message sent with the recent gift of $43 million to the Taliban rulers of Afghanistan, the most virulent anti-American violators of human rights in the world today.

"The gift, announced last Thursday by Secretary of State Colin Powell, in addition to other recent aid, makes the U.S. the main sponsor of the Taliban and rewards that 'rogue regime' for declaring that opium growing is against the will of God," Mr. Scheer continued, while noting the chances of this ban actually being enforced would be highly dependent on how many additional goodies we might be willing to send along.

"Never mind that Osama bin Laden still operates the leading anti-American terror operation from his base in Afghanistan, from which, among other crimes, he launched two bloody attacks on American embassies in Africa in 1998," Mr. Scheer reminded his readers ... four months before the events of Sept. 11 finally, permanently, raised Mr. bin Laden's name from the depths of op-ed page obscurity.

"Sadly, the Bush administration is cozying up to the Taliban regime at a time when the United Nations, at U.S. insistence, imposes sanctions on Afghanistan because the Kabul government will not turn over bin Laden.

"The war on drugs has become our own fanatics' obsession and easily trumps all other concerns," Mr. Scheer (not usually my favorite columnist) continued. "How else could we come to reward the Taliban, who has subjected the female half of the Afghan population to a continual reign of terror in a country once considered enlightened in its treatment of women?

"At no point in modern history have women and girls been more systematically abused than in Afghanistan where, in the name of madness masquerading as Islam, the government in Kabul obliterates their fundamental human rights. Women may not appear in public without being covered from head to toe with the oppressive shroud called the *burkha*. ... They've not been permitted to attend school or be treated by male doctors, yet women have been banned from practicing medicine or any profession for that matter. ..."

I hope I'm wrong. But I worry our adversaries may have it right — America is no longer virile enough, America no longer has the resolve, America has become too silly and "mommified" and caught up in Politically Correct fibs and fripperies to win a protracted struggle for our very existence against a force as elemental as the Islamic fundamentalist drive to destroy capitalism, western values ... the modern world as we know it.

September 23, 2001
Tear Down the Taliban ... Not the Bill of Rights
🌿

George Bush the Younger rose to the occasion Thursday night, marking the one-week anniversary of the World Trade Center slaughter in an effective but nuanced speech.

He was particularly successful in generating confidence that he understands the complexity of the challenge at hand.

The British attempted to subdue forbidding, mountainous Afghanistan three times in the 19th century ... without marked success. The Russians spent a decade there not long ago, committing 100,000 troops — and still failed, as they will finally fail in Chechnya.

(The Chechen independence fighters, by the way, are no more "terrorists" when they act in their own region than were George Washington and John Paul Jones, who — some may remember — carried the American Revolution to the shores of England.)

The prospect of spending the next decade attempting to subdue the Afghans with land forces, as we attempted to subdue the Vietnamese in the 1960s, thus warmed no one's heart.

It's tempting to note that the handicap of the suicidal Johnson-McNamara policy of "gradual escalation" would at least be absent. But let's recall the New York state senate delegation now consists of two socialists — a senior member who helped facilitate the massacres of Sept. 11 by fighting to guarantee that every law-abiding American on the planes in question had been thoroughly stripped of his or her Second Amendment right to keep and bear arms for the defense of himself and his nation, and a junior member who actually gave Mrs. Yasser Arafat a big hug and a smooch not long ago, right after that lady finished making a speech in which she called for shoving the Israelis into the sea. Neither Mrs. Clinton nor Mr. Schumer has been much heard from in the past 10 days. Give these Fifth Column enemies of freedom some time to build a whining chorus of defeatism and despair, though ... give them time.

On the other hand, if invasion and occupation are a daunting prospect — not least because the assailants of Sept. 11 would love to polarize the rest of the Islamic world against us — what's the alternative? Lobbing a few dozen cruise missiles at some Afghan "training camp," killing three terrorists and a camel? Dispatching Janet Reno with 98 black-clad BATF agents to pull up in front of Taliban headquarters in a cattle trailer, pump the place full of nerve gas, burn it to the ground, beat up a couple TV cameramen on the way home, and declare victory?

No, this is the kind of "war" in which Americans are going to have to be willing to settle for nodding their heads and saying "God works in mysterious ways" if Saddam Hussein and Moammar Gadhafi and Yasser Arafat all die eating bad dates while watching reruns of "Baywatch" ... whereupon a reluctant Saudi press would feel obliged to print posthumous photo spreads revealing the strange sexual habits of these departed gentlemen, apparently involving young "crusader" boys and, well ... naked pigs.

Gratifyingly, Mr. Bush indicated some theaters of this battle will consist of "covert operations which remain secret even in success."

That's encouraging.

On the other hand — it can't be said too many times — if we are fighting a battle to the death for our values, our freedoms, and our culture, we can't afford to sacrifice the very freedoms and values that make us what we are, on the pyre of a Pyrrhic victory.

The president named Gov. Tom Ridge to the new post of Secretary of Homeland Security Thursday night. It could be a harmless way to bring his 2004 vice presidential nominee into the limelight ... or Gov. Ridge could quickly become our new Wiretapping Czar.

Attorney General John Ashcroft was a miserable choice for that job — a man who will whitewash any federal atrocity for a price (do Lon Horiuchi and the Waco Killers still walk free?) and who believes along with the nation's largest gun control organization, the NRA, that the Second Amendment allows "some reasonable regulation of firearms." (Who but a lawyer could read that into "shall not be infringed"?)

Ashcroft has called for expanded FBI powers to read all our e-mail (make no mistake, the recently renamed Carnivore device can read *all* the e-mail flowing through an internet service provider, not merely those of a suspect named in a warrant). Mr. Ashcroft's proposal could force cooperation from "any communications provider in the chain of providers carrying the suspect's communications" — which also means accessing our voicemail messages ... before we ourselves have heard them.

Does this sound like the kind of free country for which American servicemen will soon be asked to fight and die?

Senator Patrick Leahy, D-Vt., responded to Mr. Ashcroft's proposals by warning, "We are not going to let our Constitution get shredded. If we let the Constitution get shredded, the terrorists win."

"A police state can do a much better job of protecting us, but unfortunately it would protect us from the very liberties that have made this country special," added Rep. Darrell Issa, R-Calif. — a member of the House Judiciary Committee, which would have to draft any such legislation.

Stick to your guns, guys. We've had enough of police state wish-lists and just-for-show "security." Time to:

1) Restore the right of all law-abiding Americans (including air crews) to carry firearms whenever and wherever they travel — I'll personally book a cross-country fare the first day the first carrier advertises I can carry my firearm aboard, even if I do have to show my "concealed carry permit" and reload with frangible ammo.

2) Encourage U.S. and British oil companies to file suits to force compliance with the original contracts under which they explored and developed the oil fields of the Middle East — contracts in many cases unilaterally abrogated 50 years ago. Enforce the resulting TROs. Cut off bin Laden's cash flow.

3) Make war in Southwest Asia by following the rules of the last fellow to successfully conquer the place. Genghis Khan graciously accepted the peaceful surrender of any city that

would send him tribute ... even allowing them to keep their religion and customs. Those who demurred were left with no stone standing atop another. Their surviving male inhabitants had their hamstrings cut so they'd be crippled for life, while their women and children were herded back to China to serve as slaves and concubines.

"The greatest happiness is to crush your enemies and drive them before you," the great Khan advised, "to see his cities reduced to ashes; to see those who love him shrouded in tears; and to gather to your bosom his wives and daughters."

We do not need to strip any American of his liberties here at home. This "airport-security" nonsense batted zero on Sept. 11. I could carry a high-tech plastic Bowie knife through the metal detectors, strapped to my thigh, tomorrow. Give it up. No terrorist could have done what was done Sept. 11 if faced with a plane full of armed American passengers.

Instead, the question now arises whether we have the strength of resolve to visit exotic lands, meet interesting people, kill them, get children on their wives and daughters, teach the resulting brats to play baseball, and barbecue their goats, leaving strangers who may happen upon the resulting piles of rubble a thousand years from now to scratch their heads and wonder if the people who once lived here had a name.

The nostalgic Taliban pray for a return to the conditions of the 13th century. Time to oblige them.

September 25, 2001
"What's Gotten Into You"?

❧

The attacks of Sept. 11, 2001 created a sharp rift among Libertarian pundits — placing me in the minority, widely accused of warmongering and a lust for murder and rapine by many — including former colleagues — who chose to argue that, since war is a matter only between states and no one could figure out on which state to declare war following the events of Sept. 11, this couldn't be a war and the only acceptable course was to treat the suicide hijack/bombings as criminal acts, seeking indictments and extradition of any surviving conspirators.

This train of argument took the very real threat to our personal liberties inherent in the wilder proposed "anti-terrorism" legislative schemes (setting federal agencies free to wiretap, freeze bank accounts, and arrest and hold suspects without due process — all the old Alien & Sedition standbys) and reached for the somewhat far-fetched conclusion that the approximately 3,000 deaths of Sept. 11 had either been set up entirely, or gleefully seized upon (Hitler's Reichstag fire being mentioned more than once) by those who had only been waiting for an excuse to turn America into a police state.

Those concerns are, again, quite valid. The statist scum are nothing if not opportunists. What is less valid, however — especially among those who have long contended each individual is responsible for his own actions; who have long rejected "collective guilt" as a justification for any number of welfare-state redistribution schemes; and who in any other context might be expected to lecture us that what we reward we only get more of (whether it be out-of-wedlock births or blowing up large buildings) — is the assertion that the only solution is for America to apologize and surrender, complying with any and all of Osama bin Laden's demands up to and including the abandonment of Israel, since after all the events of Sept. 11 were "America's own fault" for allowing our government to persist in addle-brained foreign interventions.

In this view, America gets no credit for either its good intentions or its occasional good results (rescuing the world from Hitler and Tojo seems to have worked out fairly well — must we really feel guilty and apologize for the liberation of Italy, France, the Philippines, and the low countries?), but is instead automatically convicted of every crime our enemies care to allege, up to and including the "murder by starvation" of 500,000 Iraqi infants ... through a blockade that allows Iraq to sell all the oil necessary to buy all the food and medicine it needs ... a genocide curiously lacking in photos of emaciated corpses or even supposed graveyards, in a nation where (even more curiously) there are no reports of any members of the armed forces starving, or even having to skip lunch.

I keep asking, "What is the best way to end a gunfight, once it has begun?" And the answers I keep hearing amount to, "The best way to avoid a gunfight is to not provoke your opponent, to try to see things from his point of view, to respect his sovereignty ..."

The problem is that I asked not how to *prevent* a gun fight, but how to *end* one — Osama bin Laden and his ilk having been at pains for more than a decade to convince us we are *currently at war*, for all the world like a bee trying to draw the attention of a meandering elephant by stinging through its thick and nearly oblivious hide again and again and again ...

And the best answer to the question, "What is the best way to end a gunfight" is, of course, to *win* the gunfight, typically by placing two rounds in your assailant's center of mass ... just as the most moral choice facing Harry Truman in August of 1945 was to end the war as quickly and with the fewest possible casualties to *both* sides as possible ... by dropping the atomic bombs.

❧ ❧ ❧

One of my more civil exchanges of late September was with M.L. of South Carolina who wrote in that she was "dumbfounded" by the favorable reference in my Sept. 23 column to Genghis Khan and his treatment of cities that refused to send him tribute.

I replied:

OK, M.L. —

We'll send in eight cruise missiles to destroy a couple of tents and a goat, declare victory, and come home.

Mr. Bush will speak of "war" while there is no war ... except on the privacy of our phones, e-mail, and bank accounts ... and we'll be assured we're now "safe in the air" because they're searching all passengers for toenail clippers ... even as it's revealed there were also knives and box-cutters found on *Delta* flights on Sept. 11, clearly placed there by ground crew workers, *not* carried aboard by passengers.

Is that enough "Let's pretend" for you?

Meantime, Mr. bin Laden's acts of Sept. 11 — plus the fact they'll be laughing at the U.S. throughout the Arab world — will result in his gang being able to recruit tens of thousands of new dedicated killers ... and to raise billions in new funding, now that he's demonstrated (to a previously skeptical home audience) that he can strike us successfully and with virtual impunity.

I'm sorry you are unable to discern between being "pro-war" and believing that *if* we are at war, that war must be fought to a victory, which will mean employing tactics not commonly endorsed at Georgetown cocktail parties.

(Or shall we just *pretend* that this war is to be fought with chivalry, allowing the enemy a "fair chance" to pick up his sword if he should drop it, allowing a "time out" if he has the sun in his eyes ... and then execute a few of our boys when it's all over, after we learn to our shock — our palpable shock! — that they failed to conduct themselves in this prescribed manner. In other words: Please lie to us, Mr. Government Censor; forget that "informed electorate" stuff; we're not ready to see or hear the truth.)

Frankly — as I've now said repeatedly — I believe this nation is now so dominated by soccer moms, mincing gun-grabbers, and politically correct Luddites willing to flush our entire economy into the toilet to protect some endangered mealworm that the government in Washington *will not* do what would be necessary to win this self-styled "war," precisely because as soon as they actually *do* anything (and news leaks through their increasingly heavy-handed press censorship), the East Coast media will promptly start whining about their lack of compassion for the enemy's widows and orphans, etc. etc.

Like the unarmed man who in his drunken bravado pretends to have a pistol in his jacket and tells the armed cop, "Now I'm going to kill you," we will thus end up with the worst of all worlds: We *pretend* to be fighting a war (with all the destruction of liberty on the "Home Front" that's likely to involve), while allowing our enemies to prance in the streets, bragging about their immunity and recruiting vast new battalions of funds and manpower.

The questions for you, M.L., are:

1) Do you believe there's *ever* any justification for fighting a war, or do you believe that Jefferson, Washington, young Jim Monroe — and all those guys we sent ashore on Normandy in 1944, not to mention General Curtis LeMay and Harry Truman — were moral lepers who should have been tried for "war crimes"?

2) Do you believe we have no justification for fighting a war against those who perpetrated the events of Sept. 11, and if not, why not?

3) Do you believe that, in war, the United States can and should keep up this malarkey of using the armed forces as an exercise in Political Correctness (assigning to combat units women too small to haul their comrades back to the helicopter, etc.) and that the current government can and should hamstring its *own* forces by ordering them to avoid knowingly killing noncombatant civilians ... in which case, return to question 1, because the folks who ran World War II for the United States quite knowingly and willingly engaged in causing the deaths of hundreds of thousands of noncombatant civilians via aerial bombardment in Germany and Japan ... well *before* they de-

cided to drop the nukes in August of '45.

I am not "pro-war." I am against war ... though I believe, with the Founders, that peace and freedom can only be maintained simultaneously by having a citizenry armed to the teeth with military-style weapons (which would have ended the hijackings of Sept. 11 in mere minutes and long before anyone could have reached New York or the Pentagon, of course).

I have long (and unpopularly) argued that our foolish meddling all around the globe would make us many unnecessary enemies, and would come back to haunt us. I believe that still, and favor withdrawing our ground forces from all kinds of places, from Bosnia to South Korea.

On the other hand, I'm mindful (unlike most of my fellow isolationists, including Libertarian isolationists) of the widespread conditions that applied before the Brits ... and then we ... took on the role of "world policeman": piracy and kidnap-for-ransom rampant across much of the globe. (Remember that part in the Marine hymn about the "shores of Tripoli"? How do those who contend the Muslims would leave us alone if only we'd stop supporting the state of Israel explain all that extortion and outright piracy on the north coast of Africa ... 180 years ago?)

Will we issue Letters of Marque to allow private entrepreneurs to solve such problems for us? (It doesn't sound like you'd be very happy with the tactics *they'd* be likely to use.) Will we encourage the Japanese to float a huge new war fleet to take over our current role, in this regard, in the Pacific? Libertarians seldom do well at even acknowledging such concerns, let alone answering them.

But most disturbing in your comment is the implication that we can fight a war by some kind of Marquess of Queensbury rules — particularly against the Taliban, who torture and skin alive even their own *countrymen* who decline to "get with the program."

I wish we didn't have to deal with these people. But even

if we were to cut off all (unconstitutional) aid to Israel tomorrow, announcing, "OK, radical Shi'ites, in order to get ourselves off the hook here, we invite you to slaughter every Jew in the Middle East and we promise not to interfere ... and we're also withdrawing from Saudi Arabia and inviting Saddam Hussein to reoccupy Kuwait and Riyadh while he's at it" (ah, what a proud moment of moral courage and strategic genius *that* would be), I don't think it would convince the Taliban to "make nice" with us. The problem would remain.

Most Americans remain under the illusion we can "go to war" *without* destroying cities, killing the innocent, setting rape and famine and disease to run havoc across a sizable portion of the globe.

If war can still be avoided, I'll be among the happiest of souls: Just convince me how that is now to occur ... without inviting far *worse* consequences for the forces of liberty, pluralism, and enlightenment in the decades to come. (As Charles Krauthammer correctly pointed out in mid-September, the problem of Pearl Harbor was not solved by extraditing the 145 individual Japanese pilots who bombed Pearl Harbor, trying and jailing them ... while leaving the rest of the Japanese Imperial war machine to proceed with its plans with impunity — in other words, the "bringing the criminals to justice" metaphor no longer serves. We're not after a bunch of guys who knocked off a string of 7-Elevens.)

But if there is to be war, there is surely nothing more idiotic and self-destructive than engaging in war via half-measures. Because through half-measures we will surely lose, while only goading the enemy to further exertions. And when the enemy sees the chance to strike again at *our* cities and women and children (it happened to Rome; it happened to the British enclaves in Hong Kong and Singapore in 1942; it happens to all great empires eventually), we already *know* by what dictum *he* will proceed:

"The greatest happiness is to crush your enemies and drive

them before you," the great Khan advised, "to see his cities reduced to ashes; to see those who love him shrouded in tears; and to gather to your bosom his wives and daughters."

Do you actually *not believe* these are the rules that have been adopted by our adversary? Have you seen and read *nothing* of the way the Taliban proceed against their own *countrymen*? Or is it that you think you win a gunfight by showing up with a Swiss Army knife and a court order?

By all means, let's hear your alternative plan — I know you won't lack the moral courage to dispatch it to the families of those who died on Sept. 11.

These guys have already executed plenty of their own women for such crimes as learning to read, wearing makeup, driving cars, and daring to show their faces in public (and would happily enforce just such dicta, here). They also execute foreign "guests" for the crime of "teaching Christianity." Now: Do you want to see these guys killed and their cities burned ... or surrender to them and trust to their tender mercies? The hideous majesty of war is that it *does* reduce matters to these two options — as Grant and Sherman, as wrong as their war aims may have been, successfully demonstrated even in "civilized" America in 1864.

I seriously doubt the Taliban will accept, as a compromise, a series of discussions — moderated by David Frost or Peter Jennings or Oprah Winfrey — on the importance of multicultural tolerance.

— V.S.

M.L. responded:

"Hi Vin ... I really appreciate your quick reply. Might I add that the reason I am engaging in this conversation with you is that I have long been an admirer of yours and I am truly puzzled by your stance on the 'war' on terrorism. IMO, the 'war' on *our* (freedom lovers') front right now is to fight against the Homeland Security stuff, continue (yeah, probably hopelessly) fighting for non-interventionism, fighting for individual self-defense. Already we are 'losing' some in our number who are 'signing up to fight Bush's war'. And we can't afford to lose even *one* of our freedom fighters, there ain't that many of us. So while we still can, let's us 'marshal forces' and fight the war on *our* front. Maybe it'll have some effect on Bush's war. Maybe not. But at least we'll be fighting *for* liberty, in reality, not the paranoid fantasy of a 'war on terrorism.' ...

"I don't agree that 'we are at war,' in the conventional sense, therefore I don't believe conventional tactics will prevail or give us anything but, at best, a Pyrrhic victory.

"When you ask, 'Do you believe we have no justification for fighting a war against those who perpetrated the events of Sept. 11, and if not why not?' there's the rub. Who perpetrated the events of Sept. 11? Yeah, probably Bin Laden, but even Bush isn't real sure about that. (He's not fighting a 'war against bin Laden,' he's fighting a 'war against global terrorism,' so far identified as around 27 (latest) groups with ties to 60 countries. This Orwellian 'infinite war' will be the end of us all.)

"No, I don't think dropping bombs on civilians is justified, whether nuke or not. Certainly not at this very early stage. ...

"I was not advocating 'Marquess of Queensbury' rules. In fact, I don't think I advocated anything. I do believe, however, without shame or shrinking, that using the same or worse tactics than the enemy ... whoever that enemy might be ... makes you lose in the end, even if you win. Yes, I'm an admirer of Robert E. Lee over U.S. Grant.

"The 'problem' will also not be 'solved' even if we 'slag Afghanistan.' We'd also have to slag the entire Mideast. Anywhere our 'enemies may breed.' (BTW, bin Laden hung out in Peru. Should we slag Peru?) That kind of thinking 'inside the box' will never end terrorism.

"My alternative? Well, some of us who are trying to think 'outside the box' instead of succumbing to the war frenzy ... are working on that. Fight against the Homeland Security. Press for RKBA on airlines. Fight against *any* intrusion on our liberties. That's on the home front. On the foreign front ... one idea so far, 'bomb' Afghanistan with food and crystal radios and weapons for the resistance (a la Neil's novel, *Pallas*). Try to reach the Afghan people, 'cause in the final analysis, terrorism will only end if *their* people turn against them. (Yes, I know, you want to do it with bombs ... scare them into submission. I just don't think it'll work, even if justifiable. These guys are kamikaze, and have no fear of death. So we flatten their country, send troops (in the winter, in Afghanistan), somehow are more successful than the Russians were ... and then ... move on to the next of the 60 countries? This makes Vietnam look well thought out.

"Certainly 'these guys' are horrible uncivilized bastards. (So are the Commie Chinese.) I want to see the perps brought to justice. But no, I do not want their cities burned. From a moral standpoint, we become as 'bad' as them (perhaps worse, as they are ignorant and religious fanatics and we are, presumably, civilized and know what we're doing). From a practical standpoint, against an enemy who welcomes death, we have to kill them *all*. And I doubt that's possible, even if you can stomach killing all the non-combatants as well. Usually what happens in a scenario like that, the terrorists scuttle off like roaches, the civilians stay and are killed.

"Nice talking to you, Vin; I hope you'll reconsider your position. As I said, we can't afford to lose any of our freedom fighters.

— M.L.

Hello, M.L. —

Thanks for your civil reply.

I agree that the best solution in the *long run* is to restore freedom in *this* country (armed air passengers would have prevented Sept. 11) and to return to Washington's "isolationist" advice about "foreign entanglements" (though we Libertarians *aren't* very good at explaining how the sea lanes would be kept clear, or how wise it would be to leave our Navy abandoned and rusting at the pier). What concerns me in the *short run* is that the longer we are "at war," the more the shrill majority will embrace the erosion of our freedoms here at home ... and that fighting a war by half measures — "with one hand tied behind our back," as the military would have it — is a *recipe* for an endless, draining, inconclusive, "permanent" conflict ... handing over our future to the wet dreams of the statists.

We probably should not have fought a war in Vietnam, at all. But once "we" had decided to fight that war, the historical lesson of the Vietnam war is that we only *strengthened* our enemy, *assuring* his ultimate victory, by a policy of "gradual escalation," which had the effect of *inoculating* him against each deliberate, gradual, increased measure of military might. North Vietnam could have been conquered in a matter of weeks in 1965 if we'd had the will. If the concern was that we'd end up facing the Chinese, that was an argument for *staying out*, not "fighting to lose."

The nature and goals of war were poorly understood by McNamara's "campus warriors," and thousands of young American boys — including a couple of my friends — paid with their lives or their limbs. The Washington rhetoric of the time was full of this same enlightened-sounding self-contradictory malarkey about "swaying their will," "teaching them a lesson," "demonstrating our resolve," "making them hurt," "winning their hearts and minds." Those may be good goals for TV documentaries or public-health billboard campaigns. The goals of "war," on the other hand, are to "crush your enemies and drive them before you, to see his cities reduced to ashes; to see those who love him shrouded in tears; and to gather to your bosom his wives and daughters."

If you are unwilling to do that, you have no business even going to war yourself — let alone throwing away the lives of other people's children under the illusion that war is a new kind of social service in funny-looking clothes. Beyond that, as soon as you run up against someone who *does* adopt this model of warfare ... you will lose, your sons will die, and your wives and daughters will be taken as concubines to carry on the bloodlines of those who have defeated you.

I repeat, war is to be avoided when possible because it's terrible, but *waged in as terrible a fashion as possible* once entered into to, with the goal of killing the enemy and destroying his power to make war, *utterly*, lest he do the same to you. Things burn. People die.

I have not proposed that anyone be "scared into submission," as you assert. Again, you don't seem to be able to get your mind around the realities of a war "fought to win." *If* we are going to war, our goal should be to "kill" them. K-I-L-L. To achieve a 100 percent "corpse ratio" in the camps of our enemy.

How many times did the British "make peace" with Napoleon, merely giving him a breather till he could launch new adventures? Are we happy with the results (seen in 1939 and '40) of the inconclusive armistice of 1918? How about the results of our failure to "go to Baghdad" at the premature end of the Gulf War, a decade ago?

We are *already* the largest supplier of food and other "humanitarian aid" to the Taliban. Look where it's gotten us. Do you really believe the way to soothe the bellicose beast of North Korea is to send them more food? Kim Jong Il simply uses it to feed his vastly oversized army, while leaving the peasants to eat weeds.

I agree that the good guys in Chechnya are the Chechens, not the ambitious Russians ... and have said so many times. I doubt that makes me "anti-Islamic." But I'm sorry, I fear that responding to Sept. 11 by throwing a feast for the perpetrators and hoping they die of overeating is a plan that is neither likely 1) to be adopted or 2) to work.

The notion that wars "can't be won" is a piece of postmodern decadent defeatism not justified by the historical facts. Carthage *was* destroyed and did not rise again. The North

American Indians (with many of the same advantages of terrain and disadvantages of technology now enjoyed by the Afghans) *were* military defeated, decisively and permanently. As military forces, the Picts and the Celts are *gone* (and the Europeans who complain about the current treatment of the surviving Sioux and Apache *never* answer me when I ask where they've sited their "Pict reservations"). The names of whole cities and empires which stood in the path of Genghis Khan — precisely where the Taliban now live — are now lost to the memories of man.

We live and prosper today — while the bloodlines of our enemies were subsumed or died out — because our ancestors were the *winners* in these battles. Recently, we've felt so secure that we believed we could indulge ourselves, whining with self-hating suicidal self-righteousness that the very warriors who put us where we are today were "nasty insensitive brutes" who should instead have welcomed their foes into free-love communes, sharing the buckwheat groats. Why, we even scorn the weapons and hard-won military technologies that got us where we are today, outlawing the civilian manufacture or possession of weapons technologies developed in the 1890s and simpering that all would be joyful in the land if we could merely gather up all the nasty guns and throw them into the sea, no longer even teaching our children how they're made.

But if we lose the skills of war and the will to fight — ruthlessly and to the death — the result will not be that we will live in peace ... the result will be that our *enemies* will eventually "live in peace" in our lands, after killing us, raping our women, and eating our corn.

You say: "I was not advocating 'Marquess of Queensbury' rules. In fact, I don't think I advocated anything. I do believe, however, without shame or shrinking, that using the same or worse tactics than the enemy ... whoever that enemy might be ... makes you lose in the end, even if you win. Yes, I'm an admirer of Robert E. Lee over U.S. Grant."

And here, no matter how seemingly obscure, may lie the nub of our dispute.

Lee was a great tactician ... but a terrible strategic failure. *Because* of his failure, the cause of state sovereignty and distributed power was lost, and the cause of central statism left to reign triumphant on this continent. This — even beyond the hundreds of thousands of casualties — is the brand of his failure.

What was the nature of that failure?

Lee (and Davis) saw their fight as defensive. Like Garbo, they "just wanted to be left alone." Sting the North with enough tactical defeats, the theory went, and they'll eventually withdraw and leave us alone.

No room here to go into the political and economic and geographic realities that doomed that strategy. The point is, Lee *could* have won. He started out with a *far* better officer corps and better motivated army, and the North's industrial dominance took years to make itself felt, and would have been rendered moot in a short war.

Gettysburg shows that his men would *not* walk away if asked to invade Northern territory. Therefore, early on, Lee *could* have won agreeable terms from a defeated North — imposing acknowledgement of Southern independence — by cutting loose from the defense of Richmond, attacking and burning Washington City, and then marching on Baltimore, Philadelphia, and New York City, even as Sherman eventually marched on Atlanta and Savannah (in which case, the superior Northern rail network would actually have *helped* him).

What could McClellan or McDowell have done, hung idly about in Richmond as Lee burned New Jersey?

The metastasizing police state that now squats along the Potomac, threatening all our liberties, is the unintended legacy of a man who tried to fight a positional war by the rules of proper, chivalric, 18th century conduct ... and got himself stomped by a gang of jumped-up storekeepers who were willing to burn, loot, maim, and murder even *civilians* to achieve their war aims.

Unfortunately, neither side prevailed by bombing the enemy with food and pamphlets.

This business that we can't "stoop to being as bad as our enemies" is insidious and wrong. On Iwo Jima, our leathernecks cleaned out caves full of Japanese soldiers in loincloths by using flamethrowers. That's barbaric. They "didn't give them a chance." I'm sure a lot of our guys woke up in a cold sweat for years afterwards. But if one attempted to fight that war by traditional European rules of chivalry, the little Jap bastards popped up out of their spider holes after you'd walked past and shot you in the back.

Did such tactics "make our boys as bad as the enemy"? Did our boys end up treating all the Japanese women as whores after we won the war ... the way the Japanese treated their Korean subjects? Did our G.I.s return home converted to bloodthirsty barbarians? No and no. Most of them never again did anything more violent than swinging a softball bat. They returned to rebuild a strong, peace-loving, mostly free nation with respect for the rights even of the weak and the defenseless.

If this *is* a war, it's not the kind we studied in our Modern European History classes, in which two largely mercenary armies agree to meet on some level field on Saturday morning to decide which family shall succeed to the throne of Spain or where the French-German border shall be drawn through the prosperous territories of the Ruhr and Saar river valleys — whereupon everyone agrees who won and we all go back to tanning our leather and peddling our dry goods.

Yes, it can be argued the war of the Taliban is lost from the start — just like the war of the Sioux — and for the same reason. As Neolithic hunter-gatherers, the plains Indians hadn't a clue how to manufacture or even repair firearms or kettles or knives or axes, leaving them totally dependent for the weapons of war on the very culture they were fighting.

Similarly, Osama bin Laden makes his family money from oil wells and modern construction projects that wouldn't exist without the Western world and its technologies, which he purports to despise. He then multiplies his wealth by playing our stock markets — while vowing death to Western capitalism — and finally arms his troops with rifles and explosives and jumbo jets that would not exist without the dominant Western culture and technology which he vows to destroy.

So yes, he has already lost ... from the long view. But does that mean we refrain from permanently eliminating him as a potential threat ... any more than the settlers of Arizona and New Mexico refrained from finally hounding the raiding Apache into death or submission?

Some will protest that the white man had no right to "take the land" of the Apache or the Navajo — who had come down in their turn from the Great Lakes region and seized it from the Hopi, the Pima, and the Tohono O'odham only a few centuries before. It's a good parallel. When Roman or Anglo-Saxon settlers in Britain found themselves under attack by roving bands of Picts or Celts, did they say, "Oh, well, they were here first," and offer no resistance? Someone was always there first — someone can always claim that someone on your side "initiated force" by selling axe blades or F-16s to the enemies. The "non-initiation of force" doctrine works fine in deciding who's at fault in a civilian armed robbery. But if you interpret it to mean you have no right to resist someone who comes to burn your hut and haul your wife and kids off into slavery, count me out.

It's all well and good to indulge the luxury of musing that our treatment of the Apache was unfair ... a century later, in the comfort of our air-conditioned homes and sparkling swimming pools in suburban Scottsdale and Tucson. Our ancestors had no such easy options.

September 26, 2001
Big Spenders Spot Their Chance.
As Usual, Statists Race to Dance on a
Convenient Pile of Corpses

❦

The $15 billion "bailout" of the American airline industry following the savage attacks of Sept. 11 was bad enough.

Already economically troubled, "Lucky were the airlines to be a convenient and plausible object of pity just as Washington was casting around for a way to seem in charge and armed with bottomless resources for saving the economy," mused Holman W. Jenkins Jr. in his "Business World" column in Wednesday's *Wall Street Journal.*

"What are our policy makers thinking in handing over our hard-earned billions to airlines without at least some rollback of the huge wage increases and other imprudent management decisions" that had them on the ropes even before Sept. 11, asks former *Fortune* Assistant Managing Editor Paul Weaver, author of a forthcoming book investigating management-labor collusion in the employee buyout of United.

The perceived problem on Sept. 12, of course, was that one or more airlines might be forced into bankruptcy by lawsuits from the survivors of those who died both on their aircraft and in the Pentagon and World Trade Center on Sept. 11.

Well, don't those survivors have a right to seek compensation for their losses, and let the courts decide whether anyone exhibited gross negligence? Isn't that part of the "American way" we now go to war to defend?

They had fair notice. Test after test had already demonstrated the so-called "airline security system" leaked like a sieve.

It's widely reported that federal law makes it illegal for pilots, air crews, and passengers to carry self-defense firearms on American commercial flights — firearms that could have made quick work of the madmen of Sept. 11. But that's not true. Title 14, Chapter I, Part 108 of the Code of Federal Regulations (Federal Aviation Administration) not only allows virtually any federal or other government employee to travel armed, it also allows the "certificate holder" (airline) to "authorize other persons to carry arms" in free exercise of their Second Amendment rights, providing only that said persons have "successfully completed a course of training in the use of firearms acceptable to the (FAA) Administrator."

Had United and American airlines sought clarification as to which passenger training courses would be acceptable? Would any NRA firearms safety course — or evidence of past police or honorable military service — have sufficed? Had these airlines sought approval from the FAA to recognize the concealed-carry permits of passengers from states that issue them? If not, shouldn't survivors have a right to ask — under penalty of perjury — why not? Might not the airlines in question stand doubly responsible for the fate of passengers whom it arbitrarily and capriciously rendered defenseless despite this federal regulation ... and in violation of the Bill of Rights?

Many airlines have successfully operated in bankruptcy, and plenty of entrepreneurs stand ready to buy the gate assignments and equipment of those that fail. Since it succeeded in saving numerous troubled 19th century railroads — without government bailouts or takeovers — through the innovation of "equity receivership," American bankruptcy law has remained the best in the world at protecting firms confronted with unexpected disaster.

So why should these carriers be "let off the hook" rather than allowing the free market to take its course — creating a strong incentive for their surviving competitors to restore the right of their passengers to go armed, promoting liberty and increased deterrence to criminals at the same time? (Why is it that terrorists — any criminals, for that matter — rarely attack police stations or active military bases?)

But of course, it now turns out the airlines were just the beginning.

"Now the insurance industry is asking for a bailout," Mr. Jenkins reports. "The travel agents have put in a request for $3 billion. What about hotels, restaurants, and fishing guides?" Amtrak, America's struggling subsidized passenger rail line, bellied up to the bar a few days after the terrorist assaults and asked for $3 billion to improve and extend service, and ... oh yeah, that's right, "augment security," as well.

(Americans, regardless of their Ninth Amendment right to travel, will now be asked to show a "government-issued photo ID" before boarding a train. Why? Didn't the Sept. 11 hijackers all have and show photo IDs? Is there a concern that Shi'ite hijackers will now seize a train and take it to any destination other than the one to which its tracks lead?)

After a few days of stunned silence — how do you issue the rote call for more "gun control" when the terrorists used nothing but knives, apparently pre-positioned by contract caterers? — Washington's big spenders finally seem to have regained their equilibrium and spotted an opportunity here to fill their own pre-positioned Santa sacks.

In a "spending panic," Congress has "encouraged everyone from insurance, steel, hotels, and restaurants to hold out their hands," the *Wall Street Journal* editorialized. "Ideas are also flowing fast to push money for unemployment benefits, raise the minimum wage, and undertake a whole new national effort for schools, roads, bridges, and waste disposal."

Are the mullahs of the Taliban really upset with us because the counter clerks at Wendy's are underpaid? Because garbage pick-up is slow at Cabrini Green? What, no "anti-terrorism" angle to justify expansion of the bee and mohair subsidies?

The American economy has indeed been catching its breath after the ill-considered dot.com exuberance, but a Keynesian grab-bag of tax-funded "economic stimuli" will only end up loading more debt on the shoulders of the very person whose renewed confidence and spending is now so desperately sought: the American taxpayer.

Such bailouts weaken economic discipline by creating the expectation that the federal helping hand will always be there ... before we even consider the strings that come attached to all such federal "help," leaving government regulators with powers of oversight over private-sector decision-making, which would have made Mussolini's fascist bureaucrats faint with envy.

The federal government does have a few important obligations in such an emergency — primarily those directly involved with "providing for the common defense." New outlays for sky marshals, security checks for the janitors who sweep out our planes at night, firearms safety training and courtesy pre-fragmented ammo to top off the magazines of law-abiding American travelers? Fine. Seeking out those who backed and funded the perpetrators of the events of Sept. 11 for personalized .308-caliber recognition? Sure.

These are the legitimate tasks and duties of the federal government.

But proposing that Washington fund and run the entire economy? Cynically taking cover behind the tears and pain of a grief-stricken nation as they fill their own pork pails?

Where's the House Un-American Activities Committee when we really need it?

September 30, 2001
"Stop Complying Now ... Don't Give the Government-Regulated Airlines Your Business"

"The next time someone tells you that the militia referred to in the Second Amendment has been 'superceded' by the

National Guard, ask them who it was that prevented United Airlines Flight 93 from reaching its target," writes Boston University Professor Randy E. Barnett.

"The National Guard?" asks Prof. Barnett in his Sept. 18 article for nationalreview.com, titled "Flight 93 Saved by the Militia: Arming an Army Against Terrorism."

"The regular Army? The D.C. Police Department? None of these had a presence on Flight 93 because, in a free society, professional law-enforcement and military personnel cannot be everywhere. Terrorists and criminals are well aware of this — indeed, they count on it.

"Who is everywhere? The people the Founders referred to as the 'general militia.' Cell-phone calls from the plane have now revealed that it was members of the general militia, not organized law enforcement, who successfully prevented Flight 93 from reaching its intended target at the cost of their own lives," continues Prof. Barnett, author of *The Structure of Liberty: Justice and the Rule of Law.*

"The characterization of these heroes as members of the militia is not just the opinion of one law professor. It is clearly stated in Federal statutes. Perhaps you will not believe me unless I quote Section 311 of US Code Title 10, titled, 'Militia: composition and classes' in its entirety:

"'a) The militia of the United States consists of all able-bodied males at least 17 years of age and, except as provided in section 313 of Title 32, under 45 years of age who are, or who have made a declaration of intention to become, citizens of the United States and of female citizens of the United States who are members of the National Guard.

"'b) The classes of the militia are —

"'1) the organized militia, which consists of the National Guard and the Naval Militia; and

"'2) the unorganized militia, which consists of the members of the militia who are not members of the National Guard or the Naval Militia.' ..."

It was militia members who saved whatever was the terrorists' target — whether the White House or the Capitol — at the cost of their lives. And this should help us figure out what would actually work to block the success of any such future efforts, Prof. Barnett explains.

"Asking all of us if we packed our own bags did not stop this attack. X-rays of all carry-on baggage did not stop this attack (though it may well have confined the attackers to using knives). And preventing us from using e-tickets or checking our bags at the street ... would neither have stopped this nor any future attack. ...

"Here is the cold hard fact of the matter: Often — whether on an airplane, subway, cruise ship, or in a high school — only self defense by the 'unorganized militia' will be available when domestic or foreign terrorists choose their next moment of murder. ..."

ⓦ ⓦ ⓦ

I'd booked a 7 a.m. flight to Phoenix on Oct. 6 so I could hear Aaron Zelman speak at Marc Victor's Freedom Summit in Scottsdale — my travel agent sent me a written warning to show up at the airport two hours early for a one-hour flight, so I could be diligently searched for toenail clippers by the same worthless stooges who allowed every single hijack gang to slip through their "security screens" on Sept. 11.

But within hours of booking my fare, I was shamed by the following stirring message from Mr. Zelman, executive director of Jews for the Preservation of Firearms Ownership (web site www.jpfo.org).

"Don't Finance the Murder of the Bill of Rights, or Why I Am Canceling My Appearance at the Freedom Summit:

"To reach the Summit in Arizona," my friend Aaron wrote, "I would have to fly from my home in Wisconsin. This I can no longer do — not with the latest 'heightened (and useless) airport security measures' designed to treat me like a criminal, a serf, or both.

"I will never set foot on a commercial airliner until the airlines, the airport authorities, the FAA, and all other would-be regulators of air travel respect my rights. (And I'm talking about inborn rights, the ones Americans have bled and died for. ...)

"Arbitrary searches don't halt violence. But as if they missed that entire point on September 11, 2001, the airlines and the regulators ... want more of the same. Walk through their scanners. Humbly answer their questions, praying that you don't sound nervous or 'suspicious.' Open your bags. Open your purses. Open your shaving kits or your lipstick tubes. Bend over and open whatever orifice they might wish to inspect once they've determined your willingness to submit.

"Disarming me and you doesn't make the nation's skies safe. But — tragically missing that point, also — these police-statist cowards now want to make sure that millions of people are deprived even of their razor blades, Girl Scout knives — even plastic knives from fast-food joints.

"What will they want to take next? Our shoes so that we can't kick them? Our pens so that we can't gouge them? Our teeth so that we can't bite them? ...

"Stop complying now. ... Don't give the government-regulated airlines your business. They're already in financial trouble, and they've earned it. Let them go bankrupt. Let them pay the price for conditioning us to act like cattle and lulling us into submission. ...

"Give them the Smith & Wesson treatment," Aaron advises, referring to the firearms manufacturer that signed an agreement with the Clinton administration to manufacture guns with electronic switches that could be remotely turned off by police, as well as requiring its distributors to place dangerous "trigger locks" on every gun they sold ... *not* just on S&W products.

American gun buyers boycotted once-popular S&W, forcing their British owners to sell off the company last summer for pennies on the dollar.

"So let the airlines go under," Mr. Zelman concludes. "To put it bluntly, corporations, regulators, and legislators who don't approve of free armed Americans flying on airplanes are domestic terrorists. We already saw the mass bloodshed they helped perpetrate on September 11. ...."

🌿 🌿 🌿

As this is written, I haven't yet decided whether to join Aaron's boycott and drive to Phoenix. I speak at some location or other around the country at least once a month, and I couldn't reach a lot of those places without flying. Do I do more good by setting forth and proselytizing for freedom in my own halting way ... or more harm by hanging my holster on the wall when I leave for the airport, going along with this current regime of traveler disarmament?

But Aaron is right. President Bush set his jaw and spoke firmly on Sept. 20 of defending the free market and the capitalist way — and then within hours cut a deal with Congress to authorize a $15 billion bailout of U.S. airlines, to include $5 billion in taxpayer cash, $10 billion in "loan guarantees," and unspecified "liability protection."

In fact, the airlines are and *should* be liable for whatever negligence juries decide they displayed in allowing more than 3,000 deaths on Sept. 11, all of which could have been prevented if they'd allowed their passengers (especially such disarmed heroes as Todd Beamer and Jeremy Glick of Flight 93) to fly armed, as they are required to do by the U.S. Constitution.

Enough simpering about "the right of private carriers to set the terms of their private contracts." There are dozens of major airlines — which one advertises that I'm welcome to carry my gun on board, and light up a Salem while I'm at it? Isn't the free market supposed to be about competition and diversity, rather than enforced uniformity?

FAA regulations (Title 14, Chapter I, Section 108.11) allow any government agent to carry a gun on a plane, of course. As for us second-class "civilians," the "certificate holder" (airline) can authorize anyone they like to carry firearms on their planes, providing said passenger or crew member demonstrates they have passed a gun safety course which is "acceptable to the Administrator."

But so far as I've been able to be determine, no one knows of any readily available safety course which has been so approved "by the Administrator." Thus, the FAA regulation in question is probably void for setting a requirement no one can figure out how to meet, a successful local trial attorney tells me.

The threat of bankruptcy is precisely the goad that might finally motivate some of these mincing wimps, these accessories to murder, to post signs declaring that armed passengers are welcome — please check in at the gate to top off your magazines with complimentary frangible ammo — while seeking a declaratory judgment from the courts that said FAA regulation is null and void under the clear meaning of the Second Amendment.

Instead, we now propose to put this major section of the American economy on a permanent government dole, allowing them to continue the murderous tyranny of Victim Disarmament, while their passengers die by the hundreds, taking with them thousands of innocent victims on the ground.

October 5, 2001
Not Insane

When I was a boy, we lived in a house on a hillside above the lake in Marlborough, Connecticut. This was in the days before the developers grew quite so fanciful, and so the road was merely called "Hillside Circle."

All of Connecticut had been cleared for farming by the early 19th century, of course. But then came word there was farmland in the Ohio without all these darned rocks, so there was a massive out-migration and the population of New England actually fell in the middle and late 19th century, and the land was reforested with second-growth timber.

After the Second World War, some of these woods still stood in patches between the houses on Hillside Circle. The largest critters that harbored in these little patches were, I am sure, raccoons and skunks, though at the time I imagined I might encounter lions and tigers there, or at least Sheena, the Queen of the Jungle.

I was still a small child, and one day I ventured a few yards out into the wood and sat down on a fallen log in which a swarm of yellowjackets had made their nest. The yellowjacket is an indigenous species of wasp that makes up for its modest size with its pugnacity and its territoriality. They got inside my clothes and continued stinging me even after I ran inside and my mom tried to get the clothes off me, she trying to swat the wasps and me hitting her and screaming the whole time.

I can imagine the emotions that ran through my father's mind, seeing this kind of terror and suffering in the face of his firstborn. But my father did not rush out and attempt to kill yellowjackets with a fly-swatter. Nor did he make any effort to identify the *individual* yellowjackets that had stung me, since the others were "innocent." Instead, he waited patiently till dark, poured gasoline into their hole, set it afire, and killed them all.

Ever since then, he ... and I ... watch for yellowjacket nests on our property, wait till nightfall, and burn them out. We do not feel morally obliged to wait till *individual* yellowjackets attack, and then destroy only those *individual* yellowjackets ... nor even to wait till wasps from a specific *nest* have stung us or the grandkids.

In their brief and self-mocking fling at electoral politics, California's Firesign Theatre radio troupe adopted the motto "Not Insane!"

In our decades-long systematic war on yellowjackets, in which we fully understand we can never know any "final and absolute victory," do my father and I exhibit the symptoms of insanity? I don't think so. We don't save up our vacation time and travel to parts of the country where there are lots of yellowjacket nests, to spend two weeks gleefully killing all the bees we can find. We take no particular delight in killing the pests; it's simply part of the job of a careful householder protecting his family.

Some will say, "Yellowjackets will always be with us; why bother"? So we are to huddle inside, sacrificing our yards to these pests, never again emerging into the fresh air and the light of day? Anyway, if *enough* people kill all the yellowjackets that invade their yards, Mr. Darwin will take over, and those yellowjackets that stay in the deep woods, avoiding man, will have more reproductive success. We *will* see fewer of them. Man also once said, "Smallpox will always be with us," but man was wrong. We pretty much killed *all* the smallpox bugs. Not many woolly mammoths left around these days, either.

Obviously, the objection will be raised that by comparing Islamic terrorists to insect vermin, we run the risk of making Hitler's evil mistake — identifying whole races of people as "subhuman vermin" to be destroyed.

Yes. In war, by definition, we do not treat the enemy as individuals. We attack and destroy them en masse, until they surrender. The victor rules the land, and imposes his system of social and military and economic organization. That's why war is important, and not to be entered into lightly. It is properly the subject of moral ambivalence, and even moral anguish. But having once decided to embark upon it, fate, fortune, and Mr. Darwin reward those who enter upon the venture ruthlessly, with a determination to smash the enemy's skull.

Beyond that, I'll further reply that if my dad and I set out to kill every *insect*, because "insects" had attacked me and were therefore dangerous, that would show a lack of discrimination. We'd not only be killing a lot of harmless or even beneficial butterflies, dragonflies, etc., but we'd be wasting time we could be using to watch for and go after actual aggressive wasps.

At a picnic recently in Reno, a friend took the position that "If you just leave them alone, they won't bother you." So the yellowjackets kept coming, in larger and larger numbers as word of the available feast (with no casualties being suffered) was carried back to the nest. We finally had to abandon our picnic, retreating in a rout.

A week later a Cub Scout camp-out at nearby Lake Tahoe was swarmed by the bastards, the outing nearly ruined. Why? Because no one had gone in the night before and burned them out. (It's probably illegal on government land, by now, anyway.) My dad recently saw another guest stung in the mouth after taking a swig from a can of Coke in which a yellowjacket had landed. He burned out another nest that night.

They *don't* "leave you alone if you leave them alone" — any more than the pirates of Tripoli deferred seizing our ships and ransoming our officers and buggering our cabin boys and stealing our cargoes in the 1820s, simply because we hadn't yet dreamed of "supporting the state of Israel."

George Bush has spent a lot of time recently demonstrating his "discernment," insisting we're *not* making war on all Arabs, or all Muslims, or all people with Middle Eastern accents. However, there *are* about 100 million to 165 million radical Islamicists (probably one-fifth of the world's Muslims) who dance in the streets when our planes and towers blow up. Killing and disenfranchising enough of them to dissuade the rest *is* going to be a big job. And if we all agree that "war is the health of the state" — that our liberties will progressively erode as long as we're at war — then how is it irrational to prefer that (finding ourselves at war) we conduct that war *decisively*, killing as many of them and their leaders as quickly as possible so as to paralyze their ability to harm us in future, while sustaining as few casualties on *our side* as possible ... as in the 100 hours (though it should have been 200 hours) of Desert Storm?

(Yes, I realize the Afghan terrain is different and we can't use tanks ... and that our weapon of choice must now, in many cases, be assassination. My point is about the use of *overwhelming force*, applied mercilessly and all at once and without reprieve. Think of the ballet of death at the end of Francis Coppola's original *Godfather*.)

It is precisely the weak-kneed half-serious war that the foot-dragging peaceniks will now force on us (ooh, better not produce too many body bags, public support will wane — ooh, better not bomb them during the month of Ramadan, it might offend the sensibilities of some Indonesian poobah), which is likely to generate the *most* friendly casualties and the *greatest* loss of liberty through extending the war for years and years, just like our half-hearted effort in Vietnam.

A lot of this comes back to the unresolved question of the nuking of Nagasaki and Hiroshima. When we consider that the other two options were a three-year blockade (which would have starved millions of Japanese women and children to death), or an invasion in which we would have suffered hundreds of thousands of casualties ... and the Japanese millions, among a civilian populace that was being outfitted with wooden spears with which to charge our ranks of machine-gunners ... dropping those nukes was in fact the most *moral and humane* solution available to Harry Truman.

I suspect the "peaceniks" who now call me a "murderer"

and "insane" for urging that we fight the current war to a *decisive victory*, as *soon* as possible, by using the *maximum* available force, would disagree. It begins to appear that they are, in fact, pacifists who believe no war is ever justified, even if the barbarians are coming over the hill, slaying and burning all in their path.

Before I agreed to become a Libertarian, I was careful to make sure Libertarians are not *pacificists*, that they only oppose the *initiation* of force. I agree that we should meddle less overseas, but to argue that on Sept. 11 "we only got what we deserved due to our overseas meddling," is enervating to the point of cultural and racial suicide.

We *cannot* get in a time machine and go back in time and institute a less meddlesome foreign policy. And even if we could, is there a consensus as to where we should start? 1941 — avoiding war with Hitler and Tojo, in which case we would now likely share the world with the surviving Nazi and Japanese Empires? Would that "advance the cause of freedom and individuality"? Few will answer.

"Bombing them with bread" and little crystal radio sets so they can listen to the Voice of America sounds fine in science fiction stories, but it won't end the current jihad against "The Great Satan." It's doubtful they'd stop now, even if we abandoned Israel. (In fact, that would be such a victory for their current methods — after the Arab states lost five traditional wars of aggression against Tel Aviv — it's reasonable to assume they'd merely draw tens of thousands more recruits to do more of the same. Pretty soon they'd be reduced to blowing up every American building over 10 stories. When you reward an activity, you *do* get more of it, you know.)

At one extreme I suppose there are those who do so much fighting they come to love war. I am not among them. But at the other extreme I fear what we are dealing with here are isolated academics who actually believe they can change the outside world through the magic of rearranging words and definitions. Harry Browne says in his Oct. 4 release, "What Can We Do About Terrorism":

"War is by definition a conflict between governments," and since "no government has claimed responsibility for the Sept. 11 attacks, and no government has been so accused," therefore this can't be a war.

Since it isn't war, all it can be is a crime, and, "Because the September attacks were a crime, the government's job is to locate and bring to trial any perpetrators who didn't die in the attacks," the perennial Libertarian presidential candidate continues. "If some of them are located in foreign countries, our government should request extradition" ... and just sit on our thumbs if that doesn't work out.

But will that logic affect the likelihood that the C-4 strapped around the waist of the guy next to you at the sidewalk cafe will explode when he flips the switch? Will his fuse sputter and die because you've proved we're "not at war"? Are we guests at the Mad Hatter's tea party? To believe this is to believe in magic and the power of incantation.

If your village was attacked by Mongol hordes, or raiding Kiowa Indians, would you not be justified in assuming you were "at war" with those people, just because you couldn't locate their "government"? Does that mean your only option would be to seek extradition of the *individual identified* Kiowa or Mongol hordesmen who had raped your daughter, burned your house, and stolen your horses — you couldn't just gather your forces and go burn *their* village?

Did we "become just as bad" as our enemies when we cleaned them out of the caves of Iwo Jima with flamethrowers? Those G.I.s returned home to rebuild a free and peaceful nation — not to impose a Tojo-style empire with captive women forced into "houses of comfort."

I submit that what we are seeing here is an attempt to legalistically "define" these folks' way around a reality they do not wish to face.

And reality will finally demonstrate whose course of action is more "insane."

We didn't attempt to "extradite and put on trial" the 165 individual fighter pilots who bombed Pearl Harbor. We went to war, to beat the Japanese down until they could not do that to us again. We did not go door-to-door with clipboards, asking who supported Tojo's war policies, to decide which houses to bomb in Tokyo. We bombed them all. We won. And, in the end, doing so was not insane.

October 10, 2001
The Echoing Silence of Islamic Leaders

In his latest videotaped announcement, terrorist Osama bin Laden leaves little room for anyone to still imagine he played no role in the ruthless New York and Pentagon massacres of Sept. 11, of his fanatical justification and lack of regret for the outcome, or of his intention to continue recruiting the misguided faithful to his banner, the better to conduct his ongoing jihad against all Americans, and all things American.

"This is America filled with fear from the north to south and east to west, thank God," bin Laden says. "There are civilians, innocent children being killed every day in Iraq without any guilt, and we never hear anybody," he says, referring to the U.N. claim that 500,000 children have died in Iraq thanks to an American embargo — an American embargo that allows the Iraqis *to sell as much oil as necessary to buy all the food and medicine they need.*

(Are any of Saddam Hussein's soldiers starving? Apparently not. So why don't they share their rations with the little tykes? Admittedly, if American actions are causing even one child to starve that's too many. I've long opposed all this ill-considered half-hearted Third World meddling that only earns us new enemies from Bosnia to Somalia. But shall we now accept at face value the claims of a United Nations that condemns the U.S. and Israel for racism, while offering not a word of criticism when white farmers' lands are seized in Zimbabwe due to their race — a United Nations that overwhelmingly voted terrorist Syria onto the Security Council this week, while contending the reason Communist North Korea again needs food aid is the fact that bad weather has just caused the crops to fail — for the 47th year in a row?)

"And every day we see the Israeli tanks going to Jenin, Ramallah, Beit Jalla and other lands of Islam," bin Laden the anti-capitalist Saudi multi-millionaire continues. "And, no, we never hear anybody objecting to that. So when the swords came after eight years to America, then the whole world has been crying for those criminals who attacked. This is the least which could be said about them: They supported the murder against the victim, so God has given them back what they deserve. ... Neither America nor the people who live in it will dream of security before we live it in Palestine, and not before all the infidel armies leave the land of Muhammad," threatened the killer bin Laden.

Palestine was the name of the British protectorate that was divided in half in 1948, to form a Jewish state of Israel and a Palestinian state of Jordan. Their properties largely seized without compensation, the Jews who had been living in what is now Jordan found themselves unmistakably unwelcome there and relocated to Israel — no mass of Jewish squatters has camped around the borders of that country for the past 50 years, creating a "Jewishtinian problem" and leading to U.N. condemnation of "racist Jordan" for treating them unfairly.

If the Arabs who had been living in what is now Israel left their homes it was not because the Israelis drove them out. Rather, most left before they ever saw an Israeli uniform, believing Arab promises that Israel would soon be conquered and the Jews driven into the sea. It is not America which has prevented any Palestinians from settling in Jordan or anywhere else in the Arab world, nor that prevents the Palestinian majority in Jordan — formerly "Palestine" — from living in "security."

In fact, as Paul Johnson points out in his fine history *Modern Times*, over the past 80 years one moderate Arab leader after another has been assassinated for the offense of suggesting some reasonable accommodation might be reached with the Jews. Iraq's Saddam Hussein started his career as one of those assassins.

Some of bin Laden's closest associates have now been linked even to the assassination of Egyptian president Anwar Sadat. Nor have bin Laden and his minions ever expressed a word of regret over all the Muslims and other non-Americans who died in the World Trade Center, nor for the fact that the majority of those killed in the terror bombings of the U.S. embassies in Kenya and Tanzania were not Americans, but rather Africans or Muslims — or both.

🌿 🌿 🌿

Salman Rushdie is a Muslim — the main reason Islamic fundamentalists are so outraged that he chooses to live in the West and writes in celebration of such decadent practices as "kissing in public places, bacon sandwiches, disagreement, cutting-edge fashion, literature, generosity ... movies, music, [and] freedom of thought."

Rushdie, who has survived a death sentence from Iran's Ayatollah Khomeini (imposed for the political and cultural content of his novels — not a very inspiring sign of Muslim tolerance), rejects the arguments of those who say that American foreign policy is in any way to blame for the tragedy. "Let's be clear about why this anti-American onslaught is such appalling rubbish," Mr. Rushdie writes in a current piece for the

New York Times Syndicate. "To excuse such an atrocity by blaming U.S. government policies is to deny the basic idea of all morality: that individuals are responsible for their actions.

"The fundamentalist seeks to bring down a great deal more than buildings. Such people are against, to offer just a brief list, freedom of speech, a multiparty political system, universal adult suffrage, accountable government, Jews, homosexuals, women's rights, pluralism, secularism, short skirts, dancing, beardlessness, evolution theory, sex. These are tyrants, not Muslims."

Strong words of condemnation from a man who has put his own life and safety on the line to take a stand for pluralism and freedom of speech.

But Mr. Rushdie is a mere layman. How many leaders of the Islamic faith — both abroad and on these shores — have expressed similarly strong words of rejection, revulsion, and condemnation for the practices of Mr. bin Laden and his terrorists — as well as for their interpretation of the dictates of the Koran?

Precious few.

Oh, there have been some carefully chosen words of "regret" for the casualties of Sept. 11. But any Allied military leader of the Second World War could have expressed "regret" over the casualties on both sides caused by our invasions of Sicily, Italy, Tarawa, or Iwo Jima ... without meaning that he saw the slightest thing wrong with our war aims or strategy, without meaning that he intended anything other than the further killing of a whole lot more Germans and Japanese, as soon as possible, and as long as they chose to resist.

No, an expression of "regret" is not enough, for "regret" can be felt about "collateral damage" even in a noble and necessary undertaking.

᠅ ᠅ ᠅

"Even if bin Laden was not behind the September carnage, a declaration of war against him is logical," writes my friend Dr. Imad-ad-Dean Ahmad, of the Minaret of Freedom Islamic think tank in Washington, D.C. "After all, he declared war on the United States in February of 1998. His signature appears on a fax sent to the London-based al-Quds al-Arabi of a directive that specified 'crimes and sins committed by the Americans are a clear declaration of war on God, his messenger, and Muslims' and ... that therefore 'to kill the Americans and their allies — civilians and military — is an individual duty for every Muslim who can do it in any country in which it is possible to do it. ...' (Bin Laden, et al. 1998.)

"If someone knows that bin Laden has repudiated this fax, they should produce the evidence now, otherwise it is a top priority for American Muslims to denounce it, and him.

"The fact that a man trains people to kill and tells them it is okay to use the techniques they learn against the innocent (and then gives a prayer of thanks when he hears that someone has done just that) is sufficient cause to consider him a terrorist," Dr. Ahmad continues.

"As Muslims we are obligated to use the same standard of justice with regard to bin Laden as with regard to Ariel Sharon. This is what the Qur'an means when it says: 'O ye who believe! Stand out firmly for justice as witnesses to God even as against yourselves or your parents or your kin and whether it be [against] rich or poor: for God can best protect both. Follow not the lusts [of your hearts] lest ye swerve and if ye distort [justice] or decline to do justice verily God is well-acquainted with all that ye do' (4:135)."

In a happy change from the kind of war fever that led to the rounding up and forced relocation of law-abiding Japanese-Americans in 1942, President Bush has been at great pains to show a careful discernment that America is not now at war with all the Arab peoples or with Islam in general.

But Islamic leaders could do a great deal to strengthen

this distinction by now coming forward to condemn bin Laden and his ilk as hell-bound murderers totally beyond the margins of acceptable Islamic faith when they call for the ambush and murder of the Westerners they have chosen to blame for their own failures, for the fact the Arab nations are overwhelmingly corrupt, failed, backward, and oppressive satrapies, from which millions of the best and the brightest have already escaped ... to the West.

If bin Laden's Fatwah is not the true teaching of the Koran, then leaders of the Arab and Islamic communities could be doing a whole lot better at denouncing it — making it clear that those who commit wanton mayhem and murder in this extremist cause are not true followers of their prophet at all, but rather outcasts and criminals who can expect no peace or agreeable reward for such actions, in this world or the next.

Why do they not speak up, like Mr. Rushdie and Dr. Ahmad? Because they are physically afraid of the very terrorists they have bred in their midst? Or is there some other reason?

"Only God Can Judge That" — Some Local Muslims Embrace Conspiracy Theories, Refuse to Distance Themselves from Radicalism

彩

Aziz Eddebbarh of Las Vegas, representing the Muslim Public Affairs Council, called the editors of the *Review-Journal* in November to ask if he could come in and make a presentation to the paper's news staff on the religion of Islam and some of the ways it's been misinterpreted since the events of Sept. 11.

He was invited in for an hour at lunchtime on Tuesday,

Nov. 13, 2001. The idea, clearly, was to leave the staff with the notion that the Muslim faith is one of peace and tolerance — nothing at all like the hate-filled, violent, bigoted sect that some might imagine, if they were to judge only from the actions of 19 young Egyptian and Saudi men who flew airplanes full of innocent passengers into office buildings full of innocent New Yorkers on Sept. 11, or the Muslim Palestinians videotaped dancing in the streets of the West Bank when they got the news.

But it didn't quite work out that way.

The first half of our time was taken up by a little slide show, which I daresay plays well to sixth-grade classes: photos of the faithful gathered in Mecca, listings of the five pillars of Islam, that kind of thing.

The slide show was presented by Mr. Eddebbarh's wife, Toni, a native Minnesotan of Swedish descent, who says she converted to Islam seven years ago, after 12 years of marriage. That was a nice touch, public-relations wise. But things went downhill from there.

Islam is not a religion of compulsion, the Eddebbarhs explained. Each Muslim gets to decide for himself the meaning of the dictates of their holy book, the Qu'ran (Koran.) Traditional Muslim women are not required to wear head scarves; they choose to do so in a gesture of modesty, and "so they will be viewed not as sex objects, but as intellectual equals," Mr. Eddebbarh explained.

But it didn't seem to be working out that way in Saudi Arabia, where women are barred from driving cars, or in Taliban-dominated Afghanistan, where women who sought an education — or who left the house alone to seek medical attention, or who showed an ankle or a single hair on their heads in public — were beaten with sticks, I pointed out. For that matter, Western relief workers who had been arrested and threatened with death sentences for possession of books that could be used to "teach Christianity" were released only after the fall of the Taliban. Our armed forces were discouraged from holding weekend chapel services while overseas to liberate Kuwait a decade ago; it's not even clear I could have gone to Kandahar and put on the same kind of little slide show about Christianity that Mr. Eddebbarh was staging for us here ... without being sentenced to death. Does that mean the Taliban are bad Muslims?

"Only God can judge that," responded Mr. Eddebbarh.

Nor is it just the Taliban. Less than three months before this meeting, on Aug. 25, Dr. Younis Shaikh, a medical lecturer, was sentenced to death following his conviction in a Pakistani court for violating the country's blasphemy laws.

In Pakistan, those found guilty of blasphemous statements against the Koran or the prophet are generally put to death by hanging. According to the *New York Times*, Shaikh was arrested in October 2000 after delivering a physiology lecture that included a discussion of practices prevalent in pre-Islamic 7th-century Arabia. He stated that Mohammed was not a Muslim until his revelation at age 40, and thus neither he nor his family practiced many of the customs associated with the Islamic religious tradition. According to the *London Times*, "He was also said to have made reference to certain customs of the day such as circumcision and removal of underarm hair."

A student complained to the police and a religious vigilance group known as Majilis Tahaffuz Khatm-i-Nabuwat — the Committee for the Protection of the Finality of the Prophethood. On Oct. 4, 2000, Shaikh was arrested and jailed. According to the report in the *New York Times*, "The Movement for the Finality of the Prophet, well known for pursuing blasphemers, filed a criminal complaint and sent a mob to the college and the local police station, threatening to set them on fire." As has become commonplace in the anti-blasphemy crusade in Pakistan, religious hard-liners vowed they would kill the doctor even if he should be acquitted. (See www.secularislam.org/news/shaikh.htm.)

Given all this business about tolerance and peace, I remarked how strange it is that the state-controlled Islamic press in countries like Egypt and Saudi Arabia insists on continuing to rile things up with their anti-Zionist slanders.

Writing on New York City Mayor Rudy Giuliani's rejection of Saudi Prince Al-Walid bin Talal's proffered $10 million for the families of the World Trade Center victims (less than the Saudi royals have contributed to bin Laden, if Sy Hersh of the *New Yorker* is to be believed) after the prince coupled the offer with remarks that of course it was all the fault of the Jews — Mahmoud bin Abd Al-Ghani Sabbagh, columnist for the Saudi paper *Al-Riyadh*, recently wrote (as translated by the Middle East Media Research Institute):

"Because the governor [sic] of the Big Apple is a Jew, he refused [to accept the donation] and caused a storm. ...

"Giuliani said: 'The Prince's declarations are grievous and irresponsible; these Arabs have lost the right to dictate [to us what to do]. What we [America] must do is kill 6,000 innocent people.' By Allah, I am amazed at your act, you Jew; everything Prince Al-Walid said was true. What happened proves beyond any doubt the public insolence, the open hatred and the collapse of American democratic theory. If democracy means a governor [sic] who is a homosexual in a city in which dance clubs, prostitution, homosexuality and stripping proliferate, the U.S. can keep its democracy."

Joining in the attack on Giuliani were columnists in the Palestinian Authority mouthpiece *Al-Hayat Al-Jadida*, editor Hafez Al-Barghouthi writing: "New York Mayor Rudolph Giuliani was obsessed by his hatred of Arabs even before the terrorist attacks on New York. He hides his first name, chosen for him by his Italian father, so as not to remind the Jewish voters of the infamous Rudolph Hitler [sic]. This is why he prefers to shorten it to Rudy."

(In the rough-and-tumble of New York City politics, personal secrets have short half-lives. While Mr. Giuliani has taken some political heat for consorting with a woman not his wife, it would be a considerable revelation to most New Yorkers should he turn out at this late date to be a Jewish homosexual, let alone that he has publicly called for the reprisal killings of "6,000 innocent people.")

❧ ❧ ❧

Extending this trend of moderation and well-researched reporting, some in the mainstream Arab press even go so far as to suggest the Trade Center massacre was actually planned by Israel, I pointed out to our lunchtime visitors.

"I find that extremely credible," said local physician assistant Basel Aladham, a gray-haired Palestinian who entered the room after the slide show had begun.

Now, far be it from me to underestimate the Mossad's powers of persuasion. But getting 19 Muslim religious zealots to commit suicide — and murder thousands in the process — all to the greater glory of ... Israel?

In a follow-up phone call to Mr. Aladham, who was born in Kuwait of Palestinian parents but who immigrated here 23 years ago and has been a U.S. citizen since 1988, I could not get a direct answer as to whether he believes the 19 young Muslim hijackers were duped into doing the will of the Israelis, or whether we have simply been misled about who seized those planes, altogether.

"Speaking from a purely Islamic point of view, it's hard for me to believe that any Muslim could think of doing such a thing. The teachings of Islam prevent anything like that from happening; therefore any Muslim with even half a brain or who would claim to be a Muslim, whatever happened would be from the legalistic point of view unthinkable."

Well, yes. But under this doctrine of law, we would have to dismiss charges against any murder suspect — even one found standing over the corpse with a bloody knife — if he could merely prove he was Muslim or Jewish *or* Christian, since all *three* religions prohibit murder.

"Second of all, you need resources," Mr. Aladham continued, embracing the odd "we couldn't have done it because we're so pathetic and incompetent" argument which is perhaps hardest for Westerners to understand. "And the only country that has such resources is the United States and Israel, " Mr. Aladham continued.

"Whenever you investigate any crime, the first thing the investigator asks himself is who is benefiting. Obviously not the Arabs, not the Saudis. Prior to these events, if you look at what was happening in Israel, which unfortunately has not been fully reported in this country, the Israelis on a daily basis were committing atrocities against the Palestinians, with a lot of pressure from the United States to have a dialogue or even to recognize a Palestinian state. But after this happened those pressures withered away. Since then there have been massacres — I have a satellite dish that gets 150 international channels, and there were incredible massacres in those three days [following Sept. 11] that we didn't hear about on CNN."

Where previously he was skeptical about claims that the Western press — including the BBC and French Channel 5 — are prejudiced, he now believes they are, Mr. Aladham confided. "The only beneficiary is Israel, so the notion that Israel is responsible is quite credible. Osama bin Laden's organization just doesn't have the resources. When you are in a plane going at 200 or 300 miles an hour, you have to be a pilot with 20 or 30 years experience to hit that building with accuracy. To tell me someone went to a little puddle-jumper school for six months and then hit those buildings so accurately, it's quite unbelievable."

Despite the fact it was the Palestinians — not the Israelis — who danced in the streets at word of the World Trade Center collapse (the Palestinian Authority successfully suppressing footage of at least one such celebratory rally in Ramallah by the simple expedient of threatening to kill the videographer if the footage was ever aired), he has simply "seen no evidence" that Osama bin Laden was behind the Sept. 11 attacks, Mr. Aladham continues to insist.

On Nov. 14, T.R. Reid of the *Washington Post* Foreign Service reported:

"LONDON, Nov. 14 — In an unbroadcast videotape made last month, Osama bin Laden declares that his al Qaeda network 'instigated' the Sept. 11 attacks, the British government said today, and explains that, 'If avenging the killing of our people is terrorism, let history be a witness that we are terrorists.'

"Bin Laden made the video on Oct. 20 for distribution among al Qaeda members, Prime Minister Tony Blair said today in an address to Parliament. On the tape, a British government document says, an interviewer asks bin Laden about the attacks on New York and Washington, and the Saudi replies: 'It is what we instigated, for a while, in self-defense. And it was revenge for our people killed in Palestine and Iraq. ...'

"In making his case today, Blair also said that intelligence sources have now linked a majority of the 19 men identified as Sept. 11 hijackers with al Qaeda. ... A British government statement released today also said that a senior bin Laden associate has admitted since Oct. 4 to have trained some of the hijackers in Afghanistan."

London's *Sunday Telegraph* also cited the new bin Laden video in this week's edition, saying that bin Laden used the tape to justify killing the victims in the World Trade Center.

"The twin towers were legitimate targets, they were supporting U.S. economic power," the newspaper quotes bin Laden as saying. "It is significant that throughout the video he uses the personal pronouns 'I' and 'we' to claim responsibility for the attacks. In the past, he has spoken of the attackers only in the third person," the *Telegraph* reports.

❧ ❧ ❧

Back at our lunchtime gathering, Mr. Eddebbarh grew slightly more emotional as he spoke of Islam's love of justice, immediately reaching for the "but" that so many Muslim spokesmen can't seem to help introducing after they condemn the Sept. 11 attacks ("whoever may be responsible for them ...").

"But we have to remember the 800,000 Palestinians who were driven by force from their homes," insisted Mr. Eddebbarh, who several times deflected political questions by insisting he had come to discuss only religion, not politics.

Leaving aside for a moment the question of how many Muslim Palestinians left their homes in what was to become Israel *voluntarily* in 1948 — the Arab powers, after all, were promising to "push the Jews into the sea" and shortly return them in triumph — I decided to ask Mr. Eddebbarh if there were any Jews, even a single Jewish family, that was physically forced from its home in what is now Jordan between 1922 and 1948, without being compensated for their confiscated property.

"I don't know of any examples of that," replied Mr. Eddebbarh, who presumes to lecture others on their lack of knowledge of the history of the conflict. "But if that were the case, then yes, Islam would stand for justice for those Jews too; Islam stands for justice."

Well, that explains it, then. I daresay that was the sixth demand on Mr. bin Laden's list, right after evicting all the non-believers from Saudi Arabia, throwing the Jews into the sea, and the overall discontinuance of Western culture and capitalism in general (the Eddebbarhs claim there is actually no religious restriction on non-believers visiting Mecca or Medina; the only restrictions are due to "security concerns").

Probably they just ran out of room at the bottom of the page to write, "Compensating the Jews who were booted out of Jordan after 1921."

"If that happened it is definitely an injustice," agreed Mr. Aladham on Friday. "But does that justify Jews coming from

Europe to displace an entire nation? There are three million Palestinian refugees who have been living in camps for 50 years."

In part because it does not suit the political purposes of the neighboring Arab states to welcome them and grant them citizenship, of course — unlike Israel, which gladly resettled the Jews evicted from Jordan (the Palestinian state created in 1922) rather than leave them squatting in camps around that nation's borders, the better to win U.N. resolutions condemning the Hashemite dynasty for its racist refusal to settle "the Jewishtinian problem" ... by refusing to carve out and create yet a *second* Jewish state.

Mr. Aladham goes on to detail the promises of Arab independence which the British broke after receiving Arab aid against the Turks in the First World War — Lord Balfour and company sitting down to draw completely arbitrary lines on the map to create the current nation-states of the Middle East.

But in fact, those nations now *have* had their independence for 50 years — along with the blessings of great oil wealth — and the freedom to adjust their boundaries as they saw fit. Besides which, if the British are at fault, why isn't anyone flying planes into *their* skyscrapers?

Responds Mr. Aladham: "The United States unfortunately is the only country that is capable of putting pressure on Israel, you see?"

Ah. So in this parallel universe, the Israelis engineered the events of Sept. 11 in order to force the United States to put pressure ... on Israel?

Islam is a religion of peace, Mr. Eddebbarh insisted. Muslims are never allowed to make war "except to rectify an injustice." But within moments, he was bragging that, "While Europe was in its Dark Ages, many cultures were living together in peaceful harmony" in Moorish Spain.

Precisely what injustice the Moors were seeking to "rectify" when they conquered Spain by the sword Mr. Eddebbarh did not make clear. And that ill-fated expedition over the Pyrenees, which would have led to the Moorish conquest of France were it not for the victory of Charles Martel (grandfather of Charlemagne) at Tours in 732? Why, that must have been to rectify "the French Injustice," we can only conclude.

Asked by one of the earnest young newsroom staff about this thing called "jihad," Mr. Eddebbarh replied that the term is widely misunderstood: "'Jihad' merely means struggle," he explained, and for most Muslims, "the struggle is internal, to live a proper life in the eyes of God."

Ah-hah. So when bin Laden preaches his "jihad" against Americans and all things American, apparently he merely hopes the residents of the Great Satan will get themselves signed up for 12-step programs, the better to get ourselves right with the Lord.

There are plenty of articulate spokesmen in this country for a more secular, less paranoid, less benighted practice of Islam — one that will take responsibility for the failure of the Muslim (and particularly the Arab) world in the past 50 to 80 years to build modern, tolerant, pluralistic, affluent societies, instead of blaming every failure on a conspiracy of the long-gone colonial powers and "The International Jew." I've recently quoted sensible remarks on these topics from Muslim writers like Salman Rushdie and my friend Imad-ad-Dean Ahmad of Washington's Minaret of Freedom Institute (www.minaret.org).

But if they aim to make new friends and influence people, the Muslim Public Affairs Council may want to make a few upgrades to the Aziz Eddebbarh traveling slide show.

Meet the New Boss ... Same as the Old Boss
🍂

Thirty years ago, the socialists who discovered they could successfully harness their collectivist rhetoric to the anti-Vietnam War movement (which is not to say that all who opposed that war joined the ComIntern, by any means) chafed and rebelled against the Eisenhower generation's presumption that the Dulles brothers knew what they were doing, and that any opposition to the foreign-policy status quo was thus unpatriotic. That younger generation swore that, if and when they were ever in charge, things would be different.

Well, they are, and they are.

It's just that the "difference" they promised turns out to be not so much about open debate and tolerance of minority opinions, as ... which opinions are now unpopular enough to be censored.

"Across the nation, in response to the atrocities of Sept. 11, 2001, and to the debates and discussions that have occurred in their wake, many college and university administrators are acting to inhibit the free expression of the citizens of a free society," writes Thor L. Halvorssen of the Philadelphia-based Foundation for Individual Rights in Education (FIRE) on Oct. 24.

The opinions most likely to be repressed may have shifted 180 degrees ... but not the instinct to silence those with which we do not agree.

At Holy Cross College in Worcester, Mass., "The chair of the department of sociology, Professor Royce Singleton, demanded that a secretary remove an American flag that she had hung in the departmental office," Halvorssen reports. "The flag was in memory of her friend Todd Beamer, who fought and died on the hijacked United Airlines Flight 93 over Pennsylvania. When she refused, Singleton removed it himself. After unfavorable publicity, the College apologized, but the flag in question was moved to the department of psychology."

At Duke University, the administration shut down a Web site after Prof. Gary Hull posted an article titled "Terrorism and Its Appeasement," calling for a strong military response to the terrorist attacks. The Foundation for Individual Rights in

Education took Professor's Hull's case to the print and broadcast media.

"Shamed by widespread publicity, Duke reinstated Hull's Web page, but required him to add a disclaimer that the views expressed in the article did not reflect the views of the University," a disclaimer Duke had never previously required on any other faculty Web page, Halvorssen notes.

At Florida Gulf Coast University, Dean of Library Services Kathleen Hoeth instructed her employees to remove stickers saying "Proud to be an American" from their work spaces, claiming that she did not want to "offend international students." President William Merwin revoked the policy after coming under public pressure.

In September, the University of Massachusetts granted a permit for a student rally to protest any use of force in waging the war against terrorism. The protest was held. Another student group reserved the same place to hold a rally in support of America's policy toward terrorism, but two days before the rally their permit was revoked.

"Students held the rally anyway, and their pamphlets were publicly vandalized with impunity," reports Mr. Halvorssen of FIRE.

In a widely reported case at San Diego State University, an international student, Zewdalem Kebede, overheard several other foreign students speaking loudly in Arabic in the library, expressing delight about the terrorist attacks. Kebede engaged the students and, in Arabic, challenged their positions. Kebede was accused by San Diego State University of abusive behavior toward the four students, formally admonished, and warned that "future incidents [will result in] serious disciplinary sanctions."

At Central Michigan University, an administrator told several students to remove various patriotic posters (including an American flag and a portrayal of an eagle) from their dormitory. On Oct. 8, a Residential Advisor told them that their display was "offensive," and that they had until the end of the day to remove the items.

The point here is not just how out of touch left-wing academia seems to be with heartland American opinion — though it does remain to be seen how long rank-and-file citizens will continue to pay vast sums to have their children "educated" by an intellectual class now revealed to have more sympathy with the purported grievances of Osama bin Laden than with the right of 3,000 innocent Americans to go to work in the morning without being murdered.

For it hardly solves the problem if those on "the right" grow outraged to have their flags taken down ... while asserting that suppressing the opinions of communists and Wahhabi Muslims is merely common sense.

I find the views of both the latter mentioned parties to be by turns laughable and repulsive. But the solution is to hear them out and then ridicule them mercilessly, rubbing their rhetorical faces in their own failures. If the Muslim peoples are the chosen of God, how come so many of them live in flyblown hellholes with no flush toilets while their corrupt poohbahs bask in all the oil wealth?

The pathetic buggers who cheered the mass murders of Sept. 11 cannot win a free debate — not when Exhibits A and B are their own backward, corrupt, impoverished nations and repressive social structures, manically reverting to levels of depravity and masochism not seen in the civilized world in 300 years.

But the only way to prove that is to engage them in a free debate. So-called "institutions of higher learning" that would bar these assertion of fact based on "multicultural sensitivity," curbing robust debate to avoid "offending anyone," aren't worth the fertilizer it takes to keep grass growing on the quad.

The Web site of the Foundation for Individual Rights in Education is at www.thefire.org.

❦ ❦ ❦

Fallen-away leftist Christopher Hitchens seems to have done a better job of capturing the somewhat surreal tone of our current gang of pacifists — this "dismal tide of dreary traffic, this mob of pseudo-refugees taking shelter in half-baked moral equivalence" than I've been able to. (Maybe it's something to do with picking up the cadence and inflection of a foreign language, the language in this case being not American English, but a dying tongue called Marxism.)

Writing in the December, 2001 *Atlantic* magazine (www.theatlantic.com/issues/2001/12/hitchens.htm) Hitchens reports:

"October 6, the day immediately preceding the first U.S. counterstroke against the Taliban and Osama bin Laden, found me on a panel at the New York Film Festival. The discussion, on the art of political cinema, had been arranged many months before. But as the chairman announced, the events of September 11 would now provide the atmospheric conditioning for our deliberations. I thus sat on a stage with Oliver Stone, who spoke with feeling about something he termed 'the revolt of September 11,' and with bell hooks [sic], who informed a well-filled auditorium of the Lincoln Center that those who had experienced Spike Lee's movie about the bombing of a Birmingham, Alabama, church in 1963 would understand that 'state terrorism' was nothing new in America.

"These were not off-the-cuff observations. I challenged Stone to reconsider his view of the immolation of the World Trade Center as a 'revolt.' He ignored me. Later he added that this rebellion would soon be joined by the anti-globalization forces of the Seattle protesters. When he was asked by a member of the audience to comment on the applause for the September 11 massacres in Arab streets and camps, he responded that the French Revolution, too, had been greeted by popular enthusiasm.

"These views are, sadly, not uncommon on the political left. Indeed, I would surmise that audience approval of Stone's and hooks' propositions was something near fifty-fifty. Clapping and hissing are feeble and fickle indicators, true. At different times, in combating both Stone and hooks, I got my own fair share of each. But let's say that three weeks after a mass murder had devastated the downtown district, and at a moment when the miasma from the site could still be felt and smelled, a ticket-buying audience of liberal New Yorkers awarded blame more or less evenhandedly between the members of al Qaeda and the directors of U.S. foreign policy. (And not just of foreign policy: Stone drew applause for his assertion that there was an intimate tie between the New York, Pennsylvania, and Washington attacks and the Florida ballot recount, which was, he asserted, 'a complete vindication of the fact that capitalism has destroyed democracy.')

"By this time I was entering my twenty-sixth day of active and engaged antagonism toward this sort of talk, or thought, and was impressed despite myself by the realization that I was the first person Stone and hooks and some audience members appeared to have met who did not agree with them. Or perhaps I should rephrase that: I was the first person on the political left they had met who did not echo or ratify their view. As it happens, I know enough about Marxism, for example, to state without overmuch reservation that capitalism, for all its contradictions, is superior to feudalism and serfdom, which is what bin Laden and the Taliban stand for. (Stone, when I put this to him after the event, retorted that his father had spent many years on Wall Street, and thus he knew the topic quite well.)"

Hitchens then proposes to *Atlantic* readers a "brief rhetorical experiment:

"Very well, I will stipulate that September 11 was revenge for past American crimes. Specifically, and with supporting detail, I will agree that it was revenge for the crime of past indifference to, and collusion with, the Taliban. May we now agree to cancel this crime by removing from the Taliban the power of enslavement that it exerts over Afghans, and which it hopes to extend? Dead silence from progressives. Couldn't we talk about the ozone layer instead? In other words, all the learned and conscientious objections, as well as all the silly or sinister ones, boil down to this: Nothing will make us fight against an evil if that fight forces us to go to the same corner as our own government. (The words 'our own' should of course be appropriately ironized, with the necessary quotation marks.) To do so would be a betrayal of the Cherokees. ..."

Thus endeth today's reading from Comrade Hitchens.

A certain brand of ivory-tower libertarian, too, finds it easy to duck any fruitful discussion of foreign policy by pointing out that armies and aircraft carriers and even the State Department itself are funded by taxes, and taxes are evil. That makes it morally wrong — according to this particularly sterile little academic circle-jerk — to discuss any appropriate uses of America's power, or even to acknowledge it could have more wise versus less wise uses: end of discussion.

Really? Is there really *no way* that a volunteer military couldn't be sustained by the voluntary subscription fees of, say, international shippers who benefit from our protecting the sea lanes from pirates? How do we know when it hasn't been tried in centuries? And until such time as it's tried, to be a good tax-hating Libertarian must one really take the position that the *only* policy we can recommend in response to an armed invasion of these United States is for our forces to simultaneously drop their weapons and their trousers, bending over and spreading wide, rather than firing a single "tax-funded" bullet?

If those of us who believe taxes are slavery thus forbid ourselves the chance to engage in the debate over the counterproductive waste that typifies the federal highways program, since highway funds are made up of taxes and our opposition to taxes makes it morally impossible for us to engage in any debate about how those funds are used (end of discussion), are we also forbidden to expose and criticize police misconduct and even murders by police, since police are funded by taxes and the only morally tenable position for a Libertarian concerning police brutality is, "Tax-funded police must be abolished and till that happens we have nothing to say"?

If so, it's going to be a mighty quiet year in the cave.

🍃 🍃 🍃

Let's close with excerpts a piece found at www.national post.com/home/story.html?f=/stories/20011101/765192.html.

"A lesson from the professor and the station master

"George Jonas, *National Post*

"The story of the Turkish station master was told to me by the Hungarian icon, the poet George Faludy, now in his 90s. He heard it from Rustem Vambery, the noted lawyer and diplomat, when they were both in New York at the end of the Second World War. The incident itself happened a long time ago, and it involved Vambery's father, Arminius, the 19th-century Orientalist.

"Professor Arminius Vambery was a severely crippled man who had to use crutches. This didn't stop him from becoming an explorer of note, and the author of several important books on Central Asia. ... Professor Vambery liked the Orient. He both respected and understood it.

"There were no private jets in those days, but VIPs often travelled by private railway carriage. Passing through Turkey as the Sultan's guest one year, the professor had his own carriage attached to the train. After the engine stopped at a small station in Anatolia, on the Asian side of the Marmaran Sea, a Turkish station master entered the carriage. He sized up Vambery with a sly glance, bowed perfunctorily, then informed the professor that, regrettably, his carriage needed to be uncoupled from the train.

"Vambery was travelling with a friend. They looked at

each other. 'Why?' Vambery asked.

"'Regulations, effendi,' the station master replied with a smirk. 'We need to leave your carriage behind on the siding. For a slight consideration, though, an exception can be made.' "With that, he calmly held out his hand for baksheesh.

"The station master was a huge brute, as it happened. His immense palm made a good target, so Vambery immediately whacked it with his crutch. Then he struggled to his feet, striking the Turk repeatedly with all his might.

"The station master, who could have snapped the professor in half, didn't even try to ward off the blows. 'Effendi, I didn't know, forgive me, I didn't realize,' he muttered, bowing deeply and backing off. 'In your exalted case, of course, regulations don't apply.'

"'Didn't you see the size of that fellow?' Vambery's friend asked, shaken, after the genuflecting giant had backed out of the car. 'Weren't you afraid to hit him?'

"'Of course,' replied Vambery, 'but this is the Orient. I would have been far more afraid not to hit him.'

"Vambery's assessment of what is to be feared more, firmness or appeasement, holds true in many parts of the world, not just the Orient. Except in the East it's more than a rule of thumb. It's one of the fundamentals, which Westerners, especially Americans, have trouble appreciating.

"This goes beyond the classic problem of decency or compromise being mistaken for weakness. What Americans find hard to understand is that gestures of magnanimity are not seen as such in Eastern cultures. In fact, they have the opposite effect. Stopping air attacks for Muslim religious holidays, for instance, or dropping food parcels after bombing raids, not only fail to get the United States any Brownie points, but often aggravate resentment.

"Alms alternating with bombs seem deliberately humiliating. They add insult to injury. They signal the ostentation of power. To the Oriental mind, especially, such humanitarian gestures show U.S. arrogance and swaggering tackiness, not its heart.

"They also telegraph unease, guilt, maybe even fear.

"There's a bewildered question Americans, and Westerners in general, keep asking after 9-11: 'Why do they hate us so?' The question also has an unasked corollary: 'Why don't they respect us more?'

"The answer may be that we haven't yet learned when to whack the station master and when to offer him baksheesh."

VI
Afraid of Competence,
Afraid of Freedom ...
Afraid of Guns

"The right of self-defense is the first law of nature; in most governments it has been the study of rulers to confine this right within the narrowest limits possible. Wherever standing armies are kept up, and when the right of the people to keep and bear arms is, under any color or pretext whatsoever, prohibited, liberty, if not already annihilated, is on the brink of destruction."
> — *Henry St. George Tucker, in Blackstone's 1768 "Commentaries on the Laws of England."*

Shouldn't We Repeal the Gun Laws ...
If It'll Save a Single Child?

🌿

Jessica Lynne Carpenter is 14 years old. She knows how to shoot; her father taught her. And there were adequate firearms to deal with the crisis that arose in the Carpenter home in Merced, Calif. — a San Joaquin Valley farming community 130 miles southeast of San Francisco — when 27-year-old Jonathon David Bruce came calling on Wednesday morning, Aug. 23, 2000.

There was just one problem. Under the new "safe storage" laws being enacted in California and elsewhere, parents can be held criminally liable unless they lock up their guns when their children are home alone ... so that's just what law-abiding parents John and Tephanie Carpenter had done.

Some of Jessica's siblings — Anna, 13; Vanessa, 11; Ashley, 9; and John William, 7 — were still in their bedrooms when Bruce broke into the farmhouse shortly after 9 a.m.

Bruce, who was armed with a pitchfork — but to whom police remain unable to attribute any motive — had apparently cut the phone lines. So when he forced his way into the house and began stabbing the younger children in their beds, Jessica's attempts to dial 911 didn't do much good. Next, the sensible girl ran for where the family guns were stored. But they were locked up tight.

"When the 14-year-old girl ran to a nearby house to escape the pitchfork-wielding man attacking her siblings," writes Kimi Yoshino of the *Fresno Bee*, "she didn't ask her neighbor to call 911. She begged him to grab his rifle and 'take care of this guy.'" He didn't. Jessica ended up on the phone.

By the time Merced County sheriff's deputies arrived at the home, 7-year-old John William and 9-year-old Ashley Danielle were dead. Ashley had apparently hung onto her assailant's leg long enough for her older sisters to escape. Thirteen-year-old Anna was wounded but survived.

Once the deputies arrived, Bruce rushed them with his bloody pitchfork. So they shot him dead. They shot him more than a dozen times. With their guns.

Get it?

The following Friday, the children's great-uncle, the Rev. John Hilton, told reporters: "If only [Jessica] had a gun available to her, she could have stopped the whole thing. If she had been properly armed, she could have stopped him in his tracks." Maybe John William and Ashley would still be alive, Jessica's uncle said.

"Unfortunately, 17 states now have these so-called safe storage laws," replies Yale Law School Senior Research Scholar Dr. John Lott — author of the book *More Guns, Less Crime*. "The problem is, you see *no* decrease in either juvenile accidental gun deaths or suicides when such laws are enacted, but you do see an *increase* in crime rates."

Such laws are based on the notion that young children

often "find daddy's gun" and accidentally shoot each other. But in fact only five American children under the age of 10 died of accidents involving handguns in 1997, Lott reports. "People get the impression that kids under 10 are killing each other. In fact, this is very rare: three to four per year."

The typical *shooter* in an accidental child gun death is a male in his late teens or 20s, who, statistically, is probably a drug addict or an alcoholic and has already been charged with multiple crimes, Lott reports. "These are the data that correlate. Are these the kind of people who are going to obey one more law?"

So why doesn't the national press report what happens when a victim disarmament ("gun control") law costs the lives of innocent children in a place like Merced?

"In the school shooting in Pearl, Miss.," Dr. Lott replies, "the assistant principal had formerly carried a gun to school. When the 1995 ["Gun-Free School Zones"] law passed, he took to locking his gun in his car and parking it at least a quarter-mile away from the school, in order to obey the law. When that shooting incident started he ran to his car, unlocked it, got his gun, ran back, disarmed the shooter, and held him on the ground for five minutes until the police arrived.

"There were more than 700 newspaper stories catalogued on that incident. Only 19 mentioned the assistant principal in any way, and only nine mentioned that he had a gun."

The press covers only the bad side of gun use, and only the potential benefits of victim disarmament laws — never their costs. "Basically all the current federal proposals fall into this category — trigger locks, waiting periods," Lott said. "There's not one academic study that shows any reduction in crime from measures like these. But there are good studies that show the opposite. Even with short waiting periods, crime goes up. You have women being stalked, and they can't go quickly and get a gun due to the waiting periods, so they get assaulted or they get killed."

The United States has among the world's lowest "hot" burglary rates — burglaries committed while people are in the building — at 13 percent, compared to "gun-free" Britain's rate, which is now up to 59 percent, Lott reports. "If you survey burglars, American burglars spend at least twice as long casing a joint before they break in. ... The number one reason they give for taking so much time is: They're afraid of getting shot."

The way Jonathon David Bruce, of Merced, Calif., might once have been afraid of getting shot ... before 17 states enacted laws requiring American parents to leave their kids disarmed while they're away from home.

To Reduce Crime ... Buy Your Child a Gun

It's called propaganda: Simplify your lie down to an easily recalled slogan, repeat it often enough, and people will eventually not only memorize it, but also accept it as fact.

Take: "The cause of all these school shootings is the too-easy availability of guns."

Prior to the National Firearms Act of 1934, there was no law to discourage a veteran of the Great War from keeping a fully operational souvenir machine gun in the bedroom closet. There were few towns in America where the local lads didn't know the location of at least one such weapon. Yet none was ever used in a "school shooting."

As late as the 1960s, it was not unusual in rural America for young boys to carry their .22 rifles to school with them, parking them in the principal's office until needed for the target matches after school. At age 51 I am no doddering old-timer, but I can remember young lads walking the country roads of Ohio and Connecticut after school with their rifles (or bicycling home with the weapons across their handlebars), hoping to pick off some predatory bird with the full encouragement of area farmers. A neighbor might chide you about watching where your bullets went if you missed, but no one ever called the police to report, "The Jones boy is heading down the road with his gun; come arrest him!"

When I went away to Eaglebrook School in Massachusetts (yes, "Own a gun, go to jail" Massachusetts) in 1962 at the age of 12, I took my rifle. We fired for accuracy at the range on Saturdays. I daresay we could have figured out a way to sneak them out of the lockers down at the gym for some mayhem if it ever crossed our minds ... but it never did.

The violent media? Today's TV offers nothing like "The Rifleman" or "Wanted Dead or Alive," programs of the early 1960s in which Chuck Connors and Steve McQueen ended every episode by mowing down some reprobate who had kicked the town dog or insulted Millie down at the general store, in McQueen's case using a sawed-off Winchester, which it's now a federal felony even to recreate for a museum.

This focus on "the availability of guns" — ignoring the fact they were far more accessible only 40 years ago, when you could order a 20-mm Lahti anti-tank gun through the mail from an ad in the back of a comic book — is intended not only to advance the prior agenda of those who want a disarmed and enslaved citizenry, but also to distract us from asking what it is about the mandatory behavior modification labs (public schools) that creates such rage and frustration in our incarcerated adolescent males. We don't see these shoot-em-ups in the private schools, or among home-schoolers.

It also diverts attention from the perfectly relevant question of how many of these shooters had been on drugs known to affect the judgment, like Ritalin and Luvox, prescribed and administered by their government wardens.

In the face of all this misdirection, isn't it too bad the government has never conducted an actual scientific study on how it affects a child's likelihood of committing crimes if his parents buy him a gun?

Um, actually ... they have.

The study was conducted from 1993 to 1995 by the U.S. Department of Justice's Office of Juvenile Justice and Delinquency Prevention. Child psychologists tracked 4,000 boys and girls aged 6 to 15 in Denver, Pittsburgh, and Rochester, New York. Their findings?

— Children who get guns from their parents don't commit gun crimes (0 percent), while children who get guns illegally are quite likely to do so (21 percent).

— Children who get guns from parents are less likely to commit any kind of street crime (14 percent) than children who have no gun in the house (24 percent) — and are dramatically less likely to do so than children who acquire an illegal gun (74 percent).

— Children who get guns from parents are less likely to use banned drugs (13 percent) than children who get illegal guns (41 percent).

— Most strikingly, the study found: "Boys who own legal firearms have much lower rates of delinquency and drug use [than boys who own illegal guns] and are even slightly less delinquent than non-owners of guns."

This wouldn't have surprised anyone before the rise of the modern welfare state. It used to be common knowledge that the best way to get kids to act "responsibly" was precisely to give them some "responsibility." Why would we assume a child taught by his parents to use a gun responsibly wouldn't also be more responsible in his other behaviors?

"Want to dramatically reduce the chance that your child will commit a gun-related crime or — heaven forbid — go on a shooting spree?" asked the national Libertarian Party in a May 2001 news release detailing these study results. "Buy your youngster a gun."

"Politicians are apparently more interested in demonizing guns than they are in facts," commented LP national director Steve Dasbach, himself an Indiana government schoolteacher. But "The evidence is in: The simplest way to reduce firearm-related violence among children is to buy them a gun and teach them how to use it responsibly."

"The Weapon Is to Him a Sign of Honor and Freedom"

In August 2000, Korean War veteran Bill Pickett contacted me from the little Nevada oasis of Overton, 50 miles northeast of Las Vegas, copying me part of an e-mail he'd just sent to an old army buddy of his, "a retired schoolteacher and Clinton supporter."

"Again, I'm fighting with the feds," Bill wrote. "Our local American Legion Post has four old Enfield rifles issued to the Post in 1946. The feds sent a retired colonel and a retired NCO here to 'check out the rifles.' It's reported that these two guys stayed at the local motel for three days ..." doubtless costing the Department of Defense more than the total value of the five-shot, bolt-action, 1917-vintage rifles.

"As undoubtedly pre-planned, the Post then received a 13-page letter demanding that the four rifles be stored in a vault at the police station, or at a National Guard Armory, or in a building of specified construction including bars on all openings," Bill Pickett continued.

The federals contended the post was supposed to have several more of the "Curio & Relic" rifles than members could account for. Pickett explains that members had been passing the surplus rifles from hand to hand for 50 years — many of the long guns passing through the custody of members since gone on to their heavenly reward. "A lot of those rifles were kept under people's beds and I'm sure a number of them have gone out deer hunting over the years," Pickett says, acknowledging no one is left alive who remembers exactly how many rifles the post originally had.

But the June letter, addressed to Post 38 Commander John Fetherston, a 74-year-old ex-paratrooper who served in the South Pacific, went on to set other requirements, even for those rifles that remain: Background check of the local post commander, verification of compliance with the Lautenberg Amendment — that is to say, proof that no 77-year-old vet who fires blanks through the rifles at military funerals is subject to any restraining order incident to an ongoing divorce action — even a requirement that the post submit a map of their "weapon storage" area and annual photos of the "stored weapons."

Upon compliance with the above, Pickett wrote, "The feds will issue a 'Conditional Deed of Gift' and a 'Weapons Control Register' to indicate where the weapons are 'at all times' (including use at funeral ceremonies). ... Also, there is a requirement for submission of ... a photograph of the 'weapons' clearly showing the 'blank adaptor fixed to the end of the barrel.'"

(A spokesman for the DoD TACOM has since conceded that since there's no such thing as a "blank adapter" for a World War One bolt-action rifle, the government graciously now allows as how "adaptors are not a requirement" on the Enfields.)

Most importantly, the veterans were informed, "Storage at a private residence is absolutely prohibited."

I forwarded Bill's message to *Review-Journal* Special Projects Editor A.D. Hopkins, who checked it all out and wrote up a fine story, published Aug. 13, 2000, complete with a color photo of the vets in their white helmets, firing a salute.

"They said we can store them in a bank vault, but the local bank says they don't want to fool with it," post commander Fetherston told Hopkins. "And we didn't even ask at the police substation, because we decided we're not going for the rest of it. I'm not going to ask the State Police to do any background checks on me. ... And how could I certify that some member doesn't have a domestic violence conviction 20 years ago, without doing a background check on every one?"

The government letter also included detailed instructions for sending the rifles back if the members don't want to go through all the new rigmarole — which is what John Hudrlik, 55-year-old Navy veteran and finance officer of American Legion Post 75 in Logandale, figures is the real goal.

Federal Tactical Command spokesman Ron Morton confirmed for A.D. that "accountability" for such weapons was "not fully enforced" for 50 years. Then, "During the period 1996 through 1998, the Donation Program went through a massive corrective action due to the lack of enforcement and high quantities of missing weapons throughout the U.S."

So? Uncle Sam gave away 500,000 of these same rifles to the Brits in early 1940, after they carelessly left all theirs lying on some beach in France. After the War, the crown rounded them all up and dumped them in the ocean. Why doesn't Ron go looking for *those* Enfields? Has there been a rash of inner-city gang members sneaking in and purloining these old bolt-action clunkers, sticking an original-issue 17-inch bayonet on the end of the clunky 44-inch-long rifles, hiding them under their jackets, and using them to hold up liquor stores?

Of course not. The only way this makes sense is when seen as part of the ongoing campaign to demonize possession of weapons of military usefulness, to convince a majority of urban voters that keeping firearms in one's home is as depraved as allowing a collection of venomous reptiles to crawl freely about the living room.

Of particular concern is the cited provision, "Authorized storage sites are limited to National Guard Armory, U.S. Army Reserve Center, [or] Military Installation. ... Private residences are not authorized."

During the debate over ratification of the U.S. Constitution, the anti-federalists pointed out that since the new Constitution granted Congress the power to arm the militia, the Congress would thus also have the power to *withhold* arms from the militia. (The militia being, according to Richard Henry Lee, "the people themselves.")

"Of what service would militia be to you," asked Patrick Henry, rising in the Virginia House on June 5, 1788, "when most probably you will not have a single musket in the State; for as arms are to be provided by Congress, they may or may not furnish them."

The federalists responded by promising to insert a Bill of Rights with a Second Amendment, guaranteeing that every American may keep military-style weapons *in his home*.

"Before a standing army can rule, the people must be disarmed; as they are in almost every kingdom in Europe," explained prominent federalist Noah Webster. But, "The supreme power in America cannot enforce unjust laws by the sword; because the whole body of the people are armed, and constitute a force superior to any band of regular troops that can be, on any pretense, raised in the United States."

"Congress have no power to disarm the militia," agreed Tench Coxe of Philadelphia, the friend of Madison and prominent federalist. "Their swords, and every other terrible instrument of the soldier, are the birth-right of an American. ... [T]he unlimited power of the sword is not in the hands of either the federal or the state governments, but, where I trust in God it will ever remain, in the hands of the people."

"The great object is," added Patrick Henry, "that every man be armed. Everyone who is able must have a gun."

Does that sound like the gentlemen meant our "right to bear arms" would be adequately honored simply by instructing us we're free to join the National Guard (created in 1917), reporting in federal uniform to have arms issued to us from locked federal arsenals when federal officials deem it appropriate?

Fresh in the minds of the Founding Fathers were the crucial Revolutionary War victories at Saratoga and King's Mountain, won almost entirely by militiamen/farmers — Minutemen able to respond quickly because they kept their militia weapons with them in their homes.

What is the freest nation on Earth today — the nation where the people least fear their government, because their government trusts every homeowner to keep a fully automatic assault rifle at home in the closet?

"There is probably no other country that, like Switzerland, gives the soldier his weapon to keep in the home," said Swiss President Phillipp Etter, at the opening of a local shooting festival in June of 1939. "The Swiss always has his rifle at hand. It belongs to the furnishings of his home. ... He knows what that means. With the rifle, he is liable every hour, if the country calls, to defend his hearth, his home, his family, his birthplace. The weapon is to him a pledge and sign of honor and freedom. The Swiss does not part with his rifle."

And what was the result? How was the experience of Switzerland, from 1939 to 1945, so different from that of every other little nation in central Europe?

"There was no holocaust on Swiss soil," author Stephen P. Halbrook responds, in his 1998 book *Target Switzerland*. "Swiss Jews served in the militia side by side with their fellow citizens, and kept rifles in their homes just like everyone else. It is hard to believe there could have been a holocaust had the Jews of Germany, Poland, and France had the same privilege."

"In our last Post meeting, I recommended that we fight the requirements," Bill Pickett wrote. "If we lose (and we will), then tell the army to come and get them (and they will). We hope to have TV coverage of this event: 70- and 80-year-old duffers in American Legion uniforms handing over the old war souvenirs. ...

"Hell, just dump the old guy in the ground. Forget that he might have been instrumental in saving our country and its freedom. Freedom that we enjoyed during the late forties and into the fifties. Freedom that is now in extreme jeopardy. Perhaps only the older generation is aware of the ever-tightening federal noose."

❦ ❦ ❦

I checked back a year later — in the fall of 2001 — with American Legion Post 38 Commander John Fetherston, asking whatever happened with the World War One Enfield rifles.

"What finally put a stop to it is, we had a phone call from 'em that said, 'Well, if you'll sign an affidavit that you've looked for 'em, we'll drop [the matter] on those six rifles that you didn't find,'" Fetherston told me.

"I said 'I won't do it.' They said, 'You've got to account for this government property.' So I said, 'OK, you just send me the serial numbers on those guns that's missing.'

"A couple of days later this gal called back and said, 'Unfortunately, we don't have those serial numbers,' and I said, 'Well then, you don't have any rifles.' That's been over a year ago, and I haven't heard another word. ...

"But I'll tell you one thing, it got spread around over the country; we had an interview over the telephone with a talk show in Missouri. And I had a VFW or an American Legion post up in Minnesota — I forget which one — that called and said they'd be happy to go to the expense of getting us some rifles if they took ours. We thanked 'em, but we said for now we're pretty well satisfied with what we've got."

Could It Be They Don't *Want* Us to Be Able to Obey the Law?

I honor the understandable request for anonymity of the author of this October 1998 letter:

Vin — Your Oct. 2 commentary, "And every other terrible implement of the soldier," hit home with me.

I am deeply bothered by the felony penalties hinging on trivial features of a rifle. I am currently assembling an StG58, an obsolete and beautiful Austrian rifle that is a member of the FAL family. Austria no longer has use for the things and is selling them off to U.S. importers. I bought a complete rifle, minus the receiver, which had been sawed off prior to importation as required by the BATF. Its stub was left attached to the barrel. I bought a brand new U.S.-made receiver in compliance with all local, state, and federal laws.

So far, so good. But it gets complicated once I mate the receiver to the rest of the rifle. Here is a minefield of laws and regulations, and my future well-being hinges on their trivialities.

I must remove the flash hider. And then I must either saw the threaded end off the barrel or cover it with a "muzzle brake"... but only if I solder the muzzle brake in place with solder having a melting point of 1,100 degrees Fahrenheit or higher. If I use solder with a melting point of 1,000 degrees F, for example, it's off to jail with me. Or, I could pin the muzzle brake in place. But only if the pin is in a "blind" hole that doesn't reach through to the other side. And only if the pin is strong enough to withstand the shearing torque specified by the BATF, who will try to unscrew the muzzle brake to see if it is attached in a "legal" manner. If it unscrews with 120 foot-pounds of torque, I'm a felon. If it unscrews with 130 foot-pounds, I'm free. (I made up the torque numbers — I haven't been able to find out what the real ones are. They weren't in the "assault weapon" ban that Clinton signed. Nor was anything about muzzle brake attachment methods.)

Also, the muzzle brake must have a diameter greater than 22 millimeters.

Why, you may ask? Because back when Austria used this rifle, they had grenades that would slide over the flash hider. A blank cartridge was then fired in the rifle, launching the grenade. So, depending on the diameter of my muzzle brake, I may, or may not, have replaced the original "grenade launcher" with a brand new "grenade launcher." Please don't ask where I might possibly obtain an obsolete Austrian grenade. And please don't ask why I am allowed to put a muzzle brake of "grenade launcher" diameter on any other rifle but the StG58.

And I must replace many of the original, authentic, and beautifully made parts on the rifle with U.S.-made equivalents that look and operate just like the old ones. Why? Because if I don't, I will have assembled a "non-sporting" *imported* rifle and could be thrown in jail. By substituting enough U.S.-made parts, it becomes a "sporting" *U.S.-made* rifle and is perfectly legal. How do I tell if this rifle, or any other, is "non-sporting?" Simple. According to the law, if it is "not particularly suited for sporting purposes." No ambiguities there.

The list of issues goes on and on. I am in communication with other collectors and shooters who are in similar fixes. We agonize over the legal details, sharing hearsay and rumors in valiant attempts to remain in compliance with the BATF's shifting and largely undocumented interpretations of the laws. What constitutes a pistol grip that "protrudes prominently" from the gun? What counts as a "thumbhole stock" and what doesn't? What if I put a plain unthreaded barrel on the rifle, and its (outside) diameter happens to be the same as that of the illegal "grenade launcher"? We don't know.

My opinion is that we are fools. The only reason I wade through the morass of obscure legalities is that everyone else does so, too. If we all simply ignored the absurdities, we would be free. They can't jail us all.

For that matter, I wish they *would* try to jail someone. But they never do. Given a feeble excuse of the sort mentioned, the BATF will break into your home and confiscate anything resembling a firearm, firearm accessory, and probably your computer and filing cabinet, to boot. But they will press no charges. They *know* the laws are absurd.

They *know* there is no jury in the country that will send you to jail because one part on your rifle was attached with 1,000 F solder instead of 1,100 F solder, or because the rifle had one too few U.S.-made parts on it. They'll just ransack your house, seize your property, and ruin your life. You will not get your day in court.

We should ignore them, but who will be the first to show up at the rifle range with a "flash hider"/"grenade launcher" on his rifle? Not me. I could lose my property and my life could be destroyed. Who, then, will lead the way? No one. What are the odds of *everyone* defying the laws, en masse, starting on a pre-arranged date? Zero.

And that is the beauty of the system. The screws are tightened gradually, so people are pushed over the edge and into defiance one at a time, and are thus easily vanquished.

We see the news items in the paper. "Illegal weapons cache seized." Perhaps he was the guy that had a muzzle brake with the wrong diameter, and lost everything. "Assault Weapon Found in Home." Was he the poor guy who had a bayonet lug on a rifle whose serial number implied that it was probably built the day *after* Clinton signed the celebrated Feinstein "assault weapon" ban? His neighbor, whose rifle was built the day before, was left unmolested, being a fine law-abiding citizen, you see.

It's more than the technicalities of gun regulations. Think of "standoffs." One person hits the limit of tolerance for bull and quits playing the game. He starts living in defiance of the crushing burden of the laws and regulations under which we are all groaning. Now he's a "criminal" and his place is surrounded by the thin blue line for a few days until he's hauled off, shot, or burned. Each person has a different limit, and we hit them at different times, easily taken out by the authorities singly or in tiny groups. There will never be widespread open revolt. Modern bureaucracies have learned how to avoid that.

I have never spoken my mind in public on this subject. I don't talk about this on Internet bulletin boards, or in e-mail. I am afraid to. I'm worried about sending this letter to you, even under a pseudonym. I'm not a newspaper editor. If my words attract the attention of the wrong people I could be the next faceless owner of an "illegal arms cache" that ends up as a news item at the bottom page 31. ...

As Aristotle said in *Politics*, "Both oligarch and tyrant mistrust the people, and therefore deprive them of their arms."

Please feel free to use any of this material in any way you see fit.

"Proliferation of Small Arms ... Erodes Government Authority"

⚜

U.N. Undersecretary-General for Disarmament Jayantha Dhanapala seems to have figured out he had a problem right around the Fourth of July, 2001.

"The United Nations is investigating whether irate letters and e-mails it has received from American gun enthusiasts protesting an upcoming conference on the illicit trade in small arms constitutes a security threat," reported the wide-eyed Associated Press lady at the U.N. on July 5th.

"The world body has received about 100 complaints from Americans who erroneously believe the conference seeks to infringe on their right to bear arms ... Dhanapala said Thursday."

In response, Dhanapala's office released a pamphlet called "Setting the Record Straight," stressing, "The focus of the conference is on illicit trade in small arms, not the legal trade, manufacture or ownership of weapons. ... The U.N. conference will have no effect on the rights of civilians to legally own and bear arms."

The obvious question being: how do the U.N.'s dashiki-clad potentates define "legitimate" gun ownership, as opposed to the "illicit" kind?

The U.N.'s own Web site defines "small arms" as "weapons designed for personal use. ... Examples of small arms include revolvers and self-loading pistols, rifles, sub-machine guns, assault rifles and light machine-guns."

In August 1999, a U.N. report recommended that "all small arms and light weapons which are not under legal civilian possession and which are not required for the purposes of national defense and internal security should be collected and destroyed by States as expeditiously as possible."

In March 2001, a U.N. "Committee of Governmental Experts" recommended that all nations install centralized "gun control" with detailed record-keeping and prohibitions against selling "small arms" to anyone except other governments.

Swiss Foreign Minister Joseph Deiss wrote a July 4 commentary for the *International Herald Tribune* titled, "A Plague of Small Arms Demands Action at Last."

(The irony of this guy being from Switzerland, which has stood safe from invasion for 600 years precisely because every law-abiding homeowner is required to keep a loaded machine gun in the closet, I will leave for another day.)

"BERN — More than 550 million small weapons circulate around the world and cause 500,000 deaths a year," Herr Deiss begins.

"Proliferation and misuse of small weapons imperils security and development policy as well as humanitarian efforts," the Swiss whiner continued. "They have been the weapons of choice in 46 of the 49 major conflicts since 1990."

Forty-nine wars in the 1990s? Is Herr Deiss counting the low-intensity use of small arms by folks like the Kurds, trying to defend themselves against Iraqi tanks? Is he saying they should have been disarmed — left with nothing but women and babies to throw in front of Saddam's armor?

The amazing thing about this statistic, "46 out of 49," of course, is the idea that in 8 percent of those "major conflicts" people apparently managed to find something to fight with other than small arms. This is like asserting, "Ninety-two percent of all fatal car crashes are fueled by gasoline." Before we get around to debating whether that means we should ban gasoline, I want to know how the other 8 guys managed to get their cars moving fast enough to run them into anything.

"Small arms mainly imperil civilians," Herr Deiss droned on, ignoring the fact that more than 170 million unarmed men, women, and children were actually murdered by their own governments in the course of the 20th century (Richard Poe, "The Seven Myths of Gun Control"). Which brings us to what this is really all about.

"The proliferation of small arms has contributed to a culture of violence and crime," complains U.N. Deputy Secretary-General Louise Frechette. By eroding government authority and undermining the rule of law, "the result all too often is a vicious circle in which insecurity leads to a higher demand for weapons, which itself breeds still greater insecurity," Ms. Frechette simpers.

Not to mention a reluctance to pay taxes. But notice the reversal of causality. Folks don't need self-defense weapons because the government police won't or can't protect them. No, their possession of small arms *causes* insecurity.

Anyway, poor Mr. Dhanapala hadn't seen anything yet, as U.S. Undersecretary of State for Arms Control John Bolton rose to address the opening session of his precious conference July 9, evoking actual gasps from the assembled bed-wetters

as he announced, "The United States believes that the responsible use of firearms is a legitimate aspect of national life."
Accompanied by U.S. Rep. Bob Barr, R-Ga., who sits on the board of the NRA, Bolton specifically said the U.S. won't have anything to do with a proposed prohibition on private ownership of arms designed for military purposes.

He wouldn't even buy into the notion that no one should sell arms to any group of persons not representing an established government, refusing to dismiss all such freedom fighters as "irregular forces, criminals and terrorists," in one of Ms. Frechette's favorites phrases.

(Is Ms. Frechette, by any chance, French? Has she never heard of the "French Resistance"? Think they should have been disarmed as "terrorists"? How about those guys Washington and Lafayette?)

"Perhaps most important, this proposal would preclude assistance to an oppressed non-state group defending itself from a genocidal government," Mr. Bolton pointed out.

The outpouring of outrage at Mr. Bolton's common-sense lowering of the boom on these posturing pantywaists was nearly instantaneous. Take, for example, the editorial writers of *The Washington Post*, whose fantasies apparently center on figuring out how to disarm young women in dark parking lots:

"The United Nations yesterday convened a conference that is meant to address a major global problem — the trafficking in small arms," the *Post* responded on Tuesday, July 10:

"The Bush administration's ... envoy to the conference, State Department Undersecretary John R. Bolton, delivered an opening address that appeared designed to cater to the most extreme domestic opponents of gun control, for whom the U.N. conference has conjured up the usual paranoid fantasies about international shock troops in black helicopters confiscating handguns and hunting rifles. ... The draft U.N. plan, which would be non-binding, doesn't come close to infringing the Second Amendment. ..."

Paranoid fantasies? Aren't small-arms confiscations from civilian militiamen precisely what U.S. — not merely U.N. but *U.S.* — troops are now learning about and practicing in the Balkans?

Also note the careful implication that the Second Amendment protects only registered "hunting rifles." Does the Second Amendment say, "The right of the people to keep one old-fashioned hunting rifle per person shall not be infringed, but it's OK to tax, register, ban, and otherwise infringe their right to individually own machine guns, assault rifles, hand grenades, and shoulder-launched heat-seeking missiles?"

Not in my copy.

In fact, when the federalists were busy promising our forebears, back in 1787, that their new central government would never dare try to take away our liberties, because we'd always outgun them, didn't Tench Coxe of Pennsylvania, friend of Madison and prominent federalist, write in the *Pennsylvania Gazette* of Feb. 20, 1788, "Who are the militia? Are they not ourselves? ... The militia of these free commonwealths, entitled and accustomed to their arms, when compared to any possible enemy" (here Coxe clearly referred to any hypothetical force of federal police who might eventually be fielded by outfits like the BATF or the FBI Hostage Elimination Team) "must be tremendous and irresistible. ... Congress have no power to disarm the militia. Their swords, and every other terrible instrument of the soldier, are the birth-right of an American. ... The unlimited power of the sword is not in the hands of either the federal or the state governments, but, where I trust in God it will ever remain, in the hands of the people."

"The power of the sword ... and every other terrible instrument of the soldier." Nothing about single-shot hunting rifles.

In fact, the right to keep and bear arms — in the meaningful way Madison and Coxe guaranteed us — is already perilously near elimination. Page through the ads in *Shotgun News*. Look at what it costs to import and sell a "parts kit" for a 1930s or 1940s machine gun. A couple of hundred bucks. But how much will you pay to buy a working, fully automatic, "Class 3" Browning Automatic Rifle, built in the United States and given away to one of our lesser allies as war surplus in the late 1940s?

About $10,000.

Why the price difference? Our wise federal government — staffed entirely by folks who swore on pain of hellfire and damnation to "protect and defend" the Constitution and its Bill of Rights — has effectively banned the new manufacture or re-import of fully automatic BAR receivers for civilian use. The rest they could safely leave up to "supply and demand."

If U.N. Undersecretary-General for Disarmament Jayantha Dhanapala is all in favor of the "legal trade, manufacture or ownership of weapons," why doesn't he get on Mr. Bolton's case, asking him why I can't import and keep and bear the fully-automatic BAR my uncles carried in the Second World War, without taxation, registration, or any other restriction?

For mind you, neither Mr. Bolton nor the Bush administration appears to have yet seen the light on the road to Damascus. The *Atlanta Journal-Constitution* notes, "Bolton defended the U.S. record of arms sales, citing its strong export regulations and weapons destruction programs."

What? Does every able-bodied American now own a full-auto combat rifle and a self-loading backup? If not, what is a federal government sworn to uphold the Second Amendment doing running any kind of "weapons destruction program"? The government clearly has both a fiduciary and a constitutional duty to hand out (or sell at cost) every surplus M-14, BAR, Thompson gun, water-cooled Browning, Ma Deuce, and recoilless 57mm rifle still in the inventory, to any law-abiding American citizen who wants one ... after checking them for headspace and proper function, of course.

In fact, to set an example and show I'm willing to do my part, I'm going to invite anyone who agrees with Little Miss

Frechette about how nasty and dangerous these weapons are to go ahead and turn them in ... to me.

That's right. I'm not offering to pay anything for them, mind you. But anyone out there who has a firearm that they're afraid is going to start engaging in random violence, thus "contributing to a culture of violence and crime," meantime "eroding government authority and undermining the rule of law," just package it up real good (please make sure it's not loaded) and ship it to: Vin Suprynowicz, c/o Spurlock's Gun Shop, 39 E. Basic Road, Henderson, Nev. 89015, U.S.A. We'll make sure they get handed out to law-abiding civilians who aren't afraid to keep and honor the Second Amendment in their homes, every day.

🌿 🌿 🌿

Meantime, Reuters reported in late June 2001: "One of America's leading gun control groups said Thursday it would merge with the Million Mom March. ... The Brady Campaign (formerly Handgun Control Inc.) and the Million Mom March said the two organizations would officially merge Oct. 1. ..."

Needless to say, the rape enablers tried to put a brave face on the collapse of MMM, Sarah Brady herself purring, "This alliance sends a clear message that the gun control movement is uniting and targeted."

More like: completely out of steam. The MMM's main office closed earlier in 2001 for lack of interest. With the polite and complicit silence of the mainstream press (imagine how they'd be shrieking if a major gun-rights group had to fold its tents) the merger merely spares MMM the embarrassment of hanging up the "out of business" sign.

In fact, the hysterical bleatings of folks like Ms. Frechette are daily proven more and more absurd, as the re-arming of civilian America drives down crime rates everywhere — even as crime rates skyrocket in such previously peaceful bailiwicks as Australia and England following the recent civilian gun bans and confiscations there.

It's perfectly possible the collapse of the U.N. Conference on Illicit Trade in Small Arms and Light Weapons is a harbinger of things to come. The other side has a losing hand ... and someone has finally called their bluff.

Pining for the Peaceful Paradise of an Omnipotent State
🌾

On April 20, 1999, the evening after armed culprits invaded a Colorado high school with pipe bombs and firearms in what police described as an "apparent suicide mission," an urban animal-rights activist, apparently having seen my defenses of the Second Amendment, sent me the following e-mail:

"I bet you must be very proud of those two militant freaks that murdered their fellow students and then took their own worthless lives. Hopefully you will be the next random victim of some loose cannon with an assault weapon.

"May God have mercy on your misguided soul."

I replied:

Greetings, whoever you are —

In Israel, teachers and parents who serve as school aides go armed at all times on school grounds, with semi-automatic weapons. Since this policy was put into effect, terrorist attacks in Israeli schools have dropped to zero. The only recent exception was the tragic case of a group of schoolchildren who were murdered by an Arab gunman as they visited the "Zone of Peace" on the Jordanian border. The Jordanians specifically requested that the Israeli teachers and chaperones leave their weapons behind ... which they did.

American schools are, on the other hand, "gun-free zones"

by order of our chief cowards and socialist bed-wetters, Bill and Hillary Clinton, Charles Schumer and Diane Feinstein. Therefore, our schools make ideal targets for misguided gunmen, who already violate dozens of laws when they undertake such actions — demonstrating that no number of victim disarmament laws will ever stop such creatures. (Washington, D.C. should be a peaceful paradise if "gun control" laws work. But instead that city has one of our highest murder rates — isn't that curious?)

I, too, hope the next time some nut takes it into his head to shoot an innocent child, he encounters me first. One of two things will then happen: 1) I will die, instead of an innocent child. Good trade; or 2) Being well-armed and trained in the use of the weapons that our Founding Fathers considered it our right *and* duty to own and carry (in order to protect their legacy of freedom against inevitable creeping tyranny), I will down the outlaw. An even better trade.

If someone attacks a helpless child while you're nearby, will you have the weapon and the training to stop him? (You'll dial 911, won't you? Average waiting time in Los Angeles today after dialing 911 is 20 minutes.) If the attack occurs in a school, will the nearby adults be helpless to save that child's life, due to victim disarmament laws you've supported?

In either case, are you sure God will have mercy on your soul, after you have knowingly betrayed our heritage of freedom, condemning the innocent to die without defense?

Unlike you, I do not hope you die because of your misguided faith in an armed omnipotent state — the same foolhardy faith that led many well-meaning Jews, Slavs, and Gypsies to stand by and watch their children gassed to death in Europe in the 1940s because they had foolishly "obeyed the law" and turned in their weapons, leaving only the army and the police with arms, while decent men had no recourse but to pray "that the Americans come with their Garand rifles in time to save us."

Quite to the contrary, as a member of the unorganized

militia (as are all able-bodied adult Americans), I would still use my weapons to defend your rights, your property, and the safety of your family, even after you have condemned me, vilified me, and voted to strip me of my God-given right to self-defense.

This does not make me a great man. It merely makes me a man.

What your opposite stance makes you, I'm not sure. Do I take it you oppose the existence or use of all firearms? Do you then believe our fathers, uncles, and grandfathers were wrong to hit those beaches in Normandy and Iwo Jima (yes, the names of some of my relatives are on the granite memorials), carrying these bullet-spewing machines that you hate? You would have preferred to leave things as they were in 1943, with millions condemned to fascist slavery?

And what about today in Littleton, Colorado? Would you have condemned the police to enter that building without firearms? Or do you actually believe that firearms are fine, so long as they're only in the possession of government agents ... as was the case under Stalin in 1931, under Hitler in 1942, under Mao in 1955, under Pol Pot in 1971? My, you must be very proud of *those* "militant freaks" who put *your* doctrines into effect, murdering 10 million in the Ukraine, 8 million in Germany and the Nazi empire, more millions in China, and (the piker!) a mere few hundred thousand in Cambodia.

Continue on your present course. You seem to be in the majority. So, with luck, you may yet survive — at least briefly — to live under just such a regime, yourself.

❦ ❦ ❦

On July 11, 1999, I filed a column in response to events that had occurred — well, to be more literal, that had not occurred — the week before in California. I reprint it here, along with the exchange it drew from a typically enlightened reader:

No Serial Killings This Week in Santa Clara

Racist nut Benjamin Nathaniel Smith killed two and wounded nine in a series of drive-by shootings of blacks, Asian-Americans, and Orthodox Jews in Illinois and Indiana before dying in a struggle with police on the Fourth of July.

Smith had tried to buy firearms from a federally licensed gun shop in Illinois on June 23, the AP reports, but was turned down when he failed the "background check."

Did he lie when filling out the federal form? Of course — all such forms ask whether the applicant is under a court restraining order. Is lying on that form a federal felony? It is. Did anyone try to detain, locate, arrest, or prosecute this would-be killer in the ensuing 11 days? Of course not.

So — confirming the fact that such "gun control" laws never work (confirming, in fact, that the folks who pass them have no intention of *trying* to make them work, counting on their predictable failure to justify further steps to disarm law-abiding folk by making gun ownership even *more* expensive, inconvenient, and embarrassing), Smith remained free to buy pistols in .22 and .380 caliber — not "assault weapons," as some would have it — illegally, from an unlicensed dealer already under investigation by the BATF.

Now, Benjamin Nathaniel Smith's insane crime spree brings predictable calls for more "gun control."

What do they propose to do: make it illegal to buy guns illegally?

Meantime, no one mentions that again, as in Colin Ferguson's terrible shooting spree on the Long Island Railroad a few years back (in a jurisdiction where none of the victims were allowed to carry arms), and as in the worst American mass shooting in recent memory, in which 23 occupants of the Luby's Cafeteria in Killeen, Texas were shot down like dogs because state law required them to leave their firearms out in their cars ... none of Benjamin Nathaniel Smith's victims were armed.

These "opportunity killers" are cowards at heart. Would someone like Benjamin Nathaniel Smith even have *attempted* such a thing if it was known that as many as 30 percent of blacks, Asian-Americans, and Orthodox Jews in the Midwest were now carrying concealed weapons and had received training in how to use them? I strongly doubt it.

Yet instead of urging more folks to buy and carry guns and learn how to use them, the "reformers" can only think of ways to create more disarmed victims!

"Oh, being armed is no solution," the mincing minions of genocide will surely simper. "The bad guy will only take your gun away and use it on you."

OK. Let's take a look at what really happened last week when the intended victim of such a would-be shooter turned out to be armed.

Reuters reported on July 6 from Santa Clara, California:

"A shoot-out at a California shooting range ended a bizarre hostage drama during which three gun store employees found themselves staring down the barrel of one of their own rented rifles, police said Tuesday.

"Sergeant Anton Morec of the Santa Clara Police Department said the aspiring gunman, 21-year-old Richard Gable Stevens ... 'intended to go out in a blaze of glory,' noting Stevens had accumulated more than 100 rounds of ammunition for his rented 9mm semi-automatic weapon.

"'It certainly looks like he intended to take a lot more people out.'

"Morec said Stevens arrived at the National Shooting Club Monday evening and rented the rifle for target practice. ... After several minutes on the range, however, Stevens returned to the club's gun store and shot at the ceiling. He then herded three store employees out the door into an alley, saying he intended to kill them.

"Unknown to Stevens, one store employee was carrying a .45 caliber handgun concealed beneath his shirt. When Stevens looked away, the employee fired, hitting Stevens several times in the chest and bringing him to the ground."

After police arrived, Stevens was taken to a hospital, where he was listed in critical condition. Finding a note from Stevens to his parents, predicting they would be bankrupted by lawsuits from the relatives of his intended "victims," police concluded, "The quick action by the gun club employee may have headed off a massacre," Reuters reports.

Yet which case made the front pages and the evening news — the tragedy with the unarmed victims, or the story that proves, not in theory but in real life, the best way to *stop* such crimes before they start?

Speaking of the 1991 Luby's cafeteria massacre, Dr. Suzanna Gratia Hupp was there. She had left her firearm in her car, as required by law. She therefore had to watch both her father and mother — along with 21 others — butchered before her eyes. The charming Dr. Hupp won election to the Texas legislature in 1996 on a "right to self-defense" platform. ...

🌿 🌿 🌿

In response to my July 11, 1999, column (reprinted above), pointing out there were no serial killings in Santa Clara, California, on the Fourth of July, one B.R. wrote in, asserting:

"So, if'n we arm everyone, we can have real Viet Cong-type snipers and firefights every time we get a hankerin. ..."

I replied:

Greetings —

In Switzerland, every head of household — being a member of the militia — is expected to keep a machine gun in his home. No one pretends this right and duty has anything to do with fending off bears or Wild Indians ... or even with "legitimate sporting use" (a phrase coined by Joseph Goebbels). Yet firefights are notably rare in that extremely peaceful modern industrial nation.

Before 1912, when there was no "gun control" in this nation and machine guns could be purchased through the mail, foreign visitors found America one of the most peaceful and polite nations on Earth — a condition that six decades of "gun control" and the accompanying Cult of the Omnipotent State are now, finally, beginning to destroy.

In Germany in the 1920s, most citizens — notably including the Jews — tried to prove they were "law-abiding" by turning in their firearms as required by law. Many of them found cause to regret that decision in the years after 1939. In desperation and at incalculable expense, the Jews of the Warsaw ghetto did finally fight a two-month rebellion against their *armed* oppressors.

(Why is it those who say they "want to get rid of all the guns" can only laugh at our silliness when we propose that they start by disarming their own government police? Can it be they don't really mean *everyone* would give up their guns, at all — that they instead mean to duplicate *here* the situation that prevailed in Nazi-occupied Europe from 1939 to 1944?)

Starting on April 19, 1943 (a date that Janet Reno and Bill Clinton decided to commemorate quite remarkably in 1993), those residents of the Warsaw ghetto launched a hopeless rebellion with only 14 rifles and fewer than 50 pistols. (You can still read all about it in Leon Uris' great novel, *Mila 18*.) That rebellion nonetheless proved to the world that — pushed to the limit — Jews *could* fight to defend their children and their culture from utter extinction, and fight with nearly superhuman zeal. It was, in great measure, that demonstration that made *thinkable* the birth of the sovereign modern nation of Israel, in 1948.

(Israel is another nation, by the way — like peaceful Switzerland — where no one has to worry any longer about children being shot up by terrorists or madmen in the schools. And why not? Because the Israelis finally wised up and issued their teachers semi-automatic pistols, at which point terrorism in Israeli schools stopped *overnight*. Oh, sorry, was I not supposed to bother you with any inconvenient *facts*?)

Are you saying you believe the Jews of the Warsaw ghetto had no right to revolt against those who had imposed "gun control" upon them — and who were starving their children, raping their women, shipping off hundreds of thousands to the extermination camps, and otherwise casually shooting them down in the streets like dogs? That if you had it in your power, you would see to it that they started their revolt with *fewer* than 14 rifles and a few dozen pistols?

If I had it in my power to go back to that time and place and carry along one thing, *I* would take them a .30-caliber Browning machine gun, and as many ammo belts as I could carry.

That being impossible, I can only strive to prevent it all from happening again ... here.

For what are you willing to dedicate your life? To see this becomes a nation of disarmed slaves, subject to the whim of an armed para-military police force? If so, then I am glad to discover I have finally found the person for whom I was long ago entrusted with a message. It was you, it turns out, whom Samuel Adams was addressing when he said, at the Philadelphia State House on August 1, 1776:

"If ye love wealth better than liberty, the tranquility of servitude better than the animating contest of freedom, go home from us in peace. We ask not your counsels or arms. Crouch down and lick the hands which feed you. May your chains set lightly upon you, and may posterity forget that ye were our countrymen."

You — the sniveling, smug, fascist toadie.

The Two Most Threadbare "Gun-Control" Lies
🔥

I don't know if they're the two *biggest* lies told by the victim disarmament gang, but they're easily the most threadbare, climbing out of their graves over and over to spread their stench like rotting vampires that have been killed, but never properly staked.

The first?

The year 2000 election was punctuated by Democratic presidential candidate Al Gore and others of his ilk insisting the reason we need "mandatory child safety trigger locks" is to substantially stop the "12 children killed by firearms every day in America."

Let's give a tip of the hat to historian Clayton E. Cramer (writing in the July 1, 2001, edition of *Shotgun News*) for going directly to the Web site of the Centers for Disease Control (www.cdc.gov/nchs/datawh/statab/unpubd/mortabs/gmwki.htm — search under ICD 922.0) and looking up the actual number of American children under the age of 15 who are killed in handgun accidents each year.

For 1997, that number was 21 — down from a high of 55 in 1990.

No, that's not a typo. Twenty-one children dead in handgun accidents in the whole of America in the entire year 1997.

Now, those are sad incidents. But compare them to the number of Jewish and Gypsy children who died in Europe — not as collateral casualties of war, but at the hands of "legitimate" governments — in each of the years 1939 through 1945, because their parents allowed themselves to be *disarmed* under "gun control" laws that never disarm government police or other criminals.

Government-mandated airbags seriously injure or kill more children than die in handgun accidents. Lightning and amusement-park accidents and drowning in mop buckets *each* beat out handguns in causing accidental deaths of children under 15. So why the national hysteria — and more importantly, where do Mr. Gore and the "gun control" gang come up with that "12-a-day" statistic?

They get to "12 a day" by adding in all deaths of "children" up through the age of 19 that are firearm related, including suicides, 18- and 19-year-old drug gangsters shooting each other in disputes over drug distribution turf, and even 19-year-old "children" righteously shot dead by cops or law-abiding citizens while in the act of committing rapes, murders, and armed robberies.

The question I would like to have heard someone stand up and ask candidate Gore (assuming we still had a system in which real citizens could ask *unscreened* questions of our candidates, of course) is: "Mr. Vice President, I was the victim of a sexual assault, but I managed to get to my nightstand and get my dad's old Smith and shoot my assailant after he'd blackened both my eyes and broken my jaw. You say mandatory trigger locks would stop 12 child gunshot deaths every day — I assume you're leading up to a law that would require those locks to be in place all the time.

"But the CDC says that in order to get to that number, you're including in the so-called 'children' in your statistic 18- and 19-year-olds righteously shot while committing rapes and other serious crimes. Is the death of my 19-year-old assailant one of the 'child gunshot deaths' you want to prevent? Is it your plan to require my gun to be locked up in such a way that I won't be able to use it to defend myself the next time a 19-year-old thug decides to break into my house and try to rape me? Are you saying it's 'safer' for me to be beaten and raped than for me to have an unlocked gun to defend myself, since that might cause the death of my 'child' assailant?"

🌿 🌿 🌿

The second most threadbare and putrescent "gun control" lie is that those of us who want to maintain the great American tradition of a populace armed and thus free consistently misquote and misunderstand the Second Amendment. (For the record, by the way, the Bill of Rights only acknowledges pre-existing human rights — these rights do not disappear no matter how cleverly the lawyers parse the plain English of the Constitution — nor would they even if the populace were foolish enough to attempt a repeal.)

Anyway, as this argument goes, we gun nuts insist on quoting only the second clause of the amendment: "The right of the people to keep and bear arms shall not be infringed," while purposely dropping and ignoring the introductory clause, "A well-regulated militia being necessary to the security of a free state ..."

What this introductory clause proves is that the Founding Fathers didn't want each and every law-abiding American to continue owning firearms of military usefulness, the victim disarmament gang patronizingly explains. Instead, it proves that Americans were meant to retain a right to carry firearms only when they're actively on duty in the regular army or the National Guard.

Don't laugh — this bizarre reading was actually offered up with a straight face by U.S. Attorney William B. Mateja in oral arguments before the 5th U.S. Circuit Court of Appeals in the case of U.S. vs. physician Timothy Joe Emerson, a Texan charged with illegally possessing a firearm because his wife had filed a routine restraining order against him during his divorce proceedings. But we'll get to that in a minute.

Let's start with the words of an actual reader, writing in to ask: "Why do you always sidestep the question of what the Founding Fathers meant by 'well-regulated' militias? Also, if you permit private citizens to possess heat-seeking anti-aircraft missiles as part of their Second Amendment rights, as you suggest, why not nuclear bombs?"

In fact, the Founding Fathers got the phrase "well-regulated militia" from Andrew Fletcher's 1698 *A Discourse of Government with Relation to Militias*. The original essay is available at Web site www.2ndlawlib.org/history/foreign/fletdisc.html.

Let's examine a bit of what Mr. Fletcher was actually talking about:

"A good militia is of such importance to a nation, that it is the chief part of the constitution of any free government," he writes. "For ... a good militia will always preserve the public liberty. But in the best constitution that ever was ... if the militia be not upon a right foot, the liberty of that people must perish. The militia of ancient Rome, the best that ever was in any government, made her mistress of the world: but standing armies enslaved that great people, and their excellent militia and freedom perished together. ... The Swisses at this day are the freest, happiest, and the people of all Europe who can best defend themselves, because they have the best militia. ...

"And I cannot see why arms should be denied to any man who is not a slave, since they are the only true badges of liberty; and ought never, but in times of utmost necessity, to be put into the hands of mercenaries or slaves. ...

"Is it not a shame that any man who possesses an estate, and is at the same time healthful and young, should not fit himself by all means for the defence of that, and his country, rather than to pay taxes to maintain a mercenary, who though he may defend him during a war, will be sure to insult and enslave him in time of peace? ..."

Isn't that curious? Sounds almost as though old Andrew was envisioning individual private citizens keeping their own weapons and *constituting* the militia, rather than paying professional uniformed mercenaries under orders from the seat of government — call them "Guardsmen" or whatever — to do the job for them. And remember, this is the guy from whom the Founders *got* that phrase "well-regulated militia," the guy they'd all read and were referring to.

Nahhh ... that can't be right.

Let's try something else, in this struggle to understand "well-regulated." Take a double rifle to a contemporary British gunsmith (if there are any left — all you British widows reading this, don't turn in those cast-off Webleys and Enfields and Holland & Hollands to the police: ship them to me care of Spurlock's Gun Shop, 39 E. Basic Road, Henderson, Nev. 89015) and ask him to "regulate" it. He will ask not about government restrictions, but rather for what charge of powder and weight of ball you want those two barrels "regulated."

The barrels are said to be "regulated" — adjusted for proper and predictable function — if they will both hit the same target at a predetermined range with the same loading.

As it turns out, far from "ducking the question," I defined "a well-regulated militia" back in '98, at the bottom of page 424 of my first book, *Send in the Waco Killers*: "'Well-regulated' means 'well-trained' ... in firing volleys, reloading quickly, and blowing things up. What do you think George Washington and George Mason were up to when they organized meetings of the Fairfax County Militia in the mid-1770s — trading ginger cookie recipes?"

For the record, Congress enacted the law that gave birth to the American "National Guard" as we know it in the year 1917, partially in horror at the demonstrated effectiveness of citizen militias in giving hives to the central authorities in Mexico in the recent revolution there — doing so not at all coincidentally during that same decade of hideous "progressivism" that brought us the personal income tax, the Federal Reserve Board, alcohol Prohibition, and the beginnings of our delightful and long-running Drug War via the Harrison Narcotics Act.

That the Founding Fathers gathered together in 1789, peered into their crystal ball, and wrote a Second Amendment that meant the word "militia" to be read in light of a statist ordinance that wouldn't even be written until the First World

War would require a bit of a leap of faith, even if we didn't have Richard Henry Lee of Virginia, who drafted the Second Amendment along with the rest of the Bill of Rights, on the record advising us (in 1788): "A militia, when properly formed, are in fact the people themselves. ... All regulations tending to render this militia useless and defenseless, by establishing select corps of militia or distinct bodies of military men not having permanent interests and attachments in the community [are] to be avoided. ... To preserve liberty, it is essential that the whole body of the people always possess arms, and be taught alike, especially when young, how to use them."

I, and others deluded into believing we were engaged in a rational discussion where facts and evidence might count for something, have offered up reams of documented statements from the Founding Fathers that, "No free man is to be debarred the use of arms" (Thomas Jefferson's proposed draft for the Virginia Constitution) and, "The main thing is that every man be armed — everyone who is able must have a gun" (Patrick Henry, 1788), etc.

But the other side just keeps croaking out its memorized little chant about "ignoring the first clause."

OK, guys. In a few minutes we'll see how the judges of the Fifth Circuit dealt with this argument on Oct. 16, 2001 (be forewarned — you may want to spread a drop cloth and put on a lobster bib or perhaps one of those environmental suits that covers you completely, because the blood really splatters from this one — holy cow, were they merciless).

But let's not get ahead of ourselves. It was still before the Fifth Circuit rendered its historic *Emerson* decision when I received from Yale University Press back in the summer of 2000 a copy of the weighty and definitive new 400-page tome of history and analysis, *The Bill of Rights: Creation and Reconstruction*, by that leading constitutional scholar, current Southmayd Professor of Law at Yale University, Akhil Reed Amar.

For those who have been in a cave for some little time, let me point out that the law school at Yale is not what we would call a nest of right-wing militia activism. In fact, I don't think it would be unfair to characterize professor Amar's politics as leaning somewhat to the left.

Yet how did Prof. Amar deal with the "you-forgot-the-first-clause-nyah-nyah-nyah" argument?

Writing more than a year before the Fifth Circuit's *Emerson* decision (in fact, the appeals court cited Prof. Amar in that historic ruling), beginning on page 51, Prof. Amar explains: "Several modern scholars have read the [Second] amendment as protecting only arms bearing in organized 'state militias,' like SWAT teams and National Guard units. ...

"This reading doesn't quite work. The states'-rights reading puts great weight on the word *militia*, but the word appears only in the amendment's subordinate clause. The ultimate right to keep and bear arms belongs to "the people," not the states. As the language of the Tenth Amendment shows, these two are of course not identical: when the Constitution means 'states,' it says so.

"Thus, as noted above, 'the people' at the core of the Second Amendment are the same people at the heart of the Preamble and the First Amendment. Elbridge Gerry put the point nicely in the First Congress, in language that closely tracked the populist concern about governmental self-dealing at the root of earlier amendments: 'This declaration of rights, I take it, is intended to secure *the people* against the mal-administration of the *Government*.'

"What's more, the 'militia,' as used in the amendment and in clause 16, had a very different meaning two hundred years ago than in ordinary conversation today. Nowadays, it is quite common to speak loosely of the National Guard as the 'state militia,' but two hundred years ago, any band of paid, semiprofessional, part-time volunteers, like today's Guard, would have been called "a *select* corps" or "*select* militia" —

and viewed in many quarters as little better than a standing army.

"In 1789, when used without any qualifying adjective, 'the militia' referred to all citizens capable of bearing arms. The seeming tension between the dependent and the main clauses of the Second Amendment thus evaporates on closer inspection — the 'militia' is identical to 'the people' in the core sense described above. Indeed, the version of the amendment that initially passed the House, only to be stylistically shortened in the Senate, explicitly defined the militia as 'composed of the body of the People.' This is clearly the sense in which *the militia* is used in clause 16 and throughout *The Federalist*, in keeping with standard usage confirmed by contemporaneous dictionaries, legal and otherwise. As Tench Coxe wrote in a 1788 Pennsylvania essay, 'Who are the militia? Are they not ourselves?'"

Thus endeth today's reading from professor Amar, one of the legal scholars whose writings were consulted by the U.S. Fifth Circuit Court of Appeals when confronted with the case of Dr. Timothy Emerson of Texas (we'll return to *The Bill of Rights: Creation and Reconstruction*, a little later).

Ready? Got on your heavy-weather gear? Because this does a job on the gun-grabbers that makes the rendering of a sperm whale for its oil on the high seas look downright dainty.

Federal Court Confirms
Individual Right to Bear Arms
◉

On Aug. 28, 1998, Sacha Emerson, wife of Timothy Joe Emerson, filed a petition for divorce in the District Court of Tom Green County, Texas. The petition also sought standard divorce-court boilerplate injunctions against the good doctor writing or telephoning the estranged wife, harming or threatening to harm her or their daughter, etc.

On September 4, 1998, a hearing was held to decide whether this injunction would be granted. Sacha Emerson was represented by counsel; Dr. Emerson represented himself. "There is no evidence that Emerson was unable (financially or otherwise) to retain counsel for the hearing or that he desired representation by counsel on that occasion. He announced ready at the beginning of the ... hearing," the Fifth U.S. Court of Appeals announced as a finding of fact.

"You are here today asking the Court for temporary orders regarding yourself and your daughter; is that correct?" Mrs. Emerson's attorney asked her.

"Yes," she replied.

"He has previous to today threatened to kill you; is that correct?"

"He hasn't threatened to kill me. He's threatened to kill a friend of mine," Mrs. Emerson asserted, failing to make clear whether the "friend" has been sending her flowers.

"Emerson declined an opportunity to cross-examine Sacha and presented no evidence tending to refute any of her above quoted testimony or to explain his conduct in that respect," the appeals court found. So, without "any express finding that Emerson posed a future danger to Sacha or to his daughter Logan," the temporary order was granted on Sept. 14, 1998.

On Dec. 8, 1998, a grand jury for the Northern District of Texas, San Angelo division, returned an indictment against Dr. Emerson alleging that on Nov. 16, 1998, the doctor possessed "a Beretta pistol, while subject to the above mentioned Sept. 14, 1998 order, in violation of 18 U.S.C. 922(g)(8)," the bizarre federal law known at the time of its passage as the "Violence Against Women Act," which attempts to bar possession of firearms while one is subject to such protective orders.

Since Dr. Emerson had owned the pistol prior to the divorce filing, he expressed himself "greatly surprised" to learn he may have violated any law, and sought to have the charge dismissed, arguing 18 U.S.C. 922(g)(8) infringed his Second Amendment "right to keep and bear arms," as well as his due process rights under the Fifth Amendment — his possession of the pistol had been turned into a "crime" retroactively, and he hadn't been convicted of a felony, given a chance to understand he was being disarmed, or provided a chance to argue against such an outcome.

In April 2001, U.S. District Court Judge Sam Cummings in Lubbock properly found that the law denying guns to those under a restraining order was an unconstitutional infringement of the "individual right to bear arms." The federal law, Judge Cummings wrote, "is unconstitutional because it allows a state court divorce proceeding, without particularized findings of the threat of future violence, to automatically deprive a citizen of his Second Amendment rights."

Judge Cummings granted Dr. Emerson's motion to dismiss. The government appealed.

While the case was wending its way through the federal courts, a Texas state court in October 2000 found Dr. Emerson not guilty of all allegations of violence (which means Sarah Brady and her victim-disarmament fund-raising group stooped to outright lies and slander when they responded to the Fifth Circuit's 2001 ruling in the case by asserting the good doctor "was the subject of a domestic violence restraining order and had threatened his wife with a handgun," stating as fact not merely a libel that was *unproven*, but one that had been specifically *disproven* in a Texas state court a full year before. Why am I not shocked?)

Meantime, the federal case ended up before a three-judge panel of the Fifth U.S. Court of Appeals in New Orleans.

And those three judges could barely conceal their incredulousness when the U.S. attorney told them yes, even the shotguns at home in the judges' closets could be outlawed with a flick of the wrist, since they weren't using them in the course of their National Guard duties.

On Oct, 16, 2001, that court remanded the Emerson case back to the lower court for trial, finding that Dr. Emerson's right to keep and bear arms is not absolute — the government, after all, can bar the possession of firearms by infants, idiots, and convicted felons. And so, the court contends, a judge can also disable a citizen — who has never been convicted of any crime — from bearing arms based on the uncorroborated say-so of an estranged spouse that he has threatened to harm her "friend."

Is the fact that a routine restraining order has been granted against an otherwise law-abiding and upstanding citizen during divorce proceedings equivalent, when it comes time to deprive him of his God-given and constitutionally guaranteed rights, to a finding that he is an infant, an imbecile, or a murderer serving out his final days on death row?

Of course not. This final determination by the federal appeals court is bogus, wrongheaded, and probably cynically tailored to achieve a desired political result — the judges simply didn't want to throw out all firearm regulation in the states under their jurisdiction, as they should have.

However, none of this is what will generate the most discussion about the appellate court's Oct. 16 ruling in the *Emerson* case. For no matter how they finally weaseled out of what would be the only honest, just, and equitable outcome — giving Dr. Emerson back his gun — the Fifth Circuit in the process of deciding the constitutional claims in this case did a fine and important thing: They confirmed what all careful and objective scholars (including Laurence Tribe of Harvard and Akhil Reed Amar of Yale) have long known — that the U.S. Supreme Court actually held in its 1939 *Miller* decision that Americans have an individual constitutional right to keep and bear arms of military usefulness.

The U.S. Supreme Court ruled in *Miller* (1939): "The signification attributed to the term Militia appears from the debates in the Convention, the history and legislation of Colonies and States, and the writings of approved commentators. These show plainly enough that the Militia comprised all males physically capable of acting in concert for the common defense. ... Ordinarily when called for service these men were expected to appear bearing arms supplied by themselves and of the kind in common use at the time."

"These passages from *Miller* suggest that the militia, the assurance of whose continuation and the rendering possible of whose effectiveness *Miller* says were purposes of the Second Amendment, referred to the generality of the civilian male inhabitants throughout their lives from teenage years until old age and to their personally keeping their own arms," wrote the Fifth Circuit in its decision in *U.S. vs. Emerson*, docket No. 99-10331, October 16, 2001, "and not merely to individuals during the time (if any) they might be actively engaged in actual military service or only to those who were members of special or select units.

"We conclude that *Miller* does not support the government's collective rights or sophisticated collective rights approach to the Second Amendment. Indeed, to the extent that *Miller* sheds light on the matter it cuts against the government's position. ...

"We have found no historical evidence that the Second Amendment was intended to convey militia power to the states ... or applies only to members of a select militia while on active duty," the Fifth Circuit Court continued. "All of the evidence indicates that the Second Amendment, like other parts of the Bill of Rights, applies to and protects individual Americans.

"We find that the history of the Second Amendment reinforces the plain meaning of its text, namely that it protects individual Americans in their right to keep and bear arms whether or not they are a member of a select militia or performing active military service or training," the Fifth Circuit continued.

"We reject the collective rights and sophisticated collective rights models for interpreting the Second Amendment. We hold, consistent with *Miller*, that it protects the right of individuals, including those not then actually a member of any militia or engaged in active military service or training, to privately possess and bear their own firearms, such as the pistol involved here. ..."

"We agree with the district court that the Second Amendment protects the right of individuals to privately keep and bear their own firearms that are suitable as individual, personal weapons and are not of the general kind or type excluded by *Miller*" — sawed-off shotguns — "regardless of whether the particular individual is then actually a member of a militia."

Did you want them to say it a few more times? Are you starting to get it yet? Are you *still* planning to write me another "but the introductory clause restricts gun ownership to National Guardsmen on active duty, nyah-nyah" letter?

☙ ☙ ☙

Though the mass media almost totally ignored the ground-shifting *Emerson* decision (admittedly, the Navy was bombing Afghanistan and Congress was in the middle of a terrorist anthrax scare at the time), recognition of the significance of the Oct. 16 ruling was swift from gun-rights scholars:

"A federal appeals court ruled yesterday that the Constitution guarantees individuals the right to have a gun, the first time in recent history that such a high-level legal authority has explicitly endorsed such a view," Washington's Cato Institute proclaimed in a press release the day after the decision.

Complimenting the court's "scholarly and powerfully worded opinion," Robert A. Levy, Cato Institute senior fellow in constitutional studies and a Second Amendment expert, comments:

"On Oct. 16, in *United States v. Emerson*, the United States Court of Appeals for the Fifth Circuit rejected the 'collective rights' view of the Second Amendment and affirmed the right that each of us enjoy, as individuals, to own a gun. ...

"The implications of the *Emerson* case are especially important today," Mr. Levy continued, referring to the destruction of the World Trade Center by terrorists. "On Sept. 11, we learned that the state cannot defend us against all acts of terror. It is imperative, therefore, that we be able to defend ourselves. A disarmed society, because its citizens are defenseless, tends to adopt police state tactics. That's why law-abiding inner city residents, disarmed by gun control, beg for government protection against drug gangs despite the terrible violations of civil liberties that such protection entails — like curfews and anti-loitering laws. An individual right to bear arms is thus prophylactic — it reduces the demand for a police state."

"This is truly a victory for firearms civil rights," echoed Dave LaCourse, public affairs director for the Second Amendment Foundation, of Bellevue, Washington, which lists itself as "the nation's oldest and largest tax-exempt education, research and legal action group focusing on the constitutional right and heritage to privately own and possess firearms."

"For years, gun control extremists and constitutional revisionists have insisted that there is no individual right to keep and bear arms. We now can say with the support of the federal court that we have been right, and they have been wrong, all along," Mr. LaCourse continued, in a press release the foundation headlined: "Appeals Court Confirms Second Amendment Protects an Individual Right."

"In a stunning decision," the press release begins, "the 5th Circuit Court of Appeals in New Orleans has crushed over 60 years of judicial misinterpretation and anti-gun rhetoric by finding that the Second Amendment of the U.S. Constitution protects an individual right ..."

🌾 🌾 🌾

Interestingly enough, the Fifth Circuit took particular pains to delve into that famous "introductory clause."

Again, from the Fifth Circuit's decision in *Emerson*:

"We turn now to the Second Amendment's preamble: 'A well-regulated Militia, being necessary to the security of a free State.' And, we ask ourselves whether this preamble suffices to mandate what would be an otherwise implausible collective rights or sophisticated collective rights interpretation of the amendment. We conclude that it does not. ...

"As observed in *Miller*, 'The Militia comprised all males physically capable of acting in concert for the common defense' and 'that ordinarily when called for service these men were expected to appear bearing arms supplied by themselves.' *Miller* further notes that 'In all the colonies . . . the militia systems ... implied the general obligation of all adult male inhabitants to possess arms.' There are frequent contemporaneous references to 'a well-regulated militia' being 'composed of the body of the people, trained in arms.'

"Plainly, then, 'a well-regulated Militia' refers not to a special or select subset or group taken out of the militia as a whole but rather to the condition of the militia as a whole, namely being well disciplined and trained. And, 'Militia,' just like 'well-regulated Militia,' likewise was understood to be composed of the people generally possessed of arms which they knew how to use, rather than to refer to some formal military group separate and distinct from the people at large.

"Madison also plainly shared these views, as is reflected in his Federalist No. 46 where he argued that the power of Congress under the proposed Constitution '[t]o raise and support Armies' (Art. 1, § 8, cl.12) posed no threat to liberty because any such army, if misused, 'would be opposed [by] a militia amounting to near half a million of citizens with arms in their hands' and then noting 'the advantage of being armed, which the Americans possess over the people of almost every other nation,' in contrast to 'the several kingdoms of Europe' where 'the governments are afraid to trust the people with arms.'

"Plainly, Madison saw an armed people as a foundation

of the militia which would provide security for a 'free' state, one which, like America but unlike the 'kingdoms of Europe,' was not afraid to trust its people to have their own arms," the Fifth Circuit now rules. "The militia consisted of the people bearing their own arms when called to active service, arms which they kept and hence knew how to use. If the people were disarmed there could be no militia (well-regulated or otherwise) as it was then understood.

"That expresses the proper understanding of the relationship between the Second Amendment's preamble and its substantive guarantee. As stated in Kates, "Handgun Prohibition and the Original Meaning of the Second Amendment," 'the [Second] amendment's wording, so opaque to us, made perfect sense to the Framers: believing that a militia (composed of the entire people possessed of their individually owned arms) was necessary for the protection of a free state, they guaranteed the people's right to possess those arms.'

"Similarly, Cooley, *General Principles of Constitutional Law* (Little, Brown, 1880; 1981 Rothman & Co. reprint) rejects, as 'not warranted by the intent,' an interpretation of the Second Amendment 'that the right to keep and bear arms was only guaranteed to the Militia,' and states '[t]he meaning of the provision undoubtedly is, that the people, from whom the militia must be taken, shall have the right to keep and bear arms; and they need no permission or regulation of law for the purpose. But this enables the government to have a well-regulated militia; for to bear arms implies something more than the mere keeping; it implies the learning to handle and use them in a way that makes those who keep them ready for their efficient use.'

"Much the same thought was expressed more than one hundred years later in the following passage from Tribe, American Constitutional Law:

"'Perhaps the most accurate conclusion one can reach with any confidence is that the core meaning of the Second

Amendment is a populist/republican/federalism one: Its central object is to arm "We the People" so that ordinary citizens can participate in the collective defense of their community and their state. But it does so not through directly protecting a right on the part of states or other collectivities, assertable by them against the federal government, to arm the populace as they see fit. Rather, the amendment achieves its central purpose by assuring that the federal government may not disarm individual citizens without some unusually strong justification consistent with the authority of the states to organize their own militias. That assurance in turn is provided through recognizing a right (admittedly of uncertain scope) on the part of individuals to possess and use firearms in the defense of themselves and their homes ... a right that directly limits action by Congress or by the Executive Branch ...'

"In sum," the Fifth Circuit concluded in remanding the *Emerson* case back to the lower courts, "to give the Second Amendment's preamble its full and proper due there is no need to torture the meaning of its substantive guarantee into the collective rights or sophisticated collective rights model which is so plainly inconsistent with the substantive guarantee's text, its placement within the Bill of Rights and the wording of the other articles thereof and of the original Constitution as a whole."

In this the Fifth Circuit is correct. All that is needed now is a federal bench that will match its own personal and political courage to that of the men who drew up this historic charter of freedom ... taking all 20,000 of this nation's unconstitutional "gun control" laws out behind the barn, and shooting them.

🌿 🌿 🌿

And at least one commentator holds that is precisely what the jurists of the Fifth Circuit may intend.

"The case, as the 5th Circuit left it, fairly begs for an

appeal by *Emerson* to the United States Supreme Court," writes our friend John G. Lankford, J.D., a retired Alabama attorney now resident in Belize. "The 5th Circuit indicates a desire not to establish its opinion as federal law only in the states its jurisdiction encompasses, but nationwide. Only by getting its opinion reversed by the United States Supreme Court, specifically on grounds that the case's circumstances do not suffice to deprive Mr. Emerson of his Second Amendment right, can it do so.

"Without, in this brief comment, tracing the fine points involved in that question, that appears to be what the 5th Circuit sets about doing," Mr. Langford continued in his Oct. 18 commentary. "Very generally and not all-inclusively, the question whether Emerson's circumstances suffice to allow the federal statute to deprive him of his Second Amendment right addresses itself to a very subtle and nebulous area of the law, that of whether Emerson received due process of law under the Fifth Amendment. An even greater level of complexity is imposed by the fact that the answer may involve a maddening doctrine that has borne various labels while inflicting innumerable headaches on lawyers and jurists, but is generally called 'substantive due process.' ...

"Assuming, as it appears, it is eyeing an appeal to the Supreme Court, and hopes its Second Amendment view will be adopted as rationale, not simply obiter dictum, and thus hopes to be reversed on the due-process or 'substantive due process' element of the case, the opinion rendered not only virtually guarantees an appeal by Emerson, but also shrewdly leaves the due-process issue (or substantive-due-process issue) to the Supreme Court, while making a formidable, possibly irrebuttable argument for its [the 5th Circuit's] view of the Second Amendment's meaning.

"Of two close and hard issues, it took the easier and left the harder to be resolved by its superiors. In doing so, however, the 5th Circuit virtually begged the Supreme Court for a reversal of its due-process holding."

The appeals court made "a patent reach," Mr. Lankford argues, "essentially holding that because the Texas court decided as it did, issuing the order that triggered the federal statute under which Emerson was charged and convicted, then the Texas court must have been right. It was on this shaky point, not the District Court's Second Amendment ground, that the 5th Circuit reversed — and invited the Supreme Court to reverse in turn."

Paging Clarence Thomas ...

🌿 🌿 🌿

You may now take off your lobster bibs; I believe it's done spurting and the gutted, rotting, odiferous corpse of the "You ignored the 'well-regulated militia' part, nyah nyah" argument can now be hauled out back and thrown in the dumpster ... or, if you prefer, hauled out to sea by a chain around its tail, to where the carrion-eating sharks are gathering.

But even before that thoroughly drummed-up and manufactured "problem" had been dispatched, I always asked the other side, earnestly and often: If you want to insist on the relevance of the now thoroughly explained introductory phrase, 'A well-regulated militia being necessary to the security of a free state ...' let the BATF explain to me how and where I and my buddies are *supposed* to go practice our small-unit tactics with M-16s and Squad Automatic Weapons, the better to *become* a 'well-regulated militia,' adept at shooting and killing uniformed mercenaries the next time they send in the tanks on American soil.

The answer, of course, is that they're lying. For us to form militias skilled at resisting federal tyranny or usurpation is the *last* thing they want. This is nothing but a lawyer's rhetorical trick designed to get their chorus of bed-wetters nodding in unison as they were taught in the youth propaganda camps, chanting, "Right, no guns unless they're part of the militia, which really means the National Guard" — a National Guard which the Founders warned us *against*, their warning term at the time being "special militia," describing any company of uniformed mercenaries loyal only to the seat of power.

And perhaps this brings us finally to our letter-writer's "If you permit private citizens to possess nuclear weapons ..."

Since it's not the business of Suprynowicz to "permit" private citizens to possess or not possess anything, my correspondent probably means: "If the federal government permits private citizens to possess ..."

But here we run into the same problem. All federal lawmaking authority is vested in the Congress. Is the Congress authorized to permit or ban or allow or infringe the private ownership of arms? Three provisions apply: In Article I Section 8, yes, Congress is given power to "provide for ... arming .. the militia."

May it, in turn, take away the guns? No. The Second Amendment bars any such infringement.

And what about that third, vital, relevant power of Congress (never repealed), the power to "grant Letters of Marque" — right there in Article I Section 8, directly after the power to "declare War"?

A letter of marque allows a privately owned warship to act with full authority of the government. If the First Amendment freedom of the press now applies to modern electric printing presses — not just the hand-cranked kind Ben Franklin used — then surely Congress has power to grant a letter of marque to a private billionaire who volunteers to build and operate on our behalf in time of war his own nuclear-powered aircraft carrier, with full complement of modern fighter planes ... which means he must of necessity have the right to *own* such stuff ... doesn't it?

Where did the federal government get its right, power, or authority to possess nuclear warheads? Under our system, this government can acquire no right, power, or authority except those delegated to it by the people.

Can you delegate a right, power, or authority you do not already possess? No.

Therefore, individual Americans have the right, power, and authority to own nuclear weapons. No other condition can apply, unless you submit that we now live under a form of government where all rights and powers start with the *government masters*, who then bestow upon us (their peasants and slaves) only those lesser included rights they wish *us* to have.

Few private parties would ever want a nuclear weapon, of course, or be able to afford one. Those who could or would are so rich and well-connected they could probably get one right now — law or no law — if it mattered enough to them. The real function of the argument "Oh, so you think the lunatic who talks to his shopping cart down on the corner should be able to own a nuke?" is to lure us into an ancient and familiar trap.

How tempting is the siren song: "Come on, don't you want to prove you're *reasonable*? You don't want to look like an *extremist*. Admit it: You can't possibly have any practical *need* for a nuclear weapon."

The problem, of course, is that once they've got us moving backward, they won't settle for this one concession. Oh no. They will — they always have — come right back with, "Well, then, surely you don't *need* to personally possess a 155-mm cannon ... a tank, a crew-served Ma Deuce ..." all the way down to those semi-automatic "assault rifles" that carry "more rounds than you could possibly need to shoot a deer," until all we retain is some unloaded ceremonial flintlock that we're allowed to check out from the police locker just long enough to carry in the Fourth of July parade.

The Viper Militia in Arizona? All jailed for "conspiracy" to own a few machine guns and practice blowing up a few desert sand dunes.

The leaders of the militias of Macon, Ga., and New Hampshire and West Virginia? Imprisoned after being framed by government infiltrators for conspiracy to possess bomb parts or stolen property — delivered to them by the government agents themselves.

The only answer to the argument over "need" is to refuse to enter into it. Would they apply it to any other article of the Bill of Rights? Can you prove you "need" to go to your church or temple more than once a week? Surely it would be sufficient if we only "allowed" you to attend twice a month upon presentation of your Freedom of Religion permit, wouldn't it?

Of any government that will not trust its own people with these weapons we need ask, "Then why should we trust *you* with them? Because you promise never to use them to cow us into servitude ... as you once promised, before Waco, never to use military tanks and armed helicopters against American civilians — women and children — on American soil?"

Go back and look again at what Andrew Fletcher wrote in his 1698 *Discourse of Government with Relation to Militias*. Then get yourself some new lies; the old ones are wearing thin.

Why Even Our "Victories" Aren't Really Victories

Unfortunately, so brazen and relentless have the enemies of freedom become that the impact of such fine and decisive and irrefutable research as we find in the *Emerson* decision is now akin to the tree which falls in the forest with no one there to hear.

The anti-gun hysterics immediately issued press releases, dismissing the exhaustive historical research in the appeals court decision (which they can rest assured hardly anyone in modern America will ever actually *read*) as "mere dicta" — ancillary material irrelevant to the final decision.

The main point, they assert, is that Dr. Emerson was still found guilty of threatening his wife and child with that handgun.

Which is a lie, of course. Not only was Dr. Emerson subsequently acquitted of any wrongdoing in Texas state courts, he was never even *accused* of brandishing or threatening his wife or child with a firearm. His alleged crime (created by retroactive legislation) lay in merely *possessing* the implement of self-defense.

But such calumnies still serve their intended purpose, "canceling out" any vestigial instinct to cover the news in the mainstream media. ("Have the police said they'll no longer stop some skinhead who's walking down the street with a machine gun? I didn't think so. No one can even agree on what the damned decision means, and it's much too complicated and obscure to explain in 40 or 50 words — stick with the plane crash.") Ninety-six 96 percent of our neighbors are thus sent back to mindlessly chanting the anti-gun sound bites they memorized in government school.

Try it yourself. Ask any friend or relative over dinner whether they weren't impressed by that astonishing appeals court ruling out of New Orleans — the one that confirmed once and for all that there's an *individual* right to keep and bear arms of militia usefulness — assault rifles, for heaven's sake.

Unless you're talking to a dedicated gun-rights activist, chances are you'll meet little more than a shrug and a "hunh?" Push it further, and you'll be told, "Typical Southern rednecks," or else, "That can't be right. The courts have ruled it's only a right to join the National Guard. Anyway, I watch the evening news seven nights a week; I know everything of any significance going on in this country, right down to how many panda cubs were born at the zoo last weekend, and I haven't heard a word about this so-called 'historic decision.'"

It's the same kind of blank-out you'll get from 96 percent

of your neighbors and old schoolmates if you ask whatever happened to that Randy Weaver guy who was the focus of the shoot-out and stand-off with government troops at Ruby Ridge in northern Idaho in the late summer of 1992.

If they remember Ruby Ridge at all, chances are you'll be told, "I have no idea, but from what I recall, a U.S. marshall died in that shoot-out. So I imagine this Weaver guy is still cooling his heels in some federal penitentiary with the rest of those militia types."

Inform them, "Actually, a randomly selected jury of Idaho citizens — no right-wing militia types were allowed to serve — acquitted Weaver and his friend Kevin Harris of any wrong-doing in the shooting death of federal Marshall William Degan. The jury ruled, in essence, that when Weaver and/or Harris shot and killed that federal agent, who had already killed Weaver's fleeing 12-year-old son and his dog by shooting them both in the back with his fully-automatic assault rifle, Weaver and Harris did nothing wrong — the trespassing son-of-a-bitch got exactly what he deserved.

"And not only did Randy Weaver walk free, the government then had to settle a civil suit by paying Weaver and his surviving kids $1.4 million for murdering his wife; the U.S. government took money out of what you and I pay in taxes and made him a millionaire because the government murdered an innocent woman and child."

"I don't believe that," most will say ... if they even stop watching TV long enough to hear you out. "You'd have to prove that to me."

Well, I'm a 30-year veteran newsman, my livelihood dependent on maintaining a reputation for not making up stuff out of thin air. I've met and talked with Randy Weaver and his lovely daughter Sara at conventions and gun shows here in Las Vegas in the years since the government agreed to pay them the million bucks; they're not in prison and they're doing fine. If your skeptic won't believe me, dare him to look up the facts for himself at www.davekopel.org/Waco/Arts/rrprosec.htm, or www.greatepicbooks.com/review/september98b.html, or http:/ /land.netonecom.net/tlp/ref/weaver.shtml.

And then contemplate for a moment the 200 million other Americans who don't know these things ... and don't care.

Gun-Grabbers: Masters of the New Plantation
🕊

Last time we dug into Yale Law professor Akhil Reed Amar's impressive 1998 tome *The Bill of Rights* (now out in paperback), the good professor — neither a gun owner nor in any sense a "right-wing militia nut" — demonstrated through historical research that the gun-grabbers are wrong: The Second Amendment does not merely protect firearms ownership by active-duty members of the National Guard. Rather, it acknowledges the pre-existing right of all Americans to own and carry weapons of military usefulness.

But now that this undead golem of those who despise our Bill of Rights is down, let's proceed to stake it through the heart.

For you see — while the Second Amendment is *sufficient* to guarantee the right of citizens to own machine guns (not to mention rifles, pistols, "assault weapons," and shoulder-launched missiles) — it's not even the best guarantee of this right. The whole debate over the *Second* Amendment, professor Amar points out, has largely distracted us from considering a pair of enactments even more directly on point: the 14th Amendment and the original, 1866, Civil Rights Act.

We rejoin professor Amar at page 258:

"At the Founding, the right of the people to keep and bear arms stood shoulder to shoulder with the right to vote; arms bearing in militias embodied a paradigmatic *political* right.

... But Reconstruction Republicans recast arms bearing as a core *civil* right, utterly divorced from the militia and other political rights and responsibilities. Arms were needed not as part of political and politicized militia service, but to protect one's individual homestead. Everyone — even nonvoting, nonmilitia-serving women — had a right to a gun for self-protection. ...

"The Creation vision was public, with the militia muster on the town square. The Reconstruction vision was private, with individual freedmen keeping guns at home to ward off Klansmen and other ruffians. ...

"Alongside ...the Civil Rights Act of 1866 ... Congress passed the Freedman's Bureau Act, a sister statute introduced the same day by the same sponsor. ... The Freedman's Bureau Act affirmed that 'laws ... concerning *personal* liberty, *personal* property, *personal* security, and the acquisition, enjoyment and disposition of estate, real and *personal*, including the constitutional right to bear arms, shall be secured to and enjoyed by all citizens. ...' Thus, the Reconstruction Congress expressly repudiated *Dred Scott's* claim that because free blacks could never be citizens, they lacked many of these basic rights."

Allow me to interrupt the good professor to point out that the opposite also holds true. Though modern-day black Americans tend to despise antebellum Supreme Court Chief Justice Roger Taney for ruling in *Dred Scott* that black Americans were neither citizens nor men, they might want to go back and re-read his logic. They will find the devil unintentionally gave them their due. Taney said blacks could not be considered men or citizens, because if they were so considered, *there would be no option but to allow them to own and carry arms without restriction.*

Quick, now: Which side won the Civil War? Can a law-abiding black citizen today buy a 30-caliber machine gun and drive it home in the back of his pickup truck without seeking massa's "permission"?

Why was the 14th Amendment — darling of the left when

it appears to justify the expansion of federal power — enacted? Professor Amar explains: "Southern states, ever fearful of slave insurrections, enacted sweeping antebellum laws prohibiting not just slaves but free blacks from owning guns. In response, antislavery theorists emphasized the personal right of all free citizens — white and black, male and female, northern and southern, visitor and resident — to own guns for self-protection."

Really? But what chance does a law-abiding citizen of any color have today of carrying his self-defense pistol with him if he chooses to visit the collectivist metropolises of Los Angeles, Washington, or New York City?

"In the 1846 case *Nunn vs. Georgia*," professor Amar continues, "the proslavery contrarian Chief Justice Joseph Henry Lumpkin proclaimed not only that the Second Amendment bound the states, but also, 'The right [is guaranteed to] the whole people, old and young, men, women, and boys, and not militia only, to keep and bear arms of every description, and not merely as are used by the militia.' ...

"Roger Taney and [prominent abolitionist] Joel Tiffany hardly saw eye to eye in the 1850s, but they both agreed on this: *If free blacks were citizens,* it would necessarily follow that they had a right of *private arms bearing.* According to *Dred Scott*, the 'privileges and immunities' of 'citizens' included 'full liberty of speech in public and in private ... and to keep and carry arms wherever they went.' ...

"One of the core purposes of the Civil Rights Act of 1866 and of the Fourteenth Amendment was to ... outlaw the infamous Black Codes [by which the Southern states sought to ban firearms for freed blacks], and affirm the full and equal right of every citizen to self-defense. ..."

Professor Amar quotes Sen. Samuel Pomeroy, declaring on the floor of the Senate in 1866, "Every man ... should have the right to bear arms for the defense of himself and his family and his homestead. And if the cabin door of the freedman is broken open and the intruder enters for purposes as vile as were known to slavery, then should a well-loaded musket be in the hand of the occupant." Even Rep. Henry Raymond, a founder and editor of the *New York Times*, declared that the black freedman "has a country and a home; a right to defend himself and his wife and children; a right to bear arms."

"Today's NRA," professor Amar concludes, "pays far too much attention to 1775-91 and far too little to 1830-68."

But is this curious forgetfulness about the original meaning of "civil rights" merely an accident? Where do the modern forces of "gun control" — including the nation's largest gun-control organization, the National Rifle Association, which endorsed the federal gun control acts of 1934 and 1968 and the "compromise" Brady Law with its national gun-buyer registry — now focus their energies?

What race predominates among the subsidized housing projects where HUD now claims it needs no search warrants to root out and seize "dangerous firearms" — while the cheerleader NRA urges the government to "rigorously enforce the gun laws already on the books"? Where are most of the "gun buy-back" stunts conducted? Among the racial minorities of the inner cities, of course. What is the derivation of "Saturday Night Special" — describing the inexpensive self-defense handgun the NRA says it's OK to go ahead and ban as long as we rich white folk are allowed to keep our engraved fowling pieces?

Cover your ears if you like, but the origin of this term for the inexpensive handguns most useful for self-defense to a black or Hispanic resident of the inner city is the old derogatory police slang "Niggertown Saturday Night," referring to inner city weekend violence not meriting much attention, since it mainly occurred among the black folk.

When handgun "licenses and permits" require expensive safety courses and the OK of the local sheriff, and one-third of our young black men today have experienced some kind of run-in with the legal system and are thus blocked from even applying, what percentage of these "permits" end up issued to black folk?

And when gun-grabbers try to terrify the soccer moms with visions of "inner-city street gangs armed with fully automatic AK-47s," what color skin do you imagine those soccer moms are picturing on Ernesto, Raoul, Dante, and Ahmad?

You see, those who would ban the private ownership of weapons of military usefulness to individual Americans today are not just liars ... they're also racists.

"I Became a Felon on My Last Birthday"

A sad letter arrived in March 2000. Though I will honor the request of this correspondent to keep his identity secret, this is the kind of missive that makes a columnist's job easy. All the words that follow are those of "Gun Owner in Massachusetts":

The title of your recent column, "The thugs now reign in Massachusetts," has a lot more meaning than perhaps even you realize.

Under a 1998 law, I became a felon on my last birthday. I've never had any contact with the law beyond a speeding ticket some years ago, but by the stroke of a pen I'm now a felon.

I became a felon because I own a gun and I refuse to go to the local police station every four years for mug shots and a full set of fingerprints. I also won't immediately notify the state authorities whenever I move.

If I'd been convicted of murder, the cops would have my fingerprints, but once I finished prison and parole I could live anywhere I wanted without reporting in. But because I own a gun, I am treated far worse than those convicted murderers.

Understand, I'm not talking about carrying a concealed

handgun, or even "assault weapons" (though the new law has many draconian punishments for people who dare to own a semi-auto). Under this law, possession of *any* gun, any cartridge (spent or not), any powder, primers, bullets, or shot — even a can of pepper spray — requires me to submit to fingerprinting and a mug shot. The data is kept by the state's Criminal History Systems Division — the same folks who keep the records on murderers, rapists, and other convicted criminals. ...

It gets worse. I'm not only a felon for the 25-year-old 12-gauge pump shotgun that I keep in the closet, I'm a felon for not keeping it locked (and therefore useless) at all times. Locking my front door doesn't count as "preventing unauthorized persons from gaining access to the firearm."

I have no children, but the state mandates I render myself completely defenseless to any criminal who cares to rob or kill me. God only knows what will happen to me if I ever have to use the shotgun to defend myself. I suspect I'd end up in prison, paying restitution to the home invader whose "rights" I "violated."

The penalty for each of these new crimes is 10 years in prison. Since I could get charged with a separate count for each round of ammo, that brick of .22 cartridges I bought for my granddad's single-shot match rifle could get me 50,000 years. This is not a theoretical calculation: A Wayland man is facing 70 years for "unsafe storage" of his firearms, seven counts at 10 years each. (Contact goal.org for corroboration and details of this case and my statements about the new laws.)

I go to sleep every night wondering if the door will be smashed in by ninja-suited, armored, machine-gun-toting thugs willing to kill me where I stand if I so much as reach for that shotgun. It won't really matter much to me then whether they turn out to be freelance crooks or professional, government-paid murderers. I suppose I should move out of state, but my family has been here for generations; my job is here; and I won't be run off my own property by a bunch of bullies, legal or otherwise.

I'm feeling alone here. The ACLU has abandoned Massachusetts gun owners on the left, and the NRA just betrayed them on the right. ... The ACLU fought the Georgia fingerprint-on-your-driver's-license law vigorously. But a million gun owners are forced, under penalty of fines and imprisonment, to give up their fingerprints, and the ACLU won't even answer my letters on the subject, much less file a court case.

On the right, the National Rifle Association now stands with Handgun Control Inc. in vowing to put people like me behind bars. I wouldn't have believed it if I hadn't heard and seen the video recordings on the NRA Web site. "You touch a gun in Colorado, and you're gonna have five years in a state or federal penitentiary," says Wayne LaPierre, standing on the stage with HCI representatives.

Under their Project Exile, anyone caught with an "illegal" gun gets tried in federal court. What the NRA doesn't seem to understand, or perhaps just doesn't care about, is that here in Massachusetts, my guns were made "illegal" by the stroke of a pen.

I'm scared, Mr. Suprynowicz, I'm angry, and I feel terribly alone. The ACLU turns a blind eye on massive violations of its own principles; the NRA has betrayed all gun owners ... and my own so-called representative co-sponsored this new law.

This must be something akin to what the Jews in Germany felt in the late 1930s. Gun owners have been cut out of the herd, demonized, ostracized, and blamed for everything wrong with society.

The thugs now reign in Massachusetts. They reign in the statehouse, in the courts, in the media, and in the police. One million obedient sheeple have meekly surrendered their fingerprints and now carry state-mandated papers for having the temerity to exercise their inalienable right to self-defense. They might as well make us wear special arm bands.

Thank you, and keep up the good work.

❦ ❦ ❦

By the summer of 2001, things in Massachusetts — the commonwealth where the brave Minutemen fought the first pitched battle of the American Revolution against British regulars sent to seize their powder, shot, and rifles — seem only to have gotten worse.

Writing in the Wellesley-based conservative-to-Libertarian *Massachusetts News* (www.massnews.com), published by lawyer J. Edward Pawlick (formerly of *Lawyers Weekly*) , staff writer Curt Lovelace reported: "When Alec Costerus moved back to Massachusetts in March 1999, he heard there was a new law regarding handgun licenses.

"So he innocently went to the Concord Police Department to inquire what he needed to do," Lovelace writes in a June 2001 story, headlined, "Concord Police Sued for Taking Gun of Homeowner."

Costerus "still held a Firearms Identification (FID) card which had no expiration date. But instead of being given the information on what to do, Costerus was immediately arrested by Sgt. Barry Neal and put in jail."

The charge was "illegal possession of a firearm" although Costerus didn't have any guns in his possession. Concord cops later searched his home and seized two handguns and a competition rifle.

Despite spending a night in jail and having his family frightened by an illegal search of his home, Costerus wanted to forgive and forget. He hoped to clear up the "gigantic misunderstanding," Lovelace reports. In November, the charges against him were dismissed without a trial.

Mr. Costerus then filed for a license to carry handguns. "The response was unexpected," reporter Lovelace reveals. "On Dec. 31, 1999, an officer drove up the driveway and hand delivered the chief's letter of denial. The two reasons given by Chief Leonard Wetherbee of the Concord Police Department were:

"'1. Your failure to comply with a Concord Police Department Administrative Policy requiring the completion of a state approved Firearms Safety Course when upgrading from a Firearms Identification Card to a License to Carry; and

"'2. Your recent involvement in domestic and firearms related issues in the Town of Concord.'"

Costerus told the *News* he was exempt from the necessity to complete a firearms safety course. This exemption comes straight out of the Massachusetts Gun Control Act of 1998, which exempts current FID cardholders. His FID card was still valid when he applied for his License to Carry, he says. For that matter, Costerus is qualified to *teach* the Firearms Safety Course. He's a former Massachusetts State Champion shooter, a high school and college competitive shooter, and has both ROTC and police training.

The only illegal activity regarding Costerus and firearms, he maintains, was on the part of the Town of Concord — the police illegally searched his home and confiscated his weapons without probable cause. And all charges against him were eventually dropped.

On Jan. 3, 2000, Costerus petitioned the Concord District Court to review the denial. In March a judge declared, "While the chief's discretion is certainly broad, it is not unlimited." The judge's ruling contained an order to issue Costerus a license. But Chief Wetherbee countered with a Motion for a Stay of Enforcement. Costerus received no license.

In August 2000, Costerus filed a civil rights suit in U.S. District Court in Boston against the Town of Concord and the commonwealth of Massachusetts. In the 40-count suit, Costerus, who is not an attorney but is representing himself, charged several police officers and the police chief, as well as then-Gov. Paul Cellucci and several state officials, with numerous violations of the Second, Fifth, and Fourteenth amendments to the U.S. Constitution. The suit also charges conspiracy, fraud, larceny through illegal conversion, negligence, false arrest, false imprisonment, and malicious prosecution.

"I want my property back," Costerus told the *News*. "It was illegally obtained. It was stolen from my house without due process."

In May 2001— five months before the *Emerson* ruling was handed down in New Orleans, a federal judge, Morris E. Lasker, granted a motion by the state to dismiss part of the case. According to Costerus, "The judge said I would be entitled to Prospective Injunctive relief, but only when there's a valid Constitutional claim. He said there is no individual right under the Second Amendment for an individual to keep and bear arms. So the counts of the original complaint were dismissed to the extent that they make Second Amendment claims."

Mr. Costerus has filed a Notice of Appeal to the United States Court of Appeals for the First Circuit. Mr. Costerus remains unlicensed and without his firearms, which are being held by the Concord Police Department. He awaits a ruling from the First Circuit Court of Appeals.

While Mr. Costerus has not engaged an attorney, he has amassed large legal bills. Donations can be made to the Alec S. Costerus Legal Fund, P.O. Box 705, Concord, MA 01742-0705.

Neither Sgt. (now Lt. — violating the Constitution has its rewards in modern-day Massachusetts) Barry Neal nor Chief Leonard Wetherbee of the Concord Police Department have been talking to the press.

Things I'd Like to See

❧

Although the 14th Amendment was passed just after the Civil War, for nearly a century everyone thought it was intended merely to guarantee blacks the right to vote, to keep and bear arms, to own property — that it protected them, in short, from having their elemental rights infringed by the legal enactments of recalcitrant state or local governments, anxious to overturn black emancipation.

At no point during that century did anyone suspect that the 14th Amendment overruled the much older freedom of association — that it required, say, a private white hotelkeeper or restaurateur to serve a black customer if he didn't want to.

Then, in the 1950s and '60s, the Supreme Court began to "discover" that the authors of the 14th Amendment, nearly a century before, had actually meant to grant the federal government power to enforce just such interracial good will.

Mind you, segregation was evil and we are well rid of it, if indeed we are rid of it. (The last time I visited, it was precisely the liberal universities of the Politically Correct Northeast that were most likely to consign black students to segregated dormitories, so long as they flew makeshift Ethiopian flags instead of the Confederate Stars and Bars and called themselves "Malcolm X House" or something of the sort, instead of "Darktown." Isn't Political Correctness wonderful?)

Furthermore, those legitimately interested in restoring state sovereignty can have nothing but loathing for the generation of Southern bigots and bulletheads who managed to inextricably link "states' rights" with racism in the public mind.

But, all that said, the law today does insist that the 14th Amendment forbids the private owners of "public accommodations" from depriving anyone of their "civil rights."

So here's my question: Given that the civil right to keep and bear arms is guaranteed far more explicitly in the Constitution than the right to sit at a lunch counter ("The right of the People to keep and bear Arms, shall not be infringed"), and that it was in fact one of the main rights intended to be protected by the drafters of the 14th Amendment (since Southern jurisdictions were at the time busily at work disarming black Civil War veterans), why are grocery stores, shopping malls, entire municipalities, and even the Commonwealth of Massachusetts now allowed to post signs that read, "No firearms allowed: carry a gun, go to jail"?

Why don't federal marshals immediately wrestle the people who post such signs to the ground and haul them away — no matter what color uniforms they wear — just as quickly as they would if the signs read "No coloreds, Jews, or Chinamen"?

We have whole Civil Rights Enforcement divisions with so little to do these days that they threaten to prosecute people who write letters to the editor opposing the location of halfway houses for drunks and junkies in their neighborhoods. (For once the re-interpretation of the 14th got started, it took less than 40 years for courts and Congress to "discover" that the drafters, back in 1866, also meant winos and hopheads to be a protected class among us, deserving just as much redress for past grievances as the long-suffering African-American.)

Let's re-staff these bureaus with charter members of Gun Owners of America and Jews for the Preservation of Firearms Ownership, and put them to work doing something useful.

"Just Apply for Your Permit — What Are You Worried About?"

Traveling on the East coast last year, I heard a 70-year-old resident of New York City being interviewed on the radio.

In New York City, it's illegal for a citizen to carry or even own a handgun without a government permit. The permits are granted only on the basis of demonstrable "need." This gentleman had peacefully owned and carried a handgun with a proper "permit" for decades. His "need" derived from the fact he was a jewelry store owner. The burglar alarm at his store sounded at his home as well as at the local station house, and he often arrived on the scene before police (despite the cops being already dressed and rolling and having all that fancy radio dispatch equipment — reassuring, eh?). Ergo, there was a good chance he might someday confront armed burglars, alone.

But this fellow was being interviewed on Public Radio because his permit had been cancelled. Or, to be more specific, the police had declined to renew his permit, as they had previously renewed it routinely each year. He was going to have to get rid of his gun.

The gentleman was not losing his permit because he had mishandled his weapon, or made some technical mistake in his paperwork, or even because police felt he had grown too old to handle a firearm safely. (As a matter of fact, the one thing Mayor Rudy Giuliani's NYPD could probably *not* get away with is systematically cancelling the permits of any one select group, whether it be blacks, women, or the elderly.)

No, the NYPD was perfectly up-front about it: They had decided to renew only 70 percent of the outstanding permits that year, on the theory that a general reduction in the number of legal weapons in the city would contribute to "public safety" (this despite the fact that John Lott of the Yale Law School has statistically proven that crime rates actually go down in precisely those American cities that permit the *most* law-abiding citizens to carry weapons for self-defense).

The gentleman had no recourse to the courts. The courts have held again and again that — once one applies for any government "permit" — you can forget about going back to court later and claiming you have a "right" to do that thing without restriction. Such a claim becomes "a matter that does not come before this court. Whether or not you once had such a theoretical right, you waived it when you entered into the permitting process, acknowledging the power of the state to set such restrictions on these permits as it sees fit." And a general reduction in the number of permits is well within the discretion of a government that claims to be acting "for the greater public good."

Take machine guns. It's perfectly legal for law-abiding American citizens to own machine guns. Congress has never dared to ban them, since that would blatantly violate the Second Amendment. Yet most Americans believe any machine gun is, de facto, illegal. Why?

In 1934, the federal government imposed a $200 tax on the "transfer" of any machine gun. Given government-created inflation, two hundred dollars certainly doesn't seem as large a sum today as it did 70 years ago. But as part of the "licensing and permitting" regime, the federals have effectively banned the import or manufacture of any new, functioning machine guns (except for exclusive use by police and the Army) for years. This has had the effect of driving up the price of grandpa's old Browning Automatic Rifle to $10,000. Add to that an onerous requirement for fingerprinting, a six-month wait, and the fact the BATF reserves the right to come knock on your door and "inspect" the weapon at any time — and only a few rich hobbyists persist in exercising this "right" today.

This is the perfumed trap into which we fall when we first allow any right to be "converted" into a conditional privilege.

If it was proposed that you apply for a "Freedom of Religion Permit," would you object? Why, if you were assured it was "not intended to place any kind of onerous burden on law-abiding church- and temple-goers; we only want to screen out the dangerous types, like that terrible Jim Jones who convinced all his parishioners to commit suicide down in Guyana." Just sign here and pay a buck or two.

Of course, a few years from now they might up that "religious freedom permit" fee to $200, require annual fingerprinting, and only allow churchgoing on weekends. (Can you prove a *"need"* to attend church on Tuesday?) Figure you could then go to court and claim you have some "right" to freedom of religion? Then why did you apply for a "permit" in the first place? Hmm?

People who would thus refuse to apply for a "Freedom of Religion Permit" need to be asked how they can so blithely say, "Gun owners and cattle ranchers should just shut up and get themselves in compliance with their permit requirements."

The Decline and Fall of the American Empire
🌿

At first I couldn't see anything through the rifle scope.

Growing a bit impatient at this unforeseen delay, my grandfather finally determined I was attempting to employ the wrong eye.

Once that was straightened out, the two empty soda cans sitting one atop the other up the hill appeared to leap toward me, so sharp and clear I felt I could reach out and touch them. The old man told me to center the crosshairs and shoot.

"Which can do I shoot?"

Summoning up my memory of his voice again now, I don't think the old man was as much exasperated as mildly amazed at the number of irrelevant questions that could pop into the head of a nine-year-old boy.

"It doesn't matter which one you shoot," he said.

I shifted my shoulder to draw the sling tighter, concentrated on holding the image steady, and gradually squeezed the trigger as I'd been told. The distant cans flew apart in a quite gratifying manner, the top can turning several impressive cartwheels before landing silently on the rust-colored pine needles. Emptying the rifle's chamber, we strode up to inspect the damage.

Now it was my grandfather's turn to ask a question. "Which can did you shoot at, boy?"

Hoping I hadn't done anything wrong, I told him that, lacking more specific instructions, I had aimed at the point where the two cans met. He handed me the cans. A rather impressive furrow had been sliced edge-on through the top of the bottom can, and the bottom of its mate, as the bullet had cleaved symmetrically between them. I don't recall that Clarence Edward Higginbotham said another word to me that day. He did lay his hand on my shoulder. I believe he was wearing the red, green and white plaid wool hunting jacket that now hangs in my closet, looking improbably small to have ever fit the man who towered over me that day, so that my memory is not of his face, but of that woodsman's coat, mixed with the smell of pine needles and his omnipresent pipe. We cleaned up all trace of our presence and trudged back down the hill.

My mother was waiting for us on the back porch. I realized later that — seeing us return after hearing only a single shot — she must have believed it had gone badly, her boy tearfully refusing to continue after being dumped on his butt by his first experience of the big rifle's recoil, or something of the sort.

"It didn't go well?" she asked.

We wiped our feet and marched in past her as she held the door.

"The boy can shoot," my grandfather said.

I remember it more clearly than any day they ever tried to give me some paper diploma.

But I was not raised in the gun culture. My .22 rifle was long the only gun in the house, buried deep in the closet, always unloaded. The war souvenirs — mostly Japanese Arisakas — were quickly sold off after my grandfather died, with no thought to keeping even one. It was only years later, when I found myself researching the way the protection guaranteed us by the Second and 14th Amendments has been systematically eroded — after I'd read Stephen Halbrook's *That Every Man Be Armed* and John Ross's magnificent novel of the gun culture, *Unintended Consequences* — that I decided I should begin to practice what I preached.

It's only after you start buying and owning guns that you

can truly understand how absurd it would be to accept any single gun law as "reasonable" on its face. "How can you object to just a few reasonable gun laws?" ask the mindless members of the mewling mob.

"Look," you reply. "This version of the rifle is now illegal because it has a *pistol-grip*. But this other version is legal although it's absolutely identical in range, power, and function, because the pistol grip has been replaced with a *thumbhole stock*. Does that make any *sense*?"

"But if it's such a small difference, what's your objection?" they ask.

"Look at this one," you reply. "It would have been illegal to possess with its original bayonet lug and flash hider, so to comply with the law the importer chopped off the bayonet lug, and this new metal collar was welded onto the exterior threads of the barrel so a new flash hider can't be fitted. Do you know what it can do to the accuracy of a barrel to carelessly heat the end red hot like that?"

From the expression on their faces, they clearly neither know nor care.

So you try to explain by making a comparison. The First Amendment guarantees freedom of the press in precisely the same way as the Second and 14th Amendments guarantee our right to keep and bear arms. So what if we were to pass a "modest, reasonable" law that infringed in only the most "minor and insignificant" way on the freedom of the press? What if we enacted a law that you could possess any book you wanted, except that in any book of more than 350 pages, page 346 would have to be torn out before it was sold?

What if we infringed the First Amendment freedom of religion in such a minor way that it would hardly inconvenience anyone — perhaps by making priests and ministers and rabbis fill out a simple mail-in government registration form, or banning church services between 3 and 5 a.m.? After all, no one *needs* to go to church between 3 and 5 a.m. What could be so urgent that you couldn't wait for the 7 o'clock mass? Heck, for that matter, you could even summon the minister to come pray with you in your home at 4 a.m.; it's only physically entering the *church* between 3 and 5 a.m. that we'd be banning ... for now.

"That's absurd," comes the response. "No one is even proposing such a silly law. There's no connection whatsoever. What's your point? Owning books and going to church never killed anyone; guns exist for no purpose but killing."

"Ah. So when America's hundreds of thousands of policemen strap on their duty pistols each morning, they're each hoping and intending to shoot someone that day?"

"Of course not. That's totally different. Because of their line of work they can run into the criminal element any hour of the day. They need those weapons for their own protection."

"And what is it that would prevent a criminal from assaulting an unarmed civilian like you or me — 'any hour of the day'?"

"That's crazy. If you own a gun it's more likely to be taken away and used against you. You're more likely to shoot yourself or a member of your family than ever use it to drive off a criminal."

"That's not true. Statistics gathered painstakingly, county by county, over the entire country for years, by respected university scientists and researchers like Gary Kleck and John Lott, show a woman who offers no resistance to a would-be attacker is far *more* likely to be seriously injured, than if she resists with a gun. Guns are taken away and used by attackers less than one percent of the time — and, in fact, the biggest victim of that particularly rare scenario turns out to be police officers."

"I don't believe that."

"Will you buy the books and read them if I write down the names?"

But you are unlikely to either understand or pursue such

lines of argument — against a greased-up and mighty slippery foe — unless the government is threatening to lock *you* up for possessing tomorrow what was a perfectly legal collector's firearm yesterday or last year or way back in 1933.

To the other side, it's not personal. They gradually erode our rights, simpering that it's "only a safety measure to protect the children" or "only designed to get the kind of guns most likely to be used in crimes, not legitimate sporting arms." They count on us to whine a little but finally shrug and adapt ourselves to this year's new and slightly more burdensome rules. Then they're back again next year with more, still purring, "How can you object to just one or two more *modest reasonable* gun controls if it'll save the life of just a single child? ..."

They just want the police to have the power to make everyone wear their seatbelts and change their underwear every day. They wonder why we take it so personally. And the bearded TV psychiatrists blame "the impact of right-wing talk radio and a shortage of funds for state mental-health outreach workers" when "some nut" finally flies off the handle and shoots the two city enforcement officers who come on his property without permission. Nary a word ever heard about how, maybe, "There's too much damned government. They just kept pushing him. The last time he went into town to buy ammo they asked to see his photo ID. They told him no one could have a 'legitimate need' for as much as he was trying to buy." That "neighbor interview" is quietly left on the cutting room floor. Too weird. "Not what we were looking for."

In ancient Rome, a man wearing a sword was a free man. Slaves could be recognized because they were not allowed to carry arms. Up into recent times, Swiss citizens still carried a symbolic sword with them to town meetings, symbols of their right to vote. Today, Swiss heads of household are expected to keep a loaded fully automatic assault rifle in their closets in case of invasion. Citizens of the wise and benevolent state of Vermont can carry concealed weapons without any kind of government permit. The gun control schemers would have us believe such a universal presence of "dangerous" modern arms would inevitably create societies where entire families get wiped out in a spray of machine gun fire after every fender-bending traffic accident. Yet Switzerland and Vermont are societies almost uniquely liberty-loving and crime-free.

"That's because Vermont and Switzerland are ethnically homogeneous," comes the reply.

"Are you saying blacks and Hispanics are inherently less able to be trusted with the rights of adults ... or are you instead saying we have to go back to racial segregation if we want to keep any of our other rights?"

At that point, they call us crazy and change the subject. Every time. I've never yet run into one of the "ethnically homogeneous" gang who would answer the damned question.

🌿 🌿 🌿

Free men own guns and gold. Most governments hate men who own guns and gold, especially if they sever the ties that leave most "corporate citizens" locked to a single location by a mortgaged house (loan and bank account at a government-inspected bank) and a regular paycheck (taxes withheld, and the IRS conveniently informed of "tax liability" via those familiar "employer's snitch forms," the W-2 and the 1099).

Why did the government hate the "wild Indians" ... chasing them down and massacring them even when they rode hundreds of miles from any white settlement and minded their own business up Montana way? Why have governments always loved farmers and demonized wandering hunter-gatherers?

Because the tax man always knows where to find the farmer at harvest time. But how do you audit and license and tax a wandering hunter? Where do you find him? How do you convince him that he owes you anything for "services provided"? Most of all, how do you hold down and shear the coat off a lamb who meets you with a large-caliber rifle in his hands ... one he's obviously adept with and accustomed to using?

"How could you love a gun — a sick surrogate for psychiatrically disturbed males ashamed that their penises are too small, a monstrous creation good for nothing but killing?" comes the question — usually purely rhetorical, from historically ignorant womenfolk in peasant skirts and Birkenstocks who really don't want an answer.

But, just this once, let's answer the question as though it's sincere.

Where are the surviving paleolithic tribesmen who never developed specialized flint-knappers, able to flake scores of lightweight and deadly sharp blades from a single chunk of stone?

They're all dead, all the works of their lives lost — their womenfolk raped and carried off into captivity. Did any of the victors' slave women — more "enlightened" and "sensitive" than their sisters — urge their now-dead husbands "not to make the deadly new Clovis points; they're good for nothing but killing"?

Where are the surviving neolithic tribesmen who never learned to use bronze or iron for making chariots and weaponry? A few may survive in the most remote mountains, chewing raw monkey meat as they squat in their loincloths, hoping the strange men with the smoking weapons won't find them today — about as viable a population as you might find in some fenced wild animal park. But the great empires of neolithic Mesoamerica — the Aztec and the Incas — collapsed within months of encountering small bands of Spaniards armed with primitive muzzle-loading muskets. Their temples were torn down to build modern Mexico City, their womenfolk raped and turned into slaves.

Between 1859 and 1895, the Japanese people — forbidden the use of firearms for two centuries — were able to respond to the arrival of Commodore Perry by manufacturing modern arms in a crash program to turn themselves into a modern power. Why couldn't the Indians of the Americas do that? Because they had no manufacturing or economic infrastructure that could even *envision* how to manufacture a gun. And so their works are lost to history, and their descendants, to this day, live in enervating superstition and grinding poverty. Because they lacked weapons that "are only meant to kill," they are — for all practical purposes — culturally dead.

What are these "guns"? Simply put, the soldier's weapon is the measure of his culture's technological ability. Shortly after the American Civil War, the huge Austro-Hungarian empire fielded a massively larger army to crush the upstart Prussians in the little-remembered Austro-Prussian War. The Austrian army reflected many of the problems of its cobbled-together empire — different units spoke different languages; often they couldn't even understand their own officers.

But the most concrete reflection of Hohenzollern conservatism was the insistence of the Austro-Hungarian ordnance department that their units would stick with the tried-and-true muzzle-loaders, since the new bolt-action repeaters only "encouraged the waste of ammunition."

Thus, the Austrians entered the war still trained in the tactics of Napoleonic battle: The line of infantry would fire, tediously reload their muzzle-loaders while receiving the enemy's poorly-aimed volley, fire once or twice more, then fix bayonets and advance at a measured pace to end the battle with cold steel. Superior numbers would win the day, as they always had.

They tried this against the numerically weaker Prussians, who were armed with the new bolt-action Dreyse needle-gun (so named because its fragile firing pin, shaped like a needle, had to penetrate the rifle's paper cartridge to reach the primer that ignited the whole works). The Austrians marched up the hill with bayonets fixed, hoping to take advantage of the lull as the Prussians stood upright and tediously reloaded.

Instead, the Prussians continued their aimed fire as fast as they could work their turnbolts. By the time the remnants of the Austrian army dragged themselves back to Vienna, their bodies lay so thick that no one ever bothered to sort them out and bury them. Nature took its course, and the site of the battle (in the modern Czech Republic) is known to this day as the "Forest of Skulls."

Were the Austrian and Italian and Serbian widows and orphans happy that their emperor had declined to buy the new breechloading rifles, since they were "good for nothing but killing"?

Do you think, if your life depended on it, you could design, and instruct a metal shop how to manufacture, a modern battle rifle? This instrument must sustain chamber pressures of thousands of pounds per square inch when each cartridge routinely detonates. Its finely engineered barrel must eject a lead-and-copper projectile at a speed of thousands of feet per second, with accuracy adequate that even a poorly trained peasant can place five rounds in a four-inch circle at a hundred yards. (A somewhat better-trained recruit should be able to keep all his rounds in an eight-inch circle at 300 yards — a skilled sniper using a telescopic site will perform the same feat at 600... farther away than most of us can even spot a person dressed in gray or khaki).

The rifle must maintain this performance not merely for as long as it takes to fire 10 or 20 rounds, but for tens of thousands of rounds. It must be sturdy enough that the infantryman — who *will* run out of ammunition — can finally kill his enemy with a bayonet stuck on the muzzle end of his rifle or beat him to death with the wooden buttstock — and then the rifle must still fire again as soon as it's reloaded ... first time, every time.

Think you've got it? Did I mention your weapon should weigh in at *less than 12 pounds*, since an infantryman must carry it along with a 50-pound backpack and 100 rounds of ammunition every day for months? Oh, and your design must be simple enough that it can be mass produced — thousands of copies per day — in some quickly converted third-world typewriter factory.

Think you've got it? Whoops. Did I mention that turnbolt rifles were outdated by the 1940s? Now — staying within our limits of weight and reliability — you must add a gas-diversion system that automatically ejects the spent brass case, strips a new cartridge off the magazine, runs it into the chamber, and locks the bolt behind it ... reliably reloading the weapon in the blink of an eye so all the soldier has to do to fire his next round is pull the trigger a second and then a third time, as fast as he can?

Ready? OK. We hand your rifle to a green recruit, who sleeps on the deck of a transport ship, exposing his new rifle to corrosive salt spray during his week-long transit to the combat zone. The young kid has never been to sea before, so on at least one occasion he vomits his churning stomach acids directly onto his rifle.

Arriving "over there," he finds no immediate combat, but only weeks of marching through rain and mud to get to the front. He tries to keep the mud out of the muzzle and the action of his new rifle, but the lad is, after all, sleeping on the ground, and using your weapon as his walking staff when he has to climb muddy hillsides. He finally arrives within the sound of shellfire in November, goes to sleep on the ground beneath his rude poncho, and wakes up to find it has snowed during the night, and a freezing rain has frozen his muddy rifle closed. Suddenly, the sergeant yells that combat is imminent. Line up! Load your rifles!

The young soldier has one and only one way to thaw his frozen mud-caked rifle so that he can load it — the most important action he has ever carried out in his young life, an action on which his life now literally depends. He urinates directly into the action of his rifle, snaps back the bolt, and shoves in a clip of live ammunition. Here comes the enemy over the hill. No time for a test shot, he raises his rifle to his shoulder, praying as he has never prayed before that the mud has not jammed the weapon so badly that it will explode in his hands, and pulls the trigger ...

In the early 1940s, young American soldiers faced such situations literally tens of thousands of times. The rifle they raised to their shoulders was the Springfield Armory M-1 Garand, holding eight rounds of caliber 30.06. Tens of thousands of times, an amazing thing happened. The rifle worked flawlessly, drilling enemies with the bullet of the most powerful standard shoulder-rifle cartridge then in use — the most powerful *ever* used — at ranges out to 800 yards. No less an historic personage than George S. Patton called John Garand's rifle "the weapon that won the war." You can buy a beat-up Garand today for $500 and a beautifully tuned and refinished "target" version for perhaps $1,200. I own several and enjoy building them — and their box-magazine successor, the M-14 — from parts.

Of course, American civilians must pay $4,000 (the weapons are rare, due to effective bans on manufacture and re-importation), get fingerprinted, and add on a $200 federal transfer tax to buy the M-14 our fathers carried in Korea, since that rifle has the dreaded capability to fire as many as 20 rounds with one pull of the trigger. But the Garand is "OK" for us peasants to own in the land of the Second Amendment, since it's considered a mere "historic curio and relic." The U.S. government will even sell you one at "cost" — about $500, meaning they've got the most expensive warehouse and shipping system ever known to man — if you qualify by shooting in an appropriate target match (organized by the National Rifle Association, the gun-control organization that has a government-issued monopoly over such events).

The Garand is a triumph of our culture, our technology, and our economy. So is John M. Browning's 1918 Automatic Rifle — which will cost you $10,000 (they've cut off the supply and won't allow new manufacture for "civilian use") and is again heavily regulated for "civilian ownership" by a federal government that has chosen, this time, our Second Amendment rights to urinate on. If you cannot understand why I love to hold in my hands these pieces of our nation's history, these triumphs of human engineering used in the righteous liberation of half the world from fascist tyranny — most of them actual survivors of overseas combat — then I can only assume you would value an original copy of the Declaration of Independence in Jefferson's handwriting at the same price as a bundle of fireplace kindling or a roll of toilet paper.

The Japanese speak of "the sword that takes life," and "the sword that gives life" — the latter wielded by a righteous man to preserve his family and his clan from hostile invaders. The charlatans who would disarm us are now busily rewriting history to argue that firearms really played little if any role in making us what we are, as a nation, a people, or even a species. In fact, there is some good evidence that we developed into a species with the kind of eye-hand coordination we display — and the related higher brain functions we've developed — precisely *because* these have survival value for subgroups able to develop and use superior projectile weapons ... spears, bows, and finally firearms.

A society in which only government police and soldiers are armed is, by definition, "a police state." In such cultures, young girls are routinely raped by police officers if found on the streets alone. You just have to get used to that. On the other hand, the path to *society-wide* disarmament is the path of cultural suicide. That's why, when out-of-town visitors used to ask us out to dinner (allowing *me* to pay, in many cases) and ask what we did in the evenings in Las Vegas, Jeanne used to delight in smiling her most innocent smile and replying, "At night, we clean the guns."

Where's All This Leading?

Within the next 15 years, the dumbed-down softened-up sociology experiment that the Clintonistas and their Politically Correct friends made of the once-proud U.S. military during the decade of the 1990s will fail, somewhere, catastrophically.

The best combat troops — and the best junior officers — are fleeing this new co-ed day-care Army (especially the Army) in droves. Our men used to have an esprit de corps, built on the shared survival of some mighty tough training. Now, the guys whom David Hackworth rightly calls the "perfumed princes" are proposing to give the Ranger's black beret to anyone who joins up — no survival course to "earn" this badge of honor will any longer be required.

What's going to happen when an "army" made up of today's American youth — the ones who are being taught that "guns are yucky; guns never solve anything" and are being sent home for psychological counseling if they so much as bring a squirt gun to school ... or merely point their fingers at one another and say "Bang!" — finally have to face real concerted hostile fire?

What I am predicting is not merely defeat, but something worse. Somewhere, an enemy will be smart enough to announce to our troops that there's no need to keep living in a muddy trench and taking orders from that mean old sergeant; if they'll just lay down their arms and come across the lines, they'll be given a "do-over." They'll be given hot soup and hot showers and clean sheets and a color TV and Nintendo and sent home once the attention of the American public flags and a new administration moves on to some other easier-to-solve "foreign crisis," probably in a week or two.

And these American troops will obligingly lay down their arms.

No, the result will not be a Red Chinese occupation of

Kansas City. This will happen on some distant battlefield where it can be fairly easily covered up. Like the Romans, we fight our wars far from home ... now. But the corporate and mercantile forces that depend on America's military might will get the lesson immediately. The answer will be to do the same thing the Romans did in the second century A.D. — the same thing that resulted in the fact that so many of the "British" soldiers fighting against American independence on this continent in the 1770s actually spoke German:

The United States will begin to hire an imported mercenary army, from countries where it's still considered proper and manly to learn how to hunt, and to shoot, and to kill.

Our boys fared pretty well in World War One, not only because the average farm-raised doughboy knew how to shoot *before* he joined the Army (though that was important), but also because he was armed with weapons like the Colt .45 and the Browning Automatic Rifle, dreamed up by a Mormon tinkerer named John Moses Browning, working at his *civilian* workbench in Utah — all perfectly legal — without any government license or permit.

Today, that would be a federal felony — assuming the "perpetrator" didn't "commit suicide" during the initial ATF raid. So the next generation of infantry weapons will not be developed by home-workbench tinkerers in gun-hating America or Canada or Great Britain or Australia. Instead, those weapons will be developed by the Bad Guys.

Bad guys living in the same countries from which we will soon begin to hire foreigners to fight our wars for us, promising them their coveted U.S. citizenship in exchange for four or six or eight years of faithful service. (The Romans required 20 to 30.)

Within 100 years, our "presidents" will be chosen by the members of the "foreign legions" headquartered closest to the nation's capital. If you doubt this is what happens when a nation's citizens grow too soft to fight their own battles — to carry their own weapons on their own streets every day — you can read all about it in Gibbon's *Decline and Fall of the Roman Empire.*

The Founding Fathers had read that book. Knowledge of the history of the corruption and decadence and collapse of that great civilization is one of the main reasons they sternly warned that America should always have an armed citizenry and never a professional standing army — why they stipulated, "The right of the people to keep and bear arms shall not be infringed."

But that was a long time ago. They're all dead now. Thank goodness, now we have really smart fellows like Assistant U.S. Attorney William B. Mateja to tell us that's not really what was meant by the Second Amendment, at all.

If you had any doubts about our current ruling-class's attitude toward the Second Amendment — an integral part of the Constitution they swear an oath before God to protect and defend — and about their attitude toward the armed citizenry it guarantees us, listen again to William B. Mateja's June 2001 discourse (he was officially speaking for you, remember — he's the assistant attorney for The People) with the judges of the Fifth U.S. Circuit Court in the appeals hearing of *Emerson vs. United States.*

Judge William L. Garwood asked the government: "You are saying that the Second Amendment is consistent with a position that you can take guns away from the public? You can restrict ownership of rifles, pistols, and shotguns from all people? Is that the position of the United States?"

Assistant U.S. Attorney William B. Mateja replied: "Yes."

Judge Garwood: "Is it the position of the United States that persons who are not in the National Guard are afforded no protections under the Second Amendment?"

Assistant U.S. Attorney Mateja: "Exactly."

Asked by Judge Garwood whether membership in the National Guard would qualify an American citizen to possess firearms, Mateja answered no, "The weapon in question must be used in the National Guard."

"That Scared the Crap Out of Me, That Someone Could Have a Gun in the Store"

On Monday, May 22, 2000, Sandra Suter was standing in the check-out line of the Wal-Mart in Spring Hill, Fla., when she saw several store employees wrestling with a knife-wielding man.

The employees had apprehended 50-year-old Willie J. Redding of Brookville — reported by the *St. Petersburg Times* to have previous convictions for selling drugs and dealing in stolen property — attempting to steal a VCR.

Dropping his loot, Redding pulled a small blade and lunged, cutting two employees, according to a Hernando County sheriff's report.

"Drop the knife! Drop the knife!" one of the bleeding employees was yelling.

Mrs. Suter, a 53-year-old grandmother, reacted as she had been trained.

"I have a concealed-weapons permit," she announced as she walked up to the armed assailant and presented the .40-caliber pistol she keeps in her purse. "Either drop the knife or I'll shoot you."

Getting smart in a hurry, Mr. Redding surrendered, was jailed, and gained release the next day on $3,000 bond.

"I just did what I thought was right," Grandma Suter told Jamie Malernee of the *St. Petersburg Times*. "It was the first time I've ever had to pull my gun other than at the firing range."

Suter's husband and grown children are calling the five-foot-three homemaker "a hero," reporter Malernee admits.

But then the *Times* story goes on:

"Spokesmen for the Hernando County Sheriff's Office and Wal-Mart advise civilians not to get involved in such situations. 'We want to keep our stores a pleasant place to shop, so we would never encourage our customers to arm themselves,' said Wal-Mart spokesman Tom Williams. ...

"Shopper Lorinda Smith, who was in the candy aisle during the confrontation, said Tuesday that she was more frightened by Suter's gun than the man's knife.

"'That scared the c— out of me, that someone could have a gun in the store," said Smith of Hernando Beach. 'This one lady was in there with her children and when she saw [the gun] she was like, 'Get on the ground! Get on the ground!' If I was there with my kids, I would have had a heart attack.'"

Frightened at the sight of a responsible fellow citizen — a five-foot-three grandmother — using a legally licensed handgun to stop a crime without even firing a shot.

Think about that. Would the ladies have been frightened if uniformed policemen had shown up and brandished guns in the process of arresting three-time loser Willie Redding? Of course not — even though, statistically, police officers accidentally shoot the wrong person in far more cases than do citizens with legally issued concealed-carry permits.

"NRA officials did not return phone calls," reporter Malernee continues. "Kim Mariani, spokeswoman for Handgun Control Inc., said Suter's actions, while brave, could have hurt someone.

"'God forbid something went wrong,' Mariani said. 'It just escalates the situation, and a lot of times it's unnecessary.'"

Reporter Jamie Malernee has clearly done what she thought was her job, calling all parties who might be expected to comment on the incident. (We'll leave aside for the moment the fact that the NRA, which endorsed the gun control bills of 1934 and 1968 *and* the Brady Bill, actually comprises a larger gun control advocacy group than Handgun Control — that placing a call to Gun Owners of America or JPFO might have been more appropriate in any search for "balance.")

But clearly, the formulaic structure of this story — even though it's admirably complete — seeks to "balance" any implication that the carrying and use of firearms by law-abiding citizens is natural or proper.

I believe something important is going on, here.

❧ ❧ ❧

When prominent daily newspapers can get away with lecturing us that firearms properly used by law-abiding citizens to stop crimes and prevent injuries are "more frightening than a criminal's knife," when more than 3,000 Americans can die in flames on Sept. 11, 2001, because the law-abiding civilian passengers of four hijacked airliners had been disarmed by their government and willfully deprived of their God-given constitutionally guaranteed right to self defense ... and the government's answer is not to give up its victim disarmament campaign, but instead to hire *more* clueless drones to search the citizens and take away our cuticle scissors and our nail clippers ... we have lost.

In the battle between freedom and bondage, the forces of freedom have lost. A century of wall-to-wall collectivist propaganda in the government youth camps has finally done its job.

In the past, for a hundred thousand years and into the beginning of this century, it was well understood that the education of boys past the age of 12 was best undertaken by older men, who would take the lads out into the woods and fields and teach them the courage, the cooperation, the concentration, and the skills necessary to become hunters, warriors, craftsmen, artisans, and fathers.

It is no coincidence that today most of our high school valedictorians are little girls. I bear no grudge against the ladies gaining access to college and career, but what has happened in recent decades is that our mommified socialist welfare camps now treat male adolescence as a de facto disease, dosing up nearly half of those suffering this newly diagnosed "testosterone poisoning" (yes, statistics show those who score highest on "masculinity" scales receive the lowest grades) with various mind-numbing nostrums, from Ritalin to Luvox to Prozac, primarily to get them to sit still and stop causing trouble, though each of these is acknowledged by its manufacturer to cause dementia, mania, and hallucinated voices in a statistically significant percentage of users.

Add this to the new presumption that an arrest for "child abuse" is appropriate for any father who keeps guns in the home; pulls his kids out of school for hunting trips; physically disciplines his kids; or uses psychoactive drugs in his religious observances (yes, even Indians). Then, when a small percentage of these effectively fatherless government-manufactured young morons and maniacs finally respond by shooting up those responsible for their chemical castration, the circle is closed when the Katie Couric Lapdog Press blames ... who?

The school nurse with her experimental chemical sedatives? No, no, no. We blame the evil spirits supposedly resident in those symbols of male independence, power, and freedom, the dark power of that inanimate but totemic object of wood and steel ... the gun!

What is our understanding of the difference between freedom and bondage, and what do we imagine are the prevailing conditions that bring large numbers of people into either state?

The Founding Fathers of this nation, as I've mentioned, made a close study of the Roman republic, and the way that government degenerated into despicable tyranny. They attempted to craft for us a system that would prevent the concentration of powers into a central government — a "new caesar" — warning us that it was vital that the military power be retained in the hands of a citizen militia, rather than in any mercenary "special militia" or standing legion owing personal loyalty to their general or the current caesar — like today's BATF, FBI, or National Guard.

By the time Rome fell, tax rates were so high that farmers were literally selling their daughters into prostitution to meet the onerous levies that supported the decadent court. In the provinces, the 5th century's torrent of Huns and Visigoths were probably widely greeted in much the same way the Ukraine initially welcome Hitler's troops as liberators in 1941, figuring nothing could be worse than Joe Stalin.

Then descended upon the Western world the appropriately named Dark Ages, with their stultifying codes of political and religious orthodoxy, enforced by the inquisitor and the stake.

Freedom of religion or the press? Even minor variance from the one accepted faith would get you burned after your tongue was torn out, and peasant literacy was itself grounds for suspicion of sorcery — priests graciously provided by the landed class would read you anything you needed to know out of the Bible.

Property rights? The medieval serf worked his master's land and lived in his master's cottage entirely at the baron's whim. The master of the castle could even descend and impregnate the peasant's wife on the peasant's wedding day, if the urge struck m'lord.

Why? Why?

Because for a thousand years, no village of peasants with their scythes and pitchforks could stand up to a mere handful of the helicopter gunships of that time, the mounted knight in his coat of mail.

Only the landed gentry could afford a warhorse and a suit of armor. Let even three or four of these medieval equivalents of the Abrams tank enter your village and the peasant's only hope was to drop to one knee and plead for his life. Take the cattle, take our daughters, use them as you will ...

Why did this ever change? Do you think it's because the

guys in charge just got tired of having it all their way?

Of course not. This changed in the mid-1400s, at Crecy and Agincourt, when mere English commoners found they could destroy the cream of the French aristocracy — drowning thousands of armored noble knights in the mud beneath their own toppled horses — by dint of one simple technological advance: the Welsh longbow, an inexpensive weapon best deployed by large gangs of anonymous peasants.

The French considered this so barbarous they threatened to cut off the index and middle fingers of any English archers they caught, rendering them incapable of using their dreaded bows. The Brits responded by defiantly waving these two fingers in the air — or sometimes just one of them.

Far from banning them from bearing arms, by the 16th century English law actually *required* commoners to practice their archery at least one weekend per month, to remain ready should the king need them. Suddenly — coincidentally? — the "rights of Englishmen" began to be interpreted to mean the rights of commoners under the law, not just the rights of nobles, as envisioned in the Magna Carta of 1215.

This new state of affairs reflected the new reality of the field of battle, where commoners could and did dictate terms to defeated monarchs — even going so far as to behead the King of England in 1649.

Can you imagine that? They cut off his head.

❦ ❦ ❦

Of course, some lessons take a little time to sink in. Marching south from Lake Champlain to the Hudson in the early autumn of 1777, Gentleman Johnny Burgoyne sent out mercenary Hessian scouting parties to demand fodder for his horses from the local peasantry.

The New York farmers watched the brilliantly uniformed Hessians walk into their farmyards demanding free food for the general's army ... and shot them dead, sometimes wiping out entire detachments to a man.

This was unheard of in continental Europe, where peasants were still expected to know their place.

But things only got worse for Burgoyne's army, its morale sapped by the heat, the humidity, the sudden storms, the bugs and venomous snakes of what Americans now consider the "resort district" of Glens Falls and Lake George. (Thank goodness these wimps didn't find themselves in North Florida — the Yankees would probably have ended up owning Devon, Somerset, and half of Wales.)

As the exhausted army and its overladen baggage wagons emerged from the woods and climbed toward the open lands around Saratoga, a few isolated bands of Yankee farmers in homespun took up position behind the trees, and began *"firing on the officers' persons."*

I have always loved that quotation from Johnny Burgoyne's journal. The words so succinctly capture the outrage and incredulity of a dying class. British officers knew they ran the risk of being struck, along with their men, by unaimed volley fire. But to have enemy peasants — commoners — purposely take aim at an officer's person, using a Pennsylvania or Kentucky rifle that by an outlandish historical accident proved to be more accurate than the standard-issue British Brown Bess musket ... well, it was unthinkable.

Students of American history know it was the leadership of Gen. Benedict Arnold of Connecticut — rising again and again despite his wounds to lead from the front as his horse was shot from under him — that turned the tide of battle at Saratoga, the turning point of the Revolutionary War, the battle that brought in France as America's ally and thus sealed Cornwallis' eventual fate.

But few recall the first question that occurred to both King Louis and King George when news of Burgoyne's surrender in October of '77 reached the European courts:

Who in hell had Burgoyne surrendered *to*? Washington and the entire Continental Army — excepting the aforementioned Gen. Arnold and a handful of other officers in fancy coats — were in Philadelphia, withdrawing before the successful (but finally meaningless) siege of Gen. Howe.

The answer — inconceivable to the kind of European mind that ordered the band to play "The World Turned Upside Down" at Yorktown in 1781 — was that Gentleman Johnny Burgoyne had surrendered an entire British army to the American militia, to nothing but a gang of New York and New England *farmers*.

Is there a "control sample" that tends to confirm my thesis for why commoners in America (and, to a lesser extent and until recently, places like Australia and Western Europe) managed to throw off the chains of feudal tyranny and become far more "free" in the centuries after 1500 — with all the advantages of economic, scientific, and technological progress with which we're so familiar ... even if we've forgotten how they were won?

Yes, I think so. After toying with imported European firearms in the late 1500s, the shoguns of Japan banned the instruments entirely. In fact, under the decree of the shogun Toyotomi Hideyoshi (1536-1598), issued on the 8th day of the seventh month, Tensho 16, "The people of the various provinces are strictly forbidden to have in their possession any swords, short swords, bows, spears, firearms, or other types of arms. The possession of unnecessary implements makes difficult the collection of taxes and dues, and tends to foment uprisings."

So, artificially and in an almost ideally isolated experiment, while commoners gained increasing rights in direct proportion to their importance and strength on the battlefields of the rest of the world in the next 250 years, Japan remained (until Commodore Perry brought this experiment to a crashing close in 1853) one of the few places in the world where the peasant remained in absolute feudal subservience — their very lives forfeit at a whim — to the hereditary aristocracy, with their war-horses and their deadly steel and lacquered leather armor.

Even today, the Japanese are so far behind the curve that brought the Western world the Magna Carta and the Declaration of Independence and the Bill of Rights that the average Japanese "salaryman" happily tolerates annual unannounced "courtesy police inspections" of his home to make sure he's "protected" from the danger of owning self-defense weapons, and considers it perfectly routine and even desirable that suspects frequently "commit suicide" by "jumping" out of high windows while under police interrogation, thus sparing their families further embarrassment.

Commoners "presumed innocent till proven guilty"? Not in a land where the people have no guns.

🌿 🌿 🌿

We are gathered now to inquire: Is America about to enter a new era of freedom or a new era of bondage?

Using "well-regulated" as the 18th century synonym for "oiled up and ready to go," pose yourself this question of the day:

Suppose the president of the United States got fed up tomorrow with some band of recalcitrant rebels operating in your city. For our purposes (as well as for his), it doesn't matter whether he chooses to condemn these folks as drug dealers, home schoolers, child abusers, tax resisters, or obstreperous "gun nuts" who refuse to turn in their "murderous paramilitary" arms as ordered.

The president orders the National Guard and the FBI's thousand-strong black-shirted paramilitary "Hostage Elimination Team" into your city to clean out the pockets of "antisocial bandit resistance" under an emergency decree of martial law.

Quick: With the weapons you have on hand and the degree of organization currently maintained between yourself and your neighbors (envisioned by our Founding Fathers as members along with you of your local militia), is your ability and likelihood to resist this unconstitutional incursion on your liberties by a few thousand professional soldiers armed with tanks, helicopter gunships, and fully automatic M-16 rifles more closely akin to the condition of the citizen farmers who met General Burgoyne at Saratoga, armed with weapons *better than* the standard British Army-issue musket?

Or would your circumstance be more closely akin to that of those medieval peasants we were discussing, whose only chance of survival was found in laying down their scythes and pitchforks, dropping to their knees, and begging the king's soldiers for mercy?

Now: Given your answer, are the citizens and elected "people's representatives" of this nation today crying out that, in order to be prepared to defend their liberties as they are expected to under the Constitution, they need to enter on a crash course of manufacturing and acquiring — in civilian hands, without any government license, permit, tax, registration, or paperwork — rocket-propelled anti-tank grenades, shoulder-launched heat-seeking anti-aircraft missiles, heavy mortars, and fully automatic machine guns by the millions?

Or are Wal-Mart customers now reliably reported ululating that they are "more frightened by a fellow citizen's gun than a robber's knife," while Republican members of the NRA now running for the state Assembly in once-Libertarian Nevada ask me with sneering sarcasm, "Since you're obviously in favor of private ownership of machine guns, why don't you extend your argument to the constitutionally protected right to carry a rocket-propelled grenade launcher, or shoulder launched anti-aircraft missile?"

🌾 🌾 🌾

I do not sit down today to write a call to arms. I am 51 years old, and I believe I have learned a few things.

I do not see in 96 percent of the population of this nation today the slightest hint of the smoldering fire of liberty that burst forth to illuminate our ancestors' struggles in 1775 or 1861.

Yes, the final battle of a 70-year campaign is about to be joined. But I believe it is my duty to the truth to report that this battle is, for all practical purposes, already lost.

Once they have us thoroughly accustomed to being patted down and electronically wanded and the dirty laundry in our carry-on bags rooted and rummaged by minimum-wage trolls, all to prove we're unarmed (really, won't you please check; I *want* to prove I'm disarmed), once they're done registering all Americans' firearms — rendering them expensive and hard to acquire and embarrassing to carry, arresting those who refuse to store pistol and magazine and ammunition locked in separate safes in separate rooms until their worth to defend us against jackbooted SWAT teams busting down our doors in the middle of the night is reduced to nil — when they finally get around to sending out the notices (oh, whoops, they've already done so in England, in Australia, in Staten Island, and now in California) that we have to turn in the most "dangerous" ones, first the deadly semi-auto "assault rifles" with their flash hiders and bayonet lugs, then the "cheap Saturday Night Specials" that "can only be used for crime," then the "deadly and of no legitimate use" .50-calibers (which only became popular after they outlawed everything bigger) and then the dangerous long-range scoped "sniper" rifles ...

Yes, then I suspect a few pockets of resistance will flame up, too late, in the rural South and the inland West.

For a time, a few regional IRS and BATF offices will burn, and the Army and the other increasingly indistinguishable federal police forces will get a chance to practice the urban-deployment and cauterization tactics they've been busy practicing in Mogadishu and Sarajevo and Kabul ...

But I'm sorry, I don't think it's going to look very much like the Second (or is it now the Third?) American Revolution ... especially as covered by our current lapdog collectivist press.

Instead, I figure it's going to take the federals about as long to clean us out as it took the British Army to stamp out the last traces of Highland culture after the Battle of Culloden in 1746 — after which our descendants can look forward to a couple centuries of the same kind of "liberty" the old-time Scots could tell you about, banned from even wearing their tartans or speaking their native tongue or playing their favorite music in public.

If I am not an old man yet, I soon will be. I move more slowly now and sometimes my back hurts. Glory in war is a young man's dream. I harbor no illusions about the "romance" of scampering about in the hills, sleeping on rocks or snow, dodging the gunships for as many days or weeks as I'd be likely to last before I either surrendered to the first enemy smart enough to offer me a hot bowl of soup and a shower, or else managed to take a few with me in a glorious suicidal charge against some meaningless rural roadblock ... precisely the way the real-life Crocodile Dundee died, in 2000 — newly banned rifle in hand — in North Australia. (www.newsmax.com/articles?a=2000/6/26/12629).

But frankly, what I now pray daily is that I may find the courage to somehow contrive to lie among the fallen by the time our Great Disarmament — now underway since 1934 — is finally done.

Because after it's over, a kind of "peace" will indeed descend on this land ... broken only by occasional paroxysms of cryptic violence, unintelligible to the common class whose funerals will be dismissed as "light collateral damage," as the armies of the various warlords vie for control in Washington City.

(Fans of "democracy" needn't worry — I'm sure they'll

continue the tradition of requiring the unarmed peasants to vote every four years to confirm the legitimacy of whatever warlord is currently in power.)

Face it: A working plurality of households in this increasingly urbanized and socialist land are now run by fearful women who raise their children as lost fatherless souls, who depend on Big Brother to defend them and theirs from hideous, violent, useless, smelly men, and whose propagandized view of firearms is that they cause nothing but the tragic "drive-bys" that form the main grist of their nightly television news (check out the July 3, 1998 "Lithia" episode of the revived "Outer Limits" — with Julie Harris — where they try thawing out one of the last remaining men from suspended animation, find he only breeds conflict and competition among the surviving collectivist sisterhood, and finally decide to put him down like a dog who won't stop peeing the carpet).

Meantime, the majority of gun owners shrug and say, "I guess they know best," as the National Rifle Association systematically sells us down the river, telling us "sensible" gun regulation is OK (anything that's already been enacted being, by definition, "sensible") as long as they leave each of us one (registered) deer rifle, which we dare not display in public or even keep at home unless locked in a separate cabinet from its carefully rationed ammunition.

In this environment, what can the tiny percentage of Americans who will ever read and understand these words possibly do? Call your local TV station and ask to be allowed to present these facts and arguments on the air, calmly and at reasonable length? You will be told that "doesn't make very good TV, sweetie."

Until this fearful mommified welfare state is replaced by a restored nation of self-sufficient households led by men — note the word is not "persons," but "men" — willing to sling a loaded M-14 or M-1 Garand over their shoulder (engage the safety), stride down the busiest street in town, walk up to the first armed policeman they see, and fearlessly declare, "I am an armed citizen and member of the militia; I am teaching my sons to safely and effectively keep and bear arms; are you going to congratulate and thank me, or do we shoot it out right here?" we are well on our way to becoming a nation of armed overseers and peasant slaves.

All the beauty-pageant contestants are taught to wish for "world peace." But in fact, freedom and progress have ever developed only in lands of ongoing struggle — albeit shot and shell can usually be supplanted, between pirate suppression raids, by the "creative destruction" of healthy commerce and competition: war conducted by other means.

But that's not the kind of robust, chaotic, pluralistic "peace" the victim disarmament gang have in mind. No, their vision of a peaceful world has been common to Caesar, to Stalin, to Hitler and Mao: a world at peace ... because no peasant dares raise his head or rise from his knees as they pass.

We used to wish each other health and long life. Join with me instead, now, in wishing that we do not survive to see the culmination of this new *Pax Americana*.

I've already seen enough.

The Ballad of Carl Drega

VII
Are the Gun-Rights Lobbyists Being De-Clawed?

On Jan. 16, 1968, in an address to the New York State University law school in Buffalo, Sen. Robert Kennedy, D-N.Y., stated, "I think it is a terrible indictment of the National Rifle Association that they haven't supported any legislation to try and control the misuse of rifles and pistols in this country." NRA Executive Vice President Franklin L. Orth took great umbrage at this remark in the October issue of the NRA's magazine, *The American Rifleman*, terming Sen. Kennedy's accusation "a great smear of a great American organization." Mr. Orth then went on to point out, "The National Rifle Association has been in support of workable, enforceable gun control legislation since its very inception in 1871."

Really? But the NRA has always been portrayed in the mainstream press as a radical anti-gun-control organization. Is it? Has it ever been?

In that 1968 issue of *The American Rifleman*, associate editor Alan C. Webber picked up the defense of the NRA's gun-control credentials. I quote again from the NRA's own official organ:

"Item: The late Karl T. Frederick, an NRA president, served for years as special consultant with the Commissioners on Uniform State Laws to frame the Uniform Firearms Act of 1930. ... Salient provisions of the Act require a license to carry a pistol concealed on one's person or in a vehicle; require the purchaser of a pistol to give information about himself which is submitted by the seller to the local police authorities; specify a 48-hour time lapse between application for purchase and delivery."

Remember, I'm not asking whether you think these are good ideas (though they're certainly unconstitutional — "shall not be infringed" is pretty darned clear.) I'm asking whether the NRA is the wild-eyed, take-no-prisoners, "pure language of the Second Amendment, take my gun from my cold dead fingers" radical extremist outfit that the national press corps would have us believe. In fact, can the NRA rightly be said to be a "gun rights" organization at all?

"Item," editor Webber of *The American Rifleman* continued, back in 1968: "The NRA supported the National Firearms Act of 1934 which taxes and requires registration of such firearms as machine guns, sawed-off rifles and sawed-off shotguns. ...

"NRA currently backs several Senate and House bills which, through amendment, would put new teeth into the National and Federal Firearms Acts. The essential provisions which the NRA supports ... would ...

"4) regulate the movement of handguns in interstate and foreign commerce by a) requiring a sworn statement, containing certain factual information, from the purchaser to the seller ... b) providing for notification of local police of prospective sales; c) requiring an additional 7-day waiting period by the seller after receipt of acknowledgement of notification to local police," etc. etc.

Space doesn't allow me to do as detailed a vivisection of this outfit as novelist and competitive target shooter — and 22-year NRA life member — L. Neil Smith has done on pp. 210-225 of his book *Lever Action*, culminating in his classic essay, "Am I the NRA?" which concludes, "Worse than thieves, murderers, or cannibals, those who offer compromise slow you and sap your vitality while pretending to be your friends."

"The politicians *want* the NRA, they can cut their deals with the NRA," is the way gun-rights activist Dennis Fusaro explained it to me in a phone conversation from northern Virginia in late May 2001. "The NRA has supported gun control since 1871. They admit it; I've got the 1968 issue of *The Rifleman* where NRA Executive Vice President Frank Orth is quoted saying that. The organization has never been about 'rights.' They were started by a bunch of darned Yankee generals who were pissed off that the Johnny Rebs shot their pants off in the Big War. It was all about improving marksmanship among the recruits so the army of the centralized state could keep its hobnailed boot on the throat of the people."

Until March 16, 2001, Dennis Fusaro worked for the NRA's chief competitor in the field of Washington gun-rights lobbying, the 300,000-member Gun Owners of America, training local activists to lobby against further restrictions on the Second Amendment at the state level.

He appears to have done his job too well.

"The professionals at the NRA absolutely hate it when a bunch of people start coming to the legislature and telling the politicians what they want and don't want, because it just makes an awful mess — the politicians can't figure out who they can cut a deal with.

"Compromise is the way the politicians like to play the game; you get the lobbyists in a room and everybody shakes hands on a compromise and the lobbyists go home and tell the grassroots to vote for this guy because we can work with him. A few more rights get sold down the river and everybody goes home happy and gets re-elected. In Utah [M.D. and Utah Gun Owners Alliance lobbyist] Sarah Thompson had worked to get through a good bill that would have honored concealed-carry permits from any other state without restriction."

In the final days of the 2001 session, however, NRA lobbyist Brian Judy arrived in Salt Lake and made a deal to accept an amendment that the out-of-state permits would only be honored for 60 days.

"They purposely kept Sarah out; he comes out like a knight on a white horse. Sarah had the senators pretty well under control and was pushing them with grassroots pressure, and then Brian Judy goes in the back room and accepts this bad amendment. So we left her high and dry. ..."

❦ ❦ ❦

GOA consultant Mike Rothfeld, who had worked with Fusaro since 1994 training the state-level activists and who announced he was parting company with GOA within hours of Fusaro's dismissal, confirms the tale:

"This year he cut Sarah off at the knees with a last-minute deal to undo a recognition bill she had drafted, caused to be introduced, and shepherded through the House. He blamed Sarah for making legislators 'angry.'

As opposed to the old NRA game of "Let's Make a Deal," the way Fusaro says he was training GOA's local activists to hold the feet of anti-Bill-of-Rights politicians to the fire "was to tell them, 'Do what you have to do, but you know where we stand. If you vote any way but for our gun rights, we will work against you in the next election; we will rate you with an "F"; we will run people against you; we will get all the gun owners to vote against you; we will defeat you.' Politicians respond to whoever makes their lives miserable; if they can count on your being their friend no matter what they do, they're going to start cozying up to Sarah Brady."

Fusaro says it was precisely his budding success with these tactics in 20-plus states — "a decentralized movement that couldn't be controlled; if the head went bad it couldn't poison the whole body ..." that finally led the GOA board of directors to attempt to pull in the reins on such effective lobbying, and — when that didn't work — to fire him.

"The local pols tell the lobbyists, 'Can't you control your people?' And what's more important to the [professional] lobbyists is to have these relationships with these politicians rather than saving your rights. And I said that, and for saying that I had to go."

"We're just as opposed to Project Exile as we've always been," responds GOA Executive Director Larry Pratt, Fusaro's former boss. "We're just as opposed to the instant background check as we've always been; it just isn't true that we're going to be any softer on these issues.

"There were some personality differences" that led to the removal of Fusaro and consultant Rothfeld, Pratt insists. "It's a shame" that Fusaro had "a personality difference with the chairman of the board," 73-year-old GOA founder and former California state Sen. H.L. "Bill" Richardson.

"If it had just been a personality difference that'd be great," Fusaro responds, "but if it was just a personality difference, why did [GOA] board members come out and say we can't lose the Republican majority in 2002; we have to get Bush re-elected? If that's our primary objective, then what can Bush and the Republicans in Congress do to us, or fail to do *for* us? Why should they feel obliged to do anything for gun owners?"

It's the larger NRA that cynics have long described as the "Gun Owners' Auxiliary to the Republican Party," of course, since the nation's largest gun-control organization will often award its "A" or "B" rating to GOP turncoats who have voted for half the gun-control laws to come down the pike, endorsing House incumbent Republicans over Libertarians or other third party candidates who vow to repeal every gun law on the books.

Why? Because the third-party candidate "can't win," of course, and the NRA lobbyist's real game is to "retain access" to the GOP incumbent after helping him win re-election. Why insist on the plain language of the Second Amendment ("shall not be infringed") if the end result is fewer cocktail-party invitations next year? That could make your organization appear "out of the mainstream."

"Richardson doesn't want GOA people criticizing the NRA," Fusaro explains. "Richardson yelled at me over the phone. He said they have wonderful relations with the NRA in California; we can't have this public disunity" among the supposed gun rights' groups. "Well, hell, let's look at California," which has some of the most onerous victim-disarmament laws in the country.

"They don't do anything in California; they've been going to hell for ten years. That's why I came to work for GOA a decade ago," Fusaro concludes, "because I wanted someone who'd let me fight.

"What Richardson wants most, in my opinion, is to be part of that 'respectable' conservative Republican establishment, and if that's what you want, then they own you. You have to show them you're willing to break up the country club, you're willing to be thrown into the briar patch."

I left messages for Bill Richardson both at his ranch and at the home office of Gun Owners of California over the weekend of June 1, 2001, hoping to get his response to these comments, and especially to ask him if it's true he has instructed GOA staffers to "go easy" on politicians like George W. Bush, who favor various "compromise" gun-control schemes, so long as they've "done some good for the pro-life [anti-abortion-rights] movement."

Mr. Richardson never returned my calls. His son-in-law, GOC executive director Sam Paredes, did leave a voicemail message on my work phone at 8 a.m. Monday morning June 4, informing me Mr. Richardson had asked him to field my questions. Five follow-up calls over the next three days — to Mr. Paredes' home as well as his office — failed to garner any further contact or response.

❧ ❧ ❧

"I think it's coming from Richardson," Dr. Sarah Thompson of GOA Utah agreed when I spoke to her in late May. "The NRA has never been pro-gun. They've always been interested in kind of being double agents, telling their supporters they're the strongest gun-rights group around, then going into the back rooms and cutting gun-control deals which make the NRA more powerful and allow then to go to their members and get more money. I think the NRA ultimately wants to move into taking over the gun-control bureaucracy in this country; they could become the Department of Gun Control or some such nonsense.

"The NRA's magazine *reads* like the NRA is a bunch of wild-eyed pro-gun extremists," Dr. Thompson continues. "One of their recent issues, for instance, ranted against registration — despite the fact that the NRA actually *supports* registration via NICS checks and permits." In fact, "The NRA helped write the National Firearms Act of 1934 and the Gun Control Act of 1968. They've been pushing Project Exile all these years; that's not what you do if you're a gun-rights organization. Here in Utah they backed our Olympic gun ban," restricting the right of Utah citizens to carry permitted weapons at Olympic venues while the winter Olympics are in town, so as not to offend the hoplophobic foreigners.

"We had a concealed-carry recognition bill that we were running and [that] was going to pass, and Brian Judy shows up in the closing days of the session and got it changed so that we'll honor concealed-carry permits from out of state for only sixty days.

"And mind you, the only reason Brian Judy came out here was to completely discredit our operation; there was no other reason for him to be out here. He hadn't been in the Legislature for the entire session, he had no bills running. So he shows up in the last few days, starts telling some incredibly outrageous lies about me, tells the senators if they want NRA support they can't talk to me anymore ... that I'm the reason we have gun control in Utah.

"It really had nothing to do with this bill," Dr. Thompson continues. "They don't like competition and they don't like losing control. And (Richardson son-in-law and GOA board member) Sam Paredes knew about this. Brian was in contact with Sam all of this time. Brian was calling Sam and telling him these ridiculous lies about me and Sam was calling Dennis and telling him he had to shut me down."

(Dennis Fusaro confirms receiving those calls.)

"I think we were doing some good and being effective and getting people's attention and that really was not OK with the NRA. But I have to be very clear when I'm talking to people that it's not the NRA members that I have a problem with — if you explain to them what's going on they see it and they get upset. It's the NRA leadership that's perpetrating this stuff, it's not the poor guys that send in thirty-five bucks a year."

Dr. Thompson goes on to explain how the NRA will sometimes challenge conservative Republicans like U.S. Sen. Orrin Hatch and Gov. Mike Leavitt on their miserable gun-rights records during the primary season, "but then when it comes to the general they fall very silent. We had two wonderful solid pro-gun conservative people running ... and the NRA insisted on backing Hatch and Leavitt. It's about winning, going back to your members and saying eighty percent of the people who won had NRA endorsements; never mind if they're anti-gun. ..."

"In the 2000 Legislature the NRA backed a midnight gun-control bill that vastly expanded the list of people prohibited from owning guns in the state, a retroactive ban on people who were adjudicated years ago. As a result of this, I get calls from people who have been hunters for years who now have to go through a background check, who did something wrong thirty or forty years ago, and they've lost their gun rights. ... These are not felons, but new categories of people, somebody who got into some mischief as a juvenile and was adjudicated delinquent and given some counseling or some such thing. Now it's thirty years later and the NRA helps change the law and now they can't go hunting."

Fusaro says the compromises and sell-outs are continuing, week to week. "Call [GOA Oregon field rep] Kevin Starrett; he was tipped off to a meeting that's going down next Tuesday [June 12], that's being organized in Washington with [NRA lobbyist] Brian Judy, to decide whether to fight the anti-gun-show referendum there or to do a legislative compromise. And guess who's going to be representing GOA?"

Not hard-core gun-rights activist Starrett, whom Fusaro originally brought on board and eventually put in charge of all the Northwest states, but instead Richardson son-in-law and plays-well-with-others NRA collaborator Sam Paredes.

"Their attitude is, 'We're going to lose anyway.' Well, our position was, maybe they will win, but make them spend their money; don't give them anything for free. Don't let them save their money and use it for the next campaign somewhere else. Maybe we can't win in this generation, but if you make them spend their money, maybe eventually these millionaires who fund the gun-control movement will get tired and say, 'Gee, we really haven't gotten that much for our money.'"

Ohio is another state where the NRA showed its pro-gun-control instincts in 2001, Fusaro reports. Local Gun Owners of America activist Doug Joseph was backing the 'Vermont carry' bill sponsored by state legislator Tom Brinkman, who now fills the seat once occupied by the equally pro-gun-rights Ron Hood.

(Vermont is the one state in the union where law-abiding citizens — and even visitors — are allowed to carry concealed weapons without seeking any sort of state license or permit... helping to explain the state's unusually low crime rate. The Brinkman proposal would merely acknowledge that law-abiding Ohioans enjoy the same constitutional right.)

"The Brinkman bill has twenty-two co-sponsors and it was doing fine. Well, the NRA couldn't have that. So suddenly the NRA has their own bill that would require state permits to carry a concealed weapon, and that has forty-eight co-sponsors.

"Even [Ohio legislator] Ed Jerse, who's an anti-gunner, took one look at that and asked the NRA rep, 'Wait a minute. Isn't it your position that carrying a gun is a constitutional right? Isn't it less constitutional to require a permit?'

"These NRA types are always arguing from the wrong

premise. That may win you a few battles in the short term, but the inconsistency hurts you in the end."

🌿 🌿 🌿

The test case for whether GOA *or* the NRA remains a true "gun-rights organization" will be "what's going on with [President] Bush's proposal for Project Safe Neighborhoods, and GOA has been pretty much silent on this," Thompson warns. "GOA up till now has been a pretty vocal opponent of [the NRA's] Project Exile, and Bush's new plan is just a rehash of that with a few more objectionable things thrown in."

"I wrote to (GOA Executive Director) Larry Pratt last week asking, 'Why are you being silent on this?' What I got back was a press release. But press releases are for the most part ineffective. GOA's strength has always been in going straight to the grass roots, in educating and informing and inspiring the grass roots people to get involved, and they have not sent anything out telling those people, 'Wait a minute; this is a problem. Tell President Bush you object to Project Safe Neighborhoods.'

"I can only conclude from this that GOA is not going to challenge Project Safe Neighborhoods, which goes along with Richardson's idea that we have to keep Bush in office and we cannot challenge Republicans in power."

"This thing where GOA claims to be opposing Bush's version of Project Exile; all GOA did was a press release," Dennis Fusaro confirms. "That's why we did all the seminars around the country, explaining why just doing a press release doesn't do the job — they get thrown away. That's why we do faxes and e-mails to our people because it doesn't get filtered. You have to spell it out for them. 'Look: George W. Bush pushing bad thing; maybe George W. Bush bad.' But no, they're not going to do that, according to my last message from [the GOA board of directors in] California; we want Bush elected."

Project Safe Neighborhoods "is Bush's new anti-gun proposal," Thompson explains. "Let's enforce the existing laws, and the tagline on it is, 'If you use a gun illegally, you will do hard time.' The picture they're portraying is if you use a gun and rape and murder someone you'll do hard time, and no one including me has any objection to that.

"But you don't have prosecutors saying, 'We're not going to prosecute rapists because they're really good people.' That's not the problem. Those laws are already enforced. So the people they're really going after are people who are violating one of the twenty-thousand unconstitutional gun laws, people who put a flash suppressor on their rifle, or have a high capacity magazine on their firearm, or someone who drives by the school with a hunting rifle in the back of their truck; it's all the unconstitutional, politically correct, gun-control laws they're going to be enforcing. ... They're not concerned about violent crimes that don't involve guns. ...

(The irony here should be palpable, in an era when the peer-reviewed research of such noted scholars as John Lott of Yale and Gary Kleck of Florida has conclusively demonstrated that neighborhoods are safer — that violent crime actually goes down — precisely when *more* law-abiding citizens own guns.)

"And what they're also doing with this is taking another huge step toward federalizing all crime," Dr. Thompson says.

"As far as I know, Project Exile has always come from the NRA. So, is the NRA conspiring with Sarah Brady? The conspiracy that's really going on is that the media and thus the public are defining the argument as Handgun Control being for reasonable gun control and the NRA being far-right extremists, so anyone outside of those parameters is completely dismissed. So the choice that we're left with is either Sarah Brady gun control, or NRA gun control. So the argument that there should be no gun control, and that we should be repealing gun control laws already on the books, never makes it into the discussion at all. ...

"So it's very very discouraging and frightening to me that GOA is not speaking out against Project Safe Neighborhoods," Dr. Thompson concludes. "I'm told Brian Judy is now running GOA in this state as well as NRA. Larry [Pratt] tells me, 'Well, that's just the way it is. [GOA President Bill] Richardson thinks he's the greatest thing since sliced bread.'"

🌿 🌿 🌿

Back in 1999, before Texas Gov. George W. Bush had even formally announced his candidacy for the presidency, "We thumped him in a national e-mail alert over a bad gun-show bill he was supporting, one of these bills that would shut down the gun shows by requiring background checks and waiting periods," Fusaro recalls.

"The Bush people were trying to show Bush was willing to make some compromises on gun shows, so that wouldn't be a big issue in the upcoming election. I guess Larry tried to put an article about that in the [GOA] newsletter and Richardson put the kibosh on it. I know that one for a fact and I've heard there were other cases like that.

"So Richardson called up and they kicked him over to me. He was telling me, 'We shouldn't do anything to Bush because it'll upset our people, and Bush did some very good things for the pro-lifers in Texas, and he signed that concealed-carry bill.'"

I asked Fusaro if I'd heard him right about Bush getting a bye on gun issues from the GOA — where most staffers seem to be self-avowed Christians and abortion opponents — because he'd "done some very good things for the pro-lifers."

"Oh sure, that's no secret. Neal Knox [of the NRA] told me years ago they were going to use the gun issue to get conservatives and pro-lifers elected and have the Republicans elected."

Which may give us yet another explanation for why the

so-called "gun-rights" organizations will so frequently endorse a Republican conservative who's weak-kneed on gun issues, over a Libertarian or other third-party candidate even when that third-party candidate vows to repeal every gun law on the books.

"The Bush people kept trying to triangulate the gun issue so they could get our support, but not take too many hits from the other side because they could say they were for 'reasonable' gun control," Fusaro explains. "Well, it was my job to make sure they *didn't* do that. We wanted to shape his policy positions before he became a presidential candidate, and that was short-circuited. I was disappointed, but I followed orders. I didn't make a squawk about it. ... I said, 'Yes sir, yes sir, three bags full.'

"So Bush was never really pressured to firm up his gun-rights stance before he got the nomination, and Bush kind of set the tone for a lot of Republicans. Bush's position on gun shows then became like the George Allen position in Virginia, because there's some close ties between Bush and the Virginians. ... And pretty soon they were telling us that re-authorizing the assault-weapons ban really didn't matter, so we might as well keep it because it really wouldn't make any difference."

The key to determining whether either the NRA *or* GOA remains committed to gun rights in any meaningful way will be "the reauthorization of the assault-weapons ban in Congress in 2003 or 2004," in the opinion of Dudley Brown, executive director of the 7,000-strong Rocky Mountain Gun Owners.

"You see, the original Feinstein language had a sunset provision, so it would need to be re-authorized or it will expire. Clearly the left will try. So what the NRA and GOA do will tell us the direction of gun-rights lobbying from here on. If they just roll over and say it's no big deal, you can still buy your AR-15, even though you can't have a flash hider on it and you can't have a twenty-round magazine on it and there are all these other restrictions ... if they just try to let it pass quietly, what happens with this will set the tone for the next twenty years.

"George W. Bush has already said he favors re-authorization of the assault weapons ban," Brown warns. "In the past the GOA has been very effective fighting stuff like this at the grass roots; the press says it's the NRA drumming up all these phone calls, but we all know who's really been doing it; it's GOA."

But so far in America, gun control has always been a one-way street — once a victim-disarmament law is put in place, none of the "gun-rights" organizations ever seems willing to put its credibility on the line, fighting for a repeal.

"Remember from 1990 to 1994 when the Brady Bill was the litmus test?" Brown asks. "If you supported the Brady Bill you were anti-gun. And now the NRA backs it. Are the so-called pro-gun politicians trying to repeal the Brady Bill? Bring that up and you'll pretty well get laughed out of the room."

❧ ❧ ❧

Dennis Fusaro says he hopes to put on another lobbyist training seminar in New Hampshire, in cooperation with a couple of former board members of the fine gun-rights group Jews for the Preservation of Firearms Ownership. "I'm looking for an educational group to put on the seminars," he says. But failing that, "I'm now probably pretty much out of it, Vin."

Meantime, insiders tell me there may indeed be a drop in GOA lobbying at the state legislative level this election cycle, though they place the primary blame on a shortfall in fund-raising — one that's apparently affecting most conservative organizations since the Bush election.

When it comes to conservative causes, "People are figuring with George Bush elected we've all died and gone to heaven," sighs one frustrated inside-the-Beltway fundraiser.

VIII
In Which the Author Answers Further Queries on Firearms

Wars Aren't Fought With Guns Anymore
🌿

J.D., a sincere young fellow, wrote in:

"The Second Amendment is not a hot issue for me; I'm neither a gun owner nor a hunter (I've just never been able to look into the eyes of an animal and then shoot it!). But there are some things I really don't understand:

"The supporters of the right to keep and bear arms insist that guns are needed to protect us from the government. But — they've got rockets. They've got nukes. Wars aren't fought with guns anymore. Guns didn't help at Waco or Ruby Ridge (if anything they made the problem worse). Or am I missing something here?

"Also, it seems like there's a lot of *money* greasing the RKBA movement. I tend to suspect that it's not so much that the supporters want to see us armed to protect us from the government, foreign invaders, or whatever. I suspect it's because there's a lot of profit to be made in guns, especially in ammo. Ammunition is a marketer's dream; it's a consumable!

"Nobody ever talks about how much money is made in the gun and ammunition markets. But I really wonder, personally, how much the profit motive is behind a lot of the hysteria?

"And after all, there is something to be said for keeping automatic weapons out of the hands of some nut who is about to 'go postal.' I can even understand the hunters wanting to keep their rifles, but why on Earth does anyone need an automatic or semi-automatic weapon?

"All I ever see is rhetoric — you question the RKBA and

you're branded as a pinko commie nut. But it just seems to me that people are devoid of logic in discussing this issue. Perhaps you could give it a try?

"Thanks — J.D."

A common enough inquiry, concisely summarized.

I responded:

Hi, J. D. — I've heard this argument before. It still puzzles me why those who pose it fail to see its inherent contradiction.

First, you propose: "The supporters of the RKBA insist that guns are needed to protect us from the government. But — they've got rockets. They've got nukes. Wars aren't fought with guns anymore. Guns didn't help at Waco or Ruby Ridge (if anything they made the problem worse)."

Then, you conclude: "I can even understand the hunters wanting to keep their rifles, but why on Earth does anyone need an automatic or semi-automatic weapon?"

The problem here is a faulty premise. You offer that because the "government has rockets; they've got nukes," wars "aren't fought with guns anymore."

Try telling that to the Viet Cong, the Afghans, or the Chechens.

First the Japanese (1942-1945), then the French (1945-1954), and finally the Americans fought to suppress the independence fighters of Vietnam with the aid of state-of-the-art aircraft, artillery, offshore battleships, bombs, and any other manner of high-tech warmaking stuff you care to name.

The Viet Cong had none of these, except for some 30-year-out-of-date small artillery pieces that could be disassembled and carried by hand up muddy jungle paths, their components slung over bamboo poles.

Yet the Viet Cong won. Except for the internal Marxist oppression they've foolishly imposed on *themselves*, they're free today.

The Russians had state-of-the-art Hind helicopters, fuel-air explosives, tanks, artillery, land mines, poison gas, and any other mad devices of modern war you care to name, with which to suppress a bunch of rag-tag irregular Afghani tribesmen who enjoyed the benefit of *none* of this stuff.

Yet the Afghans won. They're free of foreign domination today (unless George W. Bush and Colin Powell think *we* can rule that country by proxy, which I wouldn't advise trying).

Why? In each case, those people won their freedom with one basic implement — the very instrument of which Dianne Feinstein and Charles Schumer would deprive *us*: the select-fire hand-held assault rifle. Generally, the AK-47 with its familiar curved "banana-clip" 30-round magazine, and its variants.

Illiterate Afghan goatherds and Vietnamese rice farmers go to sleep with one of these things nestled next to the bed. Yet if I'm caught with one, I — who in 51 years have never done physical harm to another person — face 10 years in the clink. Why?

(In fact, at times the V.C. were reduced to fighting with 1891-model bolt-action Czarist-surplus Moisin-Nagants, and the Afghans with 1903-era bolt-action British Enfield rifles. Even *then* they could not be defeated.)

But let's say you're correct and the restrictions already in place on what arms can be owned by private Americans make them a less and less credible deterrent to domestic government tyranny.

Here is the heart of the inconsistency in your argument. If that's the case, surely the answer is not to take further steps to "keep automatic weapons out of our hands," but rather to sweep away all 20,000 laws currently violating the Second Amendment, making it clear that private citizens by right can *and should be encouraged to* purchase machine guns, mortars, and shoulder-launched surface-to-air missiles over the counter at Home Depot, without being asked to show any damned permit, or even so much as sign their names.

Isn't it?

I submit that the Second Amendment *ought* to be a "hot issue" to you and to all other Americans — even those who choose to own no firearms.

Those who own no firearms are at the mercy of those who do. To assume the government will always use its armed force in a way benevolent to you is naive, at best.

You may say, "But they haven't come to shoot my dog and rape my sister *yet*." Well, of course. So long as even a sizable plurality of your fellow citizens retain the *means* to resist the usurpation of *our* liberties, more than you will ever know you rely on *their* vigilance to discourage potential tyrants from stealing away *your* liberties.

These individual armed freedom-lovers needn't go around shooting IRS men — and they don't. Just as the knowledge that our NATO troops were in place — ready to resist Soviet aggression — kept the European peace from 1948 to 1991, so does the mere threat of an armed populace help keep potential *domestic* tyrants in line ... as the framers of the Second Amendment so well understood.

But if these "night watchmen" were to fall asleep and allow their "deadly destructive devices" to be lifted from their motionless hands, we'd quickly see then how kindly the last remaining armed gang — the government gang — remained.

In their book *Lethal Laws*, Aaron Zelman and his associates at Jews for the Preservation of Firearms Ownership have exhaustively documented how the genocides of the Armenians in Turkey in 1915, of the Jews, Gypsies and Slavs under Hitler from 1942-45, of the Ukrainians and others under Stalin, and of millions more under Mao and Pol Pot, *all* were preceded (usually by only a few years) by "well-meaning" laws mandating civilian victim disarmament.

Contact the JPFO in Milwaukee at 414-769-0760, or 414-769-1491. Buy and read their moderately priced books. Someday, the lives of those you love may depend upon the knowledge contained therein. John Ross's docunovel *Unintended*

Consequences, from Accurate Press in Missouri, can also be an eye-opener.

I'm not a hunter, either. I once did look into the eyes of an animal I loved, and shoot it. A cat just can't understand why the pain won't go away, after it's had its back broken and dragged itself home a mile or more, in agony, in the hopes you can help.

If I ever have to kill an armed government thug to protect a member of my family, I hope I can find it in myself to wipe away such tears again. But they will be tears of regret at what soulless creatures the government eventually makes of its own minions, not of regret at having acted to save my bloodline and their liberties.

Guns did help at Waco and Ruby Ridge. The first attacking oppressors were killed — killings so well-justified that in both cases citizen juries acquitted on all charges having to do with the shooting deaths of the federal marshal and the ninja-suited ATF assailants.

We thus learned that these enemies of freedom are not invincible, and that killing them when they attack us isn't even against the law ... no matter what the snarling choleric federal prosecutors may contend. To say "guns didn't help" is like saying "guns didn't help" in the Warsaw ghetto uprising of 1943 "because the Jews lost anyway."

Really? They should have just boarded the last trains to the death camps in quiet resignation?

Instead, troops otherwise desperately needed on the Russian front were tied up for months. And — against all odds — a few Jews escaped and survived. But most of all, an example was set, that the Nazis *could* be resisted, even by common folk with no military training — even by a supposedly "subhuman species" armed with the kind of outdated odds and ends that today would likely be melted down for scrap.

My heart thrills to think of it. God bless such "hopeless" freedom fighters. If the government isn't afraid of "a couple hundred wacko black-helicopter conspiracy nuts running around in camouflage suits with their deer rifles," why is the FBI shifting literally thousands of agents to the task of infiltrating, setting up with agents provocateurs, framing and railroading into prison the leaders of every citizen militia they can find? What are the guys with "the bombs and the nukes" so afraid of, pray tell?

You say "guns only made things worse" at Waco and Ruby Ridge. I guess so. Christians in the lions' den "only made things worse" by refusing to bow to the Roman idols; European Jews by refusing to convert to Christianity. What are our rights and principles, anyway, that we should risk our lives in their hopeless defense?

Since the Nazis would sometimes kill 10 residents of a village in occupied France or Czechoslovakia in retaliation for the death of one occupier, it could be said that such resistance to Nazi occupation "only made things worse." So, would you advise those living under the heel of such a tyrant to just collaborate and make the best of it?

After all, if the Second Amendment is a "hot issue" only for gun owners, then surely only Jews, Mormons, and Peyotists need have any concern about the freedom of religion, only those who work for newspapers or TV stations have any reason to worry about maintaining the freedom of the press, and nobody but criminals and their lawyers have any interest in preserving all that rigamarole about "trial by jury." It's all pretty much "special-interest stuff" in the end, isn't it?

The final echoes of Waco and Ruby Ridge have not yet been heard. The British lived to regret the Boston Massacre; Santa Ana the Alamo. We'll see.

As for the profitability of the gun business, given the total uncertainty about which new regulations will crop up tomorrow, either because of congressional action or because the BATF, on a whim, simply "re-interprets" existing laws (often *retroactively*, jailing a few dozen more honest gun dealers for not properly filling out some totally unnecessary and unconstitutional form), I'd hardly advise it as a lucrative investment.

Did you know I could conceivably go to jail now for mounting the wrong kind of wooden hand-grip on one of my otherwise perfectly legal rifles? Not a silencer, not a "nasty" 40-round magazine. A fixed wooden handle.

The big fortunes in the gun business have been made by inventors and marketers of new stuff, like Sam Colt in Hartford and the folks who bought out John Mose Browning's patents for Winchester in New Haven.

God bless them. I wish they'd earned twice as much. The free market is supposed to encourage invention and progress.

But you can forget about the new breakthroughs in firearm design — profitable or not — coming from this country in the next century. Federal licenses are now required to tinker with state-of-the-art military weapons on your basement workbench — licenses that are as scarce as hens' teeth.

No, our enemies will shortly have the newest, most potent, most reliable arms — and their technological lead over us will improve, decade by decade. Isn't that a pleasant thought?

Anyway, if you think the profits in manufacturing ammunition are obscene, get into the business. Anyone can reload old brass on a home workbench for the investment of only a few hundred dollars, and sell the stuff for a profit at local gun shows. The basic skills can be learned in a few hours.

Of course, you'll be competing with imported surplus foreign-made stuff, so you may not find the margins quite as high as you think. I assume if some American manufacturer could make a weapon as good as a semi-automatic Chinese SKS short rifle, or the 100-year-old surplus Swedish Mauser, and sell it for less than the $150 or so they're each now going for, such a weapon would already be offered for sale. Give it a try. It's just a steel tube and some wood.

Why complain about others making money in a field that you're perfectly free to enter yourself, in your spare time? That's like the lazy grasshopper complaining because the busy ant has stored up too much food.

For that matter, if "ammunition is a marketer's dream" because "it's a consumable!" you might also think about setting up a grocery store. As there's no expenditure less "discretionary" than food, which is 100 percent "consumable," those guys must be raking it in hand over fist.

And finally, as to "keeping automatic weapons out of the hands of some nut who is about to 'go postal'," do you have any idea what the ratio is of innocent people killed by drunks wielding Chevrolets, compared to the number of people killed by nuts wielding already heavily regulated automatic rifles — or even the kind of "assault weapons" Sen. Feinstein has been trying to ban, which aren't automatic at all?

Where is the nationwide campaign to ban "assault Chevvies"? You can't even defend your daughter against a would-be rapist with a Chevrolet ... we have no demonstrable *need* for a vehicle capable of traveling 90 mph, at all. And there certainly isn't one whole article of the Bill of Rights devoted to guaranteeing us our "right to a personal means of transportation" ... is there?

Debunking the Bad Science of the Baby-Doctors
🌿

Dr. Bernard Feldman, of the Department of Pediatrics of the University of Nevada School of Medicine, wrote to me on April 9, 1997:

"Each time the issue of gun safety and control is brought up, your editorials invoke the issue of Second Amendment rights, rather than discussing the real issue of gun-related violence and deaths due to gunfire.

"Pediatric firearm injuries are reaching epidemic proportions in the United States. In 1993, one American child (under age 20) was killed every 92 minutes by gunfire. Additionally, five more were wounded in the same time. Half of the gunshot deaths occurred with the dead kid's own finger on the trigger, being signed out by the coroner as either an accident or suicide. Handguns kept at home are 10 times more likely to injure a household occupant than an intruder. In that same household, suicide is five times more likely to occur and domestic homicide three times more likely.

"Violence due to gunfire should be treated like any other epidemic disease. If society wishes to protect children from having a slug of lead slamming into their heads or chests and succumbing to this disease ... parents should know whether guns are present in the homes of their children's friends and, if they are, ask whether the gun is locked in a safe place not accessible to children. In this way parents can make informed decisions about allowing their children to play in such a home. ...

"If your editorials would promote such preventive measures, you would be doing your readers a far better service than stirring up hysteria about the loss of constitutional rights. Certainly, our Founding Fathers would have had second thoughts about the Second Amendment if they could have predicted the consequences of allowing the citizenry to retain their right to keep a loaded musket in their homes."

🌿 🌿 🌿

Knowing that no rebuttal by a mere layman would carry much weight in the face of the kind of grasp of statistical and causative reasoning displayed here by Dr. Feldman, I contacted Dr. Edgar A. Suter, M.D., national chairman of Doctors for Integrity in Policy Research, of San Ramon, Calif., to ask if he'd be willing to briefly respond.

The next day, Dr. Suter answered via fax:

"Dear Mr. Suprynowicz: According to the latest review of the 1990 Harvard Medical Practice Study, every year 180,000 Americans die from physician negligence — nearly five times the number of Americans who die by gunshot. Careless doctors kill the equivalent of two jumbo jet crashes every three days.

"Are physicians an epidemic public-health menace? Of course not, because physicians save so many more lives than they take — and so it is with guns, where every year 2.5 million Americans use guns to protect themselves, their families, and their livelihoods. Guns are used to save lives, prevent injuries, avert medical costs, and protect property.

"Dr. Feldman's discussion of 'costs' of guns in the absence of a discussion of their benefits is poor accounting — like trying to balance a checkbook by tallying withdrawals without adding deposits. Even Dr. Feldman's claim of an 'epidemic' is false, as any careful physician can observe from FBI data. Violence has been stable to declining for every racial and demographic group in the U.S. *except* for inner-city teens and young adults involved in drug trafficking. Three-quarters of homicide 'victims' are criminals.

"Dr. Feldman's American Academy of Pediatrics pretends that 20-year-old dueling drug dealers are 'innocent children.' Sensationalized reporting of relatively rare tragedies involving 'innocent children' notwithstanding, the most certain means of avoiding homicide in the U.S. is to avoid the drug trade.

"By definition, criminals break laws. Predators who ignore laws against rape, murder, and drug trafficking also ignore gun laws. It is only the innocent victims who respect and are impeded and disarmed by gun laws. Victim disarmament is *not* a policy that saves lives.

"As to suicide, gun controls have been shown to reduce *gun* suicides, but not *total* suicide rates, because many lethal means (hanging, leaping, and auto exhaust) are even more accessible than guns. Suicide rates in the supposed gun-free paradises of Japan and Europe far outstrip U.S. suicide rates. ...

"Without exception, all 15 of the studies of the protective use of firearms demonstrate one to four million — or more! — protective uses of guns annually, saving about 400,000 lives annually. The benefits of guns far outweigh the combined detriment of criminal, suicidal, and careless gun misuse — 400,000 lives saved dwarf 38,000 gun deaths.

"The University of Chicago Lott & Mustard study of progressive reform of concealed handgun laws, allowing good citizens to protect themselves where they are at greatest risk — outside their homes — demonstrated that, rather than "blood running in the streets," the net outcome of these reforms has been thousands of lives saved and violent crimes prevented. Guns offer an overwhelming net benefit in our society.

"We can give Dr. Feldman some credit for his gun safety suggestions, but his suggestion that we treat crime as a disease is as ridiculous as treating disease as a crime."

❧ ❧ ❧

In the limited space available, Dr. Suter could only touch on the kinds of statistical manipulation now in regular use by the nation's baby doctors in their well-organized "Guns are a Disease" campaign.

For a really detailed dissection of this fraud, I recommend the Winter, 1997 special edition of *The Firearms Sentinel*, featuring the treatise "Disarming the Data Doctors: How to Debunk the 'Public Health' Argument for 'Gun Control'," by Richard W. Stevens, adjunct professor of Legal Research and Writing, George Washington University School of Law.

The publication is available at $5 (50 copies for $29.95) from Jews for the Preservation of Firearms Ownership, 2874 S. Wentworth Ave., Milwaukee, Wisc. 53207.

The JPFO Web page is at http://www.mcs.net/~lpyleprn/jpfo.html.

Infringement by Taxation
🌿

I wrote that — under the wise precedent of *Marbury vs. Madison* — no judge who honors his or her oath to protect and defend the Constitution can do anything but throw out any charge of "smuggling guns into the United States," since any such law of necessity "infringes" my right to keep and bear arms, violating that highest law of the land, the Bill of Rights.

In May 1997, long-time Texas NRA activist (now the late and lamented) J.B. responded:

"As I read the Constitution, the right to bear arms doesn't preclude the government having the right to tax them if they come into this country from a foreign port. As I remember, the only taxing and revenue rights the framers gave the [federal] government was tariff. So, yes, I can easily see how it can be illegal to smuggle arms into this country if the tariffs aren't paid. It's exactly according to the Constitution.

"Comes under the category of being right for the wrong reasons, but that's beside the point. Technically, you blew that one."

I replied:

Gee, then I guess the guarantee of "freedom of the press" in the First Amendment wouldn't prevent the government from laying a 10,000 percent "tariff" on imported Canadian newsprint, would it? Even if the effect were that the only publisher who could still afford to circulate a newspaper or magazine (now that domestically produced hemp paper is conveniently outlawed and EPA regulations effectively ban the start-up of any new domestic paper pulp plants) turned out to be the Government Printing Office?

I mean, surely, if the Second Amendment was merely intended to guarantee that each state governor could maintain an armed "National Guard" (despite widespread misunderstanding that it guarantees some kind of a right of "individuals"), then the purpose of the First Amendment was just to guarantee that *government* would retain the right to print its opinions, no?

No. The Bill of Rights is the supreme law of the land, *restricting* and *overriding* all other grants of power to the federal government, including the taxing power. When they ban the domestic manufacture of automatic weapons, then ban the *importation* of automatic weapons (except for their own "police" forces, of course), do you really want to argue the average citizen will long retain any useful "right" to "keep and bear" such weapons?

On what basis? Because I haven't been banned from praying *real hard* that the tooth fairy might leave a BAR under my pillow tonight? Because I'll eventually be "allowed" to pay $20,000 for some rusty old World War I Maxim receiver, held together by re-welds and baling wire — for which I can get arrested if I thoughtlessly carry it into another state without "permission" or discharge it within five miles of any dwelling or endangered weed or bug?

If the Chinese were allowed to ship us all the full-auto Kalashnikovs we wished to buy down at Wal-Mart, then made to pay a tariff of 4, 6, 10, or even 12 percent, they'd *pay* it, because it would be less trouble and expense, in the long run, than smuggling.

Anyway, this machine gun (and "assault rifle") import ban is no more an attempt to "raise revenue" — even if that were what the Founders intended — than is the "$200 machine gun transfer tax."

If these were *revenue* measures, we'd see public service ads on late night TV, sponsored by the ATF, urging us to buy less-expensive *domestically manufactured* machine guns for each child when he or she turns 16, and to pay the $200 tax on each weapon at their convenient 24-hour drive-through window ... and the ATF would be issuing annual press releases bragging about how much *more* they collect each year in machine gun taxes, and how many *more* licensed firearm dealers there are each year ... not bragging about how they've succeeded in cutting the number of "taxpayers" in half!

Revenue, my foot.

If you tax something, by definition you "infringe" my right to acquire it. And the daily activities of the modern ATF prove that in the case of firearms, that's not merely an unintended side-effect, but the very purpose of the agency.

The Second Amendment — adopted *after* the rest of the Constitution — does not say "shall not be infringed ... except by taxation." Did they just "forget" to add that part?

Or do you think Sen. Moynihan kept proposing a 10,000 percent tax on hollowpoint ammo in hopes we'll all go out and buy a lot of 50-shell boxes at $1,500 each, thus eliminating the national debt in no time?

But Which Arms Do We Have the Right to Keep and Bear?

M.C. wrote in June 1997, from somewhere on the Atlantic seaboard:

"I have noticed that you frequently and passionately express your support for the Constitutional right to keep and bear arms. ... I have tried my usual method of moral analysis to determine the correct position on this issue. However, I find that I am always left with a seeming quandary, and I wanted to solicit your opinion on this difficult question.

"I start with a predisposition in favor of freedom and respect for the literal meaning of the Constitution. This leads inexorably to strong support for the principle of the right to keep and bear arms. However, when I extrapolate from mere handgun ownership up through rifles and automatic weapons and continuing on to mortars, howitzers, and field artillery, and ending with nuclear weapons, it seems crystal clear to me that a line must drawn somewhere prior to nuclear weapons in this progression. And yet, from a moral perspective, I cannot seem to find the principle that makes it a right to own a pistol yet illegal to possess a cruise missile.

I assume that you do not advocate the unrestricted right to own weapons of mass destruction. If you do not, perhaps you can explain to me where you draw the line, and why."

I responded:

Thanks for your thoughtful inquiry.

Many gun-rights advocates rationalize a line between the weapons that a common foot-soldier can carry into combat and those that are "crew-served," and thus require the logistical support of a larger group of men to field effectively, such as howitzers, fighter aircraft, and, yes, nuclear weapons.

Thus, they tell us they believe the Second Amendment grants "the people" the right to own rifles, possibly up to the size of a Browning 30-caliber machine gun, which one person could conceivably carry and use in combat. This argument would also have to "allow" the citizen the use of a small mortar, but not of a wheeled 57-mm gun, etc.

An embarrassed silence usually ensues when you ask about the shoulder-launched heat-seeking anti-aircraft missile. Clearly, single Afghan "militiamen" used such weapons quite effectively against Russian Hind helicopters, but many folks get queasy about the obvious implication that some kind of "white supremacist Aryan Nation militia nut" might thus be granted the unrestricted right to take aim at any government helicopter that hies into view near his "compound."

The other approach — common among the savvier Libertarian *political* candidates, is to sidestep the issue with some kind of dismissive joke, indicating, "I'll be happy when everyone can own a handgun and an M-16; we won't be campaigning on personal ownership of atomic weapons *this* year, ha ha ha."

The problem with both approaches, as usual, is that the attempt to temper, moderate, or compromise the "principle" with whatever seems "pragmatically acceptable," only draws attention to the "fudge factor."

Like you, I don't get it. All such distinctions are arbitrary. In fact, single soldiers — admittedly not the *average* infantryman, but specially tasked SEALS and the like — are widely believed to have already carried nuclear devices in their backpacks, on special covert missions overseas. So the whole rationale of what can be "handled by a single man" will shortly collapse.

The main point is this: The federal government has no powers, except those delegated to it by the people. I cannot delegate a power that is not already mine. So how can I delegate to the government the power to build, possess, deploy, yes and even use nuclear weapons if I, as an *individual* American, do not possess that right, *prior* to its delegation to government?

(Nor do I fully give up a power when I delegate it. We each retain the right to make a citizen's arrest of a fleeing felon, even though we generally delegate this job to the police.)

Mr. Madison, and others of the Founders, said the whole idea of maintaining an armed populace is so that any potential tyrant would confront a body of the common folk, able to rise up and field a force *better* armed and equipped than the federal government. If the 82nd Airborne (under orders from some would-be dictator) descended on your town today, they would have small howitzers, 50-caliber machine guns, Kevlar vests, CS gas with protective masks and suits, and so on. To defeat them, the people would need ready access to the same stuff.

Thus in a *pragmatic* sense, as well as in principle, individual Americans not only can, but must, possess and be able to quickly and knowledgeably use in their own defense any type of weapon that they can manufacture or purchase.

The real question is: Why does this bother us?

Such weapons now exist, are widely dispersed, and are

under the control of common mortal men. What makes us think God has sent us a special race of angels, called "officers of the government," who can be better trusted with these weapons, than you or I? Do you really believe Bill Clinton or George W. Bush is of sterner moral fiber than you or I? Or some Air Force enlisted man, on a ladder in a missile silo, retrofitting new fuses on a nuclear warhead?

How about the president of France? He has nuclear weapons. Do you or I know for a fact that he isn't some kind of secret unbalanced speed freak? Didn't they just elect a bunch of giddy Socialists over there? How about the president of the Ukraine? He recently admitted one of his military missiles accidentally shot down a civilian airliner over the Black Sea.

We don't know these guys from Adam, yet we implicitly trust them, because they "work for a government."

What nonsense.

In fact, most of these people are *not* your moral equal, or mine. They all suffer from a mental disease that causes them to sacrifice all moral principles — to throw away the happiness of their families, to step on their friends — in order to gain great power over their fellow men. I submit that it is not merely a *possibility* that one of these guys may be nuts, but that, in fact, *most* of them *are* nuts.

The reason they don't unleash these weapons, therefore, is not their saintliness, but the simple fact that they know other parties, equally well armed, would kill them for their trouble. That has *always* been the strongest deterrent to the aggressive use of force.

The president of the Ukraine may be a nice and decent fellow. But the reason the French sleep soundly at night is not because their psychiatrists are allowed to interview the president of the Ukraine weekly, but because they know that *he* knows that they could and would hit back.

Do I "advocate the unrestricted right to own weapons of mass destruction"?

No, I *acknowledge* this pre-existing right of all individuals. To do otherwise is to pretend we can put the Genii back in the bottle. You might as well enact legislation "ceding to government" the right of a mother bear to use her claws in defense of her cubs.

Morally depraved zealots possess every terrible weapon you can think of, right now. Even as we speak, half the cashiered colonels of the former Red Army are operating what amounts to one giant drive-in flea market from Odessa to Tashkent, auctioning off everything from souvenir hammer-and-sickle cufflinks and RPGs to purified plutonium to any wild-eyed Iranian or Indonesian misfit who can come up with a year's salary and a couple pounds of fish eggs.

Attempts by us to "cede our self-defense rights" back to "government" will prove about as effective as King Canute standing on the shore and ordering the tide not to come in, or the attempts of various medieval states to institute the death penalty for anyone who taught their enemies how to make gunpowder.

The best way to curb the worst instincts of bad men is to let them know that men of good character possess stuff even more powerful than theirs, so they'd better not try anything.

The principle that keeps Saddam Hussein from sneaking a barge full of poison gas into New York harbor is the very same principle that makes the potential mugger look at you and go, "Uh-oh. I don't like the confident way this guy is striding around, especially out here in the dark. I'll bet dollars to donuts he's got a .45 under that jacket. I think I'll wait and pick on a more likely looking victim ..."

And that is *precisely* the thought pattern I want to see in the minds of George W. Bush and John Ashcroft when they consider seizing my guns and ordering me to line up for fingerprinting for my new "National ID card" and "internal travel permits." Which is why every loyal freedom-loving American should own a BAR ... and a couple of Stingers. To keep our leaders from the path of temptation.

If I'm given the choice between dying in a nuclear blast or leaving to my children a life of slavery to which I acquiesced on their behalf, out of fear or the mere desire for personal ease and convenience, please ... bring on your bomb.

Once the people are disarmed and terrified of their neighbors, once they believe that nothing is worse than death and that the only way to be safe is to lock their doors, cringe in terror, and dial 9-1-1 for the government police at the first sign of trouble, ... then making them into slaves becomes mere child's play.

Hoplophobia

That missive, in turn, brought the following from G.W., who files from "Business Services Accounting" at one of the nation's esteemed universities (though he doesn't specify which):

"I like your logic that the government possesses only powers delegated to it by the people, and that therefore each of us, individually, possesses the right to own nuclear weapons. I disagree that it is pragmatic for us to do so.

"Those who invest in small howitzers and 50-cal. machine guns are unlikely to use them against the 82d Airborne, as long as there are much easier targets that will provide a return on that substantial investment. The lighter military-type weapons are likely to be used in the commission of crimes; heavier weapons in the defense of a fortress to which the criminals could flee.

"Of course, it is the position of some that the best defense against this is for every citizen to own weapons with which to suppress the criminal element. However, what this does is generate an arms race, in which the criminals will trump the private citizen's pistol with an automatic weapon, and if the citizens respond by acquiring automatic weapons, the criminal acquires heavier weapons still. I think the recipe is not for an armed populace able to defend its liberties against the government, but for unruly packs of warlords descending upon targets of opportunity and then retreating to their strongholds.

"Even if by acquiring good weapons the citizenry is able to achieve some sort of uneasy truce by which the weapons are rarely used, so that the costs of the destruction caused by conflict between heavily armed groups need not be factored in, the mere cost of acquiring and maintaining such arsenals must come from funds that could have been spent on other activities, so that our quality of life must surely suffer from such an arms race.

"What seems to me to be pragmatic, then, is some sort of arms limitation treaty among all of our citizenry, by which armament (and expenditures therefor) are limited. The chief problem with a disarmament treaty among governments is enforcement; but when the treaty is among citizens, fairly effective enforcement can be achieved by delegating enforcement powers to the government. ...."

I responded:

Nearly a quarter of a million "NFA registered weapons" (that is to say — required to be registered under the 1934 National Firearms Act) are legally owned by private American citizens today. About 180,000 are full-automatic machine guns or machine pistols — nearly 1,000 of those are big tripod-mounted .50-caliber machine guns. All such hobbyists need do is register them with the government, and pay a $200 "transfer tax."

These machine gun hobbyists gather for twice-a-year machine gun shoots at sites like Knob Creek, Kentucky, demonstrating that their weapons are both functional and transportable. Yet I cannot find *any* record of any such weapon (or any of the thousands of other such weapons that have doubtless been wisely hidden away in attics and basements since passage of the National Firearms Act of 1934 — before which they were legal for private ownership *without* payment of any tax) ever being used in the commission of a crime in the past fifty years ... by anyone but police officers and federal agents, of course.

And surely your friends in the victim disarmament movement would tell us about any single such incident, endlessly, could they find one.

So, you assume the burden of predicting a crime wave on the part of what is arguably the most law-abiding segment of American society.

Meantime, the United States government has a "substantial investment" in bombers, aircraft carriers, Rapid Deployment Forces, etc. By your logic, should we expect those who control such expensive assets to forsake mere boring patrols to "keep free" the sea lanes and so forth, instead seeking "much easier targets that will provide a return on that substantial investment," by turning privateer, raiding international commerce, invading small nations and carrying off their treasuries and their attractive young women to be sold into slavery, etc.?

No? You don't expect that? Then I take it you hold the average *private* citizen to be a scurvy immoral dog who will steal at the first opportunity, while you hold that anyone who is an *officer of the government* immediately assumes angelic traits of personality.

I find no basis to share this conclusion. In fact, I suspect the opposite: The kind of people who go into the "government" business do so because they crave power over their fellow men. They quickly come to assume they have the right to seize from the purses of the peasants any level of compensation they can imagine (and woe unto any peasant who should resist), just as they quickly grow into the habit of selectively enforcing "the rules" to their own advantage, or simply rewriting them as they go along.

In fact, this type of character is by far the *more* likely to throw ethical behavior to the wind, to "do anything necessary" to maintain and expand his wealth and power, which he always manages to convince himself is exercised "for the greater good."

It's done all the time. Look at the "rescue" of "our oil" via a massive armed raid called "Desert Storm," under the absurd fiction that Kuwait — which has been far more accurately described as "a family oil company with a seat at the U.N." is some kind of "democratic republic" where the government in Washington City acted to "preserve freedom."

Ha! When do we mount our expedition to liberate Tibet?

You argue that a nation with an armed populace is "a recipe for ... unruly packs of warlords descending upon targets of opportunity and then retreating to their strongholds."

How odd, then, that America — a virtual civilian armed camp by world standards — did not degenerate into such brutal anarchy from 1790-1850, or from 1870-1910 ... that foreign visitors like de Tocqueville, in fact, found it the safest, most well-ordered, and polite nation in the known world, marveling that an unescorted woman could travel hundred of miles through rough frontier settlements without a moment's fear of harassment.

How odd that your scenario is also such a mismatch with the domestic crime situation in the only two other nations I know of that today have well-armed citizenries: Israel ... and peaceful, orderly Switzerland.

In fact, the condition you describe is the result of allowing an armed professional class to prey on an unarmed class of "producers." Following the Hundred Years War, such roving bands of out-of-control discharged soldiers, or condotierre, made life hell all across Europe. A similar phenomenon arose in Japan with the renegade "Ronin" samurai. In each case, an armed "professional soldier class," finding themselves at loose ends, was able to prey on a feebly armed common folk ... generally disarmed by law, on pain of death.

Today, we cowering underarmed peasants call these immoral bandits who see themselves as above all law, these "unruly packs of warlords descending upon targets of opportunity and then retreating to their strongholds," by the names "IRS, DEA, FBI, and ATF."

You assert that an armed populace must pay for its weapons with "funds that would have been spent on other activities, so that our quality of life must surely suffer from such an arms race."

I would call your concern for my financial well-being misplaced, if I thought it sincere. Before we start weeping tears for householders whose kids are living on stale breadcrumbs because "he spent the whole paycheck on guns," I think we have some far more prominent pathological spending habits to deal with. (Let's think beer, cigarettes, and lottery tickets.)

In fact, guns are a fairly good asset in which to invest, when it comes to "shelf life" and resale value. And much of America's success in the Industrial Revolution actually came from methods of machine-tool manufacturing developed specifically for the manufacture of firearms for the huge domestic market, by folks like Eli Whitney and Sam Colt. The industry that gave us "interchangeable parts" actually bred American prosperity, not poverty.

Anyway, I grow tired of members of the victim disarmament gang contending they "don't buy guns." They most certainly do. They merely prefer that their "gun money" be seized from their paychecks (along with ours — which of course constitutes double taxation, in the case of anyone who already spends sizable sums providing for his *own* defense) in the form of taxes, and used to arm the FBI, the DEA, the ATF, the IRS, and a hundred other federal, state, and local agencies who either are — or on short notice will quickly become — active oppressors of the dissident and the downtrodden.

I have yet to hear anyone afflicted with the "gun control" disability dial 911 and specify, "Now please be sure to send the kind of cops who are disarmed. If you can't do that, we'd rather you not send anyone at all to stop the men who are hold-

THE BALLAD OF CARL DREGA

ing my daughter at knifepoint, because in this household we don't believe that guns ever solve anything."

Meantime, are you volunteering to personally inform the descendants of the black slaves of 18th and early 19th century America how much better the "quality of life" was for their folk, since they were spared the burdensome cost of maintaining arms in defense of their rights?

Likewise, let's try to convince their surviving progeny how much less nutritious food the residents of Auschwitz, Treblinka, and Sobibor could have afforded in the difficult years 1941-1944, if they had foolishly invested more of their savings, back in the early and mid-1930s, in firearms that could have no conceivable pragmatic purpose but to "kill police officers."

Why, if they had so wasted their resources, it's quite conceivable their "quality of life would have suffered" to such an extent that some of them could actually have starved to death!

Finally, you offer: "What seems to me to be pragmatic, then, is some sort of arms limitation treaty among all of our citizenry, by which armament (and expenditures therefor) are limited. The chief problem with a disarmament treaty among governments is enforcement; but when the treaty is among citizens, fairly effective enforcement can be achieved by delegating enforcement powers to the government."

Yes. White slave owners were in a fine position to limit quarrels among their darkies, once the darkies had "consented" to be disarmed, leaving all such regulation in "Massa's" hands. Likewise, we all know there was little quarreling allowed among the inmates of the Nazi death camps.

There is no shortage of examples in our very own "modern" century: Go and look at how well the disarmed Armenians fared after "delegating enforcement powers" to the Turkish government in 1915, how well the disarmed Ukrainians fared after they put their trust in Stalin and his armed minions in the 1930s. ... Look at the legacy of bodies heaped like cordwood for which we can thank the long-term traditions of legally enforced civilian disarmament in Cambodia in the 1970s, and Rwanda a few years ago.

Once people see the wisdom of giving up their private arms and "trusting" armed government agents to keep everything peaceful and tidy, it's *amazing* what can be accomplished.

I wish you no ill, but hope you'll pack your bags and be gone from a land of free men, finding a place where you may trade your proud heritage of liberty — bought for you at the cost of so many noble lives — for another bowl of warm government porridge.

Then I want to hear you plead, "Please sir, may I have some more?"

— V.S.

In Fact, Real Rights *Are* Pretty Much Absolute
🌿

Jon Roland writes:

"We need to emphasize that CCWs ("concealed-carry" handgun permits) are not the solution, because they reduce a right to a privilege. The only document which may properly be issued would be a certificate of nondisability, signed by an official, certifying that he has searched the public records and found no court order disabling (restricting) the right to keep and bear arms for that individual. Disablement by statute, such as a statute forbidding persons convicted of a felony of doing something (vote, carry arms, whatever) are constitutionally prohibited bills of attainder."

I responded:

A good point, seldom raised.

Even our "champions" at the NRA have been known to concede: "Certainly, all reasonable people agree a mechanism is needed to keep guns out of the hands of certain people, like convicted felons ..."

Then I'm proud to be unreasonable.

Imagine being told it's "only reasonable" that an 86-year-old man, convicted of the felony of selling four bottles of rum during alcohol Prohibition back in 1931, is still not allowed to go to church, or to attend an anti-war rally, or to stand up and speak at a public meeting, since after all "no right is absolute," and convicted felons naturally lose their First Amendment rights to freedom of religion, and of speech, and of assembly, upon conviction of a felony.

Imagine being told that — even after the victim of the bureaucratic edict has served his time and been released — those rights are not automatically re-established, unless a governor or president signs a specific paper, "restoring his civil rights."

Imagine being told that — once someone convicted of embezzlement or tax evasion has served out his sentence and his parole and been set free — if he should later be arrested as a suspect in a liquor-store heist, he *no longer has a right to a public jury trial*, which he would otherwise be guaranteed by the Sixth Amendment. He lost that right when he became a convicted felon; that right has not been *specifically and expressly restored*, and therefore the courts can simply convict and sentence him in secret (any time, for the rest of his life) without a trial!

Why? Because, of course, "No right is absolute," and you lose your rights if you're a convicted felon.

All ridiculous, of course.

Remember that only a tiny *minority* of people convicted of *federal* crimes have ever done anything violent, most being locked away on purchased testimony for violating mere bureaucratic licensing edicts. So why does such a citizen not immediately regain his right to keep and bear arms, the moment he's served his time? Where in the Second Amendment does it say, "Shall not be infringed, except that those who have once in their lives been convicted of a felony, shall thereafter be forever disallowed ..."

Why can't I find that language in my copy?

The argument will be made that guns are dangerous, and a convicted felon has proved he will behave irresponsibly. Even leaving aside the (sizable) possibility of false conviction in these days of pro-government jury-stacking, or the fact that our 86-year-old man violated a law that was promptly repealed in 1933, Karl Marx proved that a printing press can kill millions. Yet do we ban someone convicted of libel from ever writing or publishing again? No.

The Rev. Jim Jones proved that religious fervor can be deadly. (As though the Crusades and the Spanish Inquisition hadn't already given us a hint.) Do we ban someone who was once convicted of a felony from becoming a preacher? No.

This is all part of a campaign to convince us that the right to keep and bear arms is somehow different from the other rights guaranteed by the Bill of Rights, not a true "unalienable individual right" but rather some conditional privilege that the state may restrict to members of a uniformed "special militia" under the command of the governor — as though the Founders, fresh from their astounding military victory over the greatest military power in the world couldn't wait to secure for their posterity the right to be *disarmed* and promptly placed under the heel of the first gang of arrogant professional government mercenaries to come along.

If by tolerating the removal of one person's rights, we inevitably erode all our own, then we must *insist* on the right of convicted felons — once they have paid their debt to society — to keep and bear arms.

What Shall We Do With the Predators?

🔥

In response to the above column, former policeman W.L. wrote in:

"An interesting and thought-provoking essay.

"I tend to find myself straddling the fence. I don't want 'violent felons' to have legal access to guns. The 81-year-old non-violent 'felon' certainly shoots down the conventional wisdom, at least for me.

"But what about the guy who was convicted of aggravated robbery at 17, 23, and 29? Okay, paroling him at the end of two years on each five-year sentence is insanity. But suppose he served all five years each time, and demonstrates that when he is free, the temptation to use force to take whatever he wants is too great to resist? Do you favor three strikes and you're out? Or one strike?

"As a former police officer, I can tell you that the barring of felons from being armed was a pro-active tool. Granted, most of my experience was in small towns. We knew who was trouble.

"And yeah, perhaps they did get stopped when someone else wouldn't. (The reality is that few can drive a mile in city or town traffic without violating some traffic law!) I am certain that you will admit that there are some violent predators in our midst. I will grant that their existence is often used as an excuse to violate the rights of others.

"When a felony was what most people think of as a felony (murder, aggravated robbery, sexual assault, burglary, car theft — no longer a real felony in Texas — aggravated assault, kidnapping, etc.), then laws banning felons from possessing arms makes sense to me. When felonies are defined as catching the wrong kind of fish, shooting a predatory bird to protect your lambs, or whatever the crime of the month is, then I agree with you.

"How do you balance it? Please don't tell me that the

balance comes by having everyone equally armed so they can resist on the street. I am a handgun instructor (CHL type, not NRA). I run our local 'combat' matches. There are very few licensed carriers (who have undergone licensing training) that I would bet on in a crisis situation. I am not against a citizen carrying a gun, but if push comes to shove, the mindset is the most important factor. Regardless of the words that are used in a training course (Have you made the decision that you could and would use a handgun in an appropriate crisis situation?), the criminal who has decided to strike has it all over a person caught flatfooted.

"Unless someone practices regularly and has had top-end advance training (Gunsite, Thunder Ranch, LFI, or something comparable), it is easy to be a danger to self and others. The greatest advantage of CHL programs is deterrence. For that reason, I support them. They put some criminals on notice that anyone may be armed. But for actually using the gun, most programs are woefully inadequate.

"I guess my bottom line is that I want some people disqualified from exercising their Second Amendment rights. However, the criteria (felony record) is most faulty. We will all soon be felons if they keep passing laws!

"But propose a workable solution that addresses the fears of those who know that simply having a gun in their pocket is not an adequate solution. ... (That law enforcement has become abusive in many areas of life, I will not argue.) I fear a totalitarian state as much as you. At the same time, I am not ready to give up on all corporate responses to the problem. Bad law makes the situation worse, but all law is not ipso facto bad."

I replied:

Thanks for your thoughtful response.

Perhaps the problem is the degree to which we have become accustomed to "(young) ex-felons in our midst," so that we are now puzzling over how to deal with this problem, instead of asking why we face such a problem.

It seems we agree that far too many things are now called "felonies." If we repealed 90 percent of the laws now on the books — mostly the stuff enacted since 1912 — the whole issue would become much clearer. (Rape, murder, and armed robbery were all illegal in every state by 1912. But why should the same leniency standards apply to a convicted multiple armed robber as we apply to someone "caught in possession of the feathers of a protected raptor," or "convicted of shifting fill dirt into a marsh" on his own property, or "structuring his cash withdrawals to avoid the cash-transaction reporting requirement," etc.?)

Hand-in-hand with *de*-criminalizing huge swatches of the federal register and the state Revised Statutes (the smallest of the 34 volumes of the Nevada Revised Statutes is titled "Criminal Laws," which always makes me wonder, "What the heck are the *other* 33 volumes for?"), we would indeed need some kind of harsh new standards for repeat violent felons.

Judges and juries need the discretion to show mercy to some waist-high kid who's just fallen into bad company, of course. Though I think getting him out of his current urban environment and associations, by requiring that he go live for two years on grandpa's farm, should be the minimum to give such a kid a real chance to change his ways.

But once we're clear that we're *not* talking about folks who have merely violated some bureaucratic edict or engaged in some form of controlled commerce without a federal license, etc., then I fear we need to get reasonably tough:

1) Libertarians, in general, favor the death penalty. With freedom must come *real* "responsibility for one's actions" — not the make-believe free-of-consequences variety cynically promoted by Bill Clinton and Janet Reno.

I have a problem with capital punishment only because it seems to get dissimilarly applied based on race and social class. Also, as currently "enforced," it's little more than a vastly more expensive form of life sentence.

However, at the very least we can and certainly should change the way we treat officers and armed civilians who kill perpetrators *in the act*. I'm thinking of medals, parades, and large cash rewards from the Chamber of Commerce.

2) End parole and probation. Some statutory sentences would have to be shortened to account for the fact that we now frequently sentence for 15 years, in hopes the jerk will serve four. But if judge and jury concur that a crime is worth 30 years, that means we don't want to see this guy outside again until his hair's white and his arthritis is too bad to allow him to even *think* of pulling a second-story job.

3) Exile. The notion that a judge should ever have to deal with a defendant back on a *third* violent felony strikes me as an admission of systemic impotence. The lenient sentence for the first offense, it should be made clear, constitutes "society giving you one more chance to 'get it.' The second time around, no such "benefit of the doubt" makes any sense. We do own the Aleutian islands, don't we? Tattoo these guys "Rapist" (the real thing — don't give me "date rape") or "Murderer," or whatever, load them up with a couple months worth of dehydrated food, a knife and a shovel, and air-drop them into a fogbound hell.

Escape? Tell them, "We don't care if you escape, but there's a $20,000 reward (the cost of a mere eight months of keeping the loser locked up) for anyone who ever finds you off this island and shoots you dead through that tattooed bulls-eye on your forehead, no questions asked."

It would be very interesting to see what kind of society would develop on that island (among those who aren't promptly murdered for their supplies by the other inmates) after a couple of years. I suspect it would be one that would make even those fellows yearn for their previous soft life in the Lower 48 ... or even for the certainties of three squares and a dry bunk in the Big Hotel.

Would they develop harpoons and kayaks and learn to hunt seal? How many would die among the ice floes? I seem to recall that after our submarines cut off their resupply ships, the Japanese we found still occupying a couple of those islands in 1943 or '44 were little more than living scarecrows, subsisting on mice, moss, and boiled boots.

The argument will be made that we've got a million people in prison, and you can't drop a million people on the Rat Islands. But as we've been discussing, the first half million go away when you legalize and pardon the pot smokers, alone. Keeping only those guilty of violating laws enacted before 1912, you could open the doors of virtually all the *federal* pens and start sending the guards their unemployment checks tomorrow. Even some professional criminals might find a different line of work, once they figure out there's no more revolving door.

How many recalcitrant feral retards do we have in this country, who just plain need killing and whom we would thus be doing a favor if we instead handed them a parachute, a book of matches, and 30 pounds of dried beans?

It may sound a little far-fetched, but what we've got now is not going to stand, and if we don't do something a *little* more bold and effective, we're going to see vigilantes lynching 20 at a time, which I do *not* favor, given the likelihood of mistaken identity, the loss of any shred of due process, etc.

Finally, I fear we must agree to disagree on Concealed Handgun Permits. The government *cannot* convert a right into a privilege, available only by permit or license. Governments have shown, again and again, that they will *not* stop at what is "modest and reasonable."

The 1916 Harrison Narcotics Act was moderate and reasonable, as such laws go. "We're not going to ban anything," the federals said, "because we have no such constitutional authority. All we're asking is that those who manufacture, sell, or prescribe opiates or marijuana sign up, get registered, get issued a license. All perfectly routine — no one will be turned down. This is *not* a precursor to regulating this part of medical practice completely out of existence; trust us. We just want to make sure we can guarantee purity, safety, and accuracy in labeling."

Yeah, sure. It took just 18 years before they broke every one of those promises, giving us a "Drug War" that has now been with us for 65 years.

Inner cities more peaceful now? Less crime and drug use? Ha! (And meantime, dying cancer patients writhe in continuous unendurable pain until they beg their families to kill them, because their M.D.s are afraid their "DEA numbers" will be pulled if they write prescriptions for "too many" painkillers.)

"We're not 'banning' the manufacture or sale of machine guns," Congress said in 1934. "That would be unconstitutional. What are you Chicken Littles squawking about? The National Firearms Act simply asks that machine gun manufacturers and retailers sign up and get a little license, perfectly routine, no one will be turned down. ..."

Write to the ATF today and tell them you're a law-abiding citizen who doesn't mind undergoing a background check and who wants to buy a license to set up a little machine shop to mill receivers for Browning Automatic Rifles in 30.06, on which you will then build up complete full-auto BARs from imported spare-parts kits, for sale to law-abiding *civilian* customers, including members of the Unorganized Montana Militia, in keeping with the intent of the Second Amendment and the 1934 National Firearms Act. Promise to collect and remit their $200 "transfer tax" on each weapon you manufacture and sell, and tell them your goal is to eventually produce and sell 10,000 new machine guns each year (militia-style, no "legitimate sporting use" that you know of), to law-abiding American *civilians*, at a cost of $900 apiece. See how far you get.

Barring a War of Western Secession — which grows increasingly likely — it'll be the same with handguns within 10 years. Pretty soon they'll pull your "firearms permit" for such crimes as trying to pay cash for medical services to someone other than your "assigned health-care provider."

And as for retaining ownership of any firearm *not* on your "concealed carry" permit ... forget it. After all, no one can legitimately "need" more than one or two, can they? And therefore we *obviously* have to do an annual "courtesy home inspection" to make sure you don't have any extras, which would only serve as a temptation to burglars. ...

Are you ready to defend your freedom? You speak of mindset, of folks being paralyzed because they really haven't considered the tough questions in advance. Well: "Have you made the decision that you could and would use a handgun to shoot and kill a uniformed government officer who was 'just following orders,' attempting to deprive you or others of your/their Second Amendment rights?" Would you aim for body mass, or for the bridge of the nose? Let her lie wounded, or quickly close in to put another round in the back of the head? Lift the hair, or shoot through it? And has it occurred to you that when that day comes, the fellow guarding your 6 may be an "armed former felon"?

The other side wants Total Victim Disarmament. Once we help them disarm "just a few dangerous ex-felons," they're going to smile and start pushing that wedge in, wider and wider. Ever been convicted of misdemeanor spouse abuse? Ever agreed to go to a mental-health-care facility for 72-hour observation to calm down a concerned loved one because you got depressed and hit the bottle for a week after a close friend or relative died? Sorry, no firearms for you.

Shooting ranges? All shut down due to noise and lead pollution. Ammo? That box of 20 shells will be $220, thanks to the Moynihan (or will it now be called the H. Clinton) thousand-percent ammo tax ... but don't worry, the extra money goes to the medical care of gang members ("little children") recovering in the hospital after being shot while committing grand theft, while the officers who shot them face million-dollar civil liability suits.

Pleasant Dreams,

— V.S.

On the Selective Doling Out of "Constitutional Rights"

❦

T.T. writes in, in response to the November 1998 column in which I admitted being a one-issue voter, rejecting any politician who won't trust me with a gun:

"Thank you, Vin, for raising the issue that has been bothering me for quite a while. When I read through the Bill of Rights, I cannot understand why a convicted felon *who has served his or her time* is, under the present selective Second Amendment rights-lifting, not automatically and permanently stripped of *all* of his or her rights, and not just the Second, plus voting:

"Felon = no free speech, freedom to assemble, or, as you say, freedom to go to the church of choice; no Third Amendment protections ... hey, quarter those soldiers at will in the forever-felon's house! ... no Fourth Amendment protections, or Fifth, or Sixth (as you point out) nor Seventh or Eighth. And of course, the 9th and 10th are moot, since they're long-gone anyway for everyone, felon and misdemeanor and non-convicted alike.

"But if the power geeks were to do this, why then, it would be too blatantly obvious what was really happening, wouldn't it?

"Best wishes, and thanks for keeping the faith so eloquently."

I responded:

Yes. Does a felon, once he has "done his time" and "paid

his debt to society," again become a member of "the people" to whom all the rights in the Bill of Rights apply, or not?

If *not*, then indeed any government agency should be able to arrest anyone who has *ever* been convicted of a felony — even a 90-year-old guy who tended bar in a speakeasy in 1930 — hold him without bond and without letting him confront his accusers, in some foreign jurisdiction, torture a confession out of him, convict him without a jury trial, and subject him to a cruel and unusual execution, all in secret. No problem with the Bill of Rights — it *doesn't apply.*

Needless to say, under this evil premise, the government should also be able to deny such a person the right to attend church, the right to publish a newspaper or magazine, the right to own property that cannot be seized on a bureaucrat's whim without compensation, etc.

On the other hand, if that is *not* the situation that does or should prevail, then it seems to me any former felon who is no longer on "parole" has a right to vote and bear arms, along with all his other pre-existing rights ... which, after all, are only *acknowledged* by the Bill of Rights as having been ordained by the Creator, not actually "granted" therein.

This business of creating different classes of citizens, with different degrees of legal "disability," is the basis for virtually *all* the invasions of our privacy — up to and including the police numbering system on our cars — so frequently justified as "allowing us to check and make sure you're not an escaping felon."

(Note what a police state South Africa became, based on the simple notion that one should have to show one's "racial identity card" to any policeman who asked, to determine whether one had a right to be on a given street at a given hour of the day — and the sad absurdities it created, as visiting Japanese businessmen were given passports declaring they were "white" so they wouldn't have to suffer the indignities visited on South Africa's native East Indian merchants, who carried second-class *internal* passports identifying them as inferior "Asians.")

There should be no *need* for me to ever "submit to a background check" to prove I'm "not a felon." Felons should be in prison, or in the graveyard.

"Parole" is the French word for "promise." If you can't trust a convict to keep his "promise" not to acquire and carry a gun and otherwise behave until his sentence expires, then don't let him out on "parole." It's not *I* who should have to suffer inconvenience or indignity because the government wardens can no longer tell the difference between me and all these convicted thugs they're allowing to wander the streets in plain clothes.

Start repealing one law a day until you have enough jail cells to keep those guilty of violating our *remaining* laws in stir for their *full sentences* (you might want to to keep murder, forcible rape, and armed robbery on the books, while tossing out drug use, "money laundering," and failure to pay gun "transfer taxes").

And set the rest of us free.

The Ballad of Carl Drega

IX
Greatest Hits from the Mailbag: Widdle Stephanie and the Princess of Rutgers

Rivaled only by the holiday columns, the pieces I most often find readers recalling with undisguised glee — even months and years after the fact — are my responses to the endlessly astonishing stuff that arrives in the daily mailbag (traditional as well as electronic).

In fairness, there are also readers who think I'm grossly unfair and insensitive to single out these correspondents for abuse — though truth be told, nobody forced them to write me in the first place ... or prevented them from setting aside their letters until they could find a few minutes for further consideration, or even routine proofreading.

A number of such exchanges are scattered throughout this book, as they best served to clarify one or another of the subjects at hand.

Herewith, however, a few that have stood the test of time and seemed to merit a special little place of their own:

The Scum Are Free to Ride It
🌾

I do not know why I was so blessed — because we show up on some list of "helpful daily newspapers over 100,000 circulation," I assume — but in October 1998 I received an unsolicited query from M.M., who identified herself as an undergraduate at Rutgers:

"My name is [M.M.], I am currently a senior at Rutgers

University in New Jersey. I am researching how to get funding for a hypothetical grant proposal. I am proposing that a monorail be built at Rutgers University so that the student congestion can be relieved between classes.

"I am curious as to who would be willing to spend the money, currently I am looking into Federal Government funding, because Rutgers is a state funded school.

"If you have any helpful advice or web pages, please feel free to relay it onto me. ..."

Though I usually ditch the "Our third grade class is doing a report on your state" inquiries, this time I replied:

Hi, M. —

Why don't you approach a private railway or trolley company, to ask what the cost of building such a system would be. If no one else comes to mind, try calling Disney World in Orlando; I believe they have some privately built "people movers." They might even be willing to estimate what the cost of debt service would be, if one were to sell private corporate bonds to raise enough money for such construction. Presumably, one would want to pay off construction costs, plus the cost of debt service, in 20 or 30 years.

Then, by a simple process of mathematical calculation, one takes the projected ridership, divides that number by four (experience shows that most advance ridership estimates will err by at least that much — they did when Los Angeles, Washington, and Miami recently built *their* mass-transit systems), and solves for the fare that you would have to charge to recover your costs within 20 to 30 years ... plus a profit, of course. Few firms are going to be willing to invest the time and money in such a project unless both they and their bondholders make some money.

Of course, you now face a new problem. Your initial ridership estimates were probably based on the notion that riding this system would be free, or perhaps would cost a quarter.

As the fare increases over $1, and then over $2, student

ridership is likely to drop off. Fewer riders mean you have to charge a higher fare. Eventually, the folks who graph such fare-versus-ridership equations refer to a point on the graph where ridership "drops off the cliff."

If you go past that point, you may have to face the possibility that *no one* will invest the requisite sums to build you such a system.

But then, your original inquiry didn't mention "investment," did it? It mentioned a "grant."

What does that mean, precisely? That the federal government should send you money taken from the paychecks of workers all over the country to build your system ... which no private investor will fund and which no student would actually pay anything to ride? You do know, I hope, that if people refuse or find themselves unable to pay those taxes, the IRS will garnish their paychecks and seize their bank accounts, leaving them unable to buy groceries, pay the rent, or take their children to the doctor.

Perhaps federal taxation can be justified to fight wars against ruthless foreign dictators or to fund courts where people can find justice. But to build a monorail to endlessly circle the campus of Rutgers University? I have just reviewed Article I Section 8 of the Constitution, which lists *all* the permissible things on which the U.S. Congress may spend money. It only takes up 431 words, if you can believe it. It says the Congress is allowed to "establish post roads." I suppose you could try to convince the Congress that the campus mailman would like to ride a monorail. Otherwise, I fear you may be out of luck, there.

Though that shouldn't mean you can't complete your assignment. Have you considered writing: "Why No Private Investors Are Likely to Willingly Fund a Monorail Proposal at Rutgers, and Why It Would Be Morally Wrong to Ask the Taxpayers to Fund a System That is Thus Revealed by the Free Market to Be a Bad Idea"?

Alternatively, have you considered bicycles?

Best Wishes ...

Within hours, young M.M. at Rutgers had responded:

"you are the biggest asshole i have ever come in contact with. I am a mere 22 year old and i am simply researching a *hypothetical* monorail to relieve the congestion on the roads of New Brunswick ...

"thanks for all your help, jerk.

"m.m."

Suspecting by this time we were onto a live one, I wrote back:

Hi, m. —

You contacted *me*, as I recall (and pretty much "out of the blue"), to ask my advice. I took time out of a busy workday to send you a polite reply. I don't remember using any abusive language.

If a "mere 22-year-old" isn't responsible to consider the moral and ethical concerns that arise from proposing a "government grant" to fund a fancy train, at what age *will* you be ready to start considering such things? And are we safe in assuming you won't be going to the polls and voting *until* you're old enough to start considering such things?

And how old do you consider you would have to be before it would be incumbent on you to assume some moral responsibility for the looting of the paychecks of others, to fund the government programs you "hypothetically" propose?

I understand it's very pleasant to attend a campus that's funded by taxes, and enjoy many other tax-funded benefits, without actually having to be the person who puts on a uniform and a gun and evicts a family from their home and puts that house up for auction to pay "back taxes." Perhaps such threats don't seem real to you, because you've never had a mortgage payment to make and a paycheck that didn't quite cover everything, then faced the trauma of losing that job and that paycheck — while the taxes still have to be paid. If not, then I suppose you are fortunate, in some ways. But do you really think your good fortune will hold forever?

At some point, we must all consider what we are asking those armed government agents to do *for* us, in our names, and whether we can forever safely assume that we don't incur any moral or ethical culpability for what we authorize them to do (every time we go to the polls), so that all our nice "grants" will still be available.

Unfortunately, m., you are far from (to use your words) "the biggest asshole i have ever come in contact with." In fact, I do understand that you are only a small, insignificant, trainee "ass - - -" ... well, perhaps it'll be OK if I just say "redistributionist." But while you are relatively young, you still have an opportunity to consider these matters, before the habits of living off ill-gotten loot becomes too ingrained to break, with all the long-term jeopardy that represents.

Why is it, by the way, that proposing you contact private railroad companies for cost estimates on your "hypothetical" monorail made me an "asshole"? Because you realize no private firm would ever be likely to fund such a project, because it isn't likely to ever be profitable?

Have you studied no economics there at Rutgers, at all? It used to be a fairly good school. Has no professor ever suggested to you that the free market helps teach us which endeavors it's wisest to spend our time on — that is to say, which will most benefit our fellow citizens — by dictating that those projects that fulfill a real demand can be done at a profit, while those for which there really *isn't* much popular demand cannot?

I find it strange that this concept causes you to take so much offense. Or did you go off to the university in hopes of never confronting any new facts or opinions that would disturb your established world-view and economic assumptions?

Best wishes, at any rate, on your continuing education. ...

❦ ❦ ❦

I guess sometimes we just live right, because the next response from M.M. was more than I could ever have hoped for:

"ok, so maybe i have been fortunate and maybe i am a naive poor little rich girl, who hasn't taken any economics classes. But, i hardly consider telling me that my idea is stupid and that building a monorail at this school is stupid ... polite ... by any means.

"I asked more along the lines of Global Defense Commission money ... something along those lines. the current bus system that we have is dirty, unreliable, and the scum of New Brunswick are free to ride it.

"Not only that but, we have to hire people to drive the buses (and let me assure you that all the bus drivers are lunatics).

"The Rutgers monorail would be set up so that only Rutgers I.D. carrying students could ride. And it would be electric so, much of the pollution pumped into this city on a daily basis, would be eliminated.

"I still maintain that you are an asshole, due to your initial demeaning response. But, maybe we are getting somewhere now???

"M."

🌿 🌿 🌿

And to think that I sometimes consider turning my hand to fiction. But who could invent as perfect a character as Ms. M. of Rutgers, the superannuated undergraduate who "hasn't taken any economics classes"?

She just gets better and better.

She wants help turning up a "government grant" — or perhaps now even some kind of U.N. eco-extremist grant (what the heck is the "Global Defense Commission"?) — to fund a monorail boondoggle so she won't have to lug her pamphlets (it doesn't appear likely she carries or reads any actual *books*) around her bloated, already subsidized, government campus. And why can't she simply hop a city bus? Because, she now reveals, "The scum of New Brunswick are free to ride it"! Oh, this is just *too* good. Having once hung around with campus socialists, I *know* they justify their self-centered demands with high-falutin' rhetoric about their solidarity with "the workers" and "the people," when in fact it is only on a giddy dare that they will stoop to rub shoulders for more than an hour or two with your actual, sweaty, beer-swilling Archie Bunkers of the working class.

But to come right out and say it — she wants a *new* government-subsidized boondoggle, with access limited to "her kind," because the problem with the *old* tax-subsidized boondoggle (the bus system) is that they let the *peasants* ride it!

A "woman of the people" to warm the heart of our late Comrade Trotsky, if no one else.

And the monorail would be electric, mind you, thus creating no pollution in posh New Brunswick. No, the pollution would instead be created by the operation of a coal-fired electric power station in some dirty low-class community miles away, down near Trenton, probably ... you know, the kind of slum inhabited by filthy tax-paying *workers*, who wouldn't know clean air if they stumbled on it!

My cup runneth over. She restoreth my soul. And yea, we shall dwell in the ivory tower of the socialists, forever.

"To Count All the People We Need to Feed"

🍃

A couple of mechanically printed schoolchild letters crossed the desk during the last week of March 2000. The most charming?

"Dear Editor,

"Hi my name is Stephanie and I am a grade 6 student at John Muir Middle Schoolin wausau,Wisconsin.I am writing this letter for Langauge Art's Class.This letter will tell you some reasons why you should fill out your census forms so read on and find out.

"One reason is so the taxis will lower.

"Second reason is to know how many job's to provide for people and how much mony to pay them.

"Third reason is you might get funding for roads or schools. Fourth reason is to count all the people we need to feed and if we need to add on to anything.Because the goverment helps pay for people that are counted and if your not you end up paying more in taxis and other things go up.

"Fifth reason is if you don't hand in your census form in time people will come to your door and ask you in person and that cost mony too.So hand in you census forms before it's to late. ...

"Sincerly, Stephanie T."

Of course I didn't write back to her directly, but in my column I replied:

Dear Stephanie:

My, how pleased the taxpayers of Wausau, Wisconsin, must be to know the "mony" looted from their paychecks is going to continue your course of government instruction (and useful civic exercises) at a school named for the founder of the Sierra Club, where after five-and-a-half years of government instruction you believe the common euphemism for those seizures of "bread from the mouth of labor" (that's Jefferson, as I'm sure you know) is spelled "taxis."

We could also go into that annoying apostrophe you keep using to form your plurals, not to mention your spelling. (The apostrophe replaces the "e" in the "es" that Old English used to form the *possessive* case, remember? Or did teacher skip that lesson to make time for the "Letter-Writing Exercise" from your shiny government-supplied "Census Kit"?)

Instead, let's concentrate on the important stuff: 1) Hit the space bar after each of those little dots called "periods," will you? 2) Since this was obviously a classroom exercise, you might also want to ask teacher to go back over the part about "proofreading."

But teacher's real error in judgment may lie in allowing you to expose to the general public the underlying assumptions you and your classmates reveal in your letters.

Listen up, Stephanie, honey: We Americans live under a system of government called a constitutional republic, in which the central government in Washington is not supposed to be "providing jobs" for people, nor figuring out how much "mony" to pay them.

Unlike those eastern European regimes fled by my grandparents and (presumably) your great-grandparents, the central government in America has a sharply limited list of powers and duties, each specifically spelled out, and I can't find the ones you mention anywhere on my list, which is called Article I, Section 8, of the Constitution. Have teacher show you her copy.

Anyway, no government can really "create" jobs, even if it claims to. Even to fund "public-works" projects, government has to take money from private persons and corporations, who could otherwise use those funds to hire more workers of their own — at far lower overhead.

Government never creates anything. It just shifts stuff around. That's called "redistribution." Like the way struggling young Wisconsin couples, now trying to save up to start families of their own, are being taxed, their wages "redistributed," to pay for your welfare education there at the John Muir Youth Propaganda Camp for the Lexicographically Deprived.

You say another reason for the census is to "count all the people we need to feed and if we need to add on to anything."

Who is this "we," Stephanie? Do they send you and your classmates envelopes full of cash from Washington, which you then use to buy food for the poor? I doubt that. I think when you say "we," you really mean "the government."

But here's another hint: The government doesn't feed anybody, either, except sometimes its own soldiers. The reason you get fed is because your parents use the money they earn at work (after our friend the government takes 40 percent off the top) to buy that food. And I doubt they need to check any census reports to figure out how many places to set at the dinner table.

In fact, Stephanie, that Constitution we were talking about no longer authorizes any federal agency to ask us about our race — let alone our earnings, our education, our mental health, or our breeding or bathroom habits — all stuff demanded on many of those census forms that teacher wants so badly for us all to return. (Have you asked her why? Have you asked her how much of her paycheck now comes from Washington? Have you asked her to explain the "Hatch Act"? Can you name any other 20th-century governments that have used their control over the children to manipulate parents' behavior?)

What the Constitution actually says is that the federal government can do its best to count us once a decade, to figure out how to apportion seats in Congress, as well as for the apportionment of "direct taxes."

That's right, Stephanie. Far from lowering our "taxis," Washington can *raise* direct taxis — uh, taxes — based on how many of us they manage to count.

Didn't teacher look that up for you? It's Article I, Section 2.

As for your final argument, that "if you don't hand in your census forms in time people will come to your door ... and that cost mony too": Awww. "Mony" they would otherwise spend funding mass torture and the burning of productive coca fields in Colombia, setting the stage for your little classmates to ship out to Bogota in a couple more years? "Mony" they would otherwise spend to launch astronauts into space, there to go around and around, studying each other's urine production? "Mony" they would otherwise spend seizing civilian firearms and locking up the most entrepreneurial 25 percent of our young black men for made-up bureaucratic crimes, until respect for the law vanishes entirely?

Money they would otherwise spend funding the John Muir Middle School, in Wausau, Wisconsin?

You're breaking my heart, Stephanie.

By the way, you didn't mention the fines. If filling out the Census forms is so good for us, why does your employer have to threaten to fine us if we don't? And did you notice where U.S. District Judge Melinda Harmon granted attorney Mark Brewer a temporary restraining order last week in that Census suit filed by five residents of Houston, Texas?

"For the moment, this will prevent prosecution against any American who chooses not to answer questions other than the number of people living at their address — that's all that's required by the Constitution," attorney Brewer told WorldNetDaily.

"Unfortunately, we know the government is capable of misusing census data," he said. "The federal government was only able to find, round up, and imprison Americans of Japanese ancestry in 1942 by the illegal use of Census Bureau data. ..."

"The Census Bureau cannot extract this information under threat of criminal prosecution — that was the issue I presented to the court," Brewer said. "The government lawyer told her that he can ask anything he darn near pleases — where does it stop?"

Please tell your teacher, Stephanie: I think millions of Americans are about to show the federal government where it stops.

Do you have a recycling program for rejected government forms, there at your Middle School? Don't you think John Muir would have wanted you to?

Damaging the Children's Self-Esteem
🌿

Plenty of response poured in to my column answering little Stephanie T. of Wausau, Wisconsin.

The best came from a schoolmarm named D.J., who attributes my ignorant "rantings and howlings" to the fact that I "went to a redneck backwater school." (The letters requesting refunds from the bursars of Eaglebrook and Wesleyan will shortly be wafting their way eastward.)

Ms. D.J., of course, contends conscripting widdle Stephanie into this propaganda project was an admirable undertaking, while simultaneously insisting any classroom discussion on whether the Census Bureau now exceeds its constitutional authorization would be "totally inappropriate for the age-group."

Funny how that works.

D.J. writes:

"A friend has been forwarding your columns to me for some time now, and most of them seem mildly interesting but annoyingly inflammatory. This column concerning Stephanie's letter, however, shows your need to stop, take a break, and decide what your message really is.

"After 15 years of working with children, I can guarantee you that with a response like that, no 'Stephanie' would ever write another letter, and no teacher of Stephanie would let their students correspond with a journalist like you for fear of quashing their students' enthusiasm.

"Sure, the spelling and grammer need attention, but that is pretty mild stuff and could be covered gently. The point is that the child had the guts to write this letter and pursue this interest, and you stepped on her like a stinkbug. You also speak back to her like a William F. Buckley wanna-be, instead of speaking in terms a young person (not a child, a young person) would understand. Your letter taught this child (and other young people who might be reading) not a lesson in civil liberties but a lesson in smart-ass response.

"I admire this kid for at least trying to pursue an interest in what her government is doing, as opposed to the common 6th grade interests of clothes, boys, and MTV icons. Do the right thing and respond in such as way as to further that interest, while gently pointing out grammer corrections that will help her communicate her ideas.

"That is, if you really want to forward your concepts and teach a younger generation, and not just sit in your pulpit and whine. — D.J.K.

I replied:

Dear D.J. —

Ha! Ha! That's great. These kids shouldn't have their errors pointed out (errors occurring in a formal, signed, classroom-produced letter to the editor of a major metropolitan newspaper), because it would damage their self-esteem!

And then you insist on seeing the problem as primarily involving "spelling and grammer" — completely ignoring the main substance of my observations, which were the outright socialist notions about government's role that she and her classmates have come to accept as foregone conclusions.

Come on, admit it, you're a paid propagandist in some branch of the youth propaganda camps, aren't you? I bet you even took your degree in "Education," after the grades you received in the more rigorous subject areas (the ones where the instructors insisted there are actually such things as "wrong answers") proved too damaging to *your* self-esteem.

The "guts to write that letter?" It was a classroom project! Her salaried government propagandist (in the USSR, at least the MVD used to forthrightly honor such efforts by handing out bronze medals) got paid that day to take her through that little "exercise" from the government-supplied "Census Kit."

"Pursue an interest in what her government is doing?" Do you think teacher led a classroom discussion on the Constitutional authorization for the census, and asked the children whether they thought the government might now be doing anything with the census *not* constitutionally authorized, and whether that would be appropriate under a constitutional government of "limited powers, specifically designated"?

Oh stop! Heeeeee haw! You're killing me!

If embarrassment was to be avoided, it was the responsibility of that salaried government propagandist, and no one else, to make sure the kids proofread their letters before sending them out.

(Should little Stephanie have been promoted from the fourth to the fifth grade without mastering at least the two-syllable words? From the fifth to the sixth?)

By the way, as to little Stephanie's "spelling and grammer" needing some attention ... you might want to look up the spelling of that word "grammer," your own self.

Thanks for making my day.

p.s. — I attach below a somewhat more thoughtful response, from a veteran *private*-school teacher.

🌿 🌿 🌿

Dear Vin,

I relish all of your columns, and have just finished reading *Send in the Waco Killers*, which has, of course, resulted in my losing even more sleep than I did before (and believe me, I wasn't sleeping so well before, since Mark and I have been researching the white squirmy things under the fed-gov rock for way too many years). But your latest column, "To count all the people we need to feed" is simply beyond wonderful.

As an ex-English teacher whom J.J. has billed as the SierraTimes.com "Local School Marm," I applaud your response to the dear public fool, "Widdle Stephanie." It touched every base and nerve, and set me positively a-tingle with admiration. I taught 6th grade and high-school English for 10 years, and I would have given that child an "F" on her pathetic missive to you — for both language use and content. Gag. — Tina Terry.

Aww, Give the Little Girl a Gold Star
🌿

One more response to my "Widdle Stephanie" column seems worth repeating. Ms. "Vivian," who writes in from one of those "EDU" e-mail addresses, asks:

"Vin — Do you have children?

"While all the points you made to Stephanie were truthful, you have lost any points you could have made by the approach you have taken with her. She is just a child, obviously fed liberal bull for breakfast, lunch, and dinner her whole life. That, however, is not her fault. Your approach will only alienate her and will not open her mind to any truths you submitted. Perhaps a softer approach, while not your style, would have made her actually think rather than react to the harshness you presented.

"When I was seven years old, I wrote to the editor of a local newspaper, the *Orange County Register*, in California. I asked him to do something about the sichooashun (situation) because the taxes (and I spelled it correctly I might add, at 7 years of age) kept going up. His response was kind, and pointed out to me that the newspaper couldn't do anything, but the people could. He carefully and patiently explained the power of the vote, etc. It was published in the local paper.

"Today I still follow his advice and try diligently to explain things to young people in a way they can understand and will give them food for thought for many years. If you loose [sic] the children of our country you will loose [sic] our country — Vivian.

I replied:

Hi, Vivian —

So the editor explained to you the power of the people to vote for lower taxes?

Funny. From my observation, folks have been voting for the "less government, lower taxes" candidate every chance they've gotten for 25 years — with the result that we now have the biggest most intrusive government in American history and the highest effective combined tax rates in the history of the world.

And let's not even get into how well federal and state and local authorities have been respecting the express wishes of the voters since Californians overwhelmingly approved Proposition 215, legalizing medical marijuana, in the year 2000. (As I write this section of this tome, in October 2001, the DEA has just raided the Cool, Calif., home and office of Dr. Mollie Fry, a physician, and her husband, Dale Schafer, a lawyer who had announced plans to run for El Dorado County district attorney. Dr. Fry is a breast-cancer survivor who is a medical marijuana patient. DEA agents seized files containing legal and medical records of more than 5,000 medicinal marijuana patients — a slight technological improvement on the way the torturers of the Inquisition got lists of suspects for *their* tender ministrations.)

As many have said, "If voting could change anything, they'd make it illegal."

It's really none of your business whether I have children. If I can prove I don't have children — or that any and all of my children are educated at my own expense, without any dependence on the government welfare schools — will that excuse me from paying the school taxes? Will that allow me to live in a nation not dominated by the thoughtless quasi-literate little pathological socialists being turned out by these nests of induced hebephrenia and "attention deficit disorder"? (Yes, induced. Read John Taylor Gatto's *Dumbing Us Down*, written *before* they started doping up a quarter of the next generation on Prozac and Ritalin.)

Where else shall we take this doctrine of yours? If you've never served in combat, does that disqualify you from criticizing our nation's military expenditures, or the use of army tanks and helicopters at Waco? After all, you "can't know the hardships facing the soldier, who needs our support, not thoughtless criticism from twits like you who probably couldn't clear a jam in an M-16 if your life depended on it. ..." blah blah blah.

Pretty soon, only astronauts and aerospace engineers on government contract will be allowed to vote on how many billions we spend on the space program.

I'm not the one who threw unprepared widdle Stephanie into this battle. Her teacher clearly assumed any editor receiving her letter would clean up her spelling and publish the letter because it's "cute," and "in the public interest," since giving the government information about our mental health and our income and our racial extraction and our breeding habits and whether we have firearms and how many and where isn't a *partisan* issue. Oh no, there can be no debate *whatever* about how fine and wonderful and helpful all these government initiatives are. Who would dare?

As though the Army never used census data to round up Japanese-Americans in 1942. As though the Rand Corporation and the highly politicized *American Journal of Public Health* didn't just release a scary study (well, actually it proves how *safe* it is to have unlocked guns lying around, since child gunshot deaths have been declining for decades, though that's hardly the way the networks are spinning it) — a study "revealing" how many households with children hold unsecured firearms, based on misinterpreted census data and distributed for political purposes. (See www.gunsandcrime.org/randucla.html.)

As though the IRS never chooses households for audit because they report substantially lower incomes than the "baseline for their neighborhoods," as determined from *census data*, which we're told will *never* be shared with other agencies or used against us. ...

Let me make sure I have this straight, now: By enlisting widdle Stephanie as their agent, the other side has rendered themselves *immune from criticism* (except of the most gentle respectful kind), lest the critic be accused of "hurting the feelings of poor defenseless children"?

Gee, that's a good one. Can we recall anyone else who has used such tactics? Ever heard about the cute little girls in long white dresses who would run up to our choppers in Nam, dumping live grenades into the doorways out of their cute little straw hats? I guess you think our guys should have just frozen up and not fired back (albeit with tears streaming down their faces) to save their buddies, so as not to "hurt the widdle children"?

People have been trying "kinder and gentler" and "working within the system for modest rational reform" of the mandatory government youth propaganda camps for 100 years. The camps just get bigger, more expensive, more arrogant, and less interested in passing along even basic historical literacy.

They have become the reproductive organ of the welfare/police state. They are the greatest enemy, bar none, to our desperately endangered traditions of liberty.

I am not interested in "a softer approach," or in "convincing" the government's little procured agents to change their ways. It's up to widdle Stephanie's parents — not me — to stop selling her propaganda services to the government in exchange for free day-care and a few daily slices of subsidized orange cheese.

The government schools don't teach children to read. They teach the vast majority to leave school at 18 vowing, "I'm finally out of there; I swear I'll never crack another book so long as I live, and *no one can make me.*" These institutions studiously and purposely teach our offspring *not* to read much beyond the soup labels and the TV listings, lest they be disturbed by evidence that all their little memorized sound bites may not be true.

("You mean Lincoln and Roosevelt *weren't* great and moral men? The income tax *doesn't* apply to in-country wages ... and the people who run the IRS know it? Juries *don't* have to follow the judges' 'instructions'? The Federal Reserve Board is some big scam, purposely institutionalizing inflation and enriching select private bankers? Government-mandated inoculations cause permanent brain damage or death in at least a dozen infants every year and the government *knows* this? There's *no* constitutional authorization for the War on Drugs? We were a happier, more peaceful, more literate nation *before* all these 'Progressive' new laws and police forces were created after 1912? Nawwww, that can't all be true. Anyone who says so is a 'Black Helicopter Nut.' Teacher says.")

My job is merely to point out how close we are approaching the way government control over conscripted children has long been used, in Hitler's Germany and in communist Russia and China, to propagandize or coerce these kids' own parents and — when it comes down to it — to turn those parents in to "the proper authorities" for listening to clandestine BBC radio broadcasts (or, in our own case, for growing pot, possessing firearms, etc.).

If you don't like my stuff, don't read it. You will find the rest of the media positively *full* of go-along-to-get-along statists, unlikely to say anything to upset you or cause you to consider how close to the precipice of state tyranny we now veer.

Or to hurt widdle Stephanie's feelings.

The Parade of Collectivism Marches On
🌿

On Nov. 12, 2000 — a week into the Bush-Gore "long count" presidential election — I penned an "items" column called "The Parade of Collectivism Marches On," that ended up triggering a dialogue with a reader named "Ed" which I could never have invented in my wildest dreams.

Here's that original column, followed by my exchanges with "Ed":

I have witnesses: I said early on Nov. 7, "This election will come down to a couple thousand Cubans sending a message to Al Gore about the way Jackboot Janet decided to 'resolve' the matter of Little Elian Gonzales."

Who, by the way — Elian, that is, not the murderess troll — will come to America and have his own talk show after Papa Fidel finally becomes the last hero of the World Socialist Revolution to be embalmed and laid out for public view. (The Russians are apparently running out of money to keep re-embalming Lenin. I'm not — as Dave Barry would say — making this up. Of course, the Russians are running out of money for pretty much everything, despite the best efforts of the thieves at the World Bank to divert an artery coursing with U.S. taxpayer cash right into the angiogenic tumor that the Kremlin has become, concluding in that secret deal recently OK'd by our point man in the kleptocommissariat, Al Gore, encouraging the Reds to unload all their leftover engines of death on Iran and other friendly powers. Not that I mind a free market in weapons, mind you. I'd just like to know, if the average barefoot goatherd from Zahedan to Samarkand can now buy his own shoulder-launched heat-seeking missile, why I can't pick one up at Home Depot. Fair is fair.)

The AP reported after the Kursk disaster this fall, "Not a single rescue system functioned on this top-of the-range submarine. ... Disasters ranging from crashing airplanes to industrial accidents have become commonplace in Russia. ... A string of plane crashes were blamed on overloading after pilots accepted bribes to take extra cargo, weighing down their aircraft. ... In rural areas, people hack holes into oil pipelines to siphon fuel, often causing fires or explosions. ... Hundreds of people are electrocuted every year while trying to pilfer communication wires, electric cable, and train and plane parts to sell as scrap metal." Airplane parts *taken out of planes that then try to fly the next day, mind you* — remember the missing parachutes in Joe Heller's *Catch-22*?

It's all thoroughly predictable, after decades of teaching a nation's youth in the government-run propaganda camps that acquiring private property and investing in hopes of future profits are both bad; that everything belongs to the first person to get there with a pair of pruning shears; that "excess earnings" should be confiscated and "redistributed." You know — the political philosophy that has been in control of Washington City since 1932, now being genetically encoded through the reproductive organs of our own collectivist state, under the secure guardianship of the National Education Association.

Give it a few more months: The Russians will try to auction off Lenin's yellowed corpse to either Disney or Madame Tussaud's. I say that in the interest of international cooperation and historical irony the State Department should approach Ringling Brothers, heirs to the great P.T. Barnum. Decked out in a top hat and Uncle Sam suit, strung up on wires, I know *I'd* pay to see the old assassin dance like the skeleton marionettes in that famous music video of the Grateful Dead's "I Will Survive" — preferably performed by the Wheaton College Department of Feminist Studies Faculty Chorale.

Meantime, from the front in the ongoing Wars on Guns and Drugs, comes word that four senior citizens, owners of Granicy's Valley Wide Feed Store in Lancaster, Calif., may become the first citizens imprisoned under another Brave New Law of the People's Republic, this one requiring merchants to record detailed personal information about people who buy iodine crystals.

Yes, iodine — you'll remember it from the Periodic Table of the Elements in Mr. Stewart's 11th-grade chemistry class. Not only is iodine the rust-colored stuff that stung when mom spread it over your childhood cuts and scrapes — it's also used to treat hoof and mouth disease in horses and to purify water. What a lot of us might not know is that the stuff is also used in the manufacture of methamphetamine, which makes it OK for the cops to kill you on the spot if you're caught with any. (Las Vegas cop Bruce Gentner, for instance, got off after emptying the magazine of his .40-caliber automatic into 32-year-old local resident John Perrin last year, when it turned out Perrin — otherwise armed only with a basketball — was in possession of a vial of iodine crystals.)

So in a way, maybe the four California oldsters should count themselves lucky. State prosecutors merely busted the four, in the words of The Associated Press, "after becoming frustrated by the store's refusal to comply with the law." Which is to say, refusing to take down the names and other intimate data of their iodine customers, thereafter turning in said data to The Proper Authorities.

If convicted, the four powderheads could spend a year in jail.

Did I mention guns? In late September, a 41-year-old Hamilton, Ontario, man was eating lunch with his family at a crowded restaurant after being fitted with a heart monitor by his cardiologist that morning. Canada being the Land of Snitches, a customer at a neighboring table noticed the bulky outline and leather strap of the heart monitor and, mistaking it for a shoulder holster concealing a handgun, summoned police.

Shattering the moment of family togetherness, a team of SWAT-clad Canadian cops suddenly dashed to the man's table, grabbed him, and threw him up against the wall. One of the thugs tore off his shirt and was trying to pull out the monitor, which was hooked to the man's belt, when he finally realized it was actually some kind of medical device.

The Hamilton chief of police later apologized for the incident, explaining it was an honest mistake.

Hey: You can't be too careful. The guy could have turned out to be an Afghan goatherd.

Like Introducing "Just a Little Sewage" in the Water Supply

❦

Some guy named Ed — my cohorts advise me he's from over the mountain in Pahrump, Nevada — wrote in to respond to my column of Nov. 12:

"Well Suprynowicz, once again, while I agree with the essence of your article and the gestalt of your philosophy, I have to voice my criticism regarding your hyperbolic use of sarcastic allegory, allusion and at times comic rhetoric. But moreso, I wish to point out a dangerously irresponsible use of your journalistic privilege.

"I was not able to discern your point regarding the Elian/ Reno debacle. It began with a 'see, I was right' message regarding the election, but devolved into a chance to cleverly and humorously dissect an easy target: the state of Russian politics.

"You said nothing new, gave no insight, offered no resolution. To what end, please? A chance for absurd comparison on the availability of arms? Really. Another needless caustic comment on the condition of the Russian infrastructure? If anything can be drawn from your detail of their disasters, perhaps it should be how fragile and delicate are the machines to which we trust our lives. If anything can be explored in more depth, might it not be better to seek ways and means whereby Russia can become a viable part of today's economy and society?

"Your cheap shot at our educational system seemed a vaudevillian attempt to get an easy laugh. I don't think anyone doubts the need to rehabilitate the system which educates and develops our youth; nor can there be many who are unaware of the problem. Could I convince you to turn your acutely analytical mind toward exploring solutions rather than getting a quick laugh at the expense of the children?

"It is easy to find the absurdly humorous among human events, so your sparkling rhetoric regarding the bust in California and the one in Canada both seemed more wasted cheap shots to get a chuckle. I was only able to discern your well-known proclivity for denouncing police as storm troopers. Tell me something: Would you want to live in today's society sans police?

"Offer me solutions, not the blades of your own personal vendettas. Really, can you do that? I think it would elevate you from a clever writer to a great writer."

I replied:

Hi, Ed —

1) The Russians deserve to be made fun of. They tried for 80 years to export at the point of a gun (successfully, in the case of the thus-tyrannized and impoverished sovereign nations of Eastern Europe, where hundreds of thousands were imprisoned, tortured, and murdered) the deadly doctrine of collectivism, which holds at its heart the notion that we don't even own our own bodies (I have a feeling Gen. McCaffrey would agree), or the products of our labors. They are now paying the price for not fighting harder for freedom — an object lesson for "go-along" cowards around the world.

We should not and shall not deferentially turn away and cover our eyes rather than add to their suffering by pointing out their failures with cackling glee: In fact, cackling glee is precisely the right approach. Hold up the mouldering corpse of the failure of socialism and wave its stinking putrescent failure in the eyes of the world, including the majority of Americans who still figure income redistribution under the threat of the gun will work better here, since we have a "more reasonable compassionate set of bureaucrats and politicians." The correct response is: "See, it *didn't work*! It *never does*, no matter how ruthlessly its credo is enforced.

As Hayek and von Mises foretold, there is no "stable mixed system" — allowing "just a little dose of collectivism" into a free country is like introducing "just a little raw sewage" into a clean water supply. And the graduated income tax was *one of the main planks of their manifesto. ...* Continue to try this here, and freedom-loving Americans will resist with whatever amount of force is necessary.

2) Yes, the comparison re the availability of arms does expose an "absurdity." It is absurd that a barefoot Afghan goatherd now has more freedom to arm himself with weapons of current military usefulness than many if not all Americans — living here in what the world used to revere as "the land of the free." Is the reason you think I no longer need to point this out your belief that all of America's 20,000 unconstitutional gun control laws have been magically repealed while we slept?

3) If the reason the Russians are suffering is the "fragility and delicacy of the machines to which we trust our lives," why are massive power outages and dam failures and plane crashes and ship sinkings so unusual in the West that their rare occurrences merit massive press attention, yet so commonplace in the "former" Soviet bloc that they hardly merit comment any more? In fact, these technologies grow ever more reliable and robust in an environment of free economic competition. All this stuff is happening in Russia because three generations were raised to *not respect ownership of private property.* Why maintain anything you do not own, and therefore from which you cannot profit? What good will be the suffering of millions of Russians, if we do not help others learn from their tragic mistake?

4) You say, "I don't think anyone doubts the need to rehabilitate the system which educates and develops our youth." Ed, you are wrong. I, along with such notables as John Taylor Gatto and Marshall Fritz of the Separation of School and State Alliance (www.sepschool.org), believe the system of mandatory monopoly government-run schooling (perhaps more appropriately dubbed our government youth propaganda camps) must be *abandoned and dismantled completely* — not "rehabilitated" — if our liberties are ever to be restored.

Should we have "rehabilitated" the Nazi death camps after overrunning them in 1945? Why rehabilitate anything that is evil in its very purpose? (Americans were more literate in the first half of the 19th century than they are now — *that's* not why Horace Mann and his gang set up the government schools.)

I respectfully suggest you may need to go read *any* of the books of Mr. Gatto, the former New York (Public School) Teacher of the Year, for some background on how the docile, doped-up, historically ignorant citizens with whom these institutions now burden us are *precisely what was intended.*

I fear you really want to hear anything *but* solutions, Ed, because (like so many) you cling to the rotting collectivist status quo (legacy of the "Progressives" of 1912-1919, and then of that world-beating confidence team, James Farley and Franklin Roosevelt) precisely as the Russians cling to Lenin's rotting corpse, assuring anyone who'll listen, "It'll be OK if you'll just give us enough funds to embalm him one more time; why are you being so *stingy*, we just need a *little more money*, it's all for for the chilllllldren, waaaaahhhh!"

I have written a 500-page book offering a first stab at the "solutions" you seek. If you live in the Las Vegas area, copies of my book are available at Master Shooter's Supply on West Sahara, at Machine Gun Kelly's Gun Vault near the airport on Sunset Road, and at Spurlock's Gun Shop on East Basic Road in Henderson (of course). Otherwise, feel free to order by dialing 800-244-2224 (locally in Nevada, 252-0655) or by visiting web site www.thespiritof76.com/wacokillers.html, where credit card and bulk orders are also accepted, as is payment in silver, gold, and other hard currencies.

And have a nice day.

"Ridicule and Emotionalism ...
Serve No Useful Purpose"
🌿

A few days later, "Ed" was back, weighing in again in our discourse based on my column of Nov. 12:

"Dear Vin, Thanks for taking the time to read and respond to my brief broadside. I was, however, somewhat disappointed when it ended with a denouement for the sale of your book. ...

"My reply will be brief; you seem to have missed my point, probably due to my inadequate explanation. I'll attempt to restate that point in clearer, more concise terms.

"Human history reveals a motherlode of inhumanity; it is easy to find acts worthy of total condemnation and easier yet to ridicule the people who committed them. This century, with its estimated 400 million violent human deaths, offers perhaps the ripest pickings. There were sufficient atrocities in the course of the 20th century to provide you with a lifelong source of material to ridicule.

"This, however, serves no useful purpose and does nothing more than inflame the emotions of a select few of the populace. ...

"I can find nothing even remotely humorous in the Russian situation. Those peoples allowed a horrible mistake and suffered tremendously for it. Tens of millions died; mothers and fathers, sons and daughters.

"We allowed and committed horrible mistakes and suffered two World Wars as a result. Tyrants and despots around the world have been — and are being — allowed to wreak unspeakable horrors on millions of people.

"This is fodder for cackling glee? I think not: Not the acts themselves nor the idiocy and immorality which allow them; it is cause for grieving and repentance. It is motivation to look for ways to raise the human mind and spirit. It is reason to examine the frailties in ourselves and advance the cause of human evolution.

"As a specific example, the facts you state about Russia would be cause to examine the Russian people, their history, their mindset, and lend logic and reason to an exposition which may help lift the yoke of their past and allow them to take a responsible and productive part in human society. Let us not kick an adversary when they are down; let us not point fingers and cackle in glee at their frailty and ignorance. Rather let those of us who are able offer a hand.

"There is a philosophy by which I have tried to live: if I give a man a fish, he can eat for a day; If I teach him to fish, he can eat for the rest of his life. I see little value pointing a finger at that man and cackling at his ignorance, regardless what he did.

"I am not suggesting that you put aside your clever and sagacious observations: they definitely draw readers. I am suggesting that once having pointed out the absurdity and horror of what you have chosen to shed your literary light upon, reveal then a path, some insight, some understanding, so reasonable, so logical, so crystal clear, that your readers will have but one thing to say: Of course.

"You are too good a writer to be mired in what I call emotionalism. Rise above it, get past it, and with your words, lead others. You have a broad readership you could lead to much greater things.

"I must comment further on two particulars in your response.

"You stated a phrase, '... if our liberties are ever to be restored ...' implying the huge misconception that any people in the world ever had the liberties of which you speak. No people anywhere have ever had such liberties. The United States was the first country to firmly establish such personal liberties, but if you look briefly at our history, those liberties took a long time, till the last half of this century, to reach the common man. The complex reality is that we have more laws governing us and more freedoms to enjoy than ever before in our brief history as a republic and as a species. ...

With warmth and respect, Ed.

I replied:

Hello again, Ed —

Do I have this straight? The idea that this was a "free country" before 1912 is just a terribly tedious and inconvenient myth — America has never been more "free" than today, under the wise, benevolent, and leveling hand of OSHA, the Dept. of Health and Human Services, the EPA, the BLM, the EEOC, the DOC, the DOE, the other DOE, the BATF, the DEA, the FBI HRT, the Fair Labor Practices boys, the Department of Housing and Urban Development, the Department of Agriculture, and the Justice Department Anti-Trust Division?

Why, come to think of it, it's a miracle Americans didn't starve, outright, before 1933!

One more time, Ed: Our personal liberties were not "established" by our Founding Fathers (let alone by Messrs. Farley and Roosevelt, or "Landslide Lyndon" Johnson). The founders were careful to note that they found mankind's natural rights to be pre-existing. (We were "endowed" with them by our "Creator," in the words of Mr. Jefferson.) The founders merely forbade the new government they were constructing from ever *infringing* on those rights. (As a matter of fact, the founders insisted that the "securing'" of those pre-existing rights is the only legitimate purpose of government.) Thus, your contention that our government has somehow brought all these wonderful rights into being, with all their new laws and agencies dreamed up in the past 70 years, renounces the founders and all their works ... in addition to being simply evil and wrong.

You advise: "Let us not kick an adversary when they are down; let us not point fingers and cackle in glee at their frailty and ignorance. Rather let those of us who are able offer a hand."

So, in the autumn of 1944, rather than "kicking the Germans when they were down," we should have arranged a negotiated peace with the leaders in Berlin, "compassionately helping" Hitler and Goebbels and Speer, "lending them a hand" with a massive American relief effort to help them "rebuild a kinder, gentler, Nazi Germany"? After all, there was nothing to be gained by ridiculing and demonizing them, after they were down and out.

It "serves no useful purpose" to identify and loudly condemn the doctrines that led to this century's 400 million civilian murders — the vast majority committed against their own populations by the very collectivist state agencies you revere?

Sounds to me like you also need to sit down and have a nice chat with Mr. Santayana.

Thanks for that bit about "teaching a man to fish, so he can eat for the rest of his life," though. Think that one up yourself?

More importantly, is that what we're doing in Russia today, Ed? Are we warning the "former" Reds we're going to stop handing them seed corn if they keep on eating it, that they must instead take a crash course in Ayn Rand and Hayek and Rothbard and von Mises, in John Locke and Adam Smith and Tom Jefferson and Richard Henry Lee — establishing a limited government and an honest and accessible court system for the sole purpose of guaranteeing personal liberties and *property rights*? Have we told them, "When you're ready to completely abandon and publicly disavow all this socialist crap, and *learn* how the free market works, come see us again"?

No, Ed. Instead we send Al Gore over there, hauling along billions in (taxpayer-backed) World Bank loans, precisely so the ruling kleptocracy *won't* get themselves hanged and replaced by some young radicals who have read Jefferson and Thomas Paine — precisely so the Russian people *won't* be radicalized enough to shoot the SOBs and open up all the former "state enterprises" to entrepreneurial homesteading, since that might breed "instability."

Freedom and independence are *so* scary. So Bill Clinton actually goes to the Ukraine and tells them *not* to become an independent nuclear power: "Instead we want you to turn over your nukes *to the Russians*"! Stability: good. Freedom and self-determination? ... wouldn't be wise; wouldn't be prudent, too many variables there. ...

Finally, your helpful advice to me (other than chiding me for urging you to read a book where all this stuff is laid out in enormous detail for only $22, instead insisting I take my time to write it all for you again longhand, in a personalized manner, and to do it all for free, since others obviously "owe" us anything we "need," and to "charge" for such "compassion" would be greedy and wrong) appears to boil down to: "Avoid emotionalism."

Ah. Now I think I get it. There's no reason to write anything *emotional*, anything that might get the peasants *upset*. I'll just write arcane footnoted research papers to be published in obscure academic journals, concluding that "the underlying premises of the Weed & Seed program, while noble in intent, may require some further double-blind fiduciary analysis in the light of the somewhat counterintuitive real-world results ... probably about seven years' worth. Our grant application is currently in the mail to the CDC in Atlanta."

Some day, Ed, I fear you may have your own run-in with our "kind, compassionate government bureaucrats" who are so busy giving us (as you gush) "more laws governing us and (thus) more freedoms to enjoy than ever before." After they have beaten you up, thrown you or your offspring in jail, seized your property, or some combination of the three, you will whine (as so many have whined), "This can't be right. That wonderful law wasn't meant for *me*! It was only meant to be used against the drug dealers and the racial minorities — you know, 'that' kind. There's obviously been some terrible mistake. I never did anything wrong. Why won't anyone listen?"

Mind you, Ed, I don't *wish* this on you — I honestly hope it never happens. But I fear it *will* happen, as it has happened to hundreds of thousands before you.

Perhaps then, you will find yourself asking, "Why isn't anyone *upset* at all this? Why do they all turn away and go back to watching the game on their wide-screen TVs? Why do even the people I thought were my friends and neighbors now tell the TV news crews, 'Well, he must have done *something* wrong. They don't send a SWAT team to your house for a parking ticket. And he always seemed like such a *quiet* guy'? Isn't there anything *anyone* can do to stir them from their bovine complacency? Can't they see what's *happening* here?"

But as Pastor Niemoller recalled, "By the time they came for me, there was no one left to speak out."

Have a nice life, Ed — here's hoping your way works out for you.

🍂 🍂 🍂

Finally, an interesting (if perhaps overly familiar) missive from one "Dowling," on the question of principles:

Dear Vinny,

I have an online friend who is a great admirer of yours. From time to time he sends your articles to me expressing how he also feels the same about certain issues. Sometimes, I agree with "Jim" wholeheartedly. On other occasions, I disagree and tell him so. It seems to me that if I speak my mind when my ideas are different than Jim's, he will not have anything to do with me. If I follow his thoughts and views to the letter, Jim accepts our friendship. I thought we had freedom of speech, even if someone doesn't like what one says. I certainly do not wish for ideas to be shunned or ignored if they are not in line with the general rules. Everyone should be able to express themselves and be heard. How does one handle those who run away, hide, or make it impossible for an individual to dispute or debate? I know you are not a Dear Abby, but I would like to know how to get along with Jim on a more consistent, even keel.

Thank you for reading, Dowling

Hi, Dowling —

Most people in this country hold a grab-bag of opinions and beliefs that they have never measured against any consistent underlying principle. This will generally be a combination of often-contradictory beliefs they were taught in school; opinions passed down by their parents; opinions that are generally met with approval in their social circle ("the Japanese should be forced to stop killing whales before they're all extinct; the greedy lumber companies should stop cutting down trees that are used to make chairs and floors like the ones that are now keeping me from falling into the basement"); and opinions that are just plain in their self-interest ("Other people should be made to pay taxes to fund the public schooling of my kids, because otherwise I couldn't afford the day care bills; young workers should be forced to keep paying into Social Security so my retirement checks will keep coming — they *promised*").

I see the impact here of the lazy thinking and "sound-bite memorization" used to indoctrinate kids in the government schools. (Literally, "They want to drill our parks for oil/That will pollute the sea and soil.")

Whether this description better suits you, or your friend Jim, I have no way to know.

Some curmudgeons are indeed so hostile to "non-believers" that you simply can't deal with them. It *may* be, however, that one of you is frustrated by the other's unwillingness to settle on a consistent principle or principles from which your beliefs stem, then to argue from that consistent baseline — admitting inconsistency or an "argument from convenience" when it's exposed.

That doesn't mean either one of you should simply cave in and accept the *other's* principles; I'd never recommend that. You each are and must remain your own person. But it may be the conversation you need to have is: "Here are my principles; here are what I gather yours must be. Since our principles are different, it's inevitable that there are subjects on which we'll disagree. We might even *think* we agree, for instance, on some generality like "the sacredness of life," but then find we disagree on the vital definitions. One of us thinks the human-to-be in the belly of a four-month pregnant woman is a "person," the other argues that the state has no right to strap that woman down in a hospital bed for the next five months and force her to bear that child against her will.

One of us holds that the "sacredness of life" means my neighbor can't cut down his tree; the other holds that "trees are property; they have no rights." And in the end, we may even have to face the fact that there are times when we all *violate our principles*, and do so knowingly, and that still doesn't make us evil trolls. I believe the income tax is an evil and invalid handmaiden of socialist redistribution that will inevitably destroy this once-free and great nation. And I *pay it anyway*, because I'd rather do that than risk being audited, fined, jailed, and made to feel like a pariah. It's a *choice* I make, OK? Call me a coward if you like, but we all make *choices* in an imperfect world. If I never — however reluctantly — violated a single principle, I'd be out living in a cave.

Libertarians, for instance, believe that it's inappropriate to use force to get anyone to do what you want them to do — that force is only justified in self-defense, in *response* to someone who uses force or the threat of force in an attempt to coerce you to *their* will.

Most people, hearing this, will say they agree. But they really don't. Tell them someone is buying the lovely Victorian house down the street and has plans to cut down the 200-year-old elms, pave the lawn into a parking lot, and turn the old place into a fast-food restaurant. They will run shrieking to their city council, demanding that an "ordinance" be passed, declaring the whole neighborhood an "historic preservation district," with penalties put in place for anyone who dares cut down an old tree or so much as paint an old Victorian home a different color without the OK of some "neighborhood historic review committee."

But what will happen if the new owners *violate* the new ordinance? "Oh, they won't," you assure everyone. "They'll have to obey the law. (Yeah, like pot-smoking stopped when it was banned in 1934.)

You just took the first step in trying to *avoid considering the consequences of your actions*, because you know in your heart they violate the principle of the non-initiation of force to which you agreed, just three paragraphs ago.

If the new owner proceeds to cut down *his* trees, which *he* has bought, he will be served with a notice to go to court and be fined. If he misses his court date, eventually men with guns will come arrest him and throw him in jail. You have just authorized the use of *armed brute force* against a person who wishes to use his own property as he sees fit, because you find the existing house and trees pretty to look at when you walk the dog in the evening.

As P.J. O'Rourke has summarized very well and in an amusing fashion in his fine books, including *Eat the Rich*, you did have two options for dealing with this "problem," which would *not* have involved the use or threat of coercive force: 1) You and your friends could have raised a few hundred thousand bucks, outbid the would-be restaurateur for the property, bought it, and run it as a museum.

"Oh, but we couldn't afford that."

2) OK then; meet with the new owner and offer to pay him hundreds of dollars per month in "tree rent," just to leave the pretty trees the way you want them. Offer to *pay* for the view you love.

"Hmm. *How* much do you think we'd have to pay?"

Now you're entering into the kind of priority-setting process that *prices* in a *free market* force on all of us, *allowing* resources to move freely to whoever values them most. Most of us could afford a Mercedes if we did without new clothes and meat and dairy products; most of us instead decide we'd rather have our families well-fed and well-clothed, and settle for a Chevrolet. But the choice is still up to us.

By the same token, you'd now be forced (but only by the

free market — only by the reality of competition for resources, not by anyone with a gun) to decide just how much the view of those nice old elms is worth to you — none of this malarkey about "trees having rights" or the "community's right to maintain its historical heritage."

Gee, isn't it much easier — and apparently cheaper — to just have the zoning-code enforcement officer do the dirty work for us? (To just have the government order the car dealer to *give* us all a new Mercedes?)

But think how *we* fume and object when they come knocking at *our* door, informing us we can't let grandma continue to live in that travel trailer out back. "What? Don't you know the old lady is sick? She has nowhere else to go; I've paid taxes for years, I have dinner at the city councilman's house, can't a special exception be made for me?"

Ah ... you mean once these decisions are "politicized," the possibility of "favoritism and political corruption" creep in? ... :-)

This is what will tend to frustrate a libertarian, or anyone who tries to justify his own positions by reference to a set of fixed core principles: Not so much the fact that his neighbor might favor limits on property rights through some "Historical Preservation Commission" — your freedom of speech certainly does guarantee your right to propose such a thing — as the dishonest refusal to acknowledge, "Yes, what I'm saying is men with guns should go arrest the guy down the street if he repaints his storm shutters in a different color I don't approve of, and yes, I acknowledge this starts us down precisely the road the Bolsheviks took in 1917. So what?"

The first thing is to know what our own principles are. I generally suggest reading Ayn Rand and P.J. O'Rourke ... or (if you're looking for something you can breeze through more quickly) Frederic Bastiat, H.L. Mencken, Lysander Spooner, and Albert J. Nock.

— Vin

X

We're From the Government; We're Here to Take Your Kids

"When an opponent declares, 'I will not come over to your side,' I calmly say, 'Your child belongs to us already. ...'"

— *Adolf Hitler*

More often than not, in recent years, Alexandera Dykes of Colorado Springs has been estranged from her husband — who works as an electrician across the mountains in Telluride.

In fact, the first place she met child welfare case worker Atilno Soltero was in the local battered women's shelter, where she sought refuge with her (then) three children in 1996.

"This shelter calls DHS on any woman who goes through there. I've seen so many women lose their children by going through the battered women shelter," Dykes says. "After that [Soltero] would check up on me, and then when the case closed he would stop by the apartment, allegedly to say hello, but then it got to the point that he was starting to get a little more friendly than he ought to have been. ...

"It got to the point where I felt like I was expected to pay for his favors. He told me if I was going to have sex again it should be with a man who had had a vasectomy and that kind of thing."

And the case worker seemed to be referring to himself?

"Oh yes, he'd had a vasectomy; he made that very clear."

Finally came the day in October 1998 when Dykes missed a food stamp appointment. When she called the welfare office to ask someone to intercede so her benefits wouldn't be cut off, she says she specifically asked to speak to anyone but Soltero. Nonetheless, he was the one who picked up the call.

"I asked if he could put me in touch with a supervisor

who could reschedule my appointment for food stamps so I wouldn't have to reapply. He asked if he should come over. I said no, but he came over anyway."

This time, the case worker was not satisfied with merely hinting around.

"He tried to get me in the bedroom, but I wouldn't go." In front of two of her children, "He did put his hands up under my sweater and was touching my breasts," Dykes reports. "He did kiss me in the, what do you call it? He did kiss me with his tongue in my mouth. He made remarks to me that he's been waiting for me for so long, why don't I just give in to it."

Dykes managed to fend off Soltero's advances and kick him out.

Later, on the advice of friends, she did report the assault and swear out a complaint. She waited two months before reporting the incident. "I was afraid of losing my children," she says. Sure enough, that's when Dykes says the visits by the child welfare agents she came to call the "housekeeping police" really seemed to accelerate.

"I started to get weekly visits from the housekeeping police, checking on a report that my 3-year-old bit my 2-year-old, that kind of thing." Dykes now has daughters aged 15, 10, and 1 year, and sons aged 4 and 3.

"I would slam the door and shout at them that they couldn't come in my house without a warrant. Obviously, they weren't very happy with my attitude."

Finally, on Feb. 5, 2000, a day when Dykes says she was suffering from the chronic fatigue associated with the Epstein-Barr virus, came the opportunity the welfare workers seemed to be waiting for.

"My 10-year-old daughter choked on a piece of candy. I dialed 9-1-1 — what would you do? The fire department came and they found the house to be messy, so later that night they came back and they took my kids."

The final raid to take the children came on a day when

her washing machine had been broken for a week, Dykes says. "The place was a mess, I admit that." The state workers contended the children were filthy and living in an unhealthy environment, citing brown stains on the carpet and (weirdly enough) "pennies scattered on the floor," according to their official report.

"My daughter is a terrible housekeeper, she admits that," replies Dykes' father, Travis "Ted" Doolin of Las Vegas. "But does that give them the right to take away her kids? The brown stains on the carpets that they referred to were candy, not feces. The kids weren't sick; they weren't malnourished."

They seized Sandra Dykes' children and sent her a notice of the date she could appear in court to contest that decision. It was the same date she was supposed to testify against case worker Soltero in his pending third-degree sexual assault trial (March 7, 2000 — case 99M2984).

"When I pointed that out they sent a cop right over to hand-deliver a summons with a new date," she laughs.

But the Soltero trial was delayed. Then, in March 2000, Dykes says she was called in to the office of Deputy District Attorney Bill Schmidt.

"Right after DHS took my children, the D.A.'s office made a deal," Dykes recalls. Her witnesses to the event — her own children — now being conveniently in the custody of the state, "They made a deal that they would not press charges against me for neglecting my children criminally because my house was dirty, and in return they would not press charges against the worker who sexually assaulted me."

"And you bought that?" I asked Dykes.

"It wasn't so much an agreement as I felt I was being blackmailed; I didn't have any choice. I did not want to drop the sexual assault charge, but the D.A.'s office made it clear they did not want to pursue that, and in return they would not pursue charges against me concerning my kids."

(Dykes supplies a copy of a May 10, 2000, letter from

Deputy District Attorney William G. Schmidt, detailing the decision to drop the charges against Soltero, who she says retained his job with the agency throughout.)

Bill Schmidt, no longer with the district attorney's office, declined to comment on Dykes' suspicion that by grabbing her kids, Soltero's office was able to maneuver prosecutors into dropping all charges as a "quid pro quo."

One of the allegations against Dykes was that, by homeschooling one of her children, she was "educationally neglecting" her kids. But, "They gave the kids an academic test and they passed with flying colors so they had to drop that," she says.

Sandi Dykes herself passed a government-mandated IQ test with flying colors.

"A large group of people that DHS deals with are the people that have average or lower IQs, and I think that's why they assume a lot of people like that will not stand up for themselves. In my case they sent me to a psychiatrist and a psychologist to have my IQ tested and it came out kind of high and that surprised them and they did not know how to deal with that."

They also hadn't figured on Sandi Dykes' tenacity when it comes to her kids. She called the press, and even put up a Web site (www.alexanderaadvocacy.com) with advice for low-income parents on how to respond to a "Health Services" or "Child Protection" raid on your own home.

Alexandera Dykes went to court on Sept. 5, 2000 and received a court order that the Colorado Dept. of Human Services must "transition" her children back to her, "which means starting with three visits before they actually come home. ... I have two of my children back as of Oct. 19," Dykes told me in November 2000. "That's the older two."

Where the younger kids are concerned, "I can't even have supervised visits here at home except for my daughter's first birthday party. They let her come home for a few hours for that. ... They are really hanging on to my other three, although they keep telling me that they're going to return them. It doesn't look like they'll be home for Christmas, though. ... It's been nine months for me now."

David Berns, director of the El Paso County Department of Human Services, declined to "discuss the specifics of any type of Children's Protection Services case" with me, including why Sandi Dykes' children were taken away from her, or whether he's happy with the way that case has worked out so far.

Allegations like those against Atilno Soltero are "taken very seriously" and "referred immediately to the police and the district attorney for an investigation," Berns told me, though he conceded Soltero remained on his department's payroll during the 15 months he faced third-degree sexual-assault charges.

As to the "tit for tat" nature of the decision to drop charges, as Dykes remembers it being explained to her by deputy D.A. Bill Schmidt, "I'm not privy to the kind of conversations that went on between the D.A. and anyone," Berns said. "The D.A. would have no authority over whether we were going to drop charges or anything of that nature. Now if there were criminal charges against her, that would be a different matter."

And Dykes' initial scheduled appearance to go to court and try to get her kids back being set on the same date she was scheduled to testify against Soltero in a sexual assault trial?

"Those dates would not be coordinated; there would be different people scheduling those appearances in different offices," Berns explains.

However, "When someone makes a serious charge, a criminal charge against one of our employees, that can't be allowed to halt the ongoing inquiry into those children's health and safety. If we allowed that to happen, obviously, they'd all be filing those kinds of charges, and avoiding their responsibility for the proper care and health and safety of those children."

Berns denies child welfare workers are "erring on the side of removing kids from the home."

"That's certainly not true in our county," he contends. "We've had a 31 percent decline in our court filings for Child Protective Services in just about a two-year period, and a 33 percent decline in the number of kids in foster care over a four-year period, from 600 on any given day down to about to 400. So our entire focus has been on strengthening and preserving families. ... We're really concentrating on finding ways to engage families whenever possible, trying to provide services that families need, trying to help them maintain the safety of their children without court involvement."

Unfortunately, when I checked back in late June 2001, Sandi — now working as a taxi dispatcher — had no good news to report. Her two older children were removed again after one missed some school due to illness, and Sandi herself was removed from her home by state authorities in March so that custody of the children could be turned over to her estranged husband. "The judge said it's better for the children to be with 'one bad parent' than to be tossed from foster home to foster home," she reported.

Her oldest daughter was placed with the child's father and the rest of the kids with her estranged husband, she reports. "My oldest daughter hasn't been able to visit her siblings, which is sad since they were once very close.

"I'm only allowed supervised visitation for a few hours a week at the Family Visitation Center. ... They say that I'm unfit and not attentive enough to the needs of my children. They also say that they don't like the idea of me being around my husband because we argue.

"I'm faced with a difficult decision here. It's not good for my children to do 'tug of war' with them. I see the pain in their eyes. They ... don't understand why I don't come and live with them. They want to know why I was bad and if I'll stop being bad. One of my children thinks that I hit him and he told me so

— the case aide at the visitation center thinks he's confusing me with a foster mother who was physically abusive to him.

"I don't want to give up on my children. But tossing them back and forth is tearing them apart. They get their little hearts ripped out every time they have to leave after our visit. They don't want to go and they refuse to be 'rounded up.' ... When they ask questions, I'm not allowed to answer them with the truth, otherwise I'm 'discussing the case.' I'm only allowed to say that I love them and that this is the way things have to be for now.

"I'm ready to walk away from this whole mess. I'm ready to say goodbye to my children and let them adjust to living with their father without me around. ... At least [the authorities] will have gotten what they wanted, which is me out of the picture. I think in the long run it will be less of a tease to my children if I stay away until they close the case."

🖋 🖋 🖋

Phillip Salisbury is a middle-class $40,000-a-year employee of Federal Express on Long Island, New York. He and his wife Damaris live in a three-bedroom home in Far Rockaway, Queens, and describe themselves as having been "Christians since we were teen-agers." As of May 1999, they had six children, ranging in age from one to 11.

On Sunday, May 17, their second oldest boy, Jared, became sick to his stomach at church and had to be fetched home. The boy continued to feel sick to his stomach Monday and Tuesday, and was kept home from school and given plenty of fluids. Since one of their other boys had the flu, the Salisburys figured that's what he had, too.

By Tuesday night, though, it was obvious something more serious was going on, and the parents called an ambulance to take their son to St. John's Episcopal Hospital, where he died of acute peritonitis from a ruptured appendix, about half an hour after he arrived.

A form filled out at the hospital by a medical examiner, whom Phillip Salisbury described as "inexperienced and very crazed" contains three fateful sentences: "Parents state their religious beliefs forbid them to seek medical care. And they state that neither Jared nor any of other 5 children at home have ever been to see a doctor. ... Due to parents failure to treat Jared's illness, Jared's cause of death is being labeled a homicide as parents' failure to seek medical care for Jared resulted in the death of the child."

But other medical testimony indicates Jared's symptoms could easily have been confused with less serious ailments, even by a physician — let alone a layman. And Philip Salisbury has been able to provide documentation that the "never been to a doctor" allegation is not true — even in the initial interviews he was able to name his children's family doctor, Dr. Margaret Safo, insisting documentation could be provided that when Jared's brother Caleb broke his arm while playing the year before, he had been immediately taken to Franklin Hospital to be examined and treated.

Nonetheless, the Salisburys stood accused of sending their children to the Church of God Christian Academy and of refusing to get them their childhood immunizations, based on the father's personal beliefs that such "shots" pose more dangers than they're worth.

That, apparently, is all it takes in New York City. Fortunately, a sympathetic D.A. refused to prosecute the so-called "homicide," and even the social worker assigned to the case reported no reason to remove the other children from the home. Nonetheless, "His superiors, after seeing what the medical examiner wrote, ordered him to remove the children," Mr. Salisbury reports. "This same social worker resigned and moved to Michigan because of the injustice he saw in our case."

The state took the five remaining Salisbury children away and placed them in foster care, despite the fact that inspectors found all the other Salisbury kids safe, happy, well-fed, and well-clothed, and the house "reasonably clean." Their one-year-old daughter, who was receiving only breast milk at the time, "was weaned by force and against our will," Salisbury says.

"We've spoken to Mayor Rudolph Giuliani in reference to this injustice, on live radio," Salisbury continues. "He stated that whereas mistakes could be made like in our case, he prefers to be too strict in removals than not strict enough, possibly causing harm to children. Our social worker told us that they have been trained by the Giuliani administration that, 'If you are in doubt, remove.'"

Damaris had the couple's seventh child last spring. I spoke to her husband Phillip when the child was just two months old. "My wife had a baby two months ago and today they took the baby," he told me. "Our children have always been 100 percent breast fed. The foster parent is a friend, so we're still going to try. She usually breast feeds the kids for two years."

The mother will have to visit the foster home several times a day to feed her child, Phillip Salisbury explained.

❦ ❦ ❦

On March 17, 2000, during the evening, four-week-old Adrian Grubb died in his crib in Lakeland, Florida.

The police were called; they investigated and found nothing amiss. The Grubbs' two older children — other than being shocked at the event — seemed happy and healthy and well-cared-for. Just another tragic case of unexplained "crib death."

(Countries that have eliminated pertussis vaccinations — or at least postponed them till children reach the age of 2 years — have seen their rates of so-called "crib death" or "Sudden Infant Death Syndrome" plummet to near-zero. But that's a story for another day.)

As it turned out, the Grubb family were not to be left alone with their grief. At 3 o'clock came another knock at the door. Amber and Michael Grubb would later recall for the *Lake-land Ledger* that among the first things they were asked by Penelope Payton, a 24-year-old investigator with Florida's Department of Children and Families, was, "Have you ever heard of the Kayla McKean Child Protection Act?"

As it turned out, Payton (just four months out of training) was misapplying the law — since largely repealed — that was named for a 6-year-old murdered by her father during a fit of anger in 1998 after she soiled herself. Blame for the Kayla McKean death had fallen on DCF investigators, found by a Lake County grand jury to have failed to act on numerous previous indications of abuse in the McKean house. That led to the 1999 law.

But "Florida law is specific," the *Ledger*'s investigation found. "It says the state can only take protective custody of a child (if) the child has suffered abuse, faces immediate danger from abuse, or if the child's parents have violated a court custody order, and there is no 'parent, legal custodian, or responsible adult relative' available to take the child," reported Billy Townsend of the *Lakeland Ledger*.

Despite this, Penelope Payton told the Grubbs that the Kayla Act left her no choice but to take 5-year-old Morgan and 19-month-old Julian from their home.

The *Ledger*'s examination also found that DCF "decided to take the Grubb children and place them with a stranger without doing an investigation of Adrian's death or the Grubbs' home environment; may have violated state law by not trying to place Morgan and Julian with relatives, one of whom was a state-licensed foster parent; and should not have investigated Adrian Grubb's death in the first place. It only became involved because the Polk Sheriff's Office called the DCF's abuse hotline as part of the routine notification process."

"When I came into the office at 8 a.m. the next morning and heard those kids had been snatched at 3 in the morning, I hit the roof," Polk sheriff's Sgt. Larry Cavallaro, who placed that initial notification call to DCF along with another detective, told the *Ledger*. "There was no need to traumatize that family any more."

The officers insist they told DCF at the time there was no suspicion of foul play in Adrian's death.

The Grubbs were lucky. They're well-to-do financially and could afford a good lawyer. They had the cops on their side. A judge quickly ordered Morgan and Julian returned.

But the Grubbs say the damage is done, anyway.

"What do I say when Morgan asks me, 'Mom, why did they have to take me away?'" Amber Grubb asks.

DCF would not tell the local newspaper whether anyone has been disciplined in connection with the case.

"The child welfare systems are arbitrary, capricious, and cruel," comments Richard Wexler, head of the National Coalition for Child Protection Reform.

In the Lakeland case, "The police came and found absolutely nothing wrong; no signs of abuse. It was a tragedy in a perfectly normal loving home. ..."

The Grubbs finally got their two remaining children back, largely because, "They were middle-class and could afford a lawyer," Wexler says. A poorer family might not have fared as well.

"The series of laws the legislature passed in 1999 in response to Kayla [McKean]'s murder sought to plug holes in the state's child protection system," writes Billy Townsend of the *Ledger*. "But the Act had a number of unintended consequences — including what a study of state figures showed as a surge in the state's removal of children from their homes with no evidence of a corresponding surge in serious child abuse.

"The actual wording of the Kayla Act doesn't even address when children should be taken from homes. But everyone in the child protection community contacted by the *Ledger* agreed that the hype and second-guessing surrounding both Kayla's murder and the law that followed had a profound effect across Florida on DCF's decision-making.

"'The system was operating under the nightmare that someone would die on their watch,' said Jack Levine, president of the Center for Florida's Children.

"Levine's organization conducted a study of state figures showing that removal of children from homes soared 75 percent in the first six months that the Kayla Act was in effect. But the study showed 'no indication that there was a 75 percent increase in serious child abuse,' said Townsend."

🍃 🍃 🍃

According to reporting by Cheryl Romo in the *Los Angeles Daily Journal*, which covers legal matters for Southern California's attorneys, little Kameron Justin Demery, aged two-and-a-half, and his twin sister Karissa appeared to be doing fine until one early morning after the Christmas holiday, 1995.

That was when Karissa was taken to the hospital emergency room by her mom, suffering with what would later be diagnosed as bronchitis.

The first thing hospital officials requested from their mom, Jacqueline Bishop (then 29), were the children's immunization records. But since Ms. Bishop had been persuaded by her own mother, a licensed vocational nurse, not to immunize the twins because of the very real health risks, she didn't have any immunization records.

(A 1985 federal report prepared for the United States Institute of Medicine concluded that if 3.6 million American children receive three pertussis vaccinations each as recommended, 22 to 36 of those infants will suffer permanent brain damage or death each year from the vaccine.

This is the vaccine intended to prevent whooping cough, mind you — a disease that can now be treated with commonly available antibiotics. Though in fact, even the level of that "protection" is highly debatable. In a recent outbreak of whooping cough in Cincinnati, more vaccinated children came down with the disease than children who'd received no shots.)

The next day, Ms. Bishop received a call from a social worker with the Los Angeles Department of Children and Family Services. She ended up getting into an argument with the bureaucrat. Next came an unannounced inspection of her Long Beach home (where Ms. Bishop was caring for the children alone, while their father was doing time in state prison). This resulted in a state finding of "dirty home" being added to the initial report of "medical neglect" (failure to volunteer for immunizations).

Jacqueline Bishop does not contest the allegation that her home was disorderly. "It was after Christmas and everything was a mess," she told Cheryl Romo of the *Journal*.

"My daughter called me and said, 'They are threatening me if I don't get their shots,' " explains Mary Ann Bishop, the twins' maternal grandmother, who lives adjacent to her daughter's home and now blames herself for what happened to little Kameron. "I told her, 'This is a free country.'"

Is it?

Frightened, Jacqueline Miller immediately made a doctor's appointment to have the twins immunized. But it was too late. Within days came the late-night government raid in which the twins and their seven-year-old brother were seized from Ms. Bishop by brute force.

The DCFS raid was carried out because the mother "basically had a personality conflict" with the social worker, contends attorney Mark Wood of Beverly Hills, later retained by the family. "Nothing else would explain the ferocity of what happened. They came in with police at 1 a.m."

Because the mother resisted when officials took her children away, the social worker reported Bishop might have a drug problem. The mother said she was advised by social workers to enter a rehabilitation program and agreed to do so because she was told it was the only way her children would ever be allowed to come home.

"I didn't have a drug problem," she explained to Cheryl Romo of the *Journal*. "But I would have done anything to get my kids back."

The twins, Kameron and Karissa, were placed in the foster care of David and Evelyn Miller, even though the Millers had previously had all foster children in their care removed by the DCFS because of "excessive discipline." The Millers had also been decertified as care providers in February 1995 by the Foster Family Network, the agency for which the couple worked at the time.

Unfortunately, reporter Romo found the previous abuse allegations against the Millers were not reported to the DCFS hotline. They "fell through the cracks." Instead, the Millers applied for, and were promptly granted, an individual state foster-care license.

Up until this time, little Kameron had been described by her mother as "a mellow laid-back" kid.

Jacqueline Bishop and her mother were allowed to visit the twins during 1996 for only one supervised hour per week, in the Millers' mobile home in Paramount, Calif., where there resided four adults, five grandchildren, and three foster children. They report they were shocked to hear the toddlers, who are part African-American, referring to each other for the first time as "niggers." They say the children "moved like robots" and had nearly stopped talking. Asked why the children had bruises, the Bishops were told the children had hit each other. The same explanation was offered when Kameron turned up with a black eye, and when on one visit they found little Karissa's arm had been broken.

After each of these incidents, the mother and grandmother told the *Daily Journal* they reported their concerns to the children's DCFS social workers.

Those reports were ignored. On Oct. 14, 1996, little Karissa looked on as her brother Kameron, against whom she had cuddled as she fell asleep each night since she was born, was beaten to death by Evelyn Miller, his state-licensed foster care provider, who reported his fatal injuries were caused by a fall from a chair.

Government forensic experts disagreed, testifying at trial that the child's fatal injuries were inconsistent with a fall from a chair. Rather, doctors testified, he had been struck six times in the head with a blunt object, most likely Evelyn Miller's cane. Little Kameron Demery became one of six children murdered in 1996 while under the supervision of the Los Angeles Department of Children and Family Services.

Evelyn Miller is now serving a sentence of 15-years-to-life for murder. Kameron's mother sued the county for failing to prevent the toddler's brutal death, in part because social workers ignored numerous child-abuse complaints against the Millers, settling for phone calls to the Miller residence in place of "mandatory, non-discretionary, face-to-face meetings with the foster children and the Millers," as required by law.

Los Angeles County responded in court briefs that the county is "immune for discretionary acts by public employees acting within the scope of their employment, and cannot be held liable for the acts of foster parents," but finally settled the Bishops' lawsuit out of court, earlier this year, for $200,000.

Finally, on Valentine's Day, 1997, the Juvenile Court ordered Karissa returned to her mother, permanently.

Ms. Romo does not report whether little Karissa ever got her shots, or whether the Juvenile Court even bothered to ask.

Karissa told reporter Romo that she and her brother don't talk any more. But every year, on her birthday cake, there's one pink candle for each year of her life, and a single blue candle for Kameron, who has gone away.

🌿 🌿 🌿

Cheryl Barnes is the national director of CPS Watch, based in her hometown of Branson, Missouri, where her husband Elvis runs a marketing company (877-CPS-WATCH; Web site www.cpswatch.com).

"We're getting an average of two new members every single day, and that's primarily people who have had their children taken," she told me in late 2000.

"Many studies have established that children are actually more likely to be injured in foster care," Barnes continues. "The National Clearing House on Child Abuse & Neglect reported that for Fiscal Year 1998 children were 11 times more prone to suffer sexual abuse in state care, that they were murdered 5.3 percent more often in state care, that they were neglected twice as often and abused three times as often in state care as children who were left in their own homes.

"We break that down to a per-100,000 figure. Four hundred-ten per 100,000 were neglected while in state care. That's compared with only 200 and something in the general population."

Cheryl Barnes was a victim, too.

"Our seventh son was taken from us. He was born prematurely while we were visiting relatives in Kansas. They asked us to apply for Medicare, and we refused. So they took our son away. Our son was severely abused while he was in foster care; he's now permanently brain damaged and legally blind." Officers of the Florida-based hospital chain, which owned Columbia Wesleyan, were subsequently the subjects of an investigation for Medicaid fraud, Barnes points out.

"If we'd known they were going to take our child we would have done it, we would have signed. We never dreamed in a million years they'd take our child. They told us to apply for Medicaid as a backup in case our insurance wouldn't cover the hospitalization costs. Well, the application they asked us to sign said we were residents of Kansas, which we weren't. He asked me to sign the application while I was in labor, and I got kind of rude with him. I told him to get out of there.

"The charge against us was unsubstantiated. Forty-one

percent of the kids they placed in foster care in Kansas that year were unsubstantiated claims; they held him 21 months despite its all being unsubstantiated.

"We have nine sons, no daughters. He was the only one that they took," [only because he was the only one in Kansas]. Taler is now 3-years-old. He had a skull fracture. Four of his ribs were fractured in foster care, and his eyes were gouged, which left him permanently blind. They agreed he'd been abused, but they couldn't tell whether it was the man or the woman, so no charges were brought. They had placed him in an unlicensed home, where the people had had their own kids taken away by the state, and they didn't do a background check or they would have known that.

"Their claim was that we refused to sign a medical consent form; the doctor signed an affidavit immediately that that wasn't true. The only thing we refused to sign was the Medicaid application. They ruled the claim was unsubstantiated, so we thought we'd get our son back right away, but they said, 'That's not the way it works, once he's in the system. ...' In the end, it took us 21 months to get him back.

"Most parents don't realize you can appeal the adjudication. The appellate court in Kansas found they didn't have a legitimate claim of 'imminent danger' to justify taking him in the first place, but all that took 21 months. On the day that ruling came down, the state Social and Rehabilitation Services filed a motion to suspend our parental rights — to allow him to be put up for adoption — so that's what would have happened if we hadn't appealed."

I asked Barnes where in hell all this madness is coming from.

"I believe it has to do with funding. If I give you $100 for blueberries and nothing for blackberries, you're going to bring me all blueberries. They give money for foster care but only a teensy bit of money for keeping kids in their own homes. ... But the states only get money if the kids are eligible" (for assistance, based on low income.) "If the parents are rich, the states don't get any money for this, so this is why they target poorer people. They establish the guidelines that just happen to fit their funding structure."

On the bright side, Barnes reports the federal Adoption and State Families Act, enacted by Congress in 1997, has been ruled unconstitutional in the Illinois state courts. "It eliminated family-preservation funding at the federal level entirely. It allows termination of parental rights at 15 months, and it shifts the burden of proof to the parents: You have to prove you're a fit parent."

Turns out that when Miss Hillary was spouting her "It takes a village" stuff, she meant it very literally, indeed.

"But the Illinois Supreme Court has agreed it's unconstitutional. So that'll now move on to the federal level ."

❧ ❧ ❧

"I'm not aware of any case where a ['child protection'] worker was ever fired, was ever prosecuted, was ever so much as slapped on the wrist for taking too *many* kids out of their homes," explains Richard Wexler, head of the National Coalition for Child Protection Reform, an outfit funded in part by the ACLU and liberal philanthropist George Soros.

"But I've seen *all* those things happen if the worker *leaves* the kids in the home and then something unfortunate happens. So the default setting is absolutely to remove the kids."

The problem with that, Wexler explains from his office in Maryland, is, "They're often taking these kids *from* safety *to* danger; the rate of abuse in foster care is significantly higher than it is in the general population. ..."

Even in the most egregious cases, where most would agree at first sight that foster care seems like a good idea — such as babies born to crack-addicted women — "The University of Florida Medical Center conducted a six-month study of crack babies left with their birth mother or taken from their moms," Wexler reports. "Both the control group and the crack babies who stayed with their birth moms did well; it was the set of children placed in foster care who had the most problems.

"For these children, removal from their moms proved to be *more toxic* than the cocaine," Wexler concludes.

The biggest problem leading to inappropriate child seizures, in Wexler's view, is "confusing poverty with neglect. The workers' definition of neglect is usually the absence of adequate food, shelter, and clothing. If the level of poverty 'affects the child,' that can be seen as neglect. ...

"Most child welfare workers are not jack-booted thugs; they want what's best for the children. But they see a filthy home and instead of helping to clean it, they don't realize the horror of taking someone's children away. In Michigan, now, they're experimenting with an alternative to that. If the women say, 'What I really need is some help cleaning this house,' they're starting to say, 'Shall we start in the kitchen?' Now, that's only a small part of what they do. ... You may need someone to do parent counseling, to help connect them with a food bank. ..."

"A lot of these cases have to do with talking back to the worker, what one lawyer in Riverside County, Calif., has called 'flunking the attitude test.' If you know enough to say, 'Thank you, I need your help, please bestow on me your wisdom and your counseling,' *that* mother is going to keep her kids; she can get away with almost anything. In Los Angeles, we had one case where a woman got into an argument with a child care worker. The issue was how to treat the child's asthma. The state took the child away, and the child died during an asthma attack."

This prejudice against the poor — and especially poor folk who won't accept the state worker's "guidance" — compounds the problem that arises when "all the incentives are for removal" from the family home, Wexler says.

"When a child died in her own home in New York recently, the *New York Daily News* wrote in an editorial that the child care worker should be 'flogged, and then fired.' What do you think that kind of rhetoric does when there's a question about whether to remove the child or not?"

All government child welfare agencies pay lip service to the notion that the first goal is to reunite a child with its birth parents or arrange an adoption by close relatives, "but they're paying private agencies a per diem, so the financial incentive is to keep them. This is one of the last open-ended entitlements."

The more children that can be seized out of their homes and moved into the system, the more money flows to all involved — essentially without limit.

Some states have grasped the problem and reversed those economic incentives, Wexler reports. "The state of Illinois said, 'Were going to penalize you for letting kids languish in foster care, and reward you for returning kids to their birth family.' The result is that their foster care population has dropped from 51,000 in 1997 to only 30,000 today, just by changing the financial incentives."

Alabama has had similar success by requiring that consent decrees place the emphasis on family restoration. That has led to a 33 percent drop in the foster care population there, "and a court observer there says the kids are safer now," he reports.

The single most important reform Wexler would like to see?

"One solution would be to open up the whole system. You get a lot of 'There's much more here than the parents are telling you; we wish we could tell you more but our hands are tied.'

"There should be a rebuttable presumption of openness at every point in the system. Only a lawyer for the parent or the child should be able to seek secrecy, the *agency* shouldn't even be allowed to *ask* to keep anything secret."

❦ ❦ ❦

What steps can you take to make sure the "Child Protection" ghouls don't single out and destroy your family — or to remedy the situation if you do find yourself the next victim of this new and ever-expanding field of government "compassion"?

Sandra Dykes of Colorado Springs replies: "The main advice I recommend is to try and avoid social services if you can possibly help it: food stamps, welfare, all of it. They offer services to you, they say [they] need to have an open account on you, and it seems innocent at first. But later they'll tell the court they have this open case on you ... so the court sees that as a record that you needed DHS intervention and they'll use that against you to prove you can't take care of yourself or your kids."

Point well taken. But not all our victims were on the dole. In fact, Cheryl Barnes of Missouri had her newborn snatched by Kansas state authorities because she *refused* to sign up for a government welfare program — Medicaid.

One could also draw the conclusion that choosing a different path than the rest of the lowing herd on matters of commonly accepted medical myths — standing up against the pertussis vaccination of newborns, for instance — seems to invite far greater risks than most of us would have supposed.

After all, the children of Phil and Damaris Salisbury were seized in part because Mr. Salisbury does not believe in vaccinations; Jacqueline Bishop saw her twins seized — one of them beaten to death — for no other reason than because she exercised her right of medical conscience. (If we don't have to give our informed consent for these injections, why do they always hand us "consent forms"?)

But then again (given that even the U.S. government has acknowledged that pertussis vaccination of young babies can and does cause permanent brain damage and death in a small number of cases — and that crib death has virtually disappeared in nations that delay pertussis vaccination till children reach the age of two years) it could very well be argued that Amber and Michael Grubb had their older children seized because they allowed little Adrian to be given his shots.

Cheryl Barnes of CPS Watch in Missouri adds:

"The biggest thing we tell people is not to deal with social services unless they present a search warrant. And that's not being uncooperative; they're asking you to circumvent procedure or asking you to do things outside of the set protocol. There's a reason why the law requires a search warrant. They generally take the children first and get a court order later. To get a search warrant they have to have some kind of credible evidence."

In the meantime, of course, you're on the phone to your lawyer.

Barnes further warns: "Don't waive your trial. Do not waive your adjudication. ... The state will do everything in their power to get you to waive adjudication; it's the only time they have to prove their case, the only time you have a presumption of innocence. ... By signing off, you sign away all your constitutional rights."

It now appears this was one of the "routine forms" that JoAnn McGuckin was asked to sign as a condition of her release from a Bonner County jail after the county government seized her own children (after locking her up to get her out of the way) in northern Idaho in June 2001. Local authorities finally relented after the case attracted national press attention; her steadfast courage in refusing to leave jail under such conditions may well be all that preserved her chance to keep that family together.

"Eighty percent of our parents sign a waiver of adjudication," Cheryl Barnes reports. "The state will go to such extremes as denial of visitation to get them to sign. But if you waive your adjudication you can't appeal; you lose your appellate rights."

Why Would Anyone Raise Their Kids to "Fear and Distrust" Government?

〰

The five McGuckin children — aged 8 to 16 — surrendered June 3, 2001, to Bonner County sheriff's deputies who had blocked off for nearly a week the dirt road leading to their home near the town of Sagle in rural northern Idaho. The children "agreed to come out Saturday after authorities said they would try to keep the family together," The AP reported.

Michael McGuckin, who died May 12 at age 61 of poverty and complications of his disease, was hardly an unschooled mountain man; the AP reports he was the son of a Harvard-educated stockbroker and an heiress of the Shreve family of the Boston jewelers Shreve Crump & Low; he was a classmate of *Washington Post* book editor and columnist Jonathan Yardley, first at the prestigious Groton prep in Massachusetts and then at the University of North Carolina.

Since they got their hands on the children, local authorities have been at pains to justify their actions, detailing the "unsanitary" conditions in which the family was living after the running water was shut off.

"The situation reached a crisis Tuesday [May 29]" — four days after her husband's burial — writes Mark Warbis of the AP, "when JoAnn McGuckin was offered cash and a trip to the store by deputies. She was subsequently arrested on a warrant charging felony injury of a child — a charge authorities have refused to elaborate on."

"After her arrest, deputies went to the house for the children, who were to be placed in state custody," The AP reports. "But one of the boys spotted them, yelled, 'Get the guns!' and set the dogs loose."

"I think they have been raised to be leery of government officials and maybe some law," said Alice Wallace, director of the local community food center, who described the children (aged 8 to 16) as 'great kids.' They're well-mannered, they're polite, they're respectful."

Following their mother's entrapment and arrest, the five — armed with rifles — had shown no inclination to either admit government agents or to be taken away. A family friend was finally allowed to bring them a note from their mother, which apparently broke the impasse.

But reports that Mrs. McGuckin, 46, was to be promptly released after the children's surrender seem to have been premature — the mother's court-appointed criminal defense lawyer, Bryce Powell, told the judge June 4 that Mrs. McGuckin refused to leave jail after her $100,000 bond was lifted. She said she would not stay away from her children as a condition of release, and has demanded the charge be dropped and that county Prosecutor Phil Robinson apologize to her.

"Those are my kids," McGuckin said in a statement read Tuesday by her attorney. "The state needs to mind its own business."

The McGuckin property, "which has a homestead exemption and is worth nearly $500,000, was seized for $5,000 in back taxes and sold at auction for $50,000," last fall, confirms Don Harkins of the *Idaho Observer*, the conservative and sometimes conspiracy-minded monthly tabloid based in nearby Spirit Lake, Idaho.

The family's "hard times began when Michael McGuckin, who had worked at a lumber mill, was diagnosed with multiple sclerosis several years ago," reports Mark Warbis of The Associated Press.

Before that, "By all accounts, the family had been relatively prosperous until their sawmill business went bankrupt in the 1980s," the wire service reports. It wasn't immediately clear how heavily federal environmental regulations — which have devastated the timber industry throughout the Pacific Northwest — contributed to that failure. Wire service reporters rarely ask about such things, of course ... even when supposedly trying to figure out why a family would raise its kids to "fear and distrust government officials."

"I think regulation did play a role — they're pretty much on a wetland there — but ... also sometime around then the IRS came down on him," recalled Don Harkins of the *Observer* when I called him on the evening of June 5.

"People who knew these guys say they were good people, polite, well-read, intelligent, people who pay their bills. The only thing they said is occasionally the kids came in and they were a little dirty."

Harkins says the property fronts on Lake Pend Oreille — largest lake in the state. The 90 percent of the sale price not needed to cover the McGuckins' back taxes was "thrown into the general fund," he says. "When I brought it up to one of the county commissioners he was ready for me; he read out of the Idaho code to me where they could do that."

"So they trick this woman into being arrested, and they go and slap $100,000 bail on her head? And [Bonner County prosecutor Phil Robinson's] comment to the press was, 'I recommended $100,000 bail to keep her from getting out of jail and going to see her children.' I don't know about you, but I thought bond was to prevent flight or perhaps because there's a threat of violence to someone in the community, not to keep a woman from seeing her children."

"If the property had been sold at auction, wasn't this really just an expedited sheriff's eviction? I asked Harkins.

"There's a lot more involved," Harkins contends. "One thing that follows this piece of property is a quit-claim" signed over to an Oregon resident in 1996. "And also there's a homestead exemption that follows this piece of property. I don't know exactly what the status of that is, whether it follows the McGuckins or the quit-claimant or if it just falls apart; I'm not really sure yet, we're looking into it."

Now, if you were Mrs. McGuckin — bankrupted by the IRS, your husband dying of a lingering disease, your half-million-dollar homestead in the process of being seized and sold off for a dime on the dollar by the county — how would you have attempted to keep government snoops and child-snatchers from getting the "nexus" the courts say they need to inspect your home and seize your children?

Well, one might refuse to sign up for any form of government welfare. One might also home-school one's children, keeping them out of the clutches of the government welfare schools, with their mandatory Ritalin and their endless assemblies on "how to turn in daddy for owning guns."

Sacrificing material comfort for freedom, Mrs. McGuckin tried both.

As a result of refusing to sign up for welfare, she is now charged with failing to properly feed and clothe her children — though independent sources say they had plenty of food in the house. As a result of home-schooling them, she is now charged with failure to provide them with a "proper education."

The only specific allegation authorities have leveled against Mrs. McGuckin to date? They say she drinks.

I don't know JoAnn McGuckin, who appears a plump but pretty, smiling redhead in family photos. Could she have psychiatric problems? We can't know. (It's hard not to note that her refusal to sign "routine" forms giving up rights to her children in order to gain a quick release from jail certainly shows some courage and presence of mind.)

But that's why people have family, neighbors, and churches. The Rev. Dennis Day of St. Joseph Catholic Church in Sandpoint says the family's eldest daughter, 19-year-old Erina, was in touch with authorities during the "siege." If there were truly a need for psychiatric or other medical intervention, it should be up to the grown daughter to seek such help ... and surely authorities seeking to discredit Mrs. McGuckin would have her safely shut away in a mental institution by now, if they thought they had any grounds.

Instead we have property seizures, tax sales, government entrapment, and arrest. For nearly a week the AP spoke of a "crisis" (without making clear it was a "crisis" almost entirely of the government's making) at the McGuckin family "compound" (uh-oh) and the "paranoia of a family that had worked hard to cut itself off from the outside world," wondering aloud how any family could possibly raise its children to so "fear and distrust" government officials.

"The specter of nearby Ruby Ridge is inescapable here," adds Mr. Warbis of the AP. "Three people died in that 1992 northern Idaho standoff — anti-government isolationist Randy Weaver's wife and son, and a federal deputy, one of several sent to arrest Weaver on a weapons charge."

Well, no. That would not be true. In fact, the federal marshals who shot and killed young Sammy Weaver were on the Weaver property for an illegal surveillance. They have admitted under oath they were not at the time in possession of any valid arrest warrant and in fact were under orders not to approach Weaver; an Idaho jury also found they started the gun fight by shooting and killing the Weaver family dog.

An Idaho jury later acquitted Weaver of any wrongdoing in the marshals' suicidal paramilitary raid; the government had to pay the Weaver family more than a million dollars for allowing Lon Horiuchi to murder Randy Weaver's unarmed wife by shooting her through the throat with a high-powered sniper rifle ("in the line of duty") as she stood holding her baby in her kitchen.

A federal appeals court in San Francisco ruled June 5, 2000, that Horiuchi may be tried in state court for killing Mrs. Weaver.

Don Harkins' *Idaho Observer* can be reached via e-mail at observer@dmi.net or by visiting Web site www.proliberty.com/observer.

"A Show of Force ... to Show
We Were in Control"

🌿

And so the Clinton administration, which began its term using tanks to knock down the walls and staircases of a plywood church in Texas, spraying in flammable nerve agent while holding firefighting equipment miles away, the better to incinerate scores of innocent women and children already choking on their own vomit, decided to go out in similar style, staging a violent and unnecessary pre-dawn raid by a massed force of bounding overweight paramilitary goons armed with German submachine guns, in order to "show who's boss" in the matter of a 6-year-old Cuban refugee.

This was the administration that wanted to take all defensive arms away from us law-abiding peasants, mind you, since "guns never solve anything." Yet when faced with even a momentary frustration in the courts (no, Elian's Florida relatives had not violated any court order to turn over the kid. In fact, it was Attorney General Janet Reno who went to court a few days before her daredevil raid, seeking a custody order, and was specifically turned down), the Clintons reverted to the old ways — MP-5 machine guns in the dawn. Unless Lon Horiuchi is available, of course.

Ms. Reno then went on TV — following the April 2000 raid — to tell us the wonderful thing about TV is that we can all see the kid was never in danger — the gunman's finger was indexed along the receiver, not actually inside the trigger guard.

Hey, good one. Actually, we couldn't see what happened inside the house on TV, Ms. Reno, because your goons slammed the pool cameraman, NBC's Tony Zumbado, in the forehead with their gun butts and stomped him so badly he had to be hospitalized (this according to NewsMax.com — NBC itself having become such a government courtesan in its electronic dotage that the network never bothered to report this, to the best of my knowledge).

Ms. Reno said her agents had to use force because the Cuban-Americans outside the house resisted the raid, "throwing ropes" around her agents. This bizarre statement led to a correction from the Justice Department a few hours later — no ropes, it turns out; the agents merely kept tripping over Mr. Zumbado's trailing video cables after they beat him to the ground.

But as for the notion that AP photographer Alan Diaz's still photo demonstrates that the kid was never in danger, take another look at the photo. Then ask anyone who's ever fired a subgun how they jump around if you discharge them, full auto, without the stock firmly tucked into your shoulder.

A friend called me after the raid to point out that, in his younger days, his ex-wife refused to obey a court order and allow him to see his kids. When he asked the court to enforce its own order, the court told him he was out of luck.

"Why didn't they send 100 guys with German submachine guns to break down her door in the middle of the night and bring me *my* kids?" he asked. "At least I had a court order."

(Though Reno's second in command at Justice initially insisted they had no arrest or custody order because "We didn't need one," the story changed within a few days. We're now informed that instead of going to Federal District Judge Michael Moore — who was familiar with the case — Reno's goons waited till after 7 p.m. Good Friday evening to obtain a "search warrant" from a low-ranking rubber-stamp magistrate, based on an absurdly perjured affidavit that young Elian was an "illegal alien" being "concealed" in the house.)

For that matter, imagine how our "justice system" would respond if someone like my friend hired armed mercenaries to go enforce his court order, seizing his kids from his ex-wife at gunpoint. If he and his hired hands were arrested, do you suppose they could count on Ms. Reno to go on TV, insisting they not be charged with any crime, since, "The pictures clearly show their index fingers lay alongside the receivers of their full-auto submachine guns, not inside the trigger guards"?

Welcome to the rule of law in modern America — one set of rules for us peasants, and no law at all to restrict the government goons.

But this was all about getting little Elian some "quiet time with his father," wasn't it? Even though, according to *The New York Times*, Juan Miguel Gonzalez divorced Elian's mom in May 1991, and Elian was born on Dec. 6, 1993. Do the math. This father — if any DNA test would even confirm he is the father — has no automatic parental rights in any American court.

Besides which, Castro's henchmen keep referring to little Elian as the "property of the Cuban state" and have made it abundantly clear that, upon return to the slave state, little Elian will be housed in a special beachfront re-education camp, 60 miles from his father, who doesn't even own a car.

"Family togetherness," Communist style.

Who was really behind the "Great Elian Raid" ... the only positive outcome of which was the fact that disgusted Floridians went for George W. Bush by a considerable margin in the ensuing fall elections, swinging the nation Republican so that an administration of grown-ups ended up occupying the White House on Sept. 11, 2001, rather than Al Gore and his freak show of green, feminist, and/or openly gay parlor queens.

Juan Miguel Gonzalez's attorney is Greg Craig. A friend of Bill Clinton since his days at Yale law school, Craig — the guy who asked the national press to "please refrain" from covering this story too closely — is the guy who helped young Bill and Hillary get their first apartment together.

This thing had more Clinton fingerprints on it than the Rose Law Firm billing records. Why are we to suppose Judge J. L. Edmondson of the 11th Circuit issued a special injunction right after Ms. Reno's latest raid, warning the administration not to spirit young Elian away "to any place ... lying beyond the power and jurisdiction of the Courts of the United States, including, but not limited to, any place that is or may be entitled to diplomatic immunity"?

Gee, I don't know. But let anyone dare speculate that Bill Clinton, the draft dodger who visited Moscow while organizing anti-war protests in London in the 1960s, the fellow who sold sensitive military satellite and missile technology to the Chinese Red Army over the objections of his own cabinet officers after accepting millions of dollars in illegally laundered Chinese bribes while hosting Red Chinese spies in the Lincoln bedroom organized this whole affair on behalf of his communist buddy Fidel Castro, and that person would surely be dismissed as just another "black-helicopter conspiracy nut," wouldn't he?

After all, it's terribly dated to pretend there's any evidence of statist leaning in the *The New York Times* and *Time* and *Newsweek* decision *not* to run Alan Diaz's dramatic photo of the child and the G-man on their covers the week after the "Elian raid" (most opting instead for the staged government-approved "happy photo" of Elian reunited with his "dad") or in the recent declaration on national TV by *Newsweek*'s Eleanor Clift that "to be a poor child in Cuba may in many instances be better than being a poor child in Miami."

So what if Human Rights Watch reports "President" Castro has made it a crime to distribute Bibles, that he "restricts such fundamental human rights as expression, association, assembly, movement, and the press," that he "imprisons or kills people for the crime of trying to leave the country" — which is why Elian's mother died in the first place.

(Though Castro did have a crucial accomplice. On the campaign trail in 1992, candidate Clinton called for an end to George Bush's "cruel and inhumane" policy of returning refugees to oppression in Haiti and Cuba. Then, once elected, Clinton promptly reversed his stance, toughening restrictions and — contrary to international law — fining private ship captains $3,000 for every refugee rescued and brought to an American shore. Ever heard Bill Clinton condemn the communist "evil empire"? I don't think so.)

So what if Cuban parents who refuse to raise their kids as good communists can now be charged with the crime of "hindering the normal development of the child"? So what if Human Rights Watch reports Castro has so far murdered 15,000 of his political opponents?

What's that, in the view of the Clintons and their media apologists, compared to the kind of "child safety" ushered in by such achievements as "modest, sensible, civilian gun control"?

And if one more child has to be sacrificed in the cause of rehabilitating state socialism in the eyes of the American public, well, who's counting anymore?

"Women Should Be Free to Choose"

On Jan. 8, 1999, lay midwife Kellie Sparkman delivered the infant Sarai Coreas-Cruz at the Las Vegas home of Ruth Coreas-Cruz and Tito Cruz. The infant survived and is now doing fine.

Shortly after the birth, midwife Sparkman worried the child was having trouble breathing. She decided to drive the infant to the emergency room at Sunrise Hospital, where little Sarai was diagnosed with respiratory problems stemming from having inhaled meconium, which happens in 15 to 25 percent of births.

Hospital physicians are required to report any suspected case of child abuse or neglect to police. Lindy Casey, a certified Boulder City midwife, explains what appears to have happened next:

"If the hospital believes a care provider has withheld the

treatment of choice, they define that as endangerment. Their protocol would have called for transporting to the hospital by ambulance, earlier. Because she didn't follow their protocol, they interpret that as delaying the treatment of choice."

And there certainly is dispute about whether an ambulance would have been the best way to go. "During an emergency newborn transport, I witnessed a paid EMS crew that did not know what to do with a baby that was not breathing, were equipped only with an adult-sized resuscitation mask, and probably failed to oxygenate a compromised baby while fumbling to do non-essential work en route to the hospital," writes Yvonne Lapp Cryns of Richmond, Ill., who is both a certified midwife and an Emergency Medical Technician.

Nonetheless, hospital physicians reported midwife Sparkman to police on a charge of child endangerment. On March 26, Las Vegas police arrested Sparkman, locking her up till she was able to post $3,000 bail.

"The police made a decision to charge her with 'child neglect with substantial bodily harm' and that makes it a felony," explains Ms. Sparkman's attorney, Kirk Kennedy. "I think this is someone trying to make an example of her. The statute requires an act of willfulness on the part of my client, but the child is doing fine, the parents of the child continue to have a good relationship with my client; they allowed my client to come over and see the child the next day. In my personal opinion, this is coming from one or two doctors at Sunrise who are trying to get rid of midwives."

A large number of e-mail correspondents to the *Las Vegas Review-Journal* in the week since Ms. Sparkman's arrest unanimously view the arrest as part of a medical conspiracy to shut down home birth and midwifery in Nevada.

"It amazes me that doctors have lost women and babies and you never hear about it, but as soon as a midwife has a complication a crime has been committed," writes a mother from Illinois. "Go on, continue the witch-hunt, but home birth is here to stay because women like me who have been sliced, diced, humiliated, and degraded are out there educating other women on the safety of home birth!"

"We thought the days when we were looked at as witches were well behind us," wrote midwife Simone Valk from Rotterdam. "It seems that on the brink of the new millennium, Nevada steps back into the dark era of the Middle Ages."

Writing from Washington, D.C., Dr. Marsden Wagner, former director of maternal and child health for the California State Department of Health, and for 15 years regional officer for women's and children's health for the World Health Organization, wrote: "The arrest ... is a clear example of doctors harassing midwives in an attempt to eliminate competition."

Reached in Washington Friday, Dr. Wagner had a lot more to say: "The doctors don't understand, much less accept, that there's another way to do births. ... There is a major obstetric lobby across the United States running around saying it's dangerous."

Studies show the "decision-to-incision" time at hospitals averages 20 to 30 minutes, reports Dr. Wagner, who was named the UCLA medical school's alumnus of the year in 1995. "So home births within 30 minutes of a hospital are just as safe."

One-third of all births in the Netherlands are planned home births, "and they lose fewer babies than we do."

Why? "We're trained to do something, when with regard to childbirth often the most important thing is to do nothing, to let nature take its course."

For example, Dr. Wagner points out more than half the women who give birth in American hospitals receive episiotomies. "They have their vaginas cut open, even though science says the rate should never be over 20 percent. The surgeons are trained to cut. They believe a cut is better than a tear, that it'll heal better, but that's wrong. It's treating birth like a surgical procedure. They put everyone in a cap and gown and a mask, including the mother and the father. They put her up on a surgical table. It predisposes everyone to do surgery. The Caesarean section rate in this country is 20 percent. It used to be 25 percent. In Sweden it's 10 percent and they lose the fewest children in the world."

Midwifery is making inroads, with as many as 5 to 6 percent of American births now occurring at home, Dr. Wagner estimates. (Lindy Casey figures only half of 1 percent of Las Vegas births are home births.)

The largest health maintenance organization in New Mexico — Lovelace — now has more midwives than obstetricians on staff, "and 80 percent of their births are midwife births," Dr. Wagner reports.

"Several years ago the president of the American College of Obstetricians and Gynecologists stood up and said, 'Home birth is child abuse'. My educated guess is this case will be dropped. But what will have happened is, the Nevada midwives will have been shot at and they will be nervous, and that's what the doctors want. And the public will have gotten the idea that home birth is not safe.

"The fundamental issue here is freedom. Women should be free to choose where they want to give birth. And the more HMOs start to promote home births, the more vigorous is the reaction you're going to get from people whose pocketbooks are threatened."

Do Our Kids Belong to Us ... or to the State?

In June 2001, a reader wrote in from Southern California:

"Well Vin, I thought you were over the line when you talked about the public schools issuing a Parents Report Card, but it has happened to me and I'm so angry I can hardly see straight.

"Just today (6/21) I received from my 3rd-grade-going-into-4th-grade son a list of requirements that have to be met over the summer in order for him to succeed in the 4th grade.

"BTW, tomorrow, 6/22, is the last day of school. Doesn't leave much time to respond, does it? Here is what our local elementary school is demanding:

"1. Every child is to keep a 'journal of their activities and thoughts' throughout the summer. Twelve quality lines 3 to 4 days per week. They 'will collect this during the first week of school.'

"2. Each child is expected to have memorized their addition, subtraction, multiplication, and division facts from 1 to 10. We're supposed to photocopy the test sheets and the kids will be tested the first day of school.

"3. Each child will read 2-6 books per month. 'Keep a record of each book and author.'

"The note says that these are requirements that will allow your child to be successful in the fourth grade.

"We (the parents) are expected to sign and return this document tomorrow to their 3rd-grade teacher.

"And what happens if we don't sign it? It doesn't say. Will this go into our 'permanent record'?

"What about future legal entanglements? Will our refusal to sign be evidence that we are not suitable parents?

"Vin, we are supposed to be running the schools, not the other way around. These professional bureaucrats are so brazen that they are dictating how we will spend our summer with our children.

"Maybe that's the problem. They are not our children, they belong to the state. Next week I'm buying more guns. — blk"

Hi, B.L.K. —

I believe there may be court decisions on point, *barring* the schools from requiring any student to read or otherwise disclose to the class or teachers or staff their private journals. I'm still checking; maybe some other readers can give us a steer.

In the meantime, though, you're not being paranoid in expressing concern. In all innocence, your child might write about feeling temporarily depressed, or upset at some punishment. Imagine a reference cropping up to his parents being angry at one another — or the presence of guns in the home. The "child welfare" authorities these days are authorized to "err on the side of removing the child from danger" if they choose to interpret such remarks as evidence of child abuse, or as a suicide threat.

I'm no expert and I can't give specific legal advice, but I'd strongly consider responding with a formal letter to the school principal — copied to the chairwoman of the school board and their attorney — demanding citations of any legislative or judicial authority for them to demand that such a journal be kept *and turned in to authorities.*

Specifically mention the reference to your child's "thoughts." Demand to know the purpose of the school system seeking disclosure of your child's "thoughts." Do they intend to submit these recorded "thoughts" for professional psychiatric evaluation? If so, demand full advance notice of who will conduct this "psychiatric examination in absentia," what his or her credentials are, and to what purpose the results of this "unauthorized medical examination" will be put.

I'd also mention the requirement that the school be told what your child is reading. Ask whether he or she would gain extra points for reading books by Ralph Nader, Paul Ehrlich, and Al Gore, or have it held against him if he reads books by Ayn Rand, Albert Jay Nock, Frederic Bastiat, or Lysander Spooner. (Don't worry about the kid only being nine. Your child will be 11 or 12 before they ever answer such a demand, and 11 or 12 is a *great* age to start reading that stuff.)

As to the notion that students on summer vacation *after* attending third grade are "expected to have memorized their addition, subtraction, multiplication, and division facts from 1 to 10. ... The kids will be tested the first day of school," I would express formal written shock at this indication that your child may not *already have these tables memorized*. This is something that has been accomplished in the schools, and by the schools, by the end of third grade since time immemorial.

Yes, you're right. "Failure to sign" is highly likely to get you identified as one of the droves of parents who "just don't care" ... as they busily try to shift blame for their failures onto others. So, far from "refusing to sign." I'd send them a *whole lot* of new reading matter. ... :-)

But then, I can't give you any specific legal advice.

Best Wishes,

— Vin

ᏏᏏᏏ

I also copied my response to BLK to Marshall Fritz of the Fresno-based Separation of School and State Alliance (sepschool@SepSchool.org.) Marshall responded:

"B.L.K., these people really want to control you and your child and you are certainly right to be upset. But I wonder... why do you keep your child in the school?

"You know they are undermining you, and by your sending the lad to the school, are you not giving him a badly mixed message? Many people have never thought it through, but the schools *are* socialism and they *are* welfare.

"If you are against both, and from the tenor of your letter I infer that is indeed the case, do you not teach the lad by your behavior in sending him to the school, that socialism and welfare aren't all that bad?

"I deeply regret the abuse I gave my children by sending them to government schools. Maybe you can wake up in time to not repeat the same mistake.

"As for helping you, I wish I could, but we have no expertise in helping people endure socialism. We mean to replace it."

XI
A Whisper They Can Ignore — Sacrificing Kids to the Government Vaccination Machine

July 25, 1994
🌿

The spring of 1979 was a happy time for Donna Burns of Gardner, Massachusetts. The young mother of three was pregnant with her fourth child.

"It was a normal pregnancy, it was a normal delivery, we all had perfectly normal healthy babies," Donna says.

Her doctor recommended immunizing little Ryan against diphtheria, pertussis, and tetanus. Burns remembers the first shot was the day before the Fourth of July. Because it was a holiday, she had several witnesses at the house: "He had a 106-degree fever, and there was this terrible screaming. Since then I've had another doctor look at the records. He says the shots did it."

Today, Ryan is 15 and "a good kid," Burns says. He's in the ninth grade, although he does third grade work. "He didn't speak till he was four years old. He has gross motor and fine motor problems. Ryan is epileptic, he has migraine headaches. He has hearing loss."

Didn't the doctor warn her this was a possible side effect of the controversial DPT shots?

"No. We were told they might be fussy, and that we should give them aspirin. I kept telling the first doctor something was wrong, but he didn't look into it." Even now, Burns says, "People sign the booklet without reading it. ... You take it on good faith the doctor knows what he's doing, the FDA is approvin' this stuff."

But the doctors kept giving Ryan the shots?

"Yes. The doctors kept measuring his head size, and it kept increasing. Then, nine months after the shots stopped, there were no more increases in his head size."

Surely records like that should help prove a connection between the immunizations and Ryan's damage?

"The original doctor wrote down that Ryan walked at 10 months. That's true. He took his first steps. Six months later, he had regressed. He'd just stumble and fall. But the doctor didn't write that. I would take him in with his hands turning blue, and the doctor wrote down 'hands chapped.' Ryan had 20 seizures a day, and the doctor wrote down, 'Mother complains of child choking.' He got to choking so bad one night I had to put my fingers down his throat and get him to vomit so he could breathe."

As a Massachusetts resident, Donna Burns is a constituent of U.S. Sen. Edward Kennedy, who was instrumental in passing the National Childhood Vaccine Compensation Act. But the act bans class-action suits, directing claims to specific panels made up of government employees. Those panels have turned down Donna Burns three times.

"All I'm asking for is the $8 a month it costs to buy the special insurance from the state. If Ryan lives 50 years that'll add up to $5,000. They've spent a lot more than that fighting me. But when you go in there the special master and both lawyers are paid for by the government. Basically the federal courts said I lied, my witnesses lied, and the doctor only said what I told him to say. ... I want a jury trial, that's my right as an American citizen."

Donna Burns has been trying to see Edward Kennedy for four years. Burns and her state representative were allowed to meet with Sen. Kennedy's health aide recently. "I asked her why aren't we using the new acellular vaccine that's been approved for older children. I asked her why we're not allowed to file class action suits. I asked, 'Isn't it easier to take us down one a time?' She said I seemed to be very cynical about the federal government."

The federal compensation plan, in Burns' opinion, "is like taking a homeless person to the supermarket in front of a lot of people and saying, 'Help yourself,' but then when you get him home you tell him, 'Hey, you didn't think we were gonna let you *eat* any of this stuff?'"

Documents acquired by Burns under the Freedom of Information Act indicate the Commonwealth of Massachusetts was telling doctors as late as 1978 that "some minor reaction may be expected," but that "the risk of injection must be weighed against the risk of the disease," even though whooping cough can now be treated with antibiotics.

By 1980, however, a revised pamphlet was warning doctors the vaccine could cause "encephalitic symptoms" (swelling of the brain), which could be followed by "severe mental or physical impairment." Also included in the 1980 information supplied to Massachusetts doctors were reports on 13 adverse reactions to the vaccine between May 1980 and December 1981, including three deaths.

A 1985 federal report prepared for the United States Institute of Medicine concluded that if 3.6 million American children receive three pertussis vaccinations each as recommended, 22 to 36 of those infants will suffer permanent brain damage each year.

Nor is the pertussis vaccine alone. Jonas and Darrel Salk warn, "The live virus against measles and mumps may produce side effects such as encephalitis." And the oral polio vaccine now favored in America over the safer Salk vaccine actually caused 94 cases of polio in this country between 1969 and 1982, according to the USIM report.

Burns says 18,000 permanent-damage claims have now been filed under the Vaccine Compensation Act. At one point, after she and her witnesses gave statements, "The stenographer told us she knew exactly what we were going to say because all the cases are the same. But one person is a whisper they can ignore."

Donna Burns' last chance for compensation may come at the Massachusetts State Legislature, where State Rep. Robert Hawke of Gardner has filed a bill that would waive the statute of limitations and allow Burns to sue the state — manufacturer of Ryan's vaccine.

"Japan uses the acellular, synthetic vaccine, and they have never had a problem. We should learn from our mistakes, not keep making the same mistakes. Ryan's a good kid but he did not have to be that way. He deserves an apology from these people."

Interested parties can reach Burns, who stresses that she is "not anti-vaccine; I'm anti-unsafe vaccine," at 449 West St., Gardner, Mass. 01440. "I'd love to hear from other people."

Parents can also try Dissatisfied Parents Together, the National Vaccine Information Center, 204-F Mill St., Vienna, Va. 22180.

"Because the Kennedy bill banned class-action suits, nobody knows who anybody is," Burns says. "We're all out here on our own."

October 2, 1994
The "SIDS Death Certificates?
They Asked Me How I Got Them"

Think the press tells you the whole truth? Then why did most outlets merely report that 1994's Miss America, 21-year-old Alabama college student Heather Whitestone, claims to have been rendered almost totally deaf at the age of 18 months by the side effects of "a shot"?

"I called her PR person, a friend of hers from Birmingham named Pat Tucker," says Donna Burns, whose own 14-

year-old son, Ryan, suffers permanent learning disability and hearing loss following the fever, seizures, and brain swelling that accompanied each of his childhood DPT vaccinations, "and she says it's true, she's deaf because of the DPT shot. God bless Miss America, she couldn't have gone on TV and given a four-hour speech and done more.''

I pointed out to Burns that those interested in keeping a lid on the side effects of the whole-cell pertussis component of the DPT vaccine rushed rebuttal witnesses onto the air in the days following Whitestone's statement, dispatching doctors in white lab coats and even Whitestone's own mom to tell TV audiences that the familiar shot couldn't possibly have caused her deafness.

"Of course they're going on TV and denying it; I'm surprised they didn't bleep it out," Burns responds. "I'm shocked they let her say it; I'm shocked they haven't shot her. I'll bet you their hair stood on end. I thank Miss America on behalf of Ryan and every other child, on behalf of thousands of other children."

The government claims serious side effects don't affect that many, of course, though they do acknowledge the shots may cause 22 to 36 cases of permanent brain damage per year. "The government numbers aren't accurate," Burns says. "How many kids are like my son, where they say, "That's not what caused it' and they blow you off? I think they've got a whole bunch of jugs of whole cell vaccine and they're waiting to use them up. It's all money."

Burns is prevented from suing the state of Massachusetts, which manufactured the vaccine she believes caused Ryan's injuries, by a three-year statute of limitations. It was more than three years before she could convince anyone his ailments were caused by the shots.

Ryan is scheduled for surgery at Massachusetts General Hospital this fall for broken eardrums and mastoiditis. "It's serious surgery. The operation is not to correct his hearing, it's just to get rid of the infections, and there's no government help with these medical costs. The doctor at the hospital asked me how long Ryan has had an ear infection and I said, 'Fourteen years'."

With a boost from Miss America, Donna Burns' lonely crusade is finally getting some attention. *The Boston Herald* ran a 15-inch story Sept. 20 under the three-column headline: "Mother Asking State to Probe Bad Reactions to Child Vaccines."

Burns is asking the Massachusetts Legislature to extend the statute of limitations to 15 years. Michael LaSalandra of the *Herald* quotes Ralph Timperi, an assistant state health commissioner, to the effect that claims against the state from a 15-year statute of limitations "would swamp ... the system potentially."

"Gee, I thought they said very few kids were damaged,'' Burns responds, "But now they say if the victims could sue, they'd be swamped. Which is it?"

The *Herald* goes on: "Burns said she knows at least two women whose babies died after DPT shots, In both cases, SIDS or crib death was listed as the cause of death, yet both women received money under the compensation program. ...''

I asked Donna Burns about those two deaths. She promptly faxed me the death certificates of Lee Ann Manley, died Wayland, Mass., age 1 year 27 days on June 2, 1983, and Michael Vincent Lindeman, died Milford, Mass., age 2 months 25 days on Jan. 16, 1985. Both death certificates list the cause of death as "Sudden Infant Death Syndrome," yet signed statements from parents in both cases state they received compensation from the federal vaccine compensation program.

Janet Manley of Wayland goes further: "Seven years after the death (of) my darling daughter Lee Ann Manley ... I had repeatedly asked for the death certificate to be changed to acknowledge death from DPT vaccine or a letter staying so. The government is allowing the medical field to get way with murder — and then not even counting how many."

What did the Massachusetts attorney general's office say when presented with the death certificates, I asked Donna Burns.

"They asked me how I got them."

I asked Dr. William Torch, a pediatric neurologist at the School of Medicine at the University of Nevada, Reno, who has published studies on the possible link between SIDS and the DPT vaccine, how the vaccine compensation program can pay parents of children whose death certificates list the cause of death as Sudden Infant Death Syndrome.

"That happens because the SIDS diagnosis is a coroner's definition," Torch explained. "Just because someone writes SIDS doesn't mean it's unrelated to DPT."

I mentioned to Dr. Torch that Donna Burns contends the safer but more expensive acellular pertussis vaccine, already recommended for American children over 18 months, is used exclusively in Japan, with none of the side effects associated with the whole cell vaccine.

"I'm not sure how effective that acellular vaccine is, but that would be an intriguing question for someone to look into," Torch responded, "whether you find less Sudden Infant Death Syndrome in populations that get the acellular vaccine exclusively."

March 22, 1995
"These Vaccinations Aren't What They're Cracked Up to Be"
🌿

In Washington, of course, "getting government out of our lives" is the script from which Republican officeholders read in between votes to continue expanding every socialist boondoggle FDR or Lyndon Johnson ever thought of. But here and there, in the state capitals, a few of the new GOP majorities are actually giving it a try.

In a close-fought 11-10 victory, the newly Republican Nevada State Senate in March 1995 gave parents the unrestricted right to exempt their offspring from the childhood immunizations long required for admission to Nevada's government schools.

The state Senate vote — the lower house must still decide — came over the objections of a vociferous minority of Democrats like State Sen. Bob Coffin of Las Vegas, who warned, "How are you going to feel? Your yes vote liberalized the law and let a child die."

"Children are already suffering from these shots," responded Republican casino executive Sue Lowden, also of Las Vegas. "This is the ultimate in government interference, saying we know better than the parents what is good for their children." Mandatory vaccination laws treat children as "sacrificial lambs" and leave parents "praying to God that their child doesn't suffer," Lowden added.

Unfortunately, most states are moving in just the opposite direction, reports Neil Z. Miller, whose *New Atlantean Press* (P.O. Box 9638, Santa Fe, New Mexico 87504) markets not only his own book, *Vaccines: Are They Really Safe and Effective*, but also such hard-to-get imports as Australian Ph.D. Viera Scheibner's *Vaccinations: A Medical Assault on the Immune System*, which reports that since 1975, when Japan raised the vaccination age from two months to 2 years, Sudden Infant Death Syndrome has virtually disappeared in those islands.

"New Jersey offers a religious exemption," Miller told me March 22. "I got a call this week from a woman there who signed a religious waiver. Everything was OK for a couple of weeks, her kid was in school, but now they've come back to her and they're demanding to know what her precise religious beliefs are."

By coincidence, the Carson City, Nev., vote follows close

on the heels of FDA Commissioner David Kessler's announcement that the government has finally OK'd Merck & Co.'s chickenpox vaccine, Varivax, ballyhooed as conqueror of the last common childhood disease.

Varivax, a live attenuated form of the varicella virus, is "expected to be 70 to 90 percent effective in preventing chickenpox," Kessler said.

"This is a vaccine that is going to go potentially into every young child in the country," enthused Kathryn C. Zoon of the FDA's center for biologics evaluation and research.

Of course, one of the problems with chickenpox is that it lies dormant in the body for years, sometimes reactivating in the form of the adult disease zoster (shingles), a painful skin condition. Is there likely to be a resulting epidemic of shingles in 40 years if we proceed to "put this vaccine into every child in the country"?

That's "not likely to happen," responds Dr. Philip Krause of the FDA's biologics center.

"It's a strong possibility," says Neil Miller in Santa Fe. "The FDA was slow to approve this vaccine because its efficacy rate is so dismal, and because of concern about potential problems down the road, when compared to the relatively innocuous nature of chickenpox itself. They say there are 50 to 100 deaths from chickenpox very year. Yet if you research the children who have died from chickenpox, you find most already had impaired immune systems from other causes."

Just as the major cause of polio in America is now the oral Sabin polio vaccine — a live attenuated vaccine like Varivax — so Varivax "will cause chickenpox and they admit that up front," Miller says.

Give them a few years, and Varivax (at $39) will be required by the government, Miller warns ... just like the measles vaccine. "They've tampered with measles and they know it. When measles hits a new population it's a dangerous disease; fatality rates are high. But once a population is exposed for awhile they develop a herd immunity. By the 1950s and '60s everybody caught measles, but you never heard about any deaths. Now we've had a measles vaccine for 30 years, and they've suppressed the natural immunity. Now the disease is mutating and their vaccine is ineffective. At one time they promised they were going to eradicate measles from the face of the Earth, by 1982 I think it was. So what's their answer now? Get booster shots. But what they've discovered is it's turning into a killer disease again."

While contracting chickenpox as a child provides lifetime immunity, the FDA admits Varivax immunity may not last that long. "In a worst-case scenario," says Dr. Philip Krause, "if immunity wanes, these kinds of problems can be dealt with by ... booster doses."

Miller is preparing his second book on vaccinations, "discussing the ploys used by the medical establishment and government officials to pull the wool over the eyes of unsuspecting parents, and then I'm off the issue. ... When you get a call from a mother whose healthy child got his first pertussis shot, and 12 hours later he's dead, what can you say? They write 'Sudden Infant Death Syndrome' on the death certificate and refuse to write down anything about the vaccination, and you're the first person that woman has been able to talk to who won't tell her she's crazy. It's too emotionally draining to me."

Casting the deciding vote in Carson City, Republican State Sen. Mark James of Las Vegas, widely touted as a future governor, said: "These vaccinations aren't what they're cracked up to be."

🌿 🌿 🌿

Disappointing followup:

The outcry — led by doctors and public health bureaucrats — against this state Senate vote, giving Nevada parents the right to choose whether their children would receive vaccinations, was so loud that the state Senate re-voted the question the following week and reversed itself. Today, Nevada children must once again prove they have received "all required immunizations" before they will be admitted to the public schools.

Not content with that, the opponents of one of the prime movers of the "vaccination choice" measure, state Sen. Sue Lowden, R-Las Vegas — already targeted by the unions because her family owns a local non-union hotel and casino — managed to defeat the 1996 re-election bid of this attractive, articulate former television news anchor, whose name had been floated for the office of lieutenant governor, in a campaign that actually claimed she had voted to "expose our children to deadly contagious diseases."

March 21, 2000
"An Almost Violent Reaction, as if I Had Just Confessed to ... Some Ritualistic Form of Child Abuse"

Dear Mr. Suprynowicz —

I am writing to thank you for your column in yesterday's paper about vaccinations. By way of introduction, I am a new mother of a daughter, Olivia. I will try and be concise but I want you to know why I appreciated your editorial so much.

Olivia was born at home last September, with the help of midwives and a birth assistant. During our preparation for our daughter's birth, my husband and I took extensive childbirth classes taught by our birth assistant and it was there that we were first introduced to information concerning the adverse effects of vaccinations.

At first I was skeptical, as I had heard about these "fringe" groups who opposed vaccinations and had always assumed that these were the same people who were always railing against the latest technology or medical innovation. I decided to at least take a look at the anti-vaccination literature before dismissing it out of hand — after all, my husband and I had chosen to have our baby at home with the help of midwives to avoid unnecessary medical interventions and because we sincerely believed that it was healthier for me and for her — certainly an unconventional decision. So why not explore the vaccination issue before making up our minds, as well?

I began reading and I found an extremely informative Web site (thinktwice.com) where I was able to order more books and I really began to immerse myself in the literature. It did not take long before I became convinced that the people who have been taking a stand against vaccinations are doing so for some very legitimate and logically sound reasons. I became absolutely convinced that there was no way I could subject my daughter to immunizations now that I knew not only about the potentially devastating side effects, but the fact that these shots do not provide real protection against the intended diseases.

That brings me to my next realization and why your editorial struck such a chord with me. Having made the decision not to immunize our daughter, it began to dawn on us that this was not just another unconventional decision, like the one we made when we decided to give birth to Olivia at home. This decision could have some really severe consequences. It will affect the schools Olivia can attend, the extracurricular activities in which she can participate, and could also impact her friendships with classmates.

I made the mistake of openly discussing our decision not to vaccinate with an acquaintance and I was met with an almost violent reaction, as if I had just confessed to participating in some ritualistic form of child abuse. The brainwashing about vaccinations is so complete that people actually believe that an unvaccinated child is a danger to the children who have had their shots.

Shortly after that experience, we had an accident with Olivia where she fell from a table while in her infant seat and we rushed her to a Quick Care. On the way in the car I told my husband that if they asked us about her vaccinations we needed to lie and tell them that she was up to date. If they pressed further, I would just tell them that I did not have the records with me. You see, I had read about the situation you detailed in your column on the Web site that I mentioned earlier and I knew that an admission to hospital personnel about Olivia's vaccination status could have some serious consequences.

I hope that I have not taken too much of your time with my story. I would love to publicly respond to your column in the paper because I think that this is a topic which needs to be discussed openly and that parents need to know the real risks before having their children vaccinated. My husband and I are both attorneys and we have decided that for now it is best to keep our decision quiet because we could be good targets for the bureaucrats wishing to grind their axe on this issue. I trust that you will keep my name confidential but feel free to reference our decision in any context you find helpful in whatever discourse you may have on this issue in the future.

— L. C.

Hi, L.C. —

Thanks for writing. I won't release your name.

Yes, all you have to do is expose anything unconventional about your child-rearing habits or plans to learn very quickly how many of our neighbors believe children are actually "the property of the state," which can and should seize them at the slightest sign of failure to train and indoctrinate them properly for life in the collective.

(It turns out simply owning firearms, or buying the wrong books, can now constitute prima facie evidence of "child abuse," as some of our unfortunate brethren east of the Mississippi are quickly learning.)

I often wonder that these folks can watch any of the "Star

Trek" spinoffs, without wondering, "But why are the Borg presented as *bad guys?*"

Personally, I have never argued that "all vaccinations are
evil." Being vaccinated against the smallpox probably made sense
at one time, and I believe the equation probably balances out in
favor of requesting a "tetanus shot" when medically indicated.

But as I'm sure you know from your research, the *known*
dangers of the pertussis vaccine far outweigh its minimal demonstrable effects in preventing the disease. And the tradeoffs
for supposed "60 percent efficacy" become more and more
weighted against "the shots" when we come to the new vaccines for measles, mumps, rubella, chicken pox, and the like.

Fortunately, home schooling — and rejection of many of
these arbitrary government edicts across the board — is growing. With any luck, those who stand up for a lot more of their
original "right to choose" will feel somewhat less lonely in the
decades to come.

Now, just wait till this next generation of kids starts to
tell cops, taxmen, and prospective employers: "No, I don't have
my vaccination records — they're optional, you know. Social
Security number? Nope. That's optional too. I simply decided
to opt out of the government 'retirement plan.' I'm also not
going to sign a form swearing under oath that I'm liable for the
income tax, since I can only find statutes applying that tax to
those who handle domestic income for off-shore investors, and
those who work in 'privileged occupations,' like machine-gun
manufacturers. Or have you found a statute that says the average wage-earner is subject to the federal income tax? Could
you show me that statute? The head of the IRS has never been
able to find it, even when Special Agent Joe Bannister said he
was going to have to resign unless they could show it to him
..." (see http://www.freedomabovefortune.com).

I fear we are doomed to live in interesting times.

Good luck to you, and to little Olivia.

XII
Burn the Schools

"A Mere Simulacrum, an Android, a Pre-Programmed Robot"

❦

I experienced one of those minor epiphanies as I grabbed lunch at the local Kentucky Fried Chicken in the fall of 1998. The owner of the franchise is public-spirited enough (savvy enough about public relations?) to co-sponsor a regular "student of the month" luncheon at the local elementary school.

The students express their gratitude by supplying the restaurant with monthly sheets of poster paper, emblazoned "Student of the Month" and "Thank You K.F.C.," which the restaurateur proudly hangs in his little dining area. The posters bear multiple color snapshots of the kids eating their KFC box lunches at school and proudly displaying their "Student of the Month" certificates and bumper stickers.

Children of the customers. Smart.

But as I sat reading the children's exotic names — Demetrius, Kinchasa, Lowanda, Sequoia, written in many different colors of felt pen — I noticed that all were printed in the same flowing hand. The children had not been judged capable of signing their own thank-you notes. Their teacher had done it for them.

Then I began to look more closely at the photographs, puzzling at how difficult it was to determine which of the many children pictured had actually been named "student of the month."

And that's when it hit me.

In a classic manifestation of the modern "self-esteem" movement, no one in our current educational establishment would *conceive* of allowing 97 percent of those kids to feel badly for 30 days because they *hadn't* been named "student of the month." So *all* the students who attend each luncheon are named "student of the month." The photos show lineups of three, four, six children at a time, all proudly showing off their identical mass-produced certificates and bumper stickers declaring "My Child is a Student of the Month at Madison Elementary."

Now, it may seem a stretch to relate this kind of "well-meaning" flim-flammery, this systematic erosion of reality-based competition and thus of the opportunity to ever be honored for any *real* individual achievement, to another event we were witnessing in the fall of 1998, the astonishing moral and political collapse of the Clinton presidency.

But I believe they are, at heart, manifestations of the same decadence — a word I use fairly carefully to mean not just accidental decay, but a willful rejection of proven values and methods, replacing them under the guise of being "progressive" with a topsy-turvy derivative celebration of everything that is false, affected, and rebellious against the truths of man's nature so painstakingly handed down to us over the past 5,000 years.

Many modern science-fiction films — *Alien* comes to mind, though there have been others before and since — contain a scene in which a character previously indistinguishable from his fellows suddenly begins to repeat the same fragmentary words or motions over and over, then to shudder and tremble, and finally to go cartwheeling across the set, gushing hydraulic fluid from "his" veins.

What we — and the other characters — had thought to be a fellow human is thus revealed to be a mere simulacrum, an android, a pre-programmed robot masterfully engineered to appear and act as a man, then infiltrated among the living as part of some nefarious ulterior scheme.

For real horror, the movies with cockroaches the size of Greyhound buses can hardly compete with films that start to convince us that — just maybe — many of our neighbors are actually alien automatons, programmed to make us think they share our thoughts and feelings, but actually incapable of feeling the slightest sympathy or compassion for us "weak waterbag organisms," instead hiding some secret, revolting, and finally unknowable agenda of the alien hive.

Some of us had realized for years that Bill and Hillary Clinton and every other progressive/redistributionist politician lies continually and as a matter of course — patting the head of some prop urchin from central casting as they justify one expansion after another of their voracious armed police state by citing "the safety of the chiiiildren."

Republican gadfly Rush Limbaugh used to show a piece of videotape on his TV show, in which Bill Clinton departed the funeral for his Secretary of Commerce, Ron Brown — whose death in a Bosnian plane crash while under investigation for bribery, having stated he was "not going to go down alone," was one of so many fortuitous deaths for this president.

Bill Clinton is seen leaving the memorial service, laughing and joking with a companion. In a flash, however, he spots the rolling camera, develops an instant expression of sadness, and wipes a tear from one eye.

It's all an act, of course. But the real reason Bill Clinton was so divisive, I think, is that those who were outraged to discover it was just an act — that no real effort was being taken to find and destroy Osama bin Laden's terror network, for example, since all that was deemed necessary was to lob a few cruise missiles at a Sudanese pharmaceutical factory long enough to drive Monica Lewinsky's stained blue dress off the front pages — couldn't understand what had possessed the slim majority of Americans (and virtually all the *soccer* moms) that prevented them from *seeing* it was all an act.

The answer — and the explanation of why the "conservative right" made itself look so silly, hopping about on one foot and holding its breath till it turned blue, trying to draw attention to the fact that the emperor had no clothes — is that the liberal left already knew the Clintons were phony as a three-dollar bill. They just didn't care.

They had come to judge politics the way we judge the Miss American pageant. No one believes some mindless little bimbo in a bathing suit and high heels is going to cure world hunger. We just find it perversely entertaining to judge them on how well they pretend to *care* about such stuff in between baton-twirling exhibitions while walking down a flight of stairs in high heels and virtually no other clothing, with a grin glued on their faces and the bright TV lights shining in their eyes.

It's called mindless decadence. Look at how quickly the soccer moms, who used to huff and puff and ridicule and storm and threaten to have us gun owners arrested for endangering the neighborhood, came knocking after the terror attacks of Sept. 11, asking for advice on how to buy a gun and where to practice.

The phrase you're looking for is "pathetic dangerously empty-headed morons."

After 30-odd years of "progressive" government schooling, America has raised two whole generations of emotionally hollow automatons whose "political opinions" are based on what teacher said and which opinions get applauded or booed on Oprah Winfrey and Jerry Springer and Dan Rather's CBS Liberal News.

How did the pod people take over while you weren't looking?

It's the government schools, stupid.

What should really frighten us is not the fact that Bill and Hillary Clinton were eventually revealed to be the moral and emotional equivalent of one of those human-looking androids in the science fictions movies, unmasked in a now-familiar scene in which they begin to stutter and shudder, and finally go cartwheeling around the spacecraft spewing white hydraulic fluid.

No, what should frighten us is that, right up through Sept. 11, 2001, and to a considerable extent thereafter, only 35 percent of Americans seemed to care. Sixty-five percent said and largely continue to say: "So what? All that moral and emotional stuff is so much make-believe, anyway. Doesn't everybody lie? Doesn't everybody fake it?"

Where did this race of pod people come from?

From the government schools, stupid.

For years, folks have been dismissing the direst of warnings about the "public-schooling" scam with exasperated disbelief.

Schools don't fight duplicity, cheating, drug use, and scorn for achievement, argued New York State Teacher of the Year John Taylor Gatto in his slim but estimable little volume *Dumbing Us Down* ($12.45, New Society Publishers, 4527 Springfield Ave., Philadelphia, Penn. 19143). Instead, Mr. Gatto discovered after a lengthy and distinguished career, these things are what the schools actually *teach*.

"Put kids in a class and they will live out their lives in an invisible cage, isolated from their chance at community," Gatto warns. "Interrupt kids with bells and horns all the time and they will learn that nothing is important; force them to plead for the natural right to the toilet and they will become liars and toadies; ridicule them and they will retreat from human association; shame them and they will find a hundred ways to get even" through exactly the kind of addictive, immature, and dependent pathologies we expect from any inmates — drugs, violence, random sex.

🌿 🌿 🌿

What caused his teachers to praise someone like the young Bill Clinton, who didn't just dodge the physical risks of Vietnam, but who (as some were shocked to discover at a very late date) apparently avoided all the emotional risks and commitments that help a boy mature into a man, leaving a 50-year-old married president at the approximate level of emotional development of a giggling, groping 13-year-old, promising to "marry" his date to the sock hop if she'll let him cop a feel?

Apparently no one believes Mr. Gatto. But the great novelist and philosopher Ayn Rand further explained the process by which children's normal mental and emotional development are now systematically and deliberately crippled in a 1970 essay called "The Comprachicos," available in the Meridian paperback *The New Left*:

"At the age of three, when his mind is almost as plastic as his bones, when his need and desire to know are more intense than they will ever be again, a child is delivered — by a Progressive nursery school — into the midst of a pack of children as helplessly ignorant as himself. ... He wants to learn; he is told to play. Why? No answer is given. He is made to understand — by the emotional vibrations permeating the atmosphere of the place ... that the most important thing in this peculiar world is not to know, but to get along with the pack. Why? No answer is given.

"He does not know what to do; he is told to do anything he feels like. He picks up a toy; it is snatched away from him by another child; he is told that he must learn to share. Why? No answer is given. He sits alone in a corner; he is told that he must join the others. Why? No answer is given. He approaches a group, reaches for their toys and is punched in the nose. He cries, in angry bewilderment; the teacher throws her arms around him and gushes that she loves him. ...

"The teacher's mechanical crib-side manner — the rigid smile, the cooing tone of voice ... the coldly unfocused, unseeing eyes — add up in the child's mind to a word he will soon learn: phony. He knows it is a disguise; a disguise hides something; he experiences suspicion — and fear.

"A small child is mildly curious about, but not greatly interested in, other children of his own age. In daily association, they merely bewilder him. He is not seeking equals, but cognitive superiors, people who *know*. Observe that young children prefer the company of older children or of adults, that they hero-worship and try to emulate an older brother or sister. A child needs to reach a certain development, a sense of his own identity, before he can enjoy the company of his 'peers.' But he is thrown into their midst and told to adjust.

"Adjust to *what*? To anything. To cruelty, to injustice, to blindness, to silliness, to pretentiousness, to snubs, to mockery, to treachery, to lies ... and to the overwhelming , overpowering presence of Whim as the ruler of everything. ...

"After a while, he adjusts. ... He learns that regardless of what he does — whether his action is right or wrong, honest or dishonest, sensible or senseless — if the pack disapproves, he is wrong and his desire is frustrated; if the pack approves, then anything goes. Thus the embryo of his concept of morality shrivels before it is born," and is replaced with the realization that the objective reality of achievement is worthless, that everything of value is instead gained through the emotional manipulation of the pack, Ms. Rand explained.

"Cut off from reality, which he has not learned fully to grasp, he is plunged into a world of fantasy playing. He may feel a dim uneasiness, at first: to him, it is not imagining, it is lying. But he loses that distinction and gets into the swing. The wilder his fantasies, the warmer the teacher's approval and concern. ... He begins to believe his own fantasies. ... Why bother facing problems if they can be solved by make-believe? ...

"The teacher prods him to self-expression, but he knows that this is a trap; he is being put on trial before the pack, to see whether he fits or not. He senses that he is constantly expected to feel, but he does not feel anything — only fear, confusion, helplessness and boredom. ...

"So he learns to hide his feelings, to simulate them, to pretend, to evade — to repress. The stronger his fear, the more aggressive his behavior; the more uncertain his assertions, the louder his voice. From playacting, he progresses easily to the skill of putting on an act. ... He cannot know by what imperceptible steps he, too, has become a phony."

☙ ☙ ☙

Is it really so hard to see how an "education" system that grades children on group projects and "how they fit in with others," that flatters them that all their uninformed opinions are equally worthy of "discussion groups," that rejects the tried and true practice of encouraging the majority to aspire to match the achievements of the best and the brightest, instead naming *every* child "student of the month," could end up producing a Bill Clinton ... or 100 million Bill Clintons? Is it really any surprise that two whole American generations are now schooled not in math, spelling, and grammar, but rather in fantasy, deception, and manipulation?

Can we really be surprised that they ignore evidence that the garbage men pour all their sorted trash into the same trucks, insisting the exercise of sorting green bottles from brown is still worthwhile if it "raises everyone's consciousness"? That they snort at statistics proving cities with gun bans actually have the highest rates of crime, or that one volcano releases more "greenhouse gases" than 1,000 years of Freon? They instead insist it doesn't matter whether an "assault weapons ban" will really reduce crime, or whether banning spray cans will really close the "ozone hole," so long as jailing the violators of such freedom-crushing edicts makes us all *feel better about ourselves*, since "at least we tried"?

Should we really be surprised to hear them now, whining, "What do you want? Everyone has affairs. Everyone lies under oath." Or, as letter-writer Bob Gore puts it in the Sept. 20, 1998, *Las Vegas Review-Journal*:

"I feel like I'm living in a country that is collectively raising an adolescent. Listen to Billy Clinton and his friends: 'I didn't do it. Nobody saw me do it. You can't prove a thing.

Everybody does it. It's no worse than anybody else. Kenny is a snitch ... and he's an old meanie. I do not have the five dollars that was on your dresser (I already spent it). I have to answer all the tough questions. I know I burnt the house down, but think of the new one we'll get. I'm sorry for what I did even though I didn't do anything.' ...

"We're living an episode of 'The Simpsons,' and Bart's in charge," Mr. Gore concludes. "I can't wait for this kid to move out — as soon as he grows up."

💥 💥 💥

Could they really have done it on purpose?

In a mere three centuries, America has written some of the most glowing chapters in the long history of man's struggle for freedom.

So how did we become — in the space of only a few generations — a nation of pathetic bed-wetters, mewling, "Oh, please don't trust me and my neighbor to save for our own retirements; we might blow it," and, "Oh, please don't trust me and my neighbor to own military-style weapons; we'd probably shoot each other."

John Taylor Gatto thinks he's found the answer: the government schools.

Gatto's thesis is one of those "big ideas" that takes a little time to wrap the mind around. The public schools cannot be reformed because they're not failing, he argues. They're succeeding beyond all expectations at precisely what they're supposed to be — not only a huge make-work jobs program and bulwark of the unionized welfare state, but also the incubators of a dependent class of conscienceless sociopaths, an entire generation with their emotional development purposely stunted, a generation (by now two or three) with little knowledge of their own nation's proud history of freedom, who instead sulk about, their short attention spans bringing them no long-term satisfaction, whining for the modern Morlocks of our welfare/ police state to do a better job feeding them and keeping them entertained.

Gatto started to develop this thesis in his 1992 book *Dumbing Us Down.* Now he's returned with a massive and far better-developed follow-up, the 400-page *Underground History of American Education*, subtitled *A Schoolteacher's Intimate Investigation Into the Problem of Modern Schooling* ($34 postpaid, Oxford Village Press, 725 McDonough Road, Oxford, N.Y. 13830).

Gatto's historical research tells him none of this is an accident — public-school pioneers like Horace Mann found the regimented system they were looking for when they visited Prussia in the 1840s, importing wholesale a scheme to tame and regiment what they saw as America's dangerously anarchist new immigrant working class, training the young of this underclass to report to a central government facility as soon as they were old enough to use the latrine, there to be trained to all hold the same shallow memorized opinions and to march around to the sound of bells.

Yes, some basic literacy and numeracy would be necessary for them to fill their intended roles in the army and in the factories ... but not too much, and certainly not the kind of critical and analytic skills that might lead them to question their new bosses.

"We want one class to have a liberal education," Gatto finds Woodrow Wilson telling a group of businessmen shortly before the First World War. "We want another class, a very much larger class of necessity, to forgo the privilege of a liberal education and fit themselves to perform specific, difficult manual tasks."

Gatto challenges the whole underlying notion that the kind of academic disciplines taught in our schools are so complicated that they have to be divvied up into small mouth-sized bits and doled out over a period of years on a careful scientific schedule arranged by highly trained experts.

Teachers should be adults over 40, Gatto argues, "people who've proven themselves at life by bearing its pain like free spirits. ... No one who hasn't known grief, challenge, success, failure, or sadness should be allowed anywhere near kids. ... "Have you noticed nobody talks to children in schools? I mean *nobody*. All verbal exchanges in school are instrumental. Person-to-person stuff is contrary to policy. That's why popular teachers are disliked or fired. They *talk* to kids. It's unacceptable."

He writes: "What if I proposed that we hand three sticks of dynamite and a detonator to anyone who asked for them. All an applicant would need is money to pay for the explosives. You'd have to be an idiot to agree with my plan — at least based on the assumptions you picked up in school about human nature and human competence.

"And yet gasoline, a spectacularly mischievous explosive, dangerously unstable and with the intriguing characteristic of an assault weapon that it can flow under locked doors and saturate bulletproof clothing, is available to anyone with a container. Five gallons of gasoline has the destructive power of a stick of dynamite. The average tank holds 15 gallons, yet no background check is necessary for dispenser or dispensee. As long as gasoline is freely available, gun control is beside the point. ... Without everybody behind the wheel, our sort of economy would be impossible, so everybody *is* here, IQ notwithstanding. ...

"We haven't even considered the battering ram aspect of cars — why are novice operators allowed to command a ton of metal capable of hurtling through school crossings at up to two miles per minute? Why do we give the power of life and death this way to everyone?

"It should strike you at once that our unstated official assumptions about human nature are dead wrong. Average people *are* competent and responsible; universal motoring proves that. ...

"The way we used to be as Americans, learning everything, breaking down social class barriers, is the way we might be again without forced schooling. Driving proves that to me."

Americans are now trained to believe that no child is capable of assuming any responsibility till he or she is 18 or 21 — and that even adults need a huge and permanent government "safety net" to protect them from their own childlike incompetence.

Yet Gatto recalls being taught in school about David Farragut — who would grow to become the U.S. Navy's first admiral — being commissioned a midshipman on the warship *Essex*, rounding the Horn and going into combat against the British. Farragut recalled in his memoirs being sent below decks for primers, at which point a gun captain on the starboard side was "struck full in the face by an 18-pound shot" and beheaded, the headless corpse falling atop Farragut.

"We tumbled down the hatch together. I lay for some moments stunned by the blow, but soon recovered consciousness enough to rush up on deck. The captain, seeing me covered in blood, asked if I were wounded; to which I replied, 'I believe not, sir.' 'Then,' said he, 'where are the primers?' This brought me to my senses and I ran below again and brought up the primers."

In such hard schools, America's young men used to receive the training for greatness.

At the time of these harrowing events recalled in his memoir, Farragut was 10. Farragut received his first command at the age of 12. Sent to the Mediterranean at 15, he had no trouble picking up French, Italian, mathematics, and literature at the home of the American consul in Tunis.

In today's government schools such a 15-year-old, locked away in a classroom, bored to tears and peering yearningly through the windows at the outside world still barred to him for years, would almost certainly be diagnosed with "Attention Deficit Disorder" and doped up on Luvox.

Gatto reminds us of another young man who left school

at an early age because he was judged "feeble-minded." Just before turning 12 he talked his mother into letting him go to work full time as an apprentice on the railroad, "a permission she gave, which would put her in jail right now," in Gatto's phrase. Claiming some old type from a printer who was about to throw it away, the young lad begged a corner in the baggage car in which to set up a little four-page newspaper about the lives of the passengers and what could be seen from the train's window. At age 12 he had 500 subscribers, earning more than his former schoolteachers.

"When the Civil War broke out, the newspaper became a goldmine. ... He sold the war to crowds at the various stops. 'The Grand Trunk Herald' sold as many as 1,000 extra copies after a battle," amassing the young man a handsome stake for his next venture.

If he tried that at age 12 today, everyone involved would be arrested and put on trial for exploitation of "child labor" ... and we would likely never have heard of the young man in question, Thomas Edison.

How does this giant jobs program known as "public schooling" work? Gatto tells the pathetic story of little Benson, Vermont, where citizens were happy with the single school that served their 137 schoolchildren.

But the state bureaucracy wasn't happy. Oh no. The state condemned the old school for lack of wheelchair ramps "and other features nobody ever considered an essential part of education before." A massively expensive new school was mandated, and into this new school the education bureaucracy piled a new non-teaching superintendent, a new non-teaching assistant superintendent, a new non-teaching principal, a new non-teaching assistant principal, a new full-time nurse, a new full-time guidance counselor, a new full-time librarian, 11 full-time teachers where eight would have sufficed — in all, a new cadre of poobahs and potentates costing an additional $250,000 per year — or $2,000 per kid.

Property taxes in the little town went up 40 percent in one year, "quite a shock to local homeowners just hanging on by their fingernails."

In nearby Walden, a town happily getting along with four 19th-century one-room schoolhouses for its 120 kids — with four teachers and *no* administrators — Gatto visited and found the story was the same. Building condemned, and then the administrators started to arrive, like clowns piling out of that little car at the circus.

"Is there a soul who believes Benson's kids are better served in their new school with its mercenary army than Walden's 120 were in four rooms with four teachers? ... What happened at Benson — the use of forced schooling to impose career ladders of unnecessary work on a poor community — has happened all over North America. School is a jobs project for a large class of people it would be difficult to find employment for otherwise. Forcible redistribution of income to others to provide work for pedagogues and for a support staff larger than the actual teaching corps is a pyramid scheme run at the expense of the children. The more 'make-work' has to be found for school employees, the worse for kids because their own enterprise is stifled by constant professional tinkering in order to justify this employment."

"Child labor" wasn't banned for humanitarian reasons, Gatto demonstrates by quoting contemporary sources. This system of stunting young people's development by locking them up in government institutions till the age of 16 or 18 was introduced to protect organized labor from unwanted competition. To this day, a complaint that a minor league baseball team is allowing youths to earn a little extra cash in the evening serving as "ball boys" is most likely to come from a nearby labor union.

Public schooling hasn't even improved literacy, Gatto demonstrates — it has, instead, considerably eroded it.

By 1840 (more than a decade before the opening of the

first tax-funded government schools on the modern model, in Massachusetts), "the incidence of complex literacy in the United States was between 93 and 100 percent. ... In Connecticut only one citizen out of every 579 was illiterate and you probably don't want to know, not really, what people in those days considered literate; it's too embarrassing. Popular novels of the period give a clue: *Last of the Mohicans*, published in 1818, sold so well a contemporary equivalent would have to move 10 million copies to match it. If you pick up an uncut version you find yourself in a dense thicket of philosophy, history, culture, politics, geography, astute analysis of human motives and actions, all conveyed in data-rich periodic sentences so formidable only a determined and well-educated reader can handle it nowadays. Yet in 1818 we were a small-farm nation without colleges or universities to speak of. Could those simple folk have had more complex minds than our own?

"By 1940 the literacy figure for all states stood at 96 percent for whites, 80 percent for blacks. Notice for all the disadvantages blacks labored under, four of five were still literate. Six decades later, at the end of the 20th century, the National Adult Literacy Survey and the National Assessment of Educational Progress say 40 percent of blacks and 17 percent of whites can't read at all. Put another way, black illiteracy doubled, white illiteracy quadrupled," despite the fact that "we spend three or four times as much real money on schooling as we did 60 years ago."

In fact, New York state spends $200,000 schooling a child through high school "when lost interest is calculated," Gatto figures. "The capital sum invested in the child's name over the past 12 years would have delivered a million dollars to each kid as a nest egg to compensate for having no school. The original $200,000 is more than the average home in New York costs. You wouldn't build a home without some idea what it would look like when finished, but you are compelled to let a corps of perfect strangers tinker with your child's mind and personality without the foggiest idea what they want to do with it."

And after they fail, "Law courts and legislatures have totally absolved school people from liability. You can sue a doctor for malpractice; not a schoolteacher. ..."

Sue the schools? What ever for?

"During World War Two, American public schools massively converted to non-phonetic ways of teaching reading," Gatto explains. "According to the justice department, 80 percent of the incarcerated *violent* criminal population is illiterate or nearly so (as are 67 percent of all criminals locked up.) There seems to be a direct connection between the humiliation poor readers experience and the life of angry criminals. As reading ability plummeted in America after World War Two, crime soared. So did out-of-wedlock births, which doubled in the 1950s and doubled again in the '60s, when bizarre violence for the first time became commonplace in daily life.

"When literacy was first abandoned as a primary goal by schools, white people were in a better position than black people because they inherited a 300-year-old American tradition of learning to read at home by matching spoken sounds with letters, thus home assistance was able to correct the deficiencies of dumbed-down schools for whites. But black people had been forbidden to learn to read during slavery, and as late as 1930 only averaged three to four years of schooling, so they were helpless when teachers suddenly stopped teaching children to read; they had no fall-back position."

In 1882, Gatto reminds us, fifth graders read in their *Appleton School Reader* the original prose of such authors as William Shakespeare, Henry Thoreau, George Washington, Sir Walter Scott, Mark Twain, Benjamin Franklin, Oliver Wendell Holmes, Daniel Webster, Lewis Carroll, Thomas Jefferson, and Ralph Waldo Emerson.

In 1995, a student teacher of fifth graders in Minneapolis wrote to the local newspaper: "I was told children are not to be expected to spell the following words correctly: back, big, call, came, can, day, did, dog, down, get, good, if, in, is, it, have, he, home, like, little, man, morning, mother, my, night, off, out, over, people, play, ran, said, saw, she, some, soon, their, them, there, time, two, too, up, us, very, water, we, went, where, when, will, would, etc. Is this nuts?"

But again, all this was no accident. Gatto finds the 1888 "Report of the Senate Committee on Education" asserting, "We believe that education is one of the principal causes of discontent of late years manifesting itself among the laboring classes. ..."

Within a few generations, working from such goals as "destruction of the narrative of American history connecting the arguments of the Founding Fathers to historical events, defining what makes Americans different from others besides wealth"; "radical dilution of the academic content of formal curriculum which familiarized students with serious literature, philosophy, theology, etc. — having the effect of curtailing any serious inquiries into economics, politics or religion"; "enlargement of the school day and year to blot up outside opportunities to acquire useful knowledge leading to independent livelihoods ..."; and "relentless low-level hostility against religious interpretations of meaning," the public schools had taken care of *that*.

Even America's smartest kids are getting dumber under the current universal government regime. Despite the fact the SAT test is easier today than it was in 1972, Gatto points out, the number of students who score above 600 has dropped by 37 percent in that time — *"an absolute decline, not a relative one. It is not affected by an increase in unsuitable minds taking the test or by an increase in numbers. The absolute body count of smart students is down drastically with a test not more difficult than yesterday's but considerably less so."*

Those scoring above 750? Down 50 percent.

Mr. Gatto's book rambles, like an old man taking you on a walk through his home town, pointing out where the old barns used to be. It swings from historical analysis to personal anecdote and reminiscence. The furthest thing from the kind of forbidding "rigorous" tomes generated by those seeking Ph.D.s in education, it invites the interested reader to sink down into it like a comfortable easy chair, to be stunned and amazed in turn by a 150-year history of the fully conscious and willful campaign to turn all but the offspring of the big banking and corporate families who would attend Hotchkiss, Choate, Kent, and Groton (the last three endowed by the Mellons, the DuPonts, and J.P. Morgan — the first by the machine gun widow) into — well, malleable morons.

Mr. Gatto's books — he promises his next will be *How to Get an Education in Spite of School* — are a wonder and a delight. It's only too bad they're true.

May 2000
Hose Out the Ant Farm

Eric Harris and Dylan Klebold planned and carried out premeditated murder at Columbine High School in Littleton, Colorado, in spring 1999. Those killings can never be justified.

But the two lads did at least have the gumption to follow through on the part of their plan that called for them to take their own lives. Harris and Klebold thus join their victims in qualifying as the latest martyrs to the greatest failed social experiment of this century, the mandatory government youth propaganda camps, still known to most of the press and public as "public schools."

We do not see private or parochial school students shooting up the joint (though the infection may yet spread there, if the strings attached to tax-funded "vouchers" succeed in turning private schools into clones of the government brand). Neither do we see home-schoolers going mad with readily available firearms.

Nonetheless, we shall now see the government youth camps dressed up with more metal detectors and armed guards. This at least has the merit of making their true nature more obvious.

The effect of such institutions on captive adolescent males was first seen when young Native American boys were kidnapped and shipped off to "Indian schools." Their hair shorn and forbidden to speak their native tongues, cut off from the fathers and uncles who could have trained them in their tribes' traditions, that generation of Indian men grew up to have fantastic rates of alcoholism, suicide, and every other form of sociopathology.

For millennia, all around the globe, human cultures have recognized that male adolescence is a dangerous necessity. The flood of hormones that turns boys into men produces the strength, aggression, and competitiveness necessary for success in the hunt, protection of the tribe against hostile neighbors, and victory in the reproductive battle to pass on these desirable characteristics.

But left unchecked, these characteristics can also produce rape and murder as in William Golding's nightmare vision from *Lord of the Flies*. Ranchers have long recognized this danger, and respond by castrating most male animals before they reach maturity.

Since that is not generally an acceptable remedy with our own children, young males in many cultures have long been taken at adolescence by their fathers and uncles into the wilderness, where they are taught the skills of war and the hunt, but also the rules that protect defenseless women and children.

Often, the older men also indoctrinate them into their religious mysteries, showing the youth how to use the hallucinogenic plants of the region to achieve a religious vision, cementing his sense of his proper role in society.

By contrast, in our modern and deeply perverted manner of raising up young men in sterile rooms full of desks and chairs, such male guidance has virtually disappeared. Young men who refuse to snitch on their fellows — observing a male code of honor — are considered disciplinary problems. Though the schools endlessly prate about the evils of "drugs," those who resist discipline are doped up — chemically castrated — with Prozac, Ritalin, or any of a whole new pharmacopeia of handy nostrums guaranteed to reduce resistance or aggression.

(Look at the energy that was poured into tracking where young Messrs. Harris and Klebold "got their guns." If they had used their cars to mow down 13 pedestrians, would we now be crying "Where on Earth did they get those Chevrolets?" Or might someone instead be spending a little time running down early reports that Eric Harris tried to join the Marines, but may have been turned down because he had been prescribed the psychiatric drug Luvox — fluvoxamine maleate — with known side effects including impaired judgement? After all, we know for a fact young Kip Kinkel of Springfield, Oregon had only recently been taken off such medications when he decided to kill his parents and shoot up that welfare awards breakfast down at his school May 20 and 21, 1998.)

This institutionalization of young males by age cohort was not a huge problem before 1945, when only a small minority finished high school, based on the sensible recognition that few had the vocation to go on to study Latin, Greek, and philosophy. There was little social stigma attached to a young lad leaving school shortly after reaching puberty to work the family farm or take up a trade, marry his sweetheart, and start a family.

But now the educrats have gone mad. Even as improved nutrition brings on puberty at an ever younger age, vast resources are mobilized to stigmatize as a "dropout and a loser" any lad who leaves the government behavior modification labs before age 18.

Herb Goldberg, Ph.D., writes in *The Hazards of Being Male*: "In the public schools, the majority of students regarded as problem cases by teachers are boys. ..."

As early as elementary school, "While there is great peer pressure to act like a boy, the teacher's coveted classroom values are traditionally 'feminine' ones. The emphasis is on politeness, neatness, docility, and cleanliness, with not much approved room being given for the boy to flex his muscles. ..."

In a study of 12,000 students, "The researcher correlated masculinity scores of the boys on the California Psychological Inventory with their school grades," Dr. Goldberg reports. "She found that the higher the boy scored on the masculine scale, the lower his report card average tended to be. ..."

The result of this institutional rejection of "maleness"? "Boys show a significantly greater prevalence of ... bizarre behavior, short attention span, [and] hyperactivity."

Mr. Goldberg's book was published 22 years ago. It's not as though we weren't warned.

Picture a steam boiler with all the safety valves welded shut. Now, picture it beginning to shudder, vibrate, and bang. These are your government schools. You have been warned.

The Mommification of America

After keeping people fed and safe from marauders, the major test of any culture is how it deals with the adolescent male.

People who keep livestock know how serious a problem testosterone can be; they denature 98 percent of the stock judged susceptible.

So far — though I hesitate to give them ideas — the women in charge of the mommification of America have not proposed castrating 98 percent of our youth. Instead, they scheme to prevent the natural maturing process of the male in more devious ways.

What do I mean by mommification?

What does the average American mom say when the police show up at her door, telling her the 16-year-old is in trouble? She says "My Sean? It can't be; Sean's a good boy. He doesn't run with that kind."

Such women are dangerous idiots who are helping to ruin our civilization.

The correct answer, in all cases when the lad has not been neutered, is: "Well, of course. He's a teenage boy. He has an irresistible craving to get laid twice a day by any tease in a skirt, use mescaline to seek a revelation and ask God why he's alive, then exhaust himself in ritual combat before wrapping up his day with a dinner of half-raw meat. We arrange things so he can't get laid, he's not allowed to fight, he'll go to prison for 20 years if he tries to talk to God with the aid of sacred plants, and he sits stir-crazy all day in some stuffy classroom. But I'm supposed to be surprised that he drank a few beers, dropped his trousers to the mayor, squeezed some girl's breasts, and ran his father's car into a tree?"

Instead, we allow these deluded mommies — and the gutless lawmakers who grovel before them — to pretend these behaviors are not natural, that what's actually happening to their dear little pantywaists is that they're falling under the influence of demons.

Since it's not in vogue to refer to real old-fashioned demons, the kind with horns, they've invented new demons called "marijuana," "LSD," and "cocaine," pretending their sons are acting this way because these drugs exist, that if we could just wipe these substances off the face of the Earth the problem would be solved.

Why is this a dangerous lie? Because no one has been killed or seriously injured by marijuana, LSD, or any other hallucinogen. Yet groups like the Partnership for a Drug-Free America devote their lives and fortunes to eliminating these useful, harmless drugs.

To the extent that they succeed, what are their teenage children doing? They are turning to "inhalants," a generic term for snorting the fumes of paint thinners and the like to get high.

These substances *are* dangerous. They cause permanent brain damage. They kill. The Partnership for a Drug-Free America held a press conference on April 14, 1995, to present just such tragic tales. Yet not a single one of the tragic moms was willing to admit, "I helped kill my son. If his dad had been allowed to provide him with marijuana or peyote or psilocybin, to teach him how to seek a transcendent experience responsibly, this need never have happened. It turns out the need to experiment, to take risks, to get high, is natural in teenage boys. My solution was wrong."

We do have rituals in our society that are designed to channel teenage violence, of course. High school sports take teenage boys, run them till they're exhausted, then reward them for silently enduring this daily pain by allowing them to go out on a field Friday night and knock each other down for two hours.

But our school boards increasingly respond to the academic failure of our schools by passing "no pass, no play" rules, "allowing" only the lads who keep up their grades to stay on the team.

Result? Young toughs from broken homes — the very ones who need "diversion" the most — get kicked off the field. Many respond by dropping out and taking up armed robbery. *That's* working well.

We may not emasculate 98 percent of our youth, but the solutions we have adopted are almost as destructive. We now incarcerate a higher percentage of our young males than any other country in the world, the majority of them normal young men whom we have *turned* into criminals by, in essence, outlawing male adolescence.

There is a solution. As our young men reach puberty, their dads should take three-month leaves of absence, pack up the lad with some rifles and camping and fishing gear and a good supply of potent hallucinogens, and head off into the wilderness for the summer to hear the voice of God and talk about life, sex, and manliness.

No, this will not "turn our sons into drug addicts." Cultures from Brazil to Africa to the Australian outback send young men on drug-assisted vision quests. When such entheogen use is part of a sacred authorized ritual, no problem has ever been discerned involving later destructive use.

The whole idea is to send young men forth to test their strength, taking risks inherently incomprehensible to most women. Try to bottle up this beast, refuse to acknowledge its existence, and in 20 or 30 years we won't have a civilization at all.

It's already happening. Any young mommy who doesn't believe me is welcome to walk a mile through the streets of the nearest big city, alone and unarmed, at midnight. This is a thing young women could do in this country with relative impunity in 1795, or 1895, when we had no drug or firearm laws at all — nor any institutionalized welfare schemes to discourage and subsidize the "Fatherless Family." If mommification works — if drugs and firearms are the cause of violence and banning them is the solution — then things must be even safer now. Care to give it a try?

"Drugs and guns are dangerous!" scream the terrified mommies, who have been taught the vicious lie that Big Government will protect them from an otherwise dangerous world.

Certainly they are. That's why you want to surround yourself with calm, stable, mature, self-confident men who have learned to tame drugs and guns and put their powers to productive use, protecting their homes and families.

The other option — like the king who vowed his daughter would never fall victim to Malevola's curse and fall into an eternal sleep after pricking her finger on a needle — is to set about finding and destroying every needle, pardon me, every firearm and consciousness-altering substance in the kingdom. How's it going?

Pharmaceutical-Blackmail: Authorities Use a Heavy Hand to Keep Kids on Drugs

About that "zero-drug-tolerance" policy in our schools: Does it really mean what it says? Or would it come closer to the truth for school administrators to admit that what they really oppose are pushers offering *competing* consciousness-altering substances?

Do our public schools today constitute a kind of official, tax-supported dope monopoly that will even threaten to take children away from parents should they refuse to go along with the mind-numbing nostrums that our schoolmasters themselves now press on nearly a quarter of our young boys, the better to keep those valuable butts planted in their seats?

The *Albany Times Union*, in a copyrighted story published May 7, 2000, tells what happened to parents Michael and Jill Carroll of Albany, N.Y., when they tried to take their son, 7-year-old Kyle, off the Ritalin:

Kyle Carroll was first prescribed Ritalin last year, after he fell behind at school. Teachers drew up an Individualized Education Plan, a standard course of action for children with "special needs." But last fall, when Kyle started second grade, the Ritalin didn't seem to be doing much good. Furthermore, the Carrolls grew concerned that Kyle was only sleeping about five hours a night and eating just one meal a day — lunch. So they told school officials they wanted to take Kyle off the Ritalin for two weeks to see if that helped.

That's when they got a call, and then a visit, from a Child Protective Services worker, based on a complaint from Kyle's school guidance counselor.

The charge? "Child abuse," in the form of "medical neglect." In plain English? Expressing doubts about keeping their child on dope.

As a result, the *Times Union* reports the Carrolls are now on a statewide list of alleged child abusers and find themselves "thrust into an Orwellian family court battle to clear their name and ensure their child isn't removed from their home."

The child remains on the medication, "in part because they fear child welfare workers will take him away if they don't," the Albany daily reports.

Furthermore, the Albany paper found the Carrolls' case is far from unique, reporting: "Public schools are increasingly accusing parents of child abuse and neglect if they balk at giving their children medication such as Ritalin, a stimulant being prescribed to more and more students."

The American Academy of Pediatrics reports as many as 3.8 million schoolchildren, mostly boys, have now been diagnosed with the newly coined "ADHD" — attention deficit/hyperactivity disorder — a psychiatric "disease" with symptoms to which most of our grandparents would have responded by simply smiling: "Boys will be boys." Or perhaps by asking, "Could it be that he finds your school boring? Does it really make sense to spend three or four years teaching reading, a skill easily mastered in six weeks if you'd just use phonics?"

At least a million children now take Ritalin for this "disorder." In two school districts near Virginia Beach, Va., for instance, a 1999 study by psychologist Gretchen LeFever found fully 20 percent of white boys in the fifth grade in the 1995-96 school year were receiving prescription drugs for ADHD. And even the AAP acknowledged in a recent study that many cases are misdiagnosed.

"This thing is so scary," says Patricia Weathers, of

Millbrook, a suburb of Poughkeepsie, New York. Officials at the Millbrook school district called police and child protective services when she took her 9-year-old son, Michael Mozer, off medications earlier this year.

Weathers reported her child's prescribed drug cocktail — including Ritalin, the anti-depressant Paxil, and Dexedrine (another stimulant, like Ritalin) caused her boy — now attending a private school — to hallucinate.

"Absent evidence that the lives of children are at stake when they're not on Ritalin," *USA Today* editorialized this week, "no arm of the state should be ramming the drug treatment down parents' — and children's — throats."

Amen to that. The underlying problem here is the notion that children belong first to the state — that they're best "socialized" in state-run institutions — and that biological parents are allowed to retain custody only at the discretion of school and "child welfare" officials, who after all have "professional diplomas," and thus "know best."

No free country can long operate under such a presumption, with its inevitable corrosive effect on the family. And this — at least as much as the corresponding *academic* failures of the public schools — is what drives the large and growing movement for separation of school and state.(See www.sepschool.org).

The Proud Profession of Mrs. Tribble
🥀

A full year after I penned the August 2000 "Pharmaceutical Blackmail" essay above (surely the Internet *is* life eternal, isn't it?), a Mrs. Tribble wrote in, commenting:

"Dear Mr. Suprynowicz,

"Your article about Ritalin which I obtained on line has a rather flippant tone. As with many diseases, ADHD is not definitively diagnosable with laboratory tests on body fluids or tissue. Yes, it is often mis-diagnosed (both too much among those without it and too little among those really affected).

"The latest scientific research, such as the PET scans, indicates obvious differences between the brain of someone with ADHD and someone without it. Ritalin is not the answer for every person with attentional difficulties (with or without hyperactivity). Rather a multi-prong approach is needed — pharmaceutical intervention, behavior management in all settings, and classroom accommodations for students.

"Careful observation must be done both before and after a medication is tried. If it is not successful, then changes in dosage, brands, and even classes of chemical composition must be tried.

"It is the 'yellow journalism' of articles such as yours which leaves concerned parents confused and guilt-ridden. I encourage you to examine the most recent research and then to address this issue again.

(signed) "C.C. Tribble, Certified learning disabilities therapist and psychometrist"

I replied:

Greetings, Miss Tribble —

"Diseases" whose traumas cannot be reliably and reproducibly measured by double-blind methods exist only in the minds of those who wish to control the behavior of others.

"Pharmaceutical interventions" into the minds and behavior of minors who do not approach the physician, seeking treatment for a self-perceived trauma or illness, deserve about as much respect as those who would tie down children and dose them with heroin against their will, the better to produce new "customers."

The notion that because the government institution is noble in its intent, any inmate who does not "fit in" is mentally ill and requires "treatment," is not new. The Soviets honed this approach for 70 years.

It is "behavior management" within the environment of the mandatory government youth propaganda camp, practiced Soviet-style by dangerous quacks such as yourself in an attempt to "accommodate" the inmate to the "classroom setting," which have left us with at least two generations of functionally illiterate sociopaths. The "different classes of chemicals" with which you so enthusiastically experiment on your young victims gave us Kip Kinkel of Springfield, Ore. (a year's worth of Prozac); Eric Harris, one of the two gentlemen at Columbine, Colo. (Luvox), and who knows how many others?

I encourage you to examine your conscience, and address your career choice again.

— Vin Suprynowicz, non-psychometrist

The lady wrote back — this time clarifying the proper honorific:

"It saddens me to note the paranoia you have expressed in your reply. We professionals who work with children must have faith in the abilities of most parents to make wise decisions for their children. I suspect you have not lived with a child who is so distractible that he spends hours doing homework which his fraternal twin from the same classroom completes in less than one hour.

"I neither diagnose nor treat ADHD, so I am not one of your "dangerous quacks." Rather I research ADHD in medical, psychological, and educational peer-reviewed journals.

"Mrs. Catherine C. Tribble, B.A., M.A.E.Ed., M.A.C.

I replied again:

Greetings —

My, my. "Paranoia," eh?

I thought that was a medical diagnosis. Have you been keeping your M.D. a secret from us? Surely that's an *excess* of modesty.

Then again, perhaps you're just the kind of person who concludes that anyone who disagrees with you must be mentally ill. I daresay psychiatry has a term for *that* system of self-validation, but I won't venture a guess as to what it is ... not being a board certified "psychometrist."

One twin takes longer to do his homework than the other, and you diagnose a "mental illness," appropriately treated with mind-altering pharmaceuticals?

For starters, I must highly recommend you consult the works of Dr. Thomas Szasz, professor emeritus of Psychiatry at the State University of New York at Syracuse and former staff member at the Chicago Institute of Psychiatry — especially his *The Myth of Mental Illness* and *The Manufacture of Madness: A Comparative Study of the Inquisition and the Mental Health Movement,* in which he refutes and decries most such "mental health treatment" schemes as "an immoral ideology of intolerance."

By the way, if "you professionals" have "faith in the abilities of most parents to make wise decisions for their children," how on Earth could you read my column of Aug. 18, 2000 (the one I must presume led to your initial communication, the one in which I detailed the case of Michael and Jill Carroll of Albany, N.Y., whose names were placed on a statewide list of alleged child abusers by state authorities when they threatened to take their son, 7-year-old Kyle, off prescribed Ritalin), without taking any taking exception to these state actions — reserving your criticism solely for my "tone" in reporting them?

If I have called you a "quack" when your delusions merely lead you to encourage the draconian quackery of others, I'm not sure an apology is quite the way to go. Hitler never personally turned the valves on a single gas chamber; did that leave him blameless?

Sincerely, V.S.

❦ ❦ ❦

The great moral and ethical question arises when a practitioner like Mrs. Tribble first confronts her "patient." Any self-respecting healer will ask: "So, young man, those who sent you to me believe you are ill. What do you think? Are you sick — is there something about yourself you perceive as an illness, and with which you want my help?"

If the "patient" answers "Yes," it's still incumbent on the practitioner to make sure that answer is freely volunteered — that the patient hasn't been beaten, threatened, shamed, or otherwise coerced into saying what he believes he's "supposed to say if he doesn't want it to go worse with him."

But if the patient responds, "There's nothing wrong with me; I just don't want to be here with you a-holes," then the great ethical watershed presents itself, immediate and unmistakable.

The ethical healer will immediately confront the subject's jailers, declaring, "This young man says he does not have any illness; he simply doesn't want to be here. Unless you can show me overwhelming evidence that upon his release he will burn buildings to the ground or wreak massive bodily harm on innocent persons, I demand that we walk him to the front door and set him on his way this instant. He does not have a 'medical problem' and 'treatment' is inappropriate; he merely doesn't want to be here ... not that I can blame him, the damned place reeks of floor wax and bad cafeteria food. I'm sure he could learn more apprenticed to some useful artisan, by the simple expedient of spending one evening a week in the college library."

The other option — I worry it's the one Mrs. Tribble might adopt — is to say, "Oh, you poor thing. You don't even know how sick you are. But surely you can see how your behavior has been disruptive to the proper functioning of this institution, can't you? Here, I want you to try these little blue pills. I think you'll be surprised at how much calmer you feel, how much easier it is for you to concentrate on your lessons."

This has all the trappings of a non-coercive "treatment," of course. That's because the Mrs. Tribbles of this world either never consider — or willfully ignore — the way their "patients" are threatened, shamed, and coerced into "taking their medicine" by authorities who are not beyond threatening to punish the parents, or to take the child out of his home, or tacitly encouraging his little schoolmates to beat the "retard" in the bathroom for his nonconformist ways, if that's what it takes.

I referred Mrs. Tribble to the works of Dr. Thomas Szasz because he specifically contends, "The ideology of mental health and illness serves an obvious and pressing moral need. Since the physician's classic mandate is to treat suffering patients with their consent and for their own benefit, it is necessary to explain and justify situations where individuals are 'treated' without their consent and to their detriment. The concept of insanity or mental illness supplies this need. ... In vain does the alleged madman insist that he is not sick; his inability to 'recognize' that he is, is regarded as a hallmark of his illness. ...

"The most important economic characteristic of Institutional Psychiatry" (which Szasz carefully differentiates from "Contractual Psychiatry," in which the patient pays for his care, enters into treatment voluntarily, and remains free to reject further treatment at any time) "is that the institutional psychiatrist is a bureaucratic employee, paid for his services by the private or public organization (not by the individual who is his ostensible client); its most important social characteristic is the use of force and fraud."

"That Cure is Freedom ..."
❦

During my speech to a group of doctors here in Las Vegas in July 2001, on the topic "Environmentalism as a State-Established Religion" (see page 195), as so often happens even when discussing subjects that far afield, my discussion with the good doctors came home to the role of the government schools in propagandizing our children on such Politically Correct topics, and I expressed the opinion that the government schools today probably cannot be reformed; they must simply be shut down and replaced with some new combination of private schools and home schooling.

Typically, this brought a quite emotional response from one of the members of the audience during the ensuing question-and-answer session. The old gent quite forcefully and angrily asserted that it was the government schools that had brought his generation — educated in the 1930s and '40s, I would presume — to their high level of education and success, that they are part of what has made America great, that shutting them down would amount to "throwing out the baby with the bathwater," and so on.

For those of a certain age — let me be more specific: those born before 1949 — who never saw first-hand the mucking about with the traditional curricula and the introduction of vast rafts of Politically Correct, touchy-feely twaddle which began in the public schools in the 1960s, there does not seem to be any quantity of factual evidence that will convince them of what the government schools have become — not just vastly expensive failures, but institutions actively and purposely poisoning the minds of our young against the notion that there is anything noble or worth keeping in our heritage of freedom, capitalism, and open discourse.

(The problem is that — at the other end of the spectrum — those born since 1960 who were not lucky enough to be home-schooled or attend private academies, are in large part wholesale victims of this fraud, and have little if anything with which to compare it, much less any learned skills of skepticism, logical proof, or discernment to apply to the problem.)

We should acknowledge this response as common and understandable — the more basic an institution we propose to abandon, the greater will be the panic of those unable to envision a future without it, shrieking that we mean to "render an entire generation illiterate," or whatever. In this case, ridicule and scorn of those clutching the schoolhouse columns and weeping and rending their clothes may be ineffective as well as unkind. For all these, I submit we must probably content ourselves with a brief answer in two parts, before moving on:

1) First, yes, the government schools were a far more useful and creditable enterprise before 1960, in a day when there was effectively no federal funding or interference. Fewer than half the students ever graduated high school, which was a good thing — no squawks about any "drop-out crisis" — because it meant some selectivity was being exercised. (An eighth grade education was all that was mandated, and that was substantially better than what we call a "high school education" today, as any honest comparison of written exams from the two eras will reveal.)

The teachers realized their job was not only to succor the young but also to measure their achievements against some objective standard — some day these aspiring graduates would be doctors and generals and architects, and if they were allowed to "slide" without mastering the basics it could eventually cost lives, if not the future of our very republic.

Now, go seek out the building which housed the local high school in 1940, and find the old photos of the graduating classes, hopefully still hanging in the halls, and you will notice one thing which was very bad. Almost all those graduates were white males. The systematic exclusion of almost all the girls and black and Hispanic students was a bad thing, and we can be happy that fault, at least, has been largely corrected.

But that doesn't mean that selectivity, in and of itself, was bad.

Though the seeds of the schools' later democratic demise were planted as soon as tax funding was introduced, the public schools as late as 1950 were still based on the 19th century model of a group of prominent local citizens gathering together to build a school and hire a schoolmarm, whereupon it was agreed that those who could afford it would contribute a little extra so the worthy children of poorer families could also attend the community school free of charge.

But there were certainly no mandates of "entitlement" handed down from the state capital — let alone from Washington. Misbehavior brought expulsion, as did academic failure or even recurrent inattention or indolence — with no malarkey about lack of motivation being a "protected disability," entitling the "sufferer" to be followed around by a special feeder with a spoon.

Those who received high school diplomas were acknowledged by all to have earned them, and now to be the custodians of the learning and tradition of the nation, charged with passing them down to a younger generation. They could recite the Bill of Rights and Washington's farewell address.

Today, we have gone over so far to the notion that everyone "deserves" a high school diploma — whether they demonstrate a vocation for learning or not, whether they even sit up smartly in class and pay attention, or instead hang out in the hallways listening to their boom boxes — that we might as well just hang our current diplomas as toe-tags on the newborns in the maternity wards, and have done with it.

Not only can our high school graduates no longer *recite* Washington's farewell address, they are not even aware that he gave one, or to whom, nor can they tell you how many amendments are in the Bill of Rights, or what document they amend, or why they were enacted, let alone recite any of them from memory.

2) But as to the second part of our answer, those offering this heartfelt assertion that the current, top-down, one-size-fits-all, mandatory youth internment and propaganda camp is the only model that will ever work, may want to take a moment to imagine what it would have been like to ask a planter in the Southern United States in the early 19th century why slavery could not be gotten rid of.

The first answers might have involved some self-serving balderdash about how the black man is like a child, who could never survive if given responsibility for his own welfare, since he knew nothing of saving and planning ahead for a rainy day, etc.

Such arguments were shattered long ago by the British abolitionist Macaulay, of course, who responded: "There is only one cure for evils which newly-acquired freedom produces, and that cure is freedom. When a prisoner first leaves his cell, he cannot bear the light of day, he is unable to discriminate colors, or recognize faces. The remedy is, to accustom him to the rays of the sun.

"The blaze of truth and liberty may at first dazzle and bewilder nations which have become half blind in the house of bondage. But let them gaze on, and they will soon be able to bear it. ...

"Many politicians of our time are in the habit of laying down as a self-evident proposition, that no people ought to be free till they are fit to use their freedom. The maxim is worthy of the fool in the old story, who resolved not to go in the water till he had learned to swim. If men are to wait for liberty till they become wise and good in slavery, they may indeed wait forever."

But then, if our Southern planter were smart, he would have advanced a far more pragmatic response:

"Here in the South, our economy is based on cash crops which cannot be profitably grown on small, family farmsteads. Profits can only be made by growing cotton, tobacco, rice and indigo on large plantations, which is a labor-intensive business. Whether we like slavery or not, it's necessary to create the wealth of America — a predominately agriculture nation — a wealth from which you have profited all your life, and the fruits of which I doubt you would want to give up.

"Eliminate the word 'slavery' — ban the practice by law — and what crops up to take its place will still acknowledge this economic reality, the need for vast platoons of unskilled agricultural labor ... even if the plantations are technically divided up among the slaves, who will then "sharecrop" for the same men they used to call "master," a system still required to take advantage of efficiencies of scale in labor pooling, purchasing, shipping, and so forth."

That turned out to be largely true. The entire nation *had* profited from agricultural chattel slavery, and what finally ended slavery — the process was already well underway by 1861 — was not the moral strength of the abolitionists' arguments, but mechanization and an industrial revolution that finally made the presence of vast hordes of permanent manual laborers unnecessary — if anything, too expensive — just as the crews of our naval and merchant ships dropped from hundreds living in virtual waterborne slavery to dozens to a handful of well-paid volunteers not because of humanitarian reforms, but because of the replacement of sail by increasingly efficient steam.

The pragmatic argument that the regimented, Prussian-style government schools worked in the past and that we cannot envision any better way to do the job — that, in fact, "everything will collapse" if we close them down — reflects the same emotional desperation as the southern planter pleading that it is not just him but the entire way of life of his nation that will collapse into dust if we dare tamper with "the peculiar institution," no matter what its failings.

And it also reflects the same blindered way of viewing the world, oblivious to the real repercussions of ongoing technological change, most significantly the home computer, and with it the freeing of the parent who was once required down at the factory for eight or 10 hours a day, now increasingly capable of working from home and thus helping to tutor his or her own child, as was the case before 1800.

The old leather-belt, waterwheel, coal-fed factories now stand almost entirely abandoned ... or converted into picturesque restaurants and shopping malls. The First Industrial Revolution has come ... and gone.

We don't do anything else the way the Prussians did it in the 1850s, when John Dewey and Horace Mann brought home to Massachusetts the current model of our regimented-by-age, jump-to-your-feet-and-race-to-the-next-classroom-at-the-sound-of-the-bell, government youth camps.

Imagine how a foreign power would do against our armed forces if it confronted us with the weapons and system of military organization practiced in the 1840s. (Heck, we don't have to *imagine* — look what happened to the Iraqis in 1991, and the Afghan Taliban in 2001.)

But there are other venues of competition between cultures besides the battlefield. How will our next generation of engineers and inventors and capitalists fare against the first upstart young nation to try a different system of schooling — one which again rewards innovation and hard work and allows the most gifted to advance as fast as they're able?

That nation will run rings around us — will probably do it with mere teen-agers (see the science fiction novels of Orson Scott Card) the way our more efficient clipper ships ran down the world in the 1840s ... the way our satellite-guided munitions shattered our enemies in the 1990s.

So: you can change now ... or you can change later.

XIII
The Drug War Murders —
Getting the Drug War
You Paid For

There was a predictable amount of hand-wringing when a hunter-killer pack of Peruvian Air Force jets — guided to their target by a U.S. "civilian" Drug War crew under contract to the CIA, who now righteously whine, "We *told* them to check their photo ID" — shot down a civilian seaplane near the Colombian border in late April 2001, murdering American missionary Veronica Bowers of Michigan and her 7-month-old daughter, Charity.

But why all this fake horror? Do the vast majority of you folks out there support the Drug War — even while admitting it can't be won, clinging to the feeble excuse that legalizing stuff less damaging than alcohol and less addictive than tobacco will somehow "send the wrong message to the children" — or don't you?

Unless you're in favor of legalizing all drugs, right now, then watching Roni Bowers and her baby choke and scream and bleed and drown in some distant muddy jungle river is exactly what you asked for, what you pay your taxes for, and what you ought to have to watch on videotape every night before you go to sleep.

Those who favor locking up hundreds of thousands of our young men for committing victimless crimes disingenuously insist: "Drug use does *too* have victims; every user is a victim."

Yeah, yeah, and everyone who's ever patronized a tattoo parlor will be victimized for the rest of his or her life by the social prejudice that assumes people with tattoos are low-income losers. What are you going to do about it — break down their doors and shoot all the tattoo artists on sight?

Like people who get tattooed — like folks who choose to kill themselves slowly with alcohol and tobacco — drug users *do it on purpose.*

The significance of turning such behaviors into "victimless crimes" is that unlike legitimate police work — we know how many armed robberies occur because the victims can generally be relied upon to call police right quick — few drug users ever dial 911 and report, "Hey, some guy just sold me drugs, and I think it may be illegal!"

So police are reduced to going undercover, reading our e-mail, bribing bank tellers to snitch on us if we deposit or withdraw large sums of money, training kids to turn in their parents like good little *Hitler Jugend*, dragging our half-naked neighbors out of their homes at 4 in the morning, and generally coarsening our once-free and polite society by getting us all accustomed to standing there like nervous sheep, avoiding eye contact and hoping we won't be next as we watch folks strip-searched and hauled away for "observed bowel movements" at the airport in an escalating (albeit fruitless) series of affronts to human decency not seen since the days of Joseph Mengele or, possibly, the heyday of the Holy Office of the Inquisition.

Our Fearless Drug Warriors have murdered thousands of innocent bystanders and carelessly misidentified "suspects" for years, and it's a rare cop who's suffered the indignity of so much as a single night in jail, providing they could claim by the furthest stretch of the imagination to have been operating "in the line of duty."

Has everyone forgotten millionaire recluse Donald Scott, 61, whose 200-acre ranch in the hills above Malibu was coveted by the bureaucrats who operated adjoining state and national recreational areas?

Has everyone forgotten the Rev. Accelyne Williams, the 75-year-old Methodist minister who was chased around his Boston apartment by police conducting a no-knock raid looking for drugs and guns in 1994? He collapsed and died of a heart attack. No guns or drugs were ever found, since police had raided an apartment on a different floor from that specified by their "snitch." In that case, the Boston police chief did, at least, apologize.

Has everyone forgotten Esequiel Hernandez, the Texas teenager shot and killed by U.S. Marines in May 1997 for the crime of plinking tin cans while out herding his family's goats near the Mexican border at a location that had been (unbeknownst to him) — staked out by our military — *operating on U.S. soil* — as a likely smugglers' point of entry?

How about 64-year-old John Adams — shot and killed in front of his wife after police broke into his Tennessee home in the fall of 2000 while serving a drug warrant — which actually named the house next door?

Annie Rae Dixon — the bedridden 84-year-old killed by police in a 1992 East Texas drug raid based on testimony from a bogus informant? No drugs were found in the home; an officer said his automatic pistol accidentally discharged as he kicked open Mrs. Dixon's bedroom door.

Need we go on? The Media Awareness Project's "Drugnews Archive" lists 57,250 such Drug War-related news clippings at www.mapinc.org/drugnews (see also www.injusticeline.com/victims.html) ... without even mentioning, so far as I can determine, the inconvenient fact that the only way our proud BATF "Gun Police" could get around restrictions on the use of military equipment on U.S. soil in order to hit the Mount Carmel Church in Waco, Texas, in 1993 with National Guard helicopters and later on FBI tanks ... pardon me, "armored personnel carriers" ... was to swear out a brazenly perjurious affidavit claiming they thought David Koresh was operating a methamphetamine lab in a Christian church community full of children, senior citizens, and men with Harvard law degrees.

It's your War on Drugs, folks. You can't vote for it, fund it, endorse it, slap on bumperstickers bragging that your kids have wasted their time in absurd programs founded on the notion that uniformed cops are best qualified to teach comparative pharmacology (Yes, I mean "D.A.R.E."), and then say, "No, we never meant for them to end up murdering some Michigan missionary and her baby in some stinking *jungle* somewhere."

Either legalize it, or stop complaining, and start looking over your shoulder. Because it's your Drug War ... and you're next.

A Rigged Game
❧

Late in the evening of April 12, 1999, Metro Police Officer Bruce Gentner pulled his cruiser to the side of the street at Rainbow and Tropicana and ordered John Perrin, 32, who was armed only with a basketball, to stop and raise his hands. At a coroner's inquest May 7, Officer Gentner testified that Mr. Perrin failed to follow his orders, instead reaching into his waistband. Officer Gentner testified he thought he saw Mr. Perrin's hands close around a weapon — he turned out to be in possession of a glass bottle containing iodine crystals, sometimes used in methamphetamine manufacture — a bottle on which investigators (curiously) could find no fingerprints.

So, Officer Gentner shot the unarmed Mr. Perrin. Officer Gentner fired until his magazine was empty, discharging 14 rounds of caliber .40 Smith & Wesson — hitting with six, one of them in the chest. But the coroner's jury voted 6-1 that Officer Gentner's killing of the unarmed Mr. Perrin was justified; there will be no criminal charges.

At the coroner's inquest, Officer Gentner — who expressed no remorse at his actions — told a tale in which the suspect Perrin made eye contact with him, then ran across the street. Meeting another man, Mr. Perrin — still in view of the police cruiser, mind you — then supposedly engaged in some furtive transfer of property that officer Gentner interpreted as a drug deal. Et cetera.

Anyone who has read the novels of Joseph Wambaugh is familiar with the carefully scripted little fairy stories police officers sometimes concoct when called to account for accosting citizens who are doing no harm. Former police officer Wambaugh shows how officers who have simply busted in a motel-room door carefully explain on the stand how they first checked the guest registry, then went to the room in question and found a marijuana seed on the carpet outside the door, which in turn gave them "reasonable cause" to search the suspect room, et cetera.

The frequent police attitude in such cases is that if the courts want to impose requirements that make no sense in the real world, we'll just get the job done, then tell them whatever fairy story they want to hear, later on.

Several in the courtroom found Officer Gentner's testimony similarly convenient and unconvincing. Brent Bryson, the attorney for the Perrin family, who filed a $25 million civil suit against Metro and Officer Gentner, called Gentner's testimony "well-rehearsed," pointing out that three civilian witnesses within earshot failed to hear him shout any commands at Perrin until after he fired.

The "second man" involved in the alleged drug deal has never been located. Until Friday, police spokesmen had never mentioned his presence in explaining details of the case. Since third parties — like the family's attorney — are granted no advance right before the inquest to discover witness lists or testimony, Mr. Bryson was obviously not prepared to challenge any of these handy new assertions.

Typical of our Khaki Killers and their fans, one Russell A. Wood wrote a letter intended for publication in the *Las Vegas Review-Journal* last week, stating in part:

"Let us remember that Police Officers are human too.

They want to go home to their families after their daily work is done. John Perrin set an awful set of circumstances in motion when he failed to comply with very simple directions. John Perrin chose to turn away from Officer Gentner and thrust his hands into an area where they could not be seen. ... John Perrin bears the bulk of the responsibility for the hurt in this case. ... Simple compliance on Perrin's part would have netted him typical Police interaction. Perrin, and not Officer Gentner took the incident to a deadly level."

This is wrong. These might be accurate statements if Mr. Perrin had been an armed felon fleeing the scene of a bank robbery or a murder. But that was not the scenario. Officer Gentner initiated this contact. He braced a citizen who was walking down the sidewalk, armed only with a basketball. If he was not calm enough, or did not have sufficient training, to deal with the possible ramifications of such a violation of Mr. Perrin's rights — yes, a citizen who is doing no harm still has a right to walk down the street without harassment in this country — if he was not brave enough to accept the risk of taking a bullet rather than shooting and killing an unarmed man, then Officer Gentner was free to let Mr. Perrin alone or to call for back-up. Instead, Officer Gentner initiated this incident, and bears full responsibility for it.

Do we really all deserve to be shot for merely "not following orders"? Are there no longer any illegal orders? If not, how do we differ from a nation where people could be shot merely for refusing to board a train to the concentration camp?

What if any normal "civilian" had acted as Officer Gentner did? Shoot someone who is unarmed and not advancing on you, and you'll be charged with manslaughter, if not second-degree murder. ...

In such a case, the very same prosecutors who steered the coroner's jury to their "warranted" verdict last Friday would be cross-examining you in court, asking sarcastically, "So you were 'in fear for your life,' because this young man armed only with a basketball refused to stand still and raise his hands? Despite the fact you had a gun and a bulletproof vest? And were you still 'in fear for your life' after you fired the sixth shot? After your ninth shot? Tell me, Mr. Defendant, what was it the defendant did after you'd fired your twelfth shot, that put you in such 'fear for your life' that you felt obliged to fire the thirteenth and fourteenth shots?"

Officer Gentner's fellow officers are now celebrating the fact that — for the 84th time out of 85 coroner's inquests into Las Vegas Metro police shootings — their guy walked free.

They shouldn't be so smug. Metro officers are outnumbered, and often alone. They depend enormously on the goodwill of the citizenry. But what does a citizenry tend to do when they discover they can find no justice in the corrupt government courts? It's ugly; it's to be opposed and regretted. But what people sometimes do is fight back, in a manner called "vigilante justice."

"What this [verdict] says is that you and I and all the tourists that come to this town ... we all have bull's-eyes on our backs, and that the police can kill you when they don't like the way you answer a question," said attorney Bryson after the verdict.

Drug War Hypocrites Kill a Troublesome Author
🦋

Peter McWilliams, 50, author of the 1993 book *Ain't Nobody's Business If You Do: The Absurdity of Consensual Crimes in Our Free Country*, and accomplished public speaker on libertarian topics, died at home in Los Angeles June 14, 2000. Struggling for breath in his bathtub, Peter choked to death on his own vomit.

But it was not an accident.

McWilliams suffered from both cancer and AIDS. A prescribed cocktail of toxic drugs was capable of holding his viral load to zero — in effect, producing complete remission. Problem was, these drugs produced such severe nausea that McWilliams was unable to keep them — or anything else — down.

Fortunately, it turned out a natural and harmless herb exists that was almost fully effective in relieving McWilliams' nausea — whereas a synthetic variant of the herb's dominant ingredient, the patented and thus pharmaceutically profitable Marinol — proved only one-third as effective.

Unfortunately, following the effective yellow-journalism campaign of William Randolph Hearst to identify this herb, Indian hemp, in the public mind as the dreaded tool of white women's seduction by minority Lotharios — "marihuana" — the forces of racism and repression managed to outlaw it, progressively if unconstitutionally, between the years 1916 and 1934.

Fortunately, the citizens of California since realized that mistake, and in the autumn of 1996 they re-legalized marijuana there for medical use on a doctor's "recommendation" — no prescription required — by a 55 percent majority. Seven other states have since followed California's sensible lead.

Unfortunately, cops operating in California — the same ones who used to snarl, "If you don't like the law, change it" — no longer pay any attention to the law. Now they just break into people's homes, trash or seize their property, and kidnap them because they feel like it.

"On Dec. 17, 1997, federal drug and tax agents raided McWilliams' home and offices, confiscating manuscripts and equipment and effectively shutting down his publishing business," according to J.D. Tuccille of Freedom Network News (www.free-market.net). "The ostensible reason for the raid was a book advance paid to Todd McCormick, an author and fellow marijuana activist who rented a home where he wrote and grew marijuana with the money."

Both men said the marijuana grown in the Bel Air mansion was intended to supply buyers' cooperatives that serve patients in California.

Mind you, this "crime" was committed, the arrests made, and the case proceeded in its entirety *after* the popular vote to legalize this activity.

Wait, it gets better. Why do you suppose the scum who run the War on Drugs in California decided to prosecute this case in federal court?

One might imagine a defendant like McWilliams would have had an open-and-shut dismissal, once he explained his deadly illness, presented medical testimony that only the medical benefits of marijuana were keeping him alive, and finally introduced evidence that he was being prosecuted in spite of the popular victory of Prop 215 in November 1996 — that is to say, "the law."

Ha ha. You see, in federal court, Judge George H. King ruled none of that information could be introduced into evidence. McWilliams couldn't even argue that the Ninth Amendment voids any and all federal drug laws. Nope. All disallowed. Any lawyer who tried to mention any of these facts to McWilliams' federal jury — carefully screened in advance to eliminate any potential juror who opposed the War on Drugs, of course — would have been arrested, jailed, and disbarred.

Deprived of the opportunity to enter any of the facts that would have constituted his only sensible, valid, and true defense, McWilliams had no choice but to cop a plea in hopes of getting a reduced sentence. He was awaiting sentencing for his "crime" at the time of his death.

"Federal Judge George King ordered him not to use medical marijuana while he was on federal bond," explains McWilliams' friend, Don Wirtshafter. "Because his mother and brother had put up their houses for this bond" — and because he was subject to periodic urine tests, of course — "Peter felt obliged to follow this order."

As a result, McWilliams' viral count soared and he spent long hours in bed, fighting nausea. Unable to work, he defaulted on bankruptcy payments and had lost his home.

By thus violating the law that holds any adult of normal intellect responsible for acts a reasonable man might expect to cause the death of another, Judge King — along with all the other sadists still prosecuting the War on Drugs — was directly responsible for the death of Peter McWilliams, whom they singled out and killed primarily for his outspoken political opinions.

"Peter McWilliams was a brilliant author and American patriot who was killed for his political beliefs — by an overdose of government," said our mutual friend Steve Kubby, California's 1996 Libertarian gubernatorial candidate and himself an adrenal cancer survivor prosecuted for using legal medical marijuana, and hounded into exile to Canada in 2001.

"McWilliams' books inspired people to believe in and fight for their rights. Those responsible for the death of Peter have only added fuel to the fire," Kubby, 53, continued. "They killed the messenger, but the very message they tried to smother will burn more brilliantly than ever."

Ironically, the Inquisition-like nature of the McWilliams prosecution was exposed by John Stossel in an interview with McWilliams that aired on ABC'c "20/20 Friday" on June 9, 2000, five days before Peter's death. Even the usually statist Barbara Walters shook her head in dismay.

But wait, we're not quite done. Scrunch down and check this out:

"Although personnel files are among the most closely guarded of police secrets, a copy of [that of] Ellis "Max" Johnson II ... was leaked to the media after he entered the academy last fall, sparking a fierce debate over the city's hiring practices," wrote Jesse Katz, under a Denver dateline, in the *Los Angeles Times* last weekend.

"Nobody expects police departments to hire saints," reporter Katz continued, but "the confessions of Johnson, one of Denver's newest officers, were startling in their candor.

"Under questioning from background investigators, Johnson admitted he had used drugs on approximately 150 occasions — not just marijuana, but also crack, LSD, speed, PCP, mescaline, Darvon, Valium. ... But Denver's Civil Service Commission, which sets the criteria for police hiring, insisted that the 40-year-old former karate instructor had been clean since 1987 and deserved a second chance. ..."

To become a cop, you understand. Busting teenagers with nickel bags of dope. Jailing and killing people like Peter McWilliams.

"With their frankness coaxed by a polygraph, 84 percent of Denver's police applicants — and at least 65 percent of its recent hires — have acknowledged past experimentation, according to civil service records," reporter Katz continued. "In some cases, officers bust people for acts they themselves have committed. ...

"That police — the ultimate symbols of order and authority — are willing to tolerate its use 'tells us that our Draconian system of drug laws bears no resemblance to reality,' said Elliott Currie, a law professor at the University of California, Berkeley and the author of *Crime and Punishment in America*. ...

"'Let's wake up,' said Paul Torres, the [Denver's Civil Service] Commission's former executive director. 'The days of Mayberry are long gone.'"

OK. I'll buy that. But it also sounds pretty much like what federal Judge George H. King should have said, in dismissing all charges against Peter McWilliams. Don't you think?

The full text of *Ain't Nobody's Business If You Do* is available on the Internet, for free, at www.mcwilliams.com/books/books/aint/.

What Bill of Rights?

❧

In California these days, the federal government is single-handedly trying to debunk two ancient myths that many well-intentioned Americans have long taught their children. To wit:

1) If you don't like the law, all you need do is follow the proper procedures to get a change before the appropriate legislative body or onto your state ballot. The majority will then determine in an orderly fashion whether your idea is a good one, and that will be that;

2) The reason the government licenses physicians is not to allow the political control of medical science — say, barring physicians from even discussing useful treatments — but simply to guarantee consumers that would-be physicians have met certain minimal and well-established standards of training and conduct. These licensing schemes, for instance, would *never* be used to allow politicians or bureaucrats to blackmail physicians into practicing medicine the way the *regulators* see fit, threatening to put our doctors out of business for, say, merely recommending natural herbs that compete with the products of politically well-connected pharmaceutical firms.

What has now happened in California is that the voters went to the polls a few years back and overwhelmingly approved the medical use of marijuana, in cases where a physician recommends that smoking the medically active herb might be of use to a specific patient — say, a glaucoma sufferer or an AIDS patient like author Peter McWilliams.

In passing the Compassionate Use Act, Californians didn't even require that a doctor write a formal "prescription" for marijuana — sidestepping the problem of how to "fill" such a prescription when federal law would still frown on a licensed pharmacy stocking the plant. Only a less formal "recommendation" is needed.

But ignoring the limitations placed on their power by the

9th and 10th Amendments — which restrict the federal government to meddling in only those affairs itemized in the U.S. Constitution (a document one searches in vain for any reference to restrictions on medicine or medical practice) — federal authorities aren't having any of it.

Answering an ACLU lawsuit seeking to block the practice, Justice Department lawyers are now arguing in U.S. District Court in San Francisco that Washington has the right to punish, put out of business, and even arrest California doctors who recommend marijuana use for specific patients, just as was envisioned by California voters when they went to the polls in 1996.

"It doesn't matter what California says," snarled Justice Department lawyer Joseph Lobue, in court in early August 2000.

The federals now threaten to take away the doctors' licenses to write prescriptions for "controlled" substances — effectively putting them out of business or forcing them to leave the country (as was the outcome of a similar regulatory coup against Las Vegas' Dr. Dietrich Stoermer, even after the good doctor was unanimously acquitted of "writing too many painkiller prescriptions" in a public trial in 1993). And that further violates the doctors' free-speech rights under the *First* Amendment, the ACLU argues.

(Not content to stop there, Drug Czar Barry McCaffrey also threatened at the same time to bar any such wayward physician from participation in the Medicare and Medicaid programs — a bit like threatening to throw Br'er Rabbit in the briar patch — and even to bring criminal charges.)

The government action here hinges on a negative, of course — the fact that the federal Food and Drug Administration has never "approved" marijuana for medical use.

But pharmaceutical firms now spend millions of dollars to usher each new nostrum through the FDA approval process — and none will bother to fund clinical trials for marijuana, since there'd be no way to patent and thus make back their investment on what is, after all, a common roadside weed.

Blue-ribbon White House panels have been recommending the de-criminalization of marijuana since the days of Richard Nixon. The herb was perfectly legal and in medical use from the Middle Ages up until the 1930s, when the current federal prohibition resulted from a combination of the yellow journalism of William Randolph Hearst (who ordered his columnists to stop calling the plant by its well-established name, Indian hemp, and instead dub it "marijuana," the better to link it with racist fears of the growing Mexican minority) and the need to find new work for recently unemployed (alcohol) Prohibition agents.

In recent years, majorities of voters in Alaska, Arizona, California, Hawaii, Maine, Nevada, Oregon, and Washington state have ruled that doctors — not police or politicians — are indeed the right folks to decide when marijuana might be medically useful for some patients.

It's the federal government that's motivated here, not by medical science or compassion for the sick, but by sheer politics.

The founders intended ours to be a pluralistic union, in which voters could always "vote with their feet" — just as religious nonconformists used to flee Massachusetts for Roger Williams' more tolerant Providence Plantation. Thomas Jefferson himself warned that we would find ourselves on the verge of Bonapartist tyranny should ever the 13 (now 50) states be reduced to mere administrative subdivisions of the central government, "like the 'departments' of France." And isn't that precisely what Gen. McCaffrey and prosecutor Lobue now have in mind?

The Justice Department's position here is wrong on every count, betraying a willingness to sacrifice even the lives of the sick for the sake of bureaucratic empire-building and political expediency.

And that's disgusting.

Another Nadir in Homicidal Hair-Splitting
🌿

In May 2001, the United States Supreme Court ruled there is no "medical necessity exception" to the federal Controlled Substances Act — a lower appellate court "erred by considering relevant the evidence that some people have 'serious medical conditions for whom the use of cannabis is necessary in order to treat or alleviate these conditions or their symptoms,' that these people 'will suffer serious harm if they are denied cannabis,' and that 'there is no legal alternative to cannabis for the effective treatment of their medical conditions.'"

Federal court prosecution of the Oakland Cannabis Buyers' Cooperative et al. shall thus proceed, Justice Clarence Thomas wrote for the unanimous court.

The California-based American Medical Marijuana Association (http://americanmarijuana.org/ — founded by former California Libertarian gubernatorial candidate Steve Kubby) was quick to reassure concerned parties that the ruling was of sharply limited scope:

"It is important to recognize that the Supreme Court decision did *not* strike down or in any way modify any state medical marijuana laws," the AMMA wrote in a press release. "The Supreme Court did *not* say that citizens don't have the right to cultivate and possess medical marijuana within their own state borders. All this decision said is that medical necessity is not a defense to federal law.

"Bottom line," the AMMA continued, "medical marijuana still stands in those states that have approved it. Even the medical marijuana clubs will be largely unaffected, because they will simply switch from distributing medical pot to helping patients grow their own. ..."

Maybe. But it turns out I wasn't the only person whose first response was to recall the high court's previous nadir of homicidal hair-splitting, when Justice Taney held in the infamous 1857 *Dred Scott* decision that black men are property, not persons entitled to the protection of the law.

The court and its defenders will whine that they're not supposed to "legislate from the bench"; that they were only asked whether there is a "medical-necessity defense" under the federal Controlled Substances Act, whereupon they looked it up, determined that there was none, and so ruled. The question of whether the Drug War as a whole is constitutional wasn't answered because it was never asked. The court simply tells us what Congress intended.

Which is a black-hearted lie, of course. If Congress in a fit of madness were to enact the Nazi race laws tomorrow, would the eight justices sit there with straight faces, instructing us, "We cannot locate within the Act any 'religious-freedom' exemption to the requirements that Jews sew yellow stars on their clothing, that Jews are no longer allowed to own businesses," etc.?

Of course not. When it's the First Amendment right of religious freedom that's involved, everyone understands the court's first duty is to determine whether the law in question is constitutional on its face.

If it isn't, under the great precedent of *Marbury vs. Madison* (in which the court answered several questions that no one had bothered to ask, by the way) the law is held to be null and void; we're instructed to treat it as though it never existed.

Besides which, attorneys for the Oakland Cannabis Buyers Cooperative et al. *did* assert (as Justice Thomas acknowledges) that the federal drug statute "exceeds Congress' Commerce Clause powers, violates the substantive due process rights of patients, and offends the fundamental liberties of the people under the Fifth, Ninth, and Tenth Amendments."

So there it is, laddies, staring the eight lawyer-politicians (Ms. Breyer retired to the powder room) square in the face.

Because, you see, the entire federal drug war — all of 21 U.S.C. — is blatantly unconstitutional, and any high court obeying its oath to preserve our government of limited power (as opposed to insisting we prostrate ourselves before the majesty of the federal government's plenary authority, holding us down by the elbows while the DEA greases up and services us from behind) would have thrown it out in its entirety the first time they got a look at it.

There are no fewer than three independently sufficient grounds on which this could and should be held. The weakest of these is the 10th Amendment, which tells us that any power not specifically delegated to the United States by the Constitution is reserved to the states or to the people. Since nowhere in the Constitution is Congress delegated any specific power to regulate drugs, the practice of medicine, or what responsible adults choose to put in their own bodies, any state law (like California's successful 1996 medical marijuana proposition) supersedes federal authority.

This is the weakest argument, simply because it would seem to authorize *state* drug wars. I personally wouldn't feel all that much better having my door kicked in and being hauled away in chains by local drug warriors based in Carson City or Sacramento or Tallahassee than by the federal variety ... would you?

Now, truth be told, even state drug wars are further banned under the 14th Amendment (the second sufficient grounds for tossing out the Drug War). Originally enacted to stop state authorities from passing "gun control" laws that could disarm black Civil War veterans, this amendment bans the several states from "abridging the privileges or immunities of citizens of the United States."

Under the 14th, the high court could and should have thrown out California's current marijuana distribution scheme, not because it allows *some* marijuana use, but because it places any restrictions on marijuana use at all.

Am I saying Americans have some kind of right to drugs?

Damned right, and here's where we come to the constitutional provision even a second-year law student could hardly ignore. The Ninth Amendment advises the justices, "The enumeration in the Constitution of certain rights shall not be construed to deny or disparage others retained by the people."

In 1787 and thenceforward, at least through 1915, did our ancestors on these shores "retain the right" to grow, produce, import, buy, and sell opium, cocaine, alcohol, and marijuana by the pound or by the ton, as and whenever they pleased, without federal restriction save the occasional modest excise?

Indeed they did. And the proof is that when Congress wanted to ban one of these forms of commerce, a separate constitutional amendment — the 18th, since repealed — had to be enacted to allow a federal ban on "intoxicating liquors."

So when was the parallel and necessary constitutional amendment ratified, authorizing the War on Drugs?

Pardon me, I didn't hear that. Could you speak up, please? What year?

There is none, of course. The Ninth Amendment stands unchallenged; the entirety of 21 U.S.C. stands invalid, and Justice Thomas acknowledges the court just had someone advise them, "Hey, that emperor has no *clothes*."

Nor is this merely some technical argument. Peter McWilliams, author of *Ain't Nobody's Business If You Do*, died vomiting in his bathtub because a California judge with a withered soul ruled he couldn't use marijuana to keep down his chemotherapy drugs while out on bail on charges of possessing medical marijuana.

They killed him, as surely as they're willing to kill Steve Kubby, whose survival of advanced adrenal cancer can only be explained by the effectiveness of his marijuana therapy. (A citizen jury quite appropriately acquitted Kubby and his wife of marijuana charges in early 2001 under California's medical marijuana law, though the Kubbys were forced to flee to Canada when a judge threatened to jail Steve on a minor related charge.)

"Today, the same Supreme Court that once ruled black slaves were the legal property of their white owners has again earned a place in infamy by ruling that no medical marijuana necessity defense is possible, simply because Congress has already decided that marijuana has no medical value," Steve Kubby wrote.

"A man sees another man drowning and steals a boat to rescue him," Kubby wrote. "What should happen to the man who stole the boat? ... For centuries, common law has upheld the right to break a law in order to protect human life. ...

"Does saving a patient's life justify a cooperative of patients in breaking federal law? According to the Supreme Court, it does not."

When Innocence Is No Excuse

Independent trucker Al Dilts, 66, had hauled eight loads for the same customer — "a clean-cut fellow, about as friendly as can be" — over a period of a year and a half. All construction equipment. It was good money for an $18,000-a-year owner-operator in an era when deregulation, high fuel costs, and the opening of the Mexican border managed to drive 5,000 trucking companies into bankruptcy over a 15-month period.

Dilts now admits he probably didn't ask enough questions.

The 40-year long-haul trucker's biggest mistake, however, came when Texas cop Ronnie Stilner pulled over his flatbed on a west Texas highway on Feb. 17, 1999, and asked if he could search the steamroller Dilts was hauling.

Dilts could have refused to consent to any search or to answer any questions until he'd seen an attorney. "If I'd have thought there was anything wrong or illegal about what I was hauling, why ... I could have pulled off somewhere and just parked it until he got out of the area," Dilts explained to Knight-Ridder reporter Matt Stearns. But, "For the life of me, I had no idea there was anything wrong." So Dilts told Stilner to go ahead and look.

As Stearns revealed in a feature that appeared in the *Las Vegas Review-Journal* on July 15, 2001, the cop found that new paint on the side of the roller covered hidden access doors. The steamroller concealed 556 pounds of marijuana.

Prosecutors later lauded the cooperation Dilts showed from that moment forward. "Defendant Dilts has continued throughout the course of this investigation to provide completely candid information to the best of his knowledge in response to all law enforcement inquiries," federal prosecutor C. Richard Baker wrote in a letter to U.S. District Court Judge Sam Cummings. "The government notes that Dilts' assistance was timely, and that his information was truthful, complete and reliable. Additionally, Dilts' cooperation involved danger and risk of injury to himself and his family."

No matter. Dilts — the only person ever charged in the case — had his truck seized and sold at auction. He spent his retirement savings — $50,000 — on lawyers. Judge Cummings sent him to Leavenworth prison for 30 months — not much different from the average sentence served by federal defendants who can actually be shown to have bought, sold, possessed, owned, and profited from large quantities of marijuana ... which is about 37 months.

What benefit do taxpayers receive for the more than $40,000 per year they will spend keeping this old man locked up (without even counting the cost of his prosecution)? Does anyone think the dope runners will have trouble finding other unwitting "mules" to haul their concealed shipments to willing buyers?

Emerging from prison in the autumn of 2002, Dilts will be a 68-year-old man with creeping arthritis, broke and with no assets. He will try to find work, driving other people's trucks (since he can't afford to replace the one the government seized and sold). A churchgoing man who neither drinks nor smokes, it's unlikely Al Dilts will turn to a permanent life of crime. But other men — barred from legitimate employment by the felony conviction on their record — do exactly that, using skills and contacts easily picked up in prison.

In 1986, 38 percent of the federal prison population was inside for drug-related convictions. Today, that figure has risen to about 60 percent, according to the group Families Against Mandatory Minimums (www.famm.org).

It's those federal mandatory-minimum sentencing laws that constitute the current Prison Guards' Full-Employment Act, guaranteeing America's booming penal system won't run out of raw material like Al Dilts.

"They're terrible," says retired U.S. District Judge Stanley Sporkin, who served on the bench in Washington, D.C., "just awful. What guidelines do is they say one size fits all. When you're dealing with people's liberty, that's not the case."

"The financial incentives created by civil asset-forfeiture laws create a very dangerous precedent," adds Robert Sharpe of the Lindesmith Center Drug Policy Foundation, focusing specifically on the seizure and sale of Dilts' truck. "When protectors of the peace become predators, society is put at risk. Both violent drug dealers and unscrupulous prosecutors share a common bond: They are both financially dependent on a never-ending drug war without victory. With so much money changing hands, it's no wonder that government institutions turn a blind eye to the parallels between the drug war and America's disastrous experiment with alcohol prohibition."

Meantime, mandatory minimum drug sentences fritter away money and resources, crowding the prisons until real violent offenders — rapists and murderers — often do less time than a guy like Al Dilts, especially when the incentive to "bargain them down to lesser charges" is taken into account.

But these laws also do something that's much harder to measure. As little as 35 years ago, an entire family would hang its head in shame if a family member fell afoul of the law and became a "jailbird." Today, with prison for so many non-violent offenses becoming commonplace, much of that stigma has fallen away. A fast-growing segment of society no longer finds courts and prisons foreign and terrifying ... nor do they hold the majesty of the law and the federal government in much awe.

If going to prison can happen to anyone — despite the testimony of police and prosecutors that the defendant had no criminal intent — it becomes a kind of reverse lottery. It could happen to anyone.

And if good intentions won't keep you *out* of prison, who but a fool would still obey the law when no one's looking? That would be like refusing to collect when your number comes up. Wouldn't it?

In a nation where we could once count on our neighbors to be decent and civil, where it was assumed most folks would pay "their" taxes and turn in lost wallets and refrain from raping or robbing a woman, child, or old person broken down at the side of the road — no matter what the chances of "getting caught" — the corrosive effects of turning a larger and larger slice of America into a subculture of hard-bitten "ex-cons" and their families, stripped of any faith in fairness or justice, has yet to be measured.

Or has it? Maybe we measure it every time we lock our doors at night, refusing to open them to strangers and forbidding our daughters to walk to the store alone after dark.

After all, "they" are out there — millions of them, the people we've imprisoned for violating laws our grandparents never dreamed of.

Waiting.

Drug Czar Aims to Infiltrate Hollywood
🌿

It turns out Drug Czar and retired Army Gen. Barry McCaffrey wasn't content with paying off TV networks to slip subliminal "anti-drug" messages into the scripts of 109 (and still counting) episodes of entertainment programs like "E.R." and "Beverly Hills, 90210" — even going so far as to preview the episodes and "suggest changes."

No, after that Orwellian scheme was exposed by the online magazine *Salon*, back in January 2000, came the April revelation that at least six major magazines and newspapers had also met the Drug Czar's "matching requirements" under 1997 legislation that requires media outlets to "match" every dollar spent by the government on anti-drug ads.

The networks were loathe to give up valuable commercial time for the stipulated free "public-service announcement or similar anti-drug message," you see. So Gen. McCaffrey's office accommodatingly allowed the networks — and the magazines and newspapers — to meet their "matching" requirement by merely running articles or entertainment programs that slipped "accurate depictions of drug-use issues" into their supposedly non-advertising content, with readers or viewers none the wiser.

Need we ask who got to define "accurate"?

Would the TV producers earn a "credit" if they ran a report on the way a federal judge in California caused the death of author Peter McWilliams? (McWilliams was posthumously awarded the Champion of Liberty Award at the Libertarian Party's national convention in Anaheim July 2.)

Somehow I doubt that's the kind of "accuracy" the Drug Czar's office has in mind — any more than it would take seriously a magazine or newspaper applying for "credit" for a story pointing out that the drug ethyl alcohol, re-legalized on a campaign promise by President Franklin Roosevelt and his Democrats in 1933 (how's that for "sending a message to the kids"?) causes thousands of times more disease, violence, social pathology, and premature death in this country than all the "controlled substances" targeted by Gen. McCaffrey's War on Drugs, combined.

But now comes a further revelation, in the July 12, 2000 edition of *The Los Angeles Times*, that the Drug Czar planned to disclose in congressional testimony this week a scheme to also "leverage popular movies" into featuring these approved anti-drug messages.

Why, even the theater owners themselves may now be able to belly up to the federal trough — just as though they'd run a 60-second "anti-drug" spot before a movie — merely by running *previews* for films that have the won the Drug Czar's "seal of approval." ("They can submit it to our contractors, after the movie is completed, for review for credit," McCaffrey spokesman Bob Weiner told the *Times*.)

It's an open secret that producers already approach commercial sponsors to subsidize film-production costs by eliciting payments for "product placement" — it's unlikely to be just a coincidence when Nicholas Cage takes a swig of Pepsi these days, or Demi Moore lights up a Marlboro.

But is this truly to be an open market? If he's so anxious to have drug issues discussed, will Gen. McCaffrey help the National Organization for the Reform of Marijuana Laws pony up a few hundred grand to influence production of a Hollywood film about millionaire recluse Donald Scott of Malibu, shot in his home by plainclothes cops? (See Chapter I, "Live Free or Die.")

Of course not. When Big Brother starts infiltrating our media to bribe the procurers into delivering propaganda messages, it's a one-way street. The general evidently envisions our film and TV industries playing the same role as those familiar Army indoctrination films in which smiling actors in tailored uniforms crack bad jokes and instruct the trainees in everything from the proper method for brushing one's teeth to the importance of avoiding VD-infected prostitutes. Eventually, no programming will be allowed that doesn't in some way "advance the interests of the state," and the notion that our "free press" can or should deliver us a healthy public debate featuring a diversity of viewpoints will evoke nothing but the kind of cynical chuckles once heard in the Soviet Union.

Americans used to snicker at the way totalitarian states

turned TV and the movies into ham-fisted propaganda organs for the regime. It shows how far we've sunk that the general response to these revelations has been a yawn and a shrug. But after all, who should be surprised — isn't a government education now reduced to 12 years of thinly-veiled socialist and "green" propaganda? "Entertainment" is now, to paraphrase Clausewitz ... or was it Zhou Enlai — state indoctrination pursued by other means?

Producers and publishers who sell out our heritage of a free and skeptical press for such paltry payoffs should be exposed. Then, the same Congress that was once wise enough to forbid the Voice of America from broadcasting government propaganda *inside* America should similarly put this Drug Czar out of the domestic propaganda business.

Either that, or we can stop struggling to help our kids understand those dusty old hard-to-read documents by guys like Jefferson and Madison in eighth-grade civics class. Instead, we'll just hand out copies of Orwell's *1984*.

Fingerprinting the Sick

Attempting to steer a course that will honor the letter of the law — Nevada voters have twice overwhelmingly OK'd a constitutional amendment authorizing the medical use of marijuana — without throwing in the towel on the entire repressive police state superstructure built on the "War on Drugs," Nevada's state Board of Agriculture in early September 2001 unanimously approved an Oct. 1 startup for the state's amazingly prissy new medical marijuana regime.

Participants were invited to send in written applications to the Department of Agriculture in Carson City beginning Sept. 24. Approved applicants (a doctor's "recommendation" is required) will be required to go get fingerprinted by a local law-enforcement agency, thereupon acquiring an appropriate government-issued photo ID, whereupon they'll be allowed to possess no more than seven plants and no more than one ounce of harvested marijuana, which may not be smoked in public.

I called Steve Kubby, 1998 California Libertarian gubernatorial nominee (Steve was instrumental in helping win passage of California's Proposition 215 on medical marijuana, and is now living in exile in Canada) to ask him his opinion of this proposed system.

Rather than requiring fingerprints, "I think it'd be a lot simpler for everyone involved if they just had us patients tattooed," Mr. Kubby advised, possibly indulging in a touch of irony. "That way they couldn't punish us for losing or forgetting our cards. ...

"Doctors regularly prescribe toxic, dangerous, lethal drugs, and no one really cares," Mr. Kubby points out. "But if it's a drug that actually makes patients feel good, now we need to fingerprint them and monitor them as criminals. ..."

Kubby — an adrenal cancer patient — was himself found innocent of all marijuana charges based on a medical defense in California earlier this year, after explaining to his jury why he needed to maintain more than 200 plants in various stages of growth at his Lake Tahoe home to successfully breed the strains which keep his adrenalin levels below toxic levels.

"The federal government sends its medical marijuana patients between seven and 10 pounds of pot each year," Kubby reports. "So why can't Nevada at least conform to the federal standard? There's no way to make the calculation (of precisely how many plants it takes to produce that volume of herb) accurately, but typically indoors you get a quarter to a half ounce per plant, according to DEA studies. And four ounces per plant outdoors."

Using those figures, producing the volume of marijuana supplied annually by the federal government to its own registered medical marijuana patients would take 28 to 40 large mature plants grown outdoors, or 224 to 640 plants grown indoors — while anyone who's ever grown lettuce or radishes knows you need to start many more seedlings than you ever expect to harvest as mature plants.

"That's according to the DEA's own study," Kubby points out. "And of course that's under optimal gardening conditions" ... for which arid Nevada is not exactly renowned.

"There's only one limit that's going to work," Mr. Kubby concludes. "The police want a bright blue line that they can identify to tell them how to enforce the law, and there's only one limit that will work, because any limit that's a set amount invites police to kick down doors and go on a fishing expedition to find some crime to charge a patient with.

"So the only limit that we recognize is the property line. There's no reason that a patient shouldn't be able to grow as much marijuana as they feel they need as long as they're not engaging in sales or diversion."

A possession limit of seven plants "shows a callous disregard for the civil rights of seriously ill people and it criminalizes a whole group of people who are simply trying to stay alive," Kubby says. "It just creates conditions where patients are forced to go over the line" — patients who will now conveniently have provided their names and addresses to arresting authorities, of course.

On the bright side, Nevada doctors may gain some de facto immunity from federal harassment for recommending marijuana — at least during the next year — under the permanent injunction issued by the federal courts in the case of *Conant vs. McCaffrey*.

California attorney Jonathan Weissglass — one of the attorneys in that case — reports the permanent injunction "technically applies only to California physicians, because the suit was brought after the federal authorities responded to California Proposition 215" by threatening to pull the DEA numbers of participating physicians, "but the same logic would apply elsewhere."

That case "is currently being briefed in the 9th Circuit" and will probably be heard there next year, at which point a ruling would have effect in all the states of the circuit (including Nevada), advises Weissglass, of the San Francisco firm Altshuler, Berzon, Nussbaum, Rubin and Demain.

"So while the injunction technically doesn't protect them, the question is whether, if the federal government went after a physician in Nevada, the same thing would happen there that happens here in California. I'm assuming that if what that physician was doing was giving a sincere recommendation within the doctor-patient relationship, it would be protected."

Still an awfully tentative "guarantee" for doctors contemplating putting their careers on the line, and a disturbing reminder that today's fearless drug warriors don't seem to have attended the same junior high school civics class as the rest of us — the one where we were told that if you want to repeal a bad law, all you have to do is a get a majority of the citizens to vote with you.

"We find the worst atrocities always occur at the end of the war," concludes Steve Kubby. "And this is the end of the war. It is over and you just have to keep out of the way of the dying dinosaur's tail — the Jurassic Narcs, as we call them."

Yes, We're at War ... Against Sick Americans

As "we watch a war unfold on the television — a 'good' war to protect us from terrorists ... taking the war to them, as we have been informed, because we cannot protect every target — it raises some questions," writes L.J. Carden of Meadow Vista, Calif., in a September 2001 letter to the editor of California's daily *Auburn Journal*.

"Why then are precious resources — specially trained,

heavily armed and already on the federal payroll 'home security types' — attacking a licensed medical physician and her attorney husband in rural El Dorado County?" asked reader Carden, whose letter was headlined: "Good War vs. Pot Raid."

"Shouldn't their goal be to protect us from really dangerous people?

"This courageous and compassionate lady doctor, Dr. Marion Fry, has brought immeasurable comfort to thousands of people and what does she get in payment? An assault by the feds, while the local law claims 'heh — they were gonna do it anyway, so I went along.' ...

"It seems to this disabled American that the resources being wasted on cannabis/marijuana/hemp prohibition should really be re-directed toward the clear and present threat of foreign terrorists."

Federal Drug Enforcement Administration agents on Sept. 28, 2001, seized files that contain legal and medical records of more than 5,000 medicinal marijuana patients in El Dorado County when they raided the home and office of Dr. Mollie Fry, a physician, and her husband, Dale Schafer, a lawyer who earlier had announced he will run for El Dorado County district attorney. Fry and Schafer run the California Medical Research Center in Cool, California. The patient files remain sealed pending a court hearing.

"In any law book you look up to answer this problem, it's going to say it's illegal in the margins," J. David Nick, a San Francisco attorney hired by CMRC, told the *Tahoe Daily Tribune*. "These types of records are confidential in the eyes of the law. It falls under attorney-client privilege. It's a huge invasion of personal privacy that chills one to the bone."

Police and prosecutors respond that the doctor-patient privilege is voided when there's fraud, and they're investigating doctors who they believe are writing recommendations for marijuana when it's not medically justified — as though police bully-boys are in any position to second-guess doctors on their medical recommendations, and as though these same goons would ever admit there are *any* legitimate medical uses of marijuana, which of course they would not.

Dr. Fry is herself a breast cancer survivor who is a medical marijuana patient. Cancer has recently reappeared in her blood, according to Jaimie Daniel, an employee of CMRC. In the Sept. 28 raid, the federal government confiscated 32 marijuana plants Fry kept for personal use.

"The two-year-old clinic in the town of Cool charges $200 to determine if people can use marijuana for medical conditions from cancer to chronic pain." The AP reports. "If they qualify under 1996's Proposition 215, which bars criminal prosecution for using marijuana for medical conditions, they are referred to cannabis 'clubs' elsewhere for marijuana."

Attorney Schafer and Dr. Fry weren't arrested during the Sept. 28 searches and remain free, with no charges filed against them.

"If you're a Prop 215 advocate and you're going to make any serious run for office, if you're any serious political threat to them they just come raid you," Kubby told me. "I'm thinking of filing a grand jury complaint that Republicans in California are using law enforcement to target political adversaries. ...

"They raided Dennis Peron when he announced he was running for governor ... as a Republican. They raided him in the summer of '96, about five months before the election, Dan Lundgren and hundreds of black-hooded goons, at 1444 Market Street, the San Francisco Cannabis Buyers Club. They raided my campaign headquarters — when I announced I was running for governor our headquarters were broken into mysteriously. We think it was police although we can't prove it — and later I was raided and persecuted.

"Even now Bill Lockyer is attempting to persuade the court to change my misdemeanor conviction into a felony. He said he couldn't get involved while I was being illegally raided and I was successfully defending Prop 215, but once I was successful he personally appealed to the appeals court to change my conviction to a felony and keep me from ever running for office again.

"Bill Lockyer is constitutionally charged by the state Constitution with enforcing the law equally. Article 3, section 3.5 specifically says if a state law is thought to conflict with a federal law, it must be challenged in appellate court to *find* it's in conflict with federal law; otherwise he's obliged to enforce the law as written and passed by the people of California." And Kubby feels the current California attorney general is failing to do that?

"Instead he's given the police and prosecutors open season by allowing them to do whatever the hell they want in their county, which is exactly what's not supposed to happen," Kubby replied.

"This is a big, big story; I can't think of another instance where police go into a doctor's office and an attorney's office and just take all their files. It's unprecedented and it's outrageous. ... It's a very important story because if the doctor-patient and attorney-client privilege is breached, then we have no more rights in this country. None. If you can't speak to your most trusted advisors without the police being able to see what was said, then the Constitution is gone, the Bill of Rights is gone, and we've just witnessed a slow-motion police coup-d'etat."

🌿 🌿 🌿

But in fact, the raid on Dr. Fry and her husband may only be the tip of the iceberg. Here's a first-hand account of a similar raid on the office of Dr. William Eidelman in Santa Monica on Wednesday, Oct. 10, 2001.

"I arrived at Dr. Eidelman's office in Santa Monica at approximately 3 p.m.," writes the witness, who is on probation and thus asks that his name not be used.

"The doctor was seeing another 'patient,' so I waited in

the lobby. A few minutes later that supposed 'patient' came out into the lobby and stopped. He smiled really big, looked down at the letter he had just received from the doctor, and said to me, 'I'm sure glad this guy is around, good luck,' then he left.

"I went into Dr. Eidelman's office and had a discussion with him. About 10 or 15 minutes later there was a knock at the front door of the office. When the doctor answered I could hear from down the hall the man introduce himself as a narcotics detective with the San Bernardino County Sheriff's department. He said he had a warrant to search the premises and seize some property. The doctor called for me to come out of the office and into the lobby. ...

"The cops said they were there to seize all his medical records, and the laptop computer the records were stored on, and to search for controlled substances. Dr. Eidelman argued with them for a few minutes about the lack of probable cause for the search and the illegality of seizing all his confidential patient records. The warrant only specified the names of two 'patients' whose records they were supposed to seize, so the doctor told them they had no right to take the computer containing all of his other patient records just to seize records for two of them. The cops told him they were going to take them all to 'make sure they got the records they needed', and told the doctor that a judge had determined there was probable cause and signed the warrant, so they had a right to take them all.

"There were approximately a dozen officers, all fully armed, outfitted, geared up, weapons showing/being carried, some wearing helmets and goggles, etc. I did not see any DEA or feds. ...

"The man who appeared to be the lead detective was the same man who had posed as a 'patient' and seen the doctor right before I did. ...

"An officer asked me for ID and I gave it to him. He then walked out into the hall and handed it to another cop and told him to 'run this guy, and try and find something so we can take him in; I'm sure you'll find something.'

"A few minutes later they sent me out into the hallway to be 'interviewed' by the cop who ran my ID. I was then face-to-face with the same guy who had been posing as a patient when I arrived. His attitude, questions and treatment of me were despicable. He asked why I was there and I told him I was meeting with my doctor. He then tried to force me to give my medical history and tell him what I had been discussing with the doctor.

"He kept asking what my medical conditions were and what treatment I was seeking from the doctor. I told him it was none of his business. He then told me I had better cooperate and stop lying to him 'or else you'll be in a lot more trouble.' He kept saying, 'You're here to buy a pot note, aren't you?' I told him I was not there to 'buy a pot note.' That went back and forth for awhile and he kept asking what my medical conditions were, in a *very* sarcastic tone, and said something to the effect of, 'You won't tell me because it's bullshit and there's nothing wrong with you.' The other cops standing around all chuckled and said, 'He looks fine to me.'

"The detective asked if I had any drugs on me and I told him no. He then said that their warrant allowed them to search any people present in the office and to search any said persons' cars. ... I was then asked how much money I had on me and told them I had around $170 in cash in my pocket. He next asked if I knew how much the doctor charged people who wanted to buy a 'pot note' and I brushed off the question. He sarcastically said, 'I'll bet it would be no surprise [to you] to know that it's $150, and you have that much in your pocket, so just stop lying and admit you're here to buy a pot note. If you bought a pot note from him we're going to find it in his records, so you better start being honest or else you'll be in more trouble when we find it,' and, 'You people think you can just come in and buy a note and then use that note to get your crack hit and call it legal medicine.'

"I found his 'crack hit' reference pretty representative of his ignorance. ...

"They acted like [Proposition] 215 recommendations were illegal. They also kept sarcastically asking me whether the doctor had ever taken x-rays, blood pressure, done an exam or any other tests.

"After more of their harassment I said I had to be somewhere and asked how much longer I had to stay. The detective gave me back my belongings and said, 'If you really have a medical condition, I recommend you go see a real doctor who will treat you with real medicine, and stop running around trying to get "a fix."' The other cops all laughed and made some comments, 'Yeah, right, like there's anything wrong with him, except that he needs his fix.'

"The detective gave me his card and then I left the office. The detective's info on his business card is: Michael Wirz, Sheriff's Detective Narcotics Division, 655 East Third St., San Bernardino, CA 92415. ...

"They did not arrest Dr. Eidelman, but are investigating him for supposed felonies. ... Please do not include my last name in any press release, as I am on probation and don't want to paint a target on my head."

🌿 🌿 🌿

Dale Gieringer of the California branch of the National Organization for the Reform of Marijuana Laws (canorml@igc.org) reported that a San Bernardino County Superior Court on Oct. 15 ordered the return of computerized patient records seized from Dr. William Eidelman. "Six patient files belonging to defendants involved in current San Bernardino medical marijuana cases were copied for use by the police," Gieringer reported in the Oct. 15 CaNORML press release. "The proceedings were monitored by a master of the state Medical Board to ensure patient confidentiality. So far, no criminal charges have been filed against Dr. Eidelman, but further investigation may be pending."

"Basically they don't like the law and they don't believe

in the legitimacy of medical marijuana," Dr. Eidelman told me on Oct. 12. "In spite of the fact the law was passed by the people of the state of California, they would like to ignore the law and contravene it. However, their investigation of me and their taking of my computer, and their thinking that I am possibly committing a felony are all against the law of Prop 215, which says that doctors cannot be punished for recommending marijuana."

There is an unalienable constitutional right to prescribe and take any medicine, Dr. Eidelman asserts. As to the government's claims that marijuana has no medical usefulness, "The only thing the DEA could say in the Cannabis Club case is that it hadn't been approved by the FDA. What they failed to mention is that marijuana was part of the U.S. pharmacopeia until 1941 with many formulations of marijuana produced by the major pharmaceutical companies. Their failure to mention that was, in my opinion, fraud. The war on drugs is really a war on citizens who use drugs, and to make war on our own American citizens, according to the Constitution, is treason. ..."

I pointed out to Dr. Eidelman that the ideal test case would be some white-haired general practitioner recommending marijuana for a life-long patient who now has to deal with chemotherapy or glaucoma, that police on the other hand will doubtless try to characterize him as some kind of "marijuana mill," with marijuana recommendations constituting the bulk of his practice.

"Well, this *is* a major part of my practice these days, because the white-haired old GP is scared to write the letters. So I'm the only one who's willing to write the letters these days in Southern California. The patients come to me and say, 'My doctor sent me to you because he says I need this, but you're the only one who's willing to write the recommendations,' so by the laws of supply and demand I've become the specialist in medical marijuana in southern California. ..."

Where are the ACLU and the federal Civil Rights authorities, as these goons now reveal themselves to be an armed gang thoroughly undeserving of any claims to being in the "law enforcement" business, instead harassing and ruining the lives of sick people, little different in their tactics from their brethren in the deep South 40 years ago, breaking heads and turning the firehoses on "uppity Negroes" who claimed to have some kind of a "right" to sit at white lunch counters?

Represented by a team of attorneys from the respected California law firm of Halpern and Halpern, Steve Kubby filed suit against Placer County in Placer County Superior Court on June 18, 2001, seeking $250 million in damages and compensation. Kubby's lawsuit charges Placer officials violated the Americans With Disabilities Act, committed assault, battery, trespass and false imprisonment, deliberately inflicted emotional distress, and violated Proposition 215. Here's hoping every one of these rabid, life-hating zealots is convicted, personally bankrupted, and given a lengthy sojourn in the gray-bar hotel.

In the Oct. 4 courtroom where Chief Magistrate Gregory Hollows set the Oct. 22 hearing in the case of Dr. Mollie Fry, wheelchair-bound Dee Blanc of Placerville told the Associated Press she had dropped to 81 lbs. before she began using marijuana to gain weight.

"I'm a chronic pain patient," she said.

Kimberly Craft of Placerville said, "We have a state law that protects us. I'm afraid they're going to put us on a list and decide who's next."

The Failed Drug War and the Real Significance of *Dune*

🌿

"A beginning is a very delicate time. Know then that it is the year 10191. The known universe is ruled by the Padishah Emperor Shaddam IV, my father.

"In this time, the most precious substance in the universe

is the spice melange. The spice extends life, the spice expands consciousness, the spice is vital to space travel. The Spacing Guild and its navigators, who the spice has mutated over four thousand years, use the orange spice gas which gives them the ability to fold space. That is travel to any part of the universe without moving.

"Oh yes, I forgot to tell you, the spice exists on only one planet in the entire universe: a desolate, dry planet with vast deserts. Hidden away within the rocks of these deserts are a people known as Fremen who have long held a prophecy, that a man would come, a messiah, who would lead them to true freedom.

"The planet is Arrakis, also known as ... Dune."

Thus begins Frank Herbert's science-fiction masterpiece — the tale of a desert religious cult and their long-prophesied messiah.

Most fans are aware of the 1984 film, directed by David Lynch and starring Kyle MacLachlan, Francesca Annis, and a supporting cast out of any director's dreams. Fewer are aware that cult director Alexandro Jodorowsky acquired the rights to the novel and began an abortive attempt to fund a production in the early 1970s — going so far as to solicit famous Swiss designer H.R. Giger (*Alien*) to dream up some custom furnishings of castle Harkonnen (http://sites.netscape.net/idahoprime/giger).

From Dec. 4 through 6, 2000, cable TV's Science Fiction Channel weighed in with a new six-hour miniseries version of the classic, starring young Scot Alec Newman as Paul Atreides and William Hurt as his father, Duke Leto.

For the record, Academy Award winner William Hurt seems to have phoned in his somnambulant portrayal, while Giancarlo Giannini as the Padishaw Emperor resembles nothing so much as the mad headmaster of some depraved finishing school for displaced Italian fashion designers, shouting most of his weirdly accented lines to the floor or the furniture while tossing about the folds and curtain rods of an outfit which I believe was last sported by Carol Burnett doing her impression of Vivien Leigh descending the grand staircase at Tara.

Our question of the moment is: What does the enduring popularity of *Dune* really signify?

Remember the reaction when the fine Mel Gibson film *The Patriot* premiered over the Fourth of July, 2000? The endlessly dismayed choirmasters of Political Correctness were appalled — appalled! — that this revolutionary war hero was depicted taking his young sons out into the woods to shoot Redcoats.

Never mind that it was historically accurate — how dare anyone glorify the evil firearm, as though it had anything to do with winning this nation's freedom?

Now let us measure this for a moment against the total lack of public objection to *Dune*, in a nation that claims to be fighting a "zero-tolerance War on Drugs."

What is *Dune* about? The future of the human race depends on the ability of a guild of interstellar navigators to mutate in themselves the ability to travel through space, a mutation they can only accomplish by consuming an hallucinogenic substance known as "the spice melange."

Our hero goes to dwell among the desert people on the spice planet, wolfing down this drug like there's no tomorrow in order to gain his religious visions, guidance for his seemingly hopeless jihad against the established political order. The spice is created by the giant sandworms. In its most potent form — the bile of a young sandworm drowned in water — this hallucinogen forms a deadly poison, which can only be transmuted inside the body of a reverend holy mother — a priestess who has learned to chemically convert the poison into an hallucinogen then consumable by the rest of her tribe.

In Herbert's book — and now again in this latest TV version — it's made clear that the tribe then drinks this regurgitated psychoactive drug, leading to a mass sexual orgy and the members' participation in the religious hallucinogenic visions that link them together in their common faith.

Herbert, it turns out, was a pretty good anthropologist.

The tribes of the Americas had no need for such complex methods to access psychoactive sacraments — the peyote cactus and the mushroom psilocybe, while hardly taste treats, are not deadly poisons. But as humans spread into northern Europe and Asia, they were not so lucky. The native hallucinogens — henbane, deadly nightshade, belladonna, foxglove, and the mushroom amanita muscaria — are indeed poisonous.

The ingenuity with which our ancestors devised ways to use these substances in order to achieve *their* religious ecstasies and guiding visions — a constant of nearly all religion until recent centuries — gives evidence of what must be considered a basic and relentless drive.

In Europe, the witches developed their "flying ointment" — a salve of herbs that would be poisonous to ingest, but that could be safely applied externally and absorbed through the mucous membranes. Stimulants like digitalis were carefully balanced against sedatives and paralytics like belladonna.

While in near Asia, ethnobotanists are now fairly sure the native shaman would indeed build up a tolerance to the hallucinogenic mushroom amanita muscaria (the red one with the white spots, which is curiously depicted in all the cute little elf collectibles), until he could consume it in large enough volume to filter the toxins through his kidneys and deliver to his parishioners a purified "water of life," which they could safely consume — pretty much as Herbert portrays the ritual in *Dune*.

So: Where are the fearless drug warriors to condemn *Dune*, with its accurate portrayal of the use of a natural hallucinogen in the search for religious ecstasy?

There are no protests, because Herbert's story seems "right" — it rings true to human nature.

I conclude that — while casual political support for the Drug War may remain wide, fed by the media drumbeat to "protect our children" against fictionalized racist stereotype black or Colombian drug dealers — public support for this failed crusade in economic and religious tyranny in fact enjoys little resonance or depth. Even that hypocrite Bill Clinton, who restored the right of his brother Roger's convicted drug dealer to carry a gun in Arkansas and had his drug-addled sibling take a bow to ecstatic applause at the Democratic National Convention, now says marijuana possession should be legal. (In fact, the goofball says he thinks it already is — ignoring the fact his administration continues to jail thousands of young black and Hispanic men for this "crime," and even went so far as to burn down a church full of women and children in Texas after the president's agents swore false affidavits that they believed David Koresh was operating a methamphetamine lab.)

I believe we'll see the War on Drugs collapse, some time in the next 15 years, with the same kind of startling suddenness and wave of public common sense that finally took alcohol Prohibition to *its* well-deserved grave in 1933.

For the unanswerable question is: In a land that supposedly cherishes individual freedom, why and how can our frenzied modern nanny state punish the possession of any hallucinogenic sacrament as the most serious "drug crime" imaginable, even though our own versions of the sandworm's "water of life" ... peyote, psilocybin, LSD ... are not addictive and are not nearly as damaging (either to the user or to "society") as plain old alcohol?

America is supposed to have freedom of religion. But the pursuit of religious vision, spiritual guidance, and a holy way of life can mean much more than singing hymns or Bingo Night at the church hall. And the fact is, for many Americans today, the search for religious vision and spiritual guidance ... is illegal.

Thoughts on the Occasion of the October Moon

🍂

Halloween is the day when many an American parent will suit up the little ones in black robes, matching 17th century conical hats, and oversized warty noses, sending them off to delight the neighbors with this impersonation of a witch, as traditionally represented from 17th century Austrian paintings of the Hexensabbat right up through Disney's *Snow White*.

Even the newspapers generally play along, running the results of polls that ask Americans how many actually believe in such mythological creatures as ghosts, trolls, and witches.

But witches are not mythological creatures, of course. They were the very real practitioners of a religion which predated Christianity in Europe and had coexisted quite peaceably with the new Christian church for more than 1,000 years, from the Council of Nicaea until the fateful year 1484 A.D., under the quite sensible rule of the Canon Episcopi, which instructed Christian clerics through all those years that — in cases where sorcery or commerce with the devil were charged but could not be proven — it was the accuser, not the accused, who was to suffer the penalty for those crimes.

Needless to say, this held false charges to a minimum.

All that changed after 1484, when an ambitious but ethically challenged Dominican friar and embezzler by the name of Heinrich Kramer managed to convince Pope Innocent VIII to set the Holy Office of the Inquisition onto the witches, using torture to extract confessions, authorizing anonymous accusations without any right for the accused to face her accuser, and granting the soon-busy witch-hunters the rights to seize and divide the estates of the accused (who were always found guilty), an invitation to systematic legal looting so foul that it was never allowed again in Western history ... until our current War on Drugs, of course.

Millions of persons — some doubtless practitioners of

the Old Craft, but many, especially in later years, just as doubtless falsely accused — were burned or hanged before the burning times faded away with a kind of embarrassed shrug in the early 1700s.

The crime of which they were accused? Worshipping a female deity, a goddess of the earth, and her male consort, the goat-horned male god of fertility.

Christian clerics, themselves mostly illiterate, called this female deity "the abomination," which has subsequently been interpreted to mean the horned devil of Hebrew tradition. But practitioners of a fertility cult would have had little reason to mock the late-comer Christianity by hanging crosses upside down or reciting masses backwards. "Satanism," to the extent that it ever existed (and I suspect more black masses were chanted on London film sets in the 1960s and '70s than anywhere in the four centuries preceding), is a very different thing.

Why should we care about the fate of the witches? For starters, it appears the witches stressed not the superiority of either sex over the other, but rather a balance between male and female principles — an obvious notion for early agriculturalists trying to come to a metaphorical understanding of the germination of crops in the "mother" earth thanks to the intervention of those primeval "male" agencies, the sun and the rain.

But the culture that destroyed the witches was not merely male-dominated. The history of our European ancestors of the 16th and 17th centuries presents a spectacle of bloodthirsty intolerance, a perverse catalogue of self-flagellation and repulsion at sexuality, which found outlet only in the frenzied drive to subjugate and enslave both the natural world and any other culture that presented itself. No matter how we may celebrate their competitive superiority from a safe distance, this was clearly a bunch of sick puppies.

Was it the plagues, which quite often left the continent literally in the hands of teenagers? Whatever the reason, using their superior technology of sail and cannon, and helped mightily by bacteriological allies to which they had developed at least partial immunity, the Europeans didn't merely conquer the indigenous populations of the Americas, they ruthlessly eradicated whole cultures, and with them any medical or other knowledge they might have had to offer, sweeping all aside as the "spawn of the devil."

Meantime, European women were being stripped of their property and other rights (many "witches," curiously, were widows of independent means), at precisely the time when their presence in the councils of church and state might have maintained some semblance of sanity.

The Europeans of the time adopted little of our hypocritical modern-day pretense of being horrified at "drug use" per se — they happily imported coffee, tobacco, opium, and cocaine. In fact, they forced the opium trade on China when it proved to be the only thing for which the Chinese would trade silver bullion.

But while they reveled in novel forms of drunkenness, what did horrify those brave conquerors was the use of any hallucinogenic substance as a means to religious revelation, a superstitious dread of alternative paths to spiritual enlightenment that still hangs on in our aforementioned and thoroughly irrational "War on Drugs."

(Which drug is involved in more incidents of spouse battery and inter-family murder by a factor of millions-to-1: alcohol or LSD? Which will get you 20 years in the federal pen, while the other now comes in convenient "wide-mouth 12-packs"?)

The wholesale eradication of the cultures of the Aztecs and the Incas was justified not because of their practice of slavery and ritual slaughter — Pizarro and Cortes would have found those familiar enough — but because they were found to be using peyotl, hallucinogenic mushrooms, and ololiuhqui (a variety of morning glory seed) in their religious rituals, sure signs of "witchcraft," and coincidentally a method of seeking direct revelations from the gods that really delivered the goods — hardly fair competition for the modest little Spanish communion wafer.

Why did the conquistadors relate such practices to the witches back home? Because the witches, too, in a triumph of empirical science (Northern Europe has no reliably safe natural hallucinogens), had found ways to turn such normally deadly poisons as henbane, monkshood, and belladonna into an externally-applied ointment, which would promote religious revelation by inducing a sensation of flying, followed by ecstatic visions.

(The stuff worked best when applied to the mucous membranes with a smooth wooden rod or staff — the "witch's broomstick" of our modern Halloween.)

This was the great evil of the witches and the justification for destroying millennia of the materia medica that they had gathered — the traditional folk knowledge of medicinal plants largely destroyed with the Wise Women of 16th and 17th century Europe, which we are only painstakingly piecing together again today.

It's commonly held that this order of midwives and herbal healers were a superstitious lot, rejecting the more "scientific" advances of the academically trained doctors of their time.

The truth is just the opposite. What could be more scientific than carefully observing and noting the effects of medicinal herbs over a period of generations? What could be a more superstitious pile of nonsense than the theories of the 2nd century quack Galen, whose theory that health is dominated by the "four humours" remained gospel for centuries, refined with the addition of harsh purgatives and the exquisite nonsense of blood-letting?

So fatal was the standard practice of medicine in the centuries after the witches were eliminated that most leading statesmen of the time — George Washington included — died while being bled by doctors. (Washington woke up with a sore throat at the age of 67, and died within 48 hours after receiving a cathartic enema, being dosed with poisonous mercury and antimony, and having literally half his blood — four pints — drained from his body, all in keeping with the best medical advice of the day.)

All three of Louis XVI's elder brothers were killed by the blood-letting of physicians during youthful illnesses. The last direct heir to the Bourbon throne was preserved only after the queen mother bundled him away to a locked room and refused on pain of death to let any of the court physicians have at him.

Superstition? Ask most modern patients whether they would rather be injected with a purified white extract, or swallow a tea made from the same herb, and see whether there isn't a "superstitious" preference for the power of the magic syringe or even for surgery over the remedy in its naturally occurring form, even when the latter offers better control of dosage and side effects. Chew up a bunch of bug-eaten leaves? How primitive!

The ancient Egyptians were fighting infection with fruit molds as early as the date of the Ebers papyrus, but thousands had to die of pneumonia, puerperal fever, and meningitis, all through the late Middle Ages and right through the 19th century, before Fleming could get anyone to take another look at penicillin. It was with similar reluctance — and not until 1795, when Napoleon seemed likely to put them all out of business unless they got practical in a hurry — that the established brotherhood of "scientific" physicians finally acknowledged that the "old wives' remedy," lemon juice, was a better cure for naval scurvy than all their acids and caustic salts put together.

This is the tradition of ignorance, intolerance, and futility that we honor when we dress up our children to ridicule warty old witches, or when we protest (as parents groups in La Mesa, Calif., and elsewhere continue to do every year) that Roald Dahl's book *The Witches* should be banned from school librar-

ies because it "portrays witches as ordinary-looking women."
Only the dimming effects of time — and the fact that the
Inquisition pretty much got them all — render this outrage acceptable. To find a modern parallel, imagine the (fully appropriate) public outcry if it were discovered that some small town
in Bavaria, from which for some undisclosed reason all the
Jewish families disappeared in 1942, had since decided to
launch a new Halloween custom, in which many of the town's
blonde-haired little children were dressed up in yarmulkes and
artificially large beaked noses, and sent out to play pranks and
demand loot under the guise of being "nasty little Jews." Imagine further that the more religious local townfolk demanded
the removal of certain children's books from the local library,
because they depicted Jews as "people of ordinary human appearance."

A healthy skepticism about many of our modern-day
"witches" and some of their New Age mumbo jumbo may be
in order ... though surely it's not up to us to choose which of
their exotic notions it's "acceptable" to explore.

But shall we extend our inherited intolerance to the many
serious researchers now trying to rediscover the healing properties of plants, to overcome centuries of medical libel designed
to convince us that mild-mannered natural remedies, which can
take weeks to rebuild our immunities, are not worth our time,
that the only valuable medicines are purified (and thus patentable) toxins that kill "bad" cells in a test tube, no matter how
much damage they cause the "host organism" in the process?

Excepting the odd mountain hamlet in Gwynedd, the
Tirol, and the Hebrides, our direct links to the Wise Women of
old are probably lost for good. But rediscovering their
worldview, a beneficent vision of humankind inextricably balanced in nature's mandala, is a journey well worth beginning
anew — perhaps even on the night of the Samhain moon.

XIV
The Regulatory State: Castrating The People Who Said 'Can Do'

Don't Just Free John Thoburn; Vindicate Him
🦋

The government of the Washington, D.C., suburb of Fairfax County, Virginia, opened a golf complex a few years back, not far from the private Reston golf driving range owned by 43-year-old native John Thoburn.

Thoburn says the tax-funded facility took away one third of his business.

But what he — and columnists for *The Washington Post* — find more interesting are the standards county officials have applied to their own facility, and how they differ from the rigorous zoning regulations enforced against Thoburn.

"To get my occupancy permit," Thoburn wrote in a guest column in the *Post* on March 15, 2001, "I planted over 700 trees around the range at a cost of $125,000 in 1994. But now Fairfax County demands that 98 trees be moved to different locations, despite prior inspections and approvals. Moving the trees provides no public benefit, but would waste thousands of dollars and damage the trees. ...

"The berm [separating Thoburn's facility from the busy Dulles Toll Road] is a Catch-22. Two contradictory zoning conditions require two different heights. Fairfax County still refuses to say which berm height they want. ... And they still haven't told me exactly which trees are in the wrong location and need to be moved. ..."

Although he is charged with not completing the berm as required, "Anyone who drives the Dulles Toll Road can see the finished berm, which has been completed for over a year," Thoburn writes.

"This zoning harassment has been going on for years. One zoning regulation ... allows a 'snack food concession.' Yet Fairfax County issued a zoning violation for selling hot dogs and Cokes. They say we can sell pre-wrapped roast beef deli sandwiches, but not microwave hot dogs. We can sell Coca-Cola in a bottle or can, but not in a cup. Meanwhile my competitors, the Fairfax County golf facilities, have carte blanche from the county to sell beer and pizza."

Post Metro columnist Marc Fisher picks up the tale: When "the county a couple of years ago opened its own golf complex not too far from the Thoburn range, the county did not require itself to plant hundreds of trees or build massive berms, and the county did permit itself to offer putting greens and miniature golf, neither of which Thoburn is allowed to offer."

When Thoburn last year balked at spending another $30,000 to move the 98 trees, he was ordered to close. He refused, was taken to court, held in contempt, and "put away until he sees the light and repents and shuts his business, or plants the trees," columnist Fisher reported on March 22.

That's right: As of the end of March, 2001, golf-park owner John Thoburn, a "family man with strong faith, an economics degree, and no criminal record" had been sitting in the Fairfax County Jail for six weeks for refusing to move his trees.

The other inmates had taken to calling Thoburn "Shrub" in acknowledgement of the nature and seriousness of his offense, columnist Fisher reports. He hadn't seen his kids since January (his wife and sons moved to Texas when the county threatened to throw Mrs. Thoburn in jail, too).

The county jailed him and was continuing to assess him fines of $1,000 per day, at last report, "for operating a legal business on my own property," Thoburn wrote to the *Post* on March 15. "So much for trying to live the American Dream of being a small business owner."

"Property rights are human rights," the inmate continued. "Fairfax County's own George Mason wrote the Virginia Declaration of Rights, adopted in 1776. It guarantees Virginians 'certain inherent rights,' including 'the means of acquiring and possessing property.' ... If I can be jailed for not moving trees, do I really possess my property? There are many ways to take away property rights. My three children are part Cherokee Indian. Their ancestors were forcibly removed from their property on the Trail of Tears. Have we really learned anything in America?"

"I have 800 years of law on my side," Thoburn told Fisher of the *Post*. "The Magna Carta says fines must be proportional to the offense. Is incarceration proportional to not moving some trees? If they say I can't sell Coke from a cup but only from a can, or I can't have a jukebox, or I've got to move a tree 10 feet, then I don't own that property anymore."

Foolishly, most Americans long ago embraced planning and zoning codes — and have given them little thought since — on the assumption they merely formalized what was common sense in the first place: "We property owners mutually agree to build only residential developments up here around the lake; those wishing to build a slaughterhouse or aluminum smelter should locate it down by the railroad tracks."

But the bureaucrats can never leave it at that, can they? Year after year they whine for bigger budgets, put their nephews and cousins on the payroll as $50,000 "enforcement officers," generate ream after ream of new "code and regulation" to keep everybody busy until shrub placement is mandatory, and everything that isn't mandatory is forbidden.

The nature of a thing is best judged by its fruit, and the evil fruit of planning and zoning is a law-abiding family man like John Thoburn sitting in prison while his wife and children flee the local jurisdiction in terror, for all the world like terrified Lincolnshire peasants fleeing the soldiers of Prince John.

The solution here is not merely to urge the Fairfax County

Board of Supervisors to back off in this particular case, while tens of thousands of other American property owners see their rights and freedoms similarly stripped away in slightly less outrageous pick-and-rolls every day.

There is no compromise with creeping fascism — an economic system in which private "owners" are allowed to continue paying taxes on "their" property, while every major decision about the *use* of that property is made by some government functionary.

One does not solve the problem of "30 percent sewage in the drinking water" by reducing the sewage level to 20 percent and announcing, "There: *much* better!" No, the solution here is to restore the property rights that lay at the heart of the free-market system, which made ours the hardest-working, most prosperous nation in the world. Every planning and zoning code in America must be abrogated and repealed, just as we would hitch a tractor to the tail of a rotting whale and haul it away from the beach where our children swim.

Don't just free John Thoburn; vindicate him.

Time to Draw the Line
🌾

Gail Atwater of Lago Vista, Tex., says she'd run into local policeman Bart Turek before.

The officer had previously stopped her for suspicion of driving without having her four-year-old son belted into her pickup truck. In that first case, however, Atwater says Turek did not cite her, since it turned out her son was, indeed, wearing his seat belt.

She wasn't as lucky the second time. A toy had fallen out of their truck, and Atwater says she'd instructed both her son and daughter — age six — to undo their belts so they could crane their heads out the window, searching for the missing item as their mother drove the truck at 15 mph down an otherwise abandoned dirt road.

Sure enough, the ever-vigilant Officer Turek chose that moment to show up again. When she was unable to produce her driver's license and registration for the officer — telling him her purse had been stolen — and especially when Mrs. Atwater asked the officer to keep his voice down because he was frightening the children, he became enraged, Atwater contends.

"You're going to jail!" she says the officer told her.

What's undisputed is that Gail Atwater, 45, was indeed arrested, handcuffed, and locked in a jail cell for about an hour on that day back in 1997, until she could post $310 bail. And all this happened even though Texas law does not stipulate any jail time even for those *convicted* of the offense of "not wearing a seat belt."

Atwater later pleaded "no contest" to three seat-belt violations, paying the maximum $50 for each. She was also charged $110 in towing fees.

She asked the city to refund the $110, but received no satisfaction. So she and her husband — an emergency-room physician — went to court.

In early December 2000 — their house long since sold and having borrowed money from their parents for $110,000 in legal fees to date — the Atwaters and their case reached the U.S. Supreme Court, which heard arguments on whether Atwater's arrest and jailing violate the Fourth Amendment, which bans unreasonable searches and seizures.

Lawyers for the city argued, "The state of Texas has a very significant interest in making sure that toddlers are wearing their seat belts so they won't be harmed or killed in accidents."

But Atwater's attorney, Robert DeCarli, responded, "Every driver, if they get caught committing a traffic violation, expects to get a ticket. Nobody expects to be handcuffed and taken to jail."

"You've got the perfect case," Justice Sandra Day O'Connor told Atwater's attorney in court. Then, turning to the city's attorney, she chided, "Even knowing it was a mother with two small children in a small town. ... This is kind of an amazing case. But you think that's fine."

Unfortunately, other justices seemed more tolerant of such oppression. "It is not a constitutional violation for a police officer to be a jerk," snarled Justice Anthony Kennedy.

Nonetheless, as Justice O'Connor seems to have sensed, in this case the state (having backed Officer Turek's call) is dead wrong.

Sure, most citizens would grant government some authority to restrict obviously dangerous behaviors on the roads. But this notion that officials can and should be empowered to stop and arrest and jail anyone, anywhere, because the authorities have some "compelling interest" in child welfare is very dangerous. In theory, don't we all collectively incur some of the "costs" if children aren't given properly balance diets? Should child welfare workers therefore be allowed to break in our doors at mealtime and conduct "spot vegetable inspections" ... without a warrant?

"They that can give up essential liberty to obtain a little temporary safety deserve neither liberty nor safety," Ben Franklin warned us in 1759.

If this is to remain a free country, responsible adults must retain a certain leeway to exercise their own discretion as to when it is or is not sensible to have their kids "buckled up." And even if it *was* appropriate to fine Ms. Atwater that $150 (which she paid without protest), arresting and jailing her — thus necessitating the towing of her truck — for such a minor offense was, by definition, "unreasonable."

But the high court has done some absurd hair-splitting of late, as in their decision in the case of the Indiana drug checkpoints, ruling police can't randomly stop drivers to look for drugs ... though it's still OK to stop us to see if we're drunk, or just to "check our papers" ... whereupon any drug offense they detect becomes fair game.

Instead of dreaming up such finer and finer distinctions — if we are indeed to restore our promised government of "powers sharply limited" — the court's job should be to re-establish a "default setting" that restricts the government from interfering in any but the most egregious threats to the public safety.

And Gail Atwater's actions did not constitute such a danger.

Nonetheless, in April 2001, the Supreme Court held, in a close 5-4 decision, that it was indeed OK to handcuff and jail Gail Atwater for failure to wear her seatbelt. Joining conservatives Anthony Kennedy, Chief Justice William Rehnquist, and Antonin Scalia in the ruling — thus showing that the court's deference to the majesty of the uniformed state overrides any supposed differences of political philosophy, were "liberal" David Souter and "small-l libertarian" Clarence Thomas.

Michele Deitch, an Austin-based attorney and criminal-justice policy consultant who co-authored an amicus brief supporting Gail Atwater's position, commented in a follow-up op-ed in the *Houston Chronicle*:

"The Supreme Court's recent decision in *Atwater vs. City of Lago Vista* — the case of the soccer mom arrested for a seat belt violation — left many observers stunned and puzzled. The court gave carte blanche to police officers who wish to arrest and place in custody, fine-only traffic offenders. Many citizens probably thought upon reading about the case, 'It could have been me!'

"How could the court, in an achingly close 5-4 decision, describe this woman's custodial arrest as 'gratuitous humiliation,' yet fail to find a constitutional violation?

"Justice David Souter's justifications boil down to two

points, neither one of which is satisfactory as an explanation and both of which are easily countered. But I think what truly underlies Souter's reasoning is a fundamental misperception about the realities of jail incarceration. He described Gail Atwater's custodial arrest as 'inconvenient and embarrassing,' but not 'unusually harmful to privacy or physical interests.'

"Most law-abiding citizens truly have no idea what happens in jails, and most don't care. But after this case, we all ought to care, because any of us could potentially find ourselves in this situation.

"Atwater was detained in a small-town police lock-up. Imagine for a moment if she had been arrested in a major metropolitan area. She could have been detained for 48 hours before even seeing a magistrate. In many jurisdictions, she would have been strip-searched, de-loused and subjected to intrusive mental health exams as part of the routine booking procedures.

"Even brief jail time carries with it a host of risks. Detention in most jails means placement in a large cell with many other offenders, who might be murderers or rapists and who might be mentally unstable. The risk of assault by other offenders is coupled with the risk of exposure to infectious diseases such as tuberculosis. The risk of suicide in the couple of hours following arrest is notoriously high. What's more, the very fact of arrest causes many to lose their jobs, and the arrest record will likely last for a lifetime.

"Most citizens would view this as an extraordinary response to a traffic offense that the Legislature determined warrants only a $50 fine as a penalty.

"Arrest, we must remember, is not and should not be confused with punishment for the crime. This case is not about whether Atwater deserved to be punished for risking her children's safety. She did deserve to be punished, and she paid the maximum penalty.

"But arrest is simply a way of ensuring that an individual will appear to answer the charges. That is why those who have been arrested usually have to post bail. Custodial arrest also provides a means of preventing immediate harm. For example, a drunk driver cannot be allowed to continue on his way after receiving a ticket. But for a person who does not present a flight risk or present an immediate harm, citations are normally sufficient to ensure the person shows up for trial. ...

"Custodial arrest in such cases is not only unjustifiable; it also puts citizens at extraordinary and unnecessary risk. That is the reality of jail incarceration, despite Souter's casual dismissal of Atwater's experience."

Making Up the Law as They Go Along
🌾

If the courts won't enforce the written law — if they simply make up whatever's necessary to protect the state's power and its revenues — why should the rest of us act as though there's any law that binds *us*? Aren't we then equally free to just make up whatever's convenient, as well?

Chad Dornsife, Nevada representative of the National Motorists Association, says, "I thought we had 'em cold, if you want to know the truth."

Las Vegas pipefitter Mike Mead, 53, gainfully employed, a father of three and a grandfather, was driving along a four-lane road in Henderson at 2:30 on the sunny afternoon of June 26, 2000, when one Officer Roy of the Henderson police department pulled him over and wrote him up for going 47 miles an hour in a 35-mph zone.

"At that time there was no school zone there. Where he got me was on a four-lane road. The weather was good. ... He absolutely did not find me doing anything dangerous; I was in a crowd of cars that I thought I was keeping up with. ... Those people leave those housing tracts and they go lickety-bob down to the K-mart — they go as fast as they can go, I'll tell you."

Mead ended up paying the municipality a total of $95. "I believe it was $45 for the fine and $50 for court fees, though it could have been the other way around."

He could have gotten off a lot cheaper if he hadn't fought the ticket, of course — the folks in charge of our courts these days apparently think "justice" is best served by offering cash rebates for paying up and not rocking the boat.

"I was offered a $25 fine and go to driving school; they offered me a deal saying I didn't do nothing wrong. It's just for revenue generation; if I went to school and paid a $25 fine there'd be no points on my drivers license, so how can they claim I was doing anything dangerous?"

But Mead had heard of a case won by Mr. Dornsife up in Reno by pointing out to the court that Nevada is bound by both state and federal law to show a written engineering study justifying any posted speed limit. And, "There's absolutely no way there'd been a study done there and justified 35 miles an hour," Mr. Mead figured.

So he called and wrote the Henderson Traffic Engineer, John Bartles, asking whether there was an engineering study for that stretch of road. And indeed, he was told — first orally and then in writing — there's no engineering study backing up *any* speed-limit sign in Henderson.

"He told me, 'We just design the road for 45 miles an hour, and then set the speed limit 10 miles an hour below the design speed,' which allows them to write their tickets and raise their revenue."

The letter submitted into evidence (as Exhibit Number One) upon appeal of Mead's conviction to the District Court of Judge Joseph Bonaventure is from the same John Bartles and clearly affirms no study was conducted.

"In your faxed letter, you inquired as to whether or not a speed limit study was ever conducted on Racetrack Road between Boulder Highway and Warm Springs Road," wrote

Bartles. "The City of Henderson has not, to my knowledge, conducted a speed limit study on this section of highway." Nevada Revised Statute 484.781, titled, "Adoption of manual and specifications for devices for control of traffic by department of transportation," covers all such devices in Nevada, *including* the speed-limit signs themselves, and (in compliance with a separate federal law requiring any state accepting federal highway funds to adopt this statute, by the way), stipulates:

"2. All devices used by local authorities or by the department of transportation shall conform with the manual and specifications adopted by the department."

The manual mentioned (the state had no choice — it's the manual they're required to adopt if they want the federal highway money) is the national *Manual on Uniform Traffic Control Devices* (*MUTCD*), published by the Federal Highway Administration.

The updated Millennium Edition of *MUTCD*, at Section 2B.11 "Speed Limit Sign (R2-1)," stipulates (remember, this has now been adopted as Nevada law): "After an engineering study has been made in accordance with established traffic engineering practices, the Speed Limit (R2-1) sign shall display the limit established by law, ordinance, regulation, or as adopted by the authorized agency. The speed limits shown shall be in multiples of 10 km/h (5 mph)."

But in the Henderson case, "They admitted there was no study done or any documentation," insists a still incredulous Chad Dornsife of Reno. "This passage couldn't be clearer."

❧ ❧ ❧

And what is the legal definition for the term 'engineering study'? "*MUTCD* 1A.13 Engineering Study: The comprehensive analysis and evaluation of available pertinent information, and the application of appropriate principles, Standards, Guidance, and practices as contained in this Manual and other sources, for the purpose of deciding upon the applicability, design, operation, or installation of a traffic control device. An engineering study shall be performed by an engineer, or by an individual working under the supervision of an engineer, through the application of procedures and criteria established by the engineer. An engineering study shall be documented."

"Documented," which in legalese always means: "in writing."

Yet on Nov. 14, 2001, putting the continued cash flow of the traffic-fine system ahead of such arcane notions as enforcing the law as it's written, District Court Judge Joseph Bonaventure ruled in the case of Mike Mead travelling 47 miles per hour, even after admitting into evidence the unrebutted letter from the city admitting there was no engineering study, as follows:

"Having read the briefs and the record below and having heard oral arguments of the parties, the Court finds that an engineering and traffic study was performed by the City and that the numeric speed limit of thirty-five miles per hours (35 mph) was reasonable and not arbitrarily set."

"There was no study done there and the judge said, 'My ruling is that there was a study done.' The city said, 'We didn't do one,'" laughs an amazed Mike Mead. "(Judge Bonaventure) said, 'I was a municipal judge for 10 years and I never heard of this manual; I never even heard that there was a rule like this.' He says, 'I do murder cases and I have never seen a brief this thick.' So he took three weeks to study it and then he sent his ruling to the city; he didn't send it to me. I was the one who appealed it and he didn't even have the courtesy to send me a ruling.

"When I went to district court I thought I would get something decent, because I know the judge in Henderson lives off of those fines," Mead explains. "That's his paycheck; that's his pension. I should have asked him to recuse himself because his pension is part of those fines. But at the district court, I would not have thought to do that. ...

"I'm amazed now that there may be thousands of cases where the city has not done an engineering study. ... I asked him, How many studies can you show me around town? And he told me on the telephone, 'None; we haven't done any.'"

Chad Dornsife of the National Motorists Association chimes in: "The letter clearly shows no study was done; federal and state law both clearly say the study has to be a written document; a 'study' can't just be some guy eyeballing the road and pulling his chin and saying, 'Looks like 35 miles an hour to me.'"

And the irony is, Dornsife insists, that accident rates are actually reduced when states like California have done the required engineering studies and posted the (often higher) legally justified limits that result, since traffic then moves more freely, without bottlenecks and the frustration that can lead to truly dangerous driving behavior.

"How can you check to see if the study was done right when there's no study? ... The last sentence of the law says 'and it shall be documented.' ... I thought we had 'em cold, if you want to know the truth. On the federal Web site it says, 'There are no exceptions.' ...

"This isn't rocket science. ... There is a national standards and practices code. We simply ask that it be followed. And when it's followed, accident rates go down! Beyond speed limits, this includes signal timing, stop-sign use ... crosswalks, speed bumps ... a whole litany of other issues."

❦ ❦ ❦

But why would Judge Bonaventure — who didn't return my calls during the week before I published a column on his ruling in the *Review-Journal* — have blatantly lied and said there was a written study done if there really isn't one?

"Because if Nevada followed the law, it would be a threat

to the paychecks of the very judges, district attorneys, city officials, traffic officers, and all the rest that depend on these fines for their very subsistence," Dornsife responds.

"And it's a clear conflict with another tenet of our laws that the trier of fact, the prosecution, and state witnesses should not have a financial interest in the outcome of a case. But contrary to this basic tenet, here they literally live off and are virtually wholly dependent on the fines collected. ...

"Moreover, in a very telling justification for the conviction, the Henderson District Attorney in his brief argued that speed traps are legal in Nevada. ...

"We do not have a rule of law. What's happened in Nevada, and it's happened in every state, is that the courts are wholly dependent on this damned traffic money. ... It's a farm system for the theft of public funds; it's just like this judge out here in Mina (Nevada) who bought the radar for the local cops to use to improve the income for his court. What kind of insanity is that?"

Legislators like Lynn Hettrick and Maurice Washington have worked with Dornsife attempting to put teeth in the state law against these illegal speed-trap schemes since 1991, he says — proposing laws that would bar the use of radar to enforce speed limits not backed up by the proper engineering studies, for instance — but Dornsife says State Sen. Bill O'Donnell has used his position on the Transportation Committee to block such reforms in three separate sessions.

"There's just too much money involved; you'd be goring too many sacred cows; the courts are too dependent on all these dollars ...

"I think it would be good for people to find out just how corrupt the courts are," Dornsife pleads. "This case in Las Vegas just put me over the edge. ... How can you go to court with such clear decisive evidence and just have them throw it out? The primary duty of the Nevada Highway Patrol now is writing speeding tickets and every court in the state lives off that;

it's a whole infrastructure now based not on safety, but on revenue. I haven't seen a single court in Nevada where you can get a fair trial [in a traffic case]."

The state Supreme Court tells him, "This is not an issue that's of interest to them," Dornsife says; Assistant Attorney General Brian Hutchins "told me their job is to protect the DMV, not the public."

(The official minutes of the meeting of state Sen. Bill O'Donnell's Nevada Senate Committee on Transportation held on May 4, 1995 — the year the states had to come up with their own new speed limits to replace the expiring national speed limit — tell us that Robey Willis, lobbyist for the Nevada Judges Association, "testified the existing speed limit bill is designed to make the fines as painless as possible for the tourists. He said Nevada has a great reputation with the tourists. He said ... it has nothing to do with safety. People are going to drive what the highway is capable of driving. Fifty dollars is not going to slow a person down. ..." In response, the official minutes tell us, Chairman O'Donnell "stated taht the committee will have to raise the fee in order to be revenue-neutral if the state is going to let people drive faster.")

"So if we can't get relief in the courts and the courts are going to rule nonsensically, where do you go? It's clear that the court is not following the law. ... Henderson acknowledges there is no study; yet the courts rule there has been an engineering study, so you can't get there from here."

Indeed, let me repeat: If the courts won't enforce the written law — if they simply make up whatever's necessary to protect the state's power and its revenues — why should the rest of us act as though there's any law that binds *us*? Why aren't we equally free to just make up whatever's convenient as we go along, as well?

Mike Mead's appeal was case C176390; Chad Dornsife can be reached at 775/851-7950 or via e-mail at chad@hwy safety.com. Judge Joseph Bonaventure never did return my calls.

"Oh, Did We Cite You Under the *Health* Regulations?"

❧

It's a head-on clash between two ways of looking at the law — between Las Vegas, the bootstrap desert town with the can-do attitude, and the New Vegas ... a suburban community where zoning is everywhere and whatever you do, you'd better have your permits.

Dan Paripovich, who served with the Sixth Special Forces Group from 1966 to 1969 when the unit was known to raise a little dust in Southeast Asia, is not a delicate guy. He's a demolition contractor — has been for decades. Back in 1997 he was retained to tear down the Harbor Freight building on Tropicana.

After breaking up the concrete pad, Paripovich freely admits, "I didn't want to pay the fees to haul the stuff all the way out to the Apex landfill," the county monopoly dump where he says he's encountered arbitrary and excessive charges with no avenue of appeal, "so I did it the way we've always done it in this town. I found a low-lying piece of property that needed clean fill. I contacted the owners, an Hispanic couple down in San Diego, faxed them an agreement, and got them to sign that it was OK to dump clean fill."

The property owners — the Ortiz Family Trust — stipulated that Paripovich's dumping and grading were OK, providing "No law [local, state or federal] ... is violated."

Paripovich dumped his broken-up concrete, grading the stuff out to extend the Ortiz property into the flood plain of a wash. A neighbor called to report "illegal dumping." The health department responded, also calling in County Code Enforcement Specialist Barry Lagan.

Paripovich insisted his dumping wasn't illegal — he had the signed permission of the property owners.

He was cited anyway, under NRS 444.630.

Paripovich looked up that law, which bans the dumping

of "garbage, swill, refuse, cans, bottles, paper, vegetable matter, carcass or any dead animal, offal from any slaughter pen or butcher shop, trash or rubbish."

"I called [County Health Department chief] Otto Ravenholt," Paripovich says, "and he had someone come out from the health department and look at the site, and I got a letter that there's no violation."

That April 28, 1998, letter is signed by Environmental Health Supervisor Victor Skaar.

At that point, according to Paripovich, "It got to be like a Jon Lovitz routine from "Saturday Night Live." They said, 'Oh, did we cite you under the *health department* regulations? We didn't mean that. We meant you violated the FEMA *floodplain* regulations, by dumping in a wash.'"

So Paripovich got hold of the appropriate "technical drainage study" for the area, along with the August 1995 FEMA flood-insurance study, which according to both Paripovich and his attorney, Robert Kossack, actually *encourages* placement of erosion-control material such as broken concrete "in the fringe of the 100-year floodway," which is what Paripovich says he did.

Anyway, the South Branch of the Tropicana Wash no longer carries major floodwaters, following the completion and May 1998 ribbon-cutting (all the big county officials were there) of the Tropicana Detention Basin, Paripovich insists.

Furthermore, Paripovich stands on the Ortiz site and points upstream, to where new homeowners have apparently filled in the wash completely and paved tennis courts across it. Farther upstream, he shows a visitor where the county has recently issued certificates of occupancy to new homes whose backyard grading completely blocks and fills the old wash — even a place where the county itself has apparently filled in the wash to extend existing roads.

County Code Enforcement Specialist Lagan responds: "You know, Vin, I hear that all the time, and what I say when

I hear that is: 'Right now as we're speaking someone is probably out robbing a bank, but that doesn't make it legal."

But can't other apparent violations — if, in fact, it is a violation to even partially fill this wash — be seen directly from the Ortiz property?

"It's not my job to go walking up and down the washes looking for violations. We respond to complaints, and this matter was brought to our attention by the health department."

But didn't the health department later state in writing there was no violation?

"The health department did drop out of the matter, because they concluded it was not organic waste, so we said, 'OK, we'll take it from here under [Clark County Codes] 2204-660 and 2204-690,'" Lagan agrees.

🌿 🌿 🌿

"So I went back in and proved to them it wasn't a flood control problem," to pick up defendant Paripovich's version of the story, "and they said, 'Oh did we say you violated the *flood-control* regulations? We didn't mean that. We meant your violation was stockpiling fill and grading without a county *permit.*'"

Paripovich contends even the cited county statutes are nothing but guidelines for grading — not penalty statutes. One of his attorneys tried to raise in court this April his contention that the entire relevant chapter 2204 was deleted by the County Commission in January 1998, though Lagan testified that was not true, and Judge Denton cut off further testimony on that question.

"If the law is being objectively administered, the Ortiz land should be liened to make them clear away the piles of asphalt on the other side of the wash, which is apparently also on their property," says attorney Kossack, an expert on defending against such county prosecutions.

"But if this is directed solely against my client, then things really become shady. If it can be shown he's being singled out for prosecution, then indeed my client may have a case. ... The real fact of the matter is that they've tried to get Dan three different ways. They tried the health code and that didn't work; they raised the flood-control issue but he was never cited for that; all they've been able to get him on is grading without a permit."

And county regulations allow for such permits to be issued even after the grading is "completed."

Although Mr. Lagan was called as an Ortiz family witness when Dan Paripovich was called back before Mark Denton's District Court on Wednesday, June 7, 2000 — and although Deputy District Attorney Steven Sweikert dutifully attends each court session as "an observer" — Lagan says the county is only "on the sidelines" of the case at this point.

How was that accomplished? The county simply contacted the Ortiz family and threatened to pick up and haul away the concrete fill, then bill the landowner for this "service" — to the tune of $50,000.

The Ortiz Family Trust thereupon brought a civil action against Paripovich and his one-man firm, Las Vegas Demolition, for $50,000 in damages should the concrete not be hauled away.

Las Vegas Demolition was to be represented on that matter by attorney Michael Weisman. But Mr. Weisman became so ill he missed two court appearances and eventually had to surrender his law license.

So Judge Kathy Hardcastle granted the plaintiffs a default judgment against Paripovich. Paripovich says this happened after Mr. Lagan journeyed down to meet with Judge Hardcastle to tell her "what an awful guy I am." Mr. Lagan says he cannot recall any such conversation. Judge Hardcastle was out of town at a conference when I called.

The matter ended up before Judge Mark Denton, who

displayed some impatience over the three-year-old matter. The judge kept ordering Mr. Paripovich to get the appropriate permits and haul the concrete away, and insists he has no intention of "re-hearing the issues of fact."

"He keeps saying 're-hear,' objects Paripovich. 'When did he ever hear them in the first place? When will the issues of fact be heard? This is supposed to be my day in court."

❦ ❦ ❦

"Finally worn down and seeking to comply with this Honorable Court's Order," Paripovich writes in an affidavit dated Monday, June 5, 2000, "I went to the Clark County Building Department on April 10, 2000, seeking a permit to remove the fill from the Ortiz property."

But Paripovich reports that when he tried to fill out an application for a permit to remove the concrete as ordered, clerk Debbie Hammond called the County Response Office, had a telephone discussion of several minutes duration with someone there, wrote "Barry" on the top of the application form, then turned back to Mr. Paripovich and told him "that because a permit was never secured prior to the placement of the fill, a permit would not be issued for the removal of the fill."

Under oath in court on June 7, Lagan denied he had ever issued such instructions to the clerk, or that he was even in the building when Ms. Hammond's call came in.

"So what's going on here, Barry?" I asked Lagan. "Is this just a case of a guy who remembers the way things used to be done in this town, and refuses to realize things have changed?"

"Vin, you've hit the nail on the head," Lagan said. "Everything this gentleman does is backwards and without permits, but he has a vendetta against this office because we're the ones that catch him and enforce it." Lagan also refers to the fact Paripovich used to receive county contracts, but has been removed from the contractors' list.

Other contractors apply for all the appropriate "dust permits and permits for hauling to the landfill, and then a person like Dan P. will undercut them (on price) because he doesn't do the stuff he's supposed to do; he dumps in the desert, literally," Lagan says.

Paripovich agrees he's had a falling out with the county, but contends that's because he was once ordered to tear down a building he believed contained asbestos tile.

Instead of obtaining an asbestos inspection as he demanded, the county fired Paripovich on the spot and brought in an unlicensed contractor to tear down the building, Paripovich contends.

"Instead of spending the time correcting the problem, he spends all this time making false accusations," Lagan responds. "He has right from the beginning accused everyone of doing him an injustice when the record speaks for itself; he just doesn't go by the book."

"Let me ask you this, Vin," said Lagan, returning to his office Monday after spending last Friday and Saturday staking out likely desert sites in his department's Fifth Annual Catch-a-Dumper Day. "Why is Dan P. the only one who can't accomplish what he wants to do; why is he the only person who has a problem with the county that's preventing him from making this correct? ... It's that simple and that easy; he just doesn't want to comply. It's not like the county hasn't tried to help him comply. He's just got a bug across his ass because we don't use him anymore."

"Nothing I've done is illegal," Paripovich responds."They threaten to throw me in jail for contempt; they're ordering me to spend $20,000 hauling this stuff away when it's good clean fill; it improved the value of the land. And they still can't show me where I broke the law."

They're Young, They're Proud, They're 'Hooters'
🌿

In 1995, the Equal Employment Opportunity Commission announced they wanted the Atlanta-based Hooters restaurant chain to replace 40 percent of their buxom young waitresses—the signature "Hooters Girls" — with men, and to pay $22 million into a fund for EEOC distribution to male "victims" of the chain's hiring policy.

But this time, for a change, the federal bean-counters did not get the docile compliance they demand. Mike McNeil, vice president for the 170-restaurant chain, held a press conference in Washington Nov. 14, 1995, to announce, "Hooters is fighting back.

"The Hooters Girls, with their charm and all-American sex appeal, are what our customers come for," McNeil said, arguing the chain would go out of business if forbidden to offer their trademark enticement. Federal law does allow some gender-based hiring, McNeil argued, including an exemption for the Playboy organization to hire all-female bunnies.

During the four years "in which we were tripping over federal regulators and investigators in our restaurants," Hooters management pointed out they had many male bartenders, dishwashers, cooks, and managers. McNeil said, "Just no waiters. But conciliation has broken down. Our attorneys tell us we're on solid ground and we're just not going to do what the commission wants."

Dawn Palarino, a Hooters bartender in Chicago, told The Associated Press women are not exploited by the chain. "Nine out of 10" Hooters Girls are aspiring models and actresses who earn as much as $75 to $150 per shift, including tips, said Palarino, who plans to advance into upper management with the firm.

With a backlog of 100,000 real sex-discrimination complaints, "It's hard to believe that forcing guys to be Hooter girls is a top government priority," McNeil said.

There were two problems with the government trying to force the chain to hire male "Hooters Girls" — mustachioed men in blonde wigs, as parodied by the restaurant chain in a full-page ad in *USA Today*.

First, the spirit of America is one of entrepreneurship. Progress only results when investors are free to venture their capital in new ways no one ever thought of before, without some higher authority — whether it be church or emperor — banning their experiments before they start.

It's really not so far from forbidding restaurateurs to try out an idea like "Hooters" to banning Dr. Fleming from experimenting with the antibiotic properties of yucky fruit molds.

But even if naming a restaurant chain with a sophomoric pun on "big breasts" were morally unacceptable, the more important question is whether Washington has any constitutional authority to correct such "tastelessness." I search the Constitution in vain for any such delegated authority.

In this case, at least, ridicule apparently worked. Within months, the EEOC quietly dropped its case against Hooters.

๛ ๛ ๛

What's in a name?

When carefully used, words can help us figure out where we are, and where we're headed.

Take "fascism." Most folks know Hitler and Mussolini were fascists. They were bad people who started wars and persecuted racial minorities. Therefore, if we hear an agency of the U.S. government accused of "fascist" behavior, since we're cognizant of no death camps, the tendency is to assume we're just listening to some rhetorical overkill.

But "fascism," as it turns out, means that form of collectivism that differs from Communism in that private economic enterprise is allowed to continue, but under government con-

THE BALLAD OF CARL DREGA

trol. While Communists actually shoot or deport business owners, under a fascist system a private business owner is generally allowed to keep title to his property — and even some of his profits — so long as his daily operations are micromanaged by bureaucrats (see: Krupp).

Let us now examine the case of Joe's Stone Crab, the well-known seafood restaurant in Miami, Florida.

On Aug. 12, 1998, Joe's Stone Crab was ordered to pay $150,000 in "lost wages" to four women who — according to the Associated Press — "accused the landmark restaurant of sex discrimination."

In addition, U.S. District Judge Daniel T.K. Hurley ruled that for the next three years, the court will review and OK any hiring decision at the 84-year-old crab house — including the busboys.

But the four women who were never hired as waitresses by the crab house — part of the proprietors' successful marketing formula since 1914 has been to offer food servers who were all men in tuxedoes — were not really the instigators of the Joe's Stone Crab court case, of course.

No, the instigator here would be our old friends at the federal Equal Employment Opportunity Commission, who were last seen crawling out of sight to public jeers of derision after the Hooters debacle.

Nor does it matter if the business owner in question hires women as chefs or managers, actually paying them more than the waiters. Nope. The goal here is to set an example, to force the defiant to grovel, self-criticize, and promise to embrace the new faith of diversity, as federally defined. If Joe's Stone Crab is eventually driven out of business, throwing all its employees on the dole — including female greeters and cooks — what's that to the EEOC?

"The Old World notion that it is 'classier' to have only male food servers is, at best, a quaint anachronism," Judge Hurley duly ruled, blithely accepting the federal assertion of some mysterious constitutional authority to review restaurant-business marketing plans. "It is not a defense to the charge of sex discrimination."

Judge Hurley calculated the four women lost between $15,000 and $71,000 each, because they were not hired at Joe's. In some cases — get this — the judge even calculated the "lost wages" starting years before the women ever interviewed for a job, on the theory that they *might* have applied there earlier, were it not for Joe's reputation for hiring only men.

(Are there not thousands of other Miami women who *might* have applied? Where does the line form?)

And how did that old misogynist, Joe, respond to the court ruling?

Joe's long gone, of course. The owner of Joe's Stone Crab, the sexist who will now have to operate the business under close court supervision like some recalcitrant local school district ordered to enforce racial busing, is — you saw this coming, didn't you? — the granddaughter of the restaurant's founder, one JoAnn Bass.

The woman-hating Ms. Bass said she would be meeting with her attorneys to discuss an appeal.

"There is no basis for the court's opinion that Joe's ever engaged in any discrimination," Ms. Bass said in a statement. "Joe's has always been an equal opportunity employer and has been a proud leader in diversity in this community."

They just wanted the "look" and style that come with male waiters ... the same way the purveyors of Maidenform bras find little use for male models in their ad campaigns.

But that's not the way the EEOC wanted to see this business managed, was it?

Yes, yes, it's wrong to systematically bar women from medical schools, from law schools, from any other profession where their physical differences are irrelevant. But — everywhere but in the benighted lands of fundamentalist Islam — those battles have almost all been won. Neither Miami nor any other American city has any shortage of female waitpersons. Instead, the EEOC looks for all the world like a frustrated soldier who misses the old campaigns, who vents his frustration and seeks to prove his "manliness" by picking fights in a barroom.

What was that word again, the one the dictionary defines as "Private economic enterprise under centralized government control"? I know I had it written down, somewhere ...

It's Your Problem
ꙮ

To hear the Las Vegas City Council tell it, the reason they've poured millions of tax dollars into redevelopment in the downtown Fremont Street area is to help local businesses.

Redevelopment of the historic Glitter Gulch will attract more paying customers, according to this line of argument, which will in turn increase business volume, eventually "paying for itself" through increased tax revenues.

So, what has been the experience of a local entrepreneur like Andre Rochat, longtime proprietor of the swanky Andre's French Restaurant on South Sixth Street, who in 1997 decided to acquire and upgrade the tavern around the corner on South Fourth Street, known in previous incarnations as Down Under and subsequently P.K. Christy's, now re-dubbed Frogeez On 4th?

Surely an upscale restaurant and tavern should be precisely the kind of tourist-friendly businesses to which the city would want to play midwife and nursemaid. No?

"There is no such a thing as redevelopment of downtown," says Mr. Rochat, a plainspoken Burgundian. "The few things happening is limited to a few people who are very well financially and politically connected.

"As for help from the city, you can forget it. Their attitude is basically, 'You can die, sucker; it's your problem.' The building department tries to put you out of business before you even get started. Talking to the Las Vegas building department is like talking to the IRS."

Under five previous owners, the downtown tavern now called Frogeez "has never made it," Mr. Rochat explains. "We wanted to go in there and re-mold it, spend $250,000, and make it a nice place."

To play it safe before starting his renovations, Rochat requested courtesy inspections from the building department, the health department, and the fire department. Only the health and fire departments cooperated. "So they came in and said there were no big problems. They saw some equipment that was outdated that they asked us to replace, just some minor changes.

"But once we started remodeling, then everyone came down on me. Because of the code it turned out I had to re-do the whole place, everything. On the exhaust system alone I spent over $300,000. That exhaust fan that was there had been there for 18 years, it had been OK for everyone else before me, and the [courtesy] fire inspector never said anything to me about it. Then after we signed the lease I had to change everything.

"We went to three meetings at the building department. First meeting, I changed the plans, the plans were signed and approved. Then when we built it according to the plans, the building inspector came in and red-tagged everything. We told him the plans were approved and signed, and he said, 'Well, I don't care.'

"We had to go to arbitration, everything was not good enough, everything had to be done with a special insulation. The fire department came back and said you need an alarm system. I said, 'Why do we need an alarm system?' They said, 'Well, your place is small enough you wouldn't need one, but because there was one there before, you need one now.'

"But they wouldn't tell me what kind of alarm system you need. 'We can't tell you.' I said, 'Don't you have a code that tells people what kind they need?' They said, 'No, just go out to bids and get one, and then we'll tell you if it's OK.'

"So I went and got bids, that took six weeks, then you have to re-do the plan and send it back, then you wait five more weeks. It goes on and on and on."

"I covered that little patio that was a glass patio. I wanted to enclose it totally. They made me build a separate building, with steel that would hold up a city bus. That cost me $100,000."

At some point, one has to ask: Does Monsieur Rochat believe the city inspectors were seeking some kind of ... special compensation?

"I'm not going to say anything. But I think if someone would investigate the building department of Las Vegas, they would have a field day. ... I just got my property tax bill last week. I pay $3,200 a year for the redevelopment of downtown in my property tax. What has the city done to me over the 19 years I've been here? They closed my street without giving me any warning. I got up one morning and the street was closed [for construction of the Fremont Street Experience]; they said, 'Tough luck, Andre.'

"I ended up spending three-quarter-million dollars on Frogeez, and I'm gonna eat it, too," Rochat told me in July 1998, just before Frogeez closed for good. "It's a beautiful place, they should be thanking us for what we did there. But you know those people that drive around in their little carts writing parking tickets? They were giving parking tickets to my customers at 11 o'clock on a Friday night. There is absolutely nobody around, downtown is empty except for my customers, and my customers were getting parking tickets. ...

"The city has put over $45 million in that Fremont Street Experience, but I can't advertise on it; it's owned by the big hotels. Everything is a game with the big people, end of story."

The Saga of the Moose's Tooth

🍃

Eight Western states outperformed the rest of the country in economic growth during much of the 1990s — while Hawaii and Alaska suffered the most pathetic growth rates, according to a Commerce Department report released in Washington June 4, 2001.

The report's authors blamed California's sub-par economic performance on slowdowns among defense contractors.

In attempting to explain Hawaii's worst-in-the-nation economic performance during the period (the Aloha State's economy actually shrank by 0.3 percent), "Government analysts said that the state ... was hard hit by the 1997-98 Asian currency crisis, which cut into the state's tourism business," reports AP economics writer Martin Crutsinger.

What "government analysts" apparently failed to note or mention is that, among the 50 American commonwealths, Hawaii is the most nearly perfect model of a high-tax single-party welfare state, where Democratic Party pork and make-work public-sector jobs proliferate unchecked by any substantial conservative or libertarian opposition, and where the now-standard run of "environmental" restrictions on business activity not only proliferate like kudzu (you can't even put up a billboard anywhere in Hawaii), but are then geometrically multiplied by restrictions on virtually any productive land use that might somehow offend aboriginal sensibilities.

That traditionally low-tax less-government havens like Idaho, New Mexico, Utah, and New Hampshire (the last proving the trend is not merely regional) would also lead the nation in job and profit growth is no surprise. At first glance, however, this would appear to leave Alaska as the largest remaining mystery in this report.

Why would the once laissez-faire northern empire place next-to-last in growth with an average increase of just 0.5 percent during the eight-year period, faring even worse than Sen. Byrd's barefoot pork palace of West Virginia, which weighed in at a predictably anemic 2.4 percent?

The answer, apparently, is that things have changed in Alaska. Matt Jones of the Bear Tooth Theater Pub explains there was no cap on microbrewery production or the number of locations he and partner Rod Hancock could open when they launched their popular upscale Anchorage venture in 1996.

But then their competitors at Alaska's Cabaret, Hotel, and Restaurant Retailers Association got busy, dispatching high-paid lobbyists to the state legislature to warn, "If we don't watch out, Alaska will have a brew pub on every corner, like they do down in Seattle!"

Oh, the humanity.

"We were never contacted or asked about it," the microbrewer told me over lunch at his spiffy new joint in early summer 2001. "Then suddenly we got this letter saying we were grandfathered in, but we can never open another restaurant, when it was written right there in our business plan that we'd always figured on expanding and opening subsequent locations."

In 1999, Jones and Hancock and the owners of Anchorage's competing Glacier Brew House were "allowed" to open second locations (Jones and Hancock started down the street at the Moose's Tooth Saloon), but only in exchange for agreeing to purchase otherwise unnecessary $150,000 full-liquor licenses for each location and accepting production caps on their microbreweries of 4,800 kegs per year.

What does this mean to Jones and Hancock's fast-growing business, which has already created 200 new Alaska jobs?

"Due to the level playing field there, Oregon is now known as the mecca of handbrewed beer, because people can live and die by their wits," Jones explains. "If you're a beer connoisseur you visit Portland. But now no one will ever come to Anchorage for that. The state is shooting itself in the foot. We just had a meeting, and it looks like we're going to have to farm out the brewing of our extra production" [to meet current-year customer demand] "to Oregon. So those jobs and that tax revenue will all go to Oregon. What we'll have to do is pace our production here so as not to reach 75,000 gallons till December so our five brewery workers don't have to get laid off in October.

"We put together a great team of brewers, and they were real excited about the chance to grow here. But now they're on pins and needles, wondering if they're even going to have their jobs."

Oregon's ranking in the same Commerce Department survey of economic growth? Third best in the nation, at 6.8 percent, interestingly enough.

The real correlation with economic growth or slowdown would appear to have far less to do with silicon chips or defense contracts — or any Asian currency crisis — than it does with whether a state's lawmakers strive to keep taxes low and stay the employment-strangling hand of the "regulatory" racketeers. Once a laissez-faire paradise for the self-sufficient, Alaska now seems to have fallen into the hands of the protection rackets and their professional legislative wheel-greasers.

Too bad. Pretty country up there ... if only they'd let a guy make a living.

OSHA Would Ban Cookie-Lifting
❧

In what is being called a "defining test of House sentiment on the issue," the House of Representatives voted 220-203 on June 8, 2000, to block the Occupational Safety and Health Administration from instituting new proposed "ergonomics" regulations — rules that would require workplaces throughout the nation to be redesigned on the theory that typing causes carpal tunnel syndrome, and so forth.

The vote split largely on partisan lines, with most Republicans voting to bar OSHA from putting the proposed new rules into effect, while most Democrats want OSHA to go to town.

"Maybe the Republicans would recognize ergonomics injuries if we applied them to tennis and golf," sneered Rep. George Miller, D-Calif.

In order to veto the "cease and desist" order, President Clinton would have had to reject the entire $339.5 billion health, education, and welfare spending bill to which it was attached.

The Labor Department estimates 1.8 million workers each year suffer injuries related to overexertion or repetitive motion — and that a third of those are injured seriously enough to be forced to take time off from work.

The proposed federal rules would cover an estimated 27 million workers.

Advocates argue the government needs to take a larger role in preventing repetitive-motion injuries, "ailments that force thousands of American workers off the job with aching muscles, tendons, and joints."

And as was the case when the workplace police were lobbying for the Americans with Disabilities Act a few years back, administration officials insist many of the proposed fixes — "some as simple as adjusting the height of a desk or a chair" — would be quick and cheap.

Business owners reply the regulations could cost employers uncounted billions, while giving government too much power to meddle in key business decisions.

Fortunately, OSHA has already brought some court cases that provide concrete examples against which to measure these conflicting claims.

In the Beverly Enterprise case, OSHA sought to prevent nursing-home employees from lifting patients. "Despite a month-long trial and a parade of OSHA experts, a judge found, 'There is no reliable epidemiological evidence establishing lifting as a cause of [lower back pain]' and that 'Science has not been successful in showing when and under what circumstances lifting presents significant risks of harm,'" writes Eugene Scalia, a labor and employment attorney in Washington D.C. and author of the Cato Institute policy analysis "OSHA's Ergonomics Litigation Record: Three Strikes and It's Out."

Seeking to correlate repetitive motion with injuries in a 1992 study of a major telecommunications firm, the government actually found complaints went down among workers who worked more overtime. "In other words, more repetitive motion meant fewer complaints," attorney Scalia reports.

In a 1998 decision in the Dayton Tire case, a judge found OSHA's expert witnesses failed to account for other possible causes of workers' reported ailments, such as sports. "The judge deemed OSHA's methods 'junk science' by the standards established in the Supreme Court's 1993 *Daubert* decision, and also found repeated inconsistencies among OSHA's own witnesses: Each of OSHA's supposed experts had a different theory about what made a job dangerous and what would fix it," Scalia reports.

OSHA looked even sillier in the 1997 Pepperidge Farm case. In that case, Mr. Scalia writes, "OSHA alleged that workers faced 'death or serious physical harm' from lifting the top of a sandwich cookie from one assembly line and placing it on the bottom of the cookie on another assembly line. OSHA also said it was dangerous to use one's thumb to flick a paper cup onto a conveyor belt and then place a cookie in the cup. It ordered the company to increase staffing, slow assembly line speeds, increase rest periods, or simply automate the entire operation."

(And here we thought the Democrats were supposed to be pro-"working man.")

"But at trial OSHA could not demonstrate that any of those measures was a feasible and effective means of reducing musculoskeletal disorders at the worksite."

Now, "Instead of backing down after those embarrassing

losses, OSHA wants to entrench the questionable science of ergonomics as a permanent rule," Mr. Scalia concludes. "But no agency should be permitted to impose on the entire American economy a costly rule premised on 'science' so mysterious that the agency itself cannot fathom it."

"When OSHA says, 'Trust us, we'll enforce it reasonably,' — well, we don't trust them," agrees Randel Johnson, a vice president of the U.S. Chamber of Commerce.

Come now, boys, haven't you learned by now? They're from the government ... they're here to help.

Employers Can No Longer Refuse You a Deadly Job

As with most "feel-good" legislation, fans of the Americans with Disabilities Act fought for passage of that original bill by attempting to brand opponents as insensitive to the plight of the blind, the disabled, and the bedridden.

The law was sold as a not-very-costly way for congressmen to "express sympathy" with the plight of the blind, the deaf, and the wheelchair-bound — since all it required was "reasonable accommodation," who on Earth could be opposed to requiring employers to provide a wheelchair ramp or a special desk or a Braille keyboard or a seeing-eye dog on the premises?

In fact, the sponsors were warned and knew darned well the act's overly broad prescriptions were bound to create a *very* expensive legal tangle. It's not too far-fetched to figure the whole idea was to pass something vague enough that the backers could then count on a much more intrusive regime of quotas and set-asides and punishments for "insufficiently sensitive" employers being crafted by the trial bar and the courts, who could be counted on to give us something *much* more onerous and intricate and expensive ... and Draconian ... than would ever have been permitted if it had all simply been written out for the congressmen and their constituents to read *before* enactment.

In the brief span of years since its adoption, the ADA has generated many times more litigation than anyone predicted, and the majority of plaintiffs have been not the deaf or those who use wheelchairs, but rather sufferers from such hard-to-measure "disabilities" as heart conditions, bad backs, migraine headaches, and the sundry manifestations of "stress."

For instance, on Jan. 8, 1999, the U.S. Supreme Court said it would review a case involving twin sisters who argue they should be protected from discrimination by their employer based on their disability — extreme farsightedness.

And what job is it Karen Sutton and Kimberly Hinston say they should not be unfairly denied? They want United Airlines to allow them to be airline pilots.

At the same time, the court agreed to hear related cases of an Oregon truck driver who says he should not have been terminated merely because it turned out he was blind in one eye, and a Kansas UPS mechanic fired for high blood pressure — which mechanic Vaughn Murphy's attorneys contend is a protected "disability" covered under the wide-reaching wingspan of the ADA.

This would all be amusing, were it not that 1) it's costing a fortune in time and legal fees; 2) even well-intentioned employers and merchants have no idea what they must do to avoid legal and financial jeopardy — a major ingredient in the rule of law; and 3) the end result is to heap suspicion and aversion even on those who are legitimately willing and able to work despite an unrelated disability — the very people this badly drafted law was initially supposed to help. (Why risk hiring a handicapped person at all, if he or she can drag you into court at any time and there are no reasonable, affordable steps you can take to prevent it?)

Ready?

Mario Echazabal, 54, found himself working at Chevron Corp.'s El Segundo refinery in Southern California a few years back, through a subcontractor.

Then Mr. Echazabal applied to work directly for Chevron. That's when it came to the company's attention that Mr. Echazabal has been diagnosed with a chronic form of hepatitis — a liver disease that could be exacerbated by exposure to the plant's chemicals.

So Chevron rejected Mr. Echazabal's job application and instructed the subcontractor to remove him from the refinery.

Having lost his refinery job, Mr. Echazabal, needless to say, sued.

In 1999, U.S. District Judge Lourdes G. Baird threw out all of Mr. Echazabal's claims, relying on guidelines promulgated by the federal Equal Employment Opportunity Commission, that employers may assert a "direct-threat" defense with regard to individuals applying for specific jobs that might pose a threat to their own health and safety.

After all, "A person who can't perform a job without being seriously injured isn't qualified for the job," as it was put — with compelling common sense — by Ann Reesman, general counsel for the Washington-based Equal Employment Advisory Council, an industry group that filed a brief in the case.

But the story doesn't end there. Oh no.

Mr. Echazabal's attorneys took their case to the Ninth Circuit Court of Appeals, which in May 2000 handed down a doozy of a new ruling that now becomes the law of the land in nine western states.

Get this: When it enacted the Americans with Disabilities Act in 1990, "Congress concluded that disabled persons should be afforded the opportunity to decide for themselves what risks to undertake," wrote Judge Stephen Reinhardt for a unanimous three-judge panel.

And here I thought proponents of the law said it would

merely require employers and retail stores to make a few "modest and sensible accommodations," like installing wheelchair ramps.

Instead, the Ninth Circuit ruled that — while employers can still refuse to assign disabled employees to jobs in which they may pose a significant risk to the lives and safety of *others* (still no blind truck drivers or airline pilots — but perhaps we should add, "so far"), it's now illegal to refuse to give a disabled person a job assignment, even if you know the job may kill him.

If grand mal epileptics want to work as topmen building skyscrapers, if people suffering potentially fatal complications from pressurized air want to work in diving bells or scuba suits, employers are now instructed to say, "OK, honey; Congress wants you to have the opportunity to make that decision for yourself."

Now, if there were general acknowledgement of the common-sense premise that a job offer is a private contract into which adult workers are free to enter or not, at their own risk — one in which the government should not be meddling in the first place — all of this might make a certain amount of sense, since honoring the freedom of adults to make their own decisions and live with the consequences is basically a good thing. *If* these same courts were routinely throwing out frivolous lawsuits that seek to blame someone else for a loved one's demise.

But are the courts routinely ruling these days that, "He chose to smoke cigarettes for 30 years despite the warning labels; your case against Big Tobacco is dismissed—and you can also pay the defendants' legal fees"?

Just the opposite. The same judges who want to be patted on the back for their defense here of the liberty of disabled folk to take whatever risks they choose are the ones who routinely allow suits to go forward in which farmers who fall off ladders are allowed to sue the ladder-makers for not putting written warnings on their products, indicating: "Do not rest foot of ladder on frozen cow manure when climbing onto roof at dawn; later in the day the stuff may melt."

Are we to imagine that hard-hearted citizen juries will now throw out the damage claims of young mothers who give birth to deformed children after being allowed to work around toxic chemicals, because the owner of the chemical factory (a fat man with a mustache, a cummerbund, and a cigar) snarls on the witness stand, "Heck, we warned her; we told her, 'It's your choice if you want to work around the pesticides, missy,' but she wanted the big bucks, and now it's her tough luck"?

That'll be the day.

And what about those EEOC guidelines, which authorize employers to defend themselves by arguing such job assignments pose a "direct threat" to an employee's life and safety?

In light of this Alice-in-Wonderland court decision, Peggy Mastroianni, the EEOC's assistant legal counsel, told the *Los Angeles Times*: "This is an issue we've been looking at, and in light of the new decision we will give it more careful consideration."

On Oct. 29, 2001 — as this book was being edited for publication — the Supreme Court agreed to hear arguments by early 2002 in Chevron's appeal of the case of Mario Echazabal.

Stay tuned.

"If We're Treated Like a Number, We're Property"

🌿

The aftermath of the terror bombings of Sept. 11, 2001, wasn't the first time the statists had proposed a "National Identity card." Back in July 1998, Lisa S. Dean, Director of the Center for Technology Policy at the Free Congress Foundation, wrote:

"I recently traveled in Russia where, despite the collapse of the Soviet Union, every citizen is still required to have an internal passport on his person at all times. If the citizen is ever stopped and asked for proper identification and fails to produce his internal passport, there are serious consequences. ...

"We in the United States always prided ourselves on the fact that we had no such internal controls. ... When Social Security was first debated in the Roosevelt Administration, the president himself assured American citizens that a Social Security number would never be used for identification purposes."

But on June 17, 1998, the U.S. Department of Transportation's National Highway Traffic Safety Administration issued proposed new rules requiring all citizens to obtain a driver's license containing a Social Security number by Oct. 1, 2000 — previous federal enactments already require this ID card to include such "biometric identifiers" as a digitized thumbprint on a magnetic strip — and requiring the states to verify those numbers with the Social Security Administration.

"Without that license," Ms. Dean warned at the time, "citizens will no longer be eligible for health care, or employment, to conduct bank transactions, to board an airplane, purchase insurance, will be ineligible for a passport and so forth. Any medical provider who takes care of you if you don't have this card will forfeit any reimbursements from federal medical programs. Fat chance that you can get medical care under these rules."

Meantime, the *Orange County Register* reported on June 24, 1998: "Immigration and Naturalization Service officials [on June 23] unveiled INSPASS, a high-tech identification system that checks a person's biometrics — such as hand and retina scans — for the purposes of getting frequent travelers quickly through Customs. ...

"Both [INSPASS and the nationalized 'driver's license'] are part of a growing trend that is unhealthy in a free society — the federal government amassing more and more information about individual citizens in centralized databases," the California daily noted in its June 24 editorial. "And this isn't a government that can be trusted with such data. Congress has been holding hearings on the abuses of taxpayers by the IRS, in which agents intimidated taxpayers and in some cases sold private tax data. The Clinton administration also is being investigated for inappropriately using the FBI files of 900 persons."

When Congress took an up-or-down vote on a national ID card during the 1998 immigration debates, our representatives emphatically rejected such a requirement, reported Ms. Dean of the Free Congress Foundation (sister think tank to Washington's Heritage Foundation.). But, "That never stops either those who would destroy our liberty in Congress or in the Clinton Administration.

"God help you if your name gets messed up in the computer," Ms. Dean warns. "You might bleed to death before you get medical treatment. You might be denied that new job you worked so hard to get."

Ms. Dean only concentrates on (highly likely) government foul-ups. The more ominous question with a national personal tracking system is what happens if some bureaucrat with time on his hands decides to cross-reference "registered gun owners" with people who write "anti-government letters" ...

Adds Cold War scholar Dave Wren of Chicago: "My first serious political discussions took place in the 1940s with DPs [Displaced Persons]. Chicago back then was filled with DPs from every part of Europe. All had one thing in common, a burning hate for the political system that had forced them to leave their homeland, homes, and family. Each hated the USSR and its socialism, built on internal passports, national identification documents, papers, pass cards, and those blue ID numbers tattooed on some arms. Fifty years later Americans are being fitted with the same chains; Americans reach their hands out for the shackles. ..."

Not everywhere, fortunately.

Do We Really Have to Show a "Government-Issued ID"?

🌿

By summer 2000, a number of folks had written in, seeking more details on the FAA security directive I often mention, which instructs airline employees to ask to see a government-issued ID from each passenger boarding a commercial aircraft — but which specifically instructs airline employees they may not refuse to let you board a plane for lack of such ID, since America still has no "mandatory internal passport."

Although airlines and the FAA may *assert* these provisions of law were changed in the aftermath of Sept. 11, they should be made to show their congressional authorization for the creation of any such de facto "internal passport." If it was not really required that we show a "government-issued photo ID" to board a commercial airliner before 9/11/01, and they merely lied about it, there's a good chance there was some *reason* they couldn't institute this requirement by mere FAA "Security Directive." As Attorney Larry Becraft documents so carefully (type his name in your search engine, or try http://www.efga.org), there is a constitutional right to unrestricted travel in this nation—such liberties are not supposed to be abridgeable without going through the purposely cumbersome process of constitutional amendment.

So, I decided to retain and present here Betsy Ross' fine research into the airport "you-must-show-a-photo-ID-to-board" scam. If her findings are now out of date, let's put the onus on the government to prove it.

🌿 🌿 🌿

It was the fine folks at Sovereign Citizens Against Numbering, operating the Fight the Fingerprint Web page at www.networkusa.org/fingerprint.shtml, who sent me the article "Flying Without Identification," printed in the May 1997 edition of Robert Kelly's *The American's Bulletin* (P.O. Box 3096, Central Point, OR 97502).

Writing under the pseudonym Betsy Ross, the author, a physician from the Pacific Northwest, reports that Northwest Airlines "was actually instrumental in advancing my education about this issue. I was so aggravated by the insolent and hostile treatment that their employee gave me (hopefully former employee, after the blistering letter I sent to the company president) that I demanded to see a supervisor on the spot.

"I then demanded that he produce the relevant federal regulations *right now*, or face personal liability for authorizing an unreasonable search and seizure, dereliction of duty, fraud, conspiracy, civil rights deprivation, and any other legal buzz words I could think of that moment, which would justify a lawsuit against him personally, as well as his employer.

"Like everyone else, he couldn't show me any statute or regulations. He even admitted that there are none. However, he did produce a copy of Security Directive 96-05, which the Federal Aviation Agency issued to all airlines in August of 1996.

"Its wording is very instructive; it reads as follows:

"IDENTIFY THE PASSENGER —

"A. All passengers who appear to be 18 years of age will present a government issued picture ID, or two other forms of ID, at least one of which must be issued by a government authority.

"B. The agent must reconcile the name on the ID and the name on the ticket — except as noted below.

"C. If the passenger cannot produce identification, or if it cannot be reconciled to match the ticket, the passenger becomes a 'selectee.' Clear all of their luggage as noted in Section 6 below. Clear selectee's checked and carry-on luggage, and suspicious articles discovered by the questions asked."

The directive then explains procedures by which luggage may be "cleared" — most of which in practice seem to involve placing matching orange stickers on boarding pass and baggage — including: "1. Empty the luggage or item and physically search its contents by a qualified screener; or, 2. Bagmatch — ensure the bag is not transported on the aircraft if the passenger does not board."

Ms. Ross writes: "This document apparently goes on for 10 or more pages; the Northwest supervisor gave me only the first page, which contains the information printed above. The next time I refused to produce ID and an agent freaked, I told her, 'Just tap up Sec-Dec 96-5 on your computer and go to Paragraph 1, Section C. Designate me as a 'selectee,' and proceed accordingly.'"

"She apparently thought I was an FAA undercover employee, because she said that she was 'tired of you federal guys coming around' and literally spying on airline agents, 'coercing us into lying to people, and essentially being the 'bag man' for an activity which has no legal requirement.' I told her I could not agree more.

"Another airline employee later confirmed that FAA agents often engage in such entrapment activities, to make sure that airline agents parrot the government party line about state-issued ID.

"I also hit paydirt in a discussion with another, much nicer Northwest agent on the East Coast. In a candid conversation, he told me that FAA personnel had held training sessions with all airline agents in the fall of 1996. Agents were informed directly by the FAA that they absolutely could not bar an American citizen from boarding a plane, even if a passenger refused to produce any identification at all! ... Anyone want to own an airline, courtesy of a judge? ...

"Yet another agent in the Midwest admitted that airline personnel were deliberately and knowingly coercing people into showing government ID by saying, 'It's the law.' According to him the reality is that the companies are simply tired of people selling their frequent-flier tickets.

"The airlines wanted to stem this practice by checking everyone's ID, but knew there would be big problems if they instituted this procedure as a private corporate policy. It was so much more convenient to say it was federal law and make the government the scapegoat.

"So this policy meets the airlines' private financial goals and the government's goal of ever-increasing social control. If no one complains or asserts their rights regarding travel, then another freedom is 'poof' gone. Our children watch this happen, and grow up thinking the state has both the right to define our identity by issuing documents saying who we are and the right to require us to produce them on demand."

Meantime, reader Brad Barnhill of Okemos, Mich., writes in that: "The pertinent security directive is now 97-01. It is worded pretty much the same. ... However, some airlines — including USAirways, Continental, and Delta — have made amendments to their 'Conditions of Contract,' which are incorporated by reference on your airline paper tickets. [These allow them] to refuse service to anyone who 'refuses to show identification.'"

And so, as Buckaroo Banzai used to say: Wherever you go, there you are.

Papers, please?

And Now ... Armed Guards at the DMV

❧

Constitutional authority for licensing cars and drivers is pretty tenuous, largely based on early legal sleight-of-hand designed to purposely confuse the excisable profession of "driving" — hauling passengers or freight for profit on the public roads — with simple civilian travel.

The image is colorful — the Slim Pickens "toll booth"

scene from the Mel Brooks film *Blazing Saddles* comes to mind — but there's no record that George Washington had to stop by each state capital along his route, signing up for the 18th century equivalent of a "photo ID" and a little metal plate to hang over his horse's rump, as he moved from Massachusetts through Connecticut, rushing to the defense of New York in 1776 and Philadelphia in 1777.

In fact, drivers' licenses are thinly disguised police ID cards. (Does one forget how to drive when moving across town or into another state? Then why isn't the license you got in another state the year you graduated from high school still as "good" as the high-school diploma you earned that same year?)

Yet we obligingly buy into the euphemism that the "customers" of the Department of Motor Vehicles want quick and efficient "service" when we go wait in line to renew these sundry government forms — as though anyone would be buying this bill of goods, absent the armed and uniformed men who stand ready to handcuff us and impound our valuable vehicles if we're caught without our "papers, please."

Now, some of the peons are apparently growing restless. Nevada Gov. Kenny Guinn announced in early December 2000 that state workers fear for their lives because "patrons" at DMV offices are going ballistic when they're told — after waiting in line for an average of more than an hour — not only that they're being refused the routine paperwork they've come to pay for, but that their vehicles are instead going to be impounded for overdue traffic or parking tickets.

DMV Director (and former Reno top cop) Richard Kirkland added that some victims have told his employees that they will be killed or that they should be looking over their shoulder when they leave work.

"Some have been grabbed around the throat," he added.

Oh, the humanity!

So the governor asked members of the Legislature's Interim Finance Committee to provide funding for armed guards in the Las Vegas and Reno DMV offices, to keep these unruly peasants in line.

The better long-term solution, of course, would be to abandon the whole system — allow Nevada's citizens to travel the highways as they please without any government "licenses," "registrations" or "permits."

In the meantime, it's tempting to suggest the new guards be given MP-40 submachine guns and fancy black uniforms with silver skulls on the collars, the better to help everyone appreciate the true nature of the transaction being effected.

XV
Practical Politics:
Don't Look for Help Here

"Where We'd Have the Haves and the Have-Nots"
❧

Candidate endorsement interviews at the *Las Vegas Review-Journal* are a tag-team affair. As my partner in the fall of 2000, I drew political columnist Steve Sebelius.

It's been years since we allowed ourselves to be surprised by the lack of any clear-cut political or economic philosophy among the main body of candidates who come trooping through. Most of these souls can't even imagine why anyone would *want* one, attempting to spin their lack of any moral or philosophical rudder into an asset, insisting it's better to "judge each matter on its merits as it comes along" than to be "doctrinaire" or captive to any "hidebound ideology" ... as though the shipping line would be more likely to hire a captain who, instead of avoiding rocks as a matter of principle in a dull and plodding way, made a fresh decision each morning whether to risk the lee shoals, depending on whether the first lobbyist to get to him that day managed to present that course of action as "moderate" and "reasonable" and "well-received by our focus groups."

October 4 was a good day. First in the door was incumbent Assemblyman Dennis Nolan, whose daytime job sees him supervising the administration of drug-testing programs to 30 different transit systems.

Mr. Nolan, a Republican who believes the salaries of state bureaucrats are too low, thinks state government "runs pretty tight" in delivering its services, and can't imagine anyplace where the state payroll could be cut.

"You keep using the word 'services,'" I noted. "If I wait in line down at the DMV and someone finally takes my money to register my car, they're rendering me a 'service,' is that right?"

"That's absolutely right," responded the neatly coiffed, diminutive lawmaker.

Advised that Mr. Nolan believes the War on Drugs can still be won, Mr. Sebelius asked how we're going to keep drugs off the streets, if we can't even keep them out of the prisons.

"I think we *can* keep drugs out of the prisons," Mr. Nolan responded. "You have personnel bringing them in."

The answer is to institute random drug testing for corrections officers, as well as for the prisoners themselves, Mr. Nolan says. Also, since "People object; it doesn't look good" to have over-eager police dogs knocking over small children in the prison waiting rooms, the new electronic "sniffing" wands should be used to check visitors for drugs, including the tiniest tots.

"Sometimes they sneak the drugs in in the babies' bibs, or the women hide them in a balloon in their mouths and then pass them to the prisoner in a kiss," Mr. Nolan explains, his eyes widening with enthusiasm as he warmed to his subject.

"But how are you going to punish prisoners when you catch them with drugs?" asked Mr. Sebelius. "I mean, they're already in jail, right? What are you going to do, put them in 'jail' jail?"

"You have to find some way to discipline them, there's no doubt about it," replied Mr. Nolan, enthusiastically.

What about the schools, I asked. Should the new electronic sniffer technology be used to randomly sweep our school-children and their lockers?

"No," Mr. Nolan replied. However, "One of the states — I can't remember which one right now — has adopted a voluntary 'no drugs' contract from the fourth grade on; both the kids and their parents sign this contract, and in the contract they volunteer for random drug testing. ... I think that's a good idea, it's a great program, because if they don't sign then they can't participate in computer labs and after-school activities and so forth."

So the kids, already dragooned under threat of jail for mom and dad if they don't report to the mandatory government propaganda camp nearest them, now further see their Fourth Amendment protections against unreasonable search and seizure neatly sidestepped as they're requested to "voluntarily" sign please-take-my-pee "contracts," with those who refuse to sign being sent home in ignominy while other kids get to go on field trips and play soccer after school and act in the school play.

Sounds plenty "voluntary" to me. After all, it's not as though little kids tend to ridicule and ostracize anyone who won't go along with the program. Surely no little kid is ever going to be asked why his parents are the only ones who refuse to "volunteer" him for the pee tests, unless, of course, they're ... on drugs, or something.

No sooner had we sent Mr. Nolan on his merry way than Democrat Terrie Stanfill showed up to fill our door.

Ms. Stanfill — recruited by the capital Democrats to challenge Ray Rawson, a solid and hard-working state senator, though not exactly Mr. Showbiz — got off to a fast start, waxing enthusiastic about the many wonderful things she hopes to accomplish up in Carson City with all our tax money, from college scholarships for poor children to visiting nurses for the infirm. The casinos "probably need to be taxed more" — though perhaps not as much as an additional 5 percent, right now — and no one should be allowed to escape from paying "their fair share," she insisted.

"So no one should get out of paying for the public schools?" even if they spend their own money to send their kids to private schools, asked Mr. Sebelius.

"No, because then we'd have the Haves and the Have-nots; if we take money away from the public schools, things would be worse."

"What is the purpose of state government?" I asked Ms. Stanfill.

"To be sure we're doing what the people are wanting, running the state business, that we're introducing laws that should be voted on by the people," she replied. "You're there for the people; at the state level you're introducing the bills."

Not a sentence, not a word (needless to say) about just governments being instituted among men to secure for us our God-given rights and liberties.

"Are there any things that the state Legislature might like to do, that it can't do?" I asked.

"I'm not sure I'm understanding your question," Ms. Stanfill replied.

"Are there any matters in which the state lawmakers might think it was a good idea to get involved, but where they're not allowed to?" I tried again.

"I'm not sure I'm understanding the question," she repeated.

Mr. Sebelius tried his hand at translating for me.

"Let's say a constituent went to a lawmaker and wanted him to, say, outlaw machine guns in Nevada, but the lawmaker said, 'Gee, I've looked at the list of powers granted to us by the state Constitution, and while I agree that's a good idea, I just don't find that we have any delegated power to do that.' What would you think about a lawmaker who said that?"

"Oh, that would be a cop-out," replied the state senate candidate.

I do not mean to imply that, when these candidates go home after a hard day knocking on doors and promising everyone a share of my purloined paycheck, Mr. Nolan changes into tall shiny boots and a sharply creased black uniform with silver skulls on the collar, nor that Ms. Stanfill secretly sneaks out late at night to attend Communist cell meetings.

I'm sure most of their neighbors would testify these are both fine folk who love their children and are always willing to bring cookies to the bake sale.

But so too were the faceless clerks and functionaries who kept the trains running on time in Italy and Germany in the 1930s, pleasant and uncomplicated folk who loved their dogs and brought flowers to church on Sunday. They did their jobs and never gave a thought to which trains were headed where, or who had been loaded aboard.

Because, after all, they didn't mean any harm. Obscure theoretical notions like governments of limited power, or the endowment of the People with certain inalienable rights — among them the right to keep what we earn — were best left to the eggheads up at the university. These were not the concerns of the kind of practical folks who merely wanted to make sure no one was ever allowed to decide what substances to put into his or her own body, while guarding against anyone who would dare "take any money from the public schools," lest the nation find itself in a situation "where we'd have the Haves and the Have-nots."

I Must Be Paranoid; I Still Believe in Communists
🌿

In June 2001, here in Las Vegas, Clark County officials finally caved in to union pressure and ended their system of merit raises. (Now the guys who sit with their feet up will get the same raises as those who stay late to get the job done ... assuming any of the latter can still be found.)

The bosses of Nevada's teachers unions have long wailed and ululated against any similar proposal to differentiate by awarding pay raises based on "merit" among their own number ... after all, this would allow school principals and other administrators to show "favoritism."

It was in this context that I received the galley proofs of the new paperback book, *Communism: A Brief History*, by

Richard Pipes, Baird Research Professor of History at Harvard University.

I thumbed through this slim volume, stumbling on a telling paragraph about a noted world leader who confronted similar proposals in 1931, when he was trying to get the factories running and his nation out of a serious economic depression.

"In 1931," Professor Pipes writes of this noted economic and political visionary, "he assailed the principle of 'egalitarianism,' which called for workers to be paid identical wages regardless of competence, as an 'ultra-left' notion. It meant, he went on to explain, that the unqualified worker had no incentive to acquire skills, while the skilled worker moved from job to job until he found one where his talents were properly rewarded; both hurt productivity. Accordingly, the new wage scale drew great distinctions between the least and most skilled workers."

Who was this enemy of worker solidarity, this promoter of dog-eat-dog competition who stood so far to the right of the enlightened leaders of today's Clark County public employee unions? Joseph Stalin.

🌿 🌿 🌿

Professor Pipes, who reminds us in his preface, "No clear distinction can be drawn between 'socialism' and 'communism'" ... in other words, that the "as much as we can get away with this year" collectivist politics of Charles Schumer and Dianne Feinstein and Shelley Berkley will lead inevitably to the same results gained by Stalin and Mao and Pol Pot, no matter how winding or flower-strewn the path ... finds that, "Just as the Holocaust expressed the quintessential nature of National Socialism, so did the Khmer Rouge rule in Cambodia (1975-78) represent the purest embodiment of Communism: what it turns into when pushed to its logical conclusion. ...

"The leaders of the Khmer Rouge received their higher

education in Paris," the good professor notes, "where they absorbed Rousseau's vision of 'natural man,' as well as the exhortations of Frantz Fanon and Jean-Paul Sartre to violence in the struggle against colonialism."

When Pol Pot's Khmer Rouge threw out the American puppet Lon Nol in 1975 and took over the nation's capital Phnom Penh, "the carnage began," Professor Pipes reports. "Unlike Mao ... Pol Pot did not waste time on 'reeducation,' but proceeded directly to extermination, by category, of ... all civilian and military employees of the old regime, former landowners, teachers, merchants, Buddhist monks, and even skilled workers. ... The executions involved entire families, including small children. ..."

Collectivism breeds such immorality — and can't stand close observation by those who reject euphemisms and stubbornly insist on calling things by their proper names — because it rests on the foundation of armed robbery, no matter how intricately disguised.

Fail to pay your school taxes or your redistributionist "income tax," and eventually armed men will set your belongings on the sidewalk and auction off your house.

What elected official in America today (possibly excepting Ron Paul of Texas) hesitates to gleefully spend the proceeds of the redistributionist income tax? They have thus embraced both the principles and the methods of the Bolsheviks. Yet neither the elected thieves nor the beneficiaries of such redistributionist (that is to say, communist) schemes face any social disapproval for "stealing our stuff." No, they're merely "receiving their entitlements"; it is *we* who are loathed as selfish anti-social deviants if we endeavor to keep some larger share of what we earn to feed and clothe our own families, shouted down for "hate speech" if we call their theft ring by its proper name.

Pipes quotes Kenneth M. Quinn from Carl D. Jackson's 1989 book *Cambodia 1975-1978: Rendezvous With Death* on the typical conduct of Pol Pot's armies:

"Khmer Rouge soldiers would rape a Vietnamese woman" (Vietnamese were a disliked racial minority in Cambodia), "then ram a stake or bayonet into her vagina. Pregnant women were cut open, their unborn babies yanked out and slapped against the dying mother's face. The Yotheas (youths) also enjoyed cutting the breasts off well-endowed Vietnamese women."

The victims could not defend themselves, because it was illegal for civilians to own firearms of military utility, of course — precisely the state of affairs that folks like Charles Schumer and Madames Feinstein and Berkley would like to see prevail on these shores. (Ever heard them propose the repeal of a single "gun control" law?)

In only 44 months, Pol Pot managed to reduce the population of the country from 7.3 million to 5.8 million, eliminating nearly a fifth (some say a quarter) of a nation's population. And it was all done in strict adherence to the doctrines they'd been taught by the most respected Leftist intellectuals of the universities of Paris, who to this day are still required reading (in translation, of course, language skills having long since been abandoned as undemocratic, elitist, and unnecessary) in the most prestigious American universities.

"It may be noted that there were no demonstrations anywhere in the world against these outrages and the United Nations passed no resolutions condemning them," Professor Pipes reports. "The world took them in stride, presumably because they were committed in what was heralded as a noble cause."

🌿 🌿 🌿

Finally, the bloodstained geriatrics who run Red China, taking time out from beating to death more imprisoned Christians, Tibetan nuns, and other "cult members," sponsored a concert (also in June 2000) in Beijing's "Forbidden City," featuring those world-class yawners, the "Three Tenors."

The concert was meant to promote Beijing's desire to host the 2008 Olympics, by showing what a civilized place it is. But a protester showed up.

American photographer Stephen Shaver, there on behalf of Agence France-Presse, photographed the protester. So, in the routine performance of their "put on a happy face" public-relations duties, Beijing police knocked Shaver down, dragged him along the ground, and hit him in the head and chest.

The United States filed a protest. From the French, who educated most of Asia's leading Communist revolutionaries? Silence.

Except that three weeks later the International Olympic Committee — the same folks who honored Hitler's little racial purification experiments by awarding him the 1936 games — announced the locale of their 2008 Olympic games.

Yep. Beijing.

You see, there are no communists. The paranoid right just imagined them. They "see them under every bush." They picture them "hiding under the bed." Poor deluded fools. Always good for a chuckle at the faculty cocktail party.

On Collaboration

❧

Correspondent E.P. sends in an inquiry that crops up from time to time:

"What practical suggestions do you have for weaning older Americans off Social Security or Medicare? Do you propose just cutting everyone off cold turkey? Do any 'privatization' plans appeal to you? If you don't like (1996 Libertarian presidential nominee) Harry Browne's idea of selling off federal assets to pay off SS debts, what specific alternatives do you support?"

I replied:

Suppose you found out your neighbor was a bank robber. Every week, he steals money that doesn't belong to him, terrorizing innocent persons at gunpoint. If he hasn't yet shot anyone — or caused some terrified teller or customer to have a heart attack or a spontaneous miscarriage — he surely will, soon.

He asks your help. Will you participate with him in developing a plan under which he will "wean himself" from his economic dependence on this activity?

You say no. Both morally and legally you would consider yourself an accessory to his crimes if you cooperated with him in an ongoing plan under which you knew he continued to rob banks (albeit gradually less frequently), while you agreed to tell no one about it, based on his "good-faith" assurance to you that he was trying to quit. He has to quit *now*.

But that would be ridiculous, he explains. "It's all well and good that you tell me I can find 'honest work' that will pay me enough to feed my children and make up for my lost bank robbery revenues. But it never worked for me before. It would be *irresponsible* for me to adopt such a radical plan — based on a mere hypothetical theory — without testing it out, gradually. Are you telling me no one has ever watched his children go hungry, while he searched for 'honest work'?

"Imagine how I'd feel as I stood over my daughter's coffin, saying, 'Gee honey, I *hoped* this new 'honest work' deal would work out for us. My buddy here *told* me it would.' Can you tell me of a single other bank robber who has ever tried this 'cold turkey theft withdrawal' plan which you're proposing ... and *succeeded*?"

Similarly, once I participate in helping the federals find some "gradual way out" of the natural and inevitable consequences of the fraudulent Ponzi schemes they've set up and promoted, I become their accessory and accomplice. I don't owe them any such favor. They're paying bribes to oldsters —

to buy their votes — with money looted from your paycheck and mine.

If the alternative thesis were true — that they're only paying the oldsters back the "premiums" stored up in their "personal accounts" over the years — then the federals should be able to cease collecting Social Security "contributions" from younger workers *today*, and keep paying the oldsters at current rates, for decades, till they die.

But of course they can't and even Bill Clinton admitted out loud they can't, at the *same* time (remember: To be a liberal you have to be able to believe two contradictory things at the same time) they insist that this is *not* an "intergenerational income-transfer Ponzi scheme."

Yes, the federal government has promised all American workers these benefits, into an indefinite future. It's too bad that many people believed and even came to depend on these lies. But if you're hired as a bank examiner, is it your responsibility — after you open the vault and show everyone it's empty — to somehow make up the missing deposits to the depositors? No!

The only honest solution is a bankruptcy. Someone needs to figure out the actual marketable assets and obligations of the United States federal government, and pay off those obligations, pro rata. Sell off the gold. Auction off the surplus warships to the highest bidder.

Of course, this will never happen. It would be politically way "too embarrassing." So what we're *really* going to have is a crash, a depression, "special police measures," another revolution, and/or wars of secession. It's inevitable.

If we posit *honest* politicians who wanted to avoid this, they could indeed auction off surplus military gear (instead of melting it), and send the pennies of proceeds to meet a prorated share of their promises to the retirees.

I wouldn't have minded if our Libertarian presidential candidates proposed selling off "federal assets"; that would indeed be wise. We could start by auctioning off all surplus military weapons ... up to and including machine guns, rocket launchers, SAMs, tanks, and howitzers ... to law-abiding private American citizens.

Instead, our current crop of Libertarian front-runners propose selling off "the federal lands," including 85 percent of Nevada ... which is quite a different thing. The U.S. government has no title to those lands; it never bought them. Even the BLM and the Forest Service call them "managed lands" — their excuse for never paying taxes or even "payments in lieu of taxes" (as military bases generally do) to local counties.

Thus, such a plan is like saying: "We're four months behind on the mortgage and we're about to be evicted? No problem. We'll just raise $6,000 selling your dad's car." When your wife objects that you have no *right* to sell her dad's car, that he's only letting us watch it while he's on vacation, you just smile and point out that you're much stronger than the old man, and you own a gun. He's alone in the world, and he's been abroad. Should he object when he returns, his body would fit real well out back, under the geraniums.

"You'd kill my dad?" she cries. Putting on your best Vito Corleone accent, you explain: "I won't have to, honey. I'm sure the old man will ... listen to reason."

Now, selling off all the disposable federal assets (state and local militias would be allowed to bid on Army and Air Force facilities — realistically, the federals would need to keep a few naval bases, the Capitol, the State Department, and the White House) probably wouldn't cover all the unfunded IOUs these congressional crooks have written. Some independent bankruptcy arbiter would have to certify that every person promised some "benefit" would get an equitable pro rated six cents on the dollar, or whatever.

Where might this leave Social Security? What pro-rated redemption plan might an honest bankruptcy referee accept? If Congress attempted to make "full restitution" of funds paid in by folks now over 62 (including retirees — though many have already drawn out more than they ever paid in, of course, at tiny 1940s contribution rates), "half restitution" to workers or veterans now aged 40 to 62, and if workers now under 40 were simply told, "It's over; it was a scam; you get nothing. But at least you've got 25 years to save for your own retirement," should we object?

I believe the answer is that it's not our responsibility to come up with a bankruptcy plan, making ourselves the targets as the focus becomes a series of vicious attacks ridiculing the perceived flaws of "our" proposed solution.

It's up to those who *made* these promises to submit a bankruptcy plan, break the bad news, and take the heat. We're just the bank examiners.

What I cannot and will not do is propose or approve a plan that begins (even if only by implication), "OK, we keep stealing money from youngsters' paychecks at current rates for another 14 years, even though they'll never get anything back. During that time, we gradually ..."

If you propose this — or sit silently by while someone else proposes it — you are engaging in a conspiracy to commit grand larceny. And once you are a co-conspirator, you will *always* be subject to the serpent's voice, saying, "Hey, we're *already* stealing. You don't want us all to get caught, do you? OK, the way we keep from getting caught is, we just commit this one *teensy* additional fraud and/or theft ..."

That is the road to hell.

And watch out for "privatization." The income people earn is theirs. It's "private." They can invest the surplus as they see fit. We don't need to "privatize" what's already private. We only need to stop stealing it.

Any plan to "re-allocate" some of these stolen funds, to "allow" the "contributor" to choose between some sharply limited set of "responsible" alternatives as to where that money gets invested, in order to create the *impression* they've been given "more control" over these funds (actually, a safety valve to relieve the pressure for violent revolution, with the blood of bureaucrats flowing in the streets) ... is like allowing the inmates of Hitler's "model concentration camp" to set up a Council of Elders that's "free" to decide whether their little orchestra will play its concerts on Wednesdays or Sundays.

It's just another cruel fraud. Collaborate as little as possible.

And Close With Love the Way You Do ...

G.B., well-meaning employee of a major aircraft-manufacturing firm, writes:

"I just had the pleasure of reading your Aug. 16 column" (on the harassment of Miami's Joe's Stone Crab by the Equal Employment Opportunity Commission). "However, without providing/allowing a general public response to the people that cause these things to happen, you're nothing more than a noisy gong; you're preaching to the choir; flapping in the wind (like the rest of us).

"Would it be too much to ask for you to include a statement at the end of each of your articles that reads something like:

"'If this bothers you, write to: Appropriate Person, Street Address, Somewhere, USA, and express your feelings (politely)'?"

I replied:

Although I will occasionally list an address to send funds, or ordering info for a book, or contacts for a relevant and admirably principled organization (the Fully Informed Jury Association, Jews for the Preservation of Firearms Ownership, Forfeiture Endangers American Rights, the Separation of School and State Alliance), I purposely do *not* do what you suggest.

Your implication is that if a reader writes to some government administrator, or his or her own congressman, it will do some good.

Let's stipulate that if they receive a thousand such letters they might "pull" or delay passage of some measure until the heat dies down ... though it'll be back under a different name, never fear.

But outweighing that, at least two *bad* things can happen: 1) The letter writer gets added to a list of "anti-government extremists," which will bring a visit from two FBI "suits," or an IRS audit, or the first ATF inspection in years of your FFL license.

This is not mere paranoia. Red Hafter, a champion Olympic pistol marksman from Arizona , recently wrote to his senator, John McCain, to protest the assault weapons ban. McCain promptly forwarded that letter to the BATF — proudly informing the 73-year-old Mr. Hafter he had thus "taken care of the matter." Within weeks, agents of the Bureau of Alcohol, Tobacco and Firearms visited Red for the first audit in decades of his Federal Firearms License. (Yes, FFL holders guilty of record-keeping errors have actually been *jailed*.)

2) But the even worse thing likely to happen is that the letter-writer's anger is thus *assuaged*. He or she feels she has "done something about that problem." With the anger thus vented, he washes his hands of the matter.

The problem is that we have gone far past the point when letters will do any good. You are merely providing the phrases they will test out in their "focus groups" and feed back to you. All that will do any good now (short of violent revolution or secession, which I do not yet endorse) is a much more active and widespread application of the principles of civil disobedience or resistance. For that to happen, people's anger and outrage have to *build* ... not be vented in fruitless mouthings, about as effective as kicking your stalled car.

So, please don't write any letters. Instead, *get mad*. And

then figure out some way — hopefully a way that will not put you, your family, or even the evil bureaucrats and tyrants themselves in the way of *real* bodily harm (yet) — to disobey, to monkey-wrench, to flout, to *resist*.

This can be as "minor" as figuring out ways to store your family's wealth in gold (untracked and unsupervised by any government agency), rather than subsidizing and patronizing the regulated banks that have become government-agencies-by-extension, with accounts the government can track or seize at will. (Thumbprint required for check-cashing? Consider marketing a flesh-colored plastic glue-on for people's thumbs, carefully scribed with the authentic thumbprint of John Dillinger. As long as there's no criminal intent ...)

The government tries to ban firearms? Make it your personal mission to stockpile 10 times more firearms — and 100 times more ammo — than your granddad ever did, and to teach five more citizens how to pick out and shoot a militia-style "assault rifle."

The government wants to stack juries with pro-government stooges? Instead of trying to get out of jury duty, shuffle down there in a bowling shirt, play dumb, and get empaneled. If you're convinced the accused is actually a violent predator who hurt a real human victim, then of course you must throw the book at the S.O.B. But if he's merely being railroaded for standing up on principle against some bureaucratic edict, doing things that wouldn't even have *been* against the law 90 years ago, then argue to acquit, or (at the very least) *hang that jury*, as is your right ... and the defendant's.

For a much longer list of suggestions, I suggest Claire Wolfe's *101 Things to Do Till the Revolution*, from Loompanics Unlimited, P.O. Box 1197, Port Townsend, Wash. 98368, at $20.90 postpaid, volume discounts available (loomps editor@olympus.net.)

But "polite letters"? Oh, please.

Postscript:
Why We're Losing
the War for Freedom

Memorial Day. The bugles blow, laughing children place flags on the graves of the fallen, the surviving comrades of the silent dead squeeze into too-tight uniforms (could they ever really have been so thin?) to march a block or two beneath the flag.

Amid the picnics and the barbecues on this first holiday of summer, who can wonder that a peaceful land spares little more thought for those who died to keep it free? Our carefree days, after all, are the very thing they died to protect.

That, and our freedoms.

How safe, today, are the liberties for which so many generations of Americans, in Mr. Lincoln's words, "gave the last full measure of devotion"?

The first Americans to take up arms to protect American liberties were the 70 militiamen who stood at Lexington on April 19, 1775, attempting to block Lt. Gen. Thomas Gage from seizing an illegal stockpile of arms and powder at nearby Concord.

The minutemen failed, at first. Eight died and 10 were wounded in the first exchange of fire. Only after Gen. Gage's troops searched the nearby village of Concord for hidden arms and turned back for Boston did the colonists exact their revenge, picking off 250. Now the British knew they had a problem.

Why were the colonists aroused? Parliament in February 1775 had declared Massachusetts to be in "open rebellion" — a declaration that made it legal for government troops to shoot troublesome rebels on sight — precisely the kind of operating orders issued to federal agents at Ruby Ridge in 1992, and at Waco in 1993.

Yet on May 10, 1996, the *Boston Globe* reported Massachusetts state authorities had finally called on the Bureau of Alcohol, Tobacco and Firearms to help clear up an 11-year backlog of paperwork generated under a Massachusetts law that now requires the registration of every firearm purchased by a law-abiding citizen, and a five-year backlog in processing permits "required to carry handguns, own rifles, or purchase ammunition."

State legislators say they're worried police officers responding to calls might be unaware which Massachusetts residents have been "stockpiling arms."

As Justice Louis Brandeis wrote in *Olmstead vs. the United States*, "The greatest dangers to liberty lurk in insidious encroachment by men of zeal, well-meaning but without understanding."

How many times, on sultry Memorial Days, have we listened to the best student in the class strive to remember Mr. Lincoln's words, without really hearing in them our own call to action? (We leave uninspected for the moment the irony that the tyrant Lincoln was personally responsible for the slaughter, having launched a ruthless military re-conquest of the South rather than allow those Americans the self-determination that Woodrow Wilson would later so graciously bestow on any Balkan backwater willing to hold a "plebiscite"):

"It is for us, the living ... to be dedicated here to the unfinished work which they who fought here have thus far so nobly advanced ... that we here highly resolve that these dead shall not have died in vain; that this nation, under God, shall have a new birth of freedom; and that government of the people, by the people, for the people, shall not perish from the earth."

Armed government forces "can never be formidable to the liberties of the people," Alexander Hamilton guaranteed in The Federalist No. 29, "while there is a large body of citizens, little if at all inferior to them in discipline and the use of arms, who stand ready to defend their rights and those of their fellow citizens."

"To preserve liberty," wrote Richard Henry Lee of Virginia, who drafted the Bill of Rights, "it is essential that the whole body of the people always possess arms, and be taught alike, especially when young, how to use them." Most Americans believe the "freedom of religion" is still sacred, but the IRS now yanks the tax exemptions of churches it finds "too political." Congress has recently passed a bill to regulate the Internet under the guise of protecting children, motivation that its members apparently believe gives them license to trash the First Amendment.

The Fourth Amendment right of the people to be "secure ... against unreasonable searches and seizures" has been eroded in the name of the War on Drugs until police forces are now rewarded with a share of the booty if they manage to seize the homes and planes of suspected criminals, even if they're never charged with a crime.

In parts of Florida, it's reached the point where county cops just pull over black motorists at random along Interstate 95, seize all their cash, and send them on their way — laughingly inviting them to return and try to "prove" they didn't intend to buy drugs, if they have some extra time and money on their hands.

Only recently have the courts started to take hesitant steps to require the compensation — required by the Fifth Amendment — of Americans whose property is rendered worthless by regulation. Jaro Baranek, a Czechoslovakian refugee, says he recognized from the old days what was happening when he was forbidden to build a home on the $20,000 piece of property he bought in Washington state. But while "The communists used to take land without compensation, at least there you didn't have to pay taxes. Here they take your land and you have to pay for it," Mr. Baranek says.

The 10th Amendment, guaranteeing the government in Washington, D.C., would remain small, limited, and distant, has vanished with the buggy whip. We now routinely dismiss from the "impartial juries" required under the Sixth Amendment any juror who admits he might not enforce what he considers to be an unjust law.

"What kind of government have you given us?" Mrs. Powel asked Mr. Franklin as he emerged, at last, from the sweltering hall in Philadelphia.

"A republic," he said ... "if you can keep it."

How Many Copies of This Book Will Be Read?

〰

From 1999 through 2001, my previous book, *Send in the Waco Killers*, went into a third printing and sold in excess of 8,000 copies — considered pretty good for a "small press" non-fiction title.

Should *The Ballad of Carl Drega* ever find its way into 20,000 hands, that would be a phenomenon.

But even if it were to match the numbers of the hottest new romance or horror or adventure tale from Anne Rice or Tom Clancy, what kind of sales does it take for a book to be considered a "bestseller" in America today? 200,000 copies?

In a nation of 200 million, that's one-tenth of 1 percent of the population.

Compare that to Tom Paine's *Common Sense*, published when James Madison estimated the number of able-bodied males in America at 2 million.

Paine's 50-page booklet took the radical stance that the American colonists should not merely revolt against taxation; they should demand independence.

Paine's book came out in early 1776. It had sold 100,000 copies within three months. Some historians estimate that by the time independence was declared on July the fourth, more than a half million copies had been sold.

Furthermore, the book was read — and then read aloud to the troops — by Revolutionary leaders including Washington himself, who said the impact of the pamphlet was of more value to the cause than an additional battalion of infantry.

No matter what the quality of our ideas, or the skill of their expression, what author today could hope to reach an eighth to a quarter of the adult population directly?

Television can reach that kind of audience. In fact, I took my degree in filmmaking, realizing early on that only the mass media really have the power to mold opinion on a large scale.

But TV and even the movies are collaborative media. Crashing in and delivering the "auteur's vision" unsullied and untrammeled to the eyes of a dumbstruck public may happen in the pages of Cahiers du Cinema, but in real life writers and directors are hired hands, thrown in like relief pitchers based on their proven (two seasons in the minors, always followed orders, shoes never untied) ability to throw 15 fading curve balls to left-hand batters on demand. You've got a creative new strategy for organizing the infield? Come talk to us after you've saved up your quarters and bought the team, champ.

Even the best script is viewed as nothing more than a skeleton on which the money-men can hang their box-office-proven celebrities and their publicity machine — and if a love scene and a car crash have to be inserted, if the film's hero has to be changed from a drug dealer to a drug cop because it plays better with the focus groups, who cares whether the original author wanted his audience to consider that maybe it's the government cops who are the villains. We've got a budget and a schedule and every minute we waste here costs us money, so we're going to do it the way it worked the last three times. You've been paid; we've got someone else to handle the rewrites and the TV pilot and the paperback "novelization"; thanks a lot and don't let that door hit your butt on the way out.

This leaves TV and even the movies almost wholly captive of the reactionary, statist, "left liberal" establishment. Check out "Dave" and "The American President" and "The West Wing" and "Spin City" — bad guys resist federally funded universal day care because they're just plain mean; they only get the girl when they play with the kids on the floor and cave in to compassion and agree to federally fund all baby food and ban all handguns even though the mean old NRA will howl over their lost ammunition profits; there *is* no problem of unintended consequences from government interventions or constitutional limits on government authority or figuring out who the hell will foot the bill; those are just made-up excuses that mean old men use to justify being, you know ... mean.

I'm not saying writers and producers wait for instructions from someone high in the tower of New World Order headquarters — they don't need to.

Everyone in the system — who wishes to keep climbing the career ladder — knows the parameters of acceptable discussion and debate. Go back and roll the earnest 24-hour head-scratching in the days following the World Trade Center bombing in September of 2001. Watch for anyone to provide a forum for any of the dozens of commentators — L. Neil Smith, me, David Kopel of the Independent Institute, Aaron Zelman of the JPFO — who started calling immediately for an abandonment of the Fred and Ethel Mertz airport security system, restoring to the average law-abiding American his constitutional right to go proudly and effectively armed aboard any means of public conveyance.

You will not find that proposal rebutted or even ridiculed, because you will find it was not allowed to be mentioned on the air at all, despite at least six news networks scrambling to fill 24 hours of coverage for a week with everything from weeping moms to a surviving Port Authority policeman describing the last time he saw his loyal golden retriever on the B-1 level of the North Tower of the World Trade Center.

Instead, the so-called "reporters" became nothing but patriotic shills for a pre-positioned and instinctively understood statist agenda. (Think you're going to get invited back to the next cocktail party if you start musing, "Gee, maybe the militia guys are right; I mean, Sept. 11 would never have happened if every passenger were allowed to pack a loaded submachine gun in their carry-on; the Delta Force *did* murder the Branch Davidians, and it's obvious *someone* moved Vince Foster's body, so given that he was Hillary's lover for years, how could she *not* have been involved? ...")

Instead, our "watchdog press" pins flags on their lapels and urges everyone to "pull together" and "sacrifice a few of your freedoms" ("Why be afraid of facial recognition cameras ... unless you've got something to hide?" asked a letter-writer to my own newspaper), waxing eloquent about how fine it was to see folks displaying American flags and joining in the singing of hymns and patriotic songs ... but not a word of dissent about the exquisite absurdity of requiring law-abiding Americans to begin searching each other's luggage for cuticle scissors and toenail clippers, not a single harsh question about how precisely all this new wiretap and e-mail snooping authority would have prevented the events of Sept. 11, let alone any harsh and repetitive questions about how we really *know* it was Osama bin Laden, in the first place.

Only 10 days later — after it was clear talk radio and the Internet were not going to let the obvious question die, and the matter might even arise in congressional hearings — did the TV "news networks" start to allow the most hesitant discussion of whether even *pilots* should be "allowed" to fly armed ... though even that question was then hushed up again as quickly as possible, and hardly mentioned since.

What does it mean to say we have no censorship in this country, when the press censors itself so effectively that the issue never arises?

🌿 🌿 🌿

If the vast majority of Americans want to read the facts and opinions and relatively radical proposed solutions offered in this book and a handful like it, and then reject them as absurd or alien or unworkable, that's fine. I have no desire to force my opinions on anyone ... it's a measure of sanity that a sensible fellow, offered God-like powers, will inquire into the time required just to do the routine maintenance once put in charge of everyone else's life, and respectfully decline.

Rare is the prophet who has any more satisfaction than knowing history will prove him right, eventually — a phenomenon for which I suspect we should all be thoroughly grateful.

But the point is that this year and next, a quantity of people statistically indistinguishable from "none" are going to read this book, or anything remotely resembling it.

I have spent 30 years "working my way up in the news media." On balance, I am "a success" — gainfully employed at a major metropolitan newspaper, my columns syndicated into a scattering of other dailies, modest dozens of eager readers gathering to hear me speak. Balancing the hours against the pay — though I'm not here to whine about how much of "a life" one has to give up, since no one forced me — I cannot recommend this course to anyone who does not feel an irresistible vocation to tell other people's stories.

Nonetheless, if you work pretty hard and sacrifice a fair bit, by the time you're at the height of your modest powers of persuasion, this is where you will be. And what does it avail our cause? How many copies of this book will be read?

Somewhere, we have lost the means of communication. And so, like those cursed by God for their presumption in the tale of the tower of Babel, the people look at one another and move their mouths; they all hear a cacophony of noise, but no one is able to understand.

Under those circumstances, how shall we few who have awakened, looked about, and seen things as they truly are, think of ourselves — given that we are riding toward the falls in a boat controlled by those who neither see nor understand, and have no interest in listening to our warnings, even if they *could* understand?

Are knowledge and understanding — even this equivalent of one-eyed sight in the land of the blind — a blessing, or a curse?

What moral obligation do we have to wave and scream and try to point out the danger? How long are we obliged to try? When are we free to decide we've done all that's required by the dictates of conscience and a decent consideration for our fellow man, and that we have no further responsibility than to find such private peace as we can?

We are losing the war for freedom because those who could have led that struggle are retiring from the field, exhausted not from battle against the collectivist, statist foe, but from their failed effort to raise even a modest cohort to stand behind their banner. Everyone is pretty busy paying their taxes. You can't fight city hall. The war is not so much lost as called on account of a lack of interest.

The few who stand up — even just to home-school and refuse to vaccinate their kids — are demonized and marginalized, if not murdered outright. The lawyers will not plead our cases for fear of disbarment, nor the judges consider our arguments for fear of being reversed. (They now attend Judicial College "continuing education" seminars on how to "deal with" Patriot and Constitutionalist "protests" — described in the course prospectus as "these attacks on the court" ... and I doubt they're advised to "start by giving straight and honest answers to their questions of jurisdiction, requiring the government agency to read out the underlying statute and then ruling on its constitutionality before proceeding, even if it means throwing out whole swatches of the federal code" — I asked to attend the Nov. 13 session at the University of Nevada in Reno, but they told me only judges are allowed.)

The news media is populated by eager Kens and Barbies

with neither the time nor the intellectual background to understand what the hell we're talking about. The Founding Fathers are not read — the government schools teach that truth is a majority consensus ("Survey says ...") or what feels good during show-and-tell ... not what some dead white male said long before you were born.

Is this what it felt like as the last Roman legion packed its wagons and headed for the ships, as the lights of learning flickered out one by one and the last of the surviving old manuscripts was rolled up and sealed in oilskin and shipped off to Ireland for safekeeping against the coming of the barbarian hordes?

Will an Arthur or a new Alfred arise? To ask the question is to explain why we are losing this war for freedom. For so long as we skulk in our hovels, hoping some hero on a white charger will come and set us free, we want what never was ... and shall never be.

V.S.

Las Vegas Nov. 9, 2001

APPENDIX I

Others seem to be realizing the truth about the "Green" movement, which has now even produced its own whistleblower.

In the February 2002 edition of *Reason* magazine online, Ronald Bailey, *Reason*'s science correspondent and editor of "Earth Report," reviews the new book, *The Skeptical Environmentalist: Measuring the Real State of the World*, by Bjorn Lomborg (Cambridge University Press) under the headline "Debunking Green Myths: An Environmentalist Gets It Right."

Mr. Bailey writes, in part:

"Modern environmentalism, born of the radical movements of the 1960s, has often made recourse to science to press its claims that the world is going to hell in a handbasket. But this environmentalism has never really been a matter of objectively describing the world and calling for the particular social policies that the description implies.

"Environmentalism is an ideology, very much like Marxism, which pretended to base its social critique on a 'scientific' theory of economic relations. Like Marxists, environmentalists have had to force the facts to fit their theory. Environmentalism is an ideology in crisis: The massive accumulating contradictions between its pretensions and the actual state of the world can no longer be easily explained away.

"The publication of *The Skeptical Environmentalist*, a magnificent and important book by a former member of Greenpeace, deals a major blow to that ideology by superbly documenting a response to environmental doomsaying. The author, Bjorn Lomborg, is an associate professor of statistics at the University of Aarhus in Denmark. On a trip to the United States a few years ago, Lomborg picked up a copy of *Wired* that included an article about the late 'doomslayer' Julian Simon.

"Simon, a professor of business administration at the University of Maryland, claimed that by most measures, the lot of humanity is improving and the world's natural environment was not critically imperiled. Lomborg, thinking it would be an amusing and instructive exercise to debunk a 'right-wing' anti-environmentalist American, assigned his students the project of finding the 'real' data that would contradict Simon's outrageous claims.

"Lomborg and his students discovered that Simon was essentially right, and that the most famous environmental alarmists (Stanford biologist Paul Ehrlich, Worldwatch Institute founder Lester Brown, former Vice President Al Gore, *Silent Spring* author Rachel Carson) and the leading environmentalist lobbying groups (Greenpeace, the World Wildlife Fund, Friends of the Earth) were wrong. It turns out that the natural environment is in good shape, and the prospects of humanity are actually quite good.

"Lomborg begins with 'the Litany' of environmentalist doom, writing: 'We are all familiar with the Litany. ... Our resources are running out. The population is ever growing, leaving less and less to eat. The air and water are becoming ever more polluted. The planet's species are becoming extinct in vast numbers. ... The world's ecosystem is breaking down. ... We all know the Litany and have heard it so often that yet another repetition is, well, almost reassuring.' Lomborg notes that there is just one problem with the Litany: 'It does not seem to be backed up by the available evidence.'

Lomborg then proceeds to demolish the Litany. He shows how, time and again, ideological environmentalists misuse, distort, and ignore the vast reams of data that contradict their dour visions.

Lomborg points out that human life expectancy in the developing world has more than doubled in the past century. Over that same time, the average amount of food per person in the developing countries has increased. And although world population has doubled, the percentage of malnourished poor people has actually fallen, and will likely fall further over the next decade. In real terms, food costs only a third of what it did a century ago. And Lomborg points out that increasing food-production trends show no sign of slackening.

Air pollution? Completely uncontroversial data show that concentrations of sulfur dioxide are down in the U.S., carbon monoxide levels are down, nitrogen oxides are down, ground level ozone is down. These trends are mirrored in all developed countries.

Lomborg shows that claims of rapid deforestation are vastly exaggerated. Eight-six percent of the Brazilian rainforests remain uncut, and the rate of clearing is falling. Lomborg also debunks the two widely circulated claims that the world will soon lose up to half of its species (in fact, the best evidence indicates that 0.3 percent of species might be lost in the next 50 years even if nothing is done) and that global warming caused by burning fossil fuels is likely to be a catastrophe.

The Green emperor has no clothes. It's bad enough we tolerate the teaching of *any* religion in our government schools, to the exclusion of all others and in violation of the strict edicts of the First Amendment. But if the bureaucrats had to choose one with which to indoctrinate our children, why on earth did they have to choose one so antithetical to the free-market system that made this country rich and free — one at the same time so transparently and self-evidently *wrong*?

APPENDIX II

The author has found the following sites, organizations, and titles useful as sources of additional information and support on topics covered in this book. (Neither the author nor the publishers are directly associated with these groups; we cannot be responsible for any future actions or positions they may take.)

In the case of the books and videos listed, your subscriptions to *Privacy Alert* help support the "Books" section of the Web site www.privacy alertonline.com, where efforts are under way to make most of these titles (particularly those less generally accessible) available in the near future. So check there first, by e-mailing privacyalert@thespiritof76.com, or dialing (775)348-8591 (Nevada business hours).

Alliance for the Separation
of School and State
Marshall Fritz, executive director
(559) 292-1776;
fax (559) 292-7582
e-mail: sepschool@psnw.com
http://www.sepschool.org/

Atlas Shrugged (the novel that destroyed socialism) and *The New Left: The Anti-Industrial Revolution* by Ayn Rand

Joe Banister
Freedom Above Fortune
e-mail: jbanister@freedomabove
fortune.com
http://www.freedomabove
fortune.com/
(Joe left the IRS when they wouldn't answer his simple questions about whether — and how — what he was doing was legal.)

Larry Becraft
http://home.hiwaay.net/~becraft/
and most importantly his
"destroyed arguments" site, at
http://home.hiwaay.net/~becraft/
deadissues.htm, (which promises,
"As more crazy ideas arise in the Freedom Movement, I will address them." Larry is an attorney who has awakened.)

The Birth of Heroin and the Demonization of the Dope Fiend by Th. Metzger
Loompanics Unlimited

Boston's Gun Bible and *Bulletproof Privacy* by Boston T. Party
Javelin Press
e-mail: javelinpress@yahoo.com
http://www.javelinpress.com/
index.html

Concerned Parents for
Vaccine Safety
http://home.sprynet.com/~sprynet/
Gyrene/home.htm

CPS Watch
and their magazine, *TCB Chronicles*
Cheryl & Elvis Barnes, directors
http://www.cpswatch.com/

Dissatisfied Parents Together (DPT)
http://www.909shot.com/

Dumbing Us Down, and
*The Underground History
of American Education*
by John Taylor Gatto
Oxford Village Press
P.O. Box 562
Oxford, NY 13830

*Emancipating Slaves, Enslaving
Free Men: A History of the
American Civil War*
by Jeffrey Rogers Hummel

Fight the Fingerprint
http://www.networkusa.org/
fingerprint.shtml

*For Good and Evil, The Impact of
Taxes on the Course of Civilization*
by Charles Adams, Madison Books

Forfeiture Endangers American
Rights Foundation (FEAR)
Brenda Grantland, president
S. Leon Felkins, executive director
415-389-8551, 888-FEAR-001
leon@fear.org, or brenda@fear.org

*Freedom in Chains: The Rise of the
State and the Demise of the Citizen*
by James Bovard, St. Martin's Press

The Fully Informed Jury
Association (FIJA)
Phone/fax (406) 793-5550
e-mail: webforeman@fija.org
http://www.fija.org/

Gun Owners of America (GOA)
Larry Pratt, executive director
703-321-8585; fax 703-321-8408
http://www.gunowners.org/

Jews for the Preservation of
Firearms Ownership (JPFO)
Aaron Zelman, executive director
(262) 673-9745; fax (262) 673-9746
e-mail: Against-Genocide@
JPFO.org
http://www.jpfo.org/
(No, it's not just for Jews:
America's *pricipled* gun-rights
organization)

The Law by Frederic Bastiat
Foundation for Economic Education
Irvington-on-Hudson, NY 10533

Lever Action (Mountain Media)
and *Pallas* (Tor) by L. Neil Smith
privacyalert@thespiritof76.com

Losing Your Illusions
by Gordon Phillips
e-mail: privacyalert@thespirit
of76.com
or info@informamerica.com
(The most complete and well-
documented analysis of the true
nature of the federal income tax;
spiral-bound)

The Matrix, 1999
written and directed by
Andy and Larry Wachowski
with Keanu Reeves and
Laurence Fishburne
(nothing you believe is true)

*Medical Warrior: Fighting
Corporate Socialized Medicine*
by Miguel A. Faria, Jr., M.D.
Hacienda Publishing, Macon, Ga.

*The Myth of Mental Illness,
Psychiatric Justice,* and
The Manufacture of Madness
by Dr. Thomas S. Szasz
Harper Torch Books

National Coalition for
Child Protection Reform
Richard Wexler, executive director
703-212-2006;
e-mail: info@NCCPR.org
http://www.nccpr.org/

101 Things to Do Till the Revolution
by Claire Wolfe
Loompanics Unlimited

The Origin of Consciousness in the Breakdown of the Bicameral Mind
by Julian Jaynes
Houghton Mifflin

The Patriot, 2000
directed by Roland Emmerich,
screenplay by Robert Rodat (*Saving Private Ryan*) with Mel Gibson,
Jason Isaacs, and Lisa Brenner

Gordon Phillips
tax research and education
http://www.informamerica.com/
news/
or http://www.informamerica.com/
e-mail: info@informamerica.com

Vin Suprynowicz's Privacy Alert
(monthly newsletter)
privacyalert@thespiritof76.com

Range (magazine)
775-884-2200, Fax 775-884-2213
E-mail: info@rangemagazine.com
http://www.rangemagazine.com/

The Save-A-Patriot Fellowship
410-857-4441; fax 410-857-5249
http://www.save-a-patriot.org/
(serious tax study and education
with a blessed minimum of the
"Buy my $119 tape and never file
again!" hucksterism now so
prevalent elsewhere)

The Sovereign Individual by James
Dale Davidson and Lord William
Rees-Mogg (Simon and Schuster)

Stewards of the Range
208-855-0707
http://www.stewardsoftherange.org/
(founded in cooperation with
Nevada rancher Wayne Hage,
whose property-rights lawsuit
against federal grazing regulations
may be the longest-running ever,
Stewards of the Range is — along
with *Range* magazine — a valuable
source for the alternative view on
the "ranchers rape the land for free"
hokum now widely circulating East
of the Mississippi)

That Every Man Be Armed
by Stephen P. Halbrook
The Independent Institute

Thinktwice Global Vaccine Institute
505-983-1856
e-mail: global@thinktwice.com
http://thinktwice.com/global.htm

Trial by Jury and *No Treason*
by Lysander Spooner

Unintended Consequences
by John Ross, Accurate Press
(the great novel of the disarming of
America)

*Vaccines: Are They Really
Safe and Effective? (A Parent's
Guide to Childhood Shots)*
by Neil Z. Miller
New Atlantean Press
P.O. Box 9638-925
Santa Fe, NM 87504

ABOUT THE AUTHOR

Vin Suprynowicz grew up in a nice Politically Correct Democratic family, fine folks who taught him that it was wrong to steal or hate people for being different from them. He still feels that way, but has expanded his idea of who those people are from merely homosexuals and members of racial minorities to machine-gun owners, militiamen, folks who choose to vote their conscience in the jury rooms in defiance of the judge's instructions, who use intoxicants other than those approved by the current government, who decline to contribute any portion of their income to support the welfare/police state, and the like.

He landed his first newspaper job at the alternative *Hartford Advocate* in 1972 after graduating from Wesleyan University. He went on to become the star reporter at the daily *Willimantic Chronicle*, wire editor of the *Norwich Bulletin*, managing editor of the daily *North Virginia Sun*, and founder and publisher of the weekly *Providence Eagle*. Suprynowicz was named three times to the Golden Dozen (the top 12 weekly editorial writers in the U.S. and Canada) by the International Society of Weekly Newspaper Editors.

He finally migrated west to Phoenix, then moved to Las Vegas. He's currently an editorial writer for the *Las Vegas Review-Journal*. He also pens a twice-a-week syndicated column that runs in 20 or so daily newspapers around the country.

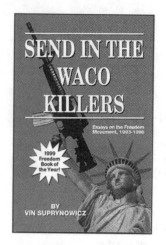

Guess What?
It's Not About Waco!

Your right to trial by a randomly selected jury — not one stacked with jurors who swear to convict in advance — is gone.

The IRS can now seize your bank account, paycheck, and house — without so much as a judge's order. Your banker will cooperate fully.

People who never sold, touched, or even saw a single gram of cocaine or marijuana are in federal prisons on "drug" charges — including plastic-vial manufacturers and hydroponic-supply store owners.

The Founders guaranteed Americans the right to keep and bear arms for defense against their own government. But the meager legal arms of the Branch Davidians were no match against government tanks and helicopters at Waco. And today, our rulers are more afraid of arming airline pilots than of having 767s fly into skyscrapers.

How did we get to this point? Is there any peaceful way back from the toboggan ride to tyranny? The answers are in *Send in the Waco Killers* (1999's Freedom Book of the Year), by America's syndicated Libertarian columnist, Vin Suprynowicz.

"... This volume by Suprynowicz is why words exist. It is the seminal work of the last five decades. It will change lives. It will direct nations. ... [The hand of Suprynowicz] points to hope and the brilliant possibilities alive in the human heart. It points past race and religion, past dogma ... It does what words were meant to do: inspire and teach. This book works a slow magic. Suprynowicz has given us the lyrics to freedom's song. It is up to us to make the music."
— Bill Branon, *author of* Let Us Prey,
Devil's Hole, Spider Snatch, *and* Timesong

Order your copy now.
Use the handy order form at the end of this section.

Ask about how you can get a *free* copy of this book with a subscription to Vin Suprynowicz's monthly newsletter, *Privacy Alert*.

And be sure to check out our Web site at
www.privacyalertonline.com

Non-Government Warning:

L. Neil Smith's vision of liberty is highly contagious and incurable. Exposure to his ideas will change your life.

This warning from the back cover pretty well sums up most people's reaction the first time they read any of L. Neil's work.

L. Neil Smith is the most prolific Libertarian writer of our time. He's the author of more than 20 science-fiction novels, including *Forge of the Elders*, named the 2000 Freedom Book of the Year by Free-Market.net.

In *Lever Action*, his first book of non-fiction, Smith again demonstrates that he's one of the strongest voices putting pressure on the Archimedes lever that will eventually lift the world to freedom — and the stars.

"Smith is best known as a science fiction author, and he's also an essayist, editorialist, activist, and speaker, and Lever Action *is the first ever print collection of his non-fiction offerings.*

It's about time.

Few books are so compelling that placing them in the hands of a friend becomes an act of revolution. Thomas Paine's Common Sense *and Vin Suprynowicz's* Send in the Waco Killers *have previously been the chronological bookends of that canon.* Lever Action *is the latest addition to it."*

— **Tom Knapp, Free-Market.Net**

An order form is included at the end of this section

Ask about how you can get a *free* copy of this book with a subscription to Vin Suprynowicz's monthly newsletter, *Privacy Alert*.

And be sure to check out our Web site at www.privacyalertonline.com

❦ Order Form ❦

Use this form to order full information on *Vin Suprynowicz's Privacy Alert* or to order copies of Vin's first book *Send in the Waco Killers,* his current book *The Ballad of Carl Drega,* or L. Neil Smith's *Lever Action.*

Send in the Waco Killers .... ___ @ $21⁹⁵ ea.

Lever Action .... ___ @ $21⁹⁵ ea.

The Ballad of Carl Drega .... ___ @ $24⁹⁵ ea.

Add $3 S&H per book _____

TOTAL ENCLOSED $_____

❑ **Send me the free information on *Privacy Alert***

Name _____

Address _____

City, State, Zip _____

❑ Visa ❑ Mastercard #: _____

Exp. date: _____

Big Discounts on Bulk Orders!

Quantity	Discount	S&H
4-7	20%	$1.00 per book,
8-15	30%	$50.00 maximum, up to 80 books.
16-32	40%	
48 or more	50%	
80 or more	50%	*Free Shipping*

To order with credit card by email: privacyalert@thespiritof76.com; at our Web site: http://www.privacyalertonline.com; or telephone: 775-348-8591

Make check payable to
"Privacy Alert," 561 Keystone Ave., #684, Reno, NV 89503